COMPLETE TRAVEL WRITING

by

D H LAWRENCE

BLACKTHORN PRESS

Blackthorn Press, Blackthorn House
Middleton Rd, Pickering YO18 8AL
United Kingdom

ISBN 978 1 906259 16 7

2009

www.blackthornpress.com

Printed and bound in Great Britain by CPI Antony Rowe, Chippenham and Eastbourne

INTRODUCTION

Lawrences and his wife Frieda left England in 1919 and for the next eleven years until Lawrence's death in 1930 in Vence in Southern France, where he is buried, they travelled and lived across the world with only occasional return visits to England. They lived in Europe, Australia and South America, taking in Italy, Switzerland, Germany, Spain, Ceylon, Australia and New Mexico.

Out of these journeys came Lawrence's collection of travel writing. The writing is gripping not only for its descriptions of people and places at a time when few but the leisured classes travelled outside of England but for Lawrence's ability to get below the surface of a place and look for the universal in the particular.

He is concerned not just with how people lived, what they ate, how they lived, what were their politics but what their relationship to the eternal was. How did they make sense of their lives? This is as true of the Etruscans who died out hundreds of years ago and whose tombs Lawrence clambered through as it is of the Indians of South America who Lawrence came to live among.

Now, when young people travel and work across the world with admirable ease, it as well to read these essays of D H Lawrence to understand the real point of travel – not just to see and indulge the senses but to challenge our own beliefs and way of life by comparing it with others. Like all great travel writing, the urge after reading one of the books is to leave the comfort of the armchair, throw a rucksack over the shoulder and follow the paths of D H Lawrence.

CONTENTS

TWILIGHT IN ITALY

THE CRUCIFIX ACROSS THE MOUNTAINS

THE imperial road to Italy goes from Munich across the Tyrol, through Innsbruck and Bozen to Verona, over the mountains. Here the great processions passed as the emperors went South, or came home again from rosy Italy to their own Germany.

And how much has that old imperial vanity clung to the German soul? Did not the German kings inherit the empire of bygone Rome? It was not a very real empire, perhaps, but the sound was high and splendid.

Maybe a certain Grössenwahn is inherent in the German nature. If only nations would realise that they have certain natural characteristics, if only they could understand and agree to each other's particular nature, how much simpler it would all be.

The imperial procession no longer crosses the mountains, going South. That is almost forgotten, the road has almost passed out of mind. But still it is there, and its signs are standing.

The crucifixes are there, not mere attributes of the road, yet still having something to do with it. The imperial processions, blessed by the Pope and accompanied by the great bishops, must have planted the holy idol like a new plant among the mountains, there where it multiplied and grew according to the soil, and the race that received it.

As one goes among the Bavarian uplands and foothills, soon one realises here is another land, a strange religion. It is a strange country, remote, out of contact. Perhaps it belongs to the forgotten, imperial processions.

Coming along the clear, open roads that lead to the mountains, one scarcely notices the crucifixes and the shrines. Perhaps one's interest is dead. The crucifix itself is nothing, a factory-made piece of sentimentalism. The soul ignores it.

But gradually, one after another looming shadowily under their hoods, the crucifixes seem to create a new atmosphere over the whole of the countryside, a darkness, a weight in the air that is so unnaturally bright and rare with the reflection from the snows above, a darkness hovering just over the earth. So rare and unearthly the light is, from the mountains, full of strange radiance. Then every now and again recurs the crucifix, at the turning of an open, grassy road, holding a shadow and a mystery under its pointed hood.

I was startled into consciousness one evening, going alone over a marshy place at the foot of the mountains, when the sky was pale and unearthly, invisible, and the hills were nearly black. At a meeting of the tracks was a crucifix, and between the feet of the Christ a handful of withered poppies. It was the poppies I saw, then the Christ.

It was an old shrine, the wood-sculpture of a Bavarian peasant. The Christ was a peasant of the foot of the Alps. He had broad cheekbones and sturdy limbs. His plain, rudimentary face stared fixedly at the hills, his neck was stiffened, as if in resistance to the fact of the nails and the cross, which he could not escape. It was a man nailed down in spirit, but set stubbornly against the bondage and the disgrace. He was a man of middle age, plain, crude, with some of the meanness of the peasant, but also with a kind of dogged nobility that does not yield its soul to the circumstances. Plain, almost blank in his soul, the middle-aged peasant of the crucifix resisted unmoving the misery of his position. He did not yield. His soul was set, his will was fixed. He was himself, let his circumstances be what they would, his life fixed down.

Across the marsh was a tiny square of orange-coloured light, from the farm-house with the low, spreading roof. I remembered how the man and his wife and the children worked on till dark, silent and intent, carrying the hay in their arms out of the streaming thunder-rain into the shed, working silent in the soaking rain.

The body bent forward towards the earth, closing round on itself; the arms clasped full of hay, clasped round the hay that presses soft and close to the breast and the body, that pricks heat into the arms and the skin of the breast, and fills the lungs with the sleepy scent of dried herbs: the rain that falls heavily and wets the shoulders, so that the shirt clings to the hot firm skin and the rain comes with heavy, pleasant coldness on the active flesh, running in a trickle down towards the loins, secretly; this is the peasant, this hot welter of physical sensation. And it is all intoxicating. It is intoxicating almost like a soporific, like a sensuous drug, to gather the burden to one's body in the rain, to stumble across the living grass to the shed, to relieve ones' arms of the weight, to throw down the hay on to the heap, to feel light and free in the dry shed, then to return again into the chill, hard rain, to stoop again under the rain, and rise to return again with the burden.

It is this, this endless heat and rousedness of physical sensation which keeps the body full and potent, and flushes the mind with a blood heat, a blood sleep. And this sleep, this heat of physical experience, becomes at length a bondage, at last a crucifixion. It is the life and the fulfilment of the peasant, this flow of sensuous experience. But at last it drives him almost mad, because he cannot escape.

For overhead there is always the strange radiance of the mountains, there is the mystery of the icy river rushing through its pink shoals into the darkness of the pine-woods, there is always the faint tang of ice on the air, and the rush of sounding water.

And the ice and the upper radiance of snow are brilliant with timeless immunity from the flux and the warmth of life. Overhead they transcend all life, all the soft, moist fire of the blood. So that a man must needs live under the radiance of his own negation.

There is a strange, clear beauty of form about the men of the Bavarian highlands, about both men and women. They are large and clear and handsome in form, with blue eyes very keen, the pupil small, tightened, the iris keen, like sharp light shining on blue ice. Their large, full-moulded limbs and erect bodies are distinct, separate, as if they were perfectly chiselled out of the stuff of life, static, cut off. Where they are everything is set back, as in a clear frosty air.

Their beauty is almost this, this strange, clean-cut isolation, as if each one of them would isolate himself still further and for ever from the rest of his fellows.

Yet they are convivial, they are almost the only race with the souls of artists. Still they act the mystery plays with instinctive fulness of interpretation, they sing strangely in the mountain fields, they love make-belief and mummery, their processions and religious festivals are profoundly impressive, solemn, and rapt.

It is a race that moves on the poles of mystic sensual delight. Every gesture is a gesture from the blood, every expression is a symbolic utterance.

For learning there is sensuous experience, for thought there is myth and drama and dancing and singing. Everything is of the blood, of the senses. There is no mind. The mind is a suffusion of physical heat, it is not separated, it is kept submerged.

At the same time, always, overhead, there is the eternal, negative radiance of the snows. Beneath is life, the hot jet of the blood playing elaborately. But above is the radiance of changeless not-being. And life passes away into this changeless radiance. Summer and the prolific blue-and-white flowering of the earth goes by, with the labour and the ecstasy of man, disappears, and is gone into brilliance that hovers overhead, the radiant cold which waits to receive back again all that which has passed for the moment into being.

The issue is too much revealed. It leaves the peasant no choice. The fate gleams transcendent above him, the brightness of eternal, unthinkable not-being. And this our life, this admixture of labour and of warm experience in the flesh, all the time it is steaming up to the changeless brilliance above, the light of the everlasting snows. This is the eternal issue.

Whether it is singing or dancing or play-acting or physical transport of love, or vengeance or cruelty, or whether it is work or sorrow or religion, the issue is always the same at last, into the radiant negation of eternity. Hence the beauty and completeness, the finality of the highland peasant. His figure, his limbs, his face, his motion, it is all formed in beauty, and it is all completed. This is no flux nor hope nor becoming, all is, once and for all. The issue is eternal, timeless, and changeless. All being and all passing away is part of the issue, which is eternal and changeless. Therefore there is no becoming and no passing away. Everything *is,* now and for ever. Hence the strange beauty and finality and isolation of the Bavarian peasant.

It is plain in the crucifixes. Here is the essence rendered in sculpture of wood. The face is blank and stiff, almost expressionless. One realises with a start how unchanging and conventionalised is the face of the living man and woman of these parts, handsome, but motionless as pure form. There is also an underlying meanness, secretive, cruel. It is all part of the beauty, the pure, plastic beauty. The body also of the Christus is stiff and conventionalised, yet curiously beautiful in proportion, and in the static tension which makes it unified into one clear thing. There is no movement, no possible movement. The being is fixed, finally. The whole body is locked in one knowledge, beautiful, complete. It is one with the nails. Not that it is languishing or dead. It is stubborn, knowing its own undeniable being, sure of the absolute reality of the sensuous experience. Though he is nailed down upon an irrevocable fate, yet, within that fate he has the power and the delight of all sensuous experience. So he accepts the fate and the mystic delight of the senses with one will, he is complete and final. His sensuous experience is supreme, a consummation of life and death at once.

It is the same at all times, whether it is the mowing with the scythe on the hill-slopes, or hewing the timber, or steering the raft down the river which is all effervescent with ice; whether it is thinking in the Gasthaus, or making love, or playing some mummer's part, or hating steadily and cruelly, or whether it is kneeling in spell-bound subjection in the incense-filled church, or walking in the strange, dark, subject-procession to bless the fields, or cutting the young birch trees for the feast of Frohenleichnam, it is always the same, the dark, powerful mystic, sensuous experience is the whole of him, he is mindless and bound within the absoluteness of the great icy not-being which holds good for ever, and is supreme.

Passing further away, towards Austria, travelling up the Isar, till the stream becomes smaller and whiter and the air is colder, the full glamour of the northern hills, which are so marvellously luminous and gleaming with flowers, wanes and gives way to a darkness, a sense of ominousness. Up there I saw another little Christ, who seemed the very soul of the place. The road went beside the river, that was seething with snowy ice-bubbles, under the rocks and the high, wolf-like pine trees, between the pinkish shoals. The air was cold and hard and high, everything was cold and separate. And in a little glass case beside the road sat a small, hewn Christ, the head resting on the hand; and he meditates, half-wearily, doggedly, the eyebrows lifted in strange abstraction, the elbow resting on the knee.

Detached, he sits and dreams and broods, wearing his little golden crown of thorns, and his little cloak of red flannel that some peasant woman has stitched for him.

No doubt he still sits there, the small, blank-faced Christ in the cloak of red flannel, dreaming, brooding, enduring, persisting. There is a wistfulness about him, as if he knew that the whole of things was too much for him. There was no solution, either, in death. Death did not give the answer to the soul's anxiety. That which is, is. It does not cease to be when it is cut. Death cannot create nor destroy. What is, is.

The little brooding Christ knows this. What is he brooding, then? His static patience and endurance is wistful. What is it that he secretly yearns for, amid all the placidity of fate? "To be, or not to be," this may be the question, but it is not a question for death to answer. It is not a question of living or not-living. It is a question of being—to be or not to be. To persist or not to persist, that is not the question; neither is it to endure or not to endure. The issue, is it eternal not-being? If not, what, then, is being? For overhead the eternal radiance of the snow gleams unfailing, it receives the efflorescence of all life and is unchanged, the issue is bright and immortal, the snowy not-being. What, then, is being?

As one draws nearer to the turning-point of the Alps, towards the culmination and the southern slope, the influence of the educated world is felt once more. Bavaria is remote in spirit, as yet unattached. Its crucifixes are old and grey and abstract, small like the kernel of the truth. Further into Austria they become new, they are painted white, they are larger, more obtrusive. They are the expressions of a later, newer phase, more introspective and self-conscious. But still they are genuine expressions of the people's soul.

Often, one can distinguish the work of a particular artist here and there in a district. In the Zemm valley, in the heart of the Tyrol, behind Innsbruck, there are five or six crucifixes by one sculptor. He is no longer a peasant working out an idea, conveying a dogma. He is an artist, trained and conscious, probably working in Vienna. He is consciously trying to convey a *feeling*, he is no longer striving awkwardly to render a truth, a religious fact.

The chief of his crucifixes stands deep in the Klamm, in the dank gorge where it is always half-night. The road runs under the rock and the trees, half-way up the one side of the pass. Below, the stream rushes ceaselessly, embroiled among great stones, making an endless loud noise. The rock face opposite rises high overhead, with the sky far up. So that one is walking in a half-night, an underworld. And just below the path, where the pack-horses go climbing to the remote, infolded villages, in the cold gloom of the pass hangs the large, pale Christ. He is larger than life-size. He has fallen forward, just dead, and the weight of the full-grown, mature body hangs on the nails of the hands. So the dead, heavy body drops forward, sags, as if it would tear away and fall under its own weight.

It is the end. The face is barren with a dead expression of weariness, and brutalised with pain and bitterness. The rather ugly, passionate mouth is set for ever in the disillusionment of death. Death is the complete disillusionment, set like a seal over the whole body and being, over the suffering and weariness and the bodily passion.

The pass is gloomy and damp, the water roars unceasingly, till it is almost like a constant pain. The driver of the pack-horses, as he comes up the narrow path in the side of the gorge, cringes his sturdy cheerfulness as if to obliterate himself, drawing near to the large, pale Christ, and he takes his hat off as he passes, though he does not look up, but keeps his face averted from the crucifix. He hurries by in the gloom, climbing the steep path after his horses, and the large white Christ hangs extended above.

The driver of the pack-horses is afraid. The fear is always there in him, in spite of his sturdy, healthy robustness. His soul is not sturdy. It is blenched and whitened with fear.

4

The mountains are dark overhead, the water roars in the gloom below. His heart is. ground between the mill-stones of dread. When he passes the extended body of the dead Christ he takes off his hat to the Lord of Death. Christ is the Deathly One, He is Death incarnate.

And the driver of the pack-horses acknowledges this deathly. Christ as supreme Lord. The mountain peasant seems grounded upon fear, the fear of death, of physical death. Beyond this he knows nothing. His supreme sensation is in physical pain, and in its culmination. His great climax, his consummation, is death. Therefore he worships it, bows down before it, and is fascinated by it all the while. It is his fulfilment, death, and his approach to fulfilment is through physical pain.

And so these monuments to physical death are found everywhere in the valleys. By the same hand that carved the big Christ, a little further on, at the end of a bridge, was another crucifix, a small one. This Christ had a fair beard, and was thin, and his body was hanging almost lightly, whereas the other Christ was large and dark and handsome. But in this, as well as in the other, was the same neutral triumph of death, complete, negative death, so complete as to be abstract, beyond cynicism in its completeness of leaving off.

Everywhere is the same obsession with the fact of physical pain, accident, and sudden death. Wherever a misfortune has befallen a man, there is nailed up a little memorial of the event, in propitiation of the God of hurt and death. A man is standing up to his waist in water, drowning in full stream, his arms in the air. The little painting in its wooden frame is nailed to the tree, the spot is sacred to the accident. Again, another little crude picture fastened to a rock: a tree, falling on a man's leg, smashes it like a stalk, while the blood flies up. Always there is the strange ejaculation of anguish and fear, perpetuated in the little paintings nailed up in the place of the disaster.

This is the worship, then, the worship of death and the approaches to death, physical violence, and pain. There is something crude and sinister about it, almost like depravity, a form of reverting, turning back along the course of blood by which we have come.

Turning the ridge on the great road to the south, the imperial road to Rome, a decisive change takes place. The Christs have been taking on various different characters, all of them more or less realistically conveyed. One Christus is very elegant, combed and brushed and foppish on his cross, as Gabriele D'Annunzio's son posing as a martyred saint. The martyrdom of this Christ is according to the most polite convention. The elegance is very important, and very Austrian. One might almost imagine the young man had taken up this striking and original position to create a delightful sensation among the ladies. It is quite in the Viennese spirit. There is something brave and keen in it, too. The individual pride of body triumphs over every difficulty in the situation. The pride and satisfaction in the clean, elegant form, the perfectly trimmed hair, the exquisite bearing, are more important than the fact of death or pain. This may be foolish, it is at the same time admirable.

But the tendency of the crucifix, as it nears the ridge to the south, is to become weak and sentimental. The carved Christs turn up their faces and roll back their eyes very piteously, in the approved Guido Reni fashion. They are overdoing the pathetic turn. They are looking to heaven and thinking about themselves, in self-commiseration. Others again are beautiful as elegies. It is dead Hyacinth lifted and extended to view, in all his beautiful, dead youth. The young, male body droops forward on the cross, like a dead flower. It looks as if its only true nature were to be dead. How lovely is death, how poignant, real, and satisfying! It is the true elegiac spirit.

5

Then there are the ordinary, factory-made Christs, which are not very significant. They are as null as the Christs we see represented in England, just vulgar nothingness. But these figures have gashes of red, a red paint of blood, which is sensational.

Beyond the Brenner, I have only seen vulgar or sensational crucifixes. There are great gashes on the breast and the knees of the Christ-figure, and the scarlet flows out and trickles down, till the crucified body has become a ghastly striped thing of red and white, just a sickly thing of striped red.

They paint the rocks at the corner of the tracks, among the mountains; a blue and white ring for the road to Ginzling, a red smear for the way to St. Jakob. So one follows the blue and white ring, or the three stripes of blue and white, or the red smear, as the case may be. And the red on the rocks, the dabs of red paint, are of just the same colour as the red upon the crucifixes; so that the red upon the crucifixes is paint, and the signs on the rocks are sensational, like blood.

I remember the little brooding Christ of the Isar, in his little cloak of red flannel and his crown of gilded thorns, and he remains real and dear to me, among all this violence of representation.

"Couvre-toi de gloire, Tartarin—couvre-toi de flanelle." Why should it please me so that his cloak is of red flannel?

In a valley near St. Jakob, just over the ridge, a long way from the railway, there is a very big, important shrine by the roadside. It is a chapel built in the baroque manner, florid pink and cream outside, with opulent small arches. And inside is the most startlingly sensational Christus I have ever seen. He is a big, powerful man, seated after the crucifixion, perhaps after the resurrection, sitting by the grave. He sits sideways, as if the extremity were over, finished, the agitation done with, only the result of the experience remaining. There is some blood on his powerful, naked, defeated body, that sits rather hulked. But it is the face which is so terrifying. It is slightly turned over the hulked, crucified shoulder, to look. And the look of this face, of which the body has been killed, is beyond all expectation horrible. The eyes look at one, yet have no seeing in them, they seem to see only their own blood. For they are bloodshot till the whites are scarlet, the iris is purpled. These red, bloody eyes with their stained pupils, glancing awfully at all who enter the shrine, looking as if to see through the blood of the late brutal death, are terrible. The naked, strong body has known death, and sits in utter dejection, finished, hulked, a weight of shame. And what remains of life is in the face, whose expression is sinister and gruesome, like that of an unrelenting criminal violated by torture. The criminal look of misery and hatred on the fixed, violated face and in the bloodshot eyes is almost impossible. He is conquered, beaten, broken, his body is a mass of torture, an unthinkable shame. Yet his will remains obstinate and ugly, integral with utter hatred.

It is a great shock to find this figure sitting in a handsome, baroque, pink-washed shrine in one of those Alpine valleys which to our thinking are all flowers and romance, like the picture in the Tate Gallery. 'Spring in the Austrian Tyrol' is to our minds a vision of pristine loveliness. It contains also this Christ of the heavy body defiled by torture and death, the strong, virile life overcome by physical violence, the eyes still looking back bloodshot in consummate hate and misery.

The shrine was well kept and evidently much used. It was hung with ex-voto limbs and with many gifts. It was a centre of worship, of a sort of almost obscene worship. Afterwards the black pine trees and the river of that valley seemed unclean, as if an unclean spirit lived there. The very flowers seemed unnatural, and the white gleam on the mountain-tops was a glisten of supreme, cynical horror.

After this, in the populous valleys, all the crucifixes were more or less tainted and vulgar. Only high up, where the crucifix becomes smaller and smaller, is there left any of the old beauty and religion. Higher and higher, the monument becomes smaller and smaller, till in the snows it stands out like a post, or a thick arrow stuck barb upwards. The crucifix itself is a small thing under the pointed hood, the barb of the arrow. The snow blows under the tiny shed, upon the little, exposed Christ. All round is the solid whiteness of snow, the awful curves and concaves of pure whiteness of the mountain top, the hollow whiteness between the peaks, where the path crosses the high, extreme ridge of the pass. And here stands the last crucifix, half buried, small and tufted with snow. The guides tramp slowly, heavily past, not observing the presence of the symbol, making no salute. Further down, every mountain peasant lifted his hat. But the guide tramps by without concern. His is a professional importance now.

On a small mountain track on the Jaufen, not far from Meran, was a fallen Christus. I was hurrying downhill to escape from an icy wind which almost took away my consciousness, and I was looking up at the gleaming, unchanging snow-peaks all round. They seemed like blades immortal in the sky. So I almost ran into a very old. Martertafel. It leaned on the cold, stony hillside surrounded by the white peaks in the upper air.

The wooden hood was silver-grey with age, and covered, on the top, with a thicket of lichen, which stuck up in hoary tufts. But on the rock at the foot of the post was the fallen Christ, armless, who had tumbled down and lay in an unnatural posture, the naked, ancient wooden sculpture of the body on the naked, living rock. It was one of the old uncouth, Christs hewn out of bare wood, having the long, wedge-shaped limbs and thin flat legs that are significant of the true spirit, the desire to convey a religious truth, not a sensational experience.

The arms of the fallen Christ had broken off at the shoulders, and they hung on their nails, as ex-voto limbs hang in the shrines. But these arms dangled from the palms, one at each end of the cross, the muscles, carved sparely in the old wood, looking all wrong, upside down. And the icy wind blew them backwards and forwards, so that they gave a painful impression, there in the stark, sterile place of rock and cold. Yet I dared not touch the fallen body of the Christ, that lay on its back in so grotesque a posture at the foot of the post. I wondered who would come and take the broken thing away, and for what purpose.

ON THE LARGO DI GARDA

I

THE SPINNER AND THE MONKS

THE Holy Spirit is a Dove, or an Eagle. In the Old Testament it was an Eagle; in the New Testament it is a Dove.

And there are, standing over the Christian world, the Churches of the Dove and the Churches of the Eagle. There are, moreover, the Churches which do not belong to the Holy Spirit at all, but which are built to pure fancy and logic; such as the Wren Churches in London.

The Churches of the Dove are shy and hidden: they nestle among trees, and their bells sound in the mellowness of Sunday; or they are gathered into a silence of their own in the very midst of the town, so that one passes them by without observing them; they are as if invisible, offering no resistance to the storming of the traffic.

But the Churches of the Eagle stand high, with their heads to the skies, as if they challenged the world below. They are the Churches of the Spirit of David, and their bells ring passionately, imperiously, falling on the subservient world below.

The Church of San Francesco was a Church of the Dove. I passed it several times, in the dark, silent little square, without knowing it was a church. Its pink walls were blind, windowless, unnoticeable, it gave no sign, unless one caught sight of the tan curtain hanging in the door, and the slit of darkness beneath. Yet it was the chief church of the village.

But the Church of San Tommaso perched over the village. Coming down the cobbled, submerged street, many a time I looked up between the houses and saw the thin old church standing above in the light, as if it perched on the house-roofs. Its thin grey neck was held up stiffly, beyond was a vision of dark foliage, and the high hillside.

I saw it often, and yet for a long time it never occurred to me that it actually existed. It was like a vision, a thing one does not expect to come close to. It was there standing away upon the house-tops, against a glamour of foliaged hillside. I was submerged in the village, on the uneven, cobbled street, between old high walls and cavernous shops and the houses with flights of steps.

For a long time I knew how the day went, by the imperious clangour of midday and evening bells striking down upon the houses and the edge of the lake. Yet it did not occur to me to ask where these bells rang. Till at last my everyday trance was broken in upon, and I knew the ringing of the Church of San Tommaso. The church became a living connection with me.

So I set out to find it, I wanted to go to it. It was very near. I could see it from the piazza by the lake. And the village itself had only a few hundreds of inhabitants. The church must be within a stone's-throw.

Yet I could not find it. I went out of the back door of the house, into the narrow gully of the back street. Women glanced down at me from the top of the flights of steps, old men stood, half-turning, half-crouching under the dark shadow of the walls, to stare. It was as if the strange creatures of the under-shadow were looking at me. I was of another element.

The Italian people are called 'Children of the Sun'. They might better be called 'Children of the Shadow'. Their souls are dark and nocturnal. If they are to be easy, they must be able to hide, to be hidden in lairs and caves of darkness. Going through these tiny chaotic back-ways of the village was like venturing through the labyrinth made by furtive creatures, who watched from out of another element. And I was pale, and clear, and evanescent, like the light, and they were dark, and close, and constant, like the shadow.

So I was quite baffled by the tortuous, tiny, deep passages of the village. I could not find my way. I hurried towards the broken end of a street, where the sunshine and the olive trees looked like a mirage before me. And there above me I saw the thin, stiff neck of old San Tommaso, grey and pale in the sun. Yet I could not get up to the church, I found myself again on the piazza.

Another day, however, I found a broken staircase, where weeds grew in the gaps the steps had made in falling, and maidenhair hung on the darker side of the wall. I went up unwillingly, because the Italians used this old staircase as a privy, as they will any deep side-passage.

But I ran up the broken stairway, and came out suddenly, as by a miracle, clean on the platform of my San Tommaso, in the tremendous sunshine.

It was another world, the world of the eagle, the world of fierce abstraction. It was all clear, overwhelming sunshine, a platform hung in the light. Just below were the confused, tiled roofs of the village, and beyond them the pale blue water, down below; and opposite, opposite my face and breast, the clear, luminous snow of the mountain across the lake, level with me apparently, though really much above.

I was in the skies now, looking down from my square terrace of cobbled pavement, that was worn like the threshold of the ancient church. Round the terrace ran a low, broad wall, the coping of the upper heaven where I had climbed.

There was a blood-red sail like a butterfly breathing down on the blue water, whilst the earth on the near side gave off a green-silver smoke of olive trees, coming up and around the earth-coloured roofs.

It always remains to me that San Tommaso and its terrace hang suspended above the village, like the lowest step of heaven, of Jacob's ladder. Behind, the land rises in a high sweep. But the terrace of San Tommaso is let down from heaven, and does not touch the earth.

I went into the church. It was very dark, and impregnated with centuries of incense. It affected me like the lair of some enormous creature. My senses were roused, they sprang awake in the hot, spiced darkness. My skin was expectant, as if it expected some contact, some embrace, as if it were aware of the contiguity of the physical world, the physical contact with the darkness and the heavy, suggestive substance of the enclosure. It was a thick, fierce darkness of the senses. But my soul shrank.

I went out again. The pavemented threshold was clear as a jewel, the marvellous clarity of sunshine that becomes blue in the height seemed to distil me into itself.

Across, the heavy mountain crouched, along the side of the lake, the upper half brilliantly white, belonging to the sky, the lower half dark and grim. So, then, that is where heaven and earth are divided. From behind me, on the left, the headland swept down out of a great, pale-grey, arid height, through a rush of russet and crimson, to the olive smoke and the water of the level earth. And between, like a blade of the sky cleaving the earth asunder, went the pale-blue lake, cleaving mountain from mountain with the triumph of the sky.

Then I noticed that a big, blue-checked cloth was spread on the parapet before me, over the parapet of heaven. I wondered why it hung there.

Turning round, on the other side of the terrace, under a caper-bush that hung like a blood-stain from the grey wall above her, stood a little grey woman whose fingers were busy. Like the grey church, she made me feel as if I were not in existence. I was wandering by the parapet of heaven, looking down. But she stood back against the solid wall, under the caper-bush, unobserved and unobserving. She was like a fragment of earth, she was a living stone of the terrace, sun-bleached. She took no notice of me, who was hesitating looking down at the earth beneath. She stood back under the sun-bleached solid wall, like a stone rolled down and stayed in a crevice.

Her head was tied in a dark-red kerchief, but pieces of hair, like dirty snow, quite short, stuck out over her ears. And she was spinning. I wondered so much, that I could not cross towards her. She was grey, and her apron, and her dress, and her kerchief, and her hands and her face were all sun-bleached and sun-stained, greyey, bluey, browny, like stones and half-coloured leaves, sunny in their colourlessness. In my black coat, I felt myself wrong, false, an outsider.

She was spinning, spontaneously, like a little wind. Under her arm she held a distaff of dark, ripe wood, just a straight stick with a clutch at the end, like a grasp of brown fingers full of a fluff of blackish, rusty fleece, held up near her shoulder. And her fingers were plucking spontaneously at the strands of wool drawn down from it. And hanging near her fret, spinning round upon a black thread, spinning busily, like a thing in a gay wind, was her shuttle, her bobbin wound fat with the coarse, blackish worsted she was making.

All the time, like motion without thought, her fingers teased out the fleece, thawing it down to a fairly uniform thickness: brown, old, natural fingers that worked as in a sleep, the thumb having a long grey nail; and from moment to moment there was a quick, downward rub, between thumb and forefinger, of the thread that hung in front of her apron, the heavy bobbin spun more briskly, and she felt again at the fleece as she drew it down, and she gave a twist to the thread that issued, and the bobbin spun swiftly.

Her eyes were clear as the sky, blue, empyrean, transcendent. They were clear, but they had no looking in them. Her face was like a sun-worn stone.

"You are spinning," I said to her.

Her eyes glanced over me, making no effort of attention.

"Yes," she said.

She saw merely a man's figure, a stranger, standing near. I was a bit of the outside, negligible. She remained as she was, dear and sustained like an old stone upon the hillside. She stood short and sturdy, looking for the most part straight in front, unseeing, but glancing from time to time, with a little, unconscious attention, at the thread. She was slightly more animated than the sunshine and the stone and the motionless caper-bush above her. Still her fingers went along the strand of fleece near her breast.

"That is an old way of spinning," I said.

"What?"

She looked up at me with eyes clear and transcendent as the heavens. But she was slightly roused. There was the slight motion of the eagle in her turning to look at me, a faint gleam of rapt light in her eyes. It was my unaccustomed Italian.

"That is an old way of spinning," I repeated.

"Yes—an old way," she repeated, as if to say the words so that they should be natural to her. And I became to her merely a transient circumstance, a man, part of the surroundings. We divided the gift of speech, that was all.

She glanced at me again, with her wonderful, unchanging eyes, that were like the visible heavens, unthinking, or like two flowers that are open in pure clear unconsciousness. To her I was a piece of the environment. That was all. Her world was clear and absolute, without consciousness of self. She was not self-conscious, because she was not aware that there was anything in the universe except *her* universe. In her universe I was a stranger, a foreign *signore*. That I had a world of my own, other than her own, was not conceived by her. She did not care.

So we conceive the stars. We are told that they are other worlds. But the stars are the clustered and single gleaming lights in the night-sky of our world. When I come home at night, there are the stars. When I cease to exist as the microcosm, when I begin to think of the cosmos, then the stars are other worlds. Then the macrocosm absorbs me. But the macrocosm is not me. It is something which I, the microcosm, am not.

So that there is something which is unknown to me and which nevertheless exists. I am finite, and my understanding has limits. The universe is bigger than I shall ever see, in mind or spirit. There is that which is not me.

If I say "The planet Mars is inhabited," I do not know what I mean by "inhabited," with reference to the planet Mars. I can only mean that that world is not my world. I can only know there is that which is not me. I am the microcosm, but the macrocosm is that also which I am not.

The old woman on the terrace in the sun did not know this. She was herself the core and centre to the world, the sun, and the single firmament. She knew that I was an inhabitant of lands which she had never seen. But what of that! There were parts of her own body which she had never seen, which physiologically she could never see. They were none the less her own because she had never seen them. The lands she had not seen were corporate parts of her own living body, the knowledge she had not attained was only the hidden knowledge of her own self. She *was* the substance of the knowledge, whether she had the knowledge in her mind or not. There was nothing which was not herself, ultimately. Even the man, the male, was part of herself. He was the mobile, separate part, but he was none the less herself because he was sometimes severed from her. If every apple in the world were cut in two, the apple would not be changed. The reality is the apple, which is just the same in the half-apple as in the whole.

And she, the old spinning-woman, was the apple, eternal, unchangeable, whole even in her partiality. It was this which gave the wonderful clear unconsciousness to her eyes. How could she be conscious of herself when all was herself?

She was talking to me of a sheep that had died, but I could not understand because of her dialect. It never occurred to her that I could not understand. She only thought me different, stupid. And she talked on. The ewes had lived under the house, and a part was divided off for the he-goat, because the other people brought their she-goats to be covered by the he-goat. But how the ewe came to die I could not make out.

Her fingers worked away all the time in a little, half-fretful movement, yet spontaneous as butterflies leaping here and there. She chattered rapidly on in her Italian that I could not understand, looking meanwhile into my face, because the story aroused her somewhat. Yet not a feature moved. Her eyes remained candid and open and unconscious as the skies. Only a sharp will in them now and then seemed to gleam at me, as if to dominate me.

Her shuttle had caught in a dead chicory plant, and spun no more. She did not notice. I stooped and broke off the twigs. There was a glint of blue on them yet. Seeing what I was doing, she merely withdrew a few inches from the plant. Her bobbin hung free.

She went on with her tale, looking at me wonderfully. She seemed like the Creation, like the beginning of the world, the first morning. Her eyes were like the first morning of the world, so ageless.

Her thread broke. She seemed to take no notice, but mechanically picked up the shuttle, wound up a length of worsted, connected the ends from her wool strand, set the bobbin spinning again, and went on talking, in her half-intimate, half-unconscious fashion, as if she were talking to her own world in me.

So she stood in the sunshine on the little platform, old and yet like the morning, erect and solitary, sun-coloured, sun-discoloured, whilst I at her elbow, like a piece of night and moonshine, stood smiling into her eyes, afraid lest she should deny me existence.

Which she did. She had stopped talking, did not look at me any more, but went on with her spinning, the brown shuttle twisting gaily. So she stood, belonging to the sunshine and the weather, taking no more notice of me than of the dark-stained caper-bush which hung from the wall above her head, whilst I, waiting at her side, was like the moon in the daytime sky, overshone, obliterated, in spite of my black clothes.

11

"How long has it taken you to do that much?" I asked.

She waited a minute, glanced at her bobbin.

"This much? I don't know. A day or two."

"But you do it quickly."

She looked at me, as if suspiciously and derisively. Then, quite suddenly, she started forward and went across the terrace to the great blue-and-white checked cloth that was drying on the wall. I hesitated. She had cut off her consciousness from me. So I turned and ran away, taking the steps two at a time, to get away from her. In a moment I was between the walls, climbing upwards, hidden.

The school-mistress had told me I should find snowdrops behind San Tommaso. If she had not asserted such confident knowledge I should have doubted her translation of *perce-neige*. She meant Christmas roses all the while.

However, I went looking for snowdrops. The walls broke down suddenly, and I was out in a grassy olive orchard, following a track beside pieces of fallen overgrown masonry. So I came to skirt the brink of a steep little gorge, at the bottom of which a stream was rushing down its steep slant to the lake. Here I stood to look for my snowdrops. The grassy, rocky bank went down steep from my feet. I heard water tittle-tattling away in deep shadow below. There were pale flecks in the dimness, but these, I knew, were primroses. So I scrambled down.

Looking up, out of the heavy shadow that lay in the cleft, I could see, right in the sky, grey rocks shining transcendent in the pure empyrean. "Are they so far up?" I thought. I did not dare to say, "Am I so far down?" But I was uneasy.

Nevertheless it was a lovely place, in the cold shadow, complete; when one forgot the shining rocks far above, it was a complete, shadowless world of shadow. Primroses were everywhere in nests of pale bloom upon the dark, steep face of the cleft, and tongues of fern hanging out, and here and there under the rods and twigs of bushes were tufts of wrecked Christmas roses, nearly over, but still, in the coldest corners, the lovely buds like handfuls of snow. There had been such crowded sumptuous tufts of Christmas roses everywhere in the stream-gullies, during the shadow of winter, that these few remaining flowers were hardly noticeable.

I gathered instead the primroses, that smelled of earth and of the weather. There were no snowdrops. I had found the day before a bank of crocuses, pale, fragile, lilac-coloured flowers with dark veins, pricking up keenly like myriad little lilac-coloured flames among the grass, under the olive trees. And I wanted very much to find the snowdrops hanging in the gloom. But there were not any.

I gathered a handful of primroses, then I climbed suddenly, quickly out of the deep watercourse, anxious to get back to the sunshine before the evening fell. Up above I saw the olive trees in their sunny golden grass, and sunlit grey rocks immensely high up. I was afraid lest the evening would fall while I was groping about like an otter in the damp and the darkness, that the day of sunshine would be over.

Soon I was up in the sunshine again, on the turf under the olive trees, reassured. It was the upper world of glowing light, and I was safe again.

All the olives were gathered, and the mills were going night and day, making a great, acrid scent of olive oil in preparation, by the lake. The little stream rattled down. A mule driver "Hued!" to his mules on the Strada Vecchia. High up, on the Strada Nuova, the beautiful, new, military high-road, which winds with beautiful curves up the mountain-side, crossing the same stream several times in clear-leaping bridges, travelling cut out of sheer slope high above the lake, winding beautifully and gracefully forward to the Austrian frontier, where it ends: high up on the lovely swinging road, in the strong evening sunshine, I saw a bullock wagon moving like a vision, though the clanking of the wagon and the crack of the bullock whip resounded close in my ears.

Everything was clear and sun-coloured up there, clear-grey rocks partaking of the sky, tawny grass and scrub, browny-green spires of cypresses, and then the mist of grey-green olives fuming down to the lake-side. There was no shadow, only clear sun-substance built up to the sky, a bullock wagon moving slowly in the high sunlight, along the uppermost terrace of the military road. It sat in the warm stillness of the transcendent afternoon.

The four o'clock steamer was creeping down the lake from the Austrian end, creeping under the cliffs. Far away, the Verona side, beyond the Island, lay fused in dim gold. The mountain opposite was so still, that my heart seemed to fade in its beating, as if it too would be still. All was perfectly still, pure substance. The little steamer on the floor of the world below, the mules down the road cast no shadow. They too were pure sun-substance travelling on the surface of the sun-made world.

A cricket hopped near me. Then I remembered that it was Saturday afternoon, when a strange suspension comes over the world. And then, just below me, I saw two monks walking in their garden between the naked, bony vines, walking in their wintry garden of bony vines and olive trees, their brown cassocks passing between the brown vine-stocks, their heads bare to the sunshine, sometimes a glint of light as their feet strode from under their skirts.

It was so still, everything so perfectly suspended, that I felt them talking. They marched with the peculiar march of monks, a long, loping stride, their heads together, their skirts swaying slowly, two brown monks with hidden hands, sliding under the bony vines and beside the cabbages, their heads always together in hidden converse. It was as if I were attending with my dark soul to their inaudible undertone. All the time I sat still in silence, I was one with them, a partaker, though I could hear no sound of their voices. I went with the long stride of their skirted feet, that slid springless and noiseless from end to end of the garden, and back again. Their hands were kept down at their sides, hidden in the long sleeves and the skirts of their robes. They did not touch each other, nor gesticulate as they walked. There was no motion save the long, furtive stride and the heads leaning together. Yet there was an eagerness in their conversation. Almost like shadow-creatures ventured out of their cold, obscure element, they went backwards and forwards in their wintry garden, thinking nobody could see them.

Across, above them, was the faint, rousing dazzle of snow. They never looked up. But the dazzle of snow began to glow as they walked, the wonderful faint, ethereal flush of the long range of snow in the heavens, at evening, began to kindle. Another world was coming to pass, the cold, rare night. It was dawning in exquisite, icy rose upon the long mountain-summit opposite. The monks walked backwards and forwards, talking, in the first undershadow.

And I noticed that up above the snow, frail in the bluish sky, a frail moon had put forth, like a thin, scalloped film of ice floated on the slow current of the coming night. And a bell sounded.

And still the monks were pacing backwards and forwards, backwards and forwards, with a strange, neutral regularity.

The shadows were coming across everything, because of the mountains in the west. Already the olive wood where I sat was extinguished. This was the world of the

13

monks, the rim of pallor between night and day. Here they paced, backwards and forwards, backwards and forwards, in the neutral, shadowless light of shadow.

Neither the flare of day nor the completeness of night reached them, they paced the narrow path of the twilight, treading in the neutrality of the law. Neither the blood nor the spirit spoke in them, only the law, the abstraction of the average. The infinite is positive and negative. But the average is only neutral. And the monks trod backward and forward down the line of neutrality.

Meanwhile, on the length of mountain-ridge, the snow grew rosy-incandescent, like heaven breaking into blossom. After all, eternal not-being and eternal being are the same. In the rosy snow that shone in heaven over a darkened earth was the ecstasy of consummation. Night and day are one, light and dark are one, both the same in the origin and in the issue, both the same in the moment of ecstasy, light fused in darkness and darkness fused in light, as in the rosy snow above the twilight.

But in the monks it was not ecstasy, in them it was neutrality, the under earth. Transcendent, above the shadowed, twilit earth was the rosy snow of ecstasy. But spreading far over *us,* down below, was the neutrality of the twilight, of the monks. The flesh neutralising the spirit, the spirit neutralising the flesh, the law of the average asserted, this was the monks as they paced backward and forward.

The moon climbed higher, away from the snowy, fading ridge, she became gradually herself. Between the roots of the olive tree was a rosy-tipped daisy just going to sleep. I gathered it and put it among the frail, moony little bunch of primroses, so that its sleep should warm the rest. Also I put in some little periwinkles, that were very blue, reminding me of the eyes of the old woman.

The day was gone, the twilight was gone, and the snow was invisible as I came down to the side of the lake. Only the moon, white and shining, was in the sky, like a woman glorying in her own loveliness as she loiters superbly to the gaze of all the world, looking sometimes through the fringe of dark olive leaves, sometimes looking at her own superb, quivering body, wholly naked in the water of the lake.

My little old woman was gone. She, all day-sunshine, would have none of the moon. Always she must live like a bird, looking down on all the world at once, so that it lay all subsidiary to herself, herself the wakeful consciousness hovering over the world like a hawk, like a sleep of wakefulness. And, like a bird, she went to sleep as the shadows came.

She did not know the yielding up of the senses and the possession of the unknown, through the senses, which happens under a superb moon. The all-glorious sun knows none of these yieldings up. He takes his way. And the daisies at once go to sleep. And the soul of the old spinning-woman also closed up at sunset, the rest was a sleep, a cessation.

It is all so strange and varied: the dark-skinned Italians ecstatic in the night and the moon, the blue-eyed old woman ecstatic in the busy sunshine, the monks in the garden below, who are supposed to unite both, passing only in the neutrality of the average. Where, then, is the meeting-point: where in mankind is the ecstasy of light and dark together, the supreme transcendence of the afterglow, day hovering in the embrace of the coming night like two angels embracing in the heavens, like Eurydice in the arms of Orpheus, or Persephone embraced by Pluto?

Where is the supreme ecstasy in mankind, which makes day a delight and night a delight, purpose an ecstasy and a concourse in ecstasy, and single abandon of the single body and soul also an ecstasy under the moon? Where is the transcendent knowledge in our hearts, uniting sun and darkness, day and night, spirit and senses? Why do we not know that the two in consummation are one; that each is only part; partial and alone for ever; but that the two in consummation are perfect, beyond the range of loneliness or solitude?

II

THE LEMON GARDENS

THE padrone came just as we were drinking coffee after dinner. It was two o'clock, because the steamer going down the lake to Desenzano had bustled through the sunshine, and the rocking water still made lights that danced up and down upon the wall among the shadows by the piano.

The signore was very apologetic. I found him bowing in the hall, cap in one hand, a slip of paper in the other, protesting eagerly, in broken French, against disturbing me.

He is a little, shrivelled man, with close-cropped grey hair on his skull, and a protruding jaw, which, with his gesticulations, always makes me think of an ancient, aristocratic monkey. The signore is a gentleman, and the last, shrivelled representative of his race. His only outstanding quality, according to the villagers, is his avarice.

"Mais—mais, monsieur—je crains que—que——que je vous dérange—"

He spreads wide his hands and bows, looking up at me with implicit brown eyes, so ageless in his wrinkled, monkey's face, like onyx. He loves to speak French, because then he feels grand. He has a queer, naïve, ancient passion to be grand. As the remains of an impoverished family, he is not much better than a well-to-do peasant. But the old spirit is eager and pathetic in him.

He loves to speak French to me. He holds his chin and waits, in his anxiety for the phrase to come. Then it stammers forth, a little rush, ending in Italian. But his pride is all on edge: we must continue in French.

The hall is cold, yet he will not come into the large room. This is not a courtesy visit. He is not here in his quality of gentleman. He is only an anxious villager.

"Voyez, monsieur—cet——cet——qu'est-ce que—qu'est-ce que veut dire cet—cela?"

He shows me the paper. It is an old scrap of print, the picture of an American patent door-spring, with directions: "Fasten the spring either end up. Wind it up. Never unwind."

It is laconic and American. The signore watches me anxiously, waiting, holding his chin. He is afraid he ought to understand my English. I stutter off into French, confounded by the laconic phrases of the directions. Nevertheless, I make it clear what the paper says.

He cannot believe me. It must say something else as well. He has not done anything contrary to these directions. He is most distressed.

"Mais, monsieur, la porte—la porte—elle ferme *pas*—elle s'ouvre—"

He skipped to the door and showed me the whole tragic mystery. The door, it is shut—ecco! He releases the catch, and pouf!—she flies open. She flies *open*. It is quite final.

The brown, expressionless, ageless eyes, that remind me of a monkey's or of onyx, wait for me. I feel the responsibility devolve upon me. I am anxious.

"Allow me," I said, "to come and look at the door."

I feel uncomfortably like Sherlock Holmes. The padrone protests—non, monsieur, non, cela vous dérange—that he only wanted me to translate the words, he does not want to disturb me. Nevertheless we go. I feel I have the honour of mechanical England in my hands.

The Casa di Paoli is quite a splendid place. It is large, pink and cream, rising up to a square tower in the centre, throwing off a painted loggia at either extreme of the façade. It stands a little way back from the road, just above the lake, and grass grows on the bay of cobbled pavement in front. When at night the moon shines full on this pale façade, the theatre is far outdone in staginess.

The hall is spacious and beautiful, with great glass doors at either end, through which shine the courtyards where bamboos fray the sunlight and geraniums glare red. The floor is of soft red tiles, oiled and polished like glass, the walls are washed grey-white, the ceiling is painted with pink roses and birds. This is half-way between the outer world and the interior world, it partakes of both.

The other rooms are dark and ugly. There is no mistake about their being interior. They are like furnished vaults. The red-tiled, polished floor in the drawing-room seems cold and clammy, the carved, cold furniture stands in its tomb, the air has been darkened and starved to death, it is perished.

Outside, the sunshine runs like birds singing. Up above, the grey rocks build the sun-substance in heaven, San Tommaso guards the terrace. But inside here is the immemorial shadow.

Again I had to think of the Italian soul, how it is dark, cleaving to the eternal night. It seems to have become so, at the Renaissance, after the Renaissance.

In the middle Ages Christian Europe seems to have been striving, out of a strong, primitive, animal nature, towards the self-abnegation and the abstraction of Christ. This brought about by itself a great sense of completeness. The two halves were joined by the effort towards the one as yet unrealised. There was a triumphant joy in the Whole.

But the movement all the time was in one direction, towards the elimination of the flesh. Man wanted more and more to become purely free and abstract. Pure freedom was in pure abstraction. The Word was absolute. When man became as the Word, a pure law, then he was free.

But when this conclusion was reached, the movement broke. Already Botticelli painted Aphrodite, queen of the senses, supreme along with Mary, Queen of Heaven. And Michael Angelo suddenly turned back on the whole Christian movement, back to the flesh. The flesh was supreme and god-like, in the oneness of the flesh, in the oneness of our physical being, we are one with God, with the Father. God the Father created man in the flesh, in His own image. Michael Angelo swung right back to the old Mosaic position. Christ did not exist. To Michael Angelo there was no salvation in the spirit. There was God the Father, the Begetter, the Author of all flesh. And there was the inexorable law of the flesh, the Last Judgment, the fall of the immortal flesh into Hell.

This has been the Italian position ever since. The mind, that is the Light; the senses, they are the Darkness. Aphrodite, the queen of the senses, she, born of the sea-foam, is the luminousness of the gleaming senses, the phosphorescence of the sea, the senses become a conscious aim unto themselves; she is the gleaming darkness, she is the luminous night, she is goddess of destruction, her white, cold fire consumes and does not create.

This is the soul of the Italian since the Renaissance. In the sunshine he basks asleep, gathering up a vintage into his veins which in the night-time he will distil into ecstatic sensual delight, the intense, white-cold ecstasy of darkness and moonlight, the

16

raucous, cat-like, destructive enjoyment, the senses conscious and crying out in their consciousness in the pangs of the enjoyment, which has consumed the southern nation, perhaps all the Latin races, since the Renaissance.

It is a lapse back, back to the original position, the Mosaic position of the divinity of the flesh, and the absoluteness of its laws. But also there is the Aphrodite-worship. The flesh, the senses, are now self-conscious. They know their aim. Their aim is in supreme sensation. They seek the maximum of sensation. They seek the reduction of the flesh, the flesh reacting upon itself, to a crisis, an ecstasy, a phosphorescent transfiguration in ecstasy.

The mind, all the time, subserves the senses. As in a cat, there is subtlety and beauty and the dignity of the darkness. But the fire is cold, as in the eyes of a cat, it is a green fire. It is fluid, electric. At its maximum it is the white ecstasy of phosphorescence, in the darkness, always amid the darkness, as under the black fur of a cat. Like the feline fire, it is destructive, always consuming and reducing to the ecstasy of sensation, which is the end in itself.

There is the I, always the I. And the mind is submerged, overcome. But the senses are superbly arrogant. The senses are the absolute, the god-like. For I can never have another man's senses. These are me, my senses absolutely me. And all that is can only come to me through my senses. So that all is me, and is administered unto me. The rest, that is not me, is nothing, it is something which is nothing. So the Italian, through centuries, has avoided our Northern purposive industry, because it has seemed to him a form of nothingness.

It is the spirit of the tiger. The tiger is the supreme manifestation of the senses made absolute. This is the

> "Tiger, tiger, burning bright,
> In the forests of the night"

of Blake. It does indeed burn within the darkness. But the *essential* fire of the tiger is cold and white, a white ecstasy. It is seen in the white eyes of the blazing cat. This is the supremacy of the flesh, which devours all, and becomes transfigured into a magnificent brindled flame, a burning bush indeed.

This is one way of transfiguration into the eternal flame, the transfiguration through ecstasy in the flesh. Like the tiger in the night, I devour all flesh, I drink all blood, until this fuel blazes up in me to the consummate fire of the Infinite. In the ecstasy I am Infinite, I become again the great Whole, I am a flame of the One White Flame which is the Infinite, the Eternal, the Originator, the Creator, the Everlasting God. in the sensual ecstasy, having drunk all blood and devoured all flesh, I am become again the eternal Fire, I am infinite.

This is the way of the tiger; the tiger is supreme. His head is flattened as if there were some great weight on the hard skull, pressing, pressing, pressing the mind into a stone, pressing it down under the blood, to serve the blood. It is the subjugate instrument of the blood. The will lies above the loins, as it were at the base of the spinal column, there is the living will, the living mind of the tiger, there in the slender loins. That is the node, there in the spinal cord.

So the Italian, so the soldier. This is the spirit of the soldier. He, too, walks with his consciousness concentrated at the base of the spine, his mind subjugated, submerged. The will of the soldier is the will of the great cats, the will to ecstasy in destruction, in absorbing life into his own life, always his own life supreme, till the ecstasy burst into the white, eternal flame, the infinite, the Flame of the Infinite. Then he is satisfied, he has been consummated in the Infinite.

This is the true soldier, this is the immortal climax of the senses. This is the acme of the flesh, the one superb tiger who has devoured all living flesh, and now paces backwards and forwards in the cage of its own infinite, glaring with blind, fierce, absorbed eyes at that which is nothingness to it.

The eyes of the tiger cannot see, except with the light from within itself, by the light of its own desire. Its own white, cold light is so fierce that the other warm light of day is outshone, it is not, it does not exist. So the white eyes of the tiger gleam to a point of concentrated vision, upon that which does not exist. Hence its terrifying sightlessness. The something which I know I am is hollow space to its vision, offers no resistance to the tiger's looking. It can only see of me that which it knows I am, a scent, a resistance, a voluptuous solid, a struggling warm violence that it holds overcome, a running of hot blood between its jaws, a delicious pang of live flesh in the mouth. This it sees. The rest is not.

And what is the rest, that which is-not the tiger, that which the tiger is-not What is this?

What is that which parted ways with the terrific eagle-like angel of the senses at the Renaissance? The Italians said, "We are one in the Father: we will go back." The Northern races said, "We are one in Christ: we will go on."

What *is* the consummation in Christ? Man knows satisfaction when he surpasses all conditions and becomes, to himself, consummate in the Infinite, when he reaches a state of infinity. in the supreme ecstasy of the flesh, the Dionysic ecstasy, he reaches this state. But how does it come to pass in Christ?

It is not the mystic ecstasy. The mystic ecstasy is a special sensual ecstasy, it is the senses satisfying themselves with a self-created object. It is self-projection into the self, the sensuous self satisfied in a projected self.

"Blessed are the poor in spirit, for theirs is the kingdom of heaven."

"Blessed are they which are persecuted for righteousness' sake, for theirs is the kingdom of heaven."

The kingdom of heaven is this Infinite into which we may be consummated, then, if we are poor in spirit or persecuted for righteousness' sake.

"Whosoever shall smite thee on the right cheek, turn to him the other also."

"Love your enemies, bless them that curse you, do good to them that hate you, and pray for them which despitefully use you, and persecute you."

"Be ye therefore perfect, even as your Father which is in heaven is perfect."

To be perfect, to be one with God, to be infinite and eternal, what shall we do? We must turn the other cheek, and love our enemies.

Christ is the lamb which the eagle swoops down upon, the dove taken by the hawk, the deer which the tiger devours.

What then, if a man come to me with a sword, to kill me, and I do not resist him, but suffer his sword and the death from his sword, what am I? Am I greater than he, am I stronger than he? Do I know a consummation in the Infinite, I, the prey, beyond the tiger who devours me? By my non-resistance I have robbed him of his consummation. For a tiger knows no consummation unless he kill a violated and struggling prey. There is no consummation merely for the butcher, nor for a hyena. I can rob the tiger of his ecstasy, his consummation, his very *raison d'être,* by my non-resistance. In my non-resistance the tiger is infinitely destroyed.

But I, what am I? "Be ye therefore perfect." Wherein am I perfect in this submission? Is there an affirmation, behind my negation, other than the tiger's affirmation of his own glorious infinity?

What is the Oneness to which I subscribe, I who offer no resistance in the flesh?

Have I only the negative ecstasy of being devoured, of becoming thus part of the Lord, the Great Moloch, the superb and terrible God? I have this also, this subject ecstasy of consummation. But there is nothing else?

The Word of the tiger is: my senses are supremely Me, and my senses are God in me. But Christ said: God is in the others, who are not-me. In all the multitude of the others is God, and this is the great God, greater than the God which is Me. God is that which is Not-Me.

And this is the Christian truth, a truth complementary to the pagan affirmation: "God is that which is Me."

God is that which is Not-Me. In realising the Not-Me I am consummated, I become infinite. In turning the other cheek I submit to God who is greater than I am, other than I am, who is in that which is not me This is the supreme consummation. To achieve this consummation I love my neighbour as myself. My neighbour is all that is not me. And if I love all this, have I not become one with the Whole is not my consummation complete, am I not one with God, have I not achieved the Infinite?

After the Renaissance the Northern races continued forward, to put into practice this religious belief in the God which is Not-Me. Even the idea of the saving of the soul was really negative: it was a question of escaping damnation. The Puritans made the last great attack on the God who is Me. When they beheaded Charles the First, the king by Divine Right, they destroyed, symbolically, for ever the supremacy of the Me who am the image of God, the Me of the flesh, of the senses, Me, the tiger burning bright, me the king, the Lord, the aristocrat, me who am divine because I am the body of God.

After the Puritans, we have been gathering data for the God Who is not-me. When Pope said: "Know then thyself, presume not God to scan, The proper study of mankind is Man," he Was stating the proposition: A man is right, he is consummated, when he is seeking to know Man, the great abstract; and the method of knowledge is by the analysis, which is the destruction, of the Self. The proposition up to that time was, a man is the epitome of the universe. He has only to express himself, to fulfil his desires, to satisfy his supreme senses.

Now the change has come to pass. The individual man is a limited being, finite in himself. Yet he is capable of apprehending that which is not himself. "The proper study of mankind is Man." This is another way of saying, "Thou shalt love thy neighbour as thyself." Which means, a man is consummated in his knowledge of that which is not himself, the abstract Man. Therefore the consummation lies in seeking that other, in knowing that other. Whereas the Stuart proposition was: "A man is consummated in expressing his own Self."

The new spirit developed into the empirical and ideal systems of philosophy. Everything that is, is consciousness. And in every man's consciousness, Man is great and illimitable, whilst the individual is small and fragmentary. Therefore the individual must sink himself in the great whole of Mankind.

This is the spirituality of Shelley, the perfectibility of man. This is the way in which we fulfil the commandment, "Be ye therefore perfect, even as your Father which is in heaven is perfect". This is Saint Paul's, "Now I know in part; but then shall I know even as I am known".

When a man knows everything and understands everything, then he will be perfect, and life will be blessed. He is capable of knowing everything and understanding everything. Hence he is justified in his hope of infinite freedom and blessedness.

The great inspiration of the new religion was the inspiration of freedom. When I have submerged or distilled away my concrete body and my limited desires, when I am like the skylark dissolved in the sky yet filling heaven and earth with song, then I am perfect, consummated in the Infinite. When I am all that is not-me, then I have perfect liberty, I know no limitation. Only I must eliminate the Self.

It was this religious belief which expressed itself in science. Science was the analysis of the outer self, the elementary substance of the self, the outer world. And the machine is the great reconstructed selfless power. Hence the active worship to which we were given at the end of the last century, the worship of mechanised force.

Still we continue to worship that which is not-me, the Selfless world, though we would fain bring in the Self to help us. We are shouting the Shakespearean advice to warriors: "Then simulate the action of the tiger." We are trying to become again the tiger, the supreme, imperial, warlike Self. At the same time our ideal is the selfless world of equity.

We continue to give service to the Selfless God, we worship the great selfless oneness in the spirit, oneness in service of the great humanity, that which is Not-Me. This selfless God is He Who works for all alike, without consideration. And His image is the machine which dominates and cows us, we cower before it, we run to serve it. For it works for all humanity alike.

At the same time, we want to be warlike tigers. That is the horror: the confusing of the two ends. We warlike tigers fit ourselves out with machinery, and our blazing tiger wrath is emitted through a machine. It is a horrible thing to see machines hauled about by tigers, at the mercy of tigers, forced to express the tiger. It is a still more horrible thing to see tigers caught up and entangled and torn in machinery. It is horrible, a chaos beyond chaos, an unthinkable hell.

The tiger is not wrong, the machine is not wrong, but we, liars, lip-servers, duplicate fools, we are unforgivably wrong. We say: "I will be a tiger because I love mankind; out of love for other people, out of selfless service to that which is not me, I will even become a tiger." Which is absurd. A tiger devours because it is consummated in devouring, it achieves its absolute self in devouring. It does not devour because its unselfish conscience bids it do so, for the sake of the other deer and doves, or the other tigers.

Having arrived at the one extreme of mechanical selflessness, we immediately embrace the other extreme of the transcendent Self. But we try to be both at once. We do not cease to be the one before we become the other. We do not even play the rôles in turn. We want to be the tiger and the deer both in one. Which is just ghastly nothingness. We try to say, "The tiger is the lamb and the lamb is the tiger." Which is nil, nihil, nought.

The padrone took me into a small room almost contained in the thickness of the wall. There the Signora's dark eyes glared with surprise and agitation, seeing me intrude. She is younger than the Signore, a mere village tradesman's daughter, and, alas, childless.

It was quite true, the door stood open. Madame put down the screw-driver and drew herself erect. Her eyes were a flame of excitement. This question of a door-spring that made the door fly open when it should make it close roused a vivid spark in her soul. It was she who was wrestling with the angel of mechanism.

She was about forty years old, and flame-like and fierily sad. I think she did not know she was sad. But her heart was eaten by some impotence in her life.

She subdued her flame of life to the little padrone. He was strange and static, scarcely human, ageless, like a monkey. She supported him with her flame, supported his static, ancient, beautiful form, kept it intact. But she did not believe in him.

Now, the Signora Gemma held her husband together whilst he undid the screw that fixed the spring. If they had been alone, she would have done it, pretending to be under his direction. But since I was there, he did it himself; a grey, shaky, highly-bred little gentleman, standing on a chair with a long screw-driver, whilst his wife stood behind him, her hands half-raised to catch him if he should fall. Yet he was strangely absolute, with a strange, intact force in his breeding.

They had merely adjusted the strong spring to the shut door, and stretched it slightly in fastening it to the door-jamb, so that it drew together the moment the latch was released, and the door flew open.

We soon made it right. There was a moment of anxiety, the screw was fixed. And the door swung to. They were delighted. The Signora Gemma, who roused in me an electric kind of melancholy, clasped her hands together in ecstasy as the door swiftly shut itself.

"Ecco!" she cried, in her vibrating, almost warlike woman's voice: "Ecco!"

Her eyes were aflame as they looked at the door. She ran forward to try it herself. She opened the door expectantly, eagerly. Pouf!—it shut with a bang.

"Ecco!" she cried, her voice quivering like bronze, overwrought but triumphant.

I must try also. I opened the door. Pouf! It shut with a bang. We all exclaimed with joy.

Then the Signor di Paoli turned to me, with a gracious, bland, formal grin. He turned his back slightly on the woman, and stood holding his chin, his strange horse-mouth grinning almost pompously at me. It was an affair of gentlemen. His wife disappeared as if dismissed. Then the padrone broke into cordial motion. We must drink.

He would show me the estate. I had already seen the house. We went out by the glass doors on the left, into the domestic courtyard.

It was lower than the gardens round it, and the sunshine came through the trellised arches on to the flagstones, where grass grew fine and green in the cracks, and all was deserted and spacious and still. There were one or two orange-tubs in the light.

Then I heard a noise, and there in the corner, among all the pink geraniums and the sunshine, the Signora Gemma sat laughing with a baby. It was a fair bonny thing of eighteen months. The Signora was concentrated upon the child as he sat perched on a bench picking at the pink geraniums.

She laughed, bent forward with her dark face out of the shadow, swift into a glitter of sunshine near the sunny baby, laughing again excitedly, making mother-noises. The child took no notice of her. She caught him swiftly into the shadow, and they were obscured; her dark head was against the baby's wool jacket, she was kissing his neck, avidly, under the creeper leaves. The pink geraniums still frilled joyously in the sunshine.

I had forgotten the padrone. Suddenly I turned to him enquiringly.

"The Signora's nephew," he explained, briefly, curtly, in a small voice. It was as if he were ashamed, or too deeply chagrined.

The woman had seen us watching, so she came across the Sunshine with the child, laughing, talking to the baby, not coming out of her own world to us, not acknowledging us, except formally.

The Signor Pietro, queer old horse, began to laugh and neigh at the child, with strange, rancorous envy. The child twisted its face to cry. The Signora caught it away, dancing back a few yards from her old husband.

"I am a stranger," I said to her across the distance. "He is afraid of a stranger."

"No, no," she cried back, her eyes flaring up. "It is the man. He always cries at the men."

She advanced again, laughing and roused, with the child in her arms. Her husband stood as if overcast, obliterated. She and I and the baby, in the sunshine, laughed a moment. Then I heard the neighing, forced laugh of the old man. He would not be left out. He seemed to force himself forward. He was bitter, acrid with chagrin and obliteration, struggling as if to assert his own existence. He was nullified.

The woman also was uncomfortable. I could see she wanted to go away with the child, to enjoy him alone, with palpitating, pained enjoyment. It was her brother's boy. And the old padrone was as if nullified by her ecstasy over the baby. He held his chin, gloomy, fretful, unimportant.

He was annulled. I was startled when I realised it. It was as though his reality were not attested till he had a child. It was as if his *raison d'être* had been to have a son. And he had no children. Therefore he had no *raison d'être*. He was nothing, a shadow that vanishes into nothing. And he was ashamed, consumed by his own nothingness.

I was startled. This, then, is the secret of Italy's attraction for us, this phallic worship. To the Italian the phallus is the symbol of individual creative immortality, to each man his own Godhead. The child is but the evidence of the Godhead.

And this is why the Italian is attractive, supple, and beautiful, because he worships the Godhead in the flesh. We envy him, we feel pale and insignificant beside him. Yet at the same time we feel superior to him, as if he were a child and we adult.

Wherein are we superior? Only because we went beyond the phallus in the search of the Godhead, the creative origin. And we found the physical forces and the secrets of science.

We have exalted Man far above the man who is in each one of us. Our aim is perfect humanity, a perfect and equable human consciousness, selfless. And we obtain it in the subjection, reduction, analysis, and destruction of the Self. So on we go, active in science and mechanics, and social reform. But we have exhausted ourselves in the process. We have found great treasures, and we are now impotent to use them. So we have said: "What good are these treasures, they are vulgar nothings." We have said: "Let us go back from this adventuring, let us enjoy our own flesh, like the Italian." But our habit of life, our very constitution, prevents our being quite like the Italian. The phallus will never serve us as a Godhead, because we do not believe in it: no Northern race does. Therefore, either we set ourselves to serve our children, calling them 'the future', or else we turn perverse and destructive, give ourselves joy in the destruction of the flesh.

The children are not the future. The living truth is the future. Time and people do not make the future. Retrogression is not the future. Fifty million children growing up purposeless, with no purpose save the attainment of their own individual desires, these are not the future, they are only a disintegration of the past. The future is in living, growing truth, in advancing fulfilment.

But it is no good. Whatever we do, it is within the greater will towards self-reduction and a perfect society, analysis on the one hand, and mechanical construction on the other. This will dominates us as a whole, and until the whole breaks down, the will must persist. So that now, continuing in the old, splendid will for a perfect selfless humanity, we have become inhuman and unable to help ourselves, we are but attributes of the great mechanised society we have created on our way to perfection. And this great mechanised society, being selfless, is pitiless. It works on mechanically and destroys us, it is our master and our God.

It is past the time we leave off, to cease entirely from what we are doing, and from what we have been doing for hundreds of years. It is past the time to cease seeking one Infinite, ignoring, striving to eliminate the other. The Infinite is twofold, the Father and the Son, the Dark and the Light, the Senses and the Mind, the Soul and the Spirit; the self and the not-self, the Eagle and the Dove, the Tiger and the Lamb. The consummation of man is twofold, in the Self and in Selflessness. By great retrogression back to the source of darkness in me, the Self, deep in the senses, I arrive at the Original, Creative Infinite. By projection forth from myself, by the elimination of my absolute sensual self, I arrive at the Ultimate Infinite, Oneness in the Spirit. They are two Infinites, twofold approach to God. And man must know both.

But he must never confuse them. They are eternally separate. The lion shall never lie down with the lamb. The lion eternally shall devour the lamb, the lamb eternally shall be devoured. Man knows the great consummation in the flesh, the sensual ecstasy, and that is eternal. Also the spiritual ecstasy of unanimity, that is eternal. But the two are separate and never to be confused. To neutralise the one with the other is unthinkable, an abomination. Confusion is horror and nothingness.

The two Infinites, negative and positive, they are always related, but they are never identical. They are always opposite, but there exists a relation between them. This is the Holy Ghost of the Christian Trinity. And it is this, the relation which is established between the two Infinites, the two natures of God, which we have transgressed, forgotten, sinned against. The Father is the Father, and the Son is the Son. I may know the Son and deny the Father, or know the Father and deny the Son. But that which I may never deny, and which I have denied, is the Holy Ghost which relates the dual Infinites into One Whole, which relates and keeps distinct the dual natures of God. To say that the two are one, this is the inadmissible lie. The two are related, by the intervention of the Third, into a Oneness.

There are two ways, there is not only One. There are two opposite ways to consummation. But that which relates them, like the base of the triangle, this is the constant, the Absolute, this makes the Ultimate Whole. And in the Holy Spirit I know the Two Ways, the Two Infinites, the Two Consummations. And knowing the Two, I admit the Whole. But excluding One, I exclude the Whole. And confusing the two, I make nullity, nihil.

"Mais," said the Signore, starting from his scene of ignominy, where his wife played with another man's child, "mais—voulez-vous vous promener dans mes petites terres?"

It came out fluently, he was so much roused in self-defence and self-assertion.

We walked under the pergola of bony vine-stocks, secure in ~the sunshine within the walls, only the long mountain, parallel with us, looking in.

I said how I liked the big vine-garden, I asked when it ended. The pride of the padrone came back with a click. He pointed me to the terrace, to the great shut lemon-houses above. They were all his. But—he shrugged his Italian shoulders—it was nothing, just a little garden, vous savez, monsieur. I protested it was beautiful, that I loved it, and that it seemed to me *very* large indeed. He admitted that to-day, perhaps, it was beautiful.

"Perchè—parce que—il fait un tempo—cosi—très bell'—très beau, ecco!"

23

He alighted on the word 'beau' hurriedly, like a bird coming to ground with a little bounce.

The terraces of the garden are held up to the sun, the sun falls full upon them, they are like a vessel slanted up, to catch the superb, heavy light. Within the walls we are remote, perfect, moving in heavy spring sunshine, under the bony avenue of vines. The padrone makes little exclamatory noises that mean nothing, and teaches me the names of vegetables. The land is rich and black.

Opposite us, looking down on our security, is the long, arched mountain of snow. We climbed one flight of steps, and we could see the little villages on the opposite side of the lake. We climbed again, and could see the water rippling.

We came to a great stone building that I had thought was a storehouse, for open-air storage, because the walls are open half-way up, showing the darkness inside and the corner pillar very white and square and distinct in front of it.

Entering carelessly into the dimness, I started, for at my feet was a great floor of water, clear and green in its obscurity, going down between the walls, a reservoir in the gloom. The Signore laughed at my surprise. It was for irrigating the land, he said. It stank, slightly, with a raw smell; otherwise, I said, what a wonderful bath it would make. The old Signore gave his little neighing laugh at the idea.

Then we climbed into a great loft of leaves, ruddy brown, stored in a great bank under the roof, seeming to give off a little red heat, as they gave off the lovely perfume of the hills. We passed through, and stood at the foot of the lemon-house. The big, blind building rose high in the sunshine before us.

All summer long, upon the mountain slopes steep by the lake, stand the rows of naked pillars rising out of the green foliage like ruins of temples: white, square pillars of masonry, standing forlorn in their colonnades and squares, rising up the mountain-sides here and there, as if they remained from some great race that had once worshipped here. And still, in the winter, some are seen, standing away in lonely places where the sun streams full, grey rows of pillars rising out of a broken wall, tier upon tier naked to the sky, forsaken.

They are the lemon plantations, and the pillars are to support the heavy branches of the trees, but finally to act as scaffolding of the great wooden houses that stand blind and ugly, covering the lemon trees in the winter.

In November, when cold winds came down and snow had fallen on the mountains, from out of the storehouses the men were carrying timber, and we heard the clang of falling planks. Then, as we walked along the military road on the mountainside, we saw below, on the top of the lemon gardens, long, thin poles laid from pillar to pillar, and we heard the two men talking and singing as they walked across perilously, placing the poles. In their clumsy zoccoli they strode easily across, though they had twenty or thirty feet to fall if they slipped. But the mountain-side, rising steeply, seemed near, and above their heads the rocks glowed high into the sky, so that the sense of elevation must have been taken away. At any rate, they went easily from pillar-summit to pillar-summit, with a great cave of space below. Then again was the rattle and clang of planks being laid in order, ringing from the mountain-side over the blue lake, till a platform of timber, old and brown, projected from the mountain-side, a floor when seen from above, a hanging roof when seen from below. And we, the road above, saw the men sitting easily on this flimsy hanging platform, hammering the planks. And all day long the sound of hammering echoed among the rocks and olive woods, and came, a faint, quick concussion, to the men on the boats far out. When the roofs were on they put in the fronts, blocked in between the white pillars with old, dark wood, in roughly made panels. And here and there, at irregular intervals, was a panel of glass, pane overlapping pane in the long strip of narrow window. So that now these enormous, unsightly buildings bulge out on the mountain-sides, rising in two or three receding tiers, blind, dark, sordid-looking places.

In the morning I often lie in bed and watch the sunrise. The lake lies dim and milky, the mountains are dark blue at the back, while over them the sky gushes and glistens with light. At a certain place on the mountain ridge the light burns gold, seems to fuse a little groove on the hill's rim. It fuses and fuses at this point, till of a sudden it comes, the intense, molten, living light. The mountains melt suddenly, the light steps down, there is a glitter, a spangle, a clutch of spangles, a great unbearable sun-track flashing across the milky lake, and the light falls on my face. Then, looking aside, I hear the little slotting noise which tells me they are opening the lemon gardens, a long panel here and there, a long slot of darkness at irregular intervals between the brown wood and the glass stripes.

"Voulez-vous"—the Signore bows me in with outstretched hand—"voulez-vous entrer, monsieur?"

I went into the lemon-house, where the poor trees seem to mope in the darkness. It is an immense, dark, cold place. Tall lemon trees, heavy with half-visible fruit, crowd together, and rise in the gloom. They look like ghosts in the darkness of the underworld, stately, and as if in life, but only grand shadows of themselves. And lurking here and there, I see one of the pillars. But he, too, seems a shadow, not one of the dazzling white fellows I knew. Here we are, trees, men, pillars, the dark earth, the sad black paths, shut in in this enormous box. It is true, here are long strips of window and slots of space, so that the front is striped, and an occasional beam of light fingers the leaves of an enclosed tree and the sickly round lemons. But it is nevertheless very gloomy.

"But it is much colder in here than outside," I said.

"Yes," replied the Signore, "now. But at night—I *think*—"

I almost wished it were night to try. I wanted to imagine the trees cosy. They seemed now in the underworld. Between the lemon trees, beside the path, were little orange trees, and dozens of oranges hanging like hot coals in the twilight. When I warm my hands at them the Signore breaks off one twig after another, till I have a bunch of burning oranges among dark leaves, a heavy bouquet. Looking down the Hades of the lemon-house, the many ruddy-clustered oranges beside the path remind me of the lights of a village along the lake at night, while the pale lemons above are the stars. There is a subtle, exquisite scent of lemon flowers. Then I notice a citron. He hangs heavy and bloated upon so small a tree, that he seems a dark green enormity. There is a great host of lemons over-head half-visible, a swarm of ruddy oranges by the paths, and here and there a fat citron. It is almost like being under the sea.

At the corners of the path were round little patches of ash and stumps of charred wood where fires had been kindled inside the house on cold nights. For during the second and third weeks in January the snow came down so low on the mountains that, after climbing for an hour, I found myself in a snow lane, and saw olive orchards on lawns of snow.

The padrone says that all lemons and sweet oranges are grafted on a bitter-orange stock. The plants raised from seed, lemon and sweet orange, fell prey to disease, so the cultivators found it safe only to raise the native bitter orange, and then to graft upon it.

And the maestra—she is the schoolmistress, who wears black gloves while she teaches us Italian—says that the lemon was brought by St. Francis of Assisi, who came to the Garda here and founded a church and a monastery. Certainly the church of San

Francesco is very old and dilapidated, and its cloisters have some beautiful and original carvings of leaves and fruit upon the pillars, which seem to connect San Francesco with lemon. I imagine him wandering here with a lemon in his pocket. Perhaps he made lemonade in the hot summer. But Bacchus had been before him in the drink trade.

Looking at his lemons, the Signore sighed. I think he hates them. They are leaving him in the lurch. They are sold retail at a halfpenny each all the year round. "But that is as dear, or dearer, than in England," I say. "Ah, but," says the maestra, "that is because your lemons are outdoor fruit from Sicily. Però—one of our lemons is as good as *two* from elsewhere."

It is true these lemons have an exquisite fragrance and perfume, but whether their force as lemons is double that of an ordinary fruit is a question. Oranges are sold at fourpence halfpenny the kilo—it comes about five for twopence, small ones. The citrons are sold also by weight in Salò for the making of that liqueur known as 'Cedro'. One citron fetches sometimes a shilling or more, but then the demand is necessarily small. So that it is evident, from these figures, the Lago di Garda cannot afford to grow its lemons much longer. The gardens are already many of them in ruins, and still more 'Da Vendere'.

We went out of the shadow of the lemon-house on to the roof of the section below us. When we came to the brink of the roof I sat down. The padrone stood behind me, a shabby, shaky little figure on his roof in the sky, a little figure of dilapidation, dilapidated as the lemon-houses themselves.

We were always level with the mountain-snow opposite. A film of pure blue was on the hills to the right and the left. There had been a wind, but it was still now. The water breathed an iridescent dust on the far shore, where the villages were groups of specks.

On the low level of the world, on the lake, an orange-sailed boat leaned slim to the dark-blue water, which had flecks of foam. A woman went down-hill quickly, with two goats and a sheep. Among the olives a man was whistling.

"Voyez," said the padrone, with distant, perfect melancholy. "There was once a lemon garden also there—you see the short pillars, cut off to make a pergola for the vine. Once there were twice as many lemons as now. Now we must have vine instead. From that piece of land I had two hundred lire a year, in lemons. From the vine I have only eighty."

"But wine is a valuable crop," I said.

"Ah—così-così! For a man who grows much. For me— poco, poco—peu."

Suddenly his face broke into a smile of profound melancholy, almost a grin, like a gargoyle. It was the real Italian melancholy, very deep, static.

"Vous voyez, monsieur—the lemon, it is all the year, all the year. But the vine— one crop—?"

He lifts his shoulders and spreads his hands with that gesture of finality and fatality, while his face takes the blank, ageless look of misery, like a monkey's. There is no hope. There is the present. Either that is enough, the present, or there is nothing.

I sat and looked at the lake. It was beautiful as paradise, as the first creation. On the shores were the ruined lemon-pillars standing out in melancholy, the clumsy, enclosed lemon-houses seemed ramshackle, bulging among vine stocks and olive trees. The villages, too, clustered upon their churches, seemed to belong to the past. They seemed to be lingering in bygone centuries.

"But it is very beautiful," I protested. "In England—"

"Ah, in England," exclaimed the padrone, the same ageless monkey-like grin of fatality, tempered by cunning, coming on his face, "in England you have the wealth—les richesses— you have the mineral coal and the machines, vous savez. Here, we have the sun—"

He lifted his withered hand to the sky, to the wonderful source of that blue day, and he smiled, in histrionic triumph. But his triumph was only histrionic. The machines were more to his soul than the sun. He did not know these mechanisms, their great, human-contrived, inhuman power, and he wanted to know them. As for the sun, that is common property, and no man is distinguished by it. He wanted machines, machine-production, money, and human power. He wanted to know the joy of man who has got the earth in his grip, bound it up with railways, burrowed it with iron fingers, subdued it. He wanted this last triumph of the ego, this last reduction. He wanted to go where the English have gone, beyond the Self into the great inhuman Not-Self, to create the great unliving creators, the machines, out of the active forces of nature that existed before flesh.

But he is too old. It remains for the young Italian to embrace his mistress, the machine.

I sat on the roof of the lemon-house, with the lake below and the snowy mountain opposite, and looked at the ruins on the old, olive-fuming shores, at all the peace of the ancient world still covered in sunshine, and the past seemed to me so lovely that one must look towards it, backwards, only backwards, where there is peace and beauty and no more dissonance.

I thought of England, the great mass of London, and the black, fuming, laborious Midlands and north-country. It seemed horrible. And yet, it was better than the padrone, this old, monkey-like cunning of fatality. It is better to go forward into error than to stay fixed inextricably in the past.

Yet what should become of the world? There was London and the industrial counties spreading like a blackness over all the world, horrible, in the end destructive. And the Garda was so lovely under the sky of sunshine, it was intolerable. For away, beyond, beyond all the snowy Alps, with the iridescence of eternal ice above them, was this England, black and foul and dry, with her soul worn down, almost worn away. And England was conquering the world with her machines and her horrible destruction of natural life. She was conquering the whole world.

And yet, was she not herself finished in this work? She had had enough. She had conquered the natural life to the end: she was replete with the conquest of the outer world, satisfied with the destruction of the Self. She would cease, she would turn round; or else expire.

If she still lived, she would begin to build her knowledge into a great structure of truth. There it lay, vast masses of rough-hewn knowledge, vast masses of machines and appliances, Vast masses of ideas and methods, and nothing done with it, only teeming swarms of disintegrated human beings seething and perishing rapidly away amongst it, till it seems as if a world will be left covered with huge ruins, and scored by strange devices of industry, and quite dead, the people disappeared, swallowed up in the last efforts towards a perfect, selfless society.

III

THE THEATRE

DURING carnival a company is playing in the theatre. On Christmas Day the padrone came in with the key of his box, and would we care to see the drama? The theatre was small, a mere nothing, in fact; a mere affair of peasants, you understand; and the Signor Di Paoli spread his hands and put his head on one side, parrot-wise; but we might find a little diversion—*un peu de divertiment.* With this he handed me the key.

I made suitable acknowledgments, and was really impressed. To be handed the key of a box at the theatre, so simply and pleasantly, in the large sitting-room looking over the grey lake on Christmas Day; it seemed to me a very graceful event. The key had a chain and a little shield of bronze, on which was beaten out a large figure 8.

So the next day we went to see *I Spettri,* expecting some good, crude melodrama. The theatre is an old church. Since that triumph of the deaf and dumb, the cinematograph, has come to give us the nervous excitement of speed,—grimace, agitation, and speed, as of flying atoms, chaos,—many an old church in Italy has taken a new lease of life.

This cast-off church made a good theatre. I realised how cleverly it had been constructed for the dramatic presentation of religious ceremonies. The east end is round, the walls are windowless, sound is well distributed. Now everything is theatrical, except the stone floor and two pillars at the back of the auditorium, and the slightly ecclesiastical seats below.

There are two tiers of little boxes in the theatre, some forty in all, with fringe and red velvet, and lined with dark red paper, quite like real boxes in a real theatre. And the padrone's is one of the best. It just holds three people.

We paid our threepence entrance fee in the stone hall and went upstairs. I opened the door of Number 8, and we were shut in our little cabin, looking down on all the world. Then I found the barber, Luigi, bowing profusely in a box opposite. It was necessary to make bows all round: ah, the chemist, on the upper tier, near the barber; how-do-you-do to the padrona of the hotel, who is our good friend, and who sits, wearing a little beaver shoulder-cape, a few boxes off; very cold salutation to the stout village magistrate with the long brown beard, who leans forward in the box facing the stage, while a grouping of faces look out from behind him; a warm smile to the family of the Signora Gemma, across next to the stage. Then we are settled.

I cannot tell why I hate the village magistrate. He looks like a family portrait by a Flemish artist, he himself weighing down the front of the picture with his portliness and his long brown beard, whilst the faces of his family are arranged in two groups for the background. I think he is angry at our intrusion. He is very republican and self-important. But we eclipse him easily, with the aid of a large black velvet hat, and black furs, and our Sunday clothes.

Downstairs the villagers are crowding, drifting like a heavy current. The women are seated, by church instinct, all together on the left, with perhaps an odd man at the end of a row, beside his wife. On the right, sprawling in the benches, are several groups of bersaglieri, in grey uniforms and slanting cock's-feather hats; then peasants, fishermen, and an odd couple or so of brazen girls taking their places on the men's side.

At the back, lounging against the pillars or standing very dark and sombre, are the more reckless spirits of the village. Their black felt hats are pulled down, their cloaks are thrown over their mouths, they stand very dark and isolated in their moments of stillness, they shout and wave to each other when anything occurs.

The men are clean, their clothes are all clean washed. The rags of the poorest porter are always well washed. But it is Sunday to-morrow, and they are shaved only on a Sunday. So that they have a week's black growth on their thins. But they have dark, soft eyes, unconscious and vulnerable. They move and balance with loose, heedless motion upon their clattering zoccoli, they lounge with wonderful ease against the wall at the back, or against the two pillars, unconscious of the patches on their clothes or of their bare throats, that are knotted perhaps with a scarlet rag. Loose and abandoned, they lounge and talk, or they watch with wistful absorption the play that is going on.

They are strangely isolated in their own atmosphere, and as if revealed. It is as if their vulnerable being was exposed and they have not the wit to cover it. There is a pathos of physical sensibility and mental inadequacy. Their mind is not sufficiently alert to run with their quick, warm senses.

The men keep together, as if to support each other, the women also are together; in a hard, strong herd. It is as if the power, the hardness, the triumph, even in this Italian village, were with the women in their relentless, vindictive unity.

That which drives men and women together, the indomitable necessity, is like a bondage upon the people. They submit as under compulsion, under constraint. They come together mostly in anger and in violence of destructive passion. There is no comradeship between men and women, none whatsoever, but rather a condition of battle, reserve, hostility.

On Sundays the uncomfortable, excited, unwilling youth walks for an hour with his sweetheart, at a little distance from her, on the public highway in the afternoon. This is a concession to the necessity for marriage. There is no real courting, no happiness of being together, only the roused excitement which is based on a fundamental hostility. There is very little flirting, and what there is is of the subtle, cruel kind, like a sex duel. On the whole, the men and women avoid each other, almost shun each other. Husband and wife are brought together in a child, which they both worship. But in each of them there is only the great reverence for the infant, and the reverence for fatherhood or motherhood, as the case may be; there is no spiritual love.

In marriage, husband and wife wage the subtle, satisfying war of sex upon each other. It gives a profound satisfaction, a profound intimacy. But it destroys all joy, all unanimity in action.

On Sunday afternoons the uncomfortable youth walks by the side of his maiden for an hour in the public highway. Then he escapes; as from a bondage he goes back to his men companions. On Sunday afternoons and evenings the married woman, accompanied by a friend or by a child—she dare not go alone, afraid of the strange, terrible sex-war between her and the drunken man—is seen leading home the wine-drunken, liberated husband. Sometimes she is beaten when she gets home. It is part of the process. But there is no synthetic love between men and women, there is only passion, and passion is fundamental hatred, the act of love is a fight.

The child, the outcome, is divine. Here the union, the oneness, is manifest. Though spirit strove with spirit, in mortal conflict, during the sex-passion, yet the flesh united with flesh in oneness. The phallus is still divine. But the spirit, the mind of man, this has become nothing.

So the women triumph. They sit down below in the theatre, their perfectly dressed hair gleaming, their backs very straight, their heads carried tensely. They are not very noticeable. They seem held in reserve. They are just as tense and stiff as the men are slack and abandoned. Some strange will holds the women taut. They seem like weapons, dangerous. There is nothing charming nor winning about them; at the best a full, prolific maternity, at the worst a yellow poisonous bitterness of the flesh that is like a narcotic. But they are too strong for the men. The male spirit, which would subdue the immediate flesh to some conscious or social purpose, is overthrown. The woman in her maternity is the law-giver, the supreme authority. The authority of the man, in work, in public affairs, is something trivial in comparison. The pathetic ignominy of the village male is complete on Sunday afternoon, on his great day of liberation, when he is accompanied home, drunk but sinister, by the erect, unswerving, slightly cowed woman. His drunken terrorising is only pitiable, she is so obviously the more constant power.

And this is why the men must go away to America. It is not the money. It is the profound desire to rehabilitate themselves, to recover some dignity as men, as producers, as workers, as creators from the spirit, not only from the flesh. It is a profound desire to get away from women altogether, the terrible subjugation to sex, the phallic worship.

The company of actors in the little theatre was from a small town away on the plain, beyond Brescia. The curtain rose, everybody was still, with that profound, naïve attention which children give. And after a few minutes I realised that *I Spettri* was Ibsen's *Ghosts*. The peasants and fishermen of the Garda, even the rows of ungovernable children, sat absorbed in watching as the Norwegian drama unfolded itself.

The actors are peasants. The leader is the son of a peasant proprietor. He is qualified as a chemist, but is unsettled, vagrant, prefers play-acting. The Signor Pietro di Paoli shrugs his shoulders and apologises for their vulgar accent. It is all same to me. I am trying to get myself to rights with the play, which I have just lately seen in Munich, perfectly produced and detestable.

It was such a change from the hard, ethical slightly mechanised characters in the German play, which was as perfect an interpretation as I can imagine, to the rather pathetic notion of the Italian peasants, that I had to wait to adjust myself.

The mother was a pleasant, comfortable woman harassed by something, she did not quite know what. The pastor was a ginger-haired caricature imitated from the northern stage, quite a lay figure. The peasants never laughed, they watched solemnly and absorbedly like children. The servant was just a slim, pert, forward hussy, much too flagrant. And then the son, the actor-manager: he was a dark, ruddy man, broad and thick-set, evidently of peasant origin, but with some education now; he was the important figure, the play was his.

And he was strangely disturbing. Dark, ruddy, and powerful, he could not be the blighted son of 'Ghosts', the hectic, unsound, northern issue of a diseased father. His flashy Italian passion for his half-sister was real enough to make one uncomfortable: something he wanted and would have in spite of his own soul, something which fundamentally he did not want.

It was this contradiction within the man that made the play so interesting. A robust, vigorous man of thirty-eight, flaunting and florid as a rather successful Italian can be, there was yet a secret sickness which oppressed him. But it was no taint in the blood, it was rather a kind of debility in the soul. That which he wanted and would have, the sensual excitement, in his soul he did not want it, no, not at all. And yet he must act from his physical desires, his physical will.

His true being, his real self, was impotent. In his soul he was dependent, forlorn. He was childish and dependent on the mother. To hear him say, "Grazia, mamma!" would have tormented the mother-soul in any woman living. Such a child crying in the night! And for what?

For he was hot-blooded, healthy, almost in his prime, and free as a man can be in his circumstances. He had his own way, he admitted no thwarting. He governed his circumstances pretty much, coming to our village with his little company, playing the plays he chose himself. And yet, that which he would have he did not vitally want, it was only a sort of inflamed obstinacy that made him so insistent, in the masculine way. He was not going to be governed by women, he was not going to be dictated to in the least by any one. And this because he was beaten by his own flesh.

His real man's soul, the soul that goes forth and builds up a new world out of the void, was ineffectual. It could only revert to the senses. His divinity was the phallic divinity. The other male divinity, which is the spirit that fulfils in the world the new germ of an idea, this was denied and obscured in him, unused. And it was this spirit which cried out helplessly in him through the insistent, inflammable flesh. Even this play-acting was a form of physical gratification for him, it had in it neither real mind nor spirit.

It was so different from Ibsen, and so much more moving. Ibsen is exciting, nervously sensational. But this was really moving, a real crying in the night. One loved the Italian nation, and wanted to help it with all one's soul. But when one sees the perfect Ibsen, how one hates the Norwegian and Swedish nations! They are detestable.

They seem to be fingering with the mind the secret places and sources of the blood, impertinent, irreverent, nasty. There is a certain intolerable nastiness about the real Ibsen: the same thing is in Strindberg and in most of the Norwegian and Swedish writings. It is with them a sort of phallic worship also, but now the worship is mental and perverted: the phallus is the real fetish, but it is the source of uncleanliness and corruption and death, it is the Moloch, worshipped in obscenity.

Which is unbearable. The phallus is a symbol of creative divinity. But it represents only part of creative divinity. The Italian has made it represent the whole. Which is now his misery, for he has to destroy his symbol in himself.

Which is why the Italian men have the enthusiasm for war, unashamed. Partly it is the true phallic worship, for the phallic principle is to absorb and dominate all life. But also it is a desire to expose themselves to death, to know death, that death may destroy in them this too strong dominion of the blood, may once more liberate the spirit of outgoing, of uniting, of making order out of chaos, in the outer world, as the flesh makes a new order from chaos in begetting a new life, set them free to know and serve a greater idea.

The peasants below sat and listened intently, like children who hear and do not understand, yet who are spellbound. The children themselves sit spellbound on the benches till the play is over. They do not fidget or lose interest. They watch with wide, absorbed eyes at the mystery, held in thrall by the sound of emotion.

But the villagers do not really care for Ibsen. They let it go. On the feast of Epiphany, as a special treat, was given a poetic drama by D'Annunzio, *La Fiaccola sotto il Moggio— The Light under the Bushel.*

It is a foolish romantic play of no real significance. There are several murders and a good deal of artificial horror. But it is all a very nice and romantic piece of make-believe, like a charade.

So the audience loved it. After the performance of Ghosts I saw the barber, and he had the curious grey clayey look of an Italian who is cold and depressed. The sterile cold inertia, which the so-called passionate nations know so well, had settled on him, and he went obliterating himself in the street, as if he were cold, dead.

31

But after the D'Annunzio play he was like a man who has drunk sweet wine and is warm.

"Ah, bellissimo, bellissimo!" he said, in tones of intoxicated reverence, when he saw me.

"Better than *I Spettri?*" I said.

He half-raised his hands, as if to imply the fatuity of the question.

"Ah, but—" he said, "it was D'Annunzio. The other . . ."

"That was Ibsen—a great Norwegian," I said, "famous all over the world."

"But, you know—D'Annunzio is a poet—oh, beautiful, beautiful!" There was no going beyond this "bello— bellissimo."

It was the language which did it. It was the Italian passion for rhetoric, for the speech which appeals to the senses and makes no demand on the mind. When an Englishman listens to a speech he wants at least to imagine that he understands thoroughly and impersonally what is meant. But an Italian only cares about the emotion. It is the movement, the physical effect of the language upon the blood which gives him supreme satisfaction. His mind is scarcely engaged at all. He is like a child, hearing and feeling without understanding. It is the sensuous gratification he asks for. Which is why D'Annunzio is a god in Italy. He can control the current of the blood with his words, and although much of what he says is bosh, yet the hearer is satisfied, fulfilled.

Carnival ends on the 5th of February, so each Thursday there is a Serata d' Onore of one of the actors. The first, and the only one for which prices were raised—to a fourpence entrance fee instead of threepence—was for the leading lady. The play was *The Wife of the Doctor*, a modern piece, sufficiently uninteresting; the farce that followed made me laugh.

Since it was her Evening of Honour, Adelaida was the person to see. She is very popular, though she is no longer young. In fact, she is the mother of the young pert person of *Ghosts*.

Nevertheless, Adelaida, stout and blonde and soft and pathetic, is the real heroine of the theatre, the prima. She is very good at sobbing; and afterwards the men exclaim involuntarily, out of their strong emotion, "bella, bella!" The women say nothing. They sit stiffly and dangerously as ever. But, no doubt, they quite agree this is the true picture of ill-used, tear-stained woman, the bearer of many wrongs. Therefore they take unto themselves the homage of the men's "bella, bella!" that follows the sobs: it is due recognition of their hard wrongs: "the woman pays." Nevertheless, they despise in their souls the plump, soft Adelaida.

Dear Adelaida, she is irreproachable. In every age, in every clime, she is dear, at any rate to the masculine soul, this soft, tear-blenched, blonde, ill-used thing. She must be ill-used and unfortunate. Dear Gretchen, dear Desdemona, dear Iphigenia, dear Dame aux Camélias, dear Lucy of Lammermoor, dear Mary Magdalene, dear, pathetic, unfortunate soul, in all ages and lands, how we love you. In the theatre she blossoms forth, she is the lily of the stage. Young and inexperienced as I am, I have broken my heart over her several times. I could write a sonnet-sequence to her, yes, the fair, pale, tear-stained thing, white-robed, with her hair down her back; I could call her by a hundred names, in a hundred languages, Mélisande, Elizabeth, Juliet, Butterfly, Phèdre, Minnehaha, etc. Each new time I hear her voice, with its faint clang of tears, my heart grows big and hot, and my bones melt. I detest her, but it is no good. My heart begins to swell like a bud under the plangent rain.

The last time I saw her was here, on the Garda, at Salò. She was the chalked, thin-armed daughter of Rigoletto. I detested her, her voice had a chalky squeak in it. And yet, by the end, my heart was over-ripe in my breast, ready to burst with loving affection. I was ready to walk on to the stage, to wipe out the odious, miscreant lover, and to offer her all myself, saying, "I can see it is real *love* you want, and you shall have it: *I* will give it to you."

Of course I know the secret of the Gretchen magic; it is all in the "Save me, Mr. Hercules!" phrase. Her shyness, her timidity, her trustfulness, her tears foster my own strength and grandeur. I am the positive half of the universe. But so I am, if it comes to that, just as positive as the other half.

Adelaide is plump, and her voice has just that moist, plangent strength which gives one a real voluptuous thrill. The moment she comes on the stage and looks round—a bit scared. She is *she,* Electra, Isolde, Sieglinde, Marguerite. She wears a dress of black voile, like the lady who weeps at the trial in the police-court. This is her modern uniform. Her antique garment is of trailing white, with a blonde pigtail and a flower. Realistically, it is black voile and a handkerchief.

Adelaida always has a handkerchief. And still I cannot resist it. I say, "There's the hanky!" Nevertheless, in two minutes it has worked its way with me. She squeezes it in her poor, plump hand as the tears begin to rise; Fate, or man, is inexorable, so cruel. There is a sob, a cry; she presses the fist and the hanky to her eyes, one eye, then the other. She weeps real tears, tears shaken from the depths of her soft, vulnerable, victimised female self. I cannot stand it. There I sit in the padrone's little red box and stifle my emotion, whilst I repeat in my heart: "What a shame, child, what a shame!" She is twice my age, but what is age in such a circumstance? "Your poor little hanky, it's sopping. There, then, don't cry, It'll be all right. *I'll* see you're all right. *All* men are not beasts, you know." So I cover her protectively in my arms, and soon I shall be kissing her, for comfort, in the heat and prowess of my compassion, kissing her soft, plump cheek and neck closely, bringing my comfort nearer and nearer.

It is a pleasant and exciting rôle for me to play, Robert Burns did the part to perfection:

> "O wert thou in the cauld blast
> On yonder lea, on yonder lea."

How many times does one recite that to all the Ophelias and Gretchens in the world:

> "Thy bield should be my bosom."

How one admires one's bosom in that capacity! Looking down at one's shirt-front, one is filled with strength and pride.

Why are the women so bad at playing this part in real life, this Ophelia-Gretchen role? Why are they so unwilling to go mad and die for our sakes? They do it regularly on the stage.

But perhaps, after all, we write the plays. What a villain I am, what a black-browed, passionate, ruthless, masculine villain I am to the leading lady on the stage; and, on the other hand, dear heart, what a hero, what a fount of chivalrous generosity and faith! I am *anything* but a dull and law-abiding citizen. I am a Galahad, full of purity and spirituality, I am the Lancelot of valour and lust; I fold my hands, or I cock my hat on one side, as the case may be: I am *myself*. Only, I am not a respectable citizen, not that, in this hour of my glory and my escape.

Dear Heaven, how Adelaida wept, her voice plashing like violin music, at my ruthless, masculine cruelty. Dear heart, how she sighed to rest on my sheltering bosom! And how I enjoyed my dual nature! How I admired myself!

Adelaida chose *La Moglie del Dottore* for her Evening of Honour. During the following week came a little storm of coloured bills: "Great Evening of Honour of Enrico Persevalli."

This is the leader, the actor-manager. What should he choose for this great occasion, this broad, thick-set, ruddy descendant of the peasant proprietors of the plain? No one knew. The title of the play was not revealed.

So we were staying at home, it was cold and wet. But the maestra came inflammably on that Thursday evening, and were we not going to the theatre, to see *Amleto?*

Poor maestra, she is yellow and bitter-skinned, near fifty, but her dark eyes are still corrosively inflammable. She was engaged to a lieutenant in the cavalry, who got drowned when she was twenty-one. Since then she has hung on the tree unripe, growing yellow and bitter-skinned, never developing.

"*Amleto!*" I say. "*Non o conosco.*"

A certain fear comes into her eyes. She is schoolmistress, and has a mortal dread of being wrong.

"Si," she cries, wavering, appealing, "una dramma inglese."

"English!" I repeated.

"Yes, an English drama."

"How do you write it?"

Anxiously, she gets a pencil from her reticule, and, with black-gloved scrupulousness, writes *Amleto*.

"*Hamlet!*" I exclaim wonderingly.

"Ecco, *Amleto!*" cries the maestra, her eyes aflame with thankful justification.

Then I knew that Signor Enrico Persevalli was looking to me for an audience - His Evening of Honour would be a bitter occasion to him if the English were not there to see his performance.

I hurried to get ready, I ran through the rain. I knew he would take it badly that it rained on his Evening of Honour. He counted himself a man who had fate against him.

"Sono un disgraziato, io."

I was late. The First Act was nearly over. The play was not yet alive, neither in the bosoms of the actors nor in the audience. I closed the door of the box softly, and came forward. The rolling Italian eyes of Hamlet glanced up at me. There came a new impulse over the Court of Denmark.

Enrico looked a sad fool in his melancholy black. The doublet sat close, making him stout and vulgar, the knee-breeches seemed to exaggerate the commonness of his thick, rather short, strutting legs. And he carried a long black rag, as a cloak, for histrionic purposes. And he had on his face a portentous grimace of melancholy and philosophic importance. His was the caricature of Hamlet's melancholy self-absorption.

I stooped to arrange my footstool and compose my countenance. I was trying not to grin. For the first time, attired in philosophic melancholy of black silk, Enrico looked a boor and a fool. His close-cropped, rather animal head was common above the effeminate doublet, his sturdy, ordinary figure looked absurd in a melancholic droop.

All the actors alike were out of their element. Their Majesties of Denmark were touching. The Queen, burly little peasant woman, was ill at ease in her pink satin. Enrico had had no mercy. He knew she loved to be the scolding servant or housekeeper, with her head tied up in a handkerchief, shrill and vulgar. Yet here she was pranked out in an expanse of satin, la Regina. Regina, indeed!

She obediently did her best to be important. Indeed, she rather fancied herself; she looked sideways at the audience, self-consciously, quite ready to be accepted as an imposing and noble person, if they would esteem her such. Her voice sounded hoarse and common, but whether it was the pink satin in contrast, or a cold, I do not know. She was almost childishly afraid to move. Before she began a speech she looked down and kicked her skirt viciously, so that she was sure it was under control. Then she let go. She was a burly, downright little body of sixty, one rather expected her to box Hamlet on the ears.

Only she liked being a queen when she sat on the throne. There she perched with great satisfaction, her train splendidly displayed down the steps. She was as proud as a child, and she looked like Queen Victoria of the Jubilee period.

The King, her noble consort, also had new honours thrust upon him, as well as new garments. His body was real enough, but it had nothing at all to do with his clothes. They established a separate identity by themselves. But wherever he went, they went with him, to the confusion of everybody.

He was a thin, rather frail-looking peasant, pathetic, and very gentle. There was something pure and fine about him, he was so exceedingly gentle and by natural breeding courteous. But he did not feel kingly, he acted the part with beautiful, simple resignation.

Enrico Persevalli had overshot himself in every direction, but worst of all in his own. He had become a hulking fellow, crawling about with his head ducked between his shoulders, pecking and poking, creeping about after other people, sniffing at them, setting traps for them, absorbed by his own self-important self-consciousness. His legs, in their black knee-breeches, had a crawling, slinking look; he always carried the black rag of a cloak, something for him to twist about as he twisted in his own soul overwhelmed by a sort of inverted perversity.

I had always felt an aversion from Hamlet: a creeping, unclean thing he seems, on the stage, whether he is Forbes Roberston or anybody else. His nasty poking and sniffing at his mother, his setting traps for the King, his conceited perversion with Ophelia make him always intolerable. The character is repulsive in its conception, based on self-dislike and a spirit of disintegration.

There is, I think, this strain of cold dislike, or self-dislike, through much of the Renaissance art, and through all the later Shakespeare. In Shakespeare it is a kind of corruption in the flesh and a conscious revolt from this. A sense of corruption in the flesh makes Hamlet frenzied, for he will never admit that it is his own flesh. Leonardo da Vinci is the same, but Leonardo loves the corruption maliciously. Michael Angelo rejects any feeling of corruption, he stands by the flesh, the flesh only. It is the corresponding reaction, but in the opposite direction. But that is all four hundred years ago. Enrico Persevalli has just reached the position. He *is* Hamlet, and evidently he has great satisfaction in the part. He is the modern Italian, suspicious, isolated, self-nauseated, labouring in a sense of physical corruption. But he will not admit it is in himself. He creeps about in self-conceit, transforming his own self-loathing. With what satisfaction did he reveal corruption— corruption in his neighbours he gloated in—letting his mother know he had discovered her incest, her uncleanness, gloated in torturing the incestuous King. Of all the unclean ones, Hamlet was the uncleanest. But he accused only the others.

Except in the 'great' speeches, and there Enrico was betrayed, Hamlet suffered the extremity of physical self-loathing, loathing of his own flesh. The play is the statement of the most significant philosophic position of the Renaissance. Hamlet is far more even than Orestes, his prototype, a mental creature, anti-physical, anti-sensual. The whole drama is the tragedy of the convulsed reaction of the mind from the flesh, of the spirit from the self, the reaction from the great aristocratic to the great democratic principle.

An ordinary instinctive man, in Hamlet's position, would either have set about murdering his uncle, by reflex action, or else would have gone right away. There would have been no need for Hamlet to murder his mother. It would have been sufficient blood-vengeance if he had killed his uncle. But that is the statement according to the aristocratic principle.

Orestes was in the same position, but the same position two thousand years earlier, with two thousand years of experience wanting. So that the question was not so intricate in him as in Hamlet, he was not nearly so conscious. The whole Greek life was based on the idea of the supremacy of the self, and the self was always male. Orestes was his father's child, he would be the same whatever mother he had. The mother was but the vehicle, the soil in which the paternal seed was planted. When Clytemnestra murdered Agamemnon, it was as if a common individual murdered God, to the Greek.

But Agamemnon, King and Lord, was not infallible. He was fallible. He had sacrificed Iphigenia for the sake of glory in war, for the fulfilment of the superb idea of self, but on the other hand he had made cruel dissension for the sake of the concubines captured in war. The paternal flesh was fallible, ungodlike. It lusted after meaner pursuits than glory, war, and slaying, it was not faithful to the highest idea of the self. Orestes was driven mad by the furies of his mother, because of the justice that they represented. Nevertheless he was in the end exculpated. The third play of the trilogy is almost foolish, with its prating gods. But it means that, according to the Greek conviction, Orestes was right and Clytemnestra entirely wrong. But for all that, the infallible King, the infallible male Self, is dead in Orestes, killed by the furies of Clytemnestra. He gains his peace of mind after the revulsion from his own physical fallibility, but he will never be an unquestioned lord, as Agamemnon was. Orestes is left at peace, neutralised. He is the beginning of non-aristocratic Christianity.

Hamlet's father, the King, is, like Agamemnon, a warrior-king. But unlike, Agamemnon, he is blameless with regard to Gertrude. Yet Gertrude, like Clytemnestra, is the potential murderer of her husband, as Lady Macbeth is murderess, as the daughters of Lear. The women murder the supreme male, the ideal Self, the King and Father.

This is the tragic position Shakespeare must dwell upon. The woman rejects, repudiates the ideal Self which the male represents to her. The supreme representative, King and Father, is murdered by the Wife and the Daughters.

What is the reason? Hamlet goes mad in a revulsion of rage and nausea. Yet the women-murderers only represent some ultimate judgment in his own soul. At the bottom of his own soul Hamlet has decided that the Self in its supremacy, Father and King, must die. It is a suicidal decision for his involuntary soul to have arrived at. Yet it is inevitable. The great religious, philosophic tide, which had been swelling all through the Middle Ages, had brought him there.

The question, to be or not to be, which Hamlet puts himself, does not mean, to live or not to live. It is not the simple human being who puts himself the question, it is the supreme I, King and Father. To be or not to be King, Father, in the Self supreme? And the decision is, not to be.

It is the inevitable philosophic conclusion of all the Renaissance. The deepest impulse in man, the religious impulse, is the desire to be immortal, or infinite, consummated. And this impulse is satisfied in fulfilment of an idea, a steady progression. In this progression man is satisfied, he seems to have reached his goal, this infinity, this immortality, this eternal being, with every step nearer which he takes.

And so, according to his idea of fulfilment, man establishes the whole order of life. If my fulfilment is the fulfilment and establishment of the unknown divine Self which I am, then I shall proceed in the realising of the greatest idea of the self, the highest conception of the I, my order of life will be kingly, imperial, aristocratic. The body politic also will culminate in this divinity of flesh, this body imbued with glory, invested with divine power and might, the King, the Emperor. In the body politic also I shall desire a king, an emperor, a tyrant, glorious, mighty, in whom I see myself consummated and fulfilled. This is inevitable!

But during the Middle Ages, struggling within this pagan, original transport, the transport of the Ego, was a small dissatisfaction, a small contrary desire. Amid the pomp of kings and popes was the Child Jesus and the Madonna. Jesus the King gradually dwindled down. There was Jesus the Child, helpless, at the mercy of all the world. And there was Jesus crucified.

The old transport, the old fulfilment of the Ego, the Davidian ecstasy, the assuming of all power and glory unto the self, the becoming infinite through the absorption of all into the Ego, this gradually became unsatisfactory. This was not the infinite, this was not immortality. This was eternal death, this was damnation.

The monk rose up with his opposite ecstasy, the Christian ecstasy. There was a death to die: the flesh, the self, must die, so that the spirit should rise again immortal, eternal, infinite. I am dead unto myself, but I live in the Infinite. The finite Me is no more, only the Infinite, the Eternal, is.

At the Renaissance this great half-truth overcame the other great half-truth. The Christian Infinite, reached by a process of abnegation, a process of being absorbed, dissolved, diffused into the great Not-Self, supplanted the old pagan Infinite, wherein the self like a root threw out branches and radicles which embraced the whole universe, became the Whole.

There is only one Infinite, the world now cried, there is the great Christian Infinite of renunciation and consummation in the not-self. The other, that old pride, is damnation. The sin of sins is Pride, it is the way to total damnation. Whereas the pagans based their life on pride.

And according to this new Infinite, reached through renunciation and dissolving into the Others, the Neighbour, man must build up his actual form of life. With Savonarola and Martin Luther the living Church actually transformed itself, for the Roman Church was still pagan. Henry VIII. simply said: "There is no Church, there is only the State?' But with Shakespeare the transformation had reached the State also. The King, the Father, the representative of the Consummate Self, the maximum of all life, the symbol of the consummate being, the becoming Supreme, Godlike, Infinite, he must perish and pass away. This Infinite was not infinite, this consummation was not consummated, all this was fallible, false. It was rotten, corrupt. It must go. But Shakespeare was also the thing itself. Hence his horror, his frenzy, his self-loathing.

The King, the Emperor is killed in the soul of man, the old order of life is over, the old tree is dead at the root. So said Shakespeare. It was finally enacted in Cromwell. Charles I. took up the old position of kingship by divine right. Like Hamlet's father, he was blameless otherwise. But as representative of the old form of life, which mankind now hated with frenzy, he must be cut down, removed. It was a symbolic act.

The world, our world of Europe, had now really turned, swung round to a new goal, a new idea, the Infinite reached through the omission of Self. God is all that which is Not-Me. I am consummate when my Self, the resistant solid, is reduced and diffused into all that which is Not-Me: my neighbour, my enemy, the great Otherness. Then I am perfect.

And from this belief the world began gradually to form a new State, a new body politic, in which the Self should be removed. There should be no king, no lords, no aristocrats. The world continued in its religious belief, beyond the French Revolution, beyond the great movement of Shelley and Godwin. There should be no Self. That which was supreme was that which was Not-Me, the other. The governing factor in the State was the idea of the good of others; that is, the Common Good. And the *vital* governing idea in the State has been this idea since Cromwell.

Before Cromwell the idea was "For the King," because every man saw himself consummated in the King. After Cromwell the idea was "For the good of my neighbour," or "For the good of the people," or "For the good of the whole." This has been our ruling idea, by which we have more or less lived.

Now this has failed. Now we say that the Christian Infinite is not infinite. We are tempted, like Nietzsche, to return back to the old pagan Infinite, to say that is supreme. Or we are inclined, like the English and the Pragmatist, to say, "There is no Infinite, there -is no Absolute. The only Absolute is expediency, the only reality is sensation and momentariness." But we may say this, even act on it, *à la Sanine.* But we never believe it.

What is really Absolute is the mystic Reason which connects both Infinites, the Holy Ghost that relates both natures of God. If we now wish to make a living State, we must build it up to the idea of the Holy Spirit, the supreme Relationship. We must say, the pagan Infinite is infinite, the Christian Infinite is infinite: these are our two Consummations, in both of these we are consummated. But that which relates them alone is absolute.

This Absolute of the Holy Ghost we may call Truth or Justice or Right. These are partial names, indefinite and unsatisfactory unless there be kept the knowledge of the two Infinites, pagan and Christian, which they go between. When both are there, they are like a superb bridge, on which one can stand and know the whole world, my world, the two halves of the universe.

"Essere, o non essere, è qui il punto."

To be or not to be was the question for Hamlet to settle. It is no longer our question, at least, not in the same sense. When it is a question of death, the fashionable young suicide declares that his self-destruction is the final proof of his own incontrovertible being. And as for not-being in our public life, we have achieved it as much as ever we want to, as much as is necessary. Whilst in private life there is a swing back to paltry selfishness as a creed. And in the war there is the position of neutralisation and nothingness. It is a question of knowing how *to be,* and how *not to be,* for we must fulfil both.

Enrico Persevalli was detestable with his "Essere, o non essere." He whispered it in a hoarse whisper as if it were some melodramatic murder he was about to commit. As a matter of fact, he knows quite well, and has known all his life, that his pagan Infinite, his transport of the flesh and the supremacy of the male in fatherhood, is all unsatisfactory. All his life he has really cringed before the northern Infinite of the Not-Self, although he has continued in the Italian habit of Self. But it is mere habit, sham.

How can he know anything about being and not-being when he is only a maudlin compromise between them, and all he wants is to be a maudlin compromise? He is neither one nor the other. He has neither being nor not-being. He is as equivocal as the monks. He was detestable, mouthing Hamlet's sincere words. He has still to let go, to know what not-being is, before he can *be*. Till he has gone through the Christian negation of himself, and has known the Christian consummation, he is a mere amorphous heap.

For the soliloquies of Hamlet are as deep as the soul of man can go, in one direction, and as sincere as the Holy Spirit itself in their essence. But thank heaven, the bog into which Hamlet struggled is almost surpassed.

It is a strange thing, if a man covers his face, and speaks with his eyes blinded, how significant and poignant he becomes. The ghost of this Hamlet was very simple. He was wrapped down to the knees in a great white cloth, and over his face was an open-work woollen shawl. But the naïve blind helplessness and verity of his voice was strangely convincing. He seemed the most real thing in the play. From the knees downward he was Laertes, because he had on Laertes' white trousers and patent leather slippers. Yet he was strangely real, a voice out of the dark.

The Ghost is really one of the play's failures, it is so trivial and unspiritual and vulgar. And it was spoilt for me from the first. When I was a child I went to the twopenny travelling theatre to see *Hamlet*. The Ghost had on a helmet and a breastplate. I sat in pale transport.

"'Amblet, 'Amblet, I *am* thy father's ghost."

Then came a voice from the dark, silent audience, like a cynical knife to my fond soul:

"Why tha arena, I can tell thy voice."

The peasants loved Ophelia: she was in white with her hair down her back. Poor thing, she was pathetic, demented. And no wonder, after Hamlet's "O, that this too, too solid flesh would melt!" What then of her young breasts and her womb? Hamlet with her was a very disagreeable sight. The peasants loved her. There was a hoarse roar, half of indignation, half of roused passion, at the end of her scene.

The graveyard scene, too, was a great success, but I could not bear Hamlet. And the grave-digger in Italian was a mere buffoon. The whole scene was farcical to me because of the Italian, "Questo cranio, Signore—" And Enrico, dainty fellow, took the skull in a corner of his black cloak. As an Italian, he would not willingly touch it. It was unclean. But be looked a fool, hulking himself in his lugubriousness. He was as self-important as D'Annunzio.

The close fell flat. The peasants had applauded the whole graveyard scene wildly. But at the end of all they got up and crowded to the doors, as if to hurry away: this in spite of Enrico's final feat: he fell backwards, smack down three steps of the throne platform, on to the stage. But planks and braced muscle will bounce, and Signor Amleto bounced quite high again.

It was the end of *Amleto,* and I was glad. But I loved the theatre, I loved to look down on the peasants, who were so absorbed. At the end of the scenes the men pushed back their black hats, and rubbed their hair across their brows with a pleased, excited movement. And the women stirred in their seats.

Just one man was with his wife and child, and he was of the same race as my old woman at San Tommaso. He was fair, thin, and clear, abstract, of the mountains. He seemed to have gathered his wife and child together into another, finer atmosphere, like the air of the mountains, and to guard them in it. This is the real Joseph, father of the child. He has a fierce, abstract look, wild and untamed as a hawk, but like a hawk at its own nest, fierce with love. He goes out and buys a tiny bottle of lemonade for a penny, and the mother and child sip it in tiny sips, whilst he bends over, like a hawk arching its wings.

It is the fierce spirit of the Ego come out of the primal infinite, but detached, isolated, an aristocrat. He is not an Italian, dark-blooded. He is fair, keen as steel, with the blood of the mountaineer in him. He is like my old spinning woman. It is curious how, with his wife and child, he makes a little separate world down there in the theatre, like a hawk's nest, high and arid under the gleaming sky.

The Bersaglieri sit close together in groups, so that there is a strange, corporal connection between them. They have close-cropped, dark, slightly bestial heads, and thick shoulders, and thick brown hands on each other's shoulders. When an act is over they pick up their cherished hats and fling on their cloaks and go into the hall. They are rather rich, the Bersaglieri.

They are like young, half-wild oxen, such strong, sturdy, dark lads, thickly built and with strange hard heads, like young male caryatides. They keep close together, as if there were some physical instinct connecting them. And they are quite womanless. There is a curious inter-absorption among themselves, a sort of physical trance that holds them all, and puts their minds to sleep. There is a strange, hypnotic unanimity among them as they put on their plumed hats and go out together, always very close, as if their bodies must touch. Then they feel safe and content in this heavy, physical trance. They are in love with one another, the young men love the young men. They shrink from the world beyond, from the outsiders, from all who are not Bersaglieri of their barracks.

One man is a sort of leader. He is very straight and solid, solid like a wall, with a dark, unblemished will. His cock-feathers slither in a profuse, heavy stream from his black oil-cloth hat, almost to his shoulder. He swings round. His feathers slip in a cascade. Then he goes out to the hall, his feather tossing and falling richly. He must be well off. The Bersaglieri buy their own cock's-plumes, and some pay twenty or thirty francs for the bunch, so the maestra said. The poor ones have only poor, scraggy plumes.

There is something very primitive about these men. They remind me really of Agamemnon's soldiers clustered on the seashore, men, all men, a living, vigorous, physical host of men. But there is a pressure on these Italian soldiers, as if they were men caryatides, with a great weight on their heads, making their brain hard, asleep, stunned. They all look as if their real brain was stunned, as if there were another centre of physical consciousness from which they lived.

Separate from them all is Pietro, the young man who lounges on the wharf to carry things from the steamer. He starts up from sleep like a wild-cat as somebody claps him on the shoulder. It is the start of a man who has many enemies. He is almost an outlaw. Will he ever find himself in prison? He is the *gamin* of the village, well detested.

He is twenty-four years old, thin, dark, handsome, with a cat-like lightness and grace, and a certain repulsive, *gamin* evil in his face. Where everybody is so clean and tidy, he is almost ragged. His week's beard shows very black in his slightly hollow cheeks. He hates the man who has waked him by clapping him on the shoulder.

Pietro is already married, yet he behaves as if he were not. He had been carrying on with a loose woman, the wife of the citron-coloured barber, the Siciliano. Then he seats himself on the women's side of the theatre, behind a young person from Bogliaco, who also has no reputation, and makes her talk to him. He leans forward, resting his arms on the seat before him, stretching his slender, cat-like, flexible loins. The padrona of the hotel hates him—"ein frecher Kerl," she says with contempt, and she looks away. Her eyes hate to see him.

In the village there is the clerical party, which is the majority; there is the anti-clerical party, and there are the ne'er-do-wells. The clerical people are dark and pious and cold; there is a curious stone-cold, ponderous darkness over them, moral and gloomy. Then the anti-clerical party, with the Syndaco at the head, is bourgeois and respectable as far as the middle-aged people are concerned, banal, respectable, shut off as by a wall from the clerical people. The young anti-clericals are the young bloods of the place, the men who gather every night in the more expensive and less-respectable café. These young men are all free-thinkers, great dancers, singers, players of the guitar. They are immoral and slightly cynical. Their leader is the young shopkeeper, who has lived in Vienna, who is a bit of a bounder, with a veneer of sneering irony on an original good nature. He is well-to-do, and gives dances to which only the looser women go, with these reckless young men. He also gets up parties of pleasure, and is chiefly responsible for the coming of the players to the theatre this carnival. These young men are disliked, but they belong to the important class, they are well-to-do, and they have the life of the village in their hands. The clerical peasants are priest-ridden and good, because they are poor and afraid and superstitious. There is, lastly, a sprinkling of loose women, one who keeps the inn where the soldiers drink. These women are a definite set. They know what they are, they pretend nothing else. They are not prostitutes, but just loose women. They keep to their own clique, among men and women, never wanting to compromise anybody else.

And beyond all these there are the Franciscan friars in their brown robes, so shy, so silent, so obliterated, as they stand back in the shop, waiting to buy the bread for the monastery, waiting obscure and neutral, till no one shall be in the shop wanting to be served. The village women speak to them in a curious neutral, official, slightly contemptuous voice. They answer neutral and humble, though distinctly.

At the theatre, now the play is over, the peasants in their black hats and cloaks crowd the hall. Only Pietro, the wharf-lounger, has no cloak, and a bit of a cap on the side of his head instead of a black felt hat. His clothes are thin and loose on his thin, vigorous, cat-like body, and he is cold, but he takes no notice. His hands are always in his pockets, his shoulders slightly raised.

The few women slip away home. In the little theatre-bar the well-to-do young atheists are having another drink. Not that they spend much. A tumbler of wine or a glass of vermouth costs a penny. And the wine is horrible new stuff. Yet the little baker, Agostino, sits on a bench with his pale baby on his knee, putting the wine to its lips. And the baby drinks, like a bird fledgling.

Upstairs, the quality has paid its visits and shaken hands: the Syndaco and the well-to-do half-Austrian owners of the woodyard, the Bertolini, have ostentatiously shown their mutual friendship; our padrone, the Signor Pietro Di Paoli, has visited his relatives the Graziani in the box next the stage, and has spent two intervals with us in our box; meanwhile, his two peasants standing down below, pathetic, thin contadini of the old school, like worn stones, have looked up at us as if we are the angels in heaven, with a reverential, devotional eye, they themselves far away below, standing in the bay at the back, below all.

The chemist and the grocer and the school-mistress pay calls. They have all sat self-consciously posed in front of their boxes, like framed photographs of themselves. The second grocer and the baker visit each other. The barber looks in on the carpenter, then drops downstairs among the crowd. Class distinctions are cut very fine. As we pass with the

41

padrona of the hotel, who is a Bavarian, we stop to speak to our own padroni, the Di Paoli. They have a warm handshake and effusive polite conversation for us; for Maria Samuelli, a distant bow. We realise our mistake.

The barber—not the Siciliano, but flashy little Luigi with the big tie-ring and the curls—knows all about the theatre. He says that Enrico Persevalli has for his mistress Carina, the servant in *Ghosts*: that the thin, gentle, old-looking king in *Hamlet* is the husband of Adelaida, and Carina is their daughter: that the old, sharp, fat little body of a queen is Adelaida's mother: that they all like Enrico Persevalli, because he is a very clever man: but that the 'Comic', Il Brillante, Francesco, is unsatisfied.

In three performances in Epiphany week, the company took two hundred and sixty-five francs, which was phenomenal. The manager, Enrico Persevalli, and Adelaida pay twenty-four francs for every performance, or every evening on which a performance is given, as rent for the theatre, including light. The company is completely satisfied with its reception on the Lago di Garda.

So it is all over. The Bersaglieri go running all the way home, because it is already half-past ten. The night is very dark. About four miles up the lake the searchlights of the Austrian border are swinging, looking for smugglers. Otherwise the darkness is complete.

IV

SAN GAUDENZIO

IN the autumn the little rosy cyclamens blossom in the shade of this west side of the lake. They are very cold and fragrant, and their scent seems to belong to Greece, to the Bacchae. They are real flowers of the past. They seem to be blossoming in the landscape of Phaedra and Helen. They bend down, they brood like little chill fires. They are little living myths that I cannot understand.

After the cyclamens the Christmas roses are in bud. It is at this season that the cacchi are ripe on the trees in the garden, whole naked trees full of lustrous, orange-yellow, paradisal fruit, gleaming against the wintery blue sky. The monthly roses still blossom frail and pink, there are still crimson and yellow roses. But the vines are bare and the lemon-houses shut. And then, in mid-winter, the lowest buds of the Christmas roses appear under the hedges and rocks and by the streams. They are very lovely, these first, large, cold, pure buds, like violets, like magnolias, but cold, lit up with the light from the snow.

The days go by, through the brief silence of winter, when the sunshine is so still and pure, like iced wine, and the dead leaves gleam brown, and water sounds hoarse in the ravines. It is so still and transcendent, the cypress trees poise like flames of forgotten darkness, that should have been blown out at the end of the summer. For as we have candles to light the darkness of night, so the cypresses are candles to keep the darkness aflame in the full sunshine.

Meanwhile, the Christmas roses become many. They rise from their budded, intact humbleness near the ground, they rise up, they throw up their crystal, they become handsome, they are heaps of confident, mysterious whiteness in the shadow of a rocky stream. It is almost uncanny to see them. They are the flowers of darkness, white and wonderful beyond belief.

Then their radiance becomes soiled and brown, they thaw, break, and scatter and vanish away. Already the primroses are coming out, and the almond is in bud. The winter is passing away. On the mountains the fierce snow gleams apricot gold as evening approaches, golden, apricot, but so bright that it is almost frightening. What can be so fiercely gleaming when all is shadowy? It is something inhuman and unmitigated between heaven and earth.

The heavens are strange and proud all the winter, their progress goes on without reference to the dim earth. The dawns come white and translucent, the lake is a moonstone in the dark hills, then across the lake there stretches a vein of fire, then a whole, orange, flashing track over the whiteness. There is the exquisite silent passage of the day, and then at evening the afterglow, a huge incandescence of rose, hanging above and gleaming, as if it were the presence of a host of angels in rapture. It gleams like a rapturous chorus, then passes away, and the stars appear, large and flashing.

Meanwhile, the primroses are dawning on the ground, their light is growing stronger, spreading over the banks and under the bushes. Between the olive roots the violets are out, large, white, grave violets, and less serious blue ones. And looking down the hill, among the grey smoke of olive leaves, pink puffs of smoke are rising up. It is the almond and the apricot trees, it is the Spring.

Soon the primroses are strong on the ground. There is a bank of small, frail crocuses shooting the lavender into this spring. And then the tussocks and tussocks of primroses are fully out, there is full morning everywhere on the banks and roadsides and stream-sides, and around the olive roots, a morning of primroses underfoot, with an invisible threading of many violets, and then the lovely blue clusters of hepatica, really like pieces of blue sky showing through a clarity of primrose. The few birds are piping thinly and shyly, the streams sing again, there is a strange flowering shrub full of incense, overturned flowers of crimson and gold, like Bohemian glass. Between the olive roots new grass is coming, day is leaping all clear and coloured from the earth, it is full Spring, full first rapture.

Does it pass away, or does it only lose its pristine quality? It deepens and intensifies, like experience. The days seem to be darker and richer, there is a sense of power in the strong air. On the banks by the lake the orchids are out, many, many pale bee-orchids standing clear from the short grass over the lake. And in the hollows are the grape hyacinths, purple as noon, with the heavy, sensual fragrance of noon. They are many-breasted, and full of milk, and ripe, and sun-darkened, like many-breasted Diana.

We could not bear to live down in the village any more, now that the days opened large and spacious and the evenings drew out in sunshine. We could not bear the indoors, when above us the mountains shone in clear air. It was time to go up, to climb with the sun.

So after Easter we went to San Gaudenzio. It was three miles away, up the winding mule-track that climbed higher and higher along the lake. Leaving the last house of the village, the path wound on the steep, cliff-like side of the lake, curving into the hollow where the landslip had tumbled the rocks in chaos, then out again on to the bluff of a headland that hung over the lake.

Thus we came to the tall barred gate of San Gaudenzio, on which was the usual little fire-insurance tablet, and then the advertisements for beer, 'Birra, Verona', which is becoming a more and more popular drink.

Through the gate, inside the high wall, is the little Garden of Eden, a property of three or four acres fairly level upon a headland over the lake. The high wall girds it on the land side, and makes it perfectly secluded. On the lake side it is bounded by the sudden drops of the land, in sharp banks and terraces, overgrown with ilex and with laurel bushes, down to the brink of the cliff, so that the thicket of the first declivities seems to safeguard the property.

The pink farmhouse stands almost in the centre of the little territory, among the olive trees. It is a solid, six-roomed place, about fifty years old, having been rebuilt by Paolo's uncle. Here we came to live for a time with the Fiori, Maria and Paolo, and their three children, Giovanni and Marco and Felicina.

Paolo had inherited, or partly inherited, San Gaudenzio, which had been in his family for generations. He was a peasant of fifty-three, very grey and wrinkled and worn-looking, but at the same time robust, with full strong limbs and a powerful chest. His face was old, but his body was solid and powerful. His eyes were blue like upper ice, beautiful. He had been a fair-haired man, now he was almost white.

He was strangely like the pictures of peasants in the northern Italian pictures, with the same curious nobility, the same aristocratic, eternal look of motionlessness, something statuesque. His head was hard and fine, the bone finely constructed, though the skin of his face was loose and furrowed with work. His temples had that fine, hard clarity which is seen in Mantegna, an almost jewel-like quality.

We all loved Paolo, he was so finished in his being, detached, with an almost classic simplicity and gentleness, an eternal kind of sureness. There was also something concluded and unalterable about him, something inaccessible.

Maria Fiori was different. She was from the plain, like Enrico Persevalli and the Bersaglieri from the Venetian district. She reminded me again of oxen, broad-boned and massive in physique, dark-skinned, slow in her soul. But, like the oxen of the plain, she knew her work, she knew the other people engaged in the work. Her intelligence was attentive and purposive. She had been a housekeeper, a servant, in Venice and Verona, before her marriage. She had got the hang of this world of commerce and activity, she wanted to master it. But she was weighted down by her heavy animal blood.

Paolo and she were the opposite sides of the universe, the light and the dark. Yet they lived together now without friction, detached, each subordinated in their common relationship. With regard to Maria, Paolo omitted himself; Maria omitted herself with regard to Paolo. Their souls were silent and detached, completely apart, and silent, quite silent. They shared the physical relationship of marriage as if it were something beyond them, a third thing.

They had suffered very much in the earlier stages of their connection. Now the storm had gone by, leaving them, as it were, spent. They were both by nature passionate, vehement. But the lines of their passion were opposite. Hers was the primitive, crude, violent flux of the blood, emotional and undiscriminating, but wanting to mix and mingle. His was the hard, clear, invulnerable passion of the bones, finely tempered and unchangeable. She was the flint and he the steel. But in continual striking together they only destroyed each other. The fire was a third thing, belonging to neither of them.

She was still heavy and full of desire. She was much younger than he.

"How long did you know your Signora before you were married?" she asked me.

"Six weeks," I said.

"Il Paolo e me, venti giorni, tre settimani," she cried vehemently. Three weeks they had known each other when they married. She still triumphed in the fact. So did Paolo. But it was past, strangely and rather terribly past.

What did they want when they came together, Paolo and she? He was a man over thirty, she was a woman of twenty-three. They were both violent in desire and of strong will. They came together at once, like two wrestlers almost matched in strength. Their

44

meetings must have been splendid. Giovanni, the eldest child, was a tall lad of sixteen, with soft brown hair and grey eyes, and a clarity of brow, and the same calm simplicity of bearing which made Paolo so complete; but the son had at the same time a certain brownness of skin, a heaviness of blood, which he had from his mother. Paolo was so clear and translucent.

In Giovanni the fusion of the parents was perfect, he was a perfect spark from the flint and steel. There was in Paolo a subtle intelligence in feeling, a delicate appreciation of the other person. But the mind was unintelligent, he could not grasp a new order. Maria Fiori was much sharper and more adaptable to the ways of the world. Paolo had an almost glass-like quality, fine and clear and perfectly tempered; but he was also finished and brittle. Maria was much coarser, more vulgar, but also she was more human, more fertile, with crude potentiality. His passion was too fixed in its motion, hers too loose and overwhelming.

But Giovanni was beautiful, gentle, and courtly like Paolo, but warm, like Maria, ready to flush like a girl with anger or confusion. He stood straight and tall, and seemed to look into the far distance with his clear grey eyes. Yet also he could look at one and touch one with his look, he could meet one. Paolo's blue eyes were like the eyes of the old spinning-woman, clear and blue and belonging to the mountains, their vision seemed to end in space, abstract. They reminded me of the eyes of the eagle, which looks into the sun, and which teaches its young to do the same, although they are unwilling.

Marco, the second son, was thirteen years old. He was his mother's favourite. Giovanni loved his father best. But Marco was his mother's son, with the same brown-gold and red complexion, like a pomegranate, and coarse black hair, and brown eyes like pebble, like agate, like an animal's eyes. He had the same broad, bovine figure, though he was only a boy. But there was some discrepancy in him. He was not unified, he had no identity.

He was strong and full of animal life, but always aimless, as though his wits scarcely controlled him. But he loved his mother with a fundamental, generous, undistinguishing love. Only he always forgot what he was going to do. He was much more sensitive than Maria, more shy and reluctant. But his shyness, his sensitiveness only made him more aimless and awkward, a tiresome clown, slack and uncontrolled, witless. All day long his mother shouted and shrilled and scolded at him, or hit him angrily. He did not mind, he came up like a cork, warm and roguish and curiously appealing. She loved him with a fierce protective love, grounded on pain. There was such a split, a contrariety in his soul, one part reacting against the other, which landed him always into trouble.

It was when Marco was a baby that Paolo had gone to America. They were poor on San Gaudenzio. There were the few olive trees, the grapes, and the fruit; there was the one cow. But these scarcely made a living. Neither was Maria content with the real peasant's lot any more, polenta at midday and vegetable soup in the evening, and no way out, nothing to look forward to, no future, only this eternal present. She had been in service, and had eaten bread and drunk coffee, and known the flux and variable chance of life. She had departed from the old static conception. She knew what one might be, given a certain chance. The fixture was the thing she militated against. So Paolo went to America, to California, into the gold mines.

Maria wanted the future, the endless possibility of life on earth. She wanted her sons to be freer, to achieve a new plane of living. The peasant's life was a slave's life, she said, railing against the poverty and the drudgery. And it was quite true, Paolo and Giovanni worked twelve and fourteen hours a day at heavy laborious work that would have broken an Englishman. And there was nothing at the end of it. Yet Paolo was even happy so. This was the truth to him.

It was the mother who wanted things different. It was she who railed and railed against the miserable life of the peasants. When we were going to throw to the fowls a dry broken penny roll of white bread, Maria said, with anger and shame and resentment in her voice: "Give it to Marco, he will eat it. It isn't too dry for him."

White bread was a treat for them even now, when everybody eats bread. And Maria Fiori hated it, that bread should be a treat to her children, when it was the meanest food of all the rest of the world. She was in opposition to this order. She did not want her sons to be peasants, fixed and static as posts driven in the earth. She wanted them to be in the great flux of life, in the midst of all possibilities. So she at length sent Paolo to America to the gold-mines. Meanwhile, she covered the wall of her parlour with picture postcards, to bring the outer world of cities and industries into her house.

Paolo was entirely remote from Maria's world. He had not yet even grasped the fact of money, not thoroughly. He reckoned in land and olive trees. So he had the old fatalistic attitude to his circumstances, even to his food. The earth was the Lord's and the fulness thereof: also the leanness thereof. Paolo could only do his part and leave the rest. If he ate in plenty, having oil and wine and sausage in the house, and plenty of maize-meal, he was glad with the Lord. If he ate meagrely, of poor polenta, that was fate, it was the skies that ruled these things, and no man ruled the skies. He took his fate as it fell from the skies.

Maria was exorbitant about money. She would charge us all she could for what we had and for what was done for us.

Yet she was not mean in her soul. In her soul she was in a state of anger because of her own closeness. It was a violation to her strong animal nature. Yet her mind had wakened to the value of money. She knew she could alter her position, the position of her children, by virtue of money. She knew it was only money that made the difference between master and servant. And this was all the difference she would acknowledge. So she ruled her life according to money. Her supreme passion was to be mistress rather than servant, her supreme aspiration for her children was that in the end they might be masters and not servants.

Paolo was untouched by all this. For him there was some divinity about a master which even America had not destroyed. If we came in for supper whilst the family was still at table he would have the children at once take their plates to the wall, he would have Maria at once set table for us, though their own meal were never finished. And this was not servility, it was the dignity of a religious conception. Paolo regarded us as belonging to the Signoria, those who were elect, near to God. And this was part of his religious service. His life was a ritual. It was very beautiful, but it made me unhappy, the purity of his spirit was so sacred and the actual facts seemed such a sacrilege to it. Maria was nearer to the actual truth when she said that money was the only distinction. But Paolo had hold of an eternal truth, where hers was temporal. Only Paolo misapplied this eternal truth. He should not have given Giovanni the inferior status and a fat, mean Italian tradesman the superior. That was false, a real falsity. Maria knew it and hated it. But Paolo could not distinguish between the accident of riches and the aristocracy of the spirit. So Maria rejected him altogether, and went to the other extreme. We were all human beings like herself; naked, there was no distinction between us, no higher nor lower. But we were possessed of more money than she. And she had to steer her course between these two conceptions. The money alone made the real distinction, the separation; the being, the life made the common level.

Paolo had the curious peasants' avarice also, but it was not meanness. It was a sort of religious conservation of his own power, his own self. Fortunately he could leave all business transactions on our account to Maria, so that his relation with us was purely ritualistic. He would have given me anything, trusting implicitly that I would fulfil my own nature as Signore, one of those more godlike, nearer the light of perfection than himself, a peasant. It was pure bliss to him to bring us the first-fruit of the garden, it was like laying it on an altar.

And his fulfilment was in a fine, subtle, exquisite relationship, not of manners, but subtle interappreciation. He worshipped a finer understanding and a subtler tact. A further fineness and dignity and freedom in bearing was to him an approach towards the divine, so he loved men best of all, they fulfilled his soul. A woman was always a woman, and sex was a low level whereon he did not esteem himself. But a man, a doer, the instrument of God, he was really god-like.

Paolo was a Conservative. For him the world was established and divine in its establishment. His vision grasped a small circle. A finer nature, a higher understanding, took in a greater circle, comprehended the whole. So that when Paolo was in relation to a man of further vision, he himself was extended towards the whole. Thus he was fulfilled. And his initial assumption was that every signore, every gentleman, was a man of further, purer vision than himself. This assumption was false. But Maria's assumption, that no one had a further vision, no one was more elect than herself, that we are all one flesh and blood and being, was even more false. Paolo was mistaken in actual life, but Maria was ultimately mistaken.

Paolo, conservative as he was, believing that a priest must be a priest of God, yet very rarely went to church. And he used the religious oaths that Maria hated, even *Porca-Maria*. He always used oaths, either Bacchus or God or Mary or the Sacrament. Maria was always offended. Yet it was she who, in her soul, jeered at the Church and at religion. She wanted the human society as the absolute, without religious abstractions. So Paolo's oaths enraged her, because of their profanity, she said. But it was really because of their subscribing to another superhuman order. She jeered at the clerical people. She made a loud clamour of derision when the parish priest of the village above went down to the big village on the lake, and across the piazza, the quay, with two pigs in a sack on his shoulder. This was a real picture of the sacred minister to her.

One day, when a storm had blown down an olive tree in front of the house, and Paolo and Giovanni were beginning to cut it up, this same priest of Mugiano came to San Gaudenzio. He was an iron-grey, thin, disreputable-looking priest, very talkative and loud and queer. He seemed like an old ne'er-do-well in priests' black, and he talked loudly, almost to himself, as drunken people do. At once *he* must show the Fiori how to cut up the tree, he must have the axe from Paolo. He shouted to Maria for a glass of wine. She brought it out to him with a sort of insolent deference, insolent contempt of the man and traditional deference to the cloth. The priest drained the tumblerful of wine at one drink, his thin throat with its Adam's apple working. And he did not pay the penny.

Then he stripped off his cassock and put away his hat, and, a ludicrous figure in ill-fitting black knee-breeches and a not very clean shirt, a red handkerchief round his neck, he proceeded to give great extravagant blows at the tree. He was like a caricature. In the doorway Maria was encouraging him rather jeeringly, whilst she winked at me. Marco was stifling his hysterical amusement in his mother's apron, and prancing with glee. Paolo and Giovanni stood by the fallen tree, very grave and unmoved, inscrutable, abstract. Then the youth came away to the doorway, with a flush mounting on his face and a grimace

47

distorting its youngness. Only Paolo, unmoved and detached, stood by the tree with unchanging, abstract face, very strange, his eyes fixed in the ageless stare which is so characteristic.

Meanwhile the priest swung drunken blows at the tree, his thin buttocks bending in the green-black broadcloth, supported on thin shanks, and thin throat growing dull purple in the red-knotted kerchief. Nevertheless he was doing the job. His face was wet with sweat. He wanted another glass of wine.

He took no notice of us. He was strangely a local, even a mountebank figure, but entirely local, an appurtenance of the district.

It was Maria who jeeringly told us the story of the priest, who shrugged her shoulders to imply that he was a contemptible figure. Paolo sat with the abstract look on his face, as of one who hears and does not hear, is not really concerned. He never opposed or contradicted her, but stayed apart. It was she who was violent and brutal in her ways. But sometimes Paolo went into a rage, and then Maria, everybody, was afraid. It was a white heavy rage, when his blue eyes shone unearthly, and his mouth opened with a curious drawn blindness of the old Furies. There was something of the cruelty of a falling mass of snow, heavy, horrible. Maria drew away, there was a silence. Then the avalanche was finished.

They must have had some cruel fights before they learned to withdraw from each other so completely. They must have begotten Marco in hatred, terrible disintegrated opposition and otherness. And it was after this, after the child of their opposition was born, that Paolo went away to California, leaving his San Gaudenzio, travelling with several companions, like blind beasts, to Havre, and thence to New York, then to California. He stayed five years in the gold-mines, in a wild valley, living with a gang of Italians in a town of corrugated iron.

All the while he had never really left San Gaudenzio. I asked him, "Used you to think of it, the lake, the Monte Baldo, the laurel trees down the slope?" He tried to see what I wanted to know. Yes, he said—but uncertainly. I could see that he had never been really homesick. It had been very wretched on the ship going from Havre to New York. That he told me about. And he told me about the gold-mines, the galleries, the valley, the huts in the valley. But he had never really fretted for San Gaudenzio whilst he was in California.

In real truth he was at San Gaudenzio all the time, his fate was riveted there. His going away was an excursion from reality, a kind of sleep-walking. He left his own reality there in the soil above the lake of Garda. That his body was in California, what did it matter? It was merely for a time, and for the sake of his own earth, his land. He would pay off the mortgage. But the gate at home was his gate all the time, his hand was on the latch.

As for Maria, he had felt his duty towards her. She was part of his little territory, the rooted centre of the world. He sent her home the money. But it did not occur to him, in his soul, to miss her. He wanted her to be safe with the children, that was all. In his flesh perhaps he missed the woman. But his spirit was even more completely isolated since marriage. Instead of having united with each other, they had made each other more terribly distinct and separate. He could live alone eternally. It was his condition. His sex was functional, like eating and thinking. To take a woman, a prostitute at the camp, or not to take her, was no more vitally important than to get drunk or not to get drunk of a Sunday. And fairly often on Sunday Paolo got drunk. His world remained unaltered.

But Maria suffered more bitterly. She was a young, powerful, passionate woman, and she was unsatisfied body and soul. Her soul's unsatisfaction became a bodily—

unsatisfaction. Her blood was heavy, violent, anarchic, insisting on the quality of the blood in all, and therefore on her own absolute right to satisfaction.

She took a wine licence for San Gaudenzio, and she sold wine. There were many scandals about her. Somehow it did not matter very much, outwardly. The authorities were too divided among themselves to enforce public opinion. Between the clerical party and the radicals and the socialists, what canons were left that were absolute? Besides, these wild villages had always been ungoverned.

Yet Maria suffered. Even she, according to her conviction, belonged to Paolo. And she felt betrayed, betrayed and deserted. The iron had gone deep into her soul. Paolo had deserted her, she had been betrayed to other men for five years. There was something cruel and implacable in life. She sat sullen and heavy, for all her quick activity. Her soul was sullen and heavy.

I could never believe that Felicina was Paolo's child. She was an unprepossessing little girl, affected, cold, selfish, foolish. Maria and Paolo, with real Italian greatness, were warm and natural towards the child in her. But they did not love her in their very souls, she was the fruit of ash to them. And this must have been the reason that she was so self-conscious and foolish and affected, small child that she was.

Paolo had come back from America a year before she was born—a year before she was born, Maria insisted. The husband and wife lived together in a relationship of complete negation. In his soul he was sad for her, and in her soul she felt annulled. He sat at evening in the chimney-seat, smoking, always pleasant and cheerful, not for a moment thinking he was unhappy. But his eyebrows and eyelids were lifted in a kind of vacancy, his blue eyes were round and somehow finished, though he was so gentle and vigorous in body. But the very quick of him was killed. He was like a ghost in the house, with his loose throat and powerful limbs, his open, blue extinct eyes, and his musical, slightly husky voice, that seemed to sound out of the past.

And Maria, stout and strong and handsome like a peasant woman, went about as if there were a weight on her, and her voice was high and strident. She, too, was finished in her life. But she remained unbroken, her will was like a hammer that destroys the old form.

Giovanni was patiently labouring to learn a little English. Paoli knew only four or five words, the chief of which were "a'right," "boss," "bread," and "day." The youth had these by heart, and was studying a little more. He was very graceful and lovable, but he found it difficult to learn. A confused light, like hot tears, would come into his eyes when he had again forgotten the phrase. But he carried the paper about with him, and he made steady progress.

He would go to America, he also. Not for anything would he stay in San Gaudenzio. His dream was to be gone. He would come back. The world was not San Gaudenzio to Giovanni.

The old order, the order of Paolo and of Pietro di Paoli, the aristocratic order of the supreme God, God the Father, the Lord, was passing away from the beautiful little territory. The household no longer receives its food, oil and wine and maize, from out of the earth in the motion of fate. The earth is annulled, and money takes its place. The landowner, who is the lieutenant of God and of Fate, like Abraham, he, too, is annulled. There is now the order of the rich, which supersedes the order of the Signoria.

It is passing away from Italy as it has passed from England. The peasant is passing away, the workman is taking his place. The stability is gone. Paolo is a ghost, Maria is the living body. And the new order means sorrow for the Italian more even than it has meant for us. But he will have the new order.

49

San Gaudenzio is already becoming a thing of the past. Below the house, where the land drops in sharp slips to the sheer cliff's edge, over which it is Maria's constant fear that Felicina will tumble, there are the deserted lemon gardens of the little territory, snug down below. They are invisible till one descends by tiny paths, sheer down into them. And there they stand, the pillars and walls erect, but a dead emptiness prevailing, lemon trees all dead, gone, a few vines in their place. It is only twenty years since the lemon trees finally perished of a disease and were not renewed. But the deserted terrace, shut between great walls, descending in their openness pull to the south, to the lake and the mountain opposite, seem more terrible than Pompeii in their silence and utter seclusion. The grape hyacinths flower in the cracks, the lizards run, this strange place hangs suspended and forgotten for ever, its erect pillars utterly meaningless.

I used to sit and write in the great loft of the lemon house, high up, far, far from the ground, the open front giving across the lake and the mountain snow opposite flush with twilight. The old matting and boards, the old disused implements of lemon culture made shadows in the deserted place. Then there would come the call from the back, away above: "Venga, venga mangiare."

We ate in the kitchen, where the olive and laurel wood burned in the open fireplace. It was always soup in the evening. Then we played games or cards, all playing; or there was singing, with the accordion, and sometimes a rough mountain peasant with a guitar.

But it is all passing away. Giovanni is in America, unless he has come back to the War. He will not want to live in San Gaudenzio when he is a man, he says. He and Marco will not spend their lives wringing a little oil and wine out of the rocky soil, even if they are not killed in the fighting which is going on at the end of the lake. In my loft by the lemon houses now I should hear the guns. And Giovanni kissed me with a kind of supplication when I went on to the steamer, as if he were beseeching for a soul. His eyes were bright and clear and lit up with courage. He will make a good fight for the new soul he wants—that is, if they do not kill him in this War.

V

THE DANCE

MARIA had no real licence for San Gaudenzio, yet the peasants always called for wine. It is easy to arrange in Italy. The penny is paid another time.

The wild old road that skirts the lake-side, scrambling always higher as the precipice becomes steeper, climbing and winding to the villages perched high up, passes under the high boundary-wall of San Gaudenzio, between that and the ruined church. But the road went just as much between the vines and past the house as outside, under the wall; for the high gates were always open, and men or women and mules come into the property to call at the door of the homestead. There was a loud shout, "Ah—a—a—ah—Mari—'a. O—O—Oh Pa'o'!" from outside, another wild, inarticulate cry from within, and one of the Fiori appeared in the doorway to hail the new-comer.

It was usually a man, sometimes a peasant from Mugiano, high up, sometimes a peasant from the wilds of the mountain, a wood-cutter, or a charcoal-burner. He came in and sat in the house-place, his glass of wine in his hand between his knees, or on the floor between his feet, and he talked in a few wild phrases, very shy, like a hawk indoors, and unintelligible in his dialect.

Sometimes we had a dance. Then, for the wine to drink, three men came with mandolines and guitars, and sat in a corner playing their rapid tunes, while all danced on the dusty brick floor of the little parlour. No strange women were invited, only men; the young bloods from the big village on the lake, the wild men from above. They danced the slow, trailing, lilting polka-waltz round and round the small room, the guitars and mandolines twanging rapidly, the dust rising from the soft bricks. There were only the two English women: so men danced with men, as the Italians love to do. They love even better to dance with men, with a dear blood-friend, than with women.

"It's better like this, two men?" Giovanni says to me, his face curiously tender.

The wood-cutters and peasants take off their coats, their throats are bare. They dance with strange intentness, particularly if they have for partner an English Signora. Their feet in thick boots are curiously swift and significant. And it is strange to see the Englishwomen, as they dance with the peasants, transfigured with a kind of brilliant surprise. All the while the peasants are very courteous, but quiet. They see the women dilate and flash, they think they have found a footing, they are certain. So the male dancers are quiet, but even grandiloquent, their feet nimble, their bodies wild and confident.

They are at a loss when the two English Signoras move together and laugh excitedly at the end of the dance.

"Isn't it fine?"

"Fine! Their arms are like iron, carrying you round."

"Yes! Yes! And the muscles on their shoulders! I never knew there were such muscles! I'm almost frightened."

"But it's fine, isn't it? I'm getting into the dance."

"Yes—yes—you've only to let them take you."

Then the glasses are put down, the guitars give their strange, vibrant, almost painful summons, and the dance begins again.

It is a strange dance, strange and lilting, and changing as the music changed. But it had always a kind of leisurely dignity, a trailing kind of polka-waltz, intimate, passionate, yet never hurried, never violent in its passion, always becoming more intense. The women's faces changed to a kind of transported wonder, they were in the very rhythm of delight. From the soft bricks of the floor the red ochre rose in a thin cloud of dust, making hazy the shadowy dancers; the three musicians, in their black hats and their cloaks, sat obscurely in the corner, making a music that came quicker and quicker, making a dance that grew swifter and more intense, more subtle, the men seeming to fly and to implicate another strange inter-rhythmic dance into the women, the women drifting and palpitating as if their souls shook and responded to a breeze that was subtly rushing upon them, through them; the men worked their feet, their thighs swifter, more vividly, the music came to an almost intolerable climax, there was a moment when the dance passed into a possession, the men caught up the women and swung them from the earth, leapt with them for a second, and then the next phase of the dance had begun, slower again, more subtly interwoven, taking perfect, oh, exquisite delight in every interrelated movement, a rhythm within a rhythm, a subtle approaching and thawing nearer to a climax, nearer, till, oh, there was the surpassing lift and swing of the women, when the woman's body seemed like a boat lifted over the powerful exquisite wave of the man's body, perfect, for a moment, and then once more the slow, intense, nearer movement of the dance began, always nearer, nearer, always to a more perfect climax.

51

And the woman waited as if in transport for the climax, when they would be flung into a movement surpassing all movement. They were flung, borne away, lifted like a boat on a supreme wave, into the zenith and nave of the heavens, consummate.

Then suddenly the dance crashed to an end, and the dancers stood stranded, lost, bewildered, on a strange shore. The air was full of red dust, half-lit by the lamp on the wall; the players in the corner were putting down their instruments to take up their glasses.

And the dancers sat round the wall, crowding in the little room, faint with the transport of repeated ecstasy. There was a subtle smile on the face of the men, subtle, knowing, so finely sensual that the conscious eyes could scarcely look at it. And the women were dazed, like creatures dazzled by too much light. The light was still on their faces, like a blindness, a reeling like a transfiguration. The men were bringing wine, on a little tin tray, leaning with their proud, vivid loins, their faces flickering with the same subtle smile. Meanwhile, Maria Fiori was splashing water, much water, on the red floor. There was the smell of water among the glowing, transfigured men and women who sat gleaming in another world, round the walls. The peasants have chosen their women. For the dark, handsome Englishwoman, who looks like a slightly malignant Madonna, comes II Duro; for the 'bella bionda', the wood-cutter. But the peasants have always to take their turn after the young well-to-do men from the village below.

Nevertheless they are confident. They cannot understand the middle-class diffidence of the young men who wear collars and ties and finger-rings.

The wood-cutter from the mountain is of medium height, dark, thin, and hard as a hatchet, with eyes that are black like the very flaming thrust of night. He is quite a savage. There is something strange about his dancing, the violent way he works one shoulder. He has a wooden leg, from the knee-joint. Yet he dances well, and is inordinately proud. He is fierce as a bird, and hard with energy as a thunderbolt. He will dance with the blonde signora. But he never speaks. He is like some violent natural phenomenon rather than a person. The woman begins to wilt a little in his possession.

"È bello—il ballo?' he asks at length, one direct, flashing question.

"Si—molto bello," cries the woman, glad to have speech again.

The eyes of the wood-cutter flash like actual possession. He seems now to have come into his own. With all his senses, he is dominant, sure.

He is inconceivably vigorous in body, and his dancing is almost perfect, with a little catch in it, owing to his lameness, which brings almost a pure intoxication. Every muscle in his body is supple as steel, supple, as strong as thunder, and yet so quick, so delicately swift, it is almost unbearable. As he draws near to the swing, the climax, the ecstasy, he seems to lie in wait, there is a sense of a great strength crouching ready. Then it rushes forth, liquid, perfect, transcendent, the woman swoons over in the dance, and it goes on, enjoyment, infinite, incalculable enjoyment. He is like a god, a strange natural phenomenon, most intimate and compelling, wonderful.

But he is not a human being. The woman, somewhere shocked in her independent soul, begins to fall away from him. She has another being, which he has not touched, and which she will fall back upon. The dance is over, she will fall back on herself. It is perfect, too perfect.

During the next dance, while she is in the power of the educated Ettore, a perfect and calculated voluptuary, who knows how much he can get out of this Northern woman, and only how much, the wood-cutter stands on the edge of the darkness, in the open doorway, and watches. He is fixed upon her, established, perfect. And all the while she is aware of the insistent hawk-like poising of the face of the wood-cutter, poised on the edge of the darkness, in the doorway, in possession, unrelinquishing.

And she is angry. There is something stupid, absurd, in the hard, talon-like eyes watching so fiercely and so confidently in the doorway, sure, unmitigated. Has the creature no sense?

The woman reacts from him. For some time she will take no notice of him. But he waits, fixed. Then she comes near to him, and his will seems to take hold of her. He looks at her with a strange, proud, inhuman confidence, as if his influence with her was already accomplished.

"Venga—venga un po'," he says, jerking his head strangely to the darkness.

"What?" she replies, and passes shaken and dilated and brilliant, consciously ignoring him, passes away among the others, among those who are safe.

There is food in the kitchen, great hunks of bread, sliced sausage that Maria has made, wine, and a little coffee. But only the quality come to eat. The peasants may not come in. There is eating and drinking in the little house, the guitars are silent. It is eleven o'clock.

Then there is singing, the strange bestial singing of these hills. Sometimes the guitars can play an accompaniment, but usually not. Then the men lift up their heads and send out the high, half-howling music, astounding. The words are in dialect. They argue among themselves for a moment: will the Signoria understand? They sing. The Signoria does not understand in the least. So with a strange, slightly malignant triumph, the men sing all the verses of their song, sitting round the walls of the little parlour. Their throats move, their faces have a slight mocking smile. The boy capers in the doorway like a faun, with glee, his straight black hair falling over his forehead. The elder brother sits straight and flushed, but even his eyes glitter with a kind of yellow light of laughter. Paolo also sits quiet, with the invisible smile on his face. Only Maria, large and active, prospering now, keeps collected, ready to order a shrill silence in the same way as she orders the peasants, violently, to keep their places.

The boy comes to me and says:

"Do you know, Signore, what they are singing?"

"No," I say.

So he capers with furious glee. The men with the watchful eyes, all roused, sit round the wall and sing more distinctly:

> "Si verrà le primavera
> Fiorann' le mandoline,
> Vienn' di basso le Trentine
> Coi 'taliani far' l'amor."

But the next verses are so improper that I pretend not to understand. The women, with wakened, dilated faces, are listening, listening hard, their two faces beautiful in their attention, as if listening to something magical, a long way off. And the men sitting round the wall sing more plainly, Coming nearer to the correct Italian. The song comes loud and vibrating and maliciously from their reedy throats, it penetrates everybody. The foreign women can understand the sound, they can feel the malicious, suggestive mockery. But they cannot catch the words. The smile becomes more dangerous on the faces of the men.

Then Maria Fiori sees that I have understood, and she cries, in her loud, overriding voice:

53

"Basta—basta."

The men get up, straighten their bodies with a curious, offering movement. The guitars and mandolines strike the vibrating strings. But the vague Northern reserve has come over the Englishwomen. They dance again, but without the fusion in the dance. They have had enough.

The musicians are thanked, they rise and go into the night. The men pass off in pairs. But the wood-cutter, whose name and whose nickname I could never hear, still hovered on the edge of the darkness.

Then Maria sent him also away, complaining that he was too wild, *proprio selvatico,* and only the 'quality' remained, the well-to-do youths from below. There was a little more coffee, and a talking, a story of a man who had fallen over a declivity in a lonely part going home drunk in the evening, and had lain unfound for eighteen hours. Then a story of a donkey who had kicked a youth in the chest and killed him.

But the women were tired, they would go to bed. Still the two young men would not go away. We all went out to look at the night.

The stars were very bright overhead, the mountain opposite and the mountains behind us faintly outlined themselves on the sky. Below, the lake was a black gulf. A little wind blew cold from the Adige.

In the morning the visitors had gone. They had insisted on staying the night. They had eaten eight eggs each and much bread at one o'clock in the morning. Then they had gone to sleep, lying on the floor in the sitting-room.

In the early sunshine they had drunk coffee and gone down to the village on the lake. Maria was very pleased. She would have made a good deal of money. The young men were rich. Her cupidity seemed like her very blossom.

VI

IL DURO

THE first time I saw Il Duro was on a sunny day when there came up a party of pleasure-makers to San Gaudenzio. They were three women and three men. The women were in cotton frocks, one a large, dark, florid woman in pink, the other two rather insignificant. The men I scarcely noticed at first, except that two were young and one elderly.

They were a queer party, even on a feast day, Coming up purely for pleasure, in the morning, strange, and slightly uncertain, advancing between the vines. They greeted Maria and Paolo in loud, coarse voices. There was something blowsy and uncertain and hesitating about the women in particular, which made one at once notice them.

Then a picnic was arranged for them out of doors, on the grass. They sat just in front of the house, under the olive tree, beyond the well. It should have been pretty, the women in their cotton frocks, and their friends, sitting with wine and food in the spring sunshine. But somehow it was not: it was hard and slightly ugly.

But since they were picnicking out of doors, we must do so too. We were at once envious. But Maria was a little unwilling, and then she set a table for us.

The strange party did not speak to us, they seemed slightly uneasy and angry at our presence. I asked Maria who they were. She lifted her shoulders, and, after a second's cold pause, said they were people from down below, and then, in her rather strident, shrill, slightly bitter, slightly derogatory voice, she added:

"They are not people for you, signore. You don't know them."

She spoke slightly angrily and Contemptuously of them, rather protectively of me. So that vaguely I gathered that they were not quite 'respectable'.

Only one man came into the house. He was very handsome, beautiful rather, a man of thirty-two or -three, with a clear golden skin, and perfectly turned face, something godlike. But the expression was strange. His hair was jet black and fine and smooth, glossy as a bird's wing, his brows were beautifully drawn, calm above his grey eyes, that had long dark lashes.

His eyes, however, had a sinister light in them, a pale, slightly repelling gleam, very much like a god's pale-gleaming eyes, with the same vivid pallor. And all his face had the slightly malignant, suffering look of a satyr. Yet he was very beautiful.

He walked quickly and surely, with his head rather down, passing from his desire to his object, absorbed, yet curiously indifferent, as if the transit were in a strange world, as if none of what he was doing were worth the while. Yet he did it for his own pleasure, and the light on his face, a pale, strange gleam through his clear skin, remained like a translucent smile, unchanging as time.

He seemed familiar with the household, he came and fetched wine at his will. Maria was angry with him. She railed loudly and violently. He was unchanged. He went out with the wine to the party on the grass. Maria regarded them all with some hostility.

They drank a good deal out there in the sunshine. The women and the older man talked floridly. Il Duro couched at the feast in his curious fashion—he had strangely flexible loins, upon which he seemed to crouch forward. But he was separate, like an animal that remains quite single, no matter where it is.

The party remained until about two o'clock. Then, slightly flushed, it moved on in a ragged group up to the village beyond. I do not know if they went to one of the inns of the stony village, or to the large strange house which belonged to the rich young grocer of the village below, a house kept only for feasts and riots, uninhabited for the most part. Maria would tell me nothing about them. Only the young well-to-do grocer, who had lived in Vienna, the Bertolotti, came later in the afternoon enquiring for the party.

And towards sunset I saw the elderly man of the group stumbling home very drunk down the path, after the two women, who had gone on in front. Then Paolo sent Giovanni to see the drunken one safely past the landslip, which was dangerous. Altogether it was an unsatisfactory business, very much like any other such party in any other country.

Then in the evening Il Duro came in. His name is Faustino, but everybody in the village has a nickname, which is almost invariably used. He came in and asked for supper. We had all eaten. So he ate a little food alone at the table, whilst we sat round the fire.

Afterwards we played 'Up, Jenkins'. That was the one game we played with the peasants, except that exciting one of thefts, which consists in shouting in rapid succession your guesses at the number of fingers rapidly spread out and shut into the hands again upon the table.

Il Duro joined in the game. And that was because he had been in America, and now was rich. He felt he could come near to the strange signori. But he was always inscrutable.

It was queer to look at the hands spread on the table: the Englishwomen, having rings on their soft fingers; the large fresh hands of the elder boy, the brown paws of the younger; Paolo's distorted great hard hands of a peasant; and the big, dark brown, animal, shapely hands of Faustino.

He had been in America first for two years and then for five years—seven years altogether—but he only spoke a very little English. He was always with Italians. He had served chiefly in a flag factory, and had very little to do save to push a trolley with flags from the dyeing-room to the drying-room— I believe it was this.

Then he had come home from America with a fair amount of money, he had taken his uncle's garden, had inherited his uncle's little house, and he lived quite alone.

He was rich, Maria said, shouting in her strident voice. He at once disclaimed it, peasant-wise. But before the signori he was glad also to appear rich. He was mean, that was more, Maria cried, half-teasing, half getting at him.

He attended to his garden, grew vegetables all the year round, lived in his little house, and in spring made good money as a vine-grafter: he was an expert vine-grafter.

After the boys had gone to bed he sat and talked to me. He was curiously attractive and curiously beautiful, but somehow like stone in his clear colouring and his clear-cut face. His temples, with the black hair, were distinct and fine as a work of art.

But always his eyes had this strange, half-diabolic, half-tortured pale gleam, like a goat's, and his mouth was shut almost uglily, his cheeks stern. His moustache was brown, his teeth strong and spaced. The women said it was a pity his moustache was brown.

"Peccato! —sa, per bellezza, i baffi neri—ah-h!"

Then a long-drawn exclamation of voluptuous appreciation.

"You live quite alone?" I said to him.

He did. And even when he had been ill he was alone. He had been ill two years before. His cheeks seemed to harden like marble and to become pale at the thought. He was afraid, like marble with fear.

"But why," I said, "why do you live alone? You are sad— ê triste."

He looked at me with his queer, pale eyes. I felt a great static misery in him, something very strange.

"Triste!" he repeated, stiffening up, hostile. I could not understand.

"Voul' dire che hai l' aria dolorosa," cried Maria, like a chorus interpreting. And there was always a sort of loud ring of challenge somewhere in her voice.

"Sad," I said in English.

"Sad!" he repeated, also in English. And he did not smile or change, only his face seemed to become more stone-like. And he only looked at me, into my eyes, with the long, pale, steady, inscrutable look of a goat, I can only repeat, something stone-like.

"Why," I said, "don't you marry? Man doesn't live alone."

"I don't marry," he said to me, in his emphatic, deliberate, cold fashion, "because I've seen too much. Ho visto troppo."

"I don't understand," I said.

Yet I could feel that Paolo, sitting silent, like a monolith also, in the chimney opening, he understood: Maria also understood.

Il Duro looked again steadily into my eyes.

"Ho visto troppo," he repeated, and the words seemed engraved on stone. "I've seen too much."

"But you can marry," I said, "however much you have seen, if you have seen all the world."

He watched me steadily, like a strange creature looking at me.

"What woman?" he said to me.

"You can find a woman—there are plenty of women," I said.

56

"Not for me," he said. "I have known too many. I've known too much, I can marry nobody."

"Do you dislike women?" I said.

"No—quite otherwise. I don't think ill of them."

"Then why can't you marry? Why must you live alone?"

"Why live with a woman?" he said to me, and he looked mockingly. "Which woman is it to be?"

"You can find her," I said. "There are many women."

Again he shook his head in the stony, final fashion.

"Not for me. I have known too much."

"But does that prevent you from marrying?"

He looked at me steadily, finally. And I could see it was impossible for us to understand each other, or for me to understand him. I could not understand the strange white gleam of his eyes, where it came from.

Also I knew he liked me very much, almost loved me, which again was strange and puzzling. It was as if he were a fairy, a faun, and had no soul. But he gave me a feeling of vivid sadness, a sadness that gleamed like phosphorescence. He himself was not sad. There was a completeness about him, about the pallid otherworld he inhabited, which excluded sadness. It was too complete, too final, too defined. There was no yearning, no vague merging off into mistiness. . . . He was as clear and fine as semi-transparent rock, as a substance in moonlight. He seemed like a crystal that has achieved its final shape and has nothing more to achieve.

That night he slept on the floor of the sitting-room. In the morning he was gone. But a week after he came again, to graft the vines.

All the morning and the afternoon he was among the vines, crouching before them, cutting them back with his sharp, bright knife, amazingly swift and sure, like a god. It filled me with a sort of panic to see him crouched flexibly, like some strange animal god, doubled on his haunches, before the young vines, and swiftly, vividly, without thought, cut, cut, cut at the young budding shoots, which fell unheeded on to the earth. Then again he strode with his curious half-goatlike movement across the garden, to prepare the lime.

He mixed the messy stuff, cow-dung and lime and water and earth, carefully with his hands, as if he understood that too. He was not a worker. He was a creature in intimate communion with the sensible world, knowing purely by touch the limey mess he mixed amongst, knowing as if by relation between that soft matter and the matter of himself.

Then again he strode over the earth, a gleaming piece of earth himself, moving to the young vines. Quickly, with a few clean cuts of the knife, he prepared the new shoot, which he had picked out of a handful which lay beside him on the ground; he went finely to the quick of the plant, inserted the graft, then bound it up, fast, hard.

It was like God grafting the life of man upon the body of the earth, intimately conjuring with his own flesh.

All the while Paolo stood by, somehow excluded from the mystery, talking to me, to Faustino. And Il Duro answered easily, as if his mind were disengaged. It was his senses that were absorbed in the sensible life of the plant, and the lime and the cow-dung he handled.

Watching him, watching his absorbed, bestial, and yet god-like crouching before the plant, as if he were the god of lower life, I somehow understood his isolation, why he did not marry. Pan and the ministers of Pan do not marry, the sylvan gods. They are single and isolated in their being.

It is in the spirit that marriage takes place. In the flesh there is connection, but only in the spirit is there a new thing created out of two different antithetic things. In the body I am conjoined with the woman. But in the spirit my conjunction with her creates a third thing, an absolute, a Word, which is neither me nor her, nor of me nor of her, but which is absolute.

And Faustino had none of this spirit. In him sensation itself was absolute—not spiritual consummation, but physical sensation. So he could not marry, it was not for him. He belonged to the god Pan, to the absolute of the senses.

All the while his beauty, so perfect and so defined, fascinated me, a strange Static perfection about him. But his movements, whilst they fascinated, also repelled. I can always see him crouched before the vines on his haunches, his haunches doubled together in a complete animal unconsciousness, his face seeming in its strange golden pallor and its hardness of line, with the gleaming black of the fine hair on the brow and temples, like something reflective, like the reflecting surface of a stone that gleams out of the depths of night. It was like darkness revealed in its steady, unchanging pallor.

Again he stayed through the evening, having quarrelled once more with the Maria about money. He quarrelled violently, yet coldly. There was something terrifying in it. And as soon as the matter of dispute was settled, all trace of interest or feeling vanished from him.

Yet he liked, above all things, to be near the English signori. They seemed to exercise a sort of magnetic attraction over him. It was something of the purely physical world, as a magnetised needle swings towards soft iron. He was quite helpless in the relation. Only by mechanical attraction he gravitated into line with us.

But there was nothing between us except our complete difference. It was like night and day flowing together.

VII

JOHN

BESIDES Il Duro, we found another Italian who could speak English, this time quite well. We had walked about four or five miles up the lake, getting higher and higher. Then quite suddenly, on the shoulder of a bluff far up, we came on a village, icy cold, and as if forgotten.

We went into the inn to drink something hot. The fire of olive sticks was burning in the open chimney, one or two men were talking at a table, a young woman with a baby stood by the fire watching something boil in a large pot. Another woman was seen in the house-place beyond.

In the chimney-seats sat a young mule-driver, who had left his two mules at the door of the inn, and opposite him an elderly stout man. They got down and offered us the seats of honour, which we accepted with due courtesy.

The chimneys are like the wide, open chimney-places of old English cottages, but the hearth is raised about a foot and a half or two feet from the floor, so that the fire is almost level with the hands; and those who sit in the chimney-seats are raised above the audience in the room, something like two gods flanking the fire, looking out of the cave of ruddy darkness into the open, lower world of the room.

We asked for coffee with milk and rum. The stout landlord took a seat near us below. The comely young woman with the baby took the tin coffee-pot that stood among the grey ashes, put in fresh coffee among the old bottoms, filled it with water, then pushed it more into the fire.

The landlord turned to us with the usual naïve, curious deference, and the usual question:

"You are Germans?"

"English."

"Ah—Inglesi."

Then there is a new note of cordiality—or so I always imagine—and the rather rough, cattle-like men who are sitting with their wine round the table look up more amicably. They do not like being intruded upon. Only the landlord is always affable.

"I have a son who speaks English," he says: he is a handsome, courtly old man, of the Falstaff sort.

"Oh!"

"He has been in America."

"And where is he now?"

"He is at home. O— Nicoletta, where is the Giovann'?" The comely young woman with the baby came in.

"He is with the band," she said.

The old landlord looked at her with pride.

"This is my daughter-in-law," he said.

She smiled readily to the Signora.

"And the baby?" we asked.

"Mio figlio," cried the young woman, in the strong, penetrating voice of these women. And she came forward to show the child to the Signora.

It was a bonny baby: the whole company was united in adoration and service of the bambino. There was a moment of suspension, when religious submission seemed to come over the inn-room.

Then the Signora began to talk, and it broke upon the Italian child-reverence.

"What is he called?"

"Oscare," came the ringing note of pride. And the mother talked to the baby in dialect. All, men and women alike, felt themselves glorified by the presence of the child.

At last the coffee in the tin coffee-pot was boiling and frothing out of spout and lid. The milk in the little copper pan was also hot, among the ashes. So we had our drink at last.

The landlord was anxious for us to see Giovanni, his son. There was a village band performing up the street, in front of the house of a colonel who had come home wounded from Tripoli. Everybody in the village was wildly proud about the colonel and about the brass band, the music of which was execrable.

We just looked into the street. The band of uncouth fellows was playing the same tune over and over again before a desolate, newish house. A crowd of desolate, forgotten villagers stood round, in the cold upper air. It seemed altogether that the place was forgotten by God and man.

But the landlord, burly, courteous, handsome, pointed out with a flourish the Giovanni, standing in the band playing a cornet. The band itself consisted only of five men, rather like beggars in the street. But Giovanni was the strangest! He was tall and thin and somewhat German-looking, wearing shabby American clothes and a very high double

59

collar and a small American crush hat. He looked entirely like a ne'er-do-well who plays a violin in the street, dressed in the most down-at-heel, sordid respectability.

"That is he—you see, Signore—the young one under the balcony."

The father spoke with love and pride, and the father was a gentleman, like Falstaff, a pure gentleman. The daughter-in-law also peered out to look at Il Giovann', who was evidently a figure of repute, in his sordid, degenerate American respectability. Meanwhile, this figure of repute blew himself red in the face, producing staccato strains on his cornet. And the crowd stood desolate and forsaken in the cold, upper afternoon.

Then there was a sudden rugged "Evviva, Evviva!" from the people, the band stopped playing, somebody valiantly broke into a line of the song:

"Tripoli, sarà italiana,
Sarà italiana al rombo del cannon."

The colonel had appeared on the balcony, a smallish man, very yellow in the face, with grizzled black hair and very shabby legs. They all seemed so sordidly, hopelessly shabby.

He suddenly began to speak, leaning forward, hot and feverish and yellow, upon the iron rail of the balcony. There was something hot and marshy and sick about him, slightly repulsive, less than human. He told his fellow-villagers how he loved them, how, when he lay uncovered on the sands of Tripoli, week after week, he had known they were watching him from the Alpine height of the village, he could feel that where he was they were all looking. When the Arabs came rushing like things gone mad, and he had received his wound, he had known that in his own village, among his own dear ones, there was recovery. Love would heal the wounds, the home country was a lover who would heal all her sons' wounds with love.

Among the grey desolate crowd were sharp, rending "Bravos!"—the people were in tears—the landlord at my side was repeating softly, abstractedly: "Caro—caro—Ettore, caro colonello—" and when, it was finished, and the little colonel with shabby, humiliated legs was gone in, he turned to me and said, with challenge that almost frightened me:

"Un brav' uomo."

"Bravissimo," I said.

Then we, too, went indoors.

It was all, somehow, grey and hopeless and acrid, unendurable.

The colonel, poor devil—we knew him afterwards—is now dead. It is strange that he is dead. There is something repulsive to me in the thought of his lying dead: such a humiliating, somehow degraded corpse. Death has no beauty in Italy, unless it be violent. The death of man or woman through sickness is an occasion of horror, repulsive. They belong entirely to life, they are so limited to life, these people.

Soon the Giovanni came home, and took his cornet upstairs. Then he came to see us. He was an ingenuous youth, sordidly shabby and dirty. His fair hair was long and uneven, his very high starched collar made one aware that his neck and his ears were not clean, his American crimson tie was ugly, his clothes looked as if they had been kicking about on the floor for a year.

Yet his blue eyes were warm and his manner and speech very gentle.

"You will speak English with us," I said.

"Oh," he said, smiling and shaking his head, "I could speak English very well. But it is two years that I don't speak it now, over two years now, so I don't speak it."

"But you speak it very well."

"No. It is two years that I have not spoke, not a word— so, you see, I have—"

"You have forgotten it? No, you haven't. It will quickly come back."

"If I hear it—when I go to America—then I shall—I shall—"

"You will soon pick it up."

"Yes—I shall pick it up."

The landlord, who had been watching with pride, now went away. The wife also went away, and we were left with the shy, gentle, dirty, and frowsily-dressed Giovanni.

He laughed in his sensitive, quick fashion.

"The women in America, when they came into the store, they said, 'Where is John, where is John?' Yes, they liked me."

And he laughed again, glancing with vague, warm blue eyes, very shy, very coiled upon himself with sensitiveness.

He had managed a store in America, in a smallish town. I glanced at his reddish, smooth, rather knuckly hands, and thin wrists in the frayed cuff. They were real shopman's hands.

The landlord brought some special feast-day cake, so overjoyed he was to have his Giovanni speaking English with the Signoria.

When we went away, we asked 'John' to come down to our villa to see us. We scarcely expected him to turn up.

Yet one morning he appeared, at about half-past nine, just as we were finishing breakfast. It was sunny and warm and beautiful, so we asked him please to come with us picnicking.

He was a queer shoot, again, in his unkempt longish hair and slovenly clothes, a sort of very vulgar down-at-heel American in appearance. And he was transported with shyness. Yet ours was the world he had chosen as his own, so he took his place bravely and simply, a hanger-on.

We climbed up the water-course in the mountain-side, up to a smooth little lawn under the olive trees, where daisies were flowering and gladioli were in bud. It was a tiny little lawn of grass in a level crevice, and sitting there we had the world below us—the lake, the distant island, the far-off low Verona shore.

Then 'John' began to talk, and he talked continuously, like a foreigner, not saying the things he would have said in Italian, but following the suggestion and scope of his limited English.

In the first place, he loved his father—it was "my father, my father" always. His father had a little shop as well as the inn in the village above. So John had had some education. He had been sent to Brescia and then to Verona to school, and there had taken his examinations to become a civil engineer. He was clever, and could pass his examinations. But he never finished his course. His mother died, and his father, disconsolate, had wanted him at home. Then he had gone back, when he was sixteen or seventeen, to the village beyond the lake, to be with his father and to look after the shop.

"But didn't you mind giving up all your work?" I said.

He did not quite understand.

"My father wanted me to come back,' he said.

It was evident that Giovanni had had no definite conception of what he was doing or what he wanted to do. His father, wishing to make a gentleman of him, had sent him to school in Verona. By accident he had been moved on into the engineering course. When it all fizzled to an end, and he returned half-baked to the remote, desolate village of the

61

mountain-side, he was not disappointed or chagrined. He had never conceived of a coherent purposive life. Either one stayed in the village, like a lodged stone, or one made random excursions into the world, across the world. It was all aimless and purposeless.

So he had stayed a while with his father, then he had gone, just as aimlessly, with a party of men who were emigrating to America. He had taken some money, had drifted about, living in the most comfortless, wretched fashion, then he had found a place somewhere in Pennsylvania, in a dry goods store. This was when he was seventeen or eighteen years old.

All this seemed to have happened to him without his being very much affected, at least consciously. His nature was simple and self-complete. Yet not so self-complete as that of Il Duro or Paolo. They had passed through the foreign world and been quite untouched. Their souls were static, it was the world that had flowed unstable by.

But John was more sensitive, he had come more into contact with his new surroundings. He had attended night classes almost every evening, and had been taught English like a child. He had loved the American free school, the teachers, the work.

But he had suffered very much in America. With his curious, over-sensitive, wincing laugh, he told us how the boys had followed him and jeered at him, calling after him, "You damn Dago, you damn Dago." They had stopped him and his friend in the street and taken away their hats, and spat into them. So that at last he had gone mad. They were youths and men who always tortured him, using bad language which startled us very much as he repeated it, there on the little lawn under the olive trees, above the perfect lake: English obscenities and abuse so coarse and startling that we bit our lips, shocked almost into laughter, whilst John, simple and natural, and somehow, for all his long hair and dirty appearance, flower-like in soul, repeated to us these things which may never be repeated in decent company.

"Oh," he said, "at last, I get mad. When they come one day, shouting, 'You damn Dago, dirty dog,' and will take my hat again, oh, I get mad, and I would kill them. I would kill them, I am so mad. I run to them, and throw one to the floor, and I tread on him while I go upon another, the biggest. Though they hit me and kick me all over, I feel nothing, I am mad. I throw the biggest to the floor, a man; he is older than I am, and I hit him so hard I would kill him. When the others see it they are afraid, they throw stones and hit me on the face. But I don't feel it—I don't know nothing. I hit the man on the floor, I almost kill him. I forget everything except I will kill him—"

"But you didn't?"

"No—I don't know—" and he laughed his queer, shaken laugh. "The other man that was with me, my friend, he came to me and we went away. Oh, I was mad, I was completely mad. I would have killed them."

He was trembling slightly, and his eyes were dilated with a strange greyish-blue fire that was very painful and elemental. He looked beside himself. But he was by no means mad.

We were shaken by the vivid, lambent excitement of the youth, we wished him to forget. We were shocked, too, in our souls to see the pure elemental flame shaken out of his gentle, sensitive nature. By his slight, crinkled laugh we could see how much he had suffered. He had gone out and faced the world, and he had kept his place, stranger and Dago though he was.

"They never came after me no more, not all the while I was there."

Then he said he became the foreman in the store—at first he was only assistant. It was the best store in the town, and many English ladies came, and some Germans. He liked the English ladies very much: they always wanted him to be in the store. He wore white clothes there, and they would say:

"You look very nice in the white coat, John"; or else:

"Let John come, he can find it"; or else they said:

"John speaks like a born American."

This pleased him very much.

In the end, he said, he earned a hundred dollars a month. He lived with the extraordinary frugality of the Italians, and had quite a lot of money.

He was not like Il Duro. Faustino had lived in a state of miserliness almost in America, but then he had had his debauches of shows and wine and carousals. John went chiefly to the schools, in one of which he was even asked to teach Italian. His knowledge of his own language was remarkable and most unusual!

"But what," I asked, "brought you back?"

"It was my father. You see, if I did not come to have my military service, I must stay till I am forty. So I think perhaps my father will be dead, I shall never see him. So I came."

He had come home when he was twenty to fulfil his military duties. At home he had married. He was very fond of his wife, but he had no conception of love in the old sense. His wife was like the past, to which he was wedded. Out of her he begot his child, as out of the past. But the future was all beyond her, apart from her. He was going away again, now, to America. He had been some nine months at home after his military service was over. He had no more to do. Now he was leaving his wife and child and his father to go to America.

"But why," I said, "why? You are not poor, you can manage the shop in your village."

"Yes," he said. "But I will go to America. Perhaps I shall go into the store again, the same."

"But is it not just the same as managing the shop at home?"

"No-no-it is quite different."

Then he told us how he bought goods in Brescia and in Salò for the shop at home, how he had rigged up a funicular with the assistance of the village, an overhead wire by which you could haul the goods up the face of the cliffs right high up, to within a mile of the village. He was very proud of this. And sometimes he himself went down the funicular to the water's edge, to the boat, when he was in a hurry. This also pleased him.

But he was going to Brescia this day to see about going again to America. Perhaps in another month he would be gone.

It was a great puzzle to me why he would go. He could not say himself. He would stay four or five years, then he would come home again to see his father—and his wife and child.

There was a strange, almost frightening destiny upon him, which seemed to take him away, always away from home, from the past, to that great, raw America. He seemed scarcely like a person with individual choice, more like a creature under the influence of fate which was disintegrating the old life and precipitating him, a fragment inconclusive, into the new chaos.

He submitted to it all with a perfect unquestioning simplicity, never even knowing that he suffered, that he must suffer disintegration from the old life. He was moved entirely from within, he never questioned his inevitable impulse.

"They say to me, 'Don't go—don't go'—" he shook his head. "But I say I will go?'

And at that it was finished.

So we saw him off at the little quay, going down the lake. He would return at evening, and be pulled up in his funicular basket. And in a month's time he would be standing on the same lake steamer going to America.

Nothing was more painful than to see him standing there in his degraded, sordid American clothes, on the deck of the steamer, waving us good-bye, belonging in his final desire to our world, the world of consciousness and deliberate action. With his candid, open, unquestioning face, he seemed like a prisoner being conveyed from one form of life to another, or like a soul in trajectory, that has not yet found a resting-place.

What were wife and child to him?—they were the last steps of the past. His father was the continent behind him; his wife and child the foreshore of the past; but his face was set outwards, away from it all—whither, neither he nor anybody knew, but he called it America.

ITALIANS IN EXILE

I was in Constance the weather was misty and enervating and depressing, it was no pleasure to travel on the big, flat desolate lake.

When I went from Constance, it was on a small steamer down the Rhine to Schaffhausen. That was beautiful. Still, the mist hung over the waters, over the wide shallows of the river and the sun, coming through the morning, made lovely yellow lights beneath the bluish haze, so that it seemed like the beginning of the world. And there was a hawk in the upper air fighting with two crows, or two rooks. Ever they rose, higher and higher, the crow flickering above the attacking hawk, the fight going on like some strange symbol in the sky, the Germans on deck watching with pleasure.

Then we passed out of sight between wooded banks and under bridges where quaint villages of old romance piled their red and coloured pointed roofs beside the water, very still, remote, lost in the vagueness of the past. It could not be that they were real. Even when the boat put in to shore, and the customs officials came to look, the village remained remote in the romantic past of High Germany, the Germany of fairy tales and minstrels and craftsmen. The poignancy of the past was almost unbearable, floating there in colour upon the haze of the river.

We went by some swimmers, whose white shadowy bodies trembled near the side of the steamer under water. One man with a round, fair head lifted his face and one arm from the water and shouted a greeting to us, as if he were a Niebelung, saluting with bright arm lifted from the water, his face laughing, the fair moustache hanging over his mouth. Then his body swirled in the water, and he was gone, swimming with the side stroke.

Schaffhausen the town, half old and bygone, half modern, with breweries and industries, that is not very real. Schaffhausen Falls, with their factory in the midst and their hotel at the bottom, and the general cinematograph effect, they are ugly.

It was afternoon when I set out to walk from the Falls to Italy, across Switzerland. I remember the big, fat, rather gloomy fields of this part of Baden, damp and unliving. I remember I found some apples under a tree in a field near a railway embankment, then some mushrooms, and I ate both. Then I came on to a long, desolate high-road, with dreary, withered trees on either side, and flanked by great fields where groups of men and women

64

were working. They looked at me as I went by down the long, long road, alone and exposed and out of the world.

I remember nobody came at the border village to examine my pack, I passed through unchallenged. All was quiet and lifeless and hopeless, with big stretches of heavy land.

Till sunset came, very red and purple, and suddenly, from the heavy spacious open land I dropped sharply into the Rhine valley again, suddenly, as if into another glamorous world.

There was the river rushing along between its high, mysterious, romantic banks, which were high as hills, and covered with vine. And there was the village of tall, quaint houses flickering its lights on to the deep-flowing river, and quite silent, save for the rushing of water.

There was a fine covered bridge, very dark. I went to the middle and looked through the opening at the dark water below, at the façade of square lights, the tall village-front towering remote and silent above the river. The hill rose on either side the flood; down here was a small, forgotten, wonderful world that belonged to the date of isolated village communities and wandering minstrels.

So I went back to the inn of 'The Golden Stag', and, climbing some steps, I made a loud noise. A woman came, and I asked for food. She led me through a room where were enormous barrels, ten feet in diameter, lying fatly on their sides; then through a large stone-clean kitchen, with bright pans, ancient as the Meistersinger; then up some steps and into the long guest-room, where a few tables were laid for supper.

A few people were eating. I asked for Abendessen, and sat by the window looking at the darkness of the river below, the covered bridge, the dark hill opposite, crested with its few lights.

Then I ate a very large quantity of knoedel soup and bread, and drank beer, and was very sleepy. Only one or two village men came in, and these soon went again; the place was dead still. Only at a long table on the opposite side of the room were seated seven or eight men, ragged, disreputable, some impudent—another came in late the landlady gave them all thick soup with dumplings and bread and meat, serving them in a sort of brief disapprobation. They sat at a long table, eight or nine tramps and beggars and wanderers out of work, and they ate with a sort of cheerful callousness and brutality for the most part, and as if ravenously, looking round and grinning sometimes, subdued, cowed, like prisoners, and yet impudent. At the end one shouted to know where he was to sleep. The landlady called to the young serving-woman, and in a classic German severity of disapprobation they were led up the stone stairs to their room. They tramped off in threes and twos, making a bad, mean, humiliated exit. It was not yet eight o'clock. The landlady sat talking to one bearded man, staid and severe, whilst, with her work on the table, she sewed steadily.

As the beggars and wanderers went slinking out of the room, some called impudently, cheerfully:

"Nacht, Frau Wirtin—G'Nacht, Wirtin—'te Nacht, Frau," to all of which the hostess answered a stereotyped "Gute Nacht," never turning her head from her sewing, or indicating by the faintest movement that she was addressing the men who were filing raggedly to the doorway.

So the room was empty, save for the landlady and her sewing, the staid, elderly villager to whom she was talking in the unbeautiful dialect, and the young serving-woman who was clearing away the plates and basins of the tramps and beggars.

65

Then the villager also went.

"Gute Nacht, Frau Seidl," to the landlady; "Gute Nacht," at random, to me.

So I looked at the newspaper. Then I asked the landlady for a cigarette, not knowing how else to begin. So she came to my table, and we talked.

It pleased me to take upon myself a sort of romantic, wandering character; she said my German was "schön"; a little goes a long way.

So I asked her who were the men who had sat at the long table. She became rather stiff and curt.

"They are the men looking for work," she said, as if the subject were disagreeable.

"But why do they come here, so many?" I asked.

Then she told me that they were going out of the country: this was almost the last village of the border: that the relieving officer in each village was empowered to give to every vagrant a ticket entitling the holder to an evening meal, bed, and bread in the morning, at a certain inn. This was the inn for the vagrants coming to this village. The landlady received four-pence per head, I believe it was, for each of these wanderers.

"Little enough," I said.

"Nothing," she replied.

She did not like the subject at all. Only her respect for me made her answer.

"Bettler, Lumpen, und Taugenichtse!" I said cheerfully.

"And men who are out of work, and are going back to their own parish;" she said stiffly.

So we talked a little, and I too went to bed.

"Gute Nacht, Frau Wirtin."

"Gute Nacht, mein Herr."

So I went up more and more stone stairs, attended by the young woman. It was a great, lofty, old deserted house, with many drab doors.

At last, in the distant topmost floor, I had my bedroom, with two beds and bare floor and scant furniture. I looked down at the river far below, at the covered bridge, at the far lights on the hill above, opposite. Strange to be here in this lost, forgotten place, sleeping under the roof with tramps and beggars. I debated whether they would steal my boots if I put them out. But I risked it. The door-latch made a loud noise on the deserted landing, everywhere felt abandoned, forgotten. I wondered where the eight tramps and beggars were asleep. There was no way of securing the door. But somehow I felt that, if I were destined to be robbed or murdered, it would not be by tramps and beggars. So I blew out the candle and lay under the big feather bed, listening to the running and whispering of the mediæval Rhine.

And when I waked up again it was sunny, it was morning on the hill opposite, though the river deep below ran in shadow.

The tramps and beggars were all gone: they must be cleared out by seven o'clock in the morning. So I had the inn to myself, I, and the landlady, and the serving-woman. Everywhere was very clean, full of the German morning energy and brightness, which is so different from the Latin morning. The Italians are dead and torpid first thing, the Germans are energetic and cheerful.

It was cheerful in the sunny morning, looking down on the swift river, the covered, picturesque bridge, the bank and the hill opposite. Then down the curving road of the facing hill the Swiss cavalry came riding, men in blue uniforms. I went out to watch them. They came thundering romantically through the dark cavern of the roofed-in bridge, and they dismounted at the entrance to the village. There was a fresh morning-cheerful newness everywhere, in the arrival of the troops, in the welcome of the villagers.

The Swiss do not look very military, neither in accoutrement nor in bearing. This little squad of cavalry seemed more like a party of common men riding out on some business of their own than like an army. They were very republican and very free. The officer who commanded them was one of themselves, his authority was by consent.

It was all very pleasant and genuine; there was a sense of ease and peacefulness, quite different from the mechanical, slightly sullen manœuvring of the Germans.

The village baker and his assistant came hot and floury from the bakehouse, bearing between them a great basket of fresh bread. The cavalry were all dismounted by the bridge-head, eating and drinking like business men. Villagers came to greet their friends: one soldier kissed his father, who came wearing a leathern apron. The school bell tang-tang-tanged from above, school children merged timidly through the grouped horses, up the narrow Street, passing unwillingly with their books. The river ran swiftly, the soldiers, very haphazard and slack in uniform, real shack-bags, chewed their bread in large mouthfuls; the young lieutenant, who seemed to be an officer only by consent of the men, stood apart by the bridge-head, gravely. They were all serious and self-contented, very unglamorous. It was like a business excursion on horseback, harmless and uninspiring. The uniforms were almost ludicrous, so ill-fitting and casual.

So I shouldered my own pack and set off, through the bridge over the Rhine, and up the hill opposite.

There is something very dead about this country. I remember I picked apples from the grass by the roadside, and some were very sweet. But for the rest, there was mile after mile of dead, uninspired country—uninspired, so neutral and ordinary that it was almost destructive.

One gets this feeling always in Switzerland, except high up: this feeling of average, of utter soulless ordinariness, something intolerable. Mile after mile, to Zurich, it was just the same. It was just the same in the tram-car going into Zurich; it was just the same in the town, in the shops, in the restaurant. All was the utmost level of ordinariness and well-being, but so ordinary that it was like a blight. All the picturesqueness of the town is as nothing, it is like a most ordinary, average, usual person in an old costume. The place was soul-killing.

So after two hours' rest, eating in a restaurant, wandering• by the quay and through the market, and sitting on a seat by the lake, I found a steamer that would take me away. That is how I always feel in Switzerland: the only possible living sensation is the sensation of relief in going away, always going away. The horrible average ordinariness of it all, something utterly without flower or soul or transcendence, the horrible vigorous ordinariness, is too much.

So I went on a steamer down the long lake, surrounded by low grey hills. It was Saturday afternoon. A thin rain came on. I thought I would rather be in fiery Hell than in this dead level of average life.

I landed somewhere on the right bank, about three-quarters of the way down the lake. It was almost dark. Yet I must walk away. I climbed a long hill from the lake, came to the crest, looked down the darkness of the valley, and descended into the deep gloom, down into a soulless village.

But it was eight o'clock, and I had had enough. One might as well sleep. I found the 'Gasthaus zur Post'.

It was a small, very rough inn, having only one common room, with bare tables, and a short, stout, grim, rather surly landlady, and a landlord whose hair stood up on end, arid who was trembling on the verge of delirium tremens.

They could only give me boiled ham: so I ate boiled ham and drank beer, and tried to digest the utter cold materialism of Switzerland.

As I sat with my back to the wall, staring blankly at the trembling landlord, who was ready at any moment to foam at the mouth, and at the dour landlady, who was quite capable of keeping him in order, there came in one of those dark, showy Italian girls with a man. She wore a blouse and skirt, and no hat. Her hair was perfectly dressed. It was really Italy. The man was soft, dark, he would get stout later, *trapu,* he would have somewhat the figure of Caruso. But as yet he was soft, sensuous, young, handsome.

They sat at the long side-table with their beer, and created another country at once within the room. Another Italian came, fair and fat and slow, one from the Venetian province; then another, a little thin young man, who might have been a Swiss save for his vivid movement.

This last was the first to speak to the Germans. The others had just said "Bier." But the little new-comer entered into a conversation with the landlady.

At last there were six Italians sitting talking loudly and warmly at the side-table. The slow, cold German-Swiss at the other tables looked at them occasionally. The landlord, with his crazed, stretched eyes, glared at them with hatred. But they fetched their beer from the bar with easy familiarity, and sat at their table, creating a bonfire of life in the callousness of the inn.

At last they finished their beer and trooped off down the passage. The room was painfully empty. I did not know what to do.

Then I heard the landlord yelling and screeching and snarling from the kitchen at the back, for all the world like a mad dog. But the Swiss Saturday evening customers at the other tables smoked on and talked in their ugly dialect, without trouble. Then the landlady came in, and soon after the landlord, he collarless, with his waistcoat unbuttoned, showing his loose throat, and accentuating his round pot-belly. His limbs were thin and feverish, the skin of his face hung loose, his eyes were glaring, his hands trembled. Then he sat down to talk to a crony. His terrible appearance was a fiasco; nobody heeded him at all, only the landlady was surly.

From the back came loud noises of pleasure and excitement and banging about. When the room door was opened I could see down the dark passage opposite another lighted door. Then the fat, fair Italian came in for more beer.

"What is all the noise?" I asked the landlady at last.

"It is the Italians," she said. "What are they doing?"

"They are doing a play."

"Where?"

She jerked her head: "In the room at the back."

"Can I go and look at them?"

"I should think so."

The landlord glaringly watched me go out. I went down the stone passage and found a great, half-lighted room that might be used to hold meetings, with forms piled at the side. At one end was a raised platform or stage. And on this stage was a table and a lamp, and the Italians grouped round the light, gesticulating and laughing. Their beer mugs were on the table and on the floor of the stage; the little sharp youth was intently looking over some papers, the others were bending over the table with him.

They looked up as I entered from the distance, looked at me in the distant twilight of the dusky room, as if I were an intruder, as if I should go away when I had seen them. But I said in German:

"May I look?"

They were still unwilling to see or to hear me.

"What do you say?" the small one asked in reply.

The others stood and watched, slightly at bay, like suspicious animals.

"If I might come and look," I said in German; then, feeling very uncomfortable, in Italian: "You are doing a drama, the landlady told me."

The big empty room was behind me, dark, the little company of Italians stood above me in the light of the lamp which was on the table. They all watched with unseeing, unwilling looks: I was merely an intrusion.

"We are only learning it," said the small youth. They wanted me to go away. But I wanted to stay. "May I listen?" I said. "I don't want to stay in there." And I indicated, with a movement of the head, the inn-room beyond.

"Yes," said the young intelligent man. "But we are only reading our parts."

They had all became more friendly to me, they accepted me.

"You are a German ?" asked one youth.

"No—English."

"English? But do you live in Switzerland?"

"No—I am walking to Italy."

"On foot?"

They looked with wakened eyes.

"Yes."

So I told them about my journey. They were puzzled. They did not quite understand why I wanted to walk. But they were delighted with the idea of going to Lugano and Como and then to Milan.

"Where do you come from?' I asked them.

They were all from the villages between Verona and Venice. They had seen the Garda. I told them of my living there.

"Those peasants of the mountains," they said at once, "they are people of little education. Rather wild folk."

And they spoke with good-humoured contempt.

I thought of Paolo, and Il Duro, and the Signor Pietro, our padrone, and I resented these factory-hands for criticising them.

So I sat on the edge of the stage whilst they rehearsed their parts. The little thin intelligent fellow, Giuseppino, was the leader. The others read their parts in the laborious, disjointed fashion of the peasant, who can only see one word at. a time, and has then to put the words together, afterwards, to make sense. The play was an amateur melodrama, printed in little penny booklets, for carnival production. This was only the second reading they had given it, and the handsome, dark fellow, who was roused and displaying himself before the girl, a hard, erect piece of callousness, laughed and flushed and stumbled, and understood nothing till it was transferred into him direct through Giuseppino. The fat, fair, slow man was more conscientious. He laboured through his part. The other two men were in the background more or less.

The most confidential was the fat, fair, slow man, who was called Alberto. His part was not very important, so he could sit by me and talk to me.

He said they were all workers in the factory—silk, I think it was—in the village. They were a whole colony of Italians, thirty or more families. They had all come at different times.

Giuseppino had been longest in the village. He had come when he was eleven, with his parents, and had attended the Swiss school. So he spoke perfect German. He was a clever man, was married, and had two children.

He himself, Alberto, had been seven years in the valley; the girl, la Maddelena, had been here ten years; the dark man, Alfredo, who was flushed with excitement of her, had been in the village about nine years—he alone of all the men was not married,

The others had all married Italian wives, and they lived in the great dwelling whose windows shone yellow by the rattling factory. They lived entirely among themselves; none of them could speak German, more than a few words except Giuseppino, who was like a native here.

It was very strange being among these Italians exiled in Switzerland. Alfredo, the dark one, the unmarried, was in the old tradition. Yet even he was curiously subject to a new purpose, as if there were some greater new will that included him, sensuous, mindless as he was. He seemed to give his consent to something beyond himself. In this he was different from Il Duro, in that he had put himself under the control of the outside conception.

It was strange to watch them on the stage, the Italians all lambent, soft, warm, sensuous, yet moving subject round Giuseppino, who was always quiet, always ready, always impersonal. There was a look of purpose, almost of devotion on his face, that singled him out and made him seem the one stable, eternal being among them. They quarrelled, and he let them quarrel up to a certain point; then he called them back. He let them do as they liked so long as they adhered more or less to the central purpose, so long as they got on in some measure with the play.

All the while they were drinking beer and smoking cigarettes. The Alberto was barman: he went out continually with the glasses. The Maddelena had a small glass. In the lamplight of the stage the little party read and smoked and practised, exposed to. the empty darkness of the big room. Queer and isolated it seemed, a tiny, pathetic magic-land far away from the barrenness of Switzerland. I could believe in the old fairy-tales where, when the rock was opened, a magic underworld was revealed.

The Alfredo, flushed, roused, handsome, but very soft and enveloping in his heat, laughed and threw himself into his pose, laughed foolishly, and then gave himself up to his part. The Alberto, slow and laborious, yet with a spark of vividness and natural intensity flashing through, replied and gesticulated; the Maddeleno laid her head on the bosom of Alfredo, the other men started into action, and the play proceeded intently for half an hour.

Quick, vivid, and sharp, the little Giuseppino was always central. But he seemed almost invisible. When I think back, I can scarcely see him, I can only see the others, the lamplight on their faces and on their full gesticulating limbs. I can see the Maddelena, rather coarse and hard and repellent, declaiming her words in a loud, half-cynical voice, falling on the breast of the Alfredo, who was soft and sensuous, more like a female, flushing, with his mouth getting wet, his eyes moist, as he was roused. I can see the Alberto, slow, laboured, yet with a kind of pristine simplicity in all his movements, that touched his fat commonplaceness with beauty. Then there were the two other men, shy, inflammable, unintelligent, with their sudden Italian rushes of hot feeling. All their faces are distinct in the lamplight, all their bodies are palpable and dramatic.

But the face of the Giuseppino is like a pale luminousness, a sort of gleam among all the ruddy glow, his body is evanescent, like a shadow. And his being seemed to cast its influence over all the others, except perhaps the woman, who was hard and resistant. The other men seemed all overcast, mitigated, in part transfigured by the will of the little leader. But they were very soft stuff, if inflammable.

The young woman of the inn, niece of the landlady, came down and called out across the room.

"We will go away from here now," said the Giuseppino to me. "They close at eleven. But we have another inn in the next parish that is open all night. Come with us and drink some wine.

"But," I said, "you would rather be alone."

No; they pressed me to go, they wanted me to go with them, they were eager, they wanted to entertain me. Alfredo, flushed, wet-mouthed, warm, protested I must drink wine, the real Italian red wine, from their own village at home. They would have no nay.

So I told the landlady. She said I must be back by twelve o'clock.

The night was very dark. Below the road the stream was rushing; there was a great factory on the other side of the water, making faint quivering lights of reflection, and one could see the working of machinery shadowy through the lighted windows. Near by was the tall tenement where the Italians lived.

We went through the straggling, raw village, deep beside the stream, then over the small bridge, and up the steep hill down which I had come earlier in the evening.

So we arrived at the café. It was so different inside from the German inn, yet it was not like an Italian café either. It was brilliantly lighted, clean, new, and there were red-and-white cloths on the tables. The host was in the room, and his daughter, a beautiful red-haired girl.

Greetings were exchanged with the quick, intimate directness of Italy. But there was another note also, a faint echo of reserve, as though they reserved themselves from the outer world, making a special inner community.

Alfredo was hot: he took off his coat. We all sat freely at a long table, while the red-haired girl brought a quart of red wine. At other tables men were playing cards, with the odd Neapolitan cards. They too were talking Italian. It was a warm, ruddy bit of Italy within the cold darkness of Switzerland.

"When you come to Italy," they said to me, "salute it from us, salute the sun, and the earth, l' Italia."

So we drank in salute of Italy. They sent their greeting by me.

"You know in Italy there is the sun, the sun," said Alfredo to me, profoundly moved, wet-mouthed, tipsy.

I was reminded of Enrico Persevalli and his terrifying cry at the end of *'Ghosts'*:

"Il sole, il sole!"

So we talked for a while of Italy. They had a pained tenderness for it, sad, reserved.

"Don't you want to go back?" I said, pressing them to tell me definitely. "Won't you go back some time?"

"Yes," they said, "we will go back."

But they spoke reservedly, without freedom. We talked about Italy, about songs, and Carnival; about the food, polenta, and salt. They laughed at my pretending to cut the slabs of polenta with a string: that rejoiced them all: it took them back to the Italian mezzo-giorno, the bells jangling in the campanile, the eating after the heavy work on the land.

But they laughed with the slight pain and contempt and fondness which every man feels towards his past, when he has struggled away from that past, from the conditions which made it.

They loved Italy passionately; but they would not go back. All their blood, all their senses were Italian, needed the Italian sky, the speech, the sensuous life. They could hardly live except through the senses. Their minds were not developed, mentally they were children, lovable, naïve, almost fragile children. But sensually they were men: sensually they were accomplished.

Yet a new tiny flower was struggling to open in them, the flower of a new spirit. The substratum of Italy has always been pagan, sensuous, the most potent symbol the sexual symbol. The child is really a non-Christian symbol: it is the symbol of man's triumph of eternal life in procreation. The worship of the Cross never really held good in Italy. The Christianity of Northern Europe has never had any place there.

And now, when Northern Europe is turning back on its own Christianity, denying it all, the Italians are struggling with might and main against the sensuous spirit which still dominates them. When Northern Europe, whether it hates Nietzsche or not, is crying out for the Dionysic ecstasy, practising on itself the Dionysic ecstasy, Southern Europe is breaking free from Dionysos, from the triumphal affirmation of life over death, immortality through procreation.

I could see these sons of Italy would never go back. Men like Paolo and Il Duro broke away only to return. The dominance of the old form was too strong for them. Call it love of country or love of the village, campanilismo, or what not, it was the dominance of the old pagan form, the old affirmation of immortality through procreation, as opposed to the Christian affirmation of immortality through self-death and social love.

But 'John' and these Italians in Switzerland were a generation younger, and they would not go back, at least not to the old Italy. Suffer as they might, and they did suffer, wincing in every nerve and fibre from the cold material insentience of the northern countries and of America, still they would endure this for the sake of something else they wanted. They would suffer a death in the flesh, as 'John' had suffered in fighting the street crowd, as these men suffered year after year cramped in their black gloomy cold Swiss valley, working in the factory. But there would come a new spirit out of it.

Even Alfredo was submitted to the new process; though he belonged entirely by nature to the sort of Il Duro, he was purely sensuous and mindless. But under the influence of Giuseppino he was thrown down, as fallow to the new spirit that would come.

And then, when the others were all partially tipsy, the Giuseppino began to talk to me. In him was a steady flame burning, burning, burning, a flame of the mind, of the spirit, something new and clear, something that held even the soft, sensuous Alfredo in submission, besides all the others, who had some little development of mind.

"Sa signore," said the Giuseppino to .me quiet, almost invisible or inaudible, as it seemed, like a spirit addressing me, "l' uomo non ha patria—a man has no country. What has the Italian Government to do with us. What does a Government mean? It makes us work, it takes part of our wages away from us, it makes us soldiers—and what for? What is government for?"

"Have you been a soldier?" I interrupted him.

He had not, none of them had: that was why they could not really go back to Italy. Now this was out; this explained partly their curious reservation in speaking about their beloved country. They had forfeited parents as well as homeland.

"What does the Government do? It takes taxes; it has an army and police, and it makes roads. But we could do without an army, and we could be our own police, and we could make our own roads. What is this Government? Who wants it? Only those who are unjust, and want to have advantage over somebody else. It is an instrument of injustice and of wrong.

"Why should we have a Government? Here, in this village, there are thirty families of Italians. There is no government for them, no Italian Government. And we live together better than in Italy. We are richer and freer, we have no policemen, no poor laws. We help each other, and there are no poor.

"Why are these Governments always doing what we don't want them to do? We should not be fighting in the Cirenaica if we were all Italians. It is the Government that does it. They talk and talk and do things with us: but we don't want them."

The others, tipsy, sat round the table with the terrified gravity of children who are somehow responsible for things they do not understand. They stirred in their seats, turning aside, with gestures almost of pain, of imprisonment. Only Alfredo, laying his hand on mine, was laughing, loosely, floridly. He would upset all the Government with a jerk of his well-built shoulder, and then he would have a spree—such a spree. He laughed wetly to me.

The Giuseppino waited patiently during this tipsy confidence, but his pale clarity and beauty was something constant and star-like in comparison with the flushed, soft handsomeness of' the other. He waited patiently, looking at me.

But I did not want him to go on: I did not want to answer. I could feel a new spirit in him, something strange and pure and slightly frightening. He wanted something which was beyond me. And my soul was somewhere in tears, crying helplessly like an infant in the night. I could not respond: I could not answer. He seemed to look at me, me, an Englishman, an educated man, for corroboration. But I could not corroborate him. I knew the purity and new struggling towards birth of a true star-like spirit. But I could not confirm him in his utterance: my soul could not respond. I did not believe in the perfectibility of man. I did not believe in infinite harmony among men. And this was his star, this belief.

It was nearly midnight. A Swiss came in and asked for beer. The Italians gathered round them a curious darkness of reserve. And then I must go.

They shook hands with me warmly, truthfully, putting a sort of implicit belief in me, as representative of some further knowledge. But there was a fixed, calm resolve over the face of the Giuseppino, a sort of steady faith, even in disappointment. He gave me a copy of a little Anarchist paper published in Geneva. *L' Anarchista,* I believe it was called. I glanced at it. It was in Italian, naïve, simple, rather rhetorical. So they were all Anarchists, these Italians.

I ran down the hill in the thick Swiss darkness to the little bridge, and along the uneven cobbled street. I did not want to think, I did not want to know. I wanted to arrest my activity, to keep it confined to the moment, to the adventure.

When I came to the flight of stone steps which led up to the door of the inn, at the side I saw in the darkness two figures. They said a low good-night and parted; the girl began to knock at the door, the man disappeared. It was the niece of the landlady parting from her lover.

We waited outside the locked door, at the top of the stone steps, in the darkness of midnight. The stream rustled below. Then came a shouting and an insane snarling within the passage; the bolts were not withdrawn.

"It is the gentleman, it is the strange gentleman," called the girl.

Then came again the furious shouting snarls, and the landlord's mad voice:

"Stop out, stop out there. The door won't be opened again."

"The strange gentleman is here," repeated the girl.

Then more movement was heard, and the door was suddenly opened, and the landlord rushed out upon us, wielding a broom. It was a strange sight, in the half-lighted passage. I stared blankly in the doorway. The landlord dropped the broom he was waving and collapsed as if by magic, looking at me, though he continued to mutter madly, unintelligibly. The girl slipped past me, and the landlord snarled. Then he picked up the brush, at the same time crying:

"You are late, the door was shut, it will not be opened. We shall have the police in the house. We said twelve o'clock; at twelve o'clock the door must be shut, and must not be opened again. If you are late you stay out—"

So he went snarling, his voice rising higher and higher, away into the kitchen.

"You are coming to your room?" the landlady said to me coldly. And she led me upstairs.

The room was over the road, clean, but rather ugly, with a large tin, that had once contained lard or Swiss-milk, to wash in. But the bed was good enough, which was all that mattered.

I heard the landlord yelling, and there was a long and systematic thumping somewhere, thump, thump, thump, and banging. I wondered where it was. I could not locate it at all, because my room lay beyond another large room: I had to go through a large room, by the foot of two beds, to get to my door; so I could not quite tell where anything was.

But I went to sleep whilst I was wondering.

I woke in the morning and washed in the tin. I could see a few people in the street, walking in the Sunday morning leisure. It felt like Sunday in England, and I shrank from it. I could see none of the Italians. The factory stood there, raw and large and sombre, by the stream, and the drab-coloured stone tenements were close by. Otherwise the village was a straggling Swiss Street, almost untouched.

The landlord was quiet and reasonable, even friendly, in the morning. He wanted to talk to me: where had I bought my boots, was his first question. I told him in Munich. And how much had they cost? I told him twenty-eight marks. He was much impressed by them: such good boots, of such soft, strong, beautiful leather; he had not seen such boots for a long time.

Then I knew it was he who had cleaned my boots. I could see him fingering them and wondering over them. I rather liked him. I could see he had had imagination once, and a certain fineness of nature. Now he was corrupted with drink, too far gone to be even a human being. I hated the village.

They set bread and butter, and a piece of cheese weighing about five pounds, and large, fresh sweet cakes for breakfast. I ate and was thankful: the food was good.

A couple of village youths came in, in their Sunday clothes. They had the Sunday stiffness. It reminded me of the stiffness and curious self-consciousness that comes over life in England on a Sunday. But the landlord sat with his waistcoat hanging open over his shirt, pot-bellied, his ruined face leaning forward, talking, always talking, wanting to know.

So in a few minutes I was out on the road again, thanking God for the blessing of a road that belongs to no man, and travels away from all men.

I did not want to see the Italians. Something had got tied up in me, and I could not bear to see them again. I liked them so much; but, for some reason or other, my mind stopped like clockwork if I wanted to think of them and of what their lives would be, their

74

future. It was as if some curious negative magnetism arrested my mind, prevented it from working, the moment I turned it towards these Italians.

I do not know why it was. But I could never write to them, or think of them, or even read the paper they gave me, though it lay in my drawer for months, in Italy, and I often glanced over six lines of it. And often, often my mind went back to the group, the play they were rehearsing, the wine in the pleasant café, and the night. But the moment my memory touched them, my whole soul stopped and was null; I could not go on. Even now I cannot really consider them in thought. I shrink involuntarily away. I do not know why this is.

THE RETURN JOURNEY

WHEN one walks, one must travel west or south. If one turns northwards or eastward it is like walking down a *cul-de-sac,* to the blind end.

So it has been since the Crusaders came home satiated, and the Renaissance saw the western sky as an archway into the future. So it is still. We must go westwards and southwards.

It is a sad and gloomy thing to travel even from Italy into France. But it is a joyful thing to walk south to Italy, south and west. It is so. And there is a certain exaltation in the thought of going west, even to Cornwall, to Ireland. It is as if the magnetic poles were south-east and north-east, for our spirits, with the south-west, under the sunset, as the positive pole. So whilst I walk through Switzerland, though it is a valley of gloom and depression, a light seems to flash out under every footstep, with the joy of progression.

It was Sunday morning when I left the valley where the Italians lived. I went quickly over the stream, heading for Lucerne. It was a good thing to be out of doors, with one's pack on one's back, climbing uphill. But the trees were thick by the roadside; I was not yet free. It was Sunday morning, very still.

In two hours I was at the top of the hill, looking out over the intervening valley at the long lake of Zurich, spread there beyond with its girdle of low hills, like a relief-map. I could not bear to look at it, it was so small and unreal. I had a feeling as if it were false, a large relief-map that I was looking down upon, and which I wanted to smash. It seemed to intervene between me and some reality. I could not believe that that was the real world. It was a figment, a fabrication, like a dull landscape painted on a wall, to hide the real landscape.

So I went on, over to the other side of the hill, and I looked out again. Again there were the smoky-looking hills and the lake like a piece of looking-glass. But the hills were higher: that big one was the Rigi. I set off down the hill.

There was fat agricultural land and several villages. And church was over. The church-goers were all coming home: men in black broadcloth and old chimney-pot silk hats, carrying their umbrellas; women in ugly dresses, carrying books and umbrellas. The streets were dotted with these black-clothed men and stiff women, all reduced to a Sunday nullity. I hated it. It reminded me of that which I knew in my boyhood, that stiff, null 'propriety' which used to come over us, like a sort of deliberate and self-inflicted cramp, on Sundays. I hated these elders in black broadcloth, with their neutral faces, going home piously to their Sunday dinners. I hated the feeling of these villages, comfortable, well-to-do, clean, and proper.

And my boot was chafing two of my toes. That always happens. I had come down to a wide, shallow valley-bed, marshy. So about a mile out of the village I sat down by a stone bridge, by a stream, and tore up my handkerchief, and bound up the toes. And as I sat binding my toes, two of the elders in black, with umbrellas under their arms, approached from the direction of the village.

They made me so furious, I had to hasten to fasten my boot, to hurry on again, before they should come near me. I could not bear the way they walked and talked, so crambling and material and mealy-mouthed.

Then it did actually begin to rain. I was just going down a short hill. So I sat under a bush and watched the trees drip. I was so glad to be there, homeless, without place or belonging, crouching under the leaves in the copse by the road, that I felt I had, like the meek, inherited the earth. Some men went by, with their coat-collars turned up, and the rain making still blacker their black broadcloth shoulders. They did not see me. I was as safe and separate as a ghost. So I ate the remains of my food that I had bought in Zurich, and waited for the rain.

Later, in the wet Sunday afternoon, I went on to the little lake, past many inert, neutral, material people, down an ugly road where trams ran. The blight of Sunday was almost intolerable near the town.

So on I went, by the side of the steamy, reedy lake, walking the length of it. Then suddenly I went in to a little villa by the water for tea. In Switzerland every house is a villa.

But this villa was kept by two old ladies and a delicate dog, who must not get his feet wet. I was very happy there. I had good jam and strange honey-cakes for tea, that I liked, and the little old ladies pattered round in a great stir, always whirling like two dry leaves after the restless dog.

"Why must he not go out?" I said.

"Because it is wet," they answered, "and he coughs and sneezes."

"Without a handkerchief, that is not *angenehm,*" I said.

So we became bosom friends.

"You are Austrian?" they said to me.

I said I was from Graz; that my father was a doctor in Graz, and that I was walking for my pleasure through the countries of Europe.

I said this because I knew a doctor from Graz who was always wandering about, and because I did not want to be myself, an Englishman, to these two old ladies. I wanted to be something else. So we exchanged confidences.

They told me, in their queer, old, toothless fashion, about their visitors, a man who used to fish all day, every day for three weeks, fish every hour of the day, though many a day he caught nothing—nothing at all—still he fished from the boat; and so on, such trivialities. Then they told me of a third sister who had died, a third little old lady. One could feel the gap in the house. They cried; and I, being an Austrian from Graz, to my astonishment felt my tears slip over on to the table. I also *was* sorry, and I would have kissed the little old ladies to comfort them.

"Only in heaven it is warm, and it doesn't rain, and no one dies," I said, looking at the wet leaves.

Then I went away. I would have stayed the night at this house: I wanted to. But I had developed my Austrian character too far.

So I went on to a detestable brutal inn in the town. And the next day I climbed over the back of the detestable Rigi, with its vile hotel, to come to Lucerne. There, on the Rigi, I met a lost young Frenchman who could speak no German, and who said he could not find people to speak French. So we sat on a stone and became close friends, and I promised faithfully to go and visit him in his barracks in Algiers: I was to sail from Naples to Algiers. He wrote me the address on his card, and told me he had friends in the regiment, to whom I should be introduced, and we could have a good time, if I would stay a week or two, down there in Algiers.

How much more real Algiers was than the rock on the Rigi where we sat, or the lake beneath, or the mountains beyond. Algiers is very real, though I have never seen it, and my friend is my friend for ever, though I have lost his card and forgotten his name. He was a Government clerk from Lyons, making this his first foreign tour before he began his military service. He showed me his 'circular excursion ticket'. Then at last we parted, for he must get to the top of the Rigi, and I must get to the bottom.

Lucerne and its lake were as irritating as ever—like the wrapper round milk chocolate. I could not sleep even one night there: I took the steamer down the lake, to the very last station. There I found a good German inn, and was happy.

There was a tall thin young man, whose face was red and inflamed from the sun. I thought he was a German tourist. He had just come in; and he was eating bread and milk. He and I were alone in the eating-room. He was looking at an illustrated paper.

"Does the steamer stop here all night?" I asked him in German, hearing the boat bustling and blowing her steam on the water outside, and glancing round at her lights, red and white, in the pitch darkness.

He only shook his head over his bread and milk, and did not lift his face.

"Are you English, then?" I said.

No one but an Englishman would have hidden his face in a bowl of milk, and have shaken his red ears in such painful confusion.

"Yes," he said, "I am."

And I started almost out of my skin at the unexpected London accent. It was as if one suddenly found oneself in the Tube.

"So am I," I said. "Where have you come from?"

Then he began, like a general explaining his plans, to tell me. He had walked round over the Furka Pass, had been on foot four or five days. He had walked tremendously. Knowing no German, and nothing of the mountains, he had set off alone on this tour: he had a fortnight's holiday. So he had come over the Rhone Glacier across the Furka and down from Andermatt to the Lake. On this last day he had walked about thirty mountain miles.

"But weren't you tired?" I said, aghast.

He was. Under the inflamed redness of his sun-and wind-and snow-burned face he was sick with fatigue. He had done over a hundred miles in the last four days.

"Did you enjoy it?" I asked.

"Oh yes. I wanted to do it all." He wanted to do it, and he *had* done it. But God knows what he wanted to do it for. He had now one day at Lucerne, one day at Interlaken and Berne, then London.

I was sorry for him in my soul, and he was so cruelly tired, so perishingly victorious.

"Why did you do so much?" I said. "Why did you come on foot all down the valley when you could have taken the train? Was it worth it?"

"I think so," he said.

Yet he was sick with fatigue and over-exhaustion. His eyes were quite dark, sightless: he seemed to have lost the power of seeing, to be virtually blind. He hung his head forward when he had to write a post card, as if he felt his way. But he turned his post card so that I should not see to whom it was addressed; not that I was interested; only I noticed his little, cautious, English movement of privacy.

"What time will you be going on?" I asked.

"When is the first steamer?" he said, and he turned out a guide-book with a time-table. He would leave at about seven.

"But why so early?" I said to him.

He must be in Lucerne at a certain hour, and at Interlaken in the evening.

"I suppose you will rest when you get to London?" I said.

He looked at me quickly, reservedly.

I was drinking beer: I asked him wouldn't he have something. He thought a moment, then said he would have another glass of hot milk. The landlord came—"And bread?" he asked.

The Englishman refused. He could not eat, really. Also he was poor; he had to husband his money. The landlord brought the milk and asked me, when would the gentleman want to go away. So I made arrangements between the landlord and the stranger. But the Englishman was slightly uncomfortable at my intervention. He did not like me to know what he would have for breakfast.

I could feel so well the machine that had him in its grip. He slaved for a year, mechanically, in London, riding in the Tube, working in the office. Then for a fortnight he was let free. So he rushed to Switzerland, with a tour planned out, and with just enough money to see him through, and to buy presents at Interlaken: bits of the edelweiss pottery: I could see him going home with them.

So he arrived, and with amazing, pathetic courage set forth on foot in a strange land, to face strange landlords, with no language but English at his command, and his purse definitely limited. Yet he wanted to go among the mountains, to cross a glacier. So he had walked on and on, like one possessed, ever forward. His name might have been Excelsior, indeed.

But then, when he reached his Furka, only to walk along the ridge and to descend on the same side My God, it was killing to the soul. And here he was, down again from the mountains, beginning his journey home again: steamer and train and steamer and train and Tube, till he was back in the machine.

It hadn't let him go. and he knew it. Hence his cruel self-torture of fatigue, his cruel exercise of courage. He who hung his head in his milk in torment when I asked him a question in German, what courage had he not needed to take this his very first trip out of England, alone, on foot!

His eyes were dark and deep with unfathomable courage. Yet he was going back in the morning. He was going back. All he had courage for was to go back. He would go back, though he died by inches. Why not? It was killing him, it was like living loaded with irons. But he had the courage to submit, to die that way, since it was the way allotted to him.

The way he sank on the table in exhaustion, drinking his milk, his will, nevertheless, so perfect and unblemished, triumphant, though his body was broken and in anguish, was almost too much to bear. My heart was wrung for my countryman, wrung till it bled.

I could not bear to understand my countryman, a man who worked for his living, as I had worked, as nearly all my countrymen work. He would not give in. On his holiday he would walk, to fulfil his purpose, walk on; no matter how cruel the effort were, he would not rest, he would not relinquish his purpose nor abate his will, not by one jot or tittle. His body must pay whatever his will demanded, though it were torture.

It all seemed to me so foolish. I was almost in tears. He went to bed. I walked by the dark lake, and talked to the girl in the inn. She was a pleasant girl: it was a pleasant inn, a homely place. One could be happy there.

In the morning it was sunny, the lake was blue. By night I should be nearly at the crest of my journey. I was glad.

The Englishman had gone. I looked for his name in the book. It was written in a fair, clerkly hand. He lived at Streatham. Suddenly I hated him. The dogged fool, to keep his nose on the grindstone like that. What was all his courage but the very tip-top of cowardice? What a vile nature—almost Sadish, proud, like the infamous Red Indians, of being able to stand torture.

The landlord came to talk to me. He was fat and comfortable and too respectful. But I had to tell him all the Englishman had done, in the way of a holiday, just to shame his own fat, ponderous, inn-keeper's luxuriousness that was too gross. Then all I got out of his enormous comfortableness was:

"Yes, that's a *very* long step to take."

So I set off myself, up the valley between the close, snow-topped mountains, whose white gleamed above me as I crawled, small as an insect, along the dark, cold valley below.

There had been a cattle fair earlier in the morning, so troops of cattle were roving down the road, some with bells tang-tanging, all with soft faces and startled eyes and a sudden swerving of horns. The grass was very green by the roads and by the streams; the shadows of the mountain slopes were very dark on either hand overhead, and the sky with snowy flanks and tips was high up.

Here, away from the world, the villages were quiet and obscure—left behind. They had the same fascinating atmosphere of being forgotten, left out of the world, that old English villages have. And buying apples and cheese and bread in a little shop that sold everything and smelled of everything, I felt at home again.

But climbing gradually higher, mile after mile, always between the shadows of the high mountains, I was glad I did not live in the Alps. The villages on the slopes, the people there, seemed as if they *must* gradually, bit by bit, slide down and tumble to the water-course, and be rolled on away, away to the sea. Straggling, haphazard little villages ledged on the slope, high up, beside their wet, green, hanging meadows, with pine trees behind and the valley bottom far below, and rocks right above, on both sides, seemed like little temporary squattings of outcast people. It seemed impossible that they should persist there, with great shadows wielded over them, like a menace, and gleams of brief sunshine, like a window. There was a sense of momentariness and expectation. It seemed as though some dramatic upheaval must take place, the mountains fall down into their own shadows. The valley beds were like deep graves, the sides of the mountains like the collapsing walls of a grave. The very mountain-tops above. bright with transcendent snow, seemed like death, eternal death.

There, it seemed, in the glamorous snow, was the source of death, which fell down in great waves of shadow and rock, rushing to the level earth. And all the people of the mountains, on the slopes, in the valleys, seemed to live upon this great, rushing wave of death, of breaking-down, of destruction.

The very pure source of breaking-down, decomposition, the very quick of cold death, is the snowy mountain-peak above. There, eternally, goes on the white foregathering of the crystals, out of the deathly cold of the heavens; this is the static nucleus where death meets life in its elementality. And thence, from their white, radiant nucleus of death in life, flows the great flux downwards, towards life and warmth. And we below, we cannot think of the flux upwards, that flows from the needle-point of snow to the unutterable cold and death.

The people under the mountains, they seem to live in the flux of death, the last, strange, overshadowed units of life. Big shadows wave over them, there is the eternal noise of water falling icily downwards from the source of death overhead.

And the people under the shadows, dwelling in the tang of snow and the noise of icy water, seem dark, almost sordid, brutal. There is no flowering or coming to flower, only this persistence, in the ice-touched air, of reproductive life.

But it is difficult to get a sense of a native population. Everywhere are the hotels and the foreigners, the parasitism. Yet there is, unseen, this overshadowed, overhung, sordid mountain population, ledged on the slopes and in the crevices. In the wider valleys there is still a sense of cowering among the people. But they catch a new tone from their contact with the foreigners. And in the towns are nothing but tradespeople.

So I climbed slowly up, for a whole day, first along the highroad, sometimes above and sometimes below the twisting, serpentine railway, then afterwards along a path on the side of the hill—a path that went through the crew-yards of isolated farms and even through the garden of a village priest. The priest was decorating an archway. He stood on a chair in the sunshine, reaching up with a garland, whilst the servingwoman stood below, talking loudly.

The valley here seemed wider, the great flanks of the mountains gave place, the peaks above were further back. So one was happier. I was pleased as I sat by the thin track of single flat stones that dropped swiftly downhill.

At the bottom was a little town with a factory or quarry, or a foundry, some place with long, smoking chimneys; which made me feel quite at home among the mountains.

It is the hideous rawness of the world of men, the horrible, desolating harshness of the advance of the industrial world upon the world of nature, that is so painful. It looks as though the industrial spread of mankind were a sort of dry disintegration advancing and advancing, a process of dry disintegration. If only we could learn to take thought for the whole world instead of for merely tiny bits of it.

I went through the little, hideous, crude factory-settlement in the high valley, where the eternal snows gleamed, past the enormous advertisements for chocolate and hotels, up the last steep slope of the pass to where the tunnel begins. Göschenen, the village at the mouth of the tunnel, is all railway sidings and haphazard villas for tourists, post cards, and touts and weedy carriages; disorder and sterile chaos, high up. How should any one stay there!

I went on up the pass itself. There were various parties of visitors on the roads and tracks, people from towns incongruously walking and driving. It was drawing on to evening. I climbed slowly, between the great cleft in the rock where are the big iron gates, through which the road winds, winds half-way down the narrow gulley of solid, living rock, the very throat of the path, where hangs a tablet in memory of many Russians killed.

Emerging through the dark rocky throat of the pass I came to the upper world, the level upper world. It was evening, livid, cold. On either side spread the sort of moorland of the wide pass-head. I drew near along the high-road to Andermatt.

Everywhere were soldiers moving about the livid, desolate waste of this upper world. I passed the barracks and the first villas for visitors. Darkness was coming on; the straggling, in-conclusive street of Andermatt looked as if it were some accident—houses, hotels, barracks, lodging-places tumbled at random as the caravan of civilisation crossed this high, cold, arid bridge of the European world.

I bought two post cards and wrote them out of doors in the cold, livid twilight. Then I asked a soldier where was the post-office. He directed me. It was something like sending post cards from Skegness or Bognor, there in the post-office.

I was trying to make myself agree to stay in Andermatt for the night. But I could not. The whole place was so terribly raw and flat and accidental, as if great pieces of furniture had tumbled out of a pantechnicon and lay discarded by the road. I hovered in the street, in the twilight, trying to make myself stay. I looked at the announcements of lodgings and boarding for visitors. It was no good. I could not go into one of these houses.

So I passed on, through the old, low, broad-eaved houses that cringe down to the very street, out into the open again. The air was fierce and savage. On one side was a moorland, level; on the other a sweep of naked hill, curved concave, and sprinkled with snow. I could see how wonderful it would all be, under five or six feet of winter snow, ski-ing and tobogganing at Christmas. But it needed the snow. In the summer there is to be seen nothing but the winter's broken detritus.

The twilight deepened, though there was still the strange, glassy translucency of the snow-lit air. A fragment of moon was in the sky. A carriage-load of French tourists passed me. There was the loud noise of water, as ever, something eternal and maddening in its sound, like the sound of Time itself, rustling and rushing and wavering, but never for a second ceasing. The rushing of Time that continues throughout eternity, this is the sound of the icy streams of Switzerland, something that mocks and destroys our warm being.

So I came, in the early darkness, to the little village with the broken castle that stands for ever frozen at the point where the track parts, one way continuing along the ridge to the Furka Pass, the other swerving over the hill to the left, over the Gotthardt.

In this village I must stay. I saw a woman looking hastily, furtively from a doorway. I knew she was looking for visitors. I went on up the hilly street. There were only a few wooden houses and a gaily lighted wooden inn, where men were laughing, and strangers, men, standing talking loudly in the doorway.

It was very difficult to go to a house this night I did not want to approach any of them. I turned back to the house of the peering woman. She had looked hen-like and anxious. She would be glad of a visitor to help her pay her rent.

It was a clean, pleasant wooden house, made to keep out the cold. That seemed its one function: to defend the inmates from the cold. It was furnished like a hut, just tables and chairs and bare wooden walls. One felt very close and secure in the room, as in a hut, shut away from the outer world.

The hen-like woman came.

"Can I have a bed," I said, "for the night?"

"Abendessen, ja!" she replied. "Will you have soup and boiled beef and vegetables?"

I said I would, so I sat down to wait, in the utter silence. I could scarcely hear the ice-stream, the silence seemed frozen, the house empty. The woman seemed to be flitting aimlessly, scurriedly, in reflex against the silence. One could almost touch the stillness as one could touch the walls, or the stove, or the table with white American oil-cloth.

Suddenly she appeared again.

"What will you drink?"

She watched my face anxiously, and her voice was pathetic, slightly pleading in its quickness.

"Wine or beer?" she said.

I would not trust the coldness of beer.

"A half of red wine," I said.

I knew she was going to keep me an indefinite time.

She appeared with the wine and bread.

"Would you like omelette after the beef?" she asked. "Omelette with cognac—I can make it *very* good."

I knew I should be spending too much, but I said yes. After all, why should I not eat, after the long walk?

So she left me again, whilst I sat in the utter isolation and stillness, eating bread and drinking the wine, which was good. And I listened for any sound: only the faint noise of the stream. And I wondered. Why am I here, on this ridge of the Alps, in the lamp-lit, wooden, close-shut room, alone? Why am I here?

Yet somehow I was glad, I was happy even: such splendid silence and coldness and clean isolation. It was something eternal, unbroachable: I was free, in this heavy, ice-cold air, this upper world, alone. London, far away below, beyond, England, Germany, France—they were all so unreal in the night. It was a sort of grief that this continent all beneath was so unreal, false, non-existent in its activity. Out of the silence one looked down on it, and it seemed to have lost all importance, all significance. It was so big, yet it had no significance: what could one do but wander about?

The woman came with my soup. I asked her, did not many people come in the summer. But she was scared away, she did not answer, she went like a leaf in the wind. However, the soup was good and plentiful.

She was a long time before she came with the next course. Then she put the tray on the table, and looking at me, then looking away, shrinking, she said:

"You must excuse me if I don't answer you—I don't hear well—I am rather deaf."

I looked at her, and I winced also. She shrank in such simple pain from the fact of her defect. I wondered if she were bullied because of it, or only afraid lest visitors would dislike it.

She put the dishes in order, set me my plate, quickly, nervously, and was gone again, like a scared chicken. Being tired, I wanted to weep over her, the nervous, timid hen, so frightened by her own deafness. The house was silent of her, empty. It was perhaps her deafness which created this empty soundlessness.

When she came with the omelette, I said to her loudly:

"That was very good, the soup and meat." So she quivered nervously, and said, "Thank you," and I managed to talk to her. She was like most deaf people, in that her terror of not hearing made her six times worse than she actually was.

She spoke with a soft, strange accent, so I thought she was perhaps a foreigner. But when I asked her she misunderstood, and I had not the heart to correct her. I can only remember she said her house was always full in the winter, about Christmas-time. People came for the winter sport. There were two young English ladies who always came to her.

She spoke of them warmly. Then, suddenly afraid, she drifted off again. I ate the omelette with cognac, which was very good, then I looked in the street. It was very dark, with bright stars, and smelled of snow. Two village men went by. I was tired, I did not want to go to the inn.

So I went to bed, in the silent, wooden house. I had a small bedroom, clean and wooden and very cold. Outside, the stream was rushing. I covered myself with a great depth of featherbed, and looked at the stars, and the shadowy upper world, and went to sleep.

In the morning I washed in the ice-cold water, and was glad to set out. An icy mist was over the noisy stream, there were a few meagre, shredded pine trees. I had breakfast and paid my bill: it was seven francs—more than I could afford; but that did not matter, once I was out in the air.

The sky was blue and perfect, it was a ringing morning, the village was very still. I went up the hill till I came to the sign-post. I looked down the direction of the Furka, and thought of my tired Englishman from Streatham, who would be on his way home. Thank God I need not go home: never, perhaps. I turned up the track to the left, to the Gothard.

Standing looking round at the mountain-tops, at the village and the broken castle below me, at the scattered debris of Andermatt on the moor in the distance, I was jumping in my soul with delight. Should one ever go down to the lower world?

Then I saw another figure striding along, a youth with knee-breeches and Alpine hat and braces over his shirt, walking manfully, his coat slung in his Rucksack behind. I laughed, and waited. He came my way.

"Are you going over the Gothard?" I said.

"Yes," he replied. "Are you also?"

"Yes," I said. "We will go together."

So we set off, climbing a track up the heathy rocks.

He was a pale, freckled town youth from Basel, seventeen years old. He was a clerk in a baggage-transport firm— Gondrand Frères, I believe. He had a week's holiday, in which time he was going to make a big circular walk, something like the Englishman's. But he was accustomed to this mountain walking: he belonged to a Sportverein. Manfully he marched in his thick hob-nailed boots, earnestly he scrambled up the rocks.

We were in the crest of the pass. Broad snow-patched slopes came down from the pure sky; the defile was full of stones, all bare stones, enormous ones as big as a house, and small ones, pebbles. Through these the road wound in silence, through this upper, transcendent desolation, wherein was only the sound of the stream. Sky and snow-patched slopes, then the stony, rocky bed of the defile, full of morning sunshine: this was all. We were crossing in silence from the northern world to the southern.

But he, Emil, was going to take the train back, through the tunnel, in the evening, to resume his circular walk at Göschenen.

I, however, was going on, over the ridge of the world, from the north into the south. So I was glad.

We climbed up the gradual incline for a long time. The slopes above became lower, they began to recede. The sky was very near, we were walking under the sky.

Then the defile widened out, there was an open place before us, the very top of the pass. Also there were low barracks, and soldiers. We heard firing. Standing still, we saw on the slopes of snow, under the radiant blue heaven, tiny puffs of smoke, then some small black figures crossing the snow patch, then another rattle of rifle-fire, rattling dry and unnatural in the upper, skyey air, between the rocks.

"Das ist schön," said my companion, in his simple admiration.

"Hübsch," I said.

"But that would be splendid, to be firing up there, manœuvring up in the snow."

And he began to tell me how hard a soldier's life was, how hard the soldier was drilled.

"You don't look forward to it?" I said.

"Oh yes, I do. I want to be a soldier, I want to serve my time."

"Why?" I said.

"For the exercise, the life, the drilling. One becomes strong."

"Do all the Swiss want to serve their time in the army?" I asked.

"Yes—they all want to. It is good for every man, and it keeps us all together. Besides, it is only for a year. For a year it is very good. The Germans have three years— that is too long, that is bad."

I told him how the soldiers in Bavaria hated the military service.

"Yes," he said, "that is true of Germans. The system is different. Ours is much better; in Switzerland a man enjoys his time as a soldier. I want to go."

So we watched the black dots of soldiers crawling over the high snow, listened to the unnatural dry rattle of guns, up there.

Then we were aware of somebody whistling, of soldiers yelling down the road. We were to come on, along the level, over the bridge. So we marched quickly forward, away from the slopes, towards the hotel, once a monastery, that stood in the distance. The light was blue and clear on the reedy lakes of this upper place; it was a strange desolation of water and bog and rocks and road, hedged by the snowy slopes round the rim, under the very sky.

The soldier was yelling again. I could not tell what he said.

"He says if we don't run we can't come at all," said Emil.

"I won't run," I said.

So we hurried forwards, over the bridge, where the soldier on guard was standing.

"Do you want to be shot?" he said angrily, as we came up.

"No, thanks," I said.

Emil was very serious.

"How long should we have had to wait if we hadn't got through now?" he asked the soldier, when we were safely out of danger.

"Till one o'clock," was the reply.

"Two hours!" said Emil, strangely elated. "We should have had to wait two hours before we could come on. He was riled that we didn't run," and he laughed with glee.

So we marched over the level to the hotel. We called in for a glass of hot milk. I asked in German. But the maid, a pert hussy, elegant and superior, was French. She served us with great contempt, as two worthless creatures, poverty-stricken. It abashed poor Emil, but we managed to laugh at her. This made her very angry. In the smoking-room she raised up her voice in French:

"Du lait chaud pour les chameaux."

"Some hot milk for the camels, she says," I translated for Emil. He was covered with confusion and youthful anger.

But I called to her, tapped the table and called:

"Mademoiselle!"

She appeared flouncingly in the doorway.

"Encore du lait pour les chameaux," I said.

Arid she whisked our glasses off the table, and flounced out without a word.

But she would not come in again with the milk. A German girl brought it. We laughed, and she smiled primly.

When we set forth again, Emil rolled up his sleeves and turned back his shirt from his neck and breast, to do the thing thoroughly. Besides, it was midday, and the sun was hot; and, with his bulky pack on his back, he suggested the camel of the French maid more than ever.

We were on the downward slope. Only a short way from the hotel, and there was the drop, the great cleft in the mountains running down from this shallow pot among the peaks.

The descent on the south side is much more precipitous and wonderful than the ascent from the north. On the south, the rocks are craggy and stupendous; the little river falls headlong down; it is not a stream, it is one broken, panting cascade far away in the gulley below, in the darkness.

But on the slopes the sun pours in, the road winds down with its tail in its mouth, always in endless loops returning on itself. The mules that travel upward seem to be treading in a mill.

Emil took the narrow tracks, and, like the water, we cascaded down, leaping from level to level, leaping, running, leaping, descending headlong, only resting now and again when we came down on to another level of the high-road.

Having begun, we could not help ourselves, we were like two stones bouncing down. Emil was highly elated. He waved his thin, bare, white arms as he leapt, his chest grew pink with the exercise. Now he felt he was doing something that became a member of his Sportverein. Down we went, jumping, running, britching.

It was wonderful on this south side, so sunny, with feathery trees and deep black shadows. It reminded me of Goethe, of the romantic period:

"Kennst du das Land, wo die Citronen blühen?"

So we went tumbling down into the south, very swiftly, along with the tumbling stream. But it was very tiring. We went at a great pace down the gully, between the sheer rocks. Trees grew in the ledges high over our heads, trees grew down below. And ever we descended.

Till gradually the gully opened, then opened into a wide valley-head, and we saw Airolo away below us, the railway emerging from its hole, the whole valley like a cornucopia full of sunshine.

Poor Emil was tired, more tired than I was. And his big boots had hurt his feet in the descent. So, having come to the open valley-head, we went more gently. He had become rather quiet.

The head of the valley had that half-tamed, ancient aspect that reminded me of the Romans. I could only expect the Roman legions to be encamped down there; and the white goats feeding on the bushes belonged to a Roman camp.

But no, we saw again the barracks of the Swiss soldiery, and again we were in the midst of rifle-fire and manœuvres. But we went evenly, tired now, and hungry. We had nothing to eat.

It is strange how different the sun-dried, ancient, southern slopes of the world are, from the northern slopes. It is as if the god Pan really had his home among these sun-bleached stones and tough, sun-dark trees. And one knows it all in one's blood, it is pure, sun-dried memory. So I was content, coming down into Airolo.

We found the streets were Italian, the houses sunny outside and dark within, like Italy, there were laurels in the road. Poor Emil was a foreigner all at once. He rolled down his shirt sleeves and fastened his shirt-neck, put on his coat and collar, and became a foreigner in his soul, pale and strange.

I saw a shop with vegetables and grapes, a real Italian shop, a dark cave.

'Quanto costa l' uva?" were my first words in the south.

"Sessanta al chilo," said the girl.

And it was as pleasant as a drink of wine, the Italian.

So Emil and I ate the sweet black grapes as we went to the station.

He was very poor. We went into the third-class restaurant at the station. He ordered beer and bread and sausage; I ordered soup and boiled beef and vegetables.

They brought me a great quantity, so, whilst the girl was serving coffee-with-rum to the men at the bar, I took another spoon and knife and fork and plates for Emil, and we had two dinners from my one. When the girl—she was a woman of thirty-five—came back, she looked at us sharply. I smiled at her coaxingly; so she gave a small, kindly smile in reply.

"Ja, dies ist reizend," said Emil, *sotto voce,* exulting. He was very shy. But we were curiously happy, in that railway restaurant.

Then we sat very still, on the platform, and waited for the train. It was like Italy, pleasant and social to wait in the railway station, all the world easy and warm in its activity, with the sun shining.

I decided to take a franc's worth of train-journey. So I chose my station. It was one franc twenty, third class. Then my train came, and Emil and I parted, he waving to me till I was out of sight. I was sorry he had to go back, he did so want to venture forth.

So I slid for a dozen miles or more, sleepily, down the Ticino valley, sitting opposite two fat priests in their feminine black.

When I got out at my station I felt for the first time ill at ease. Why was I getting out at this wayside place, on to the great, raw high-road? I did not know. But I set off walking. It was nearly tea-time.

Nothing in the world is more ghastly than these Italian roads, new, mechanical, belonging to a machine life. The old roads are wonderful, skilfully aiming their way. But these new great roads are desolating, more desolating than all the ruins in the world.

I walked on and on, down the Ticino valley, towards Bellinzona. The valley was perhaps beautiful: I don't know. I can only remember the road. It was broad and new, and it ran very often beside the railway. It ran also by quarries and by occasional factories, also through villages. And the quality of its sordidness is something that does not bear thinking of, a quality that has entered Italian life now, if it was not there before.

Here and there, where there were quarries or industries, great lodging-houses stood naked by the road, great, grey, desolate places; and squalid children were playing round the steps, and dirty men slouched in. Everything seemed under a weight.

Down the road of the Ticino valley I felt again my tenor of this new world which is coming into being on top of us. One always feels it in a suburb, on the edge of a town, where the land is being broken under the advance of houses. But this is nothing, in England, to the tenor one feels on the new Italian roads, where these great blind cubes of dwellings rise stark from the destroyed earth, swarming with a sort of verminous life, really verminous, purely destructive.

It seems to happen when the peasant suddenly leaves his home and becomes a workman. Then an entire change comes over everywhere. Life is now a matter of selling oneself to slave-work, building roads or labouring in quarries or mines or on the railways, purposeless, meaningless, really slave-work, each integer doing his mere labour, and all for no purpose, except to have money, and to get away from the old system.

These Italian navvies work all day long, their whole life is engaged in the mere brute labour. And they are the navvies of the world. And whilst they are navvying, they are almost shockingly indifferent to their circumstances, merely callous to the dirt and foulness.

It is as if the whole social form were breaking down, and the human element swarmed within the disintegration, like maggots in cheese. The roads, the railways are built, the mines and quarries are excavated, but the whole organism of life, the social organism, is slowly crumbling and caving in, in a kind of process of dry rot, most terrifying to see. So that it seems as though we should be left at last with a great system of roads and railways and industries, and a world of utter chaos seething upon these fabrications: as if we had created a steel framework, and the whole body of society were crumbling and rotting in between. It is most terrifying to realise; and I have always felt this terror upon a new Italian high-road—more there than anywhere.

The remembrance of the Ticino valley is a sort of nightmare to me. But it was better when at last, in the darkness of night I got into Bellinzona. In the midst of the town one felt the old organism still living. It is only at its extremities that it is falling to pieces, as in dry rot.

In the morning, leaving Bellinzona, again I went in terror of the new, evil high-road, with its skirting of huge cubical houses and its seething navvy population. Only the peasants driving in with fruit were consoling. But I was afraid of them: the same spirit had set in in them.

I was no longer happy in Switzerland, not even when I was eating great blackberries and looking down at the Lago Maggiore, at Locarno, lying by the lake; the terror of the callous, disintegrating process was too strong in me.

At a little inn a man was very good to me. He went into his garden and fetched me the first grapes and apples and peaches, bringing them in amongst leaves, and heaping them before me. He was Italian-Swiss; he had been in a bank in Bern; now he had retired, had bought his paternal home, and was a free man. He was about fifty years old; he spent all his time in his garden; his daughter attended to the inn.

He talked to me, as long as I stayed, about Italy and Switzerland and work and life. He was retired, he was free. But he was only nominally free. He had only achieved freedom from labour. He knew that the system he had escaped at last, persisted, and would consume his sons and his grandchildren. He himself had more or less escaped back to the old form; but as he came with me on to the hill-side, looking down the high-road at Lugano in the distance, he knew that his old order was collapsing by a slow process of disintegration.

Why did he talk to me as if I had any hope, as if I represented any positive truth as against this great negative truth that was advancing up the hill-side. Again I was afraid. I hastened down the high-road, past the houses, the grey, raw crystals of corruption.

I saw a girl with handsome bare legs, ankles shining like brass in the sun. She was working in a field, on the edge of a vineyard. I stopped to look at her, suddenly fascinated by her handsome naked flesh that shone like brass.

Then she called out to me, in a jargon I could not understand, something mocking and challenging. And her voice was raucous and challenging; I went on, afraid.

In Lugano I stayed at a German hotel. I remember sitting on a seat in the darkness by the lake, watching the stream of promenaders patrolling the edge of the water, under the trees and the lamps. I can still see many of their faces: English, German, Italian, French. And it seemed here, here in this holiday-place, was the quick of the disintegration, the dry-rot, in this dry, friable flux of people backwards and forwards on the edge of the lake, men and women from the big hotels, in evening dress, curiously sinister, and ordinary visitors, and tourists, and workmen, youths, men of the town, laughing, jeering. It was curiously and painfully sinister, almost obscene.

I sat a long time among them, thinking of the girl with her limbs of glowing brass. Then at last I went up to the hotel, and sat in the lounge looking at the papers. It was the same here as down below, though not so intense, the feeling of horror.

So I went to bed. The hotel was on the edge of a steep declivity. I wondered why the whole hills did not slide down, in some great natural catastrophe.

In the morning I walked along the side of the Lake of Lugano, to where I could take a steamer to ferry me down to the end. The lake is not beautiful, only picturesque. I liked most to think of the Romans coming to it.

So I steamed down to the lower end of the water. When I landed and went along by a sort of railway I saw a group of men. Suddenly they began to whoop and shout. They were hanging on to an immense pale bullock, which was slung up to be shod; and it was lunging and kicking with terrible energy. It was strange to see that mass of pale, soft-looking flesh working with such violent frenzy, convulsed with violent, active frenzy, whilst men and women hung on to it with ropes, hung on and weighed it down. But again it scattered some of them in its terrible convulsion. Human beings scattered into the road, the whole place was covered with hot dung. And when the bullock began to lunge again, the men set up a howl, half of triumph, half of derision.

I went on, not wanting to see. I went along a very dusty road. But it was not so terrifying, this road. Perhaps it was older.

In dreary little Chiasso I drank coffee, and watched the come and go through the Customs. The Swiss and the Italian Customs officials had their offices within a few yards of each other, and everybody must stop. I went in and showed my Rucksack to the Italian, then I mounted a tram, and went to the Lake of Como.

In the tram were dressed-up women, fashionable, but business-like. They had come by train to Chiasso, or else had been shopping in the town.

When we came to the terminus a young miss, dismounting before me, left behind her parasol. I had been conscious of my dusty, grimy appearance as I sat in the tram, I knew they thought me a workman on the roads. However, I forgot that when it was time to dismount.

"Pardon, Mademoiselle," I said to the young miss. She turned and withered me with a rather overdone contempt— "bourgeoise," I said to myself, as I looked at her— "Vous avez laissé votre parasol."

She turned, and with a rapacious movement darted upon her parasol. How her soul was in her possessions! I stood and watched her. Then she went into the road and under the trees, haughty, a demoiselle. She had on white kid boots.

I thought of the Lake of Como what I had thought of Lugano: it must have been wonderful when the Romans came there. Now it is all villas. I think only the sunrise is still wonderful, sometimes.

I took the steamer down to Como, and slept in a vast old stone cavern of an inn, a remarkable place, with rather nice people. In the morning I went out. The peace and the bygone beauty of the cathedral created the glow of the great past. And in the market-place they were selling chestnuts wholesale, great heaps of bright, brown chestnuts, and sacks of chestnuts, and peasants very eager selling and buying. I thought of Como, it must have been wonderful even a hundred years ago. Now it is cosmopolitan, the cathedral is like a relic, a museum object, everywhere stinks of mechanical money-pleasure.

I dared not risk walking to Milan: I took a train. And there, in Milan sitting in the Cathedral Square, on Saturday afternoon, drinking Bitter Campari and watching the swarm of Italian city-men drink and talk vivaciously, I saw that here the life was still vivid, here the process of disintegration was vigorous, and centred in a multiplicity of mechanical activities that engage the human mind as well as the body. But always there was the same purpose stinking in it all, the mechanising, the perfect mechanising of human life.

SEA AND SARDINIA

CHAPTER I

AS FAR AS PALERMO

COMES over one an absolute necessity to move. And what is more, to move in some particular direction. A double necessity then: to get on the move, and to know whither.

Why can't one sit still? Here in Sicily it is so pleasant: the sunny Ionian sea, the changing jewel of Calabria, like a fire-opal moved in the light; Italy and the panorama of Christmas clouds, night with the dog-star laying a long luminous gleam across the sea, as if baying at us, Orion marching above; how the dog-star Sirius looks at one, looks at one! he is the hound of heaven, green, glamorous and fierce!—and then, oh, regal evening star, hung westward flaring over the. jagged dark precipices of tall Sicily: then Etna, that wicked witch, resting her thick white snow under heaven, and slowly, slowly rolling her orange-coloured smoke. They called her the Pillar of Heaven, the Greeks. It seems wrong at first, for she trails up in a long, magical, flexible line from the sea's edge to her blunt cone, and does not seem tall. She seems rather low, under heaven. But as one knows her better, oh, awe and wizardry! Remote under heaven, aloof, so near, yet never with us. The painters try to paint her, and the photographers to photograph her, in vain. Because why? Because the near ridges, with their olives and white houses, these are with us. Because the river-bed, and Naxos under the lemon groves, Greek Naxos deep under dark-leaved, many-fruited lemon groves, Etna's skirts and, skirt-bottoms, these still are our world, our own world. Even the high villages among the oaks, on Etna. But Etna herself, Etna of the snow and secret changing winds, she is beyond a crystal wall. 'When I look at her, low, white, witch-like under heaven, slowly rolling her orange smoke and giving sometimes breath of rose-red flame, then I must look away from earth, into the ether, into the low empyrean. And there, in that remote region, Etna is alone. If you would see her, you must slowly take off your eyes from the world and go a naked seer to the strange chamber of the empyrean. Pedestal of heaven! The Greeks had a sense of the magic truth of things. Thank goodness one still knows enough about them to find one's kinship at last. There are so many photographs, there are so infinitely many water-colour drawings and oil paintings which purport to render Etna. But pedestal of heaven! You must cross the invisible border. Between the foreground, which is our own, and Etna, pivot of winds in lower heaven, there is a dividing line. You must change your state of mind. A metempsychosis. It is no use thinking you can see and behold Etna and the foreground both at once. Never. One or the other. Foreground and a transcribed Etna. Or Etna, pedestal of heaven.

Why, then, must one go? Why not stay? Ah, what a mistress, this Etna! with her strange winds prowling round her like Circe's panthers, some black, some white. With her strange, remote communications and her terrible dynamic exhalations. She makes men mad. Such terrible vibrations of wicked and beautiful electricity she throws about her, like a deadly net! Nay, sometimes, verily, one can feel a new current of her demon magnetism seize one's living tissue and change the peaceful life of one's active cells. She makes a storm in the living plasm and a new adjustment. And sometimes it is like a madness.

This timeless Grecian Etna, in her lower-heaven loveliness, so lovely, so lovely, what a torturer! Not many men can really stand her without losing their souls. She is like

Circe. Unless a man is very strong, she takes his soul away from him and leaves him not a beast, but an elemental creature, intelligent and soulless. Intelligent, almost inspired, and soulless, like the Etna Sicilians. Intelligent daimons, and humanly, according to us, the most stupid people on earth. Ach, horror! How many men, how many races; has Etna put to flight? It was she who broke the quick of the Greek soul. And after the Greeks, she gave the Romans, the Normans, the Arabs, the Spaniards, the French, the Italians, even the English, she gave them all their inspired hour and broke their souls.

Perhaps it is she one must flee from. At any rate, one must go: and at once. After having come back only at the end of October, already one must dash away. And it is only the third of January. And one cannot afford to move. Yet there you are: at the Etna bidding one goes.

Where does one go? There is Girgenti by the south. There is Tunis at hand. Girgenti, and the sulphur spirit and the Greek guarding temples, to make one madder? Never. Neither Syracuse and .the madness of its great quarries. Tunis? Africa? Not yet, not yet. Not the Arabs, not yet. Naples, Rome, Florence? No good at all. Where then?

Where then? Spain or Sardinia. Spain or Sardinia. Sardinia, which is like nowhere. Sardinia, which has no history, no date, no race, no offering. Let it be Sardinia. They say neither Romans nor Phœnicians, Greeks nor Arabs ever subdued Sardinia. It lies outside; outside the circuit of civilisation. Like the Basque lands. Sure enough, it is Italian now, with its railways and its motor omnibuses. But there is an uncaptured Sardinia still. It lies within the net of this European civilisation, but it isn't landed yet. And the net is getting old and tattered. A good many fish are slipping through the net of the old European civilisation. Like that great whale of Russia. And probably even Sardinia. Sardinia then. Let it be Sardinia.

There is a fortnightly boat sailing from Palermo—next Wednesday, three days ahead. Let us go, then. Away from abhorred Etna, and the Ionian sea, and these great stars in the water, and the almond trees in bud, and the orange trees heavy with red fruit, and these maddening, exasperating, impossible Sicilians, who never knew what truth was and have long lost all notion of what a human being is. A sort of sulphureous demons. *Andiamo!*

But let me confess, in parenthesis, that I am not at all sure whether I don't really prefer these demons to our sanctified humanity.

Why does one create such discomfort for oneself! To have to get up in the middle of the night—half-past one—to go and look at the clock. Of course this fraud of an American watch has stopped, with its impudent phosphorescent face. Half-past one! Half-past one, and a dark January night. Ah, well! Half-past one! And an uneasy sleep till at last it is five o'clock. Then light a candle and get up.

The dreary black morning, the candle-light, the house looking night-dismal. Ah, well, one does all these things for one's pleasure. So light the charcoal fire and put the kettle on. The queen bee shivering round half dressed, fluttering her unhappy candle.

"It's fun," she says, shuddering.

"Great," say I, grim as death.

First fill the thermos with hot tea. Then fry bacon—good English bacon from Malta, a god-send, indeed—and make bacon sandwiches. Make also sandwiches of scrambled eggs. Make also bread and butter. Also a little toast for breakfast—and more tea. But ugh! who wants to eat at this unearthly hour, especially when one is escaping from bewitched Sicily.

91

Fill the little bag we call the kitchenino. Methylated spirit, a small aluminium saucepan, a spirit-lamp, two spoons, two forks, a knife, two aluminium plates, salt, sugar, tea—what else The thermos flask, the various sandwiches, four apples, am a little tin of butter. So much for the kitchenino for myself and the queen bee. Then my knapsack and the q-b's hand bag.

Under the lid of the half-cloudy night sky, far away at the rim of the Ionian sea, the first light, like metal fusing. So swallow the cup of tea and the bit of toast. Hastily wash up, so that we can find the house decent when we come back. Shut the door-windows of the upper terrace and go down. Lock the door: the upper half of the house made fast.

The sky and sea are parting like an oyster shell, with a low red gape. Looking across from the veranda at it, one shivers. Not that it is cold. The morning is not at all cold. But the ominousness of it: that long red slit between a dark sky and a dark Ionian sea, terrible old bivalve which has held life between its lips so long. And here, at this house, we are ledged so awfully above the dawn, naked to it.

Fasten the door-windows of the lower veranda. One won't fasten at all. The summer heat warped it one way, the masses of autumn rain warped it another. Put a chair against it. Lock the last door and hide the key. Sling the knapsack on one's back, take the kitchenino in one's hand and look around. The dawn-red widening, between the purpling sea and the troubled sky. A light in the Capucin convent across there. Cocks crowing and the long, howling, hiccuping, melancholy bray of an ass. "All females are dead, all females-och! och! och! —hoooo! Ahaa! —there's one left." So he ends on a moaning grunt of consolation. This is what the Arabs tell us an ass is howling when he brays.

Very dark under the great carob tree as we go down the steps. Dark still the garden. Scent of mimosa, and then of jasmine. The lovely mimosa tree invisible. Dark the stony path. The goat whinnies out of her shed. The broken Roman tomb which lolls right over the garden track does not fall on me as I slip under its massive tilt. Ah, dark garden, dark garden, with your olives and your wine, your medlars and mulberries and many almond trees, your steep terraces ledged high up above the sea, I am leaving you, slinking out. Out between the rosemary hedges, out of the tall gate, on to the cruel steep stony road. So under the dark, big eucalyptus trees, over the stream, and up towards the village. There, I have got so far.

It is full dawn—dawn—not morning, the sun will not have risen. The village is nearly all dark in the red light, and asleep still. No one at the fountain by the Capucin gate: too dark still. One man leading a horse round the corner of the Palazzo Corvaia. One or two dark men along the Coso. And so over the brow, down the steep cobble-stone street between the houses, and out to the naked hill front. This is the dawn-coast of Sicily. Nay, the dawn-coast of Europe. Steep, like a vast cliff, dawn-forward. A red dawn, with mingled curdling dark clouds, and some gold. It must be seven o'clock. The station down below, by the sea. And noise of a train. Yes, a train. And we still high on the steep track, winding downwards. But it is the train from Messina to Catania, half an hour before ours, which is from Catania to Messina.

So jolt, and drop, and jolt down the old road that winds on the cliff face. Etna across there is smothered quite low, quite low in a dense puther of ink-black clouds. Playing some devilry in private, no doubt. The dawn is angry red, and yellow above, the sea takes strange colours. I hate the station, pigmy, drawn out there beside the sea. On this steep face, especially in the windless nooks, the almond blossom is already out. In little puffs and specks and stars, it looks very like bits of snow scattered by winter. Bits of snow, bits of blossom, fourth day of the year 1921. Only blossom. And Etna indescribably cloaked and secretive in her dense black clouds. She has wrapped them quite round her, quite low round her skirts.

At last we are down. We pass the pits where men are burning lime—red-hot, round pits—and are out on the highway. Nothing can be more depressing than an Italian high-road. From Syracuse to Airolo it is the same: horrible, dreary, slummy high-roads the moment you approach a village or any human habitation. Here there is an acrid smell of lemon juice. There is a factory for making citrate The houses flush on the road, under the great limestone face of the hill, open their slummy doors, and throw out dirty water and coffee dregs. We walk over the dirty water and coffee dregs. Mules rattle past with carts. Other people are going to the station. We pass the Dazio and are there.

Humanity is, externally, too much alike. Internally there are insuperable differences. So one sits and thinks, watching the people on the station: like a line of caricatures between oneself and the naked sea and the uneasy, clouding dawn.

You would look in vain this morning for the swarthy feline southerner of romance. It might, as far as features are concerned, be an early morning crowd waiting for the train or a north London suburb station. As far as features go. For some are fair and some colourless and none racially typical. The only one that is absolutely like a rare caricature is a tall stout elderly fellow with spectacles and a short nose and a bristling moustache, and he is the German of the comic papers of twenty years ago. But he is pure Sicilian.

They are mostly young fellows going up the line to Messina to their job: not artizans, lower middle class. And externally, so like any other clerks and shopmen, only rather more shabby, much less *socially* self-conscious. They are lively, they throw their arms round one another's necks, they all but kiss. One poor chap has had earache, so a black kerchief is tied round his face, and his black hat is perched above, and a comic sight he looks. No one seems to think so, however. Yet they view my arrival with a knapsack on my back with cold disapprobation, as unseemly as if I had arrived riding on a pig. I ought to be in a carriage, and the knapsack ought to be a new suitcase. I know it, but am inflexible.

That is how they are. Each one thinks he is as handsome as Adonis, and as "fetching" as Don Juan. Extraordinary! At the same time, all flesh is grass, and if a few trouser-buttons are missing or if a black hat perches above a thick black muffler and a long excruciated face, it is all in the course of nature. They seize the black-edged one by the arm, and in profound commiseration: "Do you suffer? Are you suffering?" they ask.

And that also is how they are. So terribly physically all over one another. They pour themselves one over the other like so much melted butter over parsnips. They catch each other under the chin, with a tender caress of the hand, and they smile with sunny melting tenderness into each other's face. Never in the world have I seen such melting gay tenderness as between casual Sicilians on railway platforms, whether they be young lean-checked Sicilians or huge stout Sicilians.

There must be something curious about the proximity of a volcano. Naples and Catania alike, the men are hugely fat, with great macaroni paunches, they are expansive and in a perfect drip of casual affection and love. But the Sicilians are even more wildly exuberant and fat and all over one another than the Neapolitans. They never leave off being amorously friendly with almost everybody, emitting a relentless physical familiarity that is quite bewildering to one not brought up near a volcano.

This is more true of the middle classes than of the lower. The working men are perforce thinner and less exuberant. But they hang together in clusters, and can never be physically near enough.

93

It is only thirty miles to Messina, but the train takes two hours. It winds and hurries and stops beside the lavender-grey morning sea. A flock of goats trails over the beach near the lapping wave's edge, dismally. Great wide deserts of stony river-beds run down to the sea, and men on asses are picking their way across, and women are kneeling by the small stream-channel washing clothes. The lemons hang pale and innumerable in the thick lemon groves. Lemon trees, like Italians, seem to be happiest when they are touching one another all round. Solid forests of not very tall lemon trees lie between the steep mountains and the sea, on the strip of plain. Women, vague in the orchard under-shadow, are picking the lemons, lurking as if in the undersea. There are heaps of pale yellow lemons under the trees. They look like pale primrose-smouldering fires. Curious how like fires the heaps of lemons look, under the shadow of foliage, seeming to give off a pallid burning amid the suave, naked, greenish trunks. When there comes a cluster of orange trees, the oranges are red like coals among the darker leaves. But lemons, lemons, innumerable, speckled like innumerable tiny stars in the green firmament of leaves. So many lemons! Think of all the lemonade crystals they will be reduced to! Think of America drinking them up next summer.

I always wonder why such vast wide river-beds of pale boulders come out of the heart of the high-rearing, dramatic stone mountains, a few miles to the sea. A few miles only: and never more than a few threading water-trickles in river-beds wide enough for the Rhine. But that is how it is. The landscape is ancient, and classical—romantic, as if it had known far-off days and fiercer rivers and more verdure. Steep, craggy, wild, the land goes up to its points and precipices, a tangle of heights. But all jammed on top of one another. And in old landscapes, as in old people, the flesh wears away, and the bones become prominent. Rock sticks up fantastically. The jungle of peaks in this old Sicily.

The sky is all grey. The Straits are grey. Reggio, just across the water, is white looking, under the great dark toe of Calabria, the toe of Italy. On Aspromonte there is grey cloud. It is going to rain. After such marvellous ringing blue days, it is going to rain. What luck!

Aspromonte! Garibaldi! I could always cover my face when I see it, Aspromonte. I wish Garibaldi had been prouder. Why did he go off so humbly, with his bag of seed-corn and a flea in his ear, when His Majesty King Victor Emmanuel arrived with his little short legs on the scene. Poor Garibaldi! He wanted to be a hero and a dictator of free Sicily. Well, one can't be a dictator and humble at the same time. One must be a hero, which he was, and proud, which he wasn't. Besides, people don't nowadays choose proud heroes for governors. Anything but. They prefer constitutional monarchs, who are paid servants and who know it. That is Democracy. Democracy admires its own servants and nothing else. And you couldn't make a real servant even of Garibaldi. Only of His Majesty King Victor Emmanuel. So Italy chose' Victor Emmanuel, and Garibaldi went off with a corn bag and a whack on the behind like a humble ass.

It is raining—dismally, dismally raining. And this is Messina coming. Oh, horrible Messina, earthquake-shattered and renewing your youth like a vast mining settlement, with rows and streets and miles of concrete shanties, squalor and a big street with shops and gaps and broken houses still, just behind the tram lines, and a dreary squalid earthquake-hopeless port in a lovely harbour. People don't forget and don't recover. The people of Messina seem to be to-day what they were nearly twenty years ago, after the earthquake: people who have had a terrible shock, and for whom all life's institutions are really nothing, neither civilisation nor purposes. The meaning of everything all came down with a smash in that shuddering earthquake, and nothing remains but money and the throes of some sort of sensation. Messina between the volcanoes, Etna and Stromboli, having known the death-agony's terror. I always dread coming near the awful place, yet I have found the people kind, almost feverishly so, as if they knew the awful need for kindness.

Raining, raining hard. Clambering down on to the wet platform and walking across the wet lines to the cover. Many human beings scurrying across the wet lines, among the wet trains, to get out into the ghastly town beyond. Thank heaven one need not go out into the town. Two convicts chained together among the crowd—and two soldiers. The prisoners wear fawny homespun clothes, of cloth such as the peasants weave, with irregularly occurring brown stripes. Rather nice handmade rough stuff. But linked together, dear God! And those horrid caps on their hairless foreheads. No hair. Probably they are going to a convict station on the Lipari islands. The people take no notice.

No, but convicts are horrible creatures: at least, the old one is, with his long, nasty face: his long, clean-shaven, horrible face, without emotions, or with emotions one cannot follow. Something cold, sightless. A sightless, ugly look. I should loathe to have to touch him. Of the other I am not so sure. He is younger, and with dark eyebrows. But a roundish, softish face, with a sort of leer. No, evil is horrible. I used to think there was no absolute evil. Now I know there is a great deal. So much that it threatens life altogether. That ghastly abstractedness of criminals. They don't *know* any more what other people feel. Yet some horrible force drives them.

It is a great mistake to abolish the death penalty. If I were dictator, I should order the old one to be hanged at once. I should have judges with sensitive, living hearts: not abstract intellects. And because the instinctive heart recognised a man as evil, I would have that man destroyed. Quickly. Because good warm life is now in danger.

Standing on Messina station—dreary, dreary hole—and watching the winter rain and seeing the pair of convicts, I must remember again Oscar Wilde on Reading platform, a convict. What a terrible mistake, to let oneself be martyred by a lot of canaille. A man must say his say. But *noli me tangere.*

Curious these people are. Up and down, up and down go a pair of officials. The young one in a black gold-laced cap talks to the elder in a scarlet gold-laced cap. And he walks, the young one, with a mad little hop, and his fingers fly as if he wanted to scatter them to the four winds of heaven, and his words go off like fireworks, with more than Sicilian speed. On and on, up and down, and his eye is dark and excited and unseeing, like the eye of a fleeing rabbit. Strange and beside itself is humanity.

What a lot of officials! You know them, by their caps. Elegant tubby little officials in kid and patent boots and gold-laced caps, like angels in and out of the gates of heaven they thread in and out of the various doors. As far as I can see, there are three scarlet station-masters, five black-and-gold sub-station-masters, and a countless number of principalities and powers in more or less broken boots and official caps. They are like bees round a hive, humming in an important *conversazione,* and occasionally looking at some paper or other, and extracting a little official honey. But the *conversazione* is the affair of affairs. To an Italian official, life seems to be one long and animated conversation—the Italian word is better—interrupted by casual trains and telephones. And besides the angels of heaven's gates, there are the mere ministers, porters, lamp cleaners, etc. These stand in groups and talk Socialism. A lamp man slashes along, swinging a couple of lamps. Bashes one against a barrow. Smash goes the glass. Looks down as if to say, What do you mean by it? Glances over his shoulder to see if any member of the higher hierarchies is looking. Seven members of higher hierarchies are assiduously not looking. On goes the minister with the lamp, blithely. Another pane or two gone. *Vogue la galère.*

Passengers have gathered again, some in hoods, some in nothing. Youths in thin paltry clothes stand out in the pouring rain as if they did not know it was raining. One sees their coat-shoulders soaked. And yet they do not trouble to keep under shelter. Two large station dogs run about and trot through the standing trains, just like officials. They climb up the footboard, hop into a train and hop out casually when they feel like it. Two or three port-porters, in canvas hats as big as umbrellas, literally, spreading like huge fins over their shoulders, are looking into more empty trains. More and more people appear. More and more official caps stand about. It rains and rains. The train for Palermo and the train for Syracuse are both an hour late already, coming from the port. Fleabite. Through these are the great connections from Rome.

Loose locomotives trundle back and forth, vaguely, like black dogs running and turning back. The port is only four minutes' walk. If it were not raining so hard, we would go down, walk along the lines and get into the waiting train down there. Anybody may please himself. There is the funnel of the great unwieldy ferry-object—she is just edging in. That means the connection from the mainland at last. But it is cold, standing here. We eat a bit of bread and butter from the kitchenino in resignation. After all, what is an hour and a half? It might just as easily be five hours, as it was the last time we came down from Rome. And the *wagon-lit,* booked to Syracuse, calmly left stranded in the station of Messina, to go no further. All get out and find yourselves rooms for the night in vile Messina. Syracuse or no Syracuse, Malta boat or no Malta boat. We are the *Ferrovia dello Stato.*

But there, why grumble? Noi Italiani siamo cosi buoni. Take it from their own mouths.

Ecco! Finalmente! The crowd is quite joyful as the two express trains surge proudly in, after their half a mile creep. Plenty of room, for once. Though the carriage floor is a puddle, and the roof leaks. This is second class.

Slowly, with two engines, we grunt and chuff and twist to get over the break-neck heights that shut Messina in from the north coast. The windows are opaque with steam and drops of rain. No matter—tea from the thermos flask, to the great interest of the other two passengers who had nervously contemplated the unknown object.

"Ha!" says he with joy, seeing the hot tea come out.

"It has the appearance of a bomb."

"Beautiful hot!" says she, with real admiration. All apprehension at once dissipated, peace reigns in the wet, mist-hidden compartment. We run through miles and miles of tunnel. The Italians have made wonderful roads and railways.

If one rubs the window and looks out, lemon groves with many wet-white lemons, earthquake-broken houses, new shanties, a grey weary sea on the right hand, and on the left the dim, grey complications of steep heights from which issue stone river-beds of inordinate width, and sometimes a road, a man on a mule. Sometimes near at hand, long-haired, melancholy goats leaning sideways like tilted ships under the eaves of some scabby house. They call the house-eaves the dogs' umbrellas. In town you see the dogs trotting close under the wall out of the wet. Here the goats lean like rock, listing inwards to the plaster wall. Why look out?

Sicilian railways are all single line. Hence, the *coincidenza.* A *coincidenza* is where two trains meet in a loop. You sit in a world of rain waiting until some silly engine with four trucks puffs alongside. Ecco la coincidenza! Then after brief conversazione between the two trains, *diretto* and *merce,* express and goods, the tin horn sounds and away we go, happily, towards the next coincidence. Clerks away ahead joyfully chalk up our hours of lateness on the announcement slate. All adds to the adventurous flavour of the journey, dear heart. We come to a station where we find the other diretto, the express from the other direction, awaiting our coincidental arrival. The two trains run alongside on another, like two dogs meeting in the street and snuffing one another. Every official rushes to greet every other official as if they were all David and Jonathan meeting after a crisis. They rush into each other's arms and exchange cigarettes. And the trains can't bear to part. And the station can't bear to part with us. The officials tease themselves and us wit the word *pronto,* meaning *ready!* Pronto! And again Pronto! And shrill whistles. Anywhere else a train would go off its tormented' head. But no! Here only that angel trump of an official little horn will do the business. And get them to blow that horn if you can. They can't bear to part.

Rain, continual rain, a level grey wet sky, a level grey wet sea, a wet and misty train winding round and round the little bays, diving through tunnels. Ghosts of the unpleasant-looking Lipari islands standing a little way out to sea, heaps of shadow deposited like rubbish heaps in the universal greyness.

Enter more passengers. An enormously large woman with an extraordinarily handsome face: an extraordinarily large man, quite young: and a diminutive servant, a little girl-child of about thirteen, with a beautiful face.—But the Juno—it is she who takes, my breath away. She is quite young, in her thirties still. She has that queenly stupid beauty of a classic Hera: a pure brow with level dark eyebrows, large dark, bridling eyes, a straight nose, a chiselled mouth, an air of remote self-consciousness. She sends one's heart straight back to pagan days. And—and—she is simply enormous, like a house. She wears a black toque with sticking-up wings and a black rabbit fur spread on her shoulders. She edges her way in carefully: and once seated, is terrified to rise to her feet. She sits with that motionlessness of her type, closed lips, face muted and expressionless. And she expects me to admire her: I can see that. She expects me to pay homage to her beauty: just to that: not homage to herself, but to her as a *bel pezzo.* She casts little aloof glances at me under her eyelids.

It is evident she is a country beauty become a *bourgeoise.* She speaks unwillingly to the other squint-eyed passenger, a young woman who also wears a black rabbit fur, but without pretensions.

The husband of Juno is a fresh-faced bourgeois, young fellow, and he also is simply huge. His waistcoat would make the overcoat of the fourth passenger, the unshaven companion of the squinting young woman. The young Jupiter wears kid gloves: a significant fact here. He, too, has pretensions. But he is quite affable with the unshaven one, and speaks Italian unaffectedly. Whereas Juno speaks the dialect with affectation.

No one takes any notice of the little maid. She has a gentle, virgin moon-face, and those lovely grey Sicilian eyes that are translucent, and into which the light sinks and becomes black sometimes, sometimes dark blue. She carries the bag and the extra coat of the huge Juno, and sits on the edge of the seat between me and the unshaven, Juno having motioned her there with a regal inclination of the head.

The little maid is rather frightened. Perhaps she is an orphan child—probably. Her nut-brown hair is smoothly parted and done in two pigtails. She wears no hat, as is proper for her class. On her shoulders one of those little knitted grey shoulder-capes that one associates with orphanages. Her stuff dress is dark grey, her boots are strong.

The smooth, moon-like, expressionless virgin face, rather pale and touching, rather frightened, of the girl-child. A perfect face from a mediæval picture. It moves one strangely. Why? It is so unconscious, as we are conscious. Like a little muted animal it sits there in distress. She is going to be sick. She goes into the corridor and is sick—very sick, leaning her head like a sick dog on the window-ledge. Jupiter towers above her—not unkind, and apparently feeling no repugnance. The physical convulsion of the girl does not affect him as it affects us. He looks on unmoved, merely venturing to remark that she had eaten too much before coming on to the train. An obviously true remark. After which he comes and talks a few commonplaces to me. By and by the girl-child creeps in again and sits on the edge of the seat facing Juno. But no, says Juno, if she is sick she will be sick over me. So Jupiter accommodatingly changes places with the girl-child, who is thus next to me. She sits on the edge of the seat with folded little red hands, her face pale and expressionless. Beautiful the thin line of her nut-brown eyebrows, the dark lashes of the silent, pellucid dark eyes. Silent, motionless, like a sick animal.

But Juno tells her to wipe her splashed boots. The child gropes for a piece of paper. Juno tells her to take her pocket handkerchief. Feebly the sick girl-child wipes her boots, then leans back. But no good. She has to go in the corridor and be sick again.

After a while they all get out. Queer to see people so natural. Neither Juno nor Jupiter is in the least unkind. He even seems kind, But they are just not upset. Not half as upset as we are—the q-b wanting to administer tea, and so on. We should have to hold the child's head. They just quite naturally leave it alone to its convulsions, and are neither distressed nor repelled. It is just so.

Their naturalness seems unnatural to us. Yet I am sure it is best. Sympathy would only complicate matters, and spoil that strange, remote virginal quality. The q-b says it is largely stupidity.

Nobody washes out, the corner of the corridor, though we stop at stations long enough, and there are two more hours' journey. Train officials go by and stare, passengers step over and stare, newcomers stare and step over. Somebody asks *who?* Nobody thinks of just throwing a pail of water. Why should he? It is all in the course of nature.—One begins to be a bit chary of this same "nature," in the south.

Enter two fresh passengers: a black-eyed, round-faced, bright-sharp man in corduroys and with a gun, and a long-faced, fresh-coloured man with thick snowy hair, and a new hat and a long black overcoat of smooth black cloth, lined with rather ancient, once expensive fur. He is extremely proud of this long black coat and ancient fur lining. Childishly proud he wraps it again over his knee, and gloats. The beady black eyes of the hunter look round with pleased alertness. He sits facing the one in the overcoat, who looks like the last sprout of some Norman blood. The hunter in corduroys beams abroad, with beady black eyes in a round red face, curious. And the other tucks his fur-lined long coat between his legs and gloats to himself: all to himself gloating, and looking as if he were deaf. But no, he's not. He wears muddy high-low boots.

At Termini it is already lamplight. Business men crowd in. We get five business men: all stout, respected Palermitans. The one opposite me has whiskers, and a many-coloured, patched travelling rug over his fat knees. Queer how they bring that feeling of physical intimacy with them. You are never surprised if they begin to take off their boots, or their collar and tie. The whole world is a sort of bedroom to them. One shrinks, but in vain.

There is some conversation between the black-eyed, beady hunter and the business men. Also the young white-haired one, the aristocrat, tries to stammer out, at great length, a few words. As far as I can gather the young one is mad— or deranged—and the other, the hunter, is his keeper. They are travelling over Europe together. There is some talk of "the Count." And the hunter says the unfortunate "has had an accident." But that is a southern gentleness presumably, a form of speech. Anyhow, it is queer: and the hunter in his corduroys, with his round ruddy face and strange black-bright eyes and thin black hair, is a puzzle to me, even more than the albino, long-coated, long-faced, fresh-complexioned, queer last remnant of a baron as he is. They are both muddy from the land, and pleased in a little mad way of their own.

But it is half-past six. We are at Palermo, capital of Sicily. The hunter slings his gun over his shoulder, I my knapsack, and in the throng we all disappear, into the Via Maqueda

Palermo has two great streets, the Via Maqueda, and the Corso, which cross each other at right-angles. The Maqueda is narrow, with narrow little pavements, and is always choked with carriages and foot passengers.

It had ceased raining. But the narrow road was paved with large convex slabs of hard stone, inexpressibly greasy. To cross the Via Maqueda therefore was a feat. However, once accomplished, it was done. The near end of the street was rather dark, and had mostly vegetable shops. Abundance of vegetables—piles of white and green fennel, like celery, and great sheaves of young, purplish, sea-dust-coloured artichokes, nodding their buds, piles of big radishes, scarlet and bluey purple, carrots, long strings of dried figs, mountains of big oranges, scarlet large peppers, a last slice of pumpkin, a great mass of colours and vegetable freshnesses. A mountain of black-purple cauliflowers, like niggers' heads, and a mountain of snow-white ones next to them. How the dark greasy, night-stricken street seems to beam with these vegetables, all this fresh delicate flesh of luminous vegetables piled there in the air, and in the recesses of the windowless little caverns of the shops, and gleaming forth on the dark air under the lamps. The q-b at once wants to buy vegetables "Look! Look at the snow-white broccoli. Look at the huge finocchi. Why don't we get them? I *must* have some. Look at those great clusters of dates—ten francs a kilo, and we pay sixteen. It's monstrous. Our place is simply monstrous."

For all that, one doesn't buy vegetables to take to Sardinia.

Cross the Corso at that decorated maelstrom and death-trap of the Quattro Canti. I, of course, am nearly knocked down and killed. Somebody is nearly knocked down and killed every two minutes. But there—the carriages are light, and the horses curiously aware creatures. They would never tread on one.

The second part of the Via Maqueda is the swell part: silks and plumes, and an infinite number of shirts and ties and cuff-links and mufflers and men's fancies. One realises here that man-drapery and man-underwear are quite as important as woman's, if not more.

I, of course, in a rage. The q-b stares at every rag and stitch, and crosses and re-crosses this infernal dark stream of a Via Maqueda, which, as I have said, is choked, solid with strollers and carriages. Be it remembered that I have on my back the brown knapsack, and the q-b carries the kitchenino. This is enough to make a travelling menagerie of us; If I had my shirt sticking out behind, and if the q-b had happened merely to catch up the tablecloth and wrap it round her as she came out, all well and good. But a big brown knapsack! And a basket with a thermos flask, etc.! No, one could not expect such things to pass in a southern capital.

But I am case-hardened. And I am sick of shops. True, we have not been in a town for three months. But *can* I care for the innumerable *fantasias* in the drapery line? Every wretched bit of would-be-extra chic is called a fantasia. The word goes lugubriously to my bowels.

Suddenly I am aware of the q-b darting past me like a storm. Suddenly I see her pouncing on three giggling young hussies just in front—the inevitable black velveteen tam, the inevitable white curly muffler, the inevitable lower-class flappers. "Did you want something? Have you something to say? Is there something that amuses you? Oh-h! You must laugh, must you? Oh—laugh! Oh-h! Why? Why? You ask why? Haven't I heard you! Oh—you spik Ingleesh! You spik Ingleesh! Yes—why! That's why! Yes, that's why."

The three giggling young hussies shrink together as if they would all hide behind one another, after a vain up-rearing and a demand why? Madam tells them why. So they uncomfortably squeeze together under the unexpected strokes of the q-b's sledge-hammer Italian and more than sledge-hammer retaliation, there full in the Via Maqueda. They edge round one another, each attempting to get behind the other, away from the looming q-b. I perceive that this rotary motion is equivalent to a standstill, so feel called upon to say something in the manly line.

"Beastly Palermo bad-manners," I say, and throw a nonchalant "Ignoranti" at the end, in a tone of dismissal.

Which does it. Off they go down-stream, still huddling and shrinking like boats that are taking sails in, and peeping to see if we are coming. Yes, my dears, we are coming.

"Why do you bother?" say I to the q-b, who is towering with rage.

"They've followed us the whole length of the street—with their *sacco militare* and their *parlano inglese* and their *you spik Ingleesh,* and their jeering insolence. But the English are, fools. They always put up with this Italian impudence."

Which is perhaps true.—But this knapsack! It might be full of bronze-roaring geese, it would not attract more attention!

However, and however, it is seven o'clock, and the shops are beginning to shut. No more shop-gazing. Only one lovely place: raw ham, boiled ham, chickens in aspic, chicken *vol-au-vents,* sweet curds, curd-cheese, rustic cheese-cake smoked sausages, beautiful fresh mortadella, huge Mediterranean red lobsters, and those lobsters without claws. "So good! So good!" We stand and cry it aloud.

But this shop too is shutting. I ask a man for the Hotel Pantechnico. And treating me in that gentle, strangely tender southern manner, he takes me and shows me. He make me feel such a poor, frail, helpless leaf. A foreigner, you know. A bit of an imbecile, poor dear. Hold his hand and show him the way.

To sit in the room of this young American woman, with its blue hangings, and talk and drink tea till midnight! All these naïve Americans—they are a good deal older and shrewder than we, once it nears the point. And they all seem to feel as if the world were coming to an end. And they are so truly generous of their hospitality in this cold world.

CHAPTER II

THE SEA

THE fat old porter knocks. Ah me, once more it is dark. Get up again before dawn. A dark sky outside, cloudy. The thrilling tinkle of innumerable goat-bells as the first flock enters the city, such a rippling sound. Well, it must be morning, even if one shivers at it. And at least it does not rain

That pale, bluish, theatrical light outside, of the first dawn. And a cold wind. We come on to the wide, desolate quay, the curve of the harbour Panormus. That horrible dawn-pallor of a cold sea out there. And here, port mud, greasy: and fish: and refuse. The American girl is with us, wrapped in her sweater. A coarse, cold, black-slimy world, she seems as if she would melt away before it. But these frail creatures, what a lot they can go through!

Across the great, wide, badly paved, mud-greasy, despairing road of the quay side, and to the sea. There lies our steamer, over there in the dawn-dusk of the basin, half visible. "That one who is smoking her cigarette," says the porter. She looks little, beside the huge *City of Trieste* who is lying up next her.

Our row boat is hemmed in by many empty boats, huddled to the side of the quay. She works her way out like a sheep-dog working his way out of a flock of sheep, or like a boat through pack-ice. We are on the open basin. The rower stands up and pushes the oars from him. He gives a long melancholy cry to someone on the quay. The water goes chock-chock against the urging bows. The wind is chill. The fantastic peaks behind Palermo show half-ghostly in a half-dark sky. The dawn seems reluctant to come. Our steamer still smokes her cigarette—meaning the funnel-smoke—across there. So, one sits still, and crosses the level space of half-dark water. Masts of sailing ships, and spars, cluster on the left, on the undarkening sky.

Climb up, climb up, this is our ship. Up we go up the ladder. "Oh, but!" says the American girl "Isn't she small! Isn't she impossibly small! Oh, my, will you go in such a little thing? Oh, dear! Thirty-two hours in such a little boat? Why no, I wouldn't care for it at all."

A bunch of stewards, cooks, waiters, engineers, pan cleaners and what-not, mostly in black canvas jackets. Nobody else on the ship. A little black bunch of loutish crew with nothing to do, and we the first passengers served up to be jeered at. There you are, in the grey light.

"Who is going?"

"We two—the signorina is not going."

"Tickets!"

These are casual proletarian manners.

We are taken into the one long room with a long table and many maple-golden doors, alternate panels having a wedgwood blue-and-white picture, inserted—a would-be goddess of white marble on a blue ground, like a health-salts Hygeia advertisement. One of the plain panels opens—our cabin.

"Oh, dear! Why, it isn't as big as a china-closet. However will you get in? "cries the American girl.

"One at a time," say I.

"But it's the tiniest place I *ever* saw." It really was tiny. One had to get into a bunk to shut the door. That did not matter to me, I am no titanic American. I pitched the knapsack on one bunk, the kitchenino on the other, and we shut the door. The cabin disappeared into a maplewood panel of the long subterranean state-room.

"Why, is this the only place you've got to sit in?" cried the American girl. "But how perfectly awful! No air, and so dark, and smelly. Why I never saw such a boat! Will you really go? Will you really?"

The state-room was truly rather subterranean and stuffy, with nothing but a long table and an uncanny company of screw-pin chairs seated thereat, and no outlet to the air at all, but it was not so bad otherwise, to me who have never been out of Europe. Those maplewood panels and ebony curves— and those Hygeias! They went all round, even round the curve at the dim distant end, and back up the near side. Yet how beautiful old gold-coloured maplewood is! how very lovely, with the ebony curves of the door arch! There was a wonderful old-fashioned Victorian glow in it, and a certain splendour. Even one could bear the Hygeias let in under glass—the colour was right, that wedgwood and white, in such lovely gold lustre. There was a certain homely grandeur still in the days when this ship was built: a richness of choice material. And health-salts Hygeias, wedgwood Greek goddesses on. advertisement placards! Yet they *weren't* advertisements. That was what really worried me. They never had been. Perhaps Weego's Health Salts stole her later.

We have no coffee—that goes without saying. Nothing doing so early. The crew still stands in a gang, exactly like a gang of louts at a street corner. And they've got the street all to themselves—this ship. We climb to the upper deck.

She is a long, slender, old steamer with one little funnel. And she seems so deserted, now that one can't see the street-corner gang of the casual crew. They are just below. Our ship is deserted.

The dawn is wanly blueing. The sky is a curdle of cloud, there is a bit of pale gold eastwards, beyond Monte Pellegrino. The wind blows across the harbour. The hills behind Palermo prick up their ears on the skyline. The city lies unseen, near us and level. There—a big ship is coming in: the Naples boat.

And the little boats keep putting off from the near quay, and coming to us. We watch. A stout officer, cavalry, in grey-green, with a big dark-blue cloak lined with scarlet. The scarlet lining keeps flashing. He has a little beard, and his uniform is not quite clean. He has big wooden chests, tied with rope, for luggage. Poor and of no class. Yet that scarlet, splendid lining, and the spurs. It seems a pity they must go second-class. Yet so it is, he goes forward when the dock porter has hoisted those wooden boxes. No fellow-passenger yet.

Boats still keep coming. Ha-ha! Here is the commissariat! Various sides of kid, ready for roasting: various chickens: fennel like celery: wine in a bottiglione: new bread: packages! Hand them up, hand them up. "Good food!" cries the q-b in anticipation.

It must be getting near time to go. Two more passengers—young thick men in black broadcloth standing up in the stern of a little boat, their hands in their pockets, looking a little cold about the chin: Not quite Italian, too sturdy and manly. Sardinians from Cagliari, as a matter of fact.

We go down from the chill upper-deck. It is growing full day. Bits of pale gold are flying among delicate but cold flakes of cloud from the east, over Monte Pellegrino, bits of very new turquoise sky come out. Palermo on the left crouches upon her all-harbour—a little desolate, disorderly, end-of-the-world, end-of-the-sea, along her quay front. Even from here we can see the yellow carts rattling slowly, the mules nodding their high weird plumes of scarlet along the broad weary harbour-side. Oh painted carts of Sicily, with all history on your panels!

Arrives an individual at our side. "The Captain fears it will not be possible to start. There is much wind outside. Much wind!"

How they *love* to come up with alarming, disquieting, or annoying news! The joy it gives them. What satisfaction on all the faces: of course all the other loafers are watching us, the street-corner loungers of this deck. But we have been many times bitten.

"Ah, ma!" say I, looking at the sky, "not so much wind as all that."

An air of quiet, shrugging indifference is most effectual: as if you knew all about it, a good deal more than they knew.

"Ah, si! Molto vento! Molto vento! Outside! Outside!"

With a long face and a dramatic gesture he points out -of the harbour, to the grey sea. I too look out of the harbour at the pale line of sea beyond the mole. But I do not trouble to answer, and my eye is calm. So he goes away, only half triumphant.

"Things seem to get worse and worse! "cries the American friend. "What will you do on such a boat if you have an awful time out in the Mediterranean here? Oh, no—will you risk it, really? Won't you go from Città Vecchia?"

"How awful it will be!" cries the q-b, looking round the grey harbour, the many masts clustering in the grey sky on the right; the big Naples boat turning her posterior to the quay side a little way off, and cautiously budging backwards: the almost entirely shut-in harbour: the bits of blue and flying white cloud overhead: the little boats like beetles scuttling hither and thither across the basin; the thick crowd on the quay come to meet the Naples boat.

Time! Time! The American friend must go. She bids us good-bye, more than sympathetically.

"I shall be awfully interested to hear how you get on." So down the side she goes. The boatman wants francs—wants more—but doesn't get it. He gets ten, which is five too much. And so, sitting rather small and pinched and cold-looking, huddled in her sweater; she bibbles over the ripply water to the distant stone steps. We wave farewell. But other traffic comes between us. And the q-b, feeling nervous, is rather cross because the American friend's ideas of luxury have put us in such a poor light. We feel like the poorest of poor seafaring relations.

Our ship is hooting for all she's worth. An important last-minuter comes surging up. The rope hawsers are being wound clankily in. Seagulls—they are never very many in the Mediterranean—seagulls whirl like a few flakes of snow in the upper chill air. Clouds spin. And without knowing it we are evaporating away from the shore, from our mooring, between the great *City of Trieste* and another big black steamer that lies like a wall. We breathe towards this second black wall of steamer: distinctly. And of course an individual in an official cap is standing on the bottom of our departure ladder just above the water, yelling Barca! Barca!—shouting for a boat. And an old man on the sea stands up to his oars and comes pushing his clumsy boat with gathering speed between us and the other black wall. There he stands away below there, small, firing his clumsy boat along, remote as if in a picture on the dark green water. And our black side insidiously and evilly aspires to the other huge black wall. He rows in the cañon between, and is nearly here.

When lo, the individual on the bottom step turns in the other direction. Another boat from the open basin is sweeping up: it is a race: she is near, she is nearer, she is up. With a curvet the boat from the open rounds up at the ladder. The boat between the gulf backs its oars. The official individual shouts and waves, the old man, backing his oars in the gulf below, yells expostulation, the boat from the open carries off its prey, our ship begins slowly to puddle-puddle-puddle, working her screw, the man in the gulf of green water rows for his life—we are floating into the open basin.

Slowly, slowly we turn round: and as the ship turns, our hearts turn. Palermo fades from our consciousness: the Naples boat, the disembarking crowds, the rattling carriages to the land—the great *City of Trieste,* all fade from our heart. We see only the open gap of the harbour entrance, and the level, pale-grey void of the sea beyond. There are wisps of gleamy light—out there.

And out there our heart watches—though Palermo is near us, just behind. We look round, and see it all behind us— but already it is gone, gone from our heart. The fresh wind, the gleamy wisps of light, the running, open sea beyond the harbour bars.

And so we steam out. And almost at once the ship begins to take a long, slow, dizzy dip, and a fainting swoon upwards, and a long, slow, dizzy dip, slipping away from beneath one. The q-b turns pale. Up comes the deck in that fainting swoon backwards—then down it fades in that indescribable slither forwards. It is all quite gentle—quite, quite gentle. But oh, so long, and so slow, and so dizzy.

"Rather pleasant! " say I to the q-b.

"Yes. Rather lovely *really,*" she answers wistfully. To tell the truth there is something in the long, slow lift of the ship, and her long, slow slide forwards which makes my heart beat with joy. It is the motion of freedom. To feel her come up—then slide slowly forward, with the sound of the smashing of waters, is like the magic gallop of the sky, the magic gallop of elemental space. That long, slow, waveringly rhythmic rise and fall of the ship, with waters snorting as it were from her nostrils, oh, God, what a joy it is to the wild innermost soul. One is free at last—and lilting in a slow flight of the elements, winging outwards. Oh, God, to be free of all the hemmed-in life—the horror of human tension, the absolute insanity of machine persistence. The agony which a train is to me, really. And the long-drawn-out agony of a life among tense, resistant people on land. And then to feel the long, slow lift and drop of this almost empty ship, as she took the waters. Ah, God liberty, liberty, elemental liberty. I wished in my soul the voyage might last forever, that the sea had no end, that one might float in this wavering, tremulous, yet long and surging pulsation while ever time lasted: space never exhausted, and no turning back, no looking back, even.

The ship was almost empty—save of course for the street-corner louts who hung about just below, on the deck itself. We stood alone on the weather-faded little promenade deck, which had old oak seats with old, carved little lions at the ends, for arm-rests—and a little cabin mysteriously shut, which much peeping determined as the wireless office and the operator's little curtained bed-niche.

Cold, fresh wind, a black-blue, translucent, rolling sea on which the wake rose in snapping foam, and Sicily on the left: Monte Pellegrino, a huge, inordinate mass of pinkish rock, hardly crisped with the faintest vegetation, looming up to heaven from the sea. Strangely large in mass and bulk Monte Pellegrino looks: and bare, like a Sahara in heaven: and old-looking. These coasts of Sicily are very imposing, terrific, fortifying the interior. And again one gets the feeling that age has worn them bare: as if old, old civilisations had worn away and exhausted the soil, leaving a terrifying blankness of rock, as at Syracuse in plateaus, and here in great mass.

There seems hardly anyone on board but ourselves: we alone on the little promenade deck. Strangely lonely, floating on a bare old ship past the great bare shores on a rolling sea, stooping and rising in the wind. The wood of the fittings is all bare and weather-silvered, the cabin, the seats, even the little lions of the seats. The paint wore away long ago: and this timber will never see paint any more. Strange to put one's hand on the old oaken wood, so sea-fibred. Good old delicate-threaded oak: I swear it grew in England. And everything so carefully done, so solid and everlastingly. I look at the lions, with, the perfect-fitting oaken pins through their paws chinching them down, and their little mouths open They are as solid as they were in Victorian days, as immovable. They will never wear away. What a joy in the careful, thorough, manly, everlasting work put into a ship: at least into this sixty-year-old vessel. Every bit of this oak wood so sound, so beautiful: and the whole welded together with joints and wooden pins far more beautifully and livingly than iron welds. Rustless, life-born, living-tissued old wood: rustless as flesh is rustless, and happy-seeming as iron never can be. She rides so well, she takes the sea so beautifully as a matter of course.

Various members of the crew wander past to look at us. This little promenade deck is over the first-class quarters, full in the stern. So we see first one head then another come up the ladder—mostly bare heads: and one figure after another slouches past, smoking a cigarette. All crew. At last the q-b stops one of them—it is what they are all waiting for, an opportunity to talk—and asks if the weird object on the top of Pellegrino is a ruin. Could there be a more touristy question! No, it is the semaphore station. Slap in the eye for the q-b! She doesn't mind, however, and the member of the crew proceeds to converse. He is a weedy, hollow-cheeked town-product: a Palermitan. He wears faded blue overalls and informs us he is the ship's carpenter: happily unemployed for the rest of his life, apparently, and taking it as rather less than his dues. The ship once did the Naples-Palermo course—a very important course—in the old days of the General Navigation Company. The General Navigation Company sold her for eighty thousand liras years ago, and now she was worth two million. We pretended to believe: but I make a poor show. I am thoroughly sick to death of the sound of liras. No man can overhear ten words of Italian to-day without two thousand or two million or ten or twenty or two liras flying like venomous mosquitoes round his ears. Liras—liras—liras——nothing else. Romantic, poetic, cypress-and-orange-tree Italy is gone. Remains an Italy smothered in the filthy smother of innumerable lira notes: ragged, unsavoury paper money so thick upon the air that one breathes it like some greasy fog. Behind this greasy fog some people may still see the Italian sun. I find it hard work. Through this murk of liras you peer at Michael Angelo and at Botticelli and the rest, and see them all as through a glass, darkly. For heavy around you is Italy's after-the-war atmosphere, darkly pressing you, squeezing you, milling you into dirty paper notes. King Harry was lucky that they only wanted to coin him into gold. Italy wants to mill you into filthy paper liras.

Another head—and a black alpaca jacket and a serviette this time—to tell us coffee is ready. Not before it is time, too. We go down into the subterranean state-room and sit on the screw-pin chairs, while the ship does the slide-and-slope trot under us, and we drink a couple of cups of coffee and milk, and eat a piece of bread and butter. At least one of the innumerable members of the crew gives me one cup, then casts me off. It is most obviously his intention that I shall get no more: because of course the innumerable members of the crew could all just do with another coffee and milk. However, though the ship heaves and the alpaca coats cluster menacingly in the doorway, I balance my way to the tin buffet and seize the coffee pot and the milk pot, and am quite successful in administering to the q-b and myself. Having restored the said vessels to their tin altar, I resume my spin-chair at the long and desert board. The q-b and I are alone—save that in the distance a very fat back with gold-braid collar sits sideways and a fat hand disposes of various papers—he is part of the one-and-only table, of course. The tall lean alpaca jacket, with a face of yellow stone and a big black moustache, moves from the outer doorway, glowers at our filled cups, and goes to the tin altar and touches the handles of the two vessels: just touches them to an arrangement: as one who should say: These are mine. What dirty foreigner dares help himself!

As quickly as possible we stagger up from the long dungeon where the alpaca jackets are swooping like blue-bottles upon the coffee pots, into the air. There the carpenter is waiting for us, like a spider.

"Isn't the sea a little quieter?" says the q-b wistfully. She is growing paler.

"No, Signora—how should it be?" says the gaunt-faced carpenter. "The wind is waiting for us behind Cape Gallo. You see that Cape?" he points to a tall black cliff-front in the sea ahead. "When we get to that Cape we get the wind and the sea. Here"—he makes a gesture—"it is quite moderate."

"Ugh!" says the q-b, turning paler. "I'm going to lie down."

She disappears. The carpenter, finding me stony ground, goes forward, and I see him melting into the crowd of the innumerable crew, that hovers on the lower-deck passage by the kitchen and the engines.

The clouds are flying fast overhead: and sharp and isolated come drops of rain, so that one thinks it must be spray. But no, it is a handful of rain. The ship swishes and sinks forward, gives a hollow thudding and rears slowly backward, along this pinkish lofty coast of Sicily that is just retreating into a bay. From the open sea comes the rain, come the long waves.

No shelter. One must go down. The q-b lies quietly in her bunk. The state-room is stale like a passage on the underground railway. No shelter, save near the kitchen and the engines, where there is a bit of warmth. The cook is busy cleaning fish, making the whiting bite their tails venomously at a little board just outside his kitchen-hole. A slow stream of kitchen filth swilkers back and forth along the ship's side. A gang of the crew leans near me—a larger gang further down. Heaven knows what they can all be—but they never do anything but stand in gangs and talk and eat and smoke cigarettes. They are mostly young—mostly Palermitan—with a couple of unmistakable Neapolitans, having the peculiar Neapolitan hangdog good looks, the chiselled cheek, the little black moustache, the large eyes. But they chew with their cheeks bulged out, and laugh with their fine, semi-sarcastic noses. The whole gang looks continually sideways. Nobody ever commands them—there seems to be absolutely no control. Only the fat engineer in grey linen looks as clean and as competent as his own machinery. Queer how machine-control puts the pride and self-respect into a man.

The rain over, I go and squat against the canvas that is spread over the arched sky-lights on the small promenade deck, sitting on the seat that is fixed to the sky-light sides. The wind is cold: there are snatches of sun and spits of rain. The big Cape has come and is being left behind: we are heading for a far-off Cape like a cloud in the grey air. A dimness comes over one's mind: a sort of stupefaction owing to the wind and the relentless slither and rearing of the ship. Not a sickness, but a sort of dim faintness. So much motion, such moving, powerful air. And withal a constant triumph in the long, slow sea gallop of the ship.

A great loud bell: midday and the crew going to eat, rushing to eat. After some time we are summoned. "The Signora isn't eating?" asks the waiter eagerly: hoping she is not. "Yes, she is eating," say I. I fetch the q-b from her berth. Rather wanly she comes and gets into her spin-chair. Bash comes a huge plate of thick oily cabbage soup, very full, swilkering over the sides. We do what we can with it. So does the third passenger: a young woman who never wears a hat, thereby admitting herself as one of "the people," but who has an expensive complicated dress, nigger-coloured thin silk stockings, and suede high-heeled shoes. She is handsome, sturdy, with large dark eyes and a robust, frank manner: far too robustly downright for Italy. She is from Cagliari—and can't do much with the cabbage soup: and tells the waiter so, in her deep, hail-fellow-well-met voice. In the doorway hovers a little cloud of alpaca jackets grinning faintly with malignant anticipation of food, hoping, like blowflies, we shall be too ill to eat. Away goes the soup and appears a massive. yellow omelette, like some log of bilious wood. It is hard and heavy, and cooked in the usual rank-tasting olive oil. The young woman doesn't have much truck with it: neither do we. To the triumph of the blowflies, who see the yellow monster borne to their altar. After which a

106

long slab of the inevitable meat, cut into innumerable slices, tasting of dead nothingness and having a thick sauce of brown neutrality: sufficient for twelve people at least. This, with masses of strong-tasting greenish cauliflower liberally weighted with oil, on a ship that was already heaving its heart out, made up the dinner. Accumulating malevolent triumph among the blowflies in the passage. So on to a dessert of oranges, pears with wooden hearts and thick yellowish wash-leather flesh, and apples. Then coffee.

And we had sat through it, which is something. The alpaca bluebottles buzzed over the masses of food that went back on the dishes to the tin altar. Surely it had been made deliberately so that we should not eat it! The Cagliarese young woman talked to us. Yes, she broke into that awful language which the Italians—the quite ordinary ones—call French, and which they insist on speaking for their own glorification: yet, when they get to heaven's gate they will ask St. Peter for:

"On bigliay pour ung—trozzième classe."

Fortunately or unfortunately her, inquisitiveness got the better of her, and she fell into her native Italian. What were we, where did we come from, where were we going, *why* were we going, had we any children, did we want any, etc. After every answer she nodded her head and said Ahu! and watched us with energetic dark eyes. Then she ruminated over our nationalities and said, to the unseeing witnesses: Una bella coppia, a fine couple. As at the moment we felt neither beautiful nor coupled, we only looked greener. The grim man-at-arms coming up to ask us again if we weren't going to have a little wine, she lapsed into her ten-pounder French, which was most difficult to follow. And she said that on a sea voyage one must eat, one must eat, if only a little. But—and she lapsed into Italian—one must by no means drink wine—no—no! One didn't want to, said I sadly. Whereupon the grim man-at-arms, whom, of course, we had cheated out of the bottle we refused to have opened for us, said with a lost sarcasm that wine made a man of a man, etc., etc. I was too weary of that underground, however. All I knew was that he wanted wine, wine, wine, and we hadn't ordered any. He didn't care for food.

The Cagliarese told us she came now from Naples, and her husband was following in a few days. He was doing business in Naples. I nearly asked if he was a little dogfish—this being the Italian for profiteer, but refrained in time. So the two ladies retired to lie down. I went and sat under my tarpaulin.

I felt very dim, and only a bit of myself. And I dozed blankly. The afternoon grew more sunny. The ship turned southwards, and with the wind and waves behind, it became much warmer, much smoother. The sun had the lovely strong winy warmth, golden over the dark-blue sea. The old oak- -wood looked almost white, the afternoon was sweet upon the sea. And in the sunshine and the swishing of the sea, the speedier running of the empty ship, I slept a warm, sweet hour away, and awoke anew. To see ahead pale, uplooming islands upon the right: the windy Egades: and on the right a mountain or high conical hill, with buildings on the summit: and in front against the sea, still rather far away, buildings rising upon a quay, within a harbour: and a mole, and a castle forward to sea, all small and far away, like a view. The buildings were square and fine. There was something impressive—magical under the far sunshine and the keen wind, the square and well-proportioned buildings waiting far off, waiting like a lost city in a story, a Rip van Winkle city. I knew it was Trapani, the western port of Sicily, under the western sun.

And the hill near us was Mount Eryx. I had never seen it before. So I had imagined a mountain in the sky. But it was only a hill, with an undistinguishable cluster of a village on the summit, where even now cold wisps of vapour caught. They say it is 2,500 feet high. Still it looks only a hill.

But why in the name of heaven should my heart stand still as I watch that hill which rises above the sea? It is the Etna of the west: but only a town-crowned hill. To men it must have had a magic almost greater than Etna's. Watching Africa! Africa, showing her coast on clear days. Africa the dreaded. And the great watch-temple of the summit, world-sacred, world-mystic in the world that .was. Venus of the aborigines, older than Greek Aphrodite. Venus of the aborigines, from her watch-temple looking at Africa, beyond the Egatian isles. The world mystery, the smiling Astarte. This, one of the world centres, older than old! and the woman-goddess watching Africa! *Erycina ridens.* Laughing, the woman-goddess at this centre of an ancient, quite-lost world.

I confess my heart stood still. But is mere historical fact so strong, that what one learns in bits from books can move one so? Or does the very word call an echo out of the dark blood? It seems so to me. It seems to me from the darkest recesses of my blood comes a terrible echo at the name of Mount Eryx: something quite unaccountable. The name of Athens hardly moves me. At Eryx—my darkness quivers. Eryx, looking west into Africa's sunset. *Erycina ridens.*

There is a tick-tocking in the little cabin against which I lean. The wireless operator is busy communicating with Trapani, no doubt. He is a fat young man with fairish curly hair and an important bearing. Give a man control of some machine, and at once his air of importance and more-than-human dignity develops. One of the unaccountable members of the crew lounges in the little doorway like a chicken on one foot, having nothing to do. The girl from Cagliari comes up with two young men—also Sardinians by, their thick-set, independent look, and the touch of pride in their dark eyes. She has no wraps at all: just her elegant fine-cloth dress, her bare head from which the wisps of hair blow across her brow, and the transparent "nigger" silk stockings. Yet she does not seem cold. She talks with great animation, sitting between the two young men. And she holds the hand of the one in the overcoat affectionately. She is always holding the hand of one or other of the two young men: and wiping wisps of wind-blown hair from her brow: and talking in her strong, nonchalant voice, rapidly, ceaselessly, with massive energy. Heaven knows if the two young men—they are third-class passengers—were previous acquaintances. But they hold her hand like brothers—quite, simply and nicely, not at all sticky and libidinous. It all has an air of Why not?"

She shouts at me as I pass, in her powerful, extraordinary French:

"Madame votre femme, elle est au lit?"

I say she is lying down.

"Ah!" she nods. "Elle a le mal de mer?"

No, she is not sea-sick, just lying down.

The two young men between whom she is sitting as between two pillows, watch with the curious Sardinian dark eyes that seem alert and show the white all round. They are pleasant—a bit like seals. And they have a numb look for a moment, impressed by this strange language. She proceeds energetically to translate into Sardinian, as I pass on.

We do not seem to be going to Trapani. There lies the town on the left, under the hill, the square buildings that suggest to me the factories of the East India Company shining in the sun along the curious, closed-in harbour, beyond the running dark-blue sea. We seem to be making for the island bulk of Levanzo. Perhaps we shall, steer away to Sardinia without putting in to Trapani.

On and on we run—and always as if we were going to steer between the pale blue, heaped-up islands, leaving Trapani behind us on our left. The town has been in sight for an hour or more: and still we run out to sea towards Levanzo. And the wireless operator busily tick-tocks and throbs in his little cabin on this upper-deck. Peeping in, one sees his bed and chair behind a curtain, screened off from his little office. And all so tidy and pleased-looking.

From the islands one of the Mediterranean sailing ships is beating her way, across our track, to Trapani. I don't know the names of ships but the carpenter says she is a schooner: he says it with that Italian misgiving which doesn't really know but which can't bear not to know. Anyhow, on she comes, with her tall ladder of square sails white in the afternoon light, and her lovely prow, curved in with a perfect hollow, running like a wild animal on a scent across the waters. There—the scent leads her north again. She changes her tack from the harbour mouth, and goes coursing away, passing behind us. Lovely she is, nimble and quick and palpitating, with, all her sails white and bright and eager.

We are changing our course. We have all the time been heading for the south of Levanzo. Now I see the island slowly edging back, as if clearing out of the way for us, like a man in the street. The island edges and turns aside: and. walks away. And clearly we are making for the harbour mouth. We have all this time been running, out at sea, round the back of the harbour. Now I see the fortress castle, an old thing, out forward to sea: and a little lighthouse and the way in. And beyond, the town-front with great palm trees and other curious dark trees, and behind these the large square buildings of the south rising imposingly, as if severe, big palaces upon the promenade. It all has a stately, southern, imposing appearance, withal remote from our modern centuries: standing back from the tides of our industrial life.

I remember the Crusaders, how they called here so often on their way to the East. And Trapani seems waiting for them still, with its palm trees and its silence, full in the afternoon sun. It has not much to do but wait, apparently.

The q-b emerges into the sun, crying out how lovely! And the sea is quieter: we are already in the lee of the harbour curve. From the north the many-sailed ship from the islands is running down towards us, with the wind. And away on the south, on the sea level, numerous short windmills are turning their sails briskly, windmill after windmill, rather stumpy, spinning gaily in the blue, silent afternoon, among the salt-lagoons stretching away towards Marsala. But there is a whole legion of windmills, and Don Quixote would have gone off his head. There they spin, hither and thither, upon the pale blue sea levels. And perhaps one catches a glitter of white salt-heaps. For these are the great salt lagoons which make Trapani rich.

We are entering the harbour basin, however, past the old castle out on the Spit, past the little lighthouse, then through the entrance, slipping quietly on the now tranquil water. Oh, and how pleasant the fullness of the afternoon sun flooding this round, fast-sleeping harbour, along whose side the tall palms drowse, and whose waters are fast asleep. It seems quite a small, cosy harbour, with the great buildings warm-coloured in the sun behind the dark tree-avenue of the Marina. The same silent, sleeping, endlessly sun-warmed stateliness.

In the midst of this tranquillity we slowly turn round upon the shining water, and in a few moments are moored. There are other ships moored away to the right all asleep, apparently, in the flooding of the afternoon sun. Beyond the harbour entrance run the great sea and the wind. Here all is still and hot and forgotten.

"Vous descendez en terre?" shouts the young woman, in her energetic French— she leaves off holding the young men's hands for the moment. We are not quite sure: and we don't want her to come with us, anyhow, for her French is not our French.

The land sleeps on: nobody takes any notice of us: but just one boat paddles out the dozen yards to our side. We decide to set foot on shore.

One should not, and we knew it. One should never enter into these southern towns that look so nice, so lovely, from the outside. However, we thought we would buy some cakes. So we crossed the avenue which looks so beautiful from the sea, and which, when you get into, it, is a cross between an outside place where you throw rubbish and a humpy unmade road in a raw suburb, with a few iron seats, and litter of old straw and rag. Indescribably dreary in itself: yet with noble trees, and lovely sunshine, and the sea and the islands gleaming magic beyond the harbour mouth, and the sun, the eternal sun full focused. A few mangy, nothing-to-do people stand disconsolately about, in southern fashion, as if they had been left there waterlogged, by the last flood, and were waiting for the next flood to wash them further. Round the corner along the quay a Norwegian steamer dreams that she is being loaded, in the muddle of the small port.

We looked at the cakes—heavy and wan they appeared to our sea-rolled stomachs. So we strolled into a main street, dark and dank like a sewer. A tram bumped to a standstill, as if now at last was the end of the world. Children coming from school ecstatically ran at our heels, with bated breath, to hear the vocal horrors of our foreign speech. We turned down a dark side alley, about forty paces deep: and were on the northern bay, and on a black stench that seemed like the perpetual sewer, a bank of mud.

So we got to the end of the black main street, and turned in haste to the sun. Ah— in a moment we were in it. There rose the palms, there lay our ship in the shining curving basin —and there focused the sun, so that in a moment we were drunk or dazed by it. Dazed. We sat on an iron seat in the rubbish-desolate, sun-stricken avenue.

A ragged and dirty girl was nursing a fat and moist and immovable baby and tending to a grimy, fat infant boy. She stood a yard away and gazed at us as one would gaze at a pig one was going to buy. She came nearer, and examined the q-b. I had my big hat down over my eyes. But no, she had taken her seat at my side, and poked her face right under my hat brim, so that her tousled hair touched me, and I thought she would kiss me. But again no. With her breath on my cheek she only gazed on my. face as if it were a wax mystery. I got up hastily.

"Too much for me," said I to the q-b.

She laughed, and asked what the baby was called. The baby was called Beppina, as most babies are.

Driven forth, we wandered down the desolate avenue of shade and sun towards the ship, and turned once more into the town. We had not been on shore more than ten minutes. This time we went to the right, and found more shops. The streets were dark and sunless and cold. And Trapani seemed to me to sell only two commodities: cured rabbit-skins and cat-skins, and great hideous, modern bedspread arrangements of heavy flowered silk and fabulous price. They seem to think nothing of thousands of liras in Trapani.

But most remarkable was bunny and pussy. Bunny and pussy, flattened out like pressed leaves, dangling in clusters everywhere. Furs! white bunny, black bunny in great abundance, piebald bunny, grey bunny: —then pussy, tabby pussy, and tortoiseshell pussy, but mostly black pussy, in a ghastly semblance of life, all flat, of course. Just single furs. Clusters, bunches, heaps, and dangling arrays of plain-superficies puss and bun-bun! Puss and bun by the dozen and the twenty, like dried leaves, for your choice. If a cat from a ship. should chance to find itself in Trapani streets, it would give a mortal yell, and go mad, I am sure.

We strolled for ten minutes more in this narrow, tortuous, unreal town, that seemed to have plenty of flourishing inhabitants, and a fair number of Socialists, if one was to judge by the great scrawlings on the walls: W. LENIN and ABBASSO LA BORGHESIA. Don't imagine, by the way, that Lenin is another Willie on the list. The apparent initial stands for *Evviva,* the double V.

Cakes one dared not buy, after looking at them. But we found macaroon biscuits and a sort of flat plaster-cast of the Infant Jesus under a dove, of which we bought two. The q-b ate her macaroon biscuits all through the streets, and we went towards the ship. The fat boatman hailed us to take us back. It was just about eight yards of water to row, the ship being moored to the quay: one could have jumped it. I gave the fat boatman two liras, two francs. He immediately put on the Socialist-workman indignation, and thrust the note back at me. Sixty centimes more! The fee was thirteen sous each way! In Venice or Syracuse it would be two sous. I looked at him and gave him the money and said: "Per Dio, we are in Trapani!" He muttered back something about foreigners. But the hateful, unmanly insolence of these lords of toil, now they have their various "unions" behind them and their "rights" as working men, sends my blood black. They are ordinary men no more: the human, happy Italian is most marvellously vanished. New honours come upon them, etc. The dignity of human labour is on its hind legs, busy giving every poor innocent who isn't ready for it a kick in the mouth.

But, once more, in parenthesis, let me remind myself that it is our own English fault. We have slobbered about the nobility of toil, till at last the nobles naturally insist on eating the cake. And more than that, we have set forth, politically, on such a high and Galahad quest of holy liberty, and been caught so shamelessly filling our pockets, that no wonder the naive and idealistic South turns us down with a bang.

Well, we are back on the ship. And we want tea. On the list by the door it says we are to have coffee, milk and butter at 8.30: luncheon at 11.30: tea, coffee or chocolate at 3: and dinner at 6.30. And, moreover: "The company will feed the passengers for the normal duration of the voyage only." Very well—very well. Then where is tea? Not any signs! and the alpaca jackets giving us a wide berth. But we find our man, and demand our rights: at least the q-b does.

The tickets from Palermo to Cagliari cost, together, 583 liras. Of this, 250 liras was for the ticket, and 40 liras each for the food. This, for two tickets, would make 580 liras. The odd three for usual stamps. The voyage was supposed to last about thirty or thirty-two hours: from eight of the morning of departure to two or four of the following afternoon. Surely we pay for our tea.

The other passengers have emerged: a large, pale, fat, "handsome" Palermitan who is going to be professor at Cagliari: his large, fat, but high-coloured wife: and three children, a boy of fourteen like a thin, frail, fatherly girl, a little boy in a rabbit-skin overcoat, coming rather unfluffed, and a girl-child on the mother's knee. The one-year-old girl-child being, of course, the only man in the party.

They have all been sick all day, and look washed out. We sympathise. They lament the cruelties of the journey—and *senza servizio! senza servizio!* without any maid servant. The mother asks for coffee, and a cup of milk for the children: then, seeing our tea with lemon, and knowing it by repute, she will have tea. But the rabbit-boy will have coffee—coffee and milk—and nothing else. And an orange. And the baby will have lemon, pieces of lemon. And the fatherly young "miss" of an adolescent brother laughs indulgently at all the whims of these two young ones: the father laughs and thinks it all adorable and expects us

111

to adore. He is almost too washed-out to attend properly, to give the full body of his attention.

So the mother gets her cup of tea—and puts a piece of lemon in—and then milk on top of that. The rabbit-boy sucks an orange, slobbers in the tea, insists on coffee and milk, tries a piece of lemon, and gets a biscuit. The baby, with weird faces, chews pieces of lemon: and drops them in the family cup: and fishes them out with a little sugar, and dribbles them across the table to her mouth, throws them away and reaches for a new sour piece. They all think it humorous and adorable. Arrives the milk, to be treated as another loving-cup, mingled with orange, lemon, sugar, tea, biscuit, chocolate, and cake. Father, mother, and elder brother partake of nothing, they haven't the stomach. But they are charmed, of course, by the pretty pranks and messes of the infants. They have extraordinarily amiable patience, and find the young ones a perpetual source of charming amusement. They look at one another, the elder ones, and laugh and comment, while the two young ones mix themselves and the table into a lemon-milk-orange-tea-sugar-biscuit-cake-chocolate mess. This inordinately Italian amiable patience with their young monkeys is astonishing. It makes the monkeys more monkey-like, and self-conscious incredibly, so that a baby has all the tricks of a Babylonian harlot, making eyes and trying new pranks. Till at last one sees the southern   Holy Family as an unholy triad of imbecility.

Meanwhile I munched my Infant-Jesus-and-Dove arrangement, which was rather like eating thin glass, so hard and sharp. It was made of almond and white of egg presumably, and was not so bad if you could eat it at all. It was a Christmas relic.—And I watched the Holy Family across the narrow board, and tried not to look all I felt.

Going on deck as soon as possible, we watched the loading of barrels of wine into the hold—a mild and happy-go-lucky process. The ship seemed to be almost as empty of cargo as of passengers. Of the latter, we were apparently twelve adults, all told, and the three children. And as for cargo, there were the wooden chests of the officer, and these fourteen barrels of wine from Trapani. The last were at length settled more or less firm, the owner or the responsible lands-man seeing to it. No one on the ship seemed to be responsible for anything. And four of the innumerable crew were replacing the big planks over the hold. It was curious how forlorn the ship seemed to feel, now she was ready for sea again. Her innumerable crew did not succeed in making her alive. She ran her course like a lost soul across the mid-Mediterranean.

Outside the harbour the sun was sinking, gorgeous gold and red the sky, and vast, beyond the darkening islands of the Egades group. Coming as we did from the east side of the island, where dawn beyond the Ionian sea is the day's great and familiar event: so decisive an event, that as the light appears along the sea's rim, so do my eyes invariably open and look at it, and know it is dawn, and as the night-purple is fused back, and a little scarlet thrills towards the zenith, invariably, day by day, I feel I must get up: coming from the east, shut off hermetically from the west by the steep spikes of the mountains at our back, we felt this sunset in the African sea terrible and dramatic. It seemed much more magnificent and tragic than our Ionian dawn, which has always a suggestion of a flower opening. But this great red, trumpet-flaring sunset had something African, half-sinister, upon the sea: and it seemed so far off, in an unknown land. Whereas our Ionian dawn always seems near and familiar and happy.

A different goddess the Eryx Astarte, the woman Ashtaroth, *Erycina ridens,* must have been, in her prehistoric dark smiling, watching the fearful sunsets beyond the Egades, from our gold-lighted Apollo of the Ionian east. She is a strange goddess to me, this

Erycina Venus, and the west is strange and unfamiliar and a little fearful, be it Africa or be it America.

Slowly at sunset we moved out of the harbour. And almost as we passed the bar, away in front we saw, among the islands, the pricking of a quick pointed light. Looking back, we saw the light at the harbour entrance twitching: and the remote, lost town beginning to glimmer. And night was settling down upon the sea, through the crimsoned purple of the last afterglow.

The islands loomed big as we drew nearer, dark in the thickening darkness. Overhead a magnificent evening star blazed above the open sea, giving me a pang at the heart, for I was so used to see her hang just above the spikes of the mountains, that I felt she might fall, having the space beneath.

Levanzo and the other large island were quite dark: absolutely dark, save for one beam of a lighthouse low down in the distance. The wind was again strong and cold: the ship had commenced her old slither and heave, slither and heave, which mercifully we had forgotten. Overhead were innumerable great stars active as if they were alive in the sky. I saw Orion high behind us, and the dog-star glaring. And *swish!* went the sea as we took the waves, then after a long trough, *swish!* This curious rhythmic swishing and hollow drumming of a steamer at sea have a narcotic, almost maddening effect on the spirit—a long hissing burst of waters, then the hollow roll, and again the upheaval to a sudden hiss-ss-ss!

A bell had clanged and we knew the crew were once more feeding. At every moment of the day and presumably of the night, feeding was going on—or coffee drinking.

We were summoned to dinner. Our young woman was already seated: and a fat uniformed mate or purser or official of some sort was finishing off in the distance. The pale professor also appeared and at a certain distance down the table sat a little hard-headed grey man in a long grey alpaca travelling coat. Appeared the beloved macaroni with tomato sauce: no food for the sea. I put my hopes on the fish. Had I not seen the cook making whiting bite their own tails viciously?—The fish appeared. And what was it? Fried inkpots. A *calamaio* is an inkpot: also it is a polyp, a little octopus which, alas, frequents the Mediterranean and squirts ink if offended. This polyp with its tentacles is cut up and fried, and reduced to the consistency of boiled celluloid. It is esteemed a delicacy: but is tougher than indiarubber, gristly through and through.

I have a peculiar aversion to these inkpots. Once in Liguria we had a boat of our own and paddled with the peasant paddlers. Alessandro caught inkpots: and like this. He tied up a female by a string in a cave—the string going through a convenient hole in her end. There she lived, like an Amphitrite's wire-haired terrier tied up, till Alessandro went a-fishing. Then he towed her, like a poodle, behind. And thus, like a poodly-bitch, she attracted hangers-on in the briny seas. And these poor polyp inamorati were the victims. They were lifted as prey on board, where I looked with horror on their grey, translucent tentacles and large, cold, stony eyes. The she-polyp was towed behind again. But after a few days she died.

And I think, even for creatures so awful-looking, this method is indescribably base, and shows how much lower than an octopus even is lordly man.

Well, we chewed a few ends of oil-fried inkpots, and gave it up. The Cagliari girl gave up too: the professor had not even tried. Only the hard-headed grey man in the alpaca coat chewed animatedly, with bouncing jaws. Mountains of *calamaio* remained for the joyous bluebottles.

113

Arrived the inevitable meat—this long piece of completely tasteless undercut in innumerable grey-brown slices. Oh, Italy! The professor fled.

Arrived the wash-leather pears, the apples, the oranges— we saved an apple for a happier hour.

Arrived coffee, and, as a magnificent treat, a few well-known pastries. They all taste wearily alike. The young woman shakes her head. I shake mine, but the q-b, like a child, is pleased. Most pleased of all, however, are the bluebottles, who dart in a black alpaca bunch to the tin altar, and there loudly buzz, wildly, above the sallow cakes.

The citron-checked, dry one, however, cares darkly nothing for cakes. He comes once more to twit us about wine. So much so that the Cagliari girl orders a glass of Marsala: and I must second her. So there we are, three little glasses of brown liquid. The Cagliari girl sips hers and suddenly flees. The q-b sips hers with infinite caution, and quietly retires. I finish the q-b's little glass, and my own, and the voracious blowflies buzz derisively and excited. The yellow-cheeked one has disappeared with the bottle.

From the professorial cabin faint wails, sometimes almost fierce, as one or another is going to be ill. Only a thin door is between this state-room and them. The most downtrodden, frayed, ancient rag of a man goes discreetly with basins, trying not to let out glimpses of the awful within. I climb up to look at the vivid, drenching stars, to breathe the cold wind, to see the dark sea sliding. Then I too go to the cabin, and watch the sea run past the porthole for a minute, and insert myself like the meat in a sandwich into the tight lower bunk. Oh, infinitesimal cabin, where we sway like two matches in a match box! Oh, strange, but even yet excellent gallop of a ship at sea.

I slept not so badly through the stifled, rolling night—in fact later on slept soundly. And the day was growing bright when I peered through the porthole, the sea was much smoother. It was a brilliant clear morning. I made haste and washed myself cursorily in the saucer that dribbled into a pail in a corner: there was not space even for one chair, this saucer, was by my bunk-head. And I went on deck.

Ah, the lovely morning! Away behind us the sun was just coming above the sea's horizon, and the sky all golden, all a joyous, fire-heated gold, and the sea was glassy bright, the wind gone still, the waves sunk into long, low undulations, the foam of the wake was pale ice-blue in the yellow air. Sweet, sweet wide morning on the sea, with the sun coming, swimming up, and a tall sailing barque, with her flat fore-ladder sails delicately across the light, and a far-far steamer on the electric, vivid morning horizon.

The lovely dawn: the lovely pure, wide morning in the mid-sea, so golden-aired and delighted, with the sealike sequins shaking, and the sky far, far, far above, unfathomably clear. How glad to be on a ship! What a golden hour for the heart of man! Ah, if one could sail for ever, on a small, quiet, lonely ship, from land to land and isle to isle, and saunter through the spaces of this lovely world, always through the spaces of this lovely world. Sweet it would be sometimes to come to the opaque earth, to block oneself against the stiff land, to annul the vibration of one's flight against the inertia of our terra firma! but life itself would be in the flight, the tremble of space. Ah, the trembling of never-ended space, as one moves in flight! Space, and the frail vibration of space, the glad lonely wringing of the heart. Not to be clogged to the land any more. Not to be any more like a donkey with a log on its leg, fastened to weary earth that has no answer now. But to be off.

To find three masculine, world-lost souls, and, world-lost, saunter and saunter on along with them, across the dithering space, as long as life lasts! Why come to anchor? There is nothing to anchor for. Land has no answer to the soul any more. It has gone inert. Give me a little ship, kind gods, and three world-lost comrades. Hear me! And let me wander aimless across this vivid outer world, the world empty of man, where space flies happily.

The lovely, celandine-yellow morning of the open sea, paling towards a rare sweet blue! The sun stood above the horizon, like the great burning stigma of the sacred flower of day. Mediterranean sailing ships, so mediæval, hovered on the faint morning wind, as if uncertain which way to go, curious odd-winged insects of the flower. The steamer, hull-down, was sinking towards Spain. Space rang clear about us: the level sea!

Appeared the Cagliari young woman and her two friends. She was looking handsome and restored now the sea was easy. Her two male friends stood touching her, one at either shoulder.

"Bonjour, Monsieur! " she barked across at me. "Vous avez pris le café?"

"Pas encore. Et vous?"

"Non! Madame votre femme . .."

She roared like a mastiff dog: and then translated with unction to her two uninitiated friends. How it was they did not understand her French I do not know, it was so like travestied Italian.

I went below to find the q-b.

When we came up, the faint shape of land appeared ahead, more transparent than thin pearl. Already Sardinia. Magic are high lands seen from the sea, when they are far, far off, and ghostly translucent like icebergs. This was Sardinia, looming like fascinating shadows in mid-sea. And the sailing ships, as if cut out of frailest pearl translucency, were wafting away towards Naples. I wanted to count their sails—five square ones which I call the ladder, one above the other— but how many wing-blades? That remained yet to be seen.

Our friend the carpenter spied us out: at least, he was not my friend. He didn't find me *simpatico,* I am sure. But up he came, and proceeded to entertain us with weary banality. Again the young woman called, had we had coffee? We said we were just going down. And then she said that whatever we had to-day we had to pay for: our food ended with the one day. At which the q-b was angry, feeling swindled. But I had known before.

We went down and had our coffee notwithstanding. The young woman came down, and made eyes at one of the alpaca bluebottles. After which we saw a cup of coffee and milk and two biscuits being taken to her into her cabin, discreetly. When Italians are being discreet and on. the sly, the very air about them becomes tell-tale, and seems to shout with a thousand tongues. So with a thousand invisible tongues clamouring the fact, the young woman had her coffee secretly and gratis, in her cabin.

But the morning was lovely. The q-b and I crept round the bench at the very stern of the ship and sat out of the wind and out of sight, just above the foaming of the wake. Before us was the open morning—and the glisten of our ship's track, like a snail's path, trailing across the sea: straight for a little while, then giving a bend to the left, always a bend towards the left: and coming at us from the pure horizon, like a bright snail-path. Happy it was to sit there in the stillness, with nothing but the humanless sea to shine about us.

But no, we were found out. Arrived the carpenter.

"Ah, you have found a fine place!"

"Molto bello!" This from the q-b. I could not bear the irruption.

He proceeded to talk—and as is inevitable, the war. Ah, the war—it was a terrible thing. He had become ill—very ill. Because, you see, not only do you go without proper food, without proper rest and warmth, but, you see, you are in an agony of fear for your life all the time. An agony of fear for your life. And that's what does it. Six months in hospital! The q-b, of course, was sympathetic.

The Sicilians are quite simple about it. They just tell you they were frightened to death, and it made them ill. The q-b, woman-like, loves them for being so simple about it I feel angry somewhere. For they *expect* a full-blown sympathy. And however the great god Mars may have, shrunk and gone wizened in the world, it annoys me to hear him *so* blasphemed.

Near us the automatic log was spinning, the thin rope trailing behind us in the sea. Erratically it jerked and spun, with spasmodic torsion. He explained that the little screw at the end of the line spun to the speed of travelling. We were going from ten to twelve Italian miles to the hour. Ah, yes, we *could* go twenty. But we went no faster than ten or twelve, to save the coal.

The coal—il carbone! I knew we were in for it. England —l'Inghilterra she has the coal. And what does she do? She sells it very dear. Particularly to Italy. Italy won the war and now can't even have coal. Because why! The price. The exchange! *il cambio.* Now I am doubly in for it. Two countries had been able to keep their money high—England and America. The English sovereign—la sterlina—and the American dollar—*sa,* these were money. The English and the Americans flocked to Italy, with their *sterline* and their *dollari,* and they bought what they wanted for nothing, for nothing. Ecco! Whereas we poor Italians—we are in a state of ruination—proper ruination. The Allies, etc., etc.

I am so used to it—I am so wearily used to it. I can't walk a stride without having this wretched *cambio,* the exchange, thrown at my head. And this with an injured petulant spitefulness which turns my blood. For I assure them, whatever I have in Italy I pay for: and I am not England. I am not the British Isles on two legs.

Germany—La Germania—she did wrong to make the war. But—there you are, that was war. Italy and Germany— l'Italia e la Germania—they had always been friends. In Palermo…

My God, I felt I could not stand it another second. To sit above the foam and have this miserable creature stuffing wads of chewed newspaper into my ear—no, I could not bear it. In Italy, there is no escape. Say two words, and the individual starts chewing old newspaper and stuffing it into you. No escape. You become—if you are *English—l'Inghilterra, il carbone,* and *il cambio;* and as England, coal, and exchange you are treated. It is more than useless to try to be human about it. You are a State usury system, a coal fiend and an exchange thief. Every Englishman has disappeared into this triple abstraction, in the eyes of the Italian, of the proletariat particularly. Try and get them to be human, try and get them to see that you are simply an individual if you can. After all, I am no more than a single human man wandering my lonely way across these years. But no— to an Italian I am a perfected abstraction, England—coal— exchange. The Germans were once devils for inhuman theoretic abstracting of living beings. But now the Italians beat them. I am a walking column of statistics, which adds up badly for Italy. Only this and nothing more. Which being so I shut my mouth and walk away.

For the moment the carpenter is shaken off. But I am in a rage, fool that I am. It is like being pestered by their mosquitoes. The sailing ships are near—and I count fifteen sails. Beautiful they look! Yet if I were on board somebody would be chewing newspaper at me, and addressing me as England—coal—exchange.

The mosquito hovers—and hovers. But the stony blank of the side of my cheek keeps him away. Yet he hovers. And the q-b feels sympathetic towards him: quite sympathetic. Because of course he treats her—a *bel pezzo*—as if he would lick her boots.

Meanwhile we eat the apples from yesterday's dessert, and the remains of the q-b's Infant-Jesus-and-Dove cake. The land is drawing nearer—we can see the shape of the end promontory and peninsula—and a white speck like a church. The bulk of the land is forlorn and rather shapeless, coming towards us: but attractive.

Looking ahead towards the land gives us away. The mosquito swoops on us. Yes—he is not sure—he thinks the white speck is a church—or a lighthouse. When you pass the Cape on the right, and enter the wide bay between Cape Spartivento and Cape Carbonara, then you have two hours' sail to Cagliari. We shall arrive between two and three o'clock. It is now eleven.

Yes, the sailing ships are probably going to Naples. There is not much wind for them now. When there is wind they go fast, faster than our steamer. Ah, Naples—bella, bella, eh? A little dirty, say I. But what do you want? says he. A great city! Palermo of course is better.

Ah—the Neapolitan women—he says, a propos or not. They do their hair so fine, so neat and beautiful—but underneath—sotto——sotto—they are dirty. This being received in cold silence, he continues: *Noi giriamo il mondo! Noi, che giriamo,. conosciamo il mondo. We* travel about, and *we* know the world., Who *we* are, I do not know: his highness the Palermitan carpenter lout, no doubt. But *we,* who travel, know the world. He is preparing his shot. The Neapolitan women and the English women in this are equal: that they are dirty underneath. Underneath, they are dirty. The women of London— But it is getting too much for me.

"You who look for dirty women," say I, "find dirty women everywhere."

He stops short and watches me.

"No! No! You have not understood me. No! I don't mean that. I mean that the Neapolitan women and the English women have dirty underclothing—"

To which he gets no answer but a cold look and a cold cheek. Whereupon he turns to the q-b, and proceeds to be -*simpatico*. And after a few moments he turns again to me:

"Il Signore is offended! He is offended with me."

But I turn the other way. And at last he clears out: in triumph, I must admit: like a mosquito that has bitten one in the neck. As a matter of fact one should *never* let these fellows get into conversation nowadays. They are no longer human beings. They hate one's Englishness, and leave out the individual.

We walk forward, towards the fore-deck, where the Captain's lookout cabin is. The Captain is an elderly man, silent and crushed: with the look of a gentleman. But he looks beaten down. Another, still another member of the tray-carrying department is just creeping up his ladder with a cup of black coffee. Returning, we peep down the skylight into the kitchen. And there we see roast chicken and sausages— roast chicken and sausages! Ah, this is where the sides of kid and the chickens and the good things go: all down the throats of the crew. There is no more food for us, until we land.

We have passed the Cape—and the white thing is a lighthouse. And the fattish, handsome professor has come up carrying the little girl-child, while the femaleish elder brother leads the rabbit-fluffy small boy by the hand. So *en famille:* so terribly *en famille.* They deposit themselves near us, and it threatens another conversation. But not for anything, my dears!

The sailors—not sailors, some of the street-corner loafers, are hoisting the flag, the red-white-and-green Italian tricolour. It floats at the mast-head, and the femaleish brother, in a fine burst of feeling, takes off his funny hat with a flourish and cries:

"Ecco la bandiera italiana!"

117

Ach, the hateful sentimentalism of these days.

The land passes slowly, very slowly. It is hilly, but barren looking, with a few trees. And it is not spiky and rather splendid, like Sicily. Sicily has style. We keep along the east side of the bay—away in the west is Cape Spartivento. And still no sight of Cagliari.

"Two hours yet!" cries the Cagliari girl. "Two hours before we eat. Ah, when I get on land, what a good meal I shall eat."

The men haul in the automatic log. The sky is clouding over with that icy curd which comes after midday when the bitter north wind is blowing. It is no longer warm.

Slowly, slowly we creep along the formless shore. An hour passes. We see a little fort ahead, done in enormous black-and-white checks, like a fragment of a gigantic chessboard. It stands at the end of a long spit of land—a long, barish peninsula that has no houses and looks as if it might be golf. links. But it is not golf links.

And suddenly there is Cagliari: a naked town rising steep, steep, golden-looking, piled naked to the sky from the plain at the head of the formless hollow bay. It is strange and rather wonderful, not a bit like Italy. The city piles up lofty and almost miniature, and makes me think of Jerusalem: without trees, without cover, rising rather bare and proud, remote as if back in history, like a town in a monkish, illuminated missal. One wonders how it ever got there And it seems like Spain—or Malta: not Italy. It is a steep and lonely city, treeless, as in some old illumination. Yet withal rather jewel-like: like a sudden rose-cut amber jewel naked at the depth of the vast indenture. The air is cold, blowing bleak and bitter, the sky is all curd. And that is Cagliari. It has that curious look, as if it could be seen but not entered. It is like some vision, some memory, something that has passed away. Impossible that one can actually *walk* in that city: set foot there and eat and laugh there. Ah, no! Yet the ships drift nearer, nearer, and we are looking for the actual harbour.

The usual sea front with dark trees for a promenade and palatial buildings behind, but here not so pink and gay, more reticent, more sombre of yellow stone. The harbour itself a little basin of water, into which we are slipping carefully, while three salt-barges laden with salt as white as snow creep round from the left, drawn by an infinitesimal tug. There are only two other forlorn ships in the basin. It is cold on deck. The ship turns slowly round, and is being hauled to the quay side. I go down for the knapsack, and a fat blue-bottle pounces at me.

"You pay nine francs fifty."

I pay them, and we get off that ship.

CHAPTER III

CAGLIARI

THERE is a very little crowd waiting on the quay: mostly men with their hands in their pockets. But, thank heaven, they have a certain aloofness and reserve. They are not like the tourist parasites of these post-war days, who move to the attack with a terrifying cold vindictiveness the moment one emerges from any vehicle. And some of these men look really poor. There are no poor Italians any more: at least, loafers.

Strange the feeling round the harbour: as if everybody had gone away. Yet there are people about. It is "festa" however, Epiphany. But it is so different from Sicily: none of the suave Greek-Italian charms, none of the airs and graces, none of the glamour. Rather bare, rather stark, rather cold and yellow—somehow like Malta, without Malta's foreign liveliness. Thank goodness no one wants to carry my knapsack. Thank goodness no one has a fit at the sight of it. Thank heaven no one takes any notice. They stand cold and aloof and don't move.

We make our way through the Customs: then through the Dazio, the City Customs-House. Then we are free. We set off up a steep, new, broad road, with little trees on either side. But stone, and, new, wide stone, yellowish under the cold sky—and abandoned-seeming. Though, of course, there are people about. The north wind blows bitingly.

We climb a broad flight of steps, always upwards, up the wide, precipitous, dreary boulevard with sprouts of trees. Looking for the hotel, and dying with hunger.

At last we find it, the Scala di Ferro: through a courtyard with green plants. And at last a little man with lank black hair, like an Eskimo, comes smiling. He is one brand of Sardinian—Eskimo-looking. There is no room with two beds: only single rooms. And thus we are led off, if you please, to the "bagnio": the bathing establishment wing, on the dank ground floor. Cubicles on either side a stone passage, and in every cubicle a dark stone bath, and a little bed. We can have each a little bath cubicle. If there's nothing else for it, there isn't: but it seems dank and cold and horrid, underground. And one thinks of all the unsavoury "assignations" at these old bagnio places. True, at the end of the passage are seated two carabinieri. But whether to ensure respectability or not, heaven knows. We are in the baths, that's all.

The Eskimo returns after five minutes, however. There *is* a bedroom in the house. He is pleased, because he didn't like putting us into the bagnio. Where he found the bedroom I don't know. But there it was, large, sombre, cold, and over the kitchen fumes of a small inner court like a well. But perfectly clean and all right. And the people seemed warm and good-natured, like human beings. One has got so used to the non-human ancient-souled Sicilians, who are suave and so completely callous.

After a really good meal we went out to see the town. It was after three o'clock and everywhere was shut up like an English Sunday. Cold, stony Cagliari: in summer you must be sizzling hot, Cagliari, like a kiln. The men stood about in groups, but without the intimate Italian watchfulness that never leaves a passer-by alone.

Strange, stony Cagliari. We climbed up a street like a corkscrew stairway. And we saw announcements of a children's fancy-dress ball. Cagliari is very steep. Half-way up there is a strange place called the bastions, a large level space like a drill ground with trees, curiously suspended over the town, and sending off a long shoot like a wide viaduct, across above the corkscrew street that comes climbing up. Above this bastion place the town still rises steeply to the Cathedral and the fort. What is so curious is that this terrace or bastion is so large, like some big recreation ground, that it is almost dreary, and one cannot understand its being suspended in mid-air. Down below is the little circle of the harbour. To the left a low, malarial-looking sea plain, with tufts of palm trees and Arab-looking houses. From this runs out the long spit of land towards that black-and-white watch-fort, the white road trailing forth. On the right, most curiously, a long strange spit of sand runs in a causeway far across the shallows of the bay, with the open sea on one hand, and vast, end-of-the-world lagoons on the other. There .are perky, dark mountains beyond this—just as across the vast bay are gloomy hills. It is a strange, strange landscape: as if here the world left off. The bay is vast in itself; and all these curious things happening at its head: this curious, craggy-studded town, like a great stud of house-covered rock jutting up out of the bay flats: around it on one side the weary, Arab-looking palm-desolated malarial plain, and on the other side great salt lagoons, dead beyond the sand bar: these backed again by serried, clustered mountains, suddenly, while away beyond the plain, hills rise to sea again. Land and sea both seem to give out, exhausted, at the bay head: the world's end. And into this world's end starts up Cagliari, and on either side sudden, serpent-crested hills.

But it still reminds me of Malta: lost between Europe and Africa and belonging to nowhere. Belonging to nowhere, never having belonged to anywhere. To Spain and the Arabs and the Phœnicians most. But as if it had never really had a fate. No fate. Left outside of time and history.

The spirit of the place is a strange thing. Our mechanical age tries to override it. But it does not succeed. In the end the strange, sinister spirit of the place, so diverse and adverse in differing places, will smash our mechanical oneness into smithereens, and all that we think the real thing will go off with a pop, and we shall be left staring.

On the great parapet above the Municipal Hall and above the corkscrew high-street a thick fringe of people is hanging, looking down. We go to look too: and behold, below there is the entrance to the ball. Yes, there is a china shepherdess in pale blue and powdered hair, crook, ribbons, Marie Antoinette satin daintiness and all, slowly and haughtily walking up the road, and gazing superbly round. She is not more than twelve years old, moreover. Two servants accompany her. She gazes supremely from right to Left as she goes, mincingly, and I would give her the prize for haughtiness. She is perfect—a little too haughty for Watteau, but "marquise" to a T. The people watch in silence. There is no yelling and screaming and running. They watch in a suitable silence.

Comes a carriage with two fat bay horses slithering, almost swimming up the corkscrew high-street. That in itself is a "tour de force": for Cagliari doesn't have carriages. Imagine a street like a corkscrew stair, paved with slippery stone. And imagine two bay horses rowing their way up it: they did not walk in single stride. But they arrived. And there fluttered out three strangely exquisite children, two frail, white-satin Pierrots and a white-satin Pierrette. They were like fragile winter butterflies with black spots. They had a curious, indefinable remote elegance, something conventional and "fin de siècle." But not our century. The wonderful artificial delicacy of the eighteenth. The boys had big, perfect ruffs round their necks: and behind were slung old, cream-coloured Spanish shawls, for warmth. They were frail as tobacco flowers, and with remote, cold elegance they fluttered by the carriage from which emerged a large black-satin Mama. Fluttering their queer little butterfly feet on the pavement, hovering round the large Mama like three frail-tissued ghosts, they found their way past the solid, seated carabinieri into the hall.

Arrived a primrose-brocade beau, with ruffles, and his hat under his arm: about twelve years old. Walking stately, without a qualm up the steep twist of the street. Or perhaps so perfect in his self-consciousness that it became an elegant "aplomb" in him. He was a genuine eighteenth-century exquisite, rather stiffer than the French, maybe, but completely in the spirit. Curious, curious children! They had a certain stand-offish superbness, and not a single trace of misgiving. For them, their "noblesse" was indisputable. For the first time in my life I recognised the true cold superbness of the old "noblesse." They had not a single qualm about their own perfect representing of the higher order of being.

Followed another white-satin "marquise," with a maid servant. They are strong on the eighteenth century in Cagliari. Perhaps it is the last bright reality to them. The nineteenth hardly counts.

Curious the children in Cagliari. The poor seem thoroughly poor-bare-footed urchins, gay and wild in the narrow dark streets. But the more well-to-do children are so fine: so extraordinarily elegantly dressed. It quite strikes one of a heap. Not so much the grown-ups. The children. All the *chic,* all the fashion, all the originality is expended on the children. And with a great deal of success. Better than Kensington Gardens very often. And they promenade with Papa and Mama with such alert assurance, having quite brought it off, their fashionable get-up. Who would have expected it?

Oh, narrow, dark, and humid streets going up to the Cathedral, like crevices. I narrowly miss a huge pail of slop-water which comes crashing down from heaven. A small boy who was playing in the street, and whose miss is not quite a clean miss, looks up with that naive, impersonal wonder with which children stare at a star or a lamplighter.

The Cathedral must have been a fine old pagan stone fortress once. Now it has come, as it were, through the mincing machine of the ages, and oozed out Baroque and sausagey, a bit like the horrible baldachins in St. Peter's at Rome. None the less it is homely and hole-and-cornery, with a rather ragged high mass trailing across the pavement towards the high altar, since it is almost sunset, and Epiphany. It feels as if one might squat in a corner and play marbles and eat bread and cheese and be at home: a comfortable old-time churchy feel.

There is some striking filet lace on the various altar-cloths. And St. Joseph must be a prime saint. He has an altar and a verse of invocation praying for the dying.

"Oh, St. Joseph, true potential father of Our Lord." What can it profit a man, I wonder, to be the potential father of anybody! For the rest I am not Baedeker.

The top of Cagliari is the fortress: the old gate, the old ramparts, of honeycombed, fine yellowish sandstone. Up in a great sweep goes the rampart wall, Spanish and splendid, dizzy. And the road creeping down again at the foot, down the back of the hill. There lies the country: that dead plain with its bunch of palms and a fainting sea, and inland again, hills. Cagliari must be on a single, loose, lost bluff of rock.

From the terrace just below the fortress, above the town, not behind it, we stand and look at the sunset. It is all terrible, taking place beyond the knotted, serpent-crested hills that lie, bluey and velvety, beyond the waste lagoons. Dark, sultry, heavy crimson the west is, hanging sinisterly, with those gloomy blue cloud bars and cloud banks drawn across. All behind the blue-gloomy peaks stretches the curtain of sinister, smouldering red, and away to the sea. Deep below lie the sea-meres. They seem miles and miles, and utterly waste. But the sand bar crosses like a bridge, and has a road. All the air is dark, a sombre bluish tone. The great west burns inwardly, sullenly, and gives no glow, yet a deep red. It is cold.

We go down the steep streets, smelly, dark, dank, and very cold. No wheeled vehicle can scramble up them, presumably. People live in one room. Men are combing their hair or fastening their collars in the doorways. Evening is here, and it is a feast day.

At the bottom of the street we come to a little bunch of masked youths, one in a long yellow frock and a frilled bonnet, another like an old woman, another in red twill. They are arm in arm and are accosting the passers-by. The q-b gives a cry, and looks for escape. She has a terror of maskers, a terror that comes from childhood. To say the truth, so have I. We hasten invisibly down the far side of the street, and come out under the bastions. Then we go down our own familiar wide, short, cold boulevard to the sea.

At the bottom, again, is a carriage with more maskers. Carnival is beginning. A man dressed as a peasant woman in native costume is clambering with his great wide skirts and wide strides on to the box, and, flourishing his ribboned whip, is addressing a little crowd of listeners. He opens his mouth wide and goes on with a long yelling harangue of taking a drive with his mother—another man in old woman's gaudy finery and wig who sits already bobbing on the box. The would-be daughter flourishes, yells, and prances up there on the box of the carriage. The crowd listens attentively and mildly smiles. It all seems real to them. The q-b hovers in the distance, half-fascinated, and watches. With a great flourish of whip and legs—showing his frilled drawers—the masker pulls round to drive along the boulevard by the sea—the only place where one can drive.

The big street by the sea is the Via Roma. It has the cafés on one side and across the road the thick tufts of trees intervening between the sea and us. Among these thick tufts of sea-front trees the little steam tram, like a little train, bumps to rest, after having wound round the back of the town.

The Via Roma is all social Cagliari. Including the cafés with their outdoor tables on the one side of the road, and the avenue strand on the other, it is very wide, and at evening it contains the whole town. Here and here alone carriages can spank along, very slowly, officers can ride, and the people can promenade "en masse."

We were amazed at the sudden crowd we found ourselves amongst—like a short, dense river of people streaming slowly in a mass. There is practically no vehicular traffic—only the steady dense streams of human beings of all sorts, all on a human footing. It must have been something like this in the streets of imperial Rome, where no chariots might drive and humanity was all on foot.

Little bunches of maskers, and single maskers, danced and strutted along in a thick flow under the trees. If you are a mask you don't walk like a human being: you dance and prance along extraordinarily like the life-size marionettes, conducted by wires from above. That is how you go: with that odd jauntiness as if lifted and propelled by wires from the shoulders. In front of me went a charming coloured harlequin, all in diamond-shaped colours, and beautiful as a piece of china. He tripped with the light, fantastic trip, quite alone in the thick crowd, and quite blithe. Came two little children hand in hand in brilliant scarlet and white costumes, sauntering calmly. They did not do the mask trip. After a while a sky-blue girl with a high hat and full skirts, very short, that went flip-flip-flip, as a ballet dancer's, whilst she strutted; after her a Spanish grandee capering like a monkey. They threaded among the slow stream of the crowd. Appeared Dante and Beatrice, in Paradise apparently, all in white sheet-robes, and with silver wreaths on their heads, arm in arm, and prancing very slowly and majestically, yet with the long lilt as if hitched along by wires from above. They were very good: all the well-known vision come to life, Dante incorporate, and white as a shroud, with his tow-haired, silver-crowned, immortal Beatrice on his arm, strutting the dark avenues. He had the nose and cheek bones and banded cheek, and the stupid wooden look, and offered a modern criticism on the Inferno.

It had become quite dark, the lamps were lighted. We had crossed the road to the Café Roma, and found a table on the pavement among the crowd. In a moment we had our tea. The evening was cold, with ice in the wind. But the crowd surged on, back and forth, back and forth, slowly. At the tables, were seated mostly men, taking coffee or vermouth or *aqua vitae,* all familiar and easy, without the modern self-consciousness. There was a certain pleasant, natural robustness of spirit, and something of a feudal free-and-easiness. Then arrived a family, with children, and nurse in her native costume. They all sat at table together, perfectly easy with one another, though the marvellous nurse seemed to be seated below the salt. She was as bright as a poppy, in a rose-scarlet dress of fine cloth with a curious little waistcoat of emerald green and purple, and a bodice of soft, homespun linen with great full sleeves. On her head she had a rose-scarlet and white head-dress, and she wore great studs of gold filigree, and similar ear-rings. The feudal-bourgeois family drank its syrup drinks and watched the crowd. Most remarkable is the complete absence of self-consciousness. They all have a perfect natural "sangfroid," the nurse in her marvellous native costume is as thoroughly at her ease as if she were in her own village street. She moves and speaks and calls to a passer-by without the slightest constraint, and much more, without the slightest presumption. She is below the invisible salt, the invisible but insuperable salt. And it strikes me the salt-barrier is a fine thing for both parties; they both remain natural and human on either side of it, instead of becoming devilish, scrambling and pushing at the barricade.

The crowd is across the road, under the trees near the sea. On this side stroll occasional pedestrians. And I see my first peasant in costume. He is an elderly, upright, handsome man, beautiful in the black-and-white costume. He wears the full-sleeved white shirt and the close black bodice of thick, native frieze, cut low. From this sticks out a short kilt or frill, of the same black frieze, a band of which goes between the legs, between the full loose drawers of coarse linen. The drawers are banded below the knee into tight black frieze gaiters. On his head he has the long black stocking-cap, hanging down behind. How handsome he is, and so beautifully male! He walks with his hands loose behind his back, slowly, upright, and aloof. The lovely unapproachableness, indomitable. And the flash of the black and white, .the slow stride of the full white drawers, the black gaiters and black cuirass with the bolero, then the great white sleeves and white breast again, and once more the black cap—what marvellous massing of the contrast, marvellous, and superb, as on a magpie.—How beautiful maleness is, if it finds its right expression.—And how perfectly ridiculous it is made in modern clothes.

There is another peasant too, a young one with a swift eye and hard cheek and hard, dangerous thighs. He has folded his stocking-cap, so that it comes forward to his brow like a Phrygian cap. He wears close knee-breeches and close sleeved waistcoat of thick brownish stuff that looks like leather. Over the waistcoat a sort of cuirass. of black, rusty sheepskin, the curly wool outside. So he strides, talking to a comrade. How fascinating it is, after the soft Italians, to see these limbs in their close knee-breeches, so definite, so manly, with the old fierceness in them still. One realises, with horror, that the race of men is almost extinct in Europe. Only Christ-like heroes and woman-worshipping Don Juans, and rabid equality-mongrels. The old, hardy, indomitable male is gone. His fierce singleness is quenched. The last sparks are dying out in Sardinia and Spain. Nothing left but the herd-proletariat and the herd-equality mongrelism, and the wistful, poisonous, self-sacrificial, cultured soul. How detestable.

But that curious, flashing, black-and-white costume! I seem to have known it before: to have worn it even: to have dreamed it. To have dreamed it: to have had actual contact with it. It belongs in some way to something in me—to my past, perhaps. I don't know. But the uneasy sense of blood-familiarity haunts me. I *know* I have known it before. It is something of the same uneasiness I feel before Mount Eryx: but without the awe this time.

In the morning the sun was shining from a blue, blue sky, but the shadows were deadly cold, and the wind like a flat blade of ice. We went out running to the sun. The hotel could not give us coffee and milk: only a little black coffee. So we descended to the sea front again, to the Via Roma, and to our café. It was Friday: people seemed to be bustling in from the country with huge baskets.

The Café Roma had coffee and milk, but no butter. We sat and watched the movement outside. Tiny Sardinian donkeys, the tiniest things ever seen, trotted their infinitesimally little paws along the road, drawing little wagons like handcarts. Their proportion is so small that they make a boy walking at their side look like a tall man, while a natural man looks like a Cyclops stalking hugely and cruelly. It is ridiculous for a grown man to have one of these little creatures, hardly bigger than a fly, hauling his load for him.

123

One is pulling a chest of drawers on a cart, and it seems to have a whole house behind it. Nevertheless it plods bravely away beneath the load, a wee thing.

They tell me there used to be flocks of these donkeys, feeding half wild on the wild moor-like hills of Sardinia. But the war—and also the imbecile wantonness of the war-masters—consumed these flocks too, so that few are left. The same with the cattle. Sardinia, home of cattle, hilly little Argentine of the Mediterranean, is now almost deserted. It is war, say the Italians.—And also the wanton, imbecile, foul lavishness of the war-masters. It was not alone the war which exhausted the world. It was the deliberate evil wastefulness of the war-makers in their own countries. Italy ruined Italy.

Two peasants in black and white are strolling in the sun, flashing. And my dream of last evening was not a dream. And my nostalgia for something I know not what was not an illusion. I feel it again at once, at the sight of the men in frieze and linen, a heart yearning for something I have known, and which I want back again.

It is market day. We turn up the Largo Carlo-Felice, the second wide gap of a street, a vast but very short boulevard, like the end of something. Cagliari is like that: all bits and bobs. And by the side of the pavement are many stalls, stalls selling combs and collar-studs, cheap mirrors, handkerchiefs, shoddy Manchester goods, bed-ticking, boot-paste, poor crockery and so on. But we see also Madame of Cagliari going marketing, with a servant accompanying her, carrying a huge grass-woven basket: or returning from marketing, followed by a small boy supporting one of these huge grass-woven baskets— like huge dishes—on his head, piled with bread, eggs, vegetables, a chicken, and so forth. Therefore we follow Madame going marketing, and find ourselves in the vast market-house, and it fairly glows with eggs: eggs in these great round dish-baskets of golden grass: but eggs in piles, in mounds, in heaps, a Sierra Nevada of eggs, glowing. warm white. How they glow! I have never noticed it before. But they give off a pearly effulgence into the air, almost a warmth. A pearly-gold heat seems to come out of them. Myriads of eggs, glowing avenues of eggs.

And they are marked—60 centimes, 65 centimes. Ah, cries the q-b, I must live in Cagliari—for in Sicily the eggs cost 1.50 each.

This is the meat and poultry and bread market. There are stalls of new, various-shaped bread, brown and bright: there are tiny stalls of marvellous native cakes, which I want to taste; there is a great deal of meat and kid: and there are stalls of cheese, all cheeses, all shapes, all whitenesses, all the cream colours, on into daffodil yellow. Goat's cheese, sheep's cheese, Swiss cheese, Parmeggiano, stracchino, caciocavallo, torolone, how many cheeses I don't know the names of! But they cost about the same as in Sicily, eighteen francs, twenty francs, twenty-five francs the kilo. And there is lovely ham—thirty and thirty-five francs the kilo. There is a little fresh butter too—thirty or thirty-two francs the kilo. Most of the butter, however, is tinned in Milan. It costs the same as the fresh. There are splendid piles of salted black olives, and huge bowls of green salted olives. There are chickens and ducks and wild-fowl: at eleven and twelve and fourteen francs a kilo. There is mortadella, the enormous Bologna sausage, thick as a church pillar: 16 francs: and there are various sorts of smaller sausage, salami, to be eaten in slices. A wonderful abundance of food, glowing and shining. We are rather late for fish, especially on Friday. But a barefooted man offers us two weird objects from the Mediterranean, which teems with marine monsters.

The peasant women sit behind their wares, their home-woven linen skirts, hugely full, and of various colours, ballooning round them. The yellow baskets give off a glow of light. There is a sense of profusion once more. But alas, no sense of cheapness: save the eggs. Every month up goes the price of everything.

"I must come and live in Cagliari, to do my shopping here," says the q-b. "I must have one of those big grass baskets."

We went down to the little street—but saw more baskets emerging from a broad flight of stone stairs, enclosed. So up we went—and found ourselves in the vegetable market. Here the q-b was happier still. Peasant women, sometimes barefoot, sat in their tight little bodices and voluminous, coloured skirts behind the piles of vegetables, and never have I seen a lovelier show. The intense deep green of spinach seemed to predominate, and out of that came the monuments of curd-white and black-purple cauliflowers: but marvellous cauliflowers, like a flower show, the purple ones intense as great bunches of violets. From this green, white, and purple massing struck out the vivid rose-scarlet and blue-crimson of radishes, large radishes like little turnips in piles. Then the long, slim, grey-purple buds of artichokes, and dangling clusters of dates, and piles of sugar-dusty white figs and sombre-looking black figs, and bright burnt figs: basketfuls and basketfuls of figs. A few baskets of almonds, and many huge walnuts. Basket-pans of native raisins. Scarlet peppers like trumpets: magnificent fennels, so white and big and succulent: baskets of new potatoes: scaly kohlrabi: wild asparagus in bunches, yellow-budding sparacelli: big, clean-fleshed carrots: feathery salads with white hearts: long, brown-purple onions, and then, of course, pyramids of big oranges, pyramids of pale apples, and baskets of brilliant shiny mandarini, the little tangerine oranges with their green-black leaves. The green and vivid-coloured world of fruit-gleams I have never seen in such splendour as under the market roof at Cagliari: so raw and gorgeous. And all quite cheap, the one remaining cheapness, except potatoes. Potatoes of any sort are 1.40 or 1.50 the kilo.

"Oh! "cried the q-b, "if I don't live at Cagliari and come and do my shopping here, I shall die with one of my wishes unfulfilled."

But out of the sun it was cold, nevertheless. We went into the streets to try and get warm. The sun was powerful. But alas, as in southern towns generally, the streets are as sunless as wells.

So the q-b and I creep slowly along the sunny bits, and then perforce, are swallowed by shadow. We look at the shops. But there is not much to see. Little frowsy provincial shops on the whole.

But a fair number of peasants in the streets, and peasant women in rather ordinary costume: tight-bodiced, volume-skirted dresses of hand-woven linen or thickish cotton. The prettiest is of dark-blue-and-red, stripes-and-lines, intermingled, so made that the dark blue gathers round the waist into one colour, the myriad pleats hiding all the rosy red. But when she walks, the full-petticoated peasant woman, then the red goes flash-flash-flash, like a bird showing its colours. Pretty that looks in the sombre street. She has a plain light bodice with a peak: sometimes a little vest, and great full white sleeves, and usually a handkerchief or shawl loose knotted. It is charming the way they walk, with quick, short steps. When all is said and, done, the most attractive costume for women, in my. eye, is the tight little bodice and the many-pleated skirt, full and vibrating with movement. It has a charm which modern elegance lacks completely—a bird-like play in movement.

They are amusing, these peasant girls and women: so brisk and defiant. They have straight backs like little walls, and decided, well-drawn brows. And they are amusingly on the alert. There is no Eastern creeping. Like sharp, brisk birds they dart along the streets, and you feel they would fetch you a bang over the head as lief as look at you. Tenderness, thank heaven, does not seem to be a Sardinian quality. Italy is so tender—like cooked macaroni—yards and yards of soft tenderness ravelled round everything. Here men don't idealize women, by the look of things. Here they don't make those great leering eyes, the inevitable yours-to-command look of Italian males. When the men from the country look at these women, then it is Mind-yourself, my lady. I should think the grovelling Madonna-worship is not much of a Sardinian feature. These women have to look out for themselves, keep their own backbone stiff and their knuckles hard. Man is going to be male Lord if he can. And woman isn't going to give him too much of his own way either. So there you have it, the fine old martial split between the sexes. It is tonic and splendid, really, after so much sticky intermingling and backboneless Madonna-worship. The Sardinian isn't looking for the "noble woman nobly planned." No, thank you. He wants that young madam over there, a young stiff-necked generation that she is. Far better sport than with the nobly-planned sort: hollow frauds that they are. Better sport too than with a Carmen, who gives herself away too much. In these women there is something shy and defiant and Un-get-at-able. The defiant, splendid split between the sexes, each absolutely determined to defend his side, her side from assault. So the meeting has a certain wild, salty savour, each the deadly unknown to the other. And at the same time, each his own, her own native pride and courage taking the dangerous leap and scrambling back.

Give me the old salty way of love. How I am nauseated with sentiment and nobility, the macaroni slithery-slobbery mess of modern adorations.

One sees a few fascinating faces in Cagliari: those great dark unlighted eyes. There are fascinating dark eyes in Sicily, bright, big, with an impudent point of light and a curious roll, and long lashes: the eyes of old Greece, surely. But here one sees eyes of soft, blank darkness, all velvet, with no imp looking out of them. And they strike a stranger, older note: before the soul became self-conscious: before the mentality of Greece appeared in the world. Remote, always remote, as if the intelligence lay deep within the cave, and never came forward. One searches into the gloom for one second, while the glance lasts. But without being able to penetrate to the reality. It recedes, like some unknown creature, deeper into its lair. There *is* a creature, dark and potent. But what?

Sometimes Velasquez, and sometimes Goya gives us a suggestion of these large dark unlighted eyes. And they go with fine, fleecy black hair—almost as fine as fur. I have not seen them north of Cagliari.

The q-b spies some of the blue-and-red stripe-and-line cotton stuff of which the peasants make their dress: a large roll in the doorway of a dark shop. In we go, and begin to feel it. It is just soft, thickish cotton stuff—twelve francs a metre. Like most peasant patterns, it is much more complicated and subtle than it appears: the curious placing of the stripes, the subtle proportion, and a white thread left down one side only of each broad blue block. The stripes, moreover, run *across* the cloth, not lengthwise with it. But the width would be just long enough for a skirt—though the peasant skirts have almost all a band at the bottom with the stripes running round-ways.

The man—he is the Eskimo type, simple, frank and amiable—says the stuff is made in France, and this the first roll since the war. It is the old, old pattern, quite correct—but the material not *quite* so good. The q-b takes enough for a dress.

He shows us also cashmeres, orange, scarlet, sky-blue, royal blue: good, pure wool cashmeres that were being sent to India, and were captured from a German mercantile submarine. So he says. Fifty francs a metre—very, very wide. But they are too much trouble to carry in a knapsack, though their brilliance fascinates.

So we stroll and look at the shops, at the filigree gold jewelling of the peasants, at a good bookshop. But there is little to see, and therefore the question is, shall we go on? Shall we go forward?

There are two ways of leaving Cagliari for the north: the State railway that runs up the west side of the island and the narrow-gauge secondary railway that pierces the centre. But we are too late for the big trains. So we will go by the. secondary railway, wherever it goes.

There is a train at 2.30, and we can get as far as Mandas, some fifty miles in the interior. When we tell the queer little waiter at the hotel, he says he comes from Mandas, and there are two inns. So after lunch—a strictly fish menu—we pay our bill. It comes to sixty-odd francs—for three good meals each, with wine, and the night's lodging; this is cheap, as prices now are in Italy.

Pleased with the simple and friendly Scala di Fere, I shoulder my sack and we walk off to the second station. The sun is shining hot this afternoon—burning hot by the sea. The road and the buildings look dry and desiccated, the harbour rather weary and end of the. world.

There is a great crowd of peasants at the little station. And almost every man has a pair of woven saddle-bags—a great flat strip of coarse woven wool, with flat pockets at either end, stuffed with purchases. These are almost the only carrying bags. The men sling them over their shoulders, so that one great pocket hangs in front, one behind.

These saddle-bags are most fascinating. They are coarsely woven in bands of raw black-rusty wool, with varying bands of raw white wool or hemp or cotton—the bands and stripes of varying widths going crosswise. And on the pale bands are woven sometimes flowers in most lovely colours, rose-red and blue and green, peasant patterns—and sometimes fantastic animals, beasts, in dark wool again. So that these striped zebra bags, some wonderful, gay with flowery colours on their stripes, some weird with fantastic, griffin-like animals, are a whole landscape in themselves.

The train has only first and third class. It costs about thirty francs for the two of us, third-class to Mandas, which is some sixty miles. In we crowd with the joyful saddle-bags, into the wooden carriage with its many seats.

And, wonder of wonders, punctually to the second, off we go, out of Cagliari. En route again.

CHAPTER IV

MANDAS

THE coach was fairly full of people, returning from market. On these railways the third-class coaches are not divided into compartments. They are left open, so that one sees everybody, as down a room. The attractive saddle-bags, *bercole,* were disposed anywhere, and the bulk of the people settled down to a lively conversazione. It is much nicest, on the whole, to travel third-class on the railway. There is space, there is air, and it is like being in a lively inn, everybody in good spirits.

At our end was plenty of room. Just across the gangway was an elderly couple, like two children, coming home very happily. He was fat, fat all over, with a white moustache and a little not unamiable frown. She was a tall, lean, brown woman, in a brown full-skirted dress and black apron, with huge pocket. She wore no head covering, and her iron-grey hair was parted smoothly. They were rather pleased and excited being in the train. She took all her money out of her big pocket, and counted it and gave it to him: all the ten-lira notes, and the five-lira, and the two and the one, peering at the dirty scraps of pink-backed one-lira notes to see if they were good. Then she gave him her halfpennies. And he stowed them away in the trouser pocket, standing up to push them down his fat leg. And then one saw, to one's amazement, that the whole of his shirt-tail was left out behind, like a sort of apron worn backwards. Why—a mystery. He was one of those fat, good-natured, unheeding men with a little masterful frown, such as usually have tall, lean, hard-faced, obedient wives.

They were very happy. With amazement he watched us taking hot tea from the thermos flask. I think he too had suspected it might be a bomb. He had blue eyes and standing-up white eyebrows.

"Beautiful hot! " he said, seeing the tea steam. It is the inevitable exclamation. "Does it do you good?"

"Yes," said the q-b. "Much good." And they both nodded complacently. They were going home.

The train was running over the malarial-looking sea plain—past the, down-at-heel palm trees, past mosque-looking buildings. At a level crossing the woman crossing-keeper darted out vigorously with her red flag. And we rambled into the first village. It was built of sun-dried brick-adobe houses, thick adobe garden walls, with tile ridges to keep off the rain. In the enclosures were dark orange trees. But the clay-coloured villages, clay-dry, looked foreign: the next thing to mere earth they seem, like fox-holes or coyote colonies.

Looking back, one sees Cagliari bluff on her rock, rather fine, with the thin edge of the sea's blade curving round. It is rather hard to believe in the real sea, on this sort of clay-pale plain.

But soon we begin to climb to the hills. And soon the cultivation begins to be intermittent. Extraordinary how the healthy, moor-like hills come near the sea: extraordinary how scrubby and uninhabited the great spaces of Sardinia are. It is wild, with heath and arbutus scrub and a sort of myrtle, breast-high. Sometimes one sees a few head of cattle. And then again come the greyish arable patches, where the corn is grown. It is like Cornwall, like the Land's-End region. Here and there, in the distance, are peasants working on the lonely landscape. Sometimes it is one man alone in the distance, showing so vividly in his black and white costume, small and far-off like a solitary magpie, and curiously distinct. All the strange magic of Sardinia is in this sight. Among the low, moor-like hills, away in a hollow of the wide landscape, one solitary figure, small but vivid black-and-white, working alone, as if eternally. There are patches and hollows of grey arable land, good for corn. Sardinia was once a great granary.

Usually, however, the peasants of the South have left off the costume. Usually it is the invisible soldier's grey-green cloth, the Italian khaki. Wherever you go, wherever you be, you see this khaki, this grey-green war clothing. How many millions of yards of the thick, excellent, but hateful material the Italian Government must have provided I don't know: but enough to cover Italy with a felt carpet, I should think. It is everywhere. It cases the tiny children in stiff and neutral frocks and coats, it covers their extinguished fathers, and sometimes it even encloses the women in its warmth. It is symbolic of the universal grey mist that has come over men, the extinguishing of all bright individuality, the blotting out of all wild singleness. Oh, democracy! Oh, khaki democracy!

This is very different from Italian landscape. Italy is always almost dramatic, and perhaps invariably romantic. There is drama in the Plains of Lombardy and romance in the Venetian lagoons, and sheer scenic excitement in nearly all the hilly parts of the peninsula. Perhaps it is the natural floridity of limestone formations. But Italian landscape is really eighteenth-century landscape, to be represented in that romantic-classic manner which makes everything rather marvellous and very topical: aqueducts, and ruins upon sugar-loaf mountains, and craggy ravines and Wilhelm Meister waterfalls: all up and down.

Sardinia is another thing. Much wider, much more ordinary, not up-and-down at all, but running away into the distance. Unremarkable ridges of moor-like hills running away, perhaps to a bunch of dramatic peaks on the south-west. This gives a sense of space, which is so lacking in Italy. Lovely space about one, and travelling distances—nothing finished, nothing final. It is like liberty itself, after the peaky confinement of Sicily. Room—give me room—give me room for my spirit: and you can have all the toppling crags of romance.

So we ran on through the gold of the afternoon, across a wide, almost Celtic landscape of hills, our little train winding and puffing away very nimbly. Only the heath and scrub, breast-high, man-high, are too big and brigand-like, for a Celtic land. The horns of black, wild-looking cattle show sometimes.

After a long pull, we come to a station after a stretch of loneliness. Each time it looks as if there were nothing beyond—no more habitations. And each time we come to a station.

Most of the people have left the train. And as with men driving in a gig, who get, down at every public-house, so the passengers usually alight for an airing at each station. Our old fat friend stands up and tucks his shirt tail comfortably in his trousers, which trousers all the time make one hold one's breath, for they seem at each very moment to be just dropping right down: and he clambers out, followed by the long brown stalk of a wife.

So the train sits comfortably for five or ten minutes, in the way the trains have. At last we hear whistles and horns, and our old fat friend running and clinging like a fat crab to the very end of the train as it sets off. At the same instant a loud shriek and a bunch of shouts from outside. We all jump up. There, down the line, is the long brown stalk of a wife. She had just walked back to a house some hundred yards off, for a few words, and has now seen the train moving.

Now behold her with her hands thrown to heaven, and hear the wild shriek "Madonna!" through all the hubbub. But she picks up her two skirt-knees, and with her thin legs in grey stockings starts with a mad rush after the train. In vain. The train inexorably pursues its course. Prancing, she reaches one end of the platform as we leave the other end. Then she realises it is not going to stop for her. And then, oh horror, her long arms thrown out in wild supplication after the retreating train: then flung aloft to God: then brought down in absolute despair on her head. And this is the last sight we have of her, clutching her poor head in agony and doubling forward. She is left—she is abandoned.

The poor fat husband has been all the time on the little outside platform at the end of the carriage, holding out his hand to her and shouting frenzied scolding to her and frenzied yells for the train to stop. And the train has not stopped. And she is left—left on that God-forsaken station in the waning light.

So, his face all bright, his eyes round and bright as two stars, absolutely transfigured by dismay, chagrin, anger and distress, he comes and sits in his seat, ablaze, stiff, speechless. His face is almost beautiful in its blaze of conflicting emotions. For some time he is as if unconscious in the midst of his feelings. Then anger and resentment crop out of his consternation. He turns with a flash to the long-nosed, insidious, Phœnician-looking guard. Why couldn't they stop the train for her! And immediately as if someone had set fire to him, off flares the guard. Heh!—the train can't stop for every person's convenience! The train is a train—the time-table is a time-table. What did the old woman want to take her trips down the line for? Heh! She pays the penalty for her own inconsiderateness. Had *she* paid for the train—heh? And the fat man all the time firing off his unheeding and unheeded answers. One minute—only one minute—if he, the conductor, had told the driver! if he, the conductor, had shouted! A poor woman! Not another tram! What was she going to do! Her ticket? And no money. A poor woman— There was a train back to Cagliari that night, said the conductor, at which the fat man nearly burst out of his clothing like a bursting seed-pod. He bounced on his seat. What good was that? What good was a train back to Cagliari, when their home was in Snelli! Making matters worse—

So they bounced and jerked and argued at one another to their hearts' content. Then the conductor retired, smiling subtly, in a way they have. Our fat friend looked at us with hot, angry, ashamed, grieved eyes and said it was a shame. Yes, we chimed, it *was* a shame. Whereupon a self-important miss who said she came from some Collegio, at Cagliari advanced and asked a number of impertinent questions in a tone of pert sympathy. After which our fat friend, left alone, covered his clouded face with his hand, turned his back on the world, and gloomed.

It had all been so dramatic that in spite of ourselves we laughed, even while the q-b shed a few tears.

Well, the journey lasted hours. We came to a station, and the conductor said we must get out: these coaches went no further. Only two coaches would proceed to Mandas. So we climbed out with our traps, and our fat friend with his saddle-bag, the picture of misery.

The one coach into which we clambered was rather crowded. The only other coach was most of it first-class. And the rest of the train was freight. We were two insignificant passenger wagons at the end of a long string of freight vans and trucks.

There was an empty seat, so we sat in it: only to realise after about five minutes that a thin old woman with two children—her grandchildren—was chuntering her head off because it was *her* seat—why she had left it she didn't say. And under my legs was her bundle of bread. She nearly went off her head. And over my head, on the little rack, was her *bercola,* her saddle-bag. Fat soldiers laughed at her good-naturedly, but she fluttered and flipped like a tart, featherless old hen. Since she had another seat and was quite comfortable, we smiled and let her chunter. So she clawed her bread bundle from under my legs, and, clutching it and a fat child, sat tense.

It was getting quite dark. The conductor came and said that there was no more paraffin. If what there was in the lamps gave out, we should have to sit in the dark. There was no more paraffin all along the line—So he climbed on the seats, and after a long struggle, with various boys striking matches for him, he managed to obtain a light as big as a pea. We sat in this *clairobscur,* and looked at the sombre-shadowed faces round us: the fat soldier with a gun, the handsome soldier with huge saddle-bags, the weird, dark little man who kept exchanging a baby with a solid woman who had a white cloth tied round her head, a tall peasant woman in costume, who darted out at a dark station and returned triumphant with a piece of chocolate: a young and interested young man, who told us every station. And the man who spat: there is always one.

Gradually the crowd thinned. At a station we saw our fat friend go by, bitterly, like a betrayed soul, his bulging saddle-bag hanging before and after, but no comfort in it now—no comfort. The pea of light from the paraffin lamp grew smaller. We sat in incredible dimness, and the smell of sheep's wool and peasant, with our fat and stoic young man to tell us where we were. The other dusky faces began to sink into a dead gloomy silence. Some took to sleep. And the little train ran on and on, through unknown Sardinian darkness. In despair we drained the last drop of tea and ate the last crust of bread. We knew we must arrive some time.

It was not much after seven when we came to Mandas. Mandas is a junction where these little trains sit and have a long happy chat after their arduous scramble over the downs. It had taken us somewhere about five hours to do our fifty miles. No wonder then that when the junction at last heaves in sight everybody bursts out of the train like seeds from an exploding pod, and rushes somewhere for something. To the station restaurant, of course. Hence there is a little station restaurant that does a brisk trade, and where one can have a bed.

A quite pleasant woman behind the little bar: a brown woman with brown parted hair and brownish eyes and brownish, tanned complexion and tight brown velveteen bodice. She led us up a narrow winding stone stair, as up a fortress, leading on with her candle, and ushered us into the bedroom. It smelled horrid and sourish, as shut-up bedrooms do. We threw, open the window. There were big frosty stars snapping ferociously in heaven.

The room contained a huge bed, big enough for eight people, and quite clean. And the table on which stood the candle actually had a cloth. But imagine that cloth! I think it had been originally white: now, however, it was such a web of time-eaten holes and mournful black ink stains and poor dead wine stains that it was like some 2000 B.C. mummy-cloth. I wonder if it could have been lifted from that table: or if it was mummified on to it! I for one made no attempt to try. But that table cover impressed me, as showing degrees I had not imagined—a tablecloth.

We went down the fortress-stair to the eating-room. Here was a long table with soup plates upside down and a lamp burning an uncanny naked acetylene flame. We sat at the cold table, and the lamp immediately began to wane. The room—in fact the whole of Sardinia—was stone cold, stone, stone cold. Outside the earth was freezing. Inside there was no thought of any sort of warmth: dungeon stone floors, dungeon stone walls, and a dead, corpse-like atmosphere, too heavy and icy to move.

The lamp went quite out, and the q-b gave a cry. The brown woman poked her head through a hole in the wall. Beyond her we saw the flames of the cooking, and two devil-figures stirring the pots. The brown woman came and shook the lamp—it was like a stodgy porcelain mantelpiece vase— shook it well and stirred up its innards, and started it going once more. Then she appeared with a bowl of smoking cabbage soup, in which were bits of macaroni: and would we have wine? I shuddered at the thought of death-cold red wine of the country, so asked what else there was. There was malvagia—malvoisie, the same old malmsey that did for the Duke of Clarence. So we had a pint of malvagia, and were comforted. At least we were being so—when the lamp went out again. The brown woman came and shook and smacked it, and started it off again. But as if to say "Shan't for you," it whipped out again.

Then came the host with a candle and a pin, a large, genial Sicilian with pendulous moustaches. And he thoroughly pricked the wretch with the pin, shook it, and turned little screws. So up flared the flame. We were a little nervous. He asked us where we came from, etc. And suddenly he asked us, with an excited gleam, were we Socialists. Aha, he was going to hail us as citizens and comrades. He thought we were a pair of Bolshevist agents: I could see it. And as such he was prepared to embrace us. But no, the q-b disclaimed the honour. I merely smiled and shook my head. It is a pity to rob people of their exciting illusions.

"Ah, there is too much Socialism everywhere!" cried the q-b.

131

"Ma—perhaps, perhaps—" said the discreet Sicilian. She saw which way the land lay, and added:

"Si vuole un *pochettino* di socialismo: one wants a tiny bit of Socialism in the world, a tiny bit. But not much. Not much. At present there is too much."

Our host, twinkling at this speech which treated of the sacred creed as if it were a pinch of salt in the broth, believing the q-b was throwing dust in his eyes, and thoroughly intrigued by us as a pair of deep ones, retired. No sooner had he gone than the lamp flame stood up at its full length, and started to whistle. The q-b drew back. Not satisfied by this, another flame suddenly began to whip round the bottom of the burner, like a lion lashing its tail. Unnerved, we made room: the q-b cried again: in came the host with a subtle smile and a pin and an air of benevolence, and tamed the brute.

What else was there to eat? There was a piece of fried pork for me, and boiled eggs for the q-b. As we were proceeding with these, in came the remainder of the night's entertainment: three station officials, two in scarlet peaked caps, one in a black and gold peaked cap. They sat down with a clamour, in their caps, as if there was a sort of invisible screen between us and them. They were young. The black-cap had a lean and sardonic look: one of the red-caps was little and ruddy, very young, with a little moustache: we called him the *maialino*, the gay little black pig, he was so plump and food-nourished and frisky. The third was rather puffy and pale and had spectacles. They all seemed to present us the blank side .of their cheek, and to intimate that no, they were not going to take their hats off, even if it were dinner-table and a strange signora. And they made rough quips with one another, still as if we were on the other side of the invisible screen.

Determined however to remove this invisible screen, I said good evening, and it was very cold. They muttered good evening, and yes, it was fresh. An Italian never says it is cold: it is never more than *fresco*. But this hint that it was cold they took as a hint at their caps, and they became very silent, till the woman came in with the soup-bowl. Then they clamoured at her, particularly the *maialino,* what was there to eat. She told them—beefsteaks of pork. Whereat they pulled faces. Or bits of boiled pork. They sighed, looked gloomy, cheered up, and said beefsteaks, then.

And they fell on their soup. And never, from among the steam, have I heard a more joyful trio of soup-swilkering. They sucked it in from their spoons with long gusto-rich sucks. The *maialino* was the treble—he trilled his soup into his mouth with a swift sucking vibration, interrupted by bits of cabbage, which made the lamp start to dither again. Black-cap was the baritone; good, rolling spoon-sucks. And the one in spectacles was the bass: he gave sudden deep gulps. All was led by the long trilling of the *maialino.* Then suddenly, to vary matters, he cocked up his spoon in one hand, chewed a huge mouthful of bread, and swallowed it down with a smack-smack-smack! of his tongue against his palate. As children we used to call this "clapping."

"Mother, she's clapping! "I would yell with anger, against my sister. The German word is schmatzen.

So the *maialino* clapped like a pair of cymbals, while baritone and bass rolled on. Then in chimed the swift bright treble.

At this rate, however, the soup did not last long. Arrived the beefsteaks of pork. And now the trio was a trio of castanet smacks and cymbal claps. Triumphantly the *maialino* looked round. He out-smacked all.

The bread of the country is rather coarse and brown, with a hard, hard crust. A large rock of this is perched on every damp serviette. The *maialino* tore his rock asunder, and grumbled at the black-cap, who had got a weird sort of three-cornered loaf-roll of pure white bread—starch white. He was a swell with this white bread.

Suddenly black-cap turned to me. Where had we come from, where were we going, what for? But in laconic, sardonic tone.

"I *like* Sardinia," cried the q-b.

"Why?" he asked sarcastically. And she tried to find out.

"Yes, the Sardinians please me more than the Sicilians," said I.

"Why?" he asked sarcastically.

"They are more open—more honest." He seemed to turn his nose down.

"The padrone is a' Sicilian," said the *maialino*, stuffing a huge block of bread into his mouth, and rolling his insouciant eyes of a gay, well-fed little black pig towards the background. We weren't making much headway.

"You've seen Cagliari?" the black-cap said to me, like a threat.

"Yes! oh, Cagliari pleases me—Cagliari is beautiful!" cried the q-b, who travels with a vial of melted butter ready for her parsnips.

"Yes—Cagliari is *so-so*—Cagliari is very fair," said the black-cap. *"Cagliari è discreta"* He was evidently proud of it.

"And is Mandas nice?" asked the q-b.

"In what way nice?" they asked, with immense sarcasm.

"Is there anything to see?"

"Hens," said the *maialino* briefly. They all bristled when one asked if Mandas was nice.

"What does one do here?" asked the q-b.

"Niente! At Mandas one does *nothing*. At Mandas one goes to bed when it's dark, like a chicken. At Mandas one walks down the road like a pig that is going nowhere. At Mandas a goat understands more than the inhabitants understand. At Mandas one needs socialism. . . ."

They all cried out at once. Evidently Mandas was more than flesh and blood could bear for another minute to these three conspirators.

"Then you are very bored here?" say I.

"Yes."

And the quiet intensity of that naked *yes* spoke more than volumes.

"You would like to be in Cagliari?"

"Yes"

Silence, intense, sardonic silence had intervened. The three looked at one another and made a sour joke about Mandas.

Then the black-cap turned to me.

"Can you understand Sardinian?" he said.

"Somewhat. More than Sicilian, anyhow."

"But Sardinian is more difficult than Sicilian. It is full of words utterly unknown to Italian—"

"Yes, but," say I, "it is spoken openly, in plain words, and Sicilian is spoken all stuck together, none of the words there at all."

He looks at me as if I were an impostor. Yet it is true. I find it quite easy to understand Sardinian. As a matter of fact, it is more a question of human approach than of sound. Sardinian seems open and manly and downright. Sicilian is gluey and evasive, as if the Sicilian didn't want to speak straight to you. As a matter of fact, he doesn't. He is an over-cultured, sensitive, ancient soul, and he has so many sides to his mind that he hasn't

133

got any. definite one mind at all. He's got a dozen minds, and uneasily he's aware of it, and to commit himself to any one of them is merely playing a trick on himself and his interlocutor. The Sardinian, on the other hand, still seems to have one downright mind. I bump up against a downright, smack-out belief in socialism, for example. The Sicilian is much too old in our culture to swallow socialism whole: much too ancient and *rusé* not to be sophisticated about any and every belief. He'll go off like a squib: and then he'll smoulder acridly and sceptically even against his own fire. One sympathises with him in retrospect. But in daily life it is unbearable.

"Where do you find such white bread?" say I to the black-cap, because he is proud of it.

"It comes from my home." And then he asks about the bread of Sicily. Is it any whiter than *this*—the Mandas rock? Yes, it is a little whiter. At which they gloom again. For it is a very sore point, this bread. Bread means a great deal to an Italian: it is verily his staff of life. He practically lives on bread. And instead of going by taste, he now, like all the world, goes by eye. He has got it into his head that bread should be white, so that every time he fancies a darker shade in the loaf a shadow falls on his soul. Nor is he altogether wrong. For although, personally, I don't like white bread any more, yet I do like my brown bread to be made of pure, unmixed flour. The peasants in Sicily, who have kept their own wheat and make their own natural brown bread, ah, it is amazing how fresh and sweet and *clean* their loaf seems, so perfumed, as home-bread used all to be before the war. Whereas the bread of the commune, the regulation supply, is hard, and rather coarse and rough, so rough and harsh on the palate. One gets tired to death of it. I suspect myself the maize meal mixed in. But. I don't know. And finally the bread varies immensely from town to town, from commune to commune. The so-called just and equal distribution is all-my-eye. One place has abundance of good sweet bread, another scrapes along, always stinted, on an allowance of harsh coarse stuff. And the poor suffer bitterly, really, from the bread-stinting, because they depend so on this one food. They say the inequality and the injustice of distribution come from the Camorra—la grande Camorra—which is no more nowadays than a profiteering combine, which the poor hate. But for myself, I don't know. I only know that one town—Venice, for example—seems to have an endless supply of pure bread, of sugar, of tobacco, of salt—while Florence is in one continual ferment of irritation over the stinting of these supplies—which are all Government monopolies, doled out accordingly.

We said good night to our three railway friends, and went up to bed. We had only been in the room a minute or two, when the brown woman tapped: and if you please, the black-cap had sent us one of his little white loaves. We were really touched. Such delicate little generosities have almost disappeared from the world.

It was a queer little bread—three-cornered, and almost as hard as ship's biscuit, made of starch flour. Not strictly bread at all.

The night was cold, the blankets flat and heavy, but one slept quite well till dawn. At seven o'clock it was a clear, cold morning, the sun not yet up. Standing at the bedroom window looking out, I could hardly believe my eyes, it was so like England, like Cornwall in the bleak parts, or Derbyshire uplands. There was a little paddock-garden at the back of the station, rather tumble-down, with two sheep in it. There were several forlorn-looking outbuildings, very like Cornwall. And then the wide, forlorn country road stretched away between borders of grass and low, drystone walls, towards a greystone farm with a tuft of trees, and a naked stone village in the distance. The sun came up yellow, the bleak country glimmered bluish and reluctant. The low, green hill-slopes were divided into fields, with low drystone walls and ditches. Here and there a stone barn rose alone, or with a few bare, windy trees attached. Two rough-coated winter horses pastured on the rough grass, a boy came along the naked, wide, grass-bordered high-road with, a couple of milk cans, drifting in from nowhere: and it was all Cornwall, or a part of Ireland, that the old nostalgia for the Celtic regions began to spring up in me. Ah, those old, drystone walls dividing the fields— pale and granite-blenched! Ah, the dark, sombre grass, the naked sky! the forlorn horses in the wintry morning! Strange is a Celtic landscape, far more moving, disturbing, than the lovely glamour of Italy and Greece. Before the curtains of history lifted, one feels the world was like this—this Celtic bareness and sombreness and air. But perhaps it is not Celtic at all: Iberian. Nothing is more unsatisfactory than our conception of what is Celtic and what is not Celtic. I believe there were never any Celts, as a race.—As for the Iberians—!

Wonderful to go out on a frozen road, to see the grass in shadow bluish with hoar-frost, to see the grass in the yellow winter sunrise beams melting and going cold-twinkly. Wonderful the bluish, cold air, and things standing up in cold distance. After two southern winters, with roses blooming all the time, this bleakness and this touch of frost in the ringing morning go to my soul like an intoxication. I am so glad, on this lonely naked road, I don't know what to do with myself. I walk down in the shallow grassy ditches under the loose stone walls, I walk on the little ridge of grass, the little bank on which the wall is built, I cross the road across the frozen cow-droppings: and it is all so familiar to my *feet*, my very feet in contact, that I am wild as if I had made a discovery. And I realise that I hate limestone, to live on limestone or marble or any of those limy rocks. I hate them. They are dead rocks, they have no life—thrills for the feet. Even sandstone is much better. But granite! Granite is my favourite. It is so live under the feet, it has a deep sparkle of its own. I like its roundnesses—and I hate the jaggy dryness of limestone, that burns in the sun, and withers.

After coming to a deep well in a grassy plot in a wide space of the road, I go back, across the sunny naked upland country, towards the pink station and its outbuildings. An engine is steaming its white clouds' in the new light. Away to the left there is even a row of small houses, like a row of railwaymen's dwellings. Strange and familiar sight. And the station precincts are disorderly and rather dilapidated. I think of our Sicilian host.

The brown woman gives us coffee, and very strong, rich goat's milk, and bread. After which the q-b and I set off once more along the road to the village. She, too, is thrilled. She, too, breathes deep. She, too, feels *space* around her, and freedom to move her limbs: such as one does not feel in Italy and Sicily, where all is so classic and fixed.

The village itself is just a long, winding, darkish street, in shadow, of houses and shops and a smithy. It might almost be Cornwall: not quite. Something, I don't know what, suggests the stark burning glare of summer. And then, of course, there is none of the cosiness which climbing roses and lilac trees and cottage shops and haystacks would give to an English scene. This is harder, barer, starker, more dreary. An ancient man in the black and white costume comes out of a hovel of a cottage. The butcher carries a huge side of meat. The women peer at us—but more furtive and reticent than the howling stares of Italy.

So we go on, down the rough cobbled street through the whole length of the village. And emerging on the other side, past the last cottage, we find ourselves again facing the open country, on the gentle down-slope of the rolling hill. The landscape continues the same: low, rolling upland hills, dim under the yellow sun of the January morning: stone fences, fields, grey arable land: a man slowly, slowly ploughing with a pony and a dark red cow: the road trailing empty across the distance: and then, the one violently unfamiliar note, the enclosed cemetery lying outside on the gentle hillside, closed in all round, very compact, with high walls: and on the inside face of the enclosure wall the

135

marble, slabs, like shut drawers of the sepulchres, shining white, the wall being like a chest of drawers, or pigeon-holes to hold the dead.

Tufts of dark and plumy cypresses rise among the flat graves of the enclosure. In the south, cemeteries are walled off and isolated very tight. The dead, as it were, are kept fast in pound. There is no spreading of graves over the face of the country. They are penned in a tight fold, with cypresses to fatten on the bones. This is the one thoroughly strange note in the landscape. But all-pervading there is a strangeness, that strange feeling as if the *depths* were barren, which comes in the south and the east, sun-stricken. Sun-stricken, and the heart eaten out by the dryness.

"I like it! I like it!" cries the q-b.

"But could you live here?" She would like to say yes, but daren't.

We stray back. The q-b wants to buy one of those saddle-bag arrangements. I say what for? She says to keep things in. Ach! but peeping in the shops, we see one and go in and examine it. It is quite a sound one, properly made: but plain, quite plain. On the white cross-stripes there are no lovely coloured flowers of rose and green and magenta: the three favourite Sardinian colours: nor are there any of the fantastic, griffin-like beasts. So it won't do. How much does it cost? Forty-five francs.

There is nothing to do in Mandas. So we will take the morning train and go to the terminus, to Sorgono. Thus, we shall cross the lower slopes of the great central knot of Sardinia, the mountain knot called Gennargentu. And Sorgono we feel will be lovely.

Back at the station we make tea on the spirit lamp, fill the thermos, pack the knapsack, and the kitchenino, and come out into the sun of the platform. The q-b goes to thank the black-cap for the white bread, whilst I settle the bill and ask for food for the journey. The brown woman fishes out from a huge black pot in the background sundry hunks of coarse boiled pork, and gives me two of these, hot, with bread and salt. This is the luncheon. I pay the bill: which amounts to twenty-four francs, for everything. (One says francs or liras, irrespective, in Italy.) At that moment arrives the train from Cagliari, and men rush in, roaring for the soup—or, rather, for the broth. "Ready, ready!." she cries, going to the black pot.

CHAPTER V

TO SORGONO

THE various trains in the junction squatted side by side and had long, long talks before at last we were off. It was wonderful to be running in the bright morning towards the heart of Sardinia, in the little, train that seemed so familiar. We were still going third-class, rather to the disgust of the railway officials at Mandas.

At first the country was rather open: always the long spurs of hills, steep-sided, but not high. And from our little train we looked across the country, across hill and dale. In the distance was a little town, on a low slope. But for its compact, fortified look it might have been a town on the English downs. A man in the carriage leaned out of the window holding out a white cloth, as a signal to someone in the far-off town that he was coming. The wind blew the white cloth, the town in the distance glimmered small and alone in its hollow. And the little train pelted along.

It was rather comical to see it. We were always climbing. And the line curved in great loops. So that as one looked out of the window, time and again one started, seeing a little train running in front of us, in a diverging direction, making big puffs of steam. But lo, it was our own little engine pelting off around a loop away ahead. We were quite a long train, but all trucks in front, only our two passenger coaches hitched on behind. And for this reason our own engine was always running fussily into sight, like some dog scampering in front and swerving about us, while we followed at the tail end of the thin string of trucks.

I was surprised how well the small engine took the continuous steep slopes, how bravely it emerged on the skyline. It is a queer railway. I would like to know who made it. It pelts up hill and down dale and round sudden bends in the most unconcerned fashion, not as proper big railways do, grunting inside deep cuttings and stinking their way through tunnels, but running up the hill like a panting, small dog, and having a look round, and starting off in another direction, whisking us behind unconcernedly. This is much more fun than the tunnel-and-cutting system.

They told me that Sardinia mines her own coal: and quite enough for her own needs: but very soft, not fit for steam purposes. I saw heaps of it: small, dull, dirty-looking stuff. Truck-loads of it too. And truck-loads of grain.

At every station we were left ignominiously planted. while the little engines—they had gay gold names on their black little bodies—strolled about along the side-lines, and snuffed at the various trucks. There we sat, at every station, while some truck was discarded and some other sorted out, like a. branded sheep, from the sidings and hitched on to us. It took a long time, this did.

All the stations so far had had wire netting over the windows. This means malaria-mosquitoes. The malaria climbs very high in Sardinia. The shallow upland valleys, moorland with their intense summer sun and the riverless, boggy behaviour of the water, breed the pest inevitably. But not very terribly, as far as one can make out: August and September being the danger months. The natives don't like to admit there is any malaria: a tiny bit, they say, a tiny bit. As soon as you come to the *trees* there is no more. So they say. For many miles the landscape is moorland and down-like with no trees. But wait for the trees. Ah, the woods and forests of Gennargentu: the woods and forests higher up: no malaria there!

The little engine whisks up and up, around loopy curves as if it were going to bite its own tail: we being the tail: then suddenly dives over the skyline out of sight. And the landscape changes. The famous woods begin to appear. At first it is only hazel-thickets, miles of hazel-thickets, all wild, with a few black cattle trying to peep at us out of the green myrtle and arbutus scrub which forms the undergrowth: and a couple of rare, wild peasants peering at the train. They wear the black sheepskin tunic, with the wool outside, and the long stocking-caps. Like cattle they too peer out from between deep bushes. The myrtle scrub here rises man-high, and cattle and men are smothered in it. The big hazels rise bare above. It must be difficult getting about in these parts.

Sometimes, in the distance one sees a black and white peasant riding lonely across a more open place, a tiny vivid figure. I like so much the proud instinct which makes a living creature distinguish itself from its background. I hate the rabbity khaki protection-coloration. A black-and-white peasant on his pony, only a dot in the distance beyond the foliage, still flashes and dominates the landscape. Ha-ha! proud mankind! There you ride! But alas, most of the men are still khaki-muffled, rabbit-indistinguishable, ignominious. The Italians look curiously rabbity in the grey-green uniform: just as our sand-coloured khaki men look doggy. They seem to scuffle rather abased, ignominious on the earth. Give us back the scarlet and gold, and devil take the hindmost.

The landscape really begins to change. The hillsides tilt sharper and sharper. A man is ploughing with two small red cattle on a craggy, tree-hanging slope as sharp as a roof-side. He stoops at the small wooden plough, and jerks the ploughlines. The oxen lift their noses to heaven, with a strange and beseeching snake-like movement, and taking tiny little steps with their frail feet move slantingly across the slope-face, between rocks and tree roots. Little, frail, jerky steps the bullocks take, and again they put their horns back and lift their muzzles snakily to heaven, as the man pulls the line. And he skids his wooden plough round another scoop of earth. It is marvellous how they hang upon that steep, craggy slope. An English labourer's eyes would bolt out of his head at the sight.

There is a stream: actually a long tress of a waterfall pouring into a little gorge, and a stream bed that opens a little, and shows a marvellous cluster of naked poplars away below. They are like ghosts. They have a ghostly, almost phosphorescent luminousness in the shadow of the valley, by the stream of water. If not phosphorescent, then incandescent: a grey, goldish-pale incandescence of naked limbs and myriad cold-glowing twigs, gleaming strangely. If I were a painter I would paint them: for they seem to have living, sentient flesh. And the shadow envelops them.

Another naked tree I would paint is the gleaming mauve-silver fig, which burns its cold incandescence, tangled, like some sensitive creature emerged from the rock. A fig tree come forth in its nudity gleaming over the dark winter-earth is a sight to behold. Like some white, tangled sea anemone. Ah, if it could but answer! or if we had tree-speech!

Yes, the steep valley sides become almost gorges, and there are trees. Not forests such as I had imagined, but scattered, grey, smallish oaks, and some lithe chestnuts. Chestnuts with their long whips, and oaks with their stubby boughs, scattered on steep hillsides where rocks crop out. The train perilously winding round, half-way up. Then suddenly bolting over a bridge and into a completely unexpected station. What is more, men crowd in—the station is connected with the main railway by a post motor omnibus.

An unexpected irruption of men—they may be miners or navvies or land-workers. They all have huge sacks: some lovely saddle-bags with rose-coloured flowers across the darkness. One old man is in full black-and-white costume, but very dirty and coming to pieces. The others wear the tight madder-brown breeches and sleeved waistcoats. Some have the sheepskin tunic, and all wear the long stocking-cap. And how they smell! of sheep's-wool and of men and goat. A rank scent fills the carriage.

They talk and are very lively. And they have mediæval faces, rusé, never really abandoning their defences for a moment, as a badger or a polecat never abandons its defences There is none of the brotherliness and civilised simplicity. Each man knows he must guard himself and his own: each man knows the devil is behind the next bush. They have never known the post-Renaissance Jesus. Which is rather an eye-opener.

Not that they are suspicious or uneasy. On the contrary, noisy; assertive, vigorous presences. But with none of that implicit belief that everybody will be and ought to be good to them, which is the mark of our era. They don't expect people to be good to them: they don't want it. They remind me of half-wild dogs that will love and obey, but won't be handled. They won't have their heads touched. And they won't be fondled. One can almost hear the half-savage growl.

The long stocking-caps they wear as a sort of crest, as a lizard wears his crest at mating time. They are always moving them, settling them on their heads. One fat fellow, young, with sly brown eyes and a young beard round his face, folds his stocking-foot in three, so that it rises over his brow martial and handsome. The old boy brings his stocking-foot over the left ear. A handsome fellow' with a jaw of massive teeth pushes his cap back and lets it hang a long way down his back. Then he shifts it forward over his nose and makes it have two sticking out points, like fox-ears, above his temples. It is marvellous how much expression these caps can take on. They say that only those born to them can wear them. They seem to be just long bags, nearly a yard long, of black stockinette stuff.

The conductor comes to issue them their tickets. And they all take out rolls of paper money. Even a little mothy rat of a man who sits opposite me has quite a pad of ten-franc notes. Nobody seems short of a hundred francs nowadays: nobody.

They shout and expostulate with the conductor. Full of coarse life they are: but so coarse! The handsome fellow has his sleeved waistcoat open, and his shirt-breast has come unbuttoned. Not looking, it seems as if he wears a black undervest. Then suddenly, one sees it is his own hair. He is quite black inside his shirt, like a black goat.

But there is a gulf between oneself and them. They have no inkling of our crucifixion, our universal consciousness. Each of them is pivoted and limited to himself, as the wild animals are. They look out, and they see other objects, objects to ridicule or mistrust or to sniff curiously at. But "thou shalt love thy neighbour as thyself" has never entered their souls at all, not even the thin end of it. They might love their neighbour with a hot, dark, unquestioning love. But the love would probably leave off abruptly. The fascination of what is beyond them has not seized on them. Their neighbour is a mere external. Their life is centripetal, pivoted inside itself, and does not run out towards others and mankind. One feels for the first time the real old mediæval life, which is enclosed in itself and has no interest in the world outside.

And so they lie about on the seats, play a game, shout and sleep, and settle their long stocking-caps: and spit. It is wonderful in them that at this time of day they still wear the long stocking-caps as a part of their inevitable selves. It is a sign of obstinate and powerful tenacity. They are not going to be broken in upon by world-consciousness. They are not going into the world's common clothes. Coarse, vigorous, determined, they will stick to their own coarse dark stupidity and let the big world find its own way to its own enlightened hell. Their hell is their own hell, they prefer it unenlightened.

And one cannot help wondering whether Sardinia will resist right through. Will the last waves of enlightenment and world-unity break over them and wash away the stocking-caps? Or is the tide of enlightenment and world-unity already receding fast enough?

Certainly a reaction is setting in, away from the old universality, back, away from cosmopolitanism and internationalism. Russia, with her Third International, is at the same time reacting most violently away from all other contact, back, recoiling on herself, into a fierce, unapproachable Russianism. Which motion will conquer? The workman's International, or the centripetal movement into national isolation? Are we going to merge into one grey proletarian homogeneity?—or are 'we going to swing back into more or less isolated, separate, defiant communities?

Probably both. The workman's International movement will finally break the flow towards cosmopolitanism and world-assimilation, and suddenly in a crash the world will fly back into intense separations. The moment has come when America, that extremist in world-assimilation and world-oneness, is reacting into violent egocentricity, a truly American egocentricity. As sure as fate we are on the brink of American empire.

For myself, I am glad. I am glad that the era of love and oneness is over: hateful homogeneous world-oneness. I am glad that Russia flies back into savage Russianism, Scythism, savagely self-pivoting. I am glad that America is doing the same. I shall be glad when men hate their common, world-alike clothes, when they tear them up and clothe themselves fiercely for distinction, savage distinction, savage distinction against the rest of the creeping world: when America kicks the billy-cock and the collar-and-tie into limbo, and takes to her own national costume: when men fiercely react against looking all alike, and being all alike, and betake themselves into vivid clan or nation-distinctions.

The era of love and oneness is over. The era of world-alike should be at an end. The other tide has set in. Men will set their bonnets at one another now, and fight themselves into separation and sharp distinction. The day of peace and oneness is over, the day of the great fight into multifariousness is at hand. Hasten the day, and save us from proletarian homogeneity and khaki all-alikeness.

I love my indomitable coarse men from mountain Sardinia, for their stocking-caps and their splendid, animal-bright stupidity. If only the last wave of all-alikeness won't wash those superb crests, those caps, away.

We are struggling now among the Gennargentu spurs. There is no, single peak—no Etna of Sardinia. The train, like the plough, balances on the steep, steep sides of the hill-spurs, and winds around and around. Above and below the steep slopes are all bosky. These are the woods of Gennargentu. But they aren't woods in my sense of the word. They are thin sprinkles of oaks and chestnuts and cork-trees over steep hill-slopes. And cork-trees! I see curious slim oaky-looking trees that are stripped quite naked below the boughs, standing brown-ruddy, curiously distinct among the bluey-grey pallor of the others. They remind me, again and again, of glowing, coffee-brown, naked aborigines of the South Seas. They have the naked suavity, skin-bare, and an intense coffee-red colour of unclothed savages. And these are the stripped cork-trees. Some are much stripped, some little. Some have the whole trunk and part of the lower limbs ruddy naked, some only a small part of the trunk.

It is well on in the afternoon. A peasant in black-and-white, and his young, handsome woman in rose-red costume, with gorgeous apron bordered deep with grass-green, and a little, dark-purple waistcoat over her, white, full bodice, are sitting behind me talking. The workmen peasants are subsiding into sleep. It is well on in the afternoon, we have long, ago eaten the meat. Now we finish the white loaf, the gift, and the tea. Suddenly looking out of the window, we see Gennargentu's mass behind us, a thick snow-deep knot-summit, beautiful beyond the long, steep spurs among which we are engaged. We lose the white mountain mass for half an hour: when suddenly it emerges unexpectedly almost in front, the great, snow-heaved shoulder.

How different it is from Etna, that lonely, self-conscious wonder of Sicily! This is much more human and knowable, with a deep breast and massive limbs, a powerful mountain-body. It is like the peasants.

The stations are far between—an hour from one to another. Ah, how weary one gets of these journeys, they last so long. We look across a valley—a stone's throw. But alas, the little train has no wings, and can't jump. So back turns the line. back and back towards Gennargentu, a long rocky way, till it comes at length to the poor valley-head. This, it skirts fussily, and sets off to pelt down on its traces again, gaily. And a man who was looking at us doing our roundabout has climbed down and crossed the valley in five minutes.

The peasants nearly all wear costumes now, even the women in the fields: the little fields in the half-populated valleys. These Gennargentu valleys are all half-populated, more than the moors further south.

It is past three o'clock, and cold where there is no sun. At last only one more station before the terminus. And here the peasants wake up, sling the bulging sacks over their shoulders, and get down. We see Tonara away above. We see our old grimy black-

and-white peasant greeted by his two women who have come to meet him with the pony—
daughters, handsome in vivid rose and green costume. Peasants, men in black-and-white,
men in madder-brown, with the close breeches on their compact thighs, women in rose-and-
white, ponies with saddle-bags, all begin to trail up the hill-road in silhouette, very
handsome, towards the far-off, perched, sun-bright village of Tonara, a big village, shining
like a New Jerusalem.

The train as usual leaves us standing, and shuffles with trucks—water sounds in
the valley: there are stacks of cork on the station, and coal. An idiot girl in a great full skirt
entirely made of coloured patches mops and mows. Her little waistcoat thing is also
incredibly old, and shows faint signs of having once been a lovely purple and black
brocade. The valley and steep slopes are open about us. An old shepherd has a lovely flock
of delicate merino sheep.

And at last we move. In one hour we shall be there. As we travel among the tree
slopes, many brown cork-trees, we come upon a flock of sheep. Two peasants in our
carriage, looking out, give the most weird, unnatural, high-pitched shrieks entirely
unproducible by any ordinary being. The sheep know, however, and scatter. And after ten
minutes the shrieks start again, for three young cattle. Whether the peasants do it for love, I
don't know. But it is the wildest and weirdest inhuman shepherd noise I have- ever heard.

It is Saturday afternoon and four o'clock. The country is wild and uninhabited, the
train almost empty, yet there is the leaving-off-work feeling in the atmosphere. Oh, twisty,
wooded, steep slopes, oh, glimpses of Gennargentu, oh, nigger-stripped cork-trees, oh,
smell of peasants, oh, wooden, wearisome railway carriage, we are so sick of you! Nearly
seven hours of this journey already: and a distance of sixty miles. But we are almost
there—look, look, Sorgono, nestling beautifully among the wooded slopes in front. Oh.
magic little town. Ah, you terminus and ganglion of the inland roads, we hope in you for a
pleasant inn and happy company. Perhaps we will stay a day or two at Sorgono.

The train gives a last sigh, and draws to a last standstill in the tiny terminus station.
An old fellow, fluttering with rags as a hen in the wind flutters, asked me if I wanted the
Albergo, the inn. I said yes, and let him take my knapsack. Pretty Sorgono! As we went
down the brief muddy lane between hedges, to the village high-road, we seemed almost to
have come to some little town in the English Westcountry, or in Hardy's country. There
were glades of stripling oaks and big slopes with oak-trees, and on the right a saw-mill
buzzing, and on the left the town, white and close, nestling round a Baroque church tower.
And the little lane was muddy.

Three minutes brought us to the high-road, and, a great pink-washed building
blank on the road facing the station lane, and labelled in huge letters: RISTORANTE
RISVEGLIO: the letter N being printed backwards. *Risveglio* if you please: which means
waking up or rousing, like the word *réveilé.* Into the doorway of the Risveglio bolted the
flutterer. "Half a minute," said I. "Where is the Albergo d'Italia?" I was relying on
Baedeker.

"Non c'è più," replied my rag-feather. "There isn't it any more." This answer,
being very frequent nowadays, is always most disconcerting.

"Well then, what other hotel?"

"There is no other."

Risveglio or nothing. In we go. We pass into a big dreary bar, where are
innumerable bottles behind a tin counter. Flutter-jack yells: and at length appears mine host,
a youngish fellow of the Eskimo type, but rather bigger, in a dreary black suit and a
cutaway waistcoat suggesting a dinner waistcoat, and innumerable wine stains on his shirt

front. I instantly hated him for the filthy appearance he made. He wore a battered hat and his face was long unwashed.

Was there a bedroom?

Yes.

And he led the way down the passage, just as dirty as the road outside, up the hollow, wooden stairs also just as clean as the passage, along a hollow, drum-rearing dirty corridor, and into a bedroom. Well, it contained a large bed, thin and flat with, a grey-white counterpane, like a large, poor, marble-slabbed tomb in the room's sordid emptiness; one dilapidated chair on which stood the miserablest weed of a candle I have ever seen: a broken wash-saucer in a wire ring: and for the rest, an expanse of wooden floor as dirty-grey-black as it could be, and an expanse of wall charted with the bloody deaths of mosquitoes. The window was about two feet above the level of a sort of stable yard outside, with a fowl-house just by the sash. There, at the window flew lousy feathers and dirty straw, the ground was thick with chicken droppings. An ass and two oxen comfortably chewed hay in an open shed just across, and plump in the middle of the yard lay a bristly black pig taking the last of the sun. Smells of course were varied.

The knapsack and the kitchenino were dropped on the repulsive floor, which I hated to touch with my boots even. I turned back the sheets and looked at other people's stains.

"There is nothing else?"

"Niente," said he of the lank, low forehead and beastly shirt-breast. And he sullenly departed. I gave the flutterer his tip and he too ducked and fled. Then the queen bee and I took a few mere sniffs.

"Dirty, disgusting swine! " said I, and I was in a rage.

I could have forgiven him anything, I think, except his horrible shirt-breast, his personal shamelessness.

We strolled round—saw various other bedrooms, some worse, one really better. But this showed signs of being occupied. All the doors were open: the place was quite deserted, and open to the road. The one thing that seemed definite was honesty. It must be a very honest place, for every footed beast, man or animal, could walk in at random and nobody to take the slightest regard.

So we went downstairs. The only other apartment was the open public bar, which seemed like part of the road. A muleteer, leaving his mules at the corner of the Risveglio, was drinking at the counter.

This famous inn was at the end of the village. We strolled along the road between the houses, down-hill. A dreary hole! a cold, hopeless, lifeless, Saturday-afternoon-weary village, rather sordid, with nothing to say for itself. No real shops at all. A weary-looking church, and a clutch, of disconsolate houses. We walked right through the village. In the middle was a sort of open space where stood a great, grey motor omnibus. And a bus-driver looking rather weary.

Where did the bus go?

It went to join the main railway.

When?

At half-past seven in the morning.

Only then?

Only then.

"Thank God we can get out, anyhow," said I

142

We passed on, and emerged beyond the village, still on the descending great high-road that was mended with loose stone pitched on it. This wasn't good enough. Besides, we were out of the sun, and the place being at a considerable elevation, it was very cold. So we turned back, to climb quickly uphill into the sun.

We went up a little side turning past a bunch of poor houses towards a steep little lane between banks. And before we knew where we were, we were in the thick of the public lavatory. In these villages, as I knew, there are no sanitary arrangements of any sort whatever. Every villager and villageress just betook himself at need to one of the side roads. It is the immemorial Italian custom. Why bother about privacy? The most socially-constituted people on earth, they even like to relieve themselves in company.

We found ourselves in the full thick of one of these meeting-places. To get out at any price! So we scrambled up the steep earthen banks to a stubble field above. And by this time I was in a greater rage.

Evening was falling, the sun declining. Below us clustered the Sodom apple of this vile village. Around were fair, tree-clad hills and dales, already bluish with the frost shadows. The air bit cold and strong. In a very little time the sun would be down. We were at an elevation of about 2500 feet above the sea.

No denying it was beautiful, with the oak-slopes and the wistfulness and the far-off feeling of loneliness and evening. But I was in too great a temper to admit it. We clambered frenziedly to get warm. And the sun immediately went right down, and the ice-heavy blue shadow fell over us all. The village began to send forth blue wood-smoke, and it seemed more than ever like the twilit Westcountry.

But thank you—we had to get back. And run the gauntlet of that stinking, stinking lane? Never. Towering with fury—quite unreasonable, but there you are—I marched the q-b down a declivity through a wood, over a ploughed field, along a cart-track, and so to the great high-road above the village and above the, inn.

It was cold, and evening was falling into dusk. Down the high-road came wild half-ragged men on ponies, in all degrees of costume and not costume: came four wide-eyed cows stepping down-hill round the corner, and three delicate, beautiful merino sheep which stared at us with their prominent, gold-curious eyes: came an ancient, ancient man with a stick: came a stout-chested peasant carrying a long wood pole: came a straggle of alert and triumphant goats, long-horned, long-haired, jingling their bells. Everybody greeted us hesitatingly. And everything came to a halt at the Risveglio corner, while the men had a nip.

I attacked the spotty-breast again.

Could I have milk?

No. Perhaps in an hour there would be milk. Perhaps not.

Was there anything to eat?

No—at half-past seven there would be something to eat.

Was there a fire?

No—the man hadn't made a fire.

Nothing to do but to go to that foul bedroom or walk the high-road. We turned up the high-road again. Animals stood about the road in the frost-heavy air, with heads sunk passively, waiting for the men to finish their drinks in the beastly bar—we walked slowly up the hill. In a field on the right a flock of merino sheep moved mistily, uneasily, climbing at the gaps in the broken road bank, and sounding their small fine bells with a frosty ripple of sound. A figure which in the dusk I had really thought was something inanimate broke into movement in the field. It was an old shepherd, very old, in very ragged dirty black-and-white, who had been standing like a stone there in the open field-end for heaven knows how long, utterly motionless, leaning on his stick. Now he broke into a dream-motion and hobbled after the wistful feminine, inquisitive sheep. The red was fading from the far-off west. At the corner, climbing slowly and wearily, we almost ran into a grey and lonely bull, who came stepping down-hill in his measured fashion like some god. He swerved his head and went round us.

We reached a place which we couldn't make out: then saw it was a cork-shed. There were stacks and stacks of cork-bark in the dusk, like crumpled hides.

"Now I'm going back," said the q-b flatly, and she swung round. The last red was smouldering beyond the lost, thin-wooded hills of this interior. A fleece of blue half-luminous smoke floated over the obscure village. The highway wound downhill at our feet, pale and blue.

And the q-b was angry with me for my fury.

"Why are you so indignant! Anyone would think your moral self had been outraged! Why take it morally? You petrify that man at the inn by the very way you speak to him, *such* condemnation! Why don't you take it as it comes? It's all life."

But no, my rage is black, black, black. Why, heaven knows. But I think it was because Sorgono had seemed so fascinating to me, when I imagined it beforehand. Oh, so fascinating! If I had expected nothing I should not have been so hit. Blessed is he that expecteth nothing, for he shall not be disappointed.

I cursed the degenerate aborigines, the dirty-breasted host who *dared* to keep such an inn, the sordid villagers who had the baseness to squat their beastly human nastiness in this upland valley. All my praise of the long stocking-cap—you remember?—vanished from my mouth. I cursed them all, and the q-b for an interfering female.

In the bar a wretched candle was weeping light—uneasy, gloomy men were drinking their Saturday-evening-home-coming dram. Cattle lay down in the road, in the cold air as if hopeless.

Had the milk come?

No.

When would it come?

He didn't know.

Well, what were we to do? Was there no room? Was there nowhere we could sit?

Yes, there was the stanza now.

Now! Taking the only weed of a candle, and leaving the drinkers in the dark, he led us down a dark and stumbly earthen passage, over loose stones and an odd plank, as it would seem underground, to the stanza: the room.

The stanza! It was pitch dark—but suddenly I saw a big fire of oak-root, a brilliant, flamy, rich fire, and my rage in that second disappeared.

The host, and the candle, forsook us at the door. The stanza would have been in complete darkness, save for that rushing bouquet of new flames in the chimney, like fresh flowers. By this firelight we saw the room. It was like a dungeon, absolutely empty, with an uneven earthen floor, quite dry, and high bare walls, gloomy, with a handbreadth of window high up.

There was no furniture at all, save a little wooden bench, a foot high before the fire, and several home-made-looking rush mats rolled up and leaning against the walls. Furthermore, a chair before the fire on which hung wet table-napkins. Apart from this, it was a high, dark, naked prison-dungeon.

But it was quite dry, it had an open chimney, and a gorgeous new fire rushing like a waterfall upwards among the craggy stubs of a pile of dry oak-roots. I hastily put the chair and the wet corpse-cloths to one side. We sat on the low bench side by side in the dark, in front of this rippling rich fire, in front of the cavern of the open chimney, and we did not care any more about the dungeon and the darkness. Man can live without food, but he can't live without fire. It is an Italian proverb. We had found the fire, like new gold. And we sat in front of it, a little way back, side by side on the low form, our feet on the uneven earthen floor, and felt the flame-light rippling upwards over our faces, as if we were bathing in some gorgeous stream of fieriness, I forgave the dirty-breasted host everything and was as glad as if I had come into a kingdom.

So we sat alone for half an hour smiling into the flames, bathing our faces in the glow. From time to time I was aware of steps in the tunnel-like passage outside, and of presences peering. But no one came. I was aware too of the faint steaming of the beastly table-napkins, the only other occupants of the room.

In dithers a candle, and an elderly, bearded man in gold-coloured corduroys, and an amazing object on a long, long spear. He put the candle on the mantel-ledge, and crouched at the side of the fire, arranging the oak-roots. He peered strangely and fixedly in the fire. And he held up the speared object before our faces.

It was a kid that he had come to roast. But it was a kid opened out, made quite flat, and speared like a flat fan on a long iron stalk. It was a really curious sight. And it must have taken some doing. The whole of the skinned kid was there, the head curled in against a shoulder, the stubby cut ears, the eyes, the teeth, the few hairs of the nostrils: and the feet curled curiously round, like an animal that puts its fore-paw over its ducked head: and the hind legs twisted indescribably up: and all skewered flat-wise upon the long iron rod, so that it was a complete flat pattern. It reminded me intensely of those distorted, slim-limbed, dog-like animals which figure on the old Lombard ornaments, distorted and curiously infolded upon themselves. Celtic illuminations also have these distorted, involuted creatures.

The old man flourished the flat kid like a bannerette, whilst he arranged the fire. Then in one side of the fireplace wall he poked the point of the rod. He himself crouched on the hearth-end, in the half-shadow at the other end of the fire-place, holding the further end of the long iron rod. The kid was thus extended before the fire, like a hand-screen. And he could spin it round at will.

But the hole in the masonry of the chimney-piece was not satisfactory. The point of the rod kept slipping, and the kid came down against the fire. He muttered and muttered to himself, and tried again. Then at length he reared up the kid-banner whilst he got large stones from a dark corner. He arranged these stones so that the iron point rested on them. He himself sat away on, the opposite side of the fire-place, on the shadowy hearth-end, and with queer, spellbound black eyes and completely immovable face, he watched the flames and the kid, and held the handle end of the rod.

We asked him if the kid was for the evening meal—and he said it was. It would be good! And he said yes, and looked with chagrin at the bit of ash on the meat, where it had slipped. It is a point of honour that it should never touch the ash. Did they do all their meat this way? He said they did. And wasn't it difficult to put the kid thus on the iron rod? He said it was not easy, and he eyed the joint closely, and felt one of the forelegs, and muttered that it was not fixed properly.

He spoke with a very soft mutter, hard to catch, and sideways, never to us direct. But his manner was gentle soft, muttering, reticent, sensitive. He asked us where we came from, and where we were going: always in his soft mutter. And what nation were we, were we French? Then he went on to say there was a war—but he thought it was finished. There was a war because the Austrians wanted to come into Italy again. But the French and the English came to help Italy. A lot of Sardinians had gone to it. But let us hope it is all finished. He thought it was—young men of Sorgono had been killed. He hoped it was finished.

Then he reached for the candle and peered at the kid. It was evident he was the born roaster. He held the candle and looked for a long time at the sizzling side of the meat, as if he would read portents. Then he held his spit to the fire again. And it was as if time immemorial were toasting itself another meal. I sat holding the candle.

A young woman appeared, hearing voices. Her head was swathed in a shawl, one side of which was brought across, right over the mouth, so that only her two eyes and her nose showed. The q-b thought she must have toothache—but she laughed and said no. As a matter of fact that is the way a head-dress is worn in Sardinia, even by both sexes. It is something like the folding of the Arab's burnoose. The point seems to be that the mouth and chin are thickly covered, also the ears and brow, leaving only the nose and eyes exposed. They say it keeps off the malaria. The men swathe shawls round their heads in the same way. It seems to me they want to keep their heads warm, dark and hidden: they feel secure inside.

She wore the workaday costume: a full, dark-brown skirt, the full white bodice, and a little waistcoat or corset. This little waistcoat in her case had become no more than a shaped belt, sending up graceful, stiffened points under the breasts, like long leaves standing up. It was pretty—but all dirty. She too was pretty, but with an impudent, not quite pleasant manner. She fiddled with the wet napkins, asked us various questions, and addressed herself rather jerkily to the old man;' who answered hardly at all—then she departed again. The women are self-conscious in a rather smirky way, bouncy.

When she was gone I asked the old man if she was his daughter. He said very brusquely, in his soft mutter, No. She came from a village some miles away. He did not belong to the inn. He was, as far as I understood, the postman. But I may have been mistaken about the word,

But he seemed laconic, unwilling to speak about the inn and its keepers. There seemed to be something queer. And again he asked where we were going. He told me there were now two motor-buses: a new one which ran over the mountains to Nuoro. Much better go to Nuoro than to Abbasanta. Nuoro was evidently the town towards which these villages looked as a sort of capital.

The kid-roasting proceeded very slowly, the meat never being very near the fire. From time to time the roaster arranged the cavern of red-hot roots. Then he threw on more roots. It was very hot. And he turned the long spit, and still I held the candle.

Other people came strolling in, to look at us. But they hovered behind us in the dark, so I could not make out at all clearly. They strolled in the gloom of the dungeon-like room, and watched us. One came forward—a fat, fat young soldier in uniform. I made place for him on the bench— but he put out his hand and disclaimed the attention. Then he went away again.

The old man propped up the roast, and then he too disappeared for a time. The thin candle guttered, the fire was no longer flamy but red. The roaster reappeared with a new shorter spear, thinner, and a great lump of raw hog-fat. spitted on it. This he thrust into the red fire. It sizzled and smoked and spat fat, and I wondered. He told me he wanted it to catch fire. It refused. He groped in the hearth for the bits of twigs with which the fire had been started. These twig-stumps he stuck in the fat, like an orange stuck with cloves, then he held it in the fire again. Now at last it caught, and it was a flaming torch running downwards with a thin shower of flaming fat. And now he was satisfied. He held the fat-torch with its yellow flares over the browning kid, which he turned horizontal for the occasion. All over the roast fell the flaming drops, till the meat was all shiny and browny. He put it to the fire again, holding the diminishing fat, still burning bluish, over it all the time in the upper air.

While this was in progress a man entered with a loud *Good evening.* We replied Good evening—and evidently he caught a strange note. He came and bent down and peered under my hat-brim, then under the q-b's hat-brim; we still wore hats and overcoats, as did everybody. Then he stood up suddenly and touched his cap and said *Scusi*—excuse me. I said *Niente,* which one always says, and he addressed a few jovial words to the crouching roaster: who again would hardly answer him. The omnibus was arrived from Oristano, I made out—with a few passengers.

This man brought with him a new breezy atmosphere, which the roaster did not like. However, I made place on the low bench, and the attention this time was accepted. Sitting down at the extreme end, he came into the light, and I saw a burly man in the prime of life, dressed in dark brown velvet, with a blonde little moustache and twinkling blue eyes and a tipsy look. I thought he might be some local tradesman or farmer. He asked a few questions, in a boisterous, familiar fashion, then went out again. He appeared with a small iron spit, a slim rod, in one hand, and in the other hand two joints of kid and a handful of sausages. He stuck his joints on his rod. But our roaster still held the interminable flat kid before the now red flameless fire. The fat-torch was burnt out, the cinder pushed in the fire. A moment's spurt of flame, then red, intense redness again, and our kid before it like a big, dark hand.

"Eh," said the newcomer, whom I will call the girovago, "it's done. The kid's done. It's done."

The roaster slowly shook his head, but did not answer. He sat like time and eternity at the hearth-end, his face flame-flushed, his dark eyes still fire-abstract, still sacredly intent on the roast.

"Na-na-na!" said the girovago. "Let another body see the fire." And with his pieces of meat awkwardly skewered on his iron stick he tried to poke under the authorised kid and get at the fire. In his soft mutter, the old man bade him wait for the fire till the fire was ready for him. But the girovago poked impudently and good-humouredly, and said testily that the authorised kid was done.

"Yes, surely it is done," said I, for it was already a quarter to eight.

The old roasting priest muttered, and took out his knife from his pocket. He pressed the blade slowly, slowly deep into the meat: as far as a knife will go into a piece of kid. He seemed to be feeling the meat inwardly. And he said it was not done. He shook his head, and remained there like time and eternity at the end of the rod.

The girovago said *Sangue di Dio,* but couldn't roast his meat! And he tried to poke his skewer near the coals. So doing his piece fell off into the ashes, and the invisible onlookers behind raised a shout of laughter. However, he raked it out and wiped it with his hand and said "No matter, nothing lost."

Then he turned to me and asked the usual whence and whither questions. These answered, he said wasn't I German. I said No, I was English. He looked at me many times, shrewdly, as if he wanted to make out something. Then he asked where were we domiciled—and I said Sicily. And then very pertinently, why had we come to Sardinia. I said for pleasure, and t see the island.

"Ah, per divertimento!" he repeated, half-musingly, not believing me in the least.

Various men had now come into the room, though they all remained indistinct in the background. The girovago talked and jested abroad in the company, and the half-visible men laughed in a rather hostile manner.

At last the old roaster decided the kid was done. He lifted it from the fire and scrutinized it thoroughly, holding the candle to it, as if it were some wonderful epistle from the flames. To be sure it looked marvellous, and smelled so good: brown and crisp, and hot, and savoury, not burnt in any place whatever. It was eight o'clock.

"It's done! It's done! Go away with it! Go," said the girovago, pushing the old roaster with his hand.' And at last the old man consented to depart, holding the kid like a banner.

"It looks so *good!*" cried the q-b. "And I am so hungry."

"Ha-ha! It makes one hungry to see good meat, Signora. Now it is my turn. Heh— Gino—" the girovago flourished his arm. And a handsome, unwashed man with a black moustache came forward rather sheepishly; He was dressed in soldier's clothes, neutral grey, and was a big, robust, handsome fellow with dark eyes and Mediterranean sheepishness. "Here, take it thou," said the girovago, pressing the long spit into his hand. "It is thy business, cook the supper, thou art the woman.—But I'll keep the sausages and do them."

The so-called woman sat al the end of the hearth, where the old roaster had sat, and with his brown, nervous hand piled the remaining coals together. The fire was no longer flamy: and it was sinking. The dark-browed man arranged it so that be could cook the meat. He held the spit negligently over the red mass. A joint fell off. The men laughed.

It's lost nothing," said the dark-browed man, as the girovago had said before: and he skewered it on again and thrust it to the fire. But meanwhile he was looking up from under his dark lashes at the girovago and at us.

The girovago talked continually. He turned to me, holding the handful of sausages. This makes a tasty bit," he said.

"Oh, yes—good salsiccia," said I.

"You are eating the kid? You are eating at the inn?" he said. I replied that I was.

"No," he said. "You stay and eat with me. You eat with me. The sausage is good, the kid will soon be done, the fire is grateful."

I laughed, not quite understanding him. He was certainly a bit tipsy.

"Signora," he said, turning to the q-b. She did not like him, he was impudent, and she shut a deaf ear to him as far as she could. "Signora," he said, "do you understand me what I say?"

She replied that she did.

"Signora," he said, "I sell things to the women. I sell them things."

"What do you sell?" she asked in astonishment.

"Saints," he said.

"Saints!" she cried in more astonishment.

"Yes, saints," he said with tipsy gravity.

She turned in confusion to the company in the background. The fat soldier came forward, he was the chief of the carabinieri.

"Also combs and bits of soap and little mirrors," he explained sarcastically.

"Saints!" said the girovago once more. "And also *ragazzini*—also youngsters. Wherever I go there is a little one comes running calling Babbo! Babbo! Daddy! Daddy! Wherever I go—youngsters. And I'm the babbo."

All this was received with a kind of silent sneer from the invisible assembly in the background. The candle was burning low, the fire was sinking too. In vain the dark-browed man tried to build it up. The q-b became impatient for the food. She got up wrathfully and stumbled into the dark passage, exclaiming: "Don't we eat yet?"

"Eh—Patience! Patience, Signora. It takes time in this house," said the man in the background.

The dark browed man looked up at the girovago and said:

"Are you going to cook the sausages with your fingers?"

He too was trying to be assertive and jesting but he was the kind of person no one takes any notice of. The girovago rattled on in dialect, poking fun at us and at our being there in this inn. I did not quite follow.

"Signora! " said the girovago. "Do you understand Sardinian?"

"I understand Italian—and some Sardinian," she replied rather hotly. "And I know that you are trying to laugh at us—to make fun of us."

He laughed fatly and comfortably.

"Ah, Signora," he said. "We have a language that you wouldn't understand—not one word. Nobody here would understand it but me and him—" he pointed to the black-browed one. "Everybody would want an interpreter—everybody."

But he did not say interpreter—he said *interprete,* with the accent on the penultimate, as if it were some sort of priest.

"A what?" said I.

He repeated with tipsy unction, and I saw what he meant. "Why," said I, "it is a dialect? What is your dialect?

"My dialect," he said, "is Sassari. I come from Sassari. If I spoke my dialect they would understand something. But if I speak this language they would want an interpreter."

"What language is it then?"

He leaned up to me, laughing.

"It is the language we use when the women are buying -things and we don't want them to know what we say: me and him—"

"Oh," said I. "I know. We have that language in England. It is called thieves' Latin—*Latino del furbi.*"

The men at the back suddenly laughed, glad to turn the joke against the forward girovago. He looked down his nose at me. But seeing I was laughing without malice, he leaned to me and said softly, secretly:

"What is your affair then? What affair is it, yours?"

"How? What?" I exclaimed, not understanding.

"*Che genere di affari?* What sort of business?"

"*How—affari?*" said I, still not grasping.

"What do you *sell?*" he said, flatly and rather spitefully. "What goods?"

"I don't sell anything," replied I, laughing to think he took us for some sort of strolling quacks or commercial travellers.

"Cloth—or something," he said cajolingly, slyly, as if to worm my secret out of me.

"But nothing at all. Nothing at all," said I. "We have come to Sardinia to see the peasant costumes—" I thought that might sound satisfactory.

"Ah, the costumes!" he said, evidently thinking I was a deep one. And he turned bandying words with his dark. browed mate who was still poking the meat at the embers and crouching on the hearth. The room was almost quite dark. The mate answered him back, and tried to seem witty too. But the girovago was the commanding personality! Rather too much so: too impudent for the q-b, though rather after my own secret heart. The mate was one of those handsome, passive, stupid men.

"Him!" said the girovago, turning suddenly to me and pointing at the mate. "He's my wife."

"Your wife!" said I.

"Yes. He's my wife, because we're always together."

There had become a sudden dead silence in the background. In spite of it the mate looked up under his black lashes and said, with a half smile:

"Don't talk, or I shall give thee a good *bacio* to-night."

There was an instant's fatal pause, then the girovago continued:

"To-morrow is festa of Sant' Antonio at Tonara. Tomorrow we are going to-Tonara. Where are you going?"

"To Abbasanta," said I.

"Ah, Abbasanta! You should come to Tonara. At Tonara there is a brisk trade— and there are costumes. You should come to Tonara, Come with him and me to Tonara tomorrow, and we will do business together."

I laughed, but did not answer.

"Come," said he. "You' will like Tonara! Ah, Tonara is a fine place. There is an inn: you can eat well, sleep well. I tell you, because to you ten francs don't matter. Isn't that so? Ten francs don't matter to you. Well, then come to Tonara. What? What do you say?"

I shook my head and laughed, but did not answer. To tell the truth I should have liked to go to Tonara with him and his mate and do the brisk trade: if only I knew what trade it would be.

"You are sleeping upstairs?" he said to me.

I nodded.

"This is my bed," he said, taking one of the home-made rush mats from against the wall. I did not take him seriously at any point.

"Do they make those in Sorgono?" I said.

"Yes, in Sorgono—they are the beds, you see! roll up this end a bit—so! and that is the pillow."

He laid his cheek sideways.

"Not really," said I.

He came and sat down again next to me, and my attention wandered. The q-b was raging for her dinner. It must be quite half-past eight. The kid, the perfect kid, would be cold and ruined. Both fire and candle were burning low. Someone had been out for a new candle, but there was evidently no means of replenishing the fire. The mate still crouched on the hearth, the dull red fire-glow on his handsome face, patiently trying to roast the kid and poking it against the embers. He had heavy, strong limbs in his khaki clothes, but his hand that held the spit was brown and tender and sensitive, a real Mediterranean hand. The girovago, blonde, round-faced, mature and aggressive with all his liveliness, was more like a northerner. In the background were four or five other men, of whom I had distinguished none but a stout soldier, probably chief carabiniere.

Just as the q-b was working up to the rage I had at last calmed down from, appeared the shawl-swathed girl announcing "Pronto!"

150

"Pronto! Pronto! Sad everybody

"High time, too," said the q-b, springing from the low bench before the fire. "Where do we eat? Is there another room?

"There is another room, Signora," said the carabiniere.

So we trooped out of the fire-warmed dungeon, leaving the girovago and his mate and two other men, muleteers from the road, behind us. I could see that it irked my girovago to be left behind. He was by far the strongest personality in the place, and he had the keenest intelligence. So he hated having to fall into the background, when he had been dragging all the limelight on to himself all the evening. To me, too, he was something of a kindred soul that night. But there we are: fate, in the guise of that mysterious division between a respectable life and a scamp's life, divided us. There was a gulf between me and him, between my way and his. He was a kindred spirit—but with a hopeless difference. There was something a bit sordid about him—and he knew it. That is why he was always tipsy. Yet I like the lone-wolf souls best—better than the sheep. If only they didn't feel mongrel inside themselves. Presumably a scamp is bound to be mongrel. It is a pity the untamable, lone-wolf souls should always become pariahs, almost of choice: mere scamps.

Top and bottom of it is, I regretted my girovago, though I knew it was no good thinking of him. His way was *not* my way. Yet I regretted him, I did.

We found ourselves in a dining-room with a long white table and inverted soup-plates, tomb-cold, lighted by an acetylene flare. Three men had accompanied us: the carabiniere, a little dark youth with a small black moustache, in a soldier's short, wool-lined great-coat: and a young man who looked tired round his blue eyes, and who wore a dark-blue overcoat, quite smart. The be-shawled damsel came in with the inevitable bowl of minestrone, soup with cabbage and cauliflower and other things. We helped ourselves, and the fat carabiniere started the conversation with the usual questions—and where were we going to-morrow?

I asked about buses. Then the responsible-looking, tired-eyed youth told me he was the bus-driver. He had come from Oristano, on the main line, that day. It is a distance of some forty miles. Next morning he was going on over the mountains to Nuoro—about the same distance again. The youth with the little black moustache and the Greek, large eyes, was his mate, the conductor. This was their run, from Oristano to Nuoro—a course of ninety miles or more. And every day on, on, on. No wonder he looked nerve-tired. Yet he had that kind of dignity, the wistful seriousness and pride of a man in machine control: the only god-like ones to-day, those who pull the iron levers and are the gods in the machine.

They repeated what the old roaster said: much nicer for us to go to Nuoro than to Abbasanta. So to Nuoro we decided to go, leaving at half-past nine in the morning.

Every other night the driver and his mate spent in this benighted Risveglio inn. It must have been their bedroom we saw, clean and tidy. I said was the food always so late, was everything always as bad as to-day. Always—if not worse, they said, making light of it, with sarcastic humour against the Risveglio. You spent your whole life at the Risveglio sitting, waiting, and going block-cold: unless you were content to drink *aqua vitae,* like those in there. The driver jerked his head towards the dungeon.

"Who were those in there? " said I.

The one who did all the talking was a mercante, a mercante girovago, a wandering peddler. This, was my girovago: a wandering peddler selling saints and youngsters! The other was his mate, who helped carry the pack. They went about together. Oh, my girovago was a known figure all over the, country.—And where would they sleep? There, in the room where the fire was dying.

They would unroll the mats and lie with their feet to the hearth. For this they paid threepence, or at most fourpence. And they had the privilege of cooking their own food. The Risveglio supplied them with nothing but the fire, the roof, and the rush mat.—And, of course, the drink. Oh, we need have no sympathy with the girovago and his sort. *They* lacked for nothing. They had everything they wanted: everything: and money in abundance. *They* lived for the *aqua vitae* they drank. That was all they wanted: their continual allowance of *aqua vitae*. And they got it. Ah, they were not cold. If the room became cold during the night: if they had no coverings at all: pah, they waited for morning, and as soon as it was light they drank a large glass of *aqua vitae*. That was their fire, their hearth, and their home: drink. *Aqua vitae* was hearth and home to them.

I was surprised at the contempt, tolerant and yet profound, with which these three men in the dining-room spoke of the others in the *stanza*. How contemptuous, almost bitter, the driver was against alcohol. It was evident, he hated it. And though we all had our bottles of dead-cold dark wine, anti though we all drank: still, the feeling of the, three youths against actual intoxication was deep and hostile, with a certain burning *moral* dislike that is more northern than Italian. And they curled their lip with real dislike of the girovago: his forwardness, his impudent aggressiveness.

As for the inn, yes, it was very bad. it had been quite good under the previous proprietors. But now—they shrugged their shoulders. The dirty-breast and the shawled girl were not the owners. They were merely conductors of the hotel: here a sarcastic curl of the lip. The owner was a man in the village—a young man. A week or two back, at Christmas time, there had been a roomful of men sitting drinking and roistering at this very table. When in had come the proprietor, mad-drunk, swinging a litre bottle round his head and yelling: "Out! Out! Out, all of you! Out, every one of you! I am proprietor here. And when I want to clear my house I clear my house. Every man obeys—who doesn't obey has his brains knocked out with this bottle. Out, out, I say—Out, everyone!" And the men all cleared out. "But," said the bus-driver, "I told him that when I had paid for my bed I was going to sleep in it. I was not going to be turned out by him or anybody. And so he came down."

There was a little silence from everybody after this story. Evidently there was more to it that we were not to be told. Especially the carabiniere was silent. He was a fat, not very brave fellow, though quite nice.

Ah, but—said the little dark bus-conductor, with his small-featured swarthy Greek face—you must not be angry with them. True the inn was very bad. Very bad—but you must pity them, for they are only ignorant. Poor things, they are *ignoranti!* Why be angry?

The other two men nodded their heads in agreement and repeated *ignoranti*. They are *ignoranti*. It is true. Why be angry?

And here the modern Italian spirit came out: the endless pity for the ignorant. It is only slackness. The pity makes the ignorant more ignorant, and makes the Risveglio daily more impossible. If somebody let a bottle buzz round the ears of the dirty-breast, and whipped the shawl from the head of the pert young madam and sent her flying down the tunnel with a flea in her ear, We might get some attention and they might find a little self-respect. But no: pity them, poor *ignoranti,* while they pull life down and devour it like vermin. Pity them! What they need is not pity but prods: they and all their myriad of likes.

The be-shawled appeared with a dish of kid. Needless to say, the *ignoranti* had kept all the best portions for themselves. What arrived was five pieces of cold roast, one for each of us. Mine was a sort of large comb of ribs with a thin web of meat: perhaps an ounce. That was all we got, after watching the whole process. There was moreover a dish of strong boiled cauliflower, which one ate, with the coarse bread, out of sheer hunger. After this a bilious orange. Simply one is not *fed* nowadays. In the good hotels and in the bad, one is given paltry portions of unnourishing food, and one goes unfed.

The bus-driver, the only one with an earnest soul, was talking of the Sardinians. Ah, the Sardinians! They were hopeless. Why—because they did not know how to strike. They, too, were *ignoranti*. But this form of ignorance he found more annoying. They simply did not know what a strike was. If you offered them one day ten francs a stint—he was speaking now of the miners of the Iglesias region.— No, no, no, they would not take it, they wanted twelve francs. Go to them the next day and offer them four francs for half a stint, and yes, yes, they would take it. And there they were: ignorant—ignorant Sardinians. They absolutely did not know how to strike. He was quite sarcastically hot about it. The whole tone of these three young men was the tone of sceptical irony common to the young people of our day the world over. Only they had—or at least the driver had— some little fervour for his strikes and his socialism. But it was a pathetic fervour: a *pis-aller* fervour.

We talked about the land. The war has practically gutted Sardinia of her cattle: so they said. And now the land is being deserted, the arable land is going back to fallow. Why? Why, says the driver, because the owners of the land won't spend any capital. They have got the capital locked up, and the land is dead. They find it cheaper to let all the arable go back to fallow, and raise a few head of cattle, rather than to pay high wages, grow corn and get small returns.

Yes, and also, chimes in the carabiniere, the peasants don't want to work the land. They hate the land. They'll do anything to get off the land. They want regular wages, short hours, and devil take the rest. So they will go into France as navvies, by the hundred. They flock to Rome, they besiege the labour bureaux, they will do the artificial Government navvy work at a miserable five francs a day—a railway shunter having at least eighteen francs a day—anything, anything rather than work the land.

Yes, and what does the Government do? replies the bus-driver. They pull the roads to pieces in order to find work for the unemployed, remaking them, across the campagna. But in Sardinia, where roads and bridges are absolutely wanting, will they do anything? No!

There it is, however. The bus-driver, with dark shadows under his eyes, represents the intelligent portion of the conversation. The carabiniere is soft and will go any way, though always with some interest. The little Greek-looking conductor just does not care.

Enters another belated traveller, and takes a seat at the end of the table. The be-shawled brings him soup and a skinny bit of kid. He eyes this last with contempt, and fetches out of his bag a large hunk of roast pork, and bread, and black olives, thus proceeding to make a proper meal.

We being without cigarettes, the bus-driver and his companion press them on us: their beloved Macedonia cigarettes. The driver says they are *squisitissimi*—most, most exquisite— so exquisite that all foreigners want them. In truth I believe they are exported to Germany now. And they are quite good, when they really have tobacco in them. Usually they are hollow tubes of paper which just flare away under one's nose and are done.

We decided to have a round drink: they choose the precious *aqua vitae:* the white sort I think. At last it arrives—when the little dark-eyed one has fetched it. And it tastes rather like sweetened petroleum, with a dash of aniseed: filthy. Most Italian liquors are now sweet and filthy.

At length we rise to go to bed. We shall all meet in the morning. And this room is dead cold, with frost outside. Going. out we glance into the famous stanza. One figure alone lies stretched on the floor in the almost complete darkness. A few embers still glow. The other men no doubt are in the bar.

Ah, the filthy bedroom. The q-b ties up her head in a large, clean white kerchief, to avoid contact with the unsavoury pillow. It is a cold, hard, flat bed, with two cold, hard, flat blankets. But we are very tired. Just as we are going to sleep, however, weird, high-pitched singing starts below, very uncanny—with a refrain that is a yelp-yelp-yelp! almost like a dog in angry pain. Weird, almost gruesome, this singing goes on, first one voice and then another and then a tangle of voices. Again we are roused by the pounding of heavy feet on the corridor outside, which is as hollow and resonant as a drum. And then in the infernal crew-yard outside a cock crows. Throughout the night—yea, through all the black and frosty hours this demoniac bird screams its demon griefs.

However, it is morning. I gingerly wash a bit of myself in the broken basin, and dry that bit on a muslin veil which masquerades upon the chair as a towel. The q-b contents herself with a dry wipe. And we go downstairs in hopes of the last night's milk.

There is no one to be seen. It is a cold, frost-strong, clear morning. There is no one in the bar. We stumble down, the dark tunnel passage. The stanza is as if no man had ever set foot in it: very dark, the mats against the wall, the fireplace grey with a handful of long dead ash. Just like a dungeon. The dining-room has the same long table and eternal tablecloth—and our serviettes, still wet, lying where we shovelled them aside. So back again to the bar.

And this time a man is drinking *aqua vitae,* and the dirty-shirt is officiating. He has no hat on: and extraordinary, he has no brow at all: just flat, straight black hair slanting to his eyebrows, no forehead at all.

Is there coffee?

No, there is no coffee.

Why?

Because they can't get sugar.

Ho! laughs the peasant drinking *aqua vitae.* You make coffee with sugar!

Here, say I, they make it with nothing.—Is there milk?

No.

No milk at all?,

No.

Why not?

Nobody brings it.

Yes, yes—there is milk if they like to get it, puts in the peasant. But they want you to drink *aqua vitae.*

I see myself drinking *aqua vitae.* My yesterday's rage towers up again suddenly, till it quite suffocates me. There is something in this unsavoury, black, wine-dabbled, thick, greasy young man that does for me.

"Why," say I, lapsing into the Italian rhetorical manner, "why do you keep an inn? Why do you write the word Ristorante so large, when you have nothing to offer people, and don't intend to have anything? Why do you have the impudence to take in travellers? What does it mean, that this is an inn? What, say, what does it mean? Say then—what does it mean? What does it mean, your Ristorante Risveglio, written so large?"

Getting all this out in one breath, my indignation now stifled me. He of the shirt said nothing at all. The peasant laughed. I demanded the bill. It was twenty-five francs odd. I picked up every farthing of the change.

"Won't you leave any tip at all?" asks the q-b.

"Tip!" say I, speechless.

So we march upstairs and make tea to fill the thermos flask. Then, with sack over my shoulder, I make my way out of the Risveglio.

It is Sunday morning. The frozen village street is almost empty. We march down to the wider space where the bus stands: I hope they haven't the impudence to call it a Piazza.

"Is this the Nuoro bus?" I ask a bunch of urchins.

And even they begin to jeer. But my sudden upstarting flare quenches them at once. One answers yes, and they edge away. I stow the sack and the kitchenino in the first-class part. The first-class is in front: we shall see better.

There are men standing about, with their hands in their pockets,—those who are not in costume. Some wear the black-and-white. All wear the stocking-caps. And all have the wide shirt-breasts, white, their waistcoats being just like evening dress waistcoats. Imagine one of these soft white shirt fronts well slobbered, and you have mine host of the Risveglio. But these lounging, static, white-breasted men are snowily clean, this being Sunday morning. They smoke their pipes on the .frosty air, and are none too friendly.

The bus starts at half-past nine. The campanile is clanging nine. Two or three girls go down the road in their Sunday costume of purplish brown. We go up the road, into the clear, ringing frosty air, to find the lane.

And again, from above, how beautiful it is in the sharp morning! The whole village lies in bluish shadow, the hills with their thin pale oak-trees are in bluish shadow still, only in the distance the frost-glowing sun makes a wonderful, jewel-like radiance on the pleasant hills, wild and thinly wooded, of this interior region. Real fresh wonder-beauty all around. And such humanity.

Returning to the village we find a little shop and get biscuits and cigarettes. And we find our friends the bus-men. They are shy this morning. They are ready for us when we are ready. So in we get, joyfully to leave Sorgono.

One thing I say for it, it must be an honest place. For people leave their sacks about without a qualm.

Up we go, up the road. Only to stop, alas, at the Risveglio. The little conductor goes down the lane towards the station. The driver goes and has a little drink with a comrade. There is quite a crowd round the dreary entrances of the inn. And quite a little bunch of people to clamber up into the second class, behind us.

We wait and wait. Then in climbs an old peasant, in full black-and-white costume, smiling in the pleased, naïve way of the old. After him climbs a fresh-faced young man with a suit-case.

"Na!" said the young man. "Now you are in the automobile."

And the old man gazes round with the wondering, vacant, naïve smile.

"One is all right here, eh?" the young citizen persists, patronising.

But the old man is too excited to answer. He gazes hither and thither. Then he suddenly remembers he had a parcel, and looks for it in fear. The bright-faced young man picks it from the floor and hands it him. Ah, it is all right.

I see the little conductor in his dashing, sheep-lined, short military overcoat striding briskly down the little lane with the post-bag. The driver climbs to his seat in front of me. He has a muffler round his neck and his hat pulled down to his ears. He pips at the horn, and our old peasant cranes forward to look how he does it.

And so, with a jerk and a spurt, we start uphill.

"Eh—what's that?" said the peasant, frightened.

"We're starting," explained the bright-faced young man.

"Starting! Didn't we start before?" The bright face laughs pleasedly.

"No," he said. "Did you think we had been going since you got in?"

"Yes," says the old man, simply, "since the door shut."

The young citizen looks at us for our joyful approval.

CHAPTER VI

TO NUORQ

THESE automobiles in Italy are splendid. They take the steep, looping roads so easily, they seem to run so naturally. And this one was comfortable too.

The roads of Italy always impress me. They run undaunted over the most precipitous regions, and with curious ease. In England almost any such road, among the mountains at least, would be labelled three times dangerous and would be famous throughout the land as an impossible climb. Here it is nothing. Up and down they go, swinging about with complete sangfroid. There, seems to have been no effort in their construction. They are so good, naturally, that one hardly notices what splendid gestures they represent. Of course, the surface is now often intolerably bad. And they are most of them roads which, with ten years' neglect, will become ruins. For they are cut through overhanging rock and scooped out of the sides of hills. But I think it is marvellous how the Italians have penetrated all their inaccessible regions, of which they have so many, with great high-roads: and how along these high-roads the omnibuses now keep up a perfect communication. The precipitous and craggily-involved land is threaded through and through with roads. There seems to be a passion for high-roads and for constant communication. In this the Italians have a real Roman instinct, *now*. For the roads are new

The railways, too, go piercing through rock for miles and miles, and nobody thinks anything of it. The coast railway of Calabrja, down to Reggio, would make us stand on our heads if we had it in England. Here it is a matter of course. In the same way I always have a profound admiration for their driving—whether of a great omnibus or of a motor-car.

It all seems so easy, as if. the man were part of the car. There is none of that beastly grinding, uneasy feeling one has in the north. A car behaves like a smooth, live thing, sensibly.

All the peasants have a passion for a high-road. They want their land opening out, opening out. They seem to hate the ancient Italian remoteness. They all want to be able to get out at a moment's notice, to get away—quick, quick. A village which is two miles off the high-road, even if it is perched like a hawk's nest on a peak, still chafes and chafes for the great road to come to it, chafes and chafes for the daily motor-bus connection with the railway. There is no placidity, no rest in the heart of the land. There is a fever of restless irritation all the time.

And yet the permanent way of almost every railway is falling into bad disrepair; the roads are shocking. And nothing seems to be done. Is our. marvellous mechanical era going to have so short a bloom? Is the marvellous openness, the opened-out wonder of the land going to collapse quite soon, and the remote places lapse back into inaccessibility again? Who knows! I rather hope so.

The automobile took us rushing and winding up the hill, sometimes through cold, solid-seeming shadow, sometimes' across a patch of sun. There was thin bright ice in the ruts, and deep grey hoar-frost on the grass. I cannot tell how the sight of the grass and bushes, heavy with frost and wild—in their own primitive wildness—charmed me. The slopes of the steep wild hills came down shaggy and bushy, with a few berries lingering, and the long grass stalks sere with the frost. Again, the dark valley, sank below like a ravine, but shaggy, bosky, unbroken. It came upon me how I loved the sight of the blue-shadowed, tawny-tangled winter with its frosty standstill. The young oaks keep their brown leaves. And doing so, surely they are best with a thin edge of rime.

One begins to realise how old the real Italy is, how man-gripped and how withered. England is far more wild and savage and lonely, in her country parts. Here since endless centuries man has tamed the impossible mountain-side into terraces, he has quarried the rock, he has fed his sheep among the thin woods, he has cut his boughs and burnt his charcoal, he has been half domesticated even among the wildest fastnesses. This is what is so attractive about the remote places, the Abruzzi, for example. Life is so primitive, so pagan, so strangely heathen and half-savage. And yet it is human life. And the wildest country is half humanized, half brought under. It is all conscious. Wherever one is in Italy, either one is conscious of the present, or of the mediæval influences, or of the far, mysterious gods of the early Mediterranean. Wherever one is, the place has its conscious genius. Man has lived there and brought forth his consciousness there and in some way brought that place to consciousness, given it its expression, and, really, finished it. The expression may be Proserpine, or Pan, or even the strange "shrouded gods" of the Etruscans or the Sikels, none the less it is an expression. The land has been humanized, through and through: and we in our own tissued consciousness bear the results of this humanization. So that for us to go to Italy and to *penetrate* into Italy is like a most fascinating act of self-discovery— back, back down the old ways of time. Strange and wonderful chords awake in us, and vibrate again after many hundreds of years of complete forgetfulness.

And then—and then—there is a final feeling of sterility. It is all worked out. It is all known: *connu, connu!*

This Sunday morning, seeing the frost among the tangled, still savage bushes of Sardinia, my soul thrilled again. This was not all known. This was not all worked out. Life was not only a process of rediscovering backwards, It is that, also; and it is that intensely. Italy has given me back I know not what of myself, but a very, very great deal. She has found for me so much that was lost: like a restored Osiris. But this morning in the omnibus I realise that, apart from the great rediscovery backwards, which one *must* make before one can be whole at all, there is a move forwards. There are unknown, unworked lands where the salt has not lost its savour. But one must have perfected oneself in the great past first.

If one travels one eats. We immediately began to munch biscuits, and the old peasant in his white baggy breeches and black cuirass, his old face smiling wonderingly under his old stocking-cap, although he was only going to Tonara, some seven or eight miles, began to peel himself a hard-boiled egg, which he got out of his parcel. With calm wastefulness he peeled away the biggest part of the white of the egg with the shelf—because it came away so. The citizen of Nuoro, for such the bright-faced young man was, said to him: "But see how you waste it."—"Ha!" said the old peasant, with a reckless indifferent wave of the hand. What did he care how much he wasted since he was *en voyage* and riding for the first time in his life in an automobile.

The citizen of Nuoro told us he had some sort of business in Sorgono, so he came back and forth constantly. The peasant did some work or other for him—or brought him something down from Tonara. He was a pleasant, bright-eyed young man, and he made nothing of eight hours in a motor-bus.

He told us there was still game among these hills: wild boars which were hunted in big hunts, and many hares. It was a curious and beautiful sight, he said, to see a hare at night fascinated by the flare of the lamps of the automobile, racing ahead with its ears back, always keeping in front, inside the beam, and flying like mad, on and on ahead, till at some hill it gathered speed and melted into the dark.

We descended into a deep narrow valley, to the road-junction and the canteen house, then up again, up and up sharp to Tonara, our village we had seen in the sun yesterday. But we were approaching it from the back. As we swerved into the sunlight, the road took a long curve on to the open ridge between two valleys. And there in front we saw a glitter of scarlet and white. It was in slow motion. It was a far-off procession, scarlet figures of women, and a tall image moving away from us, slowly, in the Sunday morning. It was passing along the level sunlit ridge above a deep, hollow valley. A close procession of women glittering in scarlet, white and black, moving slowly in the distance beneath the grey-yellow buildings of the village on the crest, towards an isolated old church: and all along this narrow upland saddle as on a bridge of sunshine itself.

Were we not going to see any more? The bus turned and rushed along the now level road and then veered. And there beyond, a little below, we saw the procession *coming*. The bus faded to a standstill, and we climbed out. Above us, old and mellowed among the smooth rocks and the bits of flat grass, was the church, tanging its bell. Just in front, above, were old half-broken houses of stone. The road came gently winding up to us, from what was evidently two villages ledged one above the other upon the steep summit of the south slope. Far below was the south valley, with a white puff of engine steam.

And slowly chanting in the near distance, curving slowly up to us on the white road between the grass, came the procession. The high morning was still. We stood all on this ridge above the world, with the deeps of silence below on the right. And in a strange, brief, staccato monody chanted the men, and in quick, light rustle of women's voices came the responses. Again the men's voices! The white was mostly men, not women. The priest in his robes, his boys near him, was leading the chanting. Immediately behind him came a small cluster of bare-headed, tall, sunburnt men all in golden-velveteen corduroy, mountain peasants, bowing beneath a great life-size seated image of Saint Anthony of Padua. After these a number of men in the costume, but with the white linen breeches hanging wide and loose almost to the ankles, instead of being tucked into the black gaiters. So they seemed very white beneath the black kilt frill. The black frieze body-vest was cut low, like an evening suit, and the stocking-caps were variously perched. The men chanted in low, hollow, melodic tones. Then came the rustling chime of the women. And the procession crept slowly, aimlessly forward in time with the chant. The great image rode rigid, and rather foolish.

After the men was a little gap—and then the brilliant wedge of the women. They were packed two by two, close on each other's heels, chanting inadvertently when their turn came, and all in brilliant, beautiful costume. In front were the little girl-children, two by two, immediately following the tall men in peasant black-and-white. Children demure and conventional, in vermilion, white and green—little girl-children with long skirts of scarlet cloth down to their feet, green-banded near the bottom: with white aprons bordered with vivid green and mingled colour: having little scarlet, purple-bound, open boleros over the full white skirts: and black head-cloths folded across their little chins, just leaving the lips clear, the face framed in black. Wonderful little girl-children, perfect and demure in the stiffish, brilliant costume, with black head-dress! Stiff as Velasquez princesses! The bigger girls followed, and then the mature women, a close procession. The long vermilion skirts

158

with their green bands at the bottom flashed a solid moving mass of colour, softly swinging, and the white aprons with their bands of brilliant mingled green seemed to gleam. At the throat the full-bosomed white shirts were fastened with big studs of gold filigree, two linked filigree globes: and the great white sleeves billowed from the scarlet, purplish-and-green-edged boleros. The faces came nearer to us, framed all round in the dark cloths. All the lips still sang responses, but all the eyes watched us. So the softly-swaying coloured body of the procession came up to us. The poppy-scarlet smooth cloth rocked in fusion, the bands and bars of emerald green seemed to burn across the red and the showy white, the dark eyes peered and stared at us from under the black snood, gazed back at us with raging curiosity, while the lips moved automatically in chant. The bus had run into the inner side of the road, and the procession had to press round it, towards the sky-line, the great valley lying below.

The priest stared, hideous St. Anthony cockled a bit as he passed the butt end of the big grey automobile, the peasant men in gold-coloured corduroy, old, washed soft, were sweating under the load and still singing with opened lips, the loose white breeches of the men waggled as they walked on with their hands behind their backs, turning again, to look at us. The big, hard hands, folded behind black kilt-frill! The women, too, shuffled slowly past, rocking the scarlet and the bars of green, and all twisting as they sang, to look at us still more. And so the procession edged past the bus, and was trailing upwards, curved solid against the sky-line towards the old church. From behind, the geranium scarlet was intense; one saw the careful, curiously cut backs of the shapen boleros, poppy-red, edged with mauve-purple and green, and the white of the shirt just showing at the waist. The full sleeves billowed out, the black head-cloths hung down to a point. The pleated skirts swung slowly, the broad band of green accentuating the motion. Indeed that is what it must be for, this thick, rich band of jewel green, to throw the wonderful horizontal motion back and forth, back and forth, of the suave vermilion, and give that static, Demeter splendour to a peasant motion, so magnificent in colour, geranium and malachite.

All the costumes were not exactly alike. Some had more green, some had less. In some the sleeveless boleros were of a darker red, and some had poorer aprons, without such gorgeous bands at the bottom. And some were evidently old; probably thirty years old: still perfect and in keeping, reserved for Sunday and high holidays. A few were darker, ruddier than the true vermilion. This varying of the tone intensified the beauty of the shuffling woman-host.

When they had filed into the grey, forlorn little church on the ridge-top just above us, the bus started silently to run on to the rest-point below, whilst we climbed back up the little rock-track to the church. When we came to the side-door we found the church quite full. Level with us as we stood in the open side doorway, we saw kneeling on the bare stone flags the little girl-children, and behind them all the women clustered kneeling upon their aprons, with hands negligently folded, filling the church to the further doorway, where the sun shone: the bigger west-end doorway. In the shadow of the whitewashed, bare church all these kneeling women with their colour and their black head-cloths looked like some thick bed of flowers, geranium, black-hooded above. They all knelt on the naked, solid stone of the pavement.

There was a space in front of the geranium little girl-children, then the men in corduroys, gold-soft, with dark round heads, kneeling awkwardly in reverence; and then the queer, black cuirasses and, full white sleeves of grey-headed peasant men, many bearded. Then just in front of them the priest in his white vestment, standing exposed, and just baldly beginning an address. At the side of the altar was seated, large and important, the modern,

159

simpering, black-gowned Anthony of Padua, nursing a boy-child. He looked a sort of male Madonna.

"Now," the priest was saying, "blessed Saint Anthony shows you in what way you can be Christians. It is not enough that you are not Turks. Some think they are Christians because they are not Turks. It is true you are none, of you Turks. But you have still to learn how to be good Christians. And this you can learn from our blessed Saint Anthony. Saint Anthony, etc., etc. . .

The contrast between Turks and Christians is still forceful in the Mediterranean, where the Mohammedans have left such a mark. But how the word *cristiani, cristiani,* spoken with a peculiar priestly unction, gets on my nerves. The voice is barren in its homily. And the women are all intensely watching the q-b and me in the doorway, their folded hands are very negligently held together,

"Come away!" say I. "Come away, and let them listen."

We left the church crowded with its kneeling host, and dropped down past the broken houses towards the omnibus, which stood on a sort of level outlook place, a levelled terrace with a few trees, standing silent over the valley. It should be picketed with soldiers having arquebuses. And I should have welcomed a few thorough-paced infidels, as a leaven to this dreary Christianity of ours.

But it was a wonderful place. Usually, the life-level is reckoned as sea-level. But here, in the heart of Sardinia, the life-level is high as the golden-lit plateau, and the sea-level is somewhere far away, below, in the gloom, it does not signify. The life-level is high up, high and sun-sweetened and among rocks.

We stood and looked below, at the puff of steam, far down the wooded valley where we had come, yesterday. There was an old, low house on this eagle-perching piazza. I would like to live there. The real village—or rather two villages, like an ear-ring and its pendant—lay still beyond, in front, ledging near the summit of the long, long steep wooded slope that never ended till it ran flush to the depths away below there in shadow.

And yesterday, up this slope the old peasant had come with his two brilliant daughters and the pack-pony.

And somewhere in those ledging, pearly villages in front must be my girovago and his "wife." I wish I could see their stall and drink *aqua vitae* with them.

"How beautiful the procession!" says the q-b to the driver.

"Ah yes—one of the most beautiful costumes of Sardinia, this of Tonara," he replied wistfully.

The bus sets off again—minus the old peasant. 'We retrace our road. A woman is leading a bay pony past the church,. striding with long strides, so that her maroon skirt swings like a fan, and hauling the halter rope. Apparently the geranium-red costume is Sunday only, the week-day is this maroon, or puce, or madder-brown.

Quickly and easily the bus slips down the hill into the valley. Wild, narrow valleys, with trees, and brown-legged cork-trees. Across the other side a black-and-white peasant is working alone on a tiny terrace of the hillside, a small solitary figure, for all the world like a magpie in the distance. These people like being alone——solitary——one sees a single creature so often isolated among the wilds. This is different from Sicily and Italy, where the people simply cannot be alone They *must* be in twos and threes.

But it is Sunday morning, and the worker is exceptional. Along the road we pass various pedestrians, men in their black sheepskins, boys in their soldiers' remains. They are trudging from one village to another, across the wild valleys. And there is a sense of

160

Sunday morning freedom, of roving, as in an English countryside. Only the one old peasant works alone: and a goat-herd watching his long-haired, white goats.

Beautiful the goats are: and so swift. They fly like white shadows along the road from us, then dart down-hill. I see one standing on the bough of an oak-tree, right in the tree, an enormous white tree-creature complacently munching up aloft, then rearing on her hind legs, so lengthy, and putting her slim paws far away on an upper, forward branch.

Whenever we come to a village we stop and get down, and our little conductor disappears into the post office for the post bag. This last is usually a limp affair, containing about three letters. The people crowd around—and many of them in very ragged costume. They look poor, and not attractive: perhaps a bit degenerate. It would seem as if the Italian instinct to get into rapid touch with the world were the healthy instinct after all. For in these isolated villages, which have been since time began far from any life-centre, there is an almost sordid look on the faces of the people. We must remember that the motor-bus is a great innovation. It has been running for five weeks only. I wonder for how many months it will continue.

For I am sure it cannot pay. Our first-class tickets cost, I believe, about twenty-seven francs each. The second-class costs about three-quarters the first. Some parts of the journey we were very few passengers. The distance covered is so great, the population so thin, that even granted the passion for getting out of their own villages, which possesses all people now, still the bus cannot earn much more than an average of two hundred to three hundred francs a day. Which, with two men's wages, and petrol at its enormous price, and the cost of wear-and-tear, cannot possibly pay.

I asked the driver. He did not tell me what his wages were: I did not ask him. But he said the company paid for the keep and lodging for himself and mate at the stopping-places. This being Sunday, fewer people were travelling: a statement hard to believe. Once he had carried fifty people all the way from Tonara to Nuoro. Once! But it was in vain he protested. Ah, well, he said, the bus carried the post, and the Government paid a subsidy of so many thousands of lire a year: a goodly number. Apparently then the Government was the loser as usual. And there are hundreds if not thousands of these omnibuses running in the lonely districts of Italy and Sicily—Sardinia had a network of systems. They are splendid—and they are perhaps an absolute necessity for a nervous, restless population which simply cannot keep still, and which finds some relief in being whirled about even on the *autovie*, as the bus-system is called.

The autovie are run by private companies, only subsidized by the Government.

On we rush through the morning—and at length see a large village, high on the summit beyond, stony on the high upland. But it has a magical look, as these tiny summit-cities have from the distance. They recall to me always my childish visions of Jerusalem, high against the air, and seeming to sparkle, and built in sharp cubes.

It is curious what a difference there is between the high, fresh, proud villages and the valley villages. Those that crown the world have a bright flashing air, as Tonara had. Those that lie down below, infolded in the shadow, have a gloomy, sordid feeling and a repellent population, like Sorgono and other places at which we had halted. The judgment may be all wrong: but this was the impression I got.

We were now at the highest point of the journey. The men we saw on the road were in their sheepskins, and some were even walking with their faces shawl-muffled. Glancing back, we saw up the valley clefts the snow of Gennargentu once more, a white mantle on broad shoulders, the very core of Sardinia. The bus slid to a standstill in a high valley, beside a stream where the road from Fonni joined ours. There was waiting a youth with a bicycle. I would like to go to Fonni. They say it is the highest village in Sardinia.

In front, on the broad summit, reared the towers of Gavoi. This was the half-way halt, where the buses had their *coincidenza,* and where we would stay for an hour and eat. We wound up and up the looping road, and at last entered the village. Women came to the doors to look. They were wearing the dark madder-brown costume. Men were hastening, smoking their pipes, towards our stopping place.

We saw the other bus—a little crowd of people—and we drew up at last. We were tired and hungry. We were at the door of the inn, and we entered quickly. And in an instant, what a. difference! At the clean little bar men were drinking cheerfully. A side door led into the common room. And how charming it was. In a very wide chimney, white and stone-clean, with a lovely shallow curve above, was burning a fire of long, clean-split faggots, laid horizontally on the dogs. A clean, clear bright fire, with odd little chairs in front, very low, for us to sit on. The funny, low little chairs- seem a speciality of this region.

The floor of this room was paved with round dark pebbles, beautifully clean. On the walls hung brilliant copper pans, glittering against the whitewash. And under the long, horizontal window that looked on the street was a stone slab with sockets for little charcoal fires. The curve of the chimney. arch was wide and shallow, the curve above the window was still wider, and of a. similar delicate shallowness, the white roof rose delicately vaulted. With the glitter of copper, the expanse of dark, rose-coloured, pebbled floor, the space, the few low, clean-gleaming faggots, it was really beautiful. We sat and warmed ourselves, welcomed by a plump hostess and a pleasant daughter, both in madder-brown dress and full white shirt. People strayed in and out, through the various doors. The houses are built without any plan at all, the rooms just happening, here or there. A bitch came from an inner darkness and stood looking at the fire, then looked up at me, smiling in her bitch-like, complacent fashion.

But we were dying with hunger. What was there to eat?—and was it nearly ready? There was *cinghiale,* the pleasant-hard-cheeked girl told us, and it was nearly ready. *Cinghiale* being wild boar, we sniffed the air. The girl kept tramping rather fecklessly back and forth, with a plate or a serviette; and at last it was served. We went through the dark inner place, which was apparently the windowless bit left over, inside, when the haphazard rooms were made round about, and thence into a large, bare, darkish pebbled room with a white table and inverted soup-plates. It was deathly cold. The window looked north over the wintry landscape, of the highlands, fields, stone walls and rocks. Ah, the cold, motionless air of the room.

But we were quite a party: the second bus-driver and his mate, a bearded traveller on the second bus, with his daughter, ourselves, the bright-faced citizen from Nuoro, and our driver. Our little dark-eyed conductor did not come. It dawned on me later he could not afford to pay for this meal, which was not included in his wage.

The Nuoro citizen conferred with our driver—who looked tired round the eyes—and made the girl produce a tin of sardines. These were opened at table with a large pocket-knife belonging to the second conductor. He was a reckless, odd, hot-foot fellow whom I liked very much. But I was terrified at the way he carved the sardine-box with his jack-knife. However, we could eat and drink.

Then came the *brodo,* the broth, in a great bowl. This was boiling hot and very, very strong. It was perfectly plain, strong meat-stock, without vegetables. But how good and invigorating it was, and what an abundance! We drank it down, and ate the good, cold bread.

162

Then came the boar itself. Alas, it was a bowl of hunks of dark, rather coarse boiled meat, from which the broth had been made. It was quite dry, without fat. I should have been very puzzled to know what meat it was, if I had not been told. Sad that the wild boar should have received so little culinary attention. However, we ate the hunks of hot, dry meat with bread, and were glad to get them. They were filling at least. And there was a bowl of rather bitter green olives for a condiment.

The Nuoro citizen now produced a huge bottle of wine, which he said was *finissimo,* and refused to let us go on with the dark wine on the table, of which every guest was served with a bottle. So we drank up, and were replenished with the redder, lighter, finer Sorgono wine. It was very good.

The second bus-conductor also did not eat the inn meal. He produced a vast piece of bread, good, home-made bread, and at least half of a roast lamb, and a large paper of olives. This lamb he insisted on sending round the table, waving his knife and fork with dramatic gestures at every guest, insisting that every guest should take a hunk. So one by one we all helped ourselves to the extraordinarily good cold roast lamb and to the olives. Then the bus-conductor fell to as well. There was a mass of meat still left to him.

It is extraordinary bow generous and, from the inside, well-bred these men were. To be sure the second conductor waved his knife and fork and made bitter faces if one of us took only a little bit of the lamb. He wanted us to take more. But the *essential* courtesy in all of them was quite perfect, so manly and utterly simple. Just the same with the q-b. They treated her with a sensitive, manly simplicity, which one could but be thankful for. They made none of the odious politenesses which are so detestable in well-brought-up people. They made no advances and did none of the hateful homage of the adulating male. They were quiet, and kind, and sensitive to the natural flow of life, and quite without airs. I liked them extremely. Men who can be quietly kind and simple to a woman, without wanting to show off or to make an impression, they are men still. They were neither humble nor conceited. They did not show off. And oh, God, what a blessed relief, to be with people who don't bother to show off. We sat at that table quietly and naturally as if we were by ourselves, and talked or listened to their talk, just as it had happened. When we did not want to talk, they took no notice of us. And that I call good manners. Middle-class, showing off people would have found them uncouth. I found them almost the only really well-bred people I have met. They did not show off in any way at all, not even a show of simplicity. They knew that in the beginning and in the end a man stands alone, his soul is alone in itself, and all attributes are nothing—and this curious final knowledge preserved them, in simplicity.

When we had had coffee and were going out, I found our own conductor in a little chair by the fire. He was looking a bit pathetic. I had enough sense to give him coffee, which brightened him. But it was not till afterwards, putting things together, that I realised he had wanted to be with us all at table, but that his conductor's wages probably did not allow him to spend the money. My bill for the dinner was about fifteen francs for the two of us.

In the bus again, we were quite crowded. A peasant girl in Nuoro costume sat facing me, and a dark-bearded, middle-aged man in a brown velveteen suit was next me and glowering at her. He was evidently her husband. I did not like him: one of the jealous, carping sort. She, in her way, was handsome: but a bit of a devil as well, in all probability. There were two village women become fine, in town dress and black silk scarves over their heads, fancying themselves. Then there was a wild scuffle, and three bouncing village lasses were pushed in, laughing and wild with excitement. There were wild farewells, and the bus rolled out of Gavoi between the desolate mountain fields and the rocks, on a sort of tableland. We rolled on for a mile or so: then stopped, and the excited lasses got down. I gathered they had been given a little ride for a Sunday treat. Delighted they were. And they set off, with other bare-headed women in costume, along a bare path between flat, out-cropping rocks and cold fields.

The girl facing me was a study. She was not more than twenty years old I should say: or was she? Did the delicate and fine complication of lines against her eyes mean thirty-five? But anyhow she was the wife of the velveteen man. He was thick-set and had white hairs in his coarse black beard, and little, irritable brown eyes under his irritable brows. He watched her all the time. Perhaps, she was after all a young, new girl-wife. She sat with that expressionless look of one who is watched and appears not to know it. She had her back to the engine.

She wore her black head-cloth from her brow and her hair was taken tight back from her rather hard, broad, well-shaped forehead. Her dark eyebrows were very finely drawn above her large, dark-grey, pellucid eyes, but they were drawn with a peculiar obstinate and irritating lift. Her nose was straight and small, her mouth well shut. And her big, rather hostile eyes had a withheld look in them, obstinate. Yet, being newly wed and probably newly awakened, her eyes looked sometimes at me with a provoking look, curious as to. what I was in the husband line, challenging rather defiantly with her new secrets, obstinate in opposition to the male authority, and yet intrigued by the very fact that one was man. The velveteen husband—his velveteens too had gone soft and gold-faded, yet somehow they made him look ugly, common—he watched her with, his irritable, yellow-brown eyes, and seemed to fume in his stiff beard.

She wore the costume: the full-gathered shirt fastened at the throat with the two gold filigree globes, a little dark, braided, stiff bolero just fastened at the waist, leaving a pretty pattern of white breast, and a dark maroon skirt. As the bus rushed along she turned somewhat pale, with the obstinate pinched look of a woman who is in opposition to her man. At length she flung him a few words which I did not catch—and her forehead seemed to go harder, as she drooped her lashes occasionally over her wide, alert, obstinate, rather treacherous eyes. She must have been a difficult piece of goods to deal with. And she sat with her knees touching mine, rocking against mine as the bus swayed.

We came to a village on the road: the landscape had now become wider, much more open. At the inn door the bus stopped, and the velveteen husband and the girl got down. It was cold—but in a minute I got down too. The bus-conductor, came to me and asked anxiously if the q-b were ill. The q-b said no, why? Because there was a signora whom the motion of the bus made ill. This was the girl.

There was a crowd and a great row at this inn. In the second dark room, which was bare of furniture, a man sat in a corner playing an accordion. Men in the close breeches were dancing together. Then they fell to wrestling wildly, crashing about among the others, with shouts and yells. Men in the black-and-white, but untidy, with the wide white drawers left hanging out over the black gaiters, surged here and there. All were rowdy with drink. This again was rather a squalid inn but roaring with violent, crude male life.

The Nuoro citizen said that here was very good wine, and we must try it. I did not want it, but he insisted. So we drank little glasses of merely moderate red wine. The sky had gone all grey with the afternoon curd-clouds. It was very cold and raw. Wine is no joy, cold, dead wine, in such an atmosphere.

The Nuoro, citizen insisted on paying. He would let me pay, he said, when he came to England. In him, and in our bus men, the famous Sardinian hospitality and generosity still lingers.

When the bus ran on again the q-b told the peasant girl, who again had the pinched look, to change places with me and sit with her face to the engine. This the young woman did, with that rather hard assurance common to these women. But at the next stop she got down, and made the conductor come with us into the compartment, whilst she sat in front between the driver and the citizen of Nuoro. That was what she wanted all the time. Now she was all right. She had her back to the velveteen husband, she sat close between two strange young men, who were condoling, with her. And Velveteens eyed her back, and his little eyes went littler and more pin-pointed, and his nose seemed to curl with irritation.

The costumes had changed again. There was again the scarlet, but no green. The green had given place to mauve and rose. The women in one cold, stony, rather humbled broken place were most brilliant. They had the geranium skirts, but their sleeveless boleros were made to curl out strangely from the waist, and they were edged with a puckered rose-pink, a broad edge, with lines of mauve and lavender. As they went up between the houses that were dark and grisly under the blank, cold sky, it is amazing how these women of vermilion and rose-pink seemed to melt into an almost impossible blare of colour. What a risky blend of colours! Yet how superb it could look, that dangerous hard assurance of these women as they strode along so blaring. I would not like to tackle one of them.

Wider and colder the landscape grew. As we topped a hill at the end of a village, we saw a long string of wagons, each with a pair of oxen, and laden with large sacks curving upwards in the cold, pallid Sunday afternoon. Seeing us, the procession came to a standstill at the curve of the road, and the pale oxen, the pale low wagons, the pale full sacks, all in the blenched light, each one headed by a tall man in shirt sleeves, trailing a static procession on the hillside, seemed like a vision: like a Doré drawing. The bus slid past, the man holding the wagon pole, while some oxen stood like rock, some swayed their horns. The q-b asked the Velveteener what they were carrying. For a long time he took no notice of the question. Then he volunteered, in a snappy voice, that it was the Government grain being distributed to the communes for bread. On Sunday afternoon too.

Oh, this Government corn! What a problem those sacks represent!

The country became wider as we dropped lower. But it was bleak and treeless once more. Stones cropped up in the wide hollow dales. Men on ponies passed forlorn across the distances. Men with bundles waited at the cross-roads to pick up the bus. We were drawing near to Nuoro. It was past three in the afternoon, cold with a bleached light. The landscape seemed bare and stony, wide, different from any before.

We came to the valley where the branch line runs to Nuoro. I saw little pink railway cabins at once, lonely along the valley bed. Turning sharp to the right, we ran in silence over the moorland-seeming slopes, and saw the town beyond, clustered beyond, a little below, at the end of the long declivity, with sudden mountain rising around it. There it lay, as if at the end of the world, mountains rising somber behind.

So, we stop at the Dazio, the town's customs hut, and velveteens has to pay for some meat and cheese he is bringing in. After which we slip into the cold high-street of Nuoro. I am thinking that this is the home of Grazia Deledda, the novelist, and I see a barber's shop. Deledda. And thank heaven we are at the end of the journey. It is past four o'clock.

The bus has stopped quite close to the door of the inn: Star of Italy, was it? In we go at the open door. Nobody about, free access to anywhere and everywhere, as usual;

testifying again to Sardinian honesty. We peer through a doorway to the left—through a rough little room: ah, there in a dark, biggish room beyond is a white-haired old woman with a long, ivory-coloured face standing at a large table ironing. One sees only the large whiteness of the table and the long pallid face and the querulous pale-blue eyes of the tall old woman as she looks up questioning from the gloom of the inner place.

"Is there a room, Signora?"

She looks at me with a pale, cold blue eye, and shouts into the dark for somebody. Then she advances into the passage and looks us up and down, the q-b and me.

"Are you husband and wife?" she demands, challenges.

"Yes, how shouldn't we be?" say I.

A tiny maid of about thirteen, but sturdy and brisk-looking, has appeared in answer to the shout.

"Take them to number seven," says the old dame, and she turns back to her gloom and seizes the flat-iron grimly.

We follow up two flights of cold stone stairs, disheartening narrow staircase with a cold iron rail, and corridors opening off gloomily and rather disorderly. These houses give the effect, inside, of never having been properly finished, as if, long, long ago, the inmates had crowded in, pigsty, fashion, without waiting for anything to be brought into order, and there it had been left, dreary and chaotic.

Thumbelina, the little maid, threw open the door of number seven with *éclat*. And we both exclaimed: "How fine!" It seemed to us palatial. Two good, thick white beds, a table, a chest of drawers, two mats on the tiled floor, and gorgeous oleographs on the wall—and two good wash-bowls side by side—and all perfectly clean and nice. What were we coming to! We felt we ought to be impressed.

We pulled open the latticed window doors, and looked down on the street: the only street. And it was a river of noisy life. A band was playing, rather terribly, round the corner at the end, and up and down the street jigged endless numbers of maskers in their carnival costume, with girls and young women strolling arm-in-arm to participate. And how frisky they all were, how bubbly and un-self-conscious!

The maskers were nearly all women—the street was full of women: so we thought at first. Then we saw, looking closer, that most of the women were young men dressed up. All the maskers were young men, and most of these young men, *of course,* were masquerading as women. As a rule they did not wear face-masks, only little dominoes of black cloth or green cloth or white cloth coming down to the mouth. Which is much better. For the old modelled half-masks with the lace frill, the awful proboscis sticking forward white and ghastly like the beaks of corpse-birds—such as the old Venice masks—these, I think, are simply horrifying. And the more modern "faces" are usually only repulsive. While the simple little pink half-masks with the end of black or green or white cloth, these just form a human disguise.

It was quite a game, sorting out the real women from the false. Some were easy. They had stuffed their bosoms, and stuffed their bustles, and put on hats and very various robes, and they minced along with little jigging steps like little dolls that dangle from elastic, and they put their heads on one side and dripped their hands, and danced up to flurry the actual young ladies, and sometimes they received a good clout on the head, when they broke into wild and violent gestures, whereat the *actual* young ladies scuffled wildly.

They were very lively and naïve. But some were more difficult. Every conceivable sort of "woman" was there, broad shouldered and with rather large feet. The most usual was the semi-peasant, with a very full bosom and very full skirt and a very downright bearing.

166

But one was a widow in weeds, drooping on the arm of a robust daughter. And one was an ancient crone in a crochet bed-cover. And one was in an old skirt and blouse and apron, with a broom, wildly sweeping the street from end to end. He was an animated rascal. He swept with very sarcastic assiduity in front of two town-misses in fur coats, who minced very importantly along. He swept their way very humbly, facing them and going backwards, sweeping and bowing, whilst they advanced with their noses in the air. He made his great bow, and they minced past, daughters of dog-fish, pesce-cane, no doubt. Then he skipped with a bold, gambolling flurry behind them, and with a perfectly mad frenzy began to sweep after them, as if to sweep their tracks away. He swept so madly and so blindly with his besom that he swept on to their heels and their ankles. They shrieked and glowered round, but the blind sweeper saw them not. He swept and swept and pricked their thin silk ankles. And they, scarlet with indignation and rage, gave hot skips like cats on hot bricks, and fled discomfited forwards. He bowed once more after them, and started mildly and innocently to sweep the street. A pair of lovers of fifty years ago, she in a half crinoline and poke bonnet and veil, hanging on his arm, came very coyly past, oh, so simpering, and it took me a long time to be sure that the "girl" was a youth. An old woman in a long nightdress prowled up and down, holding out her candle and peering in the street as if for burglars. She would approach the *real* young women and put her candle in their faces and peer so hard, as if she suspected them of something. And they blushed and turned their faces away and protested confusedly. This old woman searched so fearfully in the face of one strapping lass in the pink and scarlet costume, who looked for all the world like a bunch of red and rose-pink geraniums with a bit of white—a *real* peasant lass— that the latter in a panic began to beat him with her fist, furiously, quite aroused. And he made off, running comically in his long white nightdress.

There were some really beautiful dresses of rich old brocade, and some gleaming old shawls, a shimmer of lavender and silver, or of dark, rich shot colours with deep borders of white silver and primrose gold, very lovely. I believe two of them were actual women—but the q-b says no. There was a Victorian gown of thick green silk, with a creamy blotched cross-over shawl. About her we were both doubtful. There were two wistful, drooping-lily sisters, alt in white, with big feet. And there was a very successful tall miss in a narrow hobble-skirt of black satin and a toque with ospreys. The way she minced and wagged her posterior and went on her toes and peered over her shoulder and kept her elbows in was an admirable caricature. Especially the curious sagging, heaving movement of "bustle" region, a movement very characteristic of modern feminism, was hit off with a bit of male exaggeration which rejoiced me. At first she even took me in.

We stood outside our window, and leaned on the little balcony rail looking down at this flow of life. Directly opposite was the chemist's house: facing our window the best bedroom of the chemist, with a huge white matrimonial bed and muslin curtains. In the balcony sat the chemist's daughters, very elegant in high-heeled shoes and black hair done in the fluffy fashion with a big sweep sideways. Oh, very elegant! They eyed us a little and we eyed them. But without interest. The river of life was down below.

It was very cold and the day was declining. We too were cold. We decided to go into the street and look for the café. In a moment we were out of doors, walking as inconspicuously as possible near the wall. Of course there was no pavement. These maskers were very gentle and whimsical, no touch of brutality at all. Now we were level with them, how odd and funny they were. One youth wore a thin white blouse and a pair of his sister's wide, calico knickers with needlework frills near the ankle, and white stockings. He walked artlessly, and looked almost pretty. Only the q-b winced with pain: not because of the knickers, but because of that awful length, coming well below the knee. Another young man was wound into a sheet, and heaven knows if he could ever get out of it. Another was involved in a complicated entanglement of white crochet antimacassars, very troublesome to contemplate. I did not like him at all, like a fish in a net. But he strode robustly about.

We came to the end of the street, where there is a wide, desolate sort of gap. Here the little band stood braying away. There was a thick crowd of people, and on a slanting place just above, a little circle where youths and men, maskers and one or two girls were dancing, so crowded together and such a small ring that they looked like a jiggly set of upright rollers all turning ricketily against one another. They were doing a sort of intense jigging waltz. Why do they look so intense? Perhaps because they were so tight all together, like too many fish in a globe slipping through one another.

There was a café in this sort of piazza—not a piazza at all, a formless gap. But young men were drinking little drinks, and I knew it would be hopeless to ask for anything but cold drinks or black coffee: which we did not want. So we continued forwards, up the slope of the village street. These towns soon come to an end. Already we were wandering into the open. On a ledge above, a peasant family was making a huge bonfire, a tower of orange-coloured, rippling flame. Little impish boys were throwing on more rubbish. Everybody else was in town. Why were these folk at the town-end making this fire alone?

We came to the end of the houses and looked over the road-wall at the hollow, deep, interesting valley below. Away on the other side rose a blue mountain, a steep but stumpy cone. High land reared up, dusky and dark-blue, all around. Somewhere far off the sun was setting with a bit of crimson. It was a wild, unusual landscape, of unusual shape. The hills seemed so untouched, dark-blue, virgin-wild, the hollow cradle of the valley was cultivated like a tapestry away below. And there seemed so little outlying life: nothing. No castles even. In Italy and Sicily castles perching everywhere. In Sardinia none—the remote, ungrappled hills rising darkly, standing outside of life.

As we went back it was growing dark, and the little band was about to leave off its brass noise. But the crowd still surged, the maskers still jigged and frisked unweariedly. Oh, the good old energy of the bygone days, before men became so self-conscious. Here it was still on the hop.

We found no café that looked any good. Coming to the inn, we asked if there was a fire anywhere. There wasn't. We went up to our room. The chemist-daughters had lighted up opposite; one saw their bedroom as if it were one's own. In the dusk of the street the maskers were still jigging, all the youths still joyfully being women, but a little more roughly now. Away over the house-tops the purple-red of dying sunset. And it was very cold.

There was nothing for it but just to lie in bed. The q-b made a little tea on the spirit-lamp, and we sat in bed and sipped it. Then we covered ourselves up and lay still, to get warm. Outside the noise of the street came unabated. It grew quite dark, the lights reflected into the room. There was the sound of an accordion across the hoarseness of the many voices and movements in the street: and then a solid, strong singing of men's voices, singing a soldier song.

"Quando torniamo in casa nostra—"

We got up to look. Under the small electric lights the narrow, cobbled street was still running with a river of people, but fewer maskers. Two maskers beating loudly at a heavy closed door. They beat and beat. At last the door opens a crack. They rush to try to get in—but in vain. It had shut the moment it saw them, they are foiled, on they go down the street. The town is full of men, many peasants come in from the outlying parts, the black-and-white costume now showing in the streets.

We retire to bed again out of the cold. Comes a knock, and Thumbelina bursts in, in the darkness.

"Siamo qua! "says the q-b.

Thumbelina dashes at the window-doors and shuts them and shuts the casement. Then she dashes to my bedhead and turns on the light, looking down at me as if I were a rabbit in the grass. Then she flings a can of water against the wash-bowls—cold water, icy, alas. After which, small and explosive, she explodes her way out of the room again, and leaves us in the glaring light, having replied that it is now a little after six o'clock, and dinner is half-past seven.

So we lie in bed, warm and in peace, but hungry, waiting for half-past seven.

When the q-b can stand it no more she flounces up, though the clock from the Campanile has struck seven only a few minutes before. Dashing downstairs to reconnoitre, she is back in a breath to say that people are eating their heads off in the long dining-room. In the next breath we are downstairs too.

The room was brightly lighted, and at many white tables sat diners, all men. It was quite city-like. Everyone was in convivial mood. The q-b spied men opposite having chicken and salad—and she had hopes. But they were brief. When the soup came, the girl announced that there was only bistecca: which meant a bit of fried cow. So it did: a quite, quite small bit of fried beef, a few potatoes and a bit of cauliflower. Really, it was not enough for a child of twelve. But that was the end of it. A few mandarini— tangerine oranges—rolled on a plate for dessert. And there's the long and short of these infernal dinners. Was there any cheese? No, there was no cheese. So we merely masticated bread.

There came in three peasants in the black-and-white costume, and sat at the middle table. They kept on their stocking-caps. And queer they looked, coming in with slow, deliberate tread of these elderly men, and sitting rather remote, with a gap of solitude around them. The peculiar ancient loneliness of the Sardinian hills clings to them, and something stiff, static, pre-world.

. All the men at our end of the room were citizens—employees of some sort—and they were all acquaintances. A large dog, very large indeed, with a great muzzle, padded slowly from table to table, and looked at us with big wistful topaz eyes. When the meal was almost over our bus-driver and conductor came in—looking faint with hunger and cold and fatigue. They were quartered at this house. They had eaten nothing since the boar-broth at Gavoi.

In a very short time they were through their portions: and was there nothing else? Nothing! But they were half-starved. They ordered two eggs each, in padella. I ordered coffee—and asked them to come and take it with us, and a brandy. So they came when their eggs were finished.

A diversion was now created at the other side of the room. The red wine, which is good in Sardinia, had been drunk freely. Directly facing us sat a rather stout man with pleasant blue eyes and a nicely shaped head: dressed like any other town man on a Sunday. The dog had waddled up to him and sat down statuesque in front of him. And the fat man, being mellow, began to play with the big, gentle, brindled animal. He took a piece of bread and held it before the dog's nose—and the dog tried to take it. But the man, like a boy now he was ripe with wine, put the mastiff back with a restraining finger, and told him not to snatch. Then he proceeded with a little conversation with the animal. The dog again tried to

169

snatch, gently, and again the man started, saved the bread, and startled the dog, which backed and gave a sharp, sad yelp, as if to say: "Why do you tease me?"

"Now," said the man, "you are not to snatch. Come here. Come here. Vieni qua!" And he held up the piece of bread. The animal came near. "Now," said the man, "I put this bread on your nose, and you don't move, Un— Ha!"

The dog had tried to snatch the bread, the man had shouted and jerked it away, the animal had recoiled and given another expostulating yelp.

The game continued. All the room was watching, smiling. The dog did not understand at all. It came forward again, troubled. The man held the bread near its nose, and held up a warning finger. The beast dropped its head mournfully, cocking up its eye at the bread with varied feelings.

"Now—!" said the man, "not until I say three—*Uno—due* "—the dog could bear it no longer, the man in jerking let go the bread and yelled at the top of his voice—"*e tre!*" The dog gulped the piece of bread with a resigned pleasure, and the man pretended that it had all happened properly on the word "three."

So he started again. "Vieni qua! Vieni qua! " The dog, which had backed away with the bread, came hesitating, cringing forward, dropping its hind-quarters in doubt, as dogs do, advancing towards the new nugget of bread. The man preached it a little sermon.

"You sit there and look at this bread. I sit here and look at you, and I hold this bread. And you stop still, and I stop still, while I count three. Now then—uno—" The dog couldn't hear these numerals, with their awful slowness. He snatched desperately. The man yelled and lost the bread, the dog, gulping, turned to creep away.

Then it began again.

"Come here! Come here! Didn't I tell thee I would count three? Già! I said I would count three. Not one, but three. And to count three you need three numbers. Ha! Steady! Three numbers. Uno—due E TRE!" The last syllables were yelled so that the room rang again. The dog gave a mournful howl of excitement, missed the bread, groped for it and fled.

The man was red with excitement, his eyes shining. He addressed the company at large. "I had a dog," he said, a dog! And I would put a piece of bread on his nose, and say a verse. And he looked at me so!" The man put his face sideways. "And he looked at me *so!*" He gazed up under his brows. "And he talked to me so—o: Zieu! Zieu! —But he never moved. No, he never moved. If he sat with that bread on his nose for half an hour, and if tears ran down his face, he never moved—not till I said *three!*

Then—ah!" The man tossed up his face, snapped the air with his mouth, and gulped an imaginary crust. "AH, that dog was trained . . ." The man of forty shook his head.

"Vieni qua! Come here! Tweet! Come here!"

He patted his fat knee, and the dog crept forward. The man held another piece of bread.

"Now," he said to the dog, "listen! Listen. I am going to tell you something.

'Il soldato va alla guerra—'

"No—no, not yet. When I say *three!*

'Il soldato va alla guerra.

Mangia male, dorme in terra—'

"Listen. Be still. Quiet now. UNO—DUE—E—TRE!"

It came out in one simultaneous yell from the man, the dog in sheer bewilderment opened his jaws and let the bread go down his throat, and wagged his tail in agitated misery.

"Ah," said the man, "you are learning. Come! Come here! Come! Now then! Now you know. So! So! Look at me so!"

The stout, good-looking man of forty bent forward. His face was flushed, the veins in his neck stood out. He talked to the dog, and imitated the dog. And very well indeed he reproduced something of the big, gentle, wistful subservience of the animal. The dog was his totem—the affectionate, self-mistrustful, warm-hearted hound.

So he started the rigmarole again. We put it into English.

"Listen now. Listen! Let me tell it you.   -

'So the soldier goes to the war!
His food is rotten, he sleeps on the floor—'

"Now! Now! No, you are not keeping quiet. Now! Now!

'Il soldato va alla guerra
Mangia male, dorme in terra—' "

The verses, known to every Italian, were sung out in a sing-song fashion. The audience listened as one man—or as one child—the rhyme chiming in every heart. They waited with excitement for the One—Two——and Three! The last two words were always ripped out with a tearing yell. I shall never forget the force of those syllables—E TRE! But the dog made a poor show—he only gobbled the bread and was uneasy.

This game lasted us a full hour: a full hour by the clock sat the whole room in intense silence, watching the man and the dog.

Our friends told us the man was the bus-inspector—their inspector. But they liked him. "Un brav' uomo! Un bravo uomo! Eh si!" Perhaps they were a little uneasy, seeing him in his cups and hearing him yell so nakedly: AND THREE!

We talked rather sadly, wistfully. Young people, especially nice ones like the driver, are too sad and serious these days. little conductor made big brown eyes at us, wistful too, and sad we were going.

For in the morning they were driving back again to Sorgono, over the old road, and we were going on, to Terra-nova, the port. But we promised to come back in the summer, when it was warmer. Then we should all meet again.

"Perhaps you will find us on the same course still. Who knows!" said the driver sadly.

CHAPTER VII

TO TERRANOVA AND THE STEAMER

THE morning was very clear and blue. We were up betimes. The old dame of the inn very friendly this morning. We were going already! Oh, but we hadn't stayed long in Nuoro. Didn't we like it?

Yes, we like it. We would come back in the summer when it was warmer.

Ah, yes, she said, artists came in the summer. Yes, she agreed, Nuoro was a nice place—*simpatico, molto simpatico.*

And really it is. And really she was an awfully nice, capable, human old woman: and I had thought her a beldame when I saw her ironing.

She gave us good coffee and milk and bread, and we went out, into the town. There was the real Monday morning atmosphere of an old, same-as-ever provincial town: the vacant feeling of work resumed after Sunday, rather reluctantly; nobody buying anything, nobody quite at grips with anything. The doors of the old-fashioned shops stood open: in Nuoro they have hardly reached the stage of window-displays. One must go inside, into the dark caves, to see what the goods are. Near the doorways of the drapers' shops stood rolls of that fine scarlet cloth, for the women's costumes. In a large tailor's window four women sat sewing, tailoring, and looking out of the window with eyes still Sunday-emancipate and mischievous. Detached men, some in the black-and-white, stood at the street corners, as if obstinately avoiding the current of work. Having had a day off, the salt taste of liberty still lingering on their lips, they were not going to be dragged so easily back into harness. I always sympathise with these rather sulky, forlorn males who insist on making another day of it. It shows a spark of spirit, still holding out against our over-harnessed world.

There is nothing to see in Nuoro: which, to tell the truth, is always a relief. Sights are an irritating bore. Thank heaven there isn't a bit of Perugino or anything Pisan in the place: that I know of. Happy is the town that has nothing to show. What a lot of stunts and affectations it saves! Life is then life, not museum-stuffing. One could saunter along the rather inert, narrow, Monday-morning street, and see the women having a bit of a gossip, and see an old crone with a basket of bread on her head, and see the unwilling ones hanging back from work, and the whole current of industry disinclined to flow. Life is life and things are things. I am sick of gaping *things,* even Peruginos. I have had my thrills from Carpaccio and Botticelli. But now I've had enough. But I can always look at an old, grey-bearded peasant in his earthy white drawers and his black waist-frill, wearing no coat or over-garment, but just crooking along beside his little ox-wagon. I am sick of "things," even Perugino.

The sight of the woman with the basket of bread reminded us that we wanted some food. So we searched for bread. None, if you please. It was Monday morning, eaten out. There would be bread at the forno, the oven. Where was the oven? Up the road and down a passage. I thought we should smell it. But no. We wandered back. Our friends had told us to take tickets early, for perhaps the bus would be crowded. So we bought yesterday's pastry and little cakes, and slices of native sausage. And still no bread. I went and asked our old hostess.

"There is no fresh bread. It hasn't come in yet," she said.

"Never mind, give me stale."

So she went and rummaged in a drawer.

"Oh, dear, oh, dear, the women have eaten it all! But perhaps over there—" she pointed down the street—"they can give you some."

They couldn't.

I paid the bill—about twenty-eight francs, I think—and went out to look for the bus. There it was. In a dark little hole they gave me the long ticket-strips, first-class to Terra-nova. They cost some seventy francs the two. The q-b was still vainly, aimlessly looking along the street for bread.

"Ready when you are," said our new driver rather snappily. He was a pale, cross-looking young man with brown eyes and fair "ginger" hair. So in we clambered, waved farewell to our old friends, whose bus was ready to roll away in. the opposite direction. As we bumped past the "piazza" I saw Velveteens standing there, isolate, and still, apparently, scowling with unabated irritation.

I am sure he has money: why the first-class, yesterday, otherwise? And I'm sure *she* married him because he is a townsman with property..

172

Out we rolled, on our last Sardinian drive. The morning was of a bell-like beauty, blue and very lovely. Below on the right stretched the concave valley, tapestried with cultivation. Up into the morning light rose the high, humanless hills, with wild, treeless moor-slopes.

But there was no glass in the left window of the *coupé,* and the wind came howling in, cold enough. I stretched myself on the front seat, the q-b screwed herself into a corner, and we watched the land flash by. How well this new man drove! the long-nosed, freckled one with his gloomy brown eyes. How cleverly he changed gear, so that the automobile mewed and purred comfortably, like a live thing enjoying itself. And how dead he was to the rest of the world, wrapped in his gloom like a young bus-driving Hamlet. His answers to his mate were monosyllabic—or just no answers at all. He was one of those responsible, capable, morose souls, who do their work with silent perfection and look as if they were-driving along the brink of doom; say a word to them and they'll go over the edge. But gentle *au fond,* of course. Fiction used to be fond of them: a sort of ginger-haired, young, mechanic Mr. Rochester who has even lost the Jane illusion.

Perhaps it was not fair to watch him so closely from behind.

His mate was a bit of a bounder, with one of those rakish military caps whose soft tops cock sideways or backwards. He was in Italian khaki, riding-breeches and puttees. He smoked his cigarettes bounderishly: but at the same time, with peculiar gentleness, he handed one to the ginger Hamlet. Hamlet accepted it, and his mate held him a light as the bus swung on. They were like man and wife. The mate was the alert and wide-eyed Jane Eyre whom the ginger Mr. Rochester was not going to spoil in a hurry.

The landscape was different from yesterday's. As we dropped down the shallow, winding road from Nuoro, quite quickly the moors seemed to spread on either side, treeless, bushy, rocky, desert. How hot they must be in summer! One knows from Grazia Deledda's books.

A pony with a low trap was prancing unhappily in the roadside. We slowed down and slid harmlessly past. Then again, on we whizzed down the looped road, which turned back on itself as sharply as a snake that has been wounded. Hamlet darted the bus at the curves; then softly padded round like an angel: then off again for the next parabola.

We came out into wide, rather desolate, moorland valley spaces, with low rocks away to the left, and steep slopes, rocky-bushy, on the right. Sometimes groups of black-and-white men were working in the forlorn distances. A woman in the madder costume led a panniered ass along the wastes. The sun shone magnificently; already it was hotter here. The landscape had quite changed. These slopes looked east and south to the sea, they were sun-wild and sea-wild.

The first stop was where a wild, rough lane came down the hill to our road. At the corner stood a lonely house—and in the roadside the most battered, life-weary old carriage I have ever seen. The jaunty mate sorted out the post—the boy with the tattered-battered brown carriage and brown pony signed the book as we all stood in the roadway. There was a little wait for a man who was fetching up another parcel. The post-bag and parcels from the tattered carriage were received and stowed and signed for. We walked up and down in the sun to get warm. The landscape was wild and open round about.

Pip! goes Mr. Rochester, peremptorily, at the horn. Amazing how obediently we scuffle in. Away goes the bus, rushing towards the sea. Already one felt that peculiar glare in the half-way heavens, that intensification of the light in the lower sky, which is caused by the sea to sunward.

Away in front three girls in brown costume are walking along the side of the white high-road, going with panniers towards a village up a slight incline. They hear us, turn round, and instantly go off their heads, exactly like chickens in the road. They fly towards us, crossing the road, and swifter than any rabbits they scuttle, one after another, into a deep side-track, like a deep ditch at right-angles to the road. There, as we roll past, they are all crouched, peering out at us fearfully, like creatures from their hole. The bus-mate salutes them with a shout, and we roll on towards the village on the low summit.

It is a small, stony, hen-scratched place of poor people. We roll on to a standstill. There is a group of poor people. The women wear the dark-brown costume, and again the bolero has changed shape. It is a rather' fantastic low corset, curiously shapen; and originally, apparently,' made of wonderful elaborate brocade. But look at it now.

There is an altercation because a man wants to get into the bus with two little black pigs, each of which is wrapped in a little sack, with its face and ears appearing like a flower from a wrapped bouquet. He is told that he must pay the fare for each pig as if it were a Christian. *Cristo del mondo!* A pig, a little pig, and paid for as if it were a Christian. He dangles the pig-bouquets, one from each hand, and the little pigs open their black mouths and squeal with self-conscious appreciation of the excitement they are causing. *Dio benedetto!* it is a chorus. But the bus-mate is inexorable. Every animal, even if it were a mouse, must be paid for and have a ticket as if it were a Christian. The pig-master recoils stupefied with indignation, a pig-bouquet under each arm. "How much do you charge for the fleas you carry?" asks a sarcastic youth.

A woman sitting sewing a soldier's tunic into a little jacket for her urchin, and thus beating the sword into a plough-share, stitches unconcernedly in the sun. Round-checked but rather slatternly damsels giggle. The pig-master, speechless with fury, slings the pig-bouquets, like tow bottles, one on either side the saddle of the ass whose halter is held by a grinning but also malevolent girl: malevolent against pig-prices, that is. The pigs, looking abroad from their new situation, squeal the eternal pig-protest against an insufferable humanity.

"Andiamo! Andiamo!" says ginger Mr. Rochester in his quiet but intense voice. The bus-mate scrambles up and we charge once more into the strong light to seaward.

In we roll, into Orosei, a dilapidated, sun-smitten, god-forsaken little town not far from the sea. We descend to the piazza. There is a great, false baroque *façade* to a church, up a wavering vast mass of steps: and at the side a wonderful jumble of roundnesses with a jumble of round tiled roofs, peaked in the center. It must have been some sort of convent. But it is eminently what they call a "painter's bit"—that pallid, big baroque face, at the top of the slow incline, and the very curious dark building at the side of it, with its several dark-tiled round roofs, like pointed hats, at varying altitudes. The whole space has a strange Spanish look, neglected, arid, yet with a bigness and a dilapidated dignity and a stoniness which carry one back to the Middle Ages, when life was violent and Orosei was no doubt a port and a considerable place. Probably it had bishops.

The sun came hot into the wide piazza; with its pallid heavy *façade* up on the stony incline on one side, and arches and a dark great courtyard and outer stairways of some unknown building away on the other, the road entering downhill from the inland, and dropping out below to the sea-marshes, and with the impression that once some single power had had the place in grip, had given this centre an architectural unity and splendour now lost and forgotten. Orosei was truly fascinating.

But the inhabitants were churlish. We went into a sort of bar-place, very primitive, and asked for bread.

"Bread alone?" said the churl.

"If you please."

"There isn't any," he answered.

"Oh—where can we get some then?"

"You can't get any."

"Really!"

And we couldn't. People stood about glum, not friendly. There was a second great automobile, ready to set off for Tortoli, far to the south, on the east coast. Mandas is the railway junction both for Sorgono and Tortoli. The two buses stood near and communed. We prowled about the dead, almost extinct town—or call it village. Then Mr. Rochester began to pip his horn peremptorily, so we scuffled in.

The post was stowed away. A native in black broad-cloth came running and sweating, carrying an ox-blood suitcase, and said we must wait for his brother-in-law, who was a dozen yards away. Ginger Mr. Rochester sat on his driver's throne and glared in the direction whence the brother-in-law must come. His brow knitted irritably, his long, sharp nose did not promise much patience. He made the horn roar like a sea-cow. But no brother-in-law.

"I'm going to wait no longer," said he.

"Oh, a minute, a minute! That won't do us any harm," expostulated his mate. No answer from the long-faced, long-nosed ginger Hamlet. He sat statuesque, but with black eyes looking daggers down the still void, road.

"Eh va bene," he murmured through closed lips, and leaned forward grimly for the starting handle.

"Patience—patience—patience a moment—why—" cried the mate.

"Per l'amor di Dio! " cried the black broad-cloth man, simply sizzling and dancing in anguish on the road, round the suit-case, which stood in the dust. "Don't go! God's love, don't start. He's got to catch the boat. He's got to be in Rome to-morrow. He won't be a second. He's here, he's here, he's here!"

This startled the fate-fixed, sharp-nosed driver. He released the handle and looked round, with dark and glowering eyes. No one in sight. The few glum natives stood round unmoved. Thunder came into the gloomy dark eyes of the Rochester. Absolutely nobody in sight. Click! went his face into a look of almost seraphic peace, as he pulled off the brakes. We were on an incline, and insidiously, oh, most subtly the great bus started to lean forwards and steal into motion.

"Oh, *ma che!*—what a will you've got!" cried the mate, clambering into the side of the now seraphic-looking Rochester.

"Love of God—God!" yelled the broad-cloth, seeing the bus melt forward and gather momentum. He put his hands up as if to arrest it, and yelled in a wild howl: "O Beppin'!, Bepp*in*—O!"

But in vain. Already we had left the little groups of onlookers behind. — We were rolling downwards out of the piazza.

Broad-cloth had seized the bag and was running beside us in agony. Out of the piazza we rolled. Rochester had not put on the engines and we were just simply rolling down the gentle incline by the will of God. Into the dark outlet-street we melted, towards the still invisible sea.

Suddenly a yell—"OO—ahh!!"

"È qua! È qua! È qua! È qua!" gasped broad-cloth four times. "He's here!" And then: "Beppin'—she's going, she's going!"

Beppin' appeared, a middle-aged man also in black broad-cloth, with a very scrubby chin and a bundle, running *towards* us on fat legs. He was perspiring, but his face was expressionless and innocent-looking. With a sardonic flicker of a grin, half of spite, half of relief, Rochester put on the brakes again, and we stopped in the street. A woman tottered up panting and holding her breast. Now for farewells.

"Andiamo!" said Rochester curtly, looking over his shoulder and making his fine nose curl with malice. And instantly he took off the brakes again. The fat woman shoved Beppin' in, gasping farewells, the brother-in-law handed in the ox-blood-red suit-case, tottering behind, and the bus surged savagely out of Orosei.

Almost in a moment we had left the town on its slope, and there below us was a river winding through marshy flats to the sea, to where small white surf broke on. a flat isolated beach, a quarter of a mile away. The river ran rapidly between stones and then between belts of high sere reeds, high as a man. These tall reeds advanced almost into the slow, horizontal sea, from which stood up a white glare of light, massive light over the low Mediterranean.

Quickly we came down to the river level, and rolled over a bridge. Before us, between us and the sea rose another hill, almost like a wall with a flat top, running horizontal, perfectly flat, parallel with the sea edge, a sort of narrow long plateau. For a moment we were in the wide scoop of the river-bed. Orosei stood on the bluff behind us.

Away to the right the flat river marshes with the thick dead reeds met the flat and shining sea, river and sea were one water, the waves rippled tiny and soft-foot into the stream. To the left there was great loveliness. The bed of the river curved upwards and inland, and there was cultivation: but particularly, there were noble almond trees in full blossom. How beautiful they were, their pure, silvery pink gleaming so nobly, like a transfiguration, tall and perfect in that strange cradled river-bed parallel with the sea. Almond trees were in flower beneath grey Orosei, almond trees came near the road, and we could see the hot eyes of the individual blossoms, almond trees stood on the upward slope before us. And they had flowered in such noble beauty there, in that trough where the sun fell magnificent and the sea-glare whitened all the air as with a sort of God-presence, they gleamed in their incandescent sky-rosiness. One could hardly see their iron trunks, in this weird valley.

But already we had crossed, and were charging up the great road that was cut straight, slantwise along, the side of the sea-hill, like a stairway outside the side of the house. So the bus turned southward to run up this stairway slant, to get to the top of the sea's long table-land. So, we emerged: and there was the Mediterranean rippling against the black rocks not so very far away below on our right. For, once on the long table-land the road turned due north, a long white dead-straight road running between strips of moorland, wild and bushy. The sea was in the near distance, blue, blue, and beating with light. It seemed more light than watery. And on the left was the wide trough of the valley, where almond trees like clouds in a wind seemed to poise sky-rosy upon the pale, sun-pale land, and beyond which Orosei clustered its lost grey houses on the bluff. Oh, wonderful Orosei, with your almonds and your reedy river, throbbing, throbbing with light and the sea's nearness, and all so lost, in a world long gone by, lingering as legends linger on. It is hard to believe that it is real. It seems so long since life left it and memory transfigured it into pure glamour, lost away like a lost pearl on the east Sardinian coast. Yet there it is, with a few grumpy inhabitants who won't eyen give you a crust of bread. And probably there is malaria—almost sure. And it would be hell to have to live there for a month. Yet for a

176

moment, that January morning, how wonderful, oh, the timeless glamour of those Middle Ages when men were lordly and violent and shadowed with death.

"Timor mortis conturbat me."

The road ran along by the sea, above the sea, swinging gently up and down, and running on to a sea-encroaching hilly promontory in the distance. There were no high lands. The valley was left behind, and moors surrounded us, wild, desolate, uninhabited and uninhabitable moors sweeping up gently on the left, and finishing where the land dropped low and cliff-like to the sea on the right. No life was now in sight: even no ship upon the pale blue sea. The great globe of the sky was unblemished and royal in its blueness and its ringing cerulean light. Over the moors a great hawk hovered. Rocks cropped out. It was a savage, dark-bushed,, sky-exposed land, forsaken to the sea and the sun.

We were alone in the *coupé*. The bus-mate had made one or two sets at us, but he rather confused us. He was young—about twenty-two or three. He was quite good-looking, with his rakish military cap and his well-knitted figure in military clothes. But he had dark eyes that seemed to ask too much, and his manner of approach was abrupt, persistent, and disconcerting. Already he had asked us where we were going, where we lived, whence we came, of what nationality we were, and was I a painter. Already he knew so much. Further we rather fought shy of him. We ate those pale Nuoro pastries—they were just flaky pastry, good, with nothing inside but a breath of air. And we gnawed slices of very highly flavoured Nuoro sausage. And we drank the tea. And we were very hungry, for it was past noon, and we had eaten as good as nothing. The sun was magnificent in heaven; we rushed at a great, purring speed along that moorland road just above the sea.

And then the bus-mate climbed in to share the *coupé* with us. He put his dark, beseeching and yet persistent eyes on us, sat plumb in front of us, his knees squared, and began to shout awkward questions in a strong curious voice. Of course it was very difficult to hear, for the great rushing bus made much noise. We had to try to yell in our Italian— and he was as awkward as we were.

However, although it said "Smoking Forbidden" he offered us both cigarettes, and insisted we should smoke with him. Easiest to submit. He tried to point us out features in the landscape; but there were none to point, except that, where the hill ran to sea out of the moor, and formed a cape, he said there was a house away under the cliffs where coast-guards lived. Nothing else.

Then, however, he launched. He asked once more was I English and was the q-b German. We said it was so. And then he started the old story. Nations popped up and down again like Punch and Judy. Italy—l'Italia—she had no quarrel with La Germania—never had had—no—no, good friends the two nations. But once the war was started, Italy had to come in. For why. Germany would beat France, occupy her lands, march down and invade Italy. Best then join the war whilst the enemy was only invading somebody else's territory.

They are perfectly naïve about it. That's what I like. He went on to say that he was a soldier: he had served eight years in the Italian cavalry. Yes, he was a cavalryman, and had been all through the war. But he had not therefore any quarrel with Germany. No—war was war, and it was over. So let it be over.

But France—*ma la Francia!* Here he sat forward on his seat, with his face near ours, and his pleading-dog's eyes suddenly took a look of quite irrational blazing rage. France! There wasn't a man in Italy who wasn't dying to get at the throat of France. France! Let there be war, and every Italian would leap to arms, even the old. Even the old— *anche i vecchi.* Yes, there must be war—with France. It was coming: it was bound to come. Every

Italian was waiting for it. Waiting to fly at the French throat. For why? Why? He had served two years on the French front, and he knew why. Ah, the French! For arrogance, for insolence, Dio! —they were not to be borne. The French— they thought themselves lords of the world—*signori del mondo!* Lords of the world, and masters of the world. Yes. They thought themselves no less—and what are they? Monkeys! Monkeys! Not better than' monkeys. But let there be war, and Italy would show them. Italy would give them *signori del mondo!* Italy was pining for war—all, all, pining for war. With no one, with no one but France. All, with no one—Italy loved everybody else—but France! France!

We let him shout it all out, till he was at the end of it. The passion and energy of him was amazing. He was like one possessed. I could only wonder. And wonder again. For it is curious what fearful passions these pleading, wistful souls fall into when they feel they have been insulted. It was evident he felt he had been insulted, and he went just beside himself. But dear chap, he shouldn't speak so loudly for all Italy—even the old. The bulk of Italian men are only too anxious to beat their bayonets into cigarette-holders, and smoke the cigarette of eternal and everlasting peace, to coincide at all with our friend. Yet there he was—raging at me in the bus as we dashed along the coast.

And then, after a space of silence, he became sad again, wistful, and looked at us once more with those pleading brown eyes, beseeching, beseeching—he knew not what: and I'm sure I didn't know. Perhaps what he really wants is to be back on a horse in a cavalry regiment: even at war.

But no, it comes out, what he thinks he wants.

When are we going to London? And are there many motor-cars in. England?—many, many? In America too? Do they want men in America? I say no, they have unemployment out there: they are going to stop immigration in April: or at least cut it down. Why? he asks sharply. Because they have their own unemployment problem. And the q-b quotes how many millions of Europeans want to emigrate to the United States. His eye becomes gloomy. Are all nations of Europe going to be forbidden? he asks. Yes—and already the Italian Government will give no more passports for America—to emigrants. No passports? then you can't go? You can't go, say I.

By this time his hot-souled eagerness and his hot, beseeching eyes have touched the q-b. She asks him what he wants. And from his gloomy face it comes out in a rap. *"Andare fuori dell' Italia."* To go out of Italy. To go out—away—to go away—to go away. It has become a craving, a neurasthenia with them.

Where is his home? His home is at a village a few miles ahead—here on this coast. We are coming to it soon. There is his home. And a few miles inland from the village he also has a property: he also has land. But he doesn't want to work it. He doesn't want it. In fact he won't, bother with it. He hates the land, he detests looking after vines. He can't even bring himself to try any more.

What does he want then?

He wants to leave Italy, to go abroad—as a chauffeur. Again the long beseeching look, as of a distraught, pleading animal. He would prefer to be the chauffeur of a gentleman. But he would drive a bus, he would do anything—in England.

Now he has launched it. Yes, I say, but in England also we have more men than jobs. Still he looks at me with his beseeching eyes—so desperate, too—and so young—and so full of energy—and so longing to *devote* himself—to devote himself: or else to go off in an unreasonable paroxysm against the French. To my horror I feel he is believing in my goodness of heart. And as for motor-cars, it is all I can do to own a pair of boots, so how am I to set about employing a *chauffeur?*

We have all gone quiet again. So at last he climbs back and takes his seat with the driver once more. The road is straight, swinging on through the moorland strip by the sea. And he leans to the silent, nerve-tense Mr. Rochester, pleading again. And at length Mr. Rochester edges aside, and lets him take the driving wheel. And so now we are all in the hands of our friend the bus-mate. He drives—not very well, it is evident he is learning. The bus can't quite keep in the grooves of this wild bare road. And he shuts off when we slip down a hill—and there is a great muddle on the upslope when he tries to change gear. But Mr. Rochester sits squeezed and silently attentive in his corner. He puts out his hand and swings the levers. There is no, fear that he will let anything go wrong. I would trust him to drive me down the bottomless pit and up the other side. But still the beseeching mate holds the steering wheel. And on we rush, rather uncertainly and hesitatingly now. And thus we come to the bottom of a hill where the road gives a sudden curve. My heart rises an inch in my breast. I know he can't do it. And he can't oh, Lord—but the quiet hand of the freckled Rochester takes the wheel, we swerve on. And the bus-mate gives up, and the nerve-silent driver resumes control.

But the bus-mate now feels at home with us. He clambers back into the coupé, and when it is too painfully noisy to talk, he simply sits and looks at us with brown, pleading eyes. Miles and miles and miles goes this coast road, and never a village. Once or twice a sort of lonely watch-house and soldiers lying about by the road. But never a halt. Everywhere moorland and desert, uninhabited.

And we are faint with fatigue and hunger and this relentless travelling. When, oh, when shall we come to Siniscola, where we are due to eat our midday meal? Oh, yes, says the mate. There is an inn at Siniscola where we can eat what we like. Siniscola—Siniscola! We feel we must get down, we must eat, it is past one o'clock and the glaring light and the rushing loneliness are still about us.

But it is behind the hill in front. We see the hill. Yes. Behind it is Siniscola. And down there on the beach are the Bagni di Siniscola, where many forestieri, strangers, come in the summer. Therefore we set high hopes on Siniscola. From the town to the sea, two miles, the bathers ride on asses. Sweet place. And it is coming near—really near. There are stone-fenced fields—even stretches of moor fenced off. There are vegetables in a little field with a stone wall—there is a strange white track through the moor to a forsaken sea coast. We are near.

Over the brow of the low hill—and there it is, a grey huddle of a village with two towers: There it is, we are there. Over the cobbles we bump, and pull up by the side of the street. This is Siniscola, and here we eat.

We drop out of the weary bus. The mate asks a man to show us the inn—the man says he won't, muttering. So a boy is deputed—and he consents. This is the welcome.

And I can't say much for Siniscola. It is just a narrow, crude, stony place, hot in the sun, cold in the shade. In a minute or two we were at the inn, where a fat young man was just dismounting from his brown pony and fastening it to a ring beside the door.

The inn did not look promising—the usual cold room opening gloomily on the gloomy street. The usual long table, with this time a foully blotched tablecloth.. And two young peasant madams in charge, in the brown costume, rather sordid, and with folded white cloths on their heads. The younger was in attendance. She was a full-bosomed young hussy, and would be very queenly and cocky. She held her nose in the air, and seemed ready to jibe at any order. It takes one some time to get used to this cocky, assertive behaviour of the young damsels, the who'll-tread-on-the-tail-of-my-skirt bearing of the hussies. But it is partly a sort of. crude defensiveness and shyness, partly it is barbaric *méfiance* or mistrust, and partly, without doubt, it is a tradition with Sardinian women that they must hold their own and be ready to hit first. This young sludge-queen was all hit. She flounced her posterior round the table, planking down the lumps of bread on the foul cloth with an air of take-it-as-a-condescension-that-I-wait-on-you, a subdued grin lurking somewhere on her face. It is not meant to be offensive: yet it is so. Truly, it is just uncouthness. But when one is tired and hungry . . .

We were not the only feeders. There was the man off the pony, and a sort of workman or porter or dazio official with him—and a smart young man: and later our Hamlet driver. Bit by bit the young damsel planked down bread, plates, spoons, glasses, bottles of black wine, whilst we sat at the dirty table in uncouth constraint and looked at the hideous portrait of His reigning Majesty of Italy. And at length came the inevitable soup. And with it the sucking chorus. The little *maialino* at Mandas had been a good one. But the smart young man in the country beat him. As water clutters and slavers down a choky gutter, so did his soup travel upwards into his mouth with one long sucking stream of noise, intensified as the bits of cabbage, etc., found their way through the orifice.

They did all the talking—the young men. They addressed the sludge-queen curtly and disrespectfully as if to say: "What's she up to?" Her airs were finely thrown away. Still she showed off. What else was there to eat? There was the meat that had been boiled for the soup. We knew what that meant. I had as lief eat the foot of an old worsted stocking. Nothing else, you sludge-queen? No, what do you want anything else for? Beefsteak— what's the good of asking for beefsteak or any other steak on a Monday? Go to the butcher's and see for yourself.

The Hamlet, the pony rider, and the porter had the faded and tired chunks of boiled meat. The smart young man ordered eggs in padella—two eggs fried with a little butter. We asked for the same. The smart young man got his first— and of course they were warm and liquid. So he fell upon them with a fork, and once he had got hold of one end of the eggs he just sucked them up in a prolonged and violent suck, like a long, thin, ropy drink being sucked upwards from the little pan. It was a genuine exhibition. Then he fell upon the bread with loud chews.

What else was there? A miserable little common orange. So much for the dinner. Was there cheese? No. But the sludge-queen—they are quite good-natured really—held a conversation in dialect with the young men, which I did not try to follow. Our pensive driver translated that there *was* cheese, but it wasn't good so they wouldn't offer it us. And the pony man interpolated that they didn't like to offer us anything that was not of the best. He said it in all sincerity—after such a meal. This roused my curiosity, so I asked for the cheese whether or not. And it wasn't so bad after all.

This meal cost fifteen francs, for the pair of us.

We made our way back to the bus, through the uncouth men who stood about. To tell the truth, strangers are not popular nowadays—not anywhere. Everybody has a grudge against them at first sight. This grudge may or may not wear off on acquaintance.

The afternoon had become hot—hot as an English June. And we had various other passengers—for one a dark-eyed, long-nosed priest who showed his teeth when he talked. There was not much room in the *coupé,* so the goods were stowed upon the little rack.

With the strength of the sun, and the six or seven people in it, the *coupé* became stifling. The q-b opened her window. But the priest, one of the loud-talking sort, said that a draught was harmful, very harmful, so he put it up again. He was' one of the gregarious sort, a loud talker, nervy really, very familiar with all the passengers. And everything did one harm—*fa male, fa male.* A draught *fa male, fa molto male. Non è vero?* this to all the men from Siniscola. And they all said "Yes—yes."

The bus-mate clambered into the coupé, to take the tickets of the second-class passengers in the rotondo, through the little wicket. There was great squeezing and shouting and reckoning change. And then we stopped at a halt, and he dashed down with the post and the priest got down for a drink with the other men. The Hamlet driver sat stiff in his seat. He pipped the horn. He pipped again, with decision. Men came clambering in. But it looked as if the offensive priest would be left behind. The bus started venomously, the priest came running, his gown flapping, wiping his lips.

He dropped into his seat with a cackling laugh, showing his long teeth. And he said that it was as well to take a drink, to fortify the stomach. To travel with the stomach uneasy did one harm: *fa male, fa male—non è vero?* Chorus of "Yes."

The bus-mate resumed his taking the tickets through the little wicket, thrusting his rear amongst us. As he stood like this, down fell his sheepskin-lined military overcoat on the q-b's head. He was filled with grief. He folded it and placed it on the seat as a sort of cushion for her, oh, so gently! And how he would love to devote himself to a master and mistress.

He sat beside me, facing the q-b, and offered us an acid-drop. We took the acid-drop. He smiled with zealous yearning at the q-b, and resumed his conversations. Then he offered us cigarettes—insisted on our taking cigarettes.

The priest with the long teeth looked sideways at the q-b, seeing her smoking. Then he fished out a long cigar, bit it, and spat. He was offered a cigarette.—But no, cigarettes were harmful: *fanno male.* The paper was bad for the health: oh, very bad. A pipe or a cigar. So he lit his long cigar and spat large spits on the floor, continually.

Beside me sat a big, bright-eyed, rather good-looking but foolish man. Hearing me speak to the q-b, he said in confidence to the priest: "Here are two Germans—eh? Look at them. The woman smoking. These are a couple of those who were interned here. Sardinia can do without them now."

Germans in Italy at the outbreak of the war were interned in Sardinia, and as far as one hears, they were left very free and happy, and treated very well, the Sardinians having been generous as all proud people are. But now our bright-eyed fool made a great titter through the bus: quite unaware that we understood. He said nothing offensive: but that sort of tittering exultation of common people who think they have you at a disadvantage annoyed me. However, I kept still to hear what they would say. But it was only trivialities about the Germans having nearly all gone now, their being free to travel, their coming back to Sardinia because they liked it better than Germany. Oh, yes—they all wanted to come back. They all wanted to come back to Sardinia. Oh, yes, they knew where they were well off. They knew their own advantage. Sardinia was this, that, and the other of advantageousness, and the Sardi were decent people. It is just as well to put in a word on one's own behalf occasionally. As for la Germania—she was down, down: bassa. What did one pay for bread in Germany? Five francs a kilo, my boy.

The bus stopped again, and they trooped out into the hot sun. The priest scuffled round the corner this time. Not to go round the corner was no doubt harmful. We waited. A frown came between the bus Hamlet's brows. He looked nerve-worn and tired. It was about three o'clock. We had to wait for a man from a village, with the post. And he did not appear.

"I am going! I won't wait," said the driver.

"Wait—wait a minute," said the mate, pouring oil. And he went round to look. But suddenly the bus started, with a vicious lurch. The mate came flying and hung on to the footboard. He had really almost been left. The driver glanced round sardonically to see if he were there. The bus flew on. The mate shook his head in deprecation.

"He's a bit *nervoso,* the driver," said the q-b. "A bit out of temper!"

"Ah, poor chap!" said the good-looking young mate, leaning forward and making such beseeching eyes of hot tolerance. "One has to be sorry for him. Persons like him, they suffer so much from themselves, how should one be angry with them! *Poverino.* We must have sympathy."

Never was such a language of sympathy as the Italian. *Poverino! Poverino!* They are never happy unless they are sympathising pityingly with somebody. And I rather felt that I was thrown in with the *poverini* who had to be pitied for being *nervosi.* Which did not improve my temper.

However, the bus-mate suddenly sat on the opposite seat between the priest and the q-b. He turned over his official notebook, and began to write on the back cover very carefully, in the flourishing Italian hand. Then he tore off what he had written, and with a very bright and zealous look he handed me the paper saying: "You will find me a post in England, when you go in the-summer? You will find me a place in London as a chauffeur!"

"If I can," said I. "But it is not easy."

He nodded his head at me with the most complete bright confidence, quite sure now that he had settled his case perfectly.

On the paper he had written his name and his address, and if anyone would like him as chauffeur he had only to say so. On the back of the scrap of paper the inevitable goodwill: *Auguri infiniti e buon viaggio.* Infinite good wishes and a good journey.

I folded the paper and put it in my waistcoat pocket, feeling a trifle disconcerted by my new responsibility. He was such a dear fellow and such bright trustful eyes.

This much achieved, there was a moment of silence. And the bus-mate turned to take a ticket of a fat, comfortable man who had got in at the last stop. There was a bit of flying conversation.

"Where are they from?" asked the good-looking stupid man next to me, inclining his head in our direction.

"Londra," said our friend, with stern satisfaction: and they have said so often to one another that London is the greatest city in the world, that now the very word Londra conveys it all. You should have seen the blank little-boy look come over the face of the big handsome fellow on hearing that we were citizens of the greatest city in the world.

"And they understand Italian?" he asked, rather nipped.

"Sicuro!" said our friend scornfully. "How shouldn't they?"

"Ah!" My large neighbour left his mouth open for a few moments. And then another sort of smile came on his face. He began to peep at us sideways from his brown eyes, brightly, and was henceforth itching to get into conversation with the citizens of the world's mistress-city. His look of semi-impudence was quite gone, replaced by a look of ingratiating admiration.

Now I ask you, is this to be borne? Here I sit, and he talks half-impudently and patronisingly about me. And here I sit, and he is glegging at me as if he saw signs of an aureole under my grey hat. All in ten minutes. And just because, instead of *la Germania* I turn out to be *l'Inghilterra.* I might as well be a place on a map, or a piece of goods with a trade-mark. So little perception of the actual me! so much going by labels! I now could have kicked him harder. I would have liked to say I was ten times German, to see the fool change his smirk again.

The priest now chimed in, that he had been to America. He had been to America and hence he dreaded not the crossing from Terranuova di Sardegna to Cività Vecchia. For he had crossed the great Atlantic.

Apparently, however, the natives had all heard this song of the raven before, so he spat largely on the floor. Whereupon the new fat neighbour asked him was it true that the Catholic Church was now becoming the one Church in the United States? And the priest said there was no doubt about it.

The hot afternoon wore on. The coast was rather more inhabited, but we saw practically no villages. The view was rather desolate. From time to time we stopped at a sordid-looking canteen house. From time to time we passed natives riding on their ponies, and sometimes there was an equestrian exhibition as the rough, strong little beasts reared and travelled rapidly backwards, away from the horrors of our great automobile. But the male riders sat heavy and unshakeable, with Sardinian male force. Everybody in the bus laughed, and we passed, looking back to see the pony still corkscrewing, but in vain, in the middle of the lonely, grass-bordered high-road.

The bus-mate climbed in and out, coming in to sit near us. He was like a dove which has at last found an olive bough to nest in. And we were the olive bough in this world of waste waters. Alas, I felt a broken reed. But he sat so serenely near us, now, like a dog that has found a master.

The afternoon was declining, the bus pelted on at a great rate. Ahead we saw the big lump of the island of Tavolara, a magnificent mass of rock which fascinated me by its splendid, weighty form. It looks like a headland, for it apparently touches the land. There it rests at the sea's edge, in this lost afternoon world. Strange how this coast-country does not belong to our present-day world. As we rushed along we saw steamers, two steamers, steering south, and one sailing ship coming from Italy. And instantly, the steamers seemed like our own familiar world. But still this coast-country was forsaken, forgotten, not included. It just is not included.

How tired one gets of these long, long rides! It seemed we should never come up to Tavolara. But we did. We came right near to it, and saw the beach with the waves rippling undisturbed, saw the narrow waters between the rock-lump and the beach. For now the road was down at sea-level. And we are not very far from Terranova. Yet all seemed still forsaken, outside of the world's life.

The sun was going down, very red and strong, away inland. In the bus all were silent, subsiding into the pale travel-sleep. We charged along the flat road, down on a plain now. And dusk was gathering heavily over the land.

We saw the high-road curve flat upon the plain. It was the harbour head. We saw a magic, land-locked harbour, with masts and dark land encircling a glowing basin. We even saw a steamer lying at the end of a long, thin bank of land, in the shallow, shining, wide harbour, as if wrecked there. And this was our steamer. But no, it looked in the powerful glow of the sunset like some lonely steamer laid up in some land-locked bay away at Spitsbergen, towards the North Pole: a solemn, mysterious, blue-landed bay, lost, lost to mankind.

Our bus-mate came and told us we were to sit in the bus till the post-work was done, then we should be driven to the hotel where we could eat, and then he would accompany us on the town omnibus to the boat. We need not be on board till eight o'clock: and now it was something after five. So we sat still while the bus rushed and the road curved and the view of the weird, land-locked harbour changed, though the bare masts of ships in a bunch still pricked the upper glow, and the steamer lay away out, as if wrecked on a sandbank, and dark, mysterious land with bunchy hills circled round, dark blue and wintry in a golden after-light, while the great, shallow-seeming bay of water shone like a mirror.

In we charged, past a railway, along the flat darkening road into a flat God-lost town of dark houses, on the marshy bay-head. It felt more like a settlement than a town. But it was Terranova-Pausanias. And after bumping and rattling down a sombre, uncouth, barren-seeming street, we came up -with a jerk at a doorway—which was the post office. Urchins, mud-larks, were screaming for the luggage. Everybody got out and set off towards the sea, the urchins carrying luggage. We sat still.

Till I couldn't bear it. I did not want to stay in the automobile another moment, and I did not, I did not want to be accompanied by our new-found friend to the steamer. So I burst out, and the q-b followed. She too was relieved to escape the new attachment, though she had a great *tendre* for him. But in the end one runs away from one's *tendrei* much harder and more precipitately than from one's *durs*.

The mud-larking urchins fell upon us. Had we any more luggage—were we going to the steamer? I asked how one went to the steamer—did one walk? I thought perhaps it would be necessary to row out. You go on foot, or in a carriage, or in an aeroplane, said an impudent brat. How far? Ten minutes. Could one go on board at once? Yes, certainly.

So, in spite of the q-b's protests, I handed the sack to a wicked urchin, to be led. She wanted us to go alone—but I did not know the way, and am wary of stumbling into entanglements in these parts.

I told the bus-Hamlet, who was abstract with nerve fatigue, please to tell his comrade that I would not forget the commission: and I tapped my waistcoat pocket, where the paper lay over my heart. He briefly promised—and we escaped. We escaped any further friendship.

I bade the mud-lark lead me to the telegraph office: which of course was quite remote from the post office. Shouldering the sack, and clamouring for the kitchenino, which the q-b stuck to, he marched forward. By his height he was ten years old: by his face with its evil mud-lark pallor and good looks, he was forty. He wore a cut-down soldier's tunic which came nearly to his knees, was barefoot, and sprightly with that alert mud-larking quickness which has its advantages.

So we went down a passage and climbed a stair and came to an office where one would expect to register births and deaths. But the urchin said it was the telegraph office. No sign of life. Peering through the wicket I saw a fat individual seated writing in the distance. Feeble lights relieved the big, barren, official spaces—I wonder the fat official wasn't afraid to be up here alone.

He made no move. I banged the shutter and demanded a telegraph blank. His shoulders went up to his ears, and he plainly intimated his intention to let us wait. But I said loudly to the urchin: "Is *that* the telegraph official?" and the urchin said: "Si, signore"—so the fat individual had to come.

After which considerable delay we set off again. The bus, thank heaven, had gone, the savage dark street was empty of friends. We turned away to the harbour front. It was dark now. I saw a railway near at hand—a bunch of dark masts—the steamer showing a few lights, far down at the tip of a long spit of land, remote in mid-harbour. And so off we went, the barefoot urchin twinkling a few yards ahead, on the road that followed the spit of land. The spit was wide enough to carry this road, and a railway. On the right was a silent house apparently built on piles in the harbour. Away far down in front leaned our glimmering steamer, and a little train was shunting trucks among the low sheds beside it. Night had fallen, and the great stars flashed. Orion was in the air, and his dog-star after him. We followed on down the dark bar between the silent, lustrous water. The harbour was smooth as glass, and gleaming like a mirror. Hills came round encircling it entirely—dark land ridging up and lying away out, even to seaward. One was not sure which was exactly seaward. The dark encircling of the land seemed stealthy, the hills had a remoteness, guarding the waters in the silence. Perhaps the great mass away beyond was Tavolara again. It seemed like some lumpish berg guarding an arctic, locked-up bay where ships lay dead.

On and on we followed the urchin, till the town was left behind, until it also twinkled a few meagre lights out of its low, confused blackness at the bay-head, across the waters. We had left the ship-masts and the settlement. The urchin padded on, only turning now and again and extending a thin, eager hand towards the kitchenino. Especially when some men were advancing down the railway he wanted it: the q-b's carrying it was a slur on his prowess. So the kitchenino was relinquished, and the lark strode on satisfied.

Till at last we came to the low sheds that squatted between the steamer and the railway-end. The lark led me into one, where a red-cap was writing. The cap let me wait some minutes before informing me that this was the goods office—the ticket office was further on. The lark flew at him and said "Then you've changed it, have you?." And he led me on to another shed, which was just going to shut up. Here they finally had the condescension to give me two tickets— a hundred and fifty francs the two. So we followed the lark, who strode like Scipio Africanus up the gangway with the sack.

It was quite a small ship. The steward put me in number one cabin—the q-b in number seven. Each cabin had four berths. Consequently man and woman must separate rigorously on this ship. Here was a blow for the q-b, who knows what Italian female fellow-passengers can be. However, there we were. All the cabins were down below, and all, for some reason, inside—no portholes outside. It was hot and close down below already. I pitched the sack on my berth, and there stood the lark on the red carpet at the door.

I gave him three francs. He looked at it as if it were my death-warrant. He peered at the paper in the light of the lamp. Then he extended his arm with a gesture of superb insolence, flinging me back my gold without a word.

"How!" said I. "Three francs are quite enough."

"Three francs—two kilometres—and three pieces of luggage! No, signore. No! Five francs. Cinque franchi!"

And averting his pallid old mud-larking face, and flinging his hand out at me, he stood the image of indignant repudiation. And truly, he was no taller than my upper waistcoat pocket. The brat! The brat! He was such an actor, and so impudent, that I wavered between wonder- and amusement and a great inclination to. kick him up the steps. I decided not to waste my energy being angry.

"What a beastly little boy! What a horrid little boy! What a *horrid* little boy! Really—a little thief. A little swindler!" I mused aloud.

"Swindler!" he quavered after me. And he was beaten.

"Swindler" doubled him up: that and the quiet mildness of my tone of invocation. Now he would have gone with his three francs. And now, in final contempt, I gave him the other two.

He disappeared like a streak of lightning up the gangway, terrified lest the steward should come and catch him at his tricks. For later on I saw the steward send other larks flying for demanding more than one-fifty. The brat.

The question was now the cabin: for the q-b simply refused to entertain the idea of sharing a cabin with three Italian women, who would all be sick simply for the fuss of it, though the sea was smooth as glass. We hunted up the steward. He said all the first-class cabins had four berths—the second had three, but much smaller. How that was possible I don't know. However, if no one came, he would give us a cabin to ourselves.

The ship was clean and civilised, though very poky. And there we were.

We went on deck. Would we eat on board, asked another person. No, we wouldn't. We went out to a fourth little shed, which was a refreshment stall, and bought bread and sardines and chocolate and apples. Then we went on the upper deck to make our meal. In a sheltered place I lit the spirit lamp, and put on water to boil. The water we had taken from the cabin. Then we sat down alone in the darkness, on a seat which had its back against the deck cabins, now appropriated by the staff. A thin, cold wind was travelling: We wrapped the one plaid round us both and snugged together, waiting for the tea to boil. I could just see the point of the spirit-flame licking up from where we sat.

The stars were marvellous in the soundless sky, so big, that one could see them hanging orb-like and alone in their, own space, yet all the myriads. Particularly bright the evening star. And he hung flashing in the lower night with a power that made me hold my breath. Grand and powerful he sent out his flashes, so sparkling that he seemed more intense than any sun or moon. And from the dark, uprising land he sent his way of light to us across the water, a marvellous star-road. So all above us the stars soared and pulsed, over that silent, night-dark, land-locked harbour.

After a long time the water boiled, and we drank our hot tea and ate our sardines and bread and bits of remaining Nuoro sausage, sitting there alone in the intense starry darkness of that upper deck. I said alone: but no, two ghoulish ship's cats came howling at us for the bits. And even when everything was eaten, and the sardine tin thrown in the sea, still they circled and prowled and howled.

We sat on, resting under the magnificent deep heavens, wrapped together in the old shepherd's shawl for which I have blessed so often a Scottish friend, half sheltered from the cold night wind, and recovering somewhat from the sixty miles bus-ride we had done that day.

As yet there was nobody on the ship—we were the very first, at least in the first-class. Above, all was silent and deserted. Below, all was lit up and deserted. But it was a little ship, with accommodation for some thirty first-class and forty second-class passengers.

In the low deck forward stood two rows of cattle—eighteen cattle. They stood tied up side by side, and quite motionless, as if stupefied. Only two had lain down. The rest stood motionless, with tails dropped and heads dropped, as if drugged or gone insensible. These cattle on the ship fascinated the q-b. She insisted on going down to them, and examining them minutely. But there they were—stiff almost as Noah's Ark cows. What she could not understand was that they neither cried nor struggled. Motionless—terribly motionless. In her idea cattle are wild and indomitable creatures. She will not realise the horrid strength of passivity and inertia which is almost the preponderant force in domesticated creatures, men and beast alike. There are fowls too in various coops—flappy and agitated these.

At last, at about half-past seven the train from the island arrived, and the people surged out in a mass. We stood hanging over the end of the upper deck, looking down. On they poured, in a thick mass, up the gangway, with all conceivable sorts of luggage: bundles, embroidered carry-alls, bags, saddle-bags—the q-b lamenting she had not bought one—a sudden surging mass of people and goods. There are soldiers too—but these are lined upon the bit of a quay, to wait.

Our interest is to see whether there will be any more first-class passengers. Coming up the wide board which serves as gangway each individual hands a ticket to the man at the top, and is shooed away to his own region—usually second-class. There are three sorts of tickets—green first-class, white second, and pink third. The second-class passengers go aft, the third-class go forward, along the passage past our cabins, into the steerage. And so we watch and watch the excited people come on board and divide. Nearly all are second-class—and a great many are women. We have seen a few first-class men. But as yet no women. And every hat with ospreys gives the q-b a qualm.

For a long time we are safe. The women flood to the second-class. One, who is third, begs and beseeches to go with her friends in the second. I am glad to say without success. And then, alas, an elderly man with a daughter, first-class. They are very respectable and pleasant looking. But the q-b wails: "I'm sure she will be sick."

Towards the end come three convicts, chained together. They wear the brownish striped homespun, and do not look evil. They seem to be laughing together, not at all in distress. The two young soldiers who guard them, and who have gunsus. So the convicts go forward to the steerage, past our cabins.

At last the soldiers are straightened up, and turned on board. There almost at once they start making a tent: drawing a huge tarpaulin over, a cross rope in the mid-deck below us, between the first and second-class regions. The great tarpaulin is pulled down well on either side and fastened down, and it makes a big dark tent. The soldiers creep in and place their bundles.

And now it is the soldiers who fascinate the q-b. She hangs over the bar above, and peers in. The soldiers arrange themselves in two rows. They will sleep with their heads on their bundles on either side of the tent, the two rows of feet coming together inwards. But first they must eat, for it is eight o'clock and more.

Out come their suppers: a whole roast fowl, hunks of kid, legs of lamb, huge breads. The fowl is dismembered with a jackknife in a twinkling, and shared. Everything among the soldiers is shared. There they sit in their pent-house with its open ends, crowded together and happy, chewing with all their might and clapping one another on the shoulder lovingly, and taking swigs at the wine bottles. We envy them their good food.

At last all are on board—the omnibus has driven up from town and gone back. A last young lout dashes up in a carriage and scuffles aboard. The crew begins to run about. The quay-porters have trotted on board with the last bales and packages—all is stowed safely. The steamer hoots and hoots. Two men and a girl kiss their friends all round and get off the ship. The night re-echoes the steamer's hoots. The sheds have gone all dark. Far off the town twinkles very sparsely. All is night-deserted. And so the gangway is hauled up, and the rope hawsers quickly wound in. We are drifting away from the quay side. The few watchers wave, their white handkerchiefs, standing diminutive and forlorn on the dark little quay, in the heart of the dark, deserted harbour. One woman cries and waves and weeps. A man makes exaggerated flag-wagging signals with his white hanky, and feels important. We drift—and the engines begin to beat. We are moving in the land-locked harbour.

Everybody watches. The commander and the crew shout orders. And so, very slowly, and without any fuss at all, like a man wheeling a barrow out of a yard gate, we throb very slowly out of the harbour, past one point, then past another, away from the encircling hills, away from the great lump of Tavolara which is to southward, away from, the outreaching land to the north, and over the edge of the open sea.

187

And now to try for a cabin to ourselves. I approach the steward. Yes, he says, he has it in mind. But there are eighty second-class passengers, in an accommodation space for forty. The transit-controller is now considering it. Most probably he will transfer some second-class women to the vacant first-class cabins. If he does not do so, then the steward will accommodate us.

I know what this means—this equivocation. We decide not to bother any more. So we make a tour of the ship—to look at the soldiers, who have finished eating, sitting yarning to one another, while some are already stretched out in the shadow, for sleep. Then to look at the cattle, which stand rooted to the deck—which is now all messy. To look at the unhappy fowls in their coops. And a peep at the third-class—rather horrifying.

And so to bed. Already the other three berths in my cabin are occupied, the lights are switched off. As I enter I hear one young man tenderly inquiring of the berth below: "Dost thou feel ill?" "Er—not much—not much!" says the other faintly.

Yet the sea is like glass, so smooth.

I am quickly rolled in my lower berth, where I feel the trembling of the machine-impelled ship, and hear the creaking of the berth above me as its occupant rolls over: I listen to the sighs of the others, the wash of dark water. And so, uneasily, rather hot and very airless, uneasy with the machine-throbbing and the sighing of my companions, and with a cock that crows shrilly from one of the coops, imagining the ship's lights to be dawn, the night goes by. One sleeps—but a bad sleep. If only there were cold air, not this lower-berth, inside cabin airlessness.

CHAPTER VIII
BACK

THE sea being steady as a level road, nobody succeeded in being violently sick. My young men rose at dawn—I was not long in following. It was a grey morning on deck, a grey sea, a grey sky, and a grey, spider-cloth, unimportant coast of Italy not far away. The q-b joined me: and quite delighted with her fellow-passenger: such a nice girl, she said! who, when she let down her ordinary-looking brown hair, it reached rippling right to her feet! Voilà! You never know your luck.

The cock that had crowed all night crowed again, hoarsely, with a sore throat. The miserable cattle looked more wearily miserable, but still were motionless, as sponges that grow at the bottom of the sea. The convicts were out for air: grinning. Someone told us they were war-deserters. Considering the light in which these people look on war, desertion seemed to me the only heroism. But the q-b, brought up in a military air, gazed upon them as upon men miraculously alive within the shadow of death. According to her code they had been shot when recaptured. The soldiers had unslung the tarpaulin, their home for the night had melted with the darkness, they were mere fragments of grey transit smoking cigarettes and staring overboard.

We drew near to Cività Vecchia: the old, mediæval-looking port, with its castle, and a round fortress-barracks at the entrance. Soldiers aboard shouted and waved to soldiers on the ramparts. We backed insignificantly into the rather scrubby, insignificant harbour. And in five minutes we were out, and walking along the wide, desolate boulevard to the station. The cabmen looked hard at us: but no doubt owing to the knapsack, took us for poor Germans.

Coffee and milk—and then, only about three-quarters of an hour late, the train from the north. It is the night express from Turin. There was plenty of room—so in we got, followed by half a dozen Sardinians. We found a large, heavy Torinese in the carriage, his eyes dead with fatigue. It seemed quite a new world on the mainland: and at once one breathed again the curious suspense that is in the air. Once more I read the "Corriere della Sera" from end to end. Once more we knew ourselves in the real active world, where the air seems like a lively wine dissolving the pearl of the old order. I hope, dear reader, you like the metaphor. Yet I cannot forbear repeating how strongly one is sensible of the solvent property of the atmosphere, suddenly arriving on the mainland again. And in an hour one changes one's psyche. The human being is a most curious creature. He thinks he has got one soul, and he has got dozens. I felt my sound Sardinian soul melting off me, I felt myself evaporating into the real Italian uncertainty and momentaneity. So I perused the, "Corriere" whilst the metamorphosis took place. I like Italian newspapers because they say what they mean, and not merely what is most convenient to say. We call it naïveté—I call it manliness. Italian newspapers read as if they were written by men, and not by calculating eunuchs.

The train ran very heavily along the Maremma. It began to rain. Then we stopped at a station where we should not stop—somewhere in the Maremma country, the invisible sea not far off, the low country cultivated and yet forlorn. Oh, how the Turin man sighed, and wearily shifted his feet as the train stood meaningless. There it sat—in the rain. Oh, express!

At last on again, till we were winding through the curious long troughs of the Roman Campagna. There the shepherds minded the sheep: the slender-footed merino sheep. In Sardinia the merinos were very white and glistening, so that one thought of the scriptural "white as wool." And the black sheep among the flock were very black. But these Campagna were no longer white, but dingy. And though the wildness of the Campagna is a real wildness still, it is a historic wildness, familiar in its way as a fireside is familiar.

So we approach the hopeless sprawling of modern Rome— over the yellow Tiber, past the famous pyramid tomb, skirting the walls of the city, till at last we plunge in, into the well-known station, out of all the chaos.

We are late. It is a quarter to twelve. And I have to go out and change money, and I hope to find my two friends.—The q-b and I dash down the platform—no friends at the barrier. The station moderately empty. We bolt across to the departure platforms. The Naples train stands ready. In we pitch our bags, ask a naval man not to let anyone steal them, then I fly out into town while the q-b buys food and wine at the buffet.

It no longer rains, and Rome feels as ever—rather holiday-like and not inclined to care about anything. I get a hundred and three lira for each pound note: pocket my money at two minutes past twelve, and bolt back, out of the Piazza delle Terme. Aha, there are the two missing ones, just descending vaguely from a carriage, the one gazing inquiringly through his monocle across the tram-lines, the other very tall and alert and elegant, looking as if he expected us to appear out of the air for his convenience.

Which is exactly what happens. We fly into each other's arms. "Oh, there you *are!* Where's the q-b? Why are you here? We've been to the arrival platform—no *sign* of you. Of course I only got your wire half an hour ago. We *flew* here. Well, how nice to see you.— Oh, let the man wait.— What, going on at once to Naples? But must you? Oh, but how flighty you are! Birds of passage *veramente!* Then let us find the q-b, quick !—And they won't let us on the platform. No, they're not issuing platform tickets to-day. — Oh, merely

189

the guests returning from the Savoy-Bavarian wedding in the north, a few royal Duchesses about. Oh, well, we must try and wangle him."

At the barrier a woman trying in vain to be let on to the station. But what a Roman matron can't do, an elegant young Englishman can. So our two heroes wangle their way in, and fall into the arms of the q-b by the Naples train. Well, now, tell us all about it! So we rush into a four-branched candlestick of conversation. In my ear murmurs he of the monocle about the Sahara—he is back from the Sahara a week ago: the winter sun in the Sahara! He with the smears of paint on his elegant trousers is giving the q-b a sketchy outline of his now *grande passion*. Click—goes the exchange, and he of the monocle is detailing to the q-b his trip to Japan, on which he will start in six weeks' time, while he of the paint-smears is expatiating on the thrills of the etching needle, and concocting a plan for a month in Sardinia in May, with me doing the scribbles and he the pictures. What sort of pictures? Out flies the name of Goya. And well now, a general rush into oneness, and won't they come down to Sicily to us for the almond blossom: in about ten days' time. Yes, they will—wire them when the almond blossom is just stepping on the stage and making its grand bow, and they will come next day. Somebody has smitten the wheel of a coach two ringing smacks with a hammer. This is a sign to get in. The q-b is terrified the train will slip through her fingers. "I'm frightened, I must get in."—"Very well then! You're sure you have everything you want? Everything? A fiasco of vino? Oh, *two!* All the better! Well then—ten days' time. All right—quite sure—how nice to have seen you, if only a *glimpse.*—Yes, yes, poor q-b! Yes, you're quite safe. Good-bye! Good-bye!

The door is shut—we are seated—the train moves out of the station. And quickly on this route Rome disappears. We are out on the wintry Campagna, where crops are growing. Away on the left we see the Tivoli hills, and think of the summer that is gone, the heat, the fountains of the Villa D'Este. The train rolls heavily over the Campagna, towards the Alban Mounts, homewards.

So we fall on our food, and devour the excellent little beefsteaks and rolls and boiled eggs, apples and oranges and dates, and drink the good red wine, and wildly discuss plans and the latest news, and are altogether thrilled about things. So thrilled that we are well away among the romantic mountains of the south-centre before we realise that there are other passengers besides ourselves in the carriage. Half the journey is over. Why, there is the monastery on its high hill! In a wild moment I suggest we shall get down and spend a night up there at Montecassino, and see the other friend, the monk who knows so much about the world, being out of it. But the q-b shudders, thinking of the awful winter coldness of that massive stone monastery, which has no spark of heating apparatus. And therefore the plan subsides, and at Cassino station I only get down to procure coffee and sweet cakes. They always have good things to eat at Cassino station: in summer, big fresh ices and fruits and iced water, in winter toothsome sweet cakes which make an awfully good finish to a meal.

I count Cassino half-way to Naples. After Cassino the excitement of being in the north begins quite to evaporate. The southern heaviness descends upon us. Also the sky begins to darken: and the rain falls. I think of the night before us, on the sea again. And I am vaguely troubled lest we may not get a berth. However, we may spend the night in Naples: or even sit on in this train, which goes forward, all through the long, long night, to the Straits of Messina. We must decide as we near Naples.

Half-dozing, one becomes aware of the people about one. We are travelling second-class. Opposite is a little, hold-your-own school-mistressy young person in pince-nez. Next her a hollow-cheeked white soldier with ribbons on his breast. Then a fat man in a corner. Then a naval officer of low rank. The naval officer is coming from Fiume, and is dead with sleep and perhaps mortification. D'Annunzio had just given up. Two compartments away we hear soldiers singing, martial still though bruised with fatigue, the D'Annunzio-bragging songs of Fiume. They are soldiers of the D'Annunzio legion. And one of them, I hear the sick soldier saying, is very hot and republican still. Private soldiers are not allowed, with their reduced tickets, to travel on the express trains. But these legionaries are not penniless: they have paid the excess and come along. For the moment they are sent to their homes. And with heads dropping with fatigue, we hear them still defiantly singing down the carriage for D'Annunzio.

A regular officer went along—a captain of the Italian, not the Fiume army. He heard the chants and entered the carriage. The legionaries were quiet, but they lounged and ignored the entry of the Officer. "On your feet! " he yelled, Italian fashion. The vehemence did it. Reluctantly as may be, they stood up in the compartment. "Salute!" And though it was bitter, up went their hands in the salute, whilst he stood and watched them. And then, very superb, he sauntered away again. They sat down glowering. Of course they were beaten. Didn't they know it! The men in our carriage smiled curiously: in slow, and futile mockery of both parties.

The rain was falling outside, the windows were steamed quite dense, so that we were shut in from the world. Throughout the length of the train, which was not very full, could be felt the exhausted weariness and the dispirited dejection of the poor D'Annunzio legionaries. In the afternoon silence of the mist-enclosed, half-empty train the snatches of song broke out again, and faded in sheer dispirited fatigue. We ran on blindly and heavily. But one young fellow was not to be abashed. He was well built, and his thick black hair was brushed up, like a great fluffy crest upon his head. He came slowly and unabated down the corridor, and on every big, mist-opaque pane he scrawled with his finger W D'ANNUNZIO GABRIELE—W D'ANNUNZIO GABRIELE.

The sick soldier laughed thinly, saying to the schoolmistress: "Oh, yes, they are fine chaps. But it was folly. D'Annunzio is a world poet—a world wonder—but Fiume was a mistake, you know. And these chaps have got to learn a lesson. They got beyond themselves. Oh, they aren't short of money. D'Annunzio had wagon-loads of money there in Fiume, and he wasn't altogether mean with it." The schoolmistress, who was one of the sharp ones, gave a little disquisition to show *why* it was a mistake, and wherein she knew better than the world's poet and wonder.

It always makes me sick to hear people chewing over newspaper pulp.

The sick soldier was not a legionary. He had been wounded through the lung. But it was healed, he said. He lifted the flap of his breast pocket, and there hung a little silver medal, It was his wound-medal. He wore it concealed: and over the place of the wound. He and the schoolmistress looked at one another significantly.

Then they talked pensions: and soon were on the old topic. The schoolmistress had her figures pat, as a schoolmistress should. Why, the ticket-collector, the man who punches one's tickets on the train, now had twelve thousand lire a year: twelve thousand lire. Monstrous! Whilst a fully qualified *professore,* a schoolmaster who had been through all his training and had all his degrees, was given five thousand. Five thousand for a fully qualified *professore,* and twelve thousand for a ticket puncher. The soldier agreed, and quoted other figures. But the railway was the outstanding grievance Every boy who left school now, said the schoolmistress wanted to go on the railway. Oh, but—said the soldier—the train-men—!

The naval officer, who collapsed into the most uncanny positions, blind with sleep, got down at Capua to get into a little train that would carry him back to his own station, where our train had not stopped. At Caserta the sick soldier got out. Down the great avenue of trees the rain was falling. A young man entered. Remained also the schoolmistress and the stout man. Knowing, we had been listening, the schoolmistress spoke to us about the soldier. Then—she had said she was catching the night boat for Palermo—I asked her if she thought the ship would be very full. Oh, yes, very full, she said. Why, hers was one of the last cabin numbers, and she had got her ticket early that morning. The fat man now joined in. He too was crossing to Palermo. The ship was sure to be quite full by now. Were we depending on booking berths at the port of Naples? We were. Whereupon he and the schoolmistress shook their heads and said it was more than doubtful—nay, it was as good as impossible. For the boat was the renowned *Città di Trieste,* that floating palace, and such was the fame of her gorgeousness that everybody wanted to travel by her.

"First and second-class alike?" I asked.

"Oh, yes, also first-class," replied the school-marm rather spitefully. So I knew she had a white ticket—second.

I cursed the *Città di Trieste* and her gorgeousness, and looked down my nose. We had now two alternatives: to spend the night in Naples, or to sit on all through the night and next morning, and arrive home, with heaven's aid, in the early afternoon. Though these long-distance trains think nothing of six hours late. But we were tired already. What we should be like after another twenty-four hours sitting, heaven knows. And yet to struggle for a bed in a Naples hotel this night, in the rain, all the hotels being at present crammed with foreigners, that was no rosy prospect. Oh, dear!

However, I was not going to take their discouragement so easily. One has been had that way before. They love to make the case look desperate.

Were we English? asked the schoolmistress. We were. Ah, a fine thing to be English in Italy now. Why?—rather tart from me. Because of the *cambio,* the exchange. You English, with your money exchange, you come here and buy everything for nothing, you take the best of everything, and with your money you pay nothing for it. Whereas we poor Italians we pay heavily for everything at an exaggerated price, and we can have nothing. Ah, it is all very nice to be English in Italy now. You can travel, you go to the hotels, you can see everything and buy everything, and it costs you nothing. What is the exchange to-day? She whipped it out. A hundred and four, twenty.

This she told me to my nose. And the fat man murmured bitterly già! già!—ay! ay! Her impertinence and the fat man's quiet bitterness stirred my bile. Has not this song been sung at me once too often, by these people?

You are mistaken, said I to the schoolmistress. We don't by any means live in Italy for nothing. Even with the exchange at a hundred and three, we don't live for nothing. We pay, and pay through the nose, for whatever we have in Italy: and you Italians see that we pay. What! You put all the tariff you do on foreigners, and then say we live here for nothing. I tell you I could live in England just as well, on the same money—perhaps better. Compare the cost of things in England with the cost here in Italy, and even considering the exchange Italy costs nearly as much as England. Some things are cheaper here—the railway comes a little cheaper. and is infinitely more miserable. Travelling is usually a misery. But other things, clothes of all sorts, and a good deal of food, are even more expensive here than in England, exchange considered.

Oh, yes, she said, England had had to bring her prices down this last fortnight. In her own interests indeed.

"This last fortnight! This last six months," said I. "Whereas prices rise every single day here."

Here a word from the quiet young man who had got in Caserta.

"Yes," he said, "yes. I say, every nation pays in its own money, no matter what the exchange. And it works out about equal."

But I felt angry. Am I always to have the exchange flung in my teeth, as if I were a personal thief? But the woman persisted.

"Ah," she said, "we Italians, we are so nice, we are so good. Noi siamo cosi buoni. We are so good-natured. But others, they are not buoni, they are not good-natured to us." And she nodded her head. And truly, I did not feel at all good-natured towards her: which she knew. And as for the Italian good-nature, it forms a sound and unshakable basis nowadays for their extortion and self-justification and spite.

Darkness was falling over the rich flat plains that lie around Naples, over the tall uncanny vines with their brown thongs in the intensely cultivated black earth. It was night by the time we were in that vast and thievish station. About half-past five. We were not very late. Should we sit on in our present carriage, and go down in it to the port; along with the schoolmistress, and risk it? But first look at the coach which was going on to Sicily. So we got down and ran along the train to the Syracuse coach. Hubbub, confusion, a wedge in the corridor, and for sure no room. Certainly no room to lie down a bit. We *could* not sit tight for twenty-four hours more.

So we decided to go to the port—and to walk. Heaven knows when the railway carriage would be shunted down. Back we went therefore for the sack, and told the school-mistress our intention.

"You can but try," she said frostily.

So there we are, with the sack over my shoulder and the kitchenino in the q-b's hand, bursting out of that thrice-damned and annoying station, and running through the black wet gulf of a Naples night, in a slow rain. Cabmen look at us. But my sack saved me. I am weary of that boa-constrictor, a Naples cabman after dark. By day there is more or less a tariff.

It is about a mile from the station to the quay where the ship lies. We make our way through the deep, gulf-like streets; over the slippery black cobbles. The black houses rise massive to a great height on either side, but the streets are not in this part very narrow. We plunge forwards in the unearthly half-darkness of this great uncontrolled city. There are no lights at all from the buildings—only the small electric lamps of the streets.

So we emerge on the harbour front, and hurry past the great storehouses in the rainy night, to where the actual entrances begin. The tram bangs past us. We scuffle along that pavement-ridge which lies like an isthmus down the vast black quicksands of that harbour road. One feels peril all round. But at length we come to a gate by the harbour railway. No, not that: On to the next iron gate of the railway crossing. And so we run out past the great sheds and the buildings of the port station, till we see a ship rearing in front, and the sea all black. But now where is that little hole where one gets the tickets? We are at the back of everywhere in this desert jungle of the harbour darkness.

A man directs us round the corner—and actually does not demand money. It is the sack again. So—there, I see the knot of men, soldiers chiefly, fighting in a bare room round a tiny wicket. I recognise the place where I have fought before.

So while the q-b stands guard over sack and bag, I plunge into the fray. It literally is a fight. Some thirty men all at once want to get at a tiny wicket in a blank wall. There are no queue-rails, there is no order: just a hole in a blank wall and thirty fellows, mostly military, pressing at it in a mass. But I have done this before. The way is to insert the thin end of oneself, and without any violence, by deadly pressure and pertinacity come at the goal. One hand must be kept fast over the money pocket, and one must be free to clutch the wicket-side when one gets there. And thus one is ground small in those mills of God, Demos struggling for tickets. It isn't very nice—so close, so incomparably crushed. And never for a second must one be off one's guard for one's watch and money and even hanky. When I first came to Italy after the war I was robbed twice in three weeks, floating round in the sweet old innocent confidence in mankind. Since then I have never ceased to be on my guard. Somehow or other, waking and sleeping one's spirit must be on its guard nowadays. Which is really what I prefer, now I have learnt it. Confidence in the goodness of mankind is a very thin protection indeed. *Integer vitae scelerisque purus* will do nothing for you when it comes to humanity, however efficacious it may be with lions and wolves. Therefore, tight on my guard, like a screw biting into a bit of wood, I bite my way through that knot of fellows, to the wicket, and shout for two first-class. The clerk inside ignores me for some time, serving soldiers. But if you stand like Doomsday you get your way. Two firsts, says the clerk. Husband and wife, say I, in case there is a two-berth cabin. Jokes behind. But I get my tickets. Impossible to put my hand to my pocket. The tickets cost about a hundred and five francs each. Clutching paper change and the green slips, with a last gasp I get out of the knot. So—we've done it. As I sort my money and stow away, I hear another ask for one first-class. Nothing left, says the clerk. So you see how one must fight.

I must say for these dense and struggling crowds, they are only intense, not violent, and not in the least brutal. I always feel a certain sympathy with the men in them.

Bolt through the pouring rain to the ship. And in two flutes we are aboard. And behold, each of us has a deck cabin, I one to myself, the q-b to herself next door. Palatial— not a cabin at all, but a proper little bedroom with a curtained bed under the porthole windows, a comfortable sofa, chairs, table, carpets, big wash-bowls with silver taps—a whole *de luxe*. I dropped the sack on the sofa with a gasp, drew back the yellow curtains of the bed, looked out of the porthole at the lights of Naples, and sighed with relief. One could wash thoroughly, refreshingly, and change one's linen. Wonderful!

The state-room is like an hotel lounge, many little tables with flowers and periodicals, arm-chairs, warm carpet, bright but soft lights, and people sitting about chatting. A loud group of English people in one corner, very assured, two quiet English ladies: various Italians seeming quite modest. Here one could sit in peace and rest, pretending to look at an illustrated magazine. So we rested. After about an hour there entered a young Englishman and his wife, whom we had seen on our train. So, at last the coach had been shunted down to the port. Where should we have been had we waited!

The waiters began to flap the white tablecloths and spread the tables nearest the walls. Dinner would begin at half-past seven, immediately the boat started. We sat in silence, till eight or nine tables were spread. Then we let the other people take their choice. After which we chose a table by ourselves, neither of us wanting company. So we sat before the plates and the wine bottles and sighed in the hopes of a decent meal. Food by the way is not included in the hundred and five francs.

Alas, we were not to be alone: two young Neapolitans, pleasant, quiet, blond, or semi-blond. They were well bred, and evidently of northern extraction. Afterwards we found out they were jewellers. But I liked their quiet, gentle manners. The dinner began, and we were through the soup, when up pranced another young fellow, rather strapping and loud, a commercial traveller, for sure. He had those cocky assured manners of one who is not sure of his manners. He had a rather high forehead, and black hair brushed up in a showy wing, and a large ring on his finger. Not that a ring signifies anything. Here most of the men wear several, all massively jewelled. If one believed in all the jewels, why, Italy would be more fabulous than fabled India. But our friend the bounder was smart, and smelled of cash. Not money, but cash.

I had an inkling of what to expect when he handed the salt and said in English "Salt, thenk you." But I ignored the advance. However, he did not wait long. Through the windows across the room the q-b saw the lights of the harbour slowly moving. "Oh," she cried, "are we going?" And also in Italian: "Partiamo?" All watched the lights, the bounder screwing round. He had one of the fine, bounderish backs.

"Yes," he said. "We—*going.*"

"Oh," cried she. "Do you speak English?"

"Ye-es. Some English—I speak."

As a matter of fact he spoke about forty disconnected words. But his accent was so good for these forty. He did not speak English, he imitated an English voice making sounds. And the effect was startling. He had served on the Italian front with the Scots Guards—so he told us in Italian. He was Milanese. Oh, he had had a time with the Scots Guards. Wheesky—eh? Wheesky.

"Come along, *bhoys!*" he shouted.

And it was such a Scotch voice shouting, so loud-mouthed and actual, I nearly went under the table. It struck us both like a blow.

Afterwards he rattled away without misgiving. He was a traveller for a certain type of machine, and was doing Sicily. Shortly he was going to England—and he asked largely about first-class hotels. Then he asked was the q-b French?—Was she Italian?—No, she was German. Ah—German. And immediately out he came with the German word: "Deutsch! Deutsch, eh? From Deutschland. Oh, yes! Deutschland über alles! Ah, I know. No more—what? Deutschland unter alles now? Deutschland unter alles." And he bounced on his seat with gratification of the words. Of German as of English he knew half a dozen phrases.

"No," said the q-b, "not Deutschland unter alles. Not for long, anyhow."

"How? Not for long? You think so? I think so too," said the bounder. And in Italian: "La Germania won't stand under all for long. No, no. At present it is England über alles. *England über alles.* But Germany will rise up again."

"Of course," said the q-b. "How shouldn't she?"

"Ah," said the bounder, "while England keeps the money in her pocket, we shall none of us rise up. Italy won the war, and Germany lost it. And Italy and Germany they both are down, and England is up. They both are down, and England is up. England and France. Strange, isn't it? Ah, the allies. What are the allies for? To keep England up, and France half-way, and Germany and Italy down."

"Ah they won't stay down for ever," said the q-b.

"You think not? Ah! We will see. We will see how England goes on now"

"England is not going on so marvellously, after all," say I.

"How not? You mean Ireland?"

"No, not only Ireland. Industry altogether. England is as near to ruin as other countries."

"Ma! With all the money, and we others with no money? How will she be ruined?"

"And what good would it be to you if she were?"

"Oh, well—who knows? If England were ruined—" a slow smile of anticipation spread over his face. How he would love it—how they would all love it, if England were ruined. That is, the business part of them, perhaps, would not love it. But the human part would. The human part fairly licks its lips at the thought of England's ruin. The commercial part, however, quite violently disclaims the anticipations of the human part. And there it is. The newspapers chiefly speak with the commercial voice. But individually, when you are got at in a railway carriage or as now on a ship, up speaks the human voice, and you know how they love you. This is no doubt inevitable. When the exchange stands at a hundred and six men go humanly blind, I suppose, however much they may keep the commercial eye open. And having gone humanly blind they bump into one's human self nastily: a nasty jar. You know then how they bate you. Underneath, they hate us, and as human beings we are objects of envy and malice. They hate us, with envy, and despise us, with jealousy. Which perhaps doesn't hurt commercially. Humanly it is to me unpleasant.

The dinner was over, and the bounder was lavishing cigarettes—Murattis, if you please. We had all drunk two bottles of wine. Two other commercial travellers had joined the bounder at our table—two smart young fellows, one a bounder and one gentle and nice. Our two jewellers remained quiet, talking their share, but quietly and so sensitively. One could not help liking them. So we were seven people, six men.

"Wheesky! Will you drink wheesky, Mister?" said our original bounder. "Yes, one small Scotch! One Scotch wheesky." All this in a perfect Scotty voice of a man standing at a bar calling for a drink. It was comical, one could not but laugh: and very impertinent. He called for the waiter, took him by the button-hole, and with a breast-to-breast intimacy asked if there was whisky. The waiter, with the same tone of you-and-I-are-men-who-have-the-same-feelings, said he didn't think there was whisky, but he would look. Our bounder went round the table inviting us all to whiskies, and pressing on us his expensive English cigarettes with great aplomb.

The whisky came—and five persons partook. It was fiery, oily stuff from heaven knows where. The bounder rattled away, spouting his bits of English and his four words of German. He was in high feather, wriggling his large haunches on his chair and waving his hands. He had a peculiar manner of wriggling from the bottom of his back, with fussy self-assertiveness. It was my turn to offer whisky.

I was able in a moment's lull to peer through the windows and see the dim lights of Capri—the glimmer of Anacapri up on the black shadow—the lighthouse. We had passed the island. In the midst of the babel I sent out a few thoughts to a few people on the island. Then I had to come back.

The bounder had once more resumed his theme of l'Inghilterra, l'Italia, la Germania. He swanked England as hard as he could. Of course England was the top dog, and if he could speak some English, if he were talking to English people, and if, as he said, he was going to England in April, why, he was so much the more top-doggy than his companions, who could not rise to all these heights. At the same time, my nerves had too much to bear.

Where were we going and where had we been and where did we live? And ah, yes, English people lived in Italy. Thousands, thousands of English people lived in Italy. Yes, it was very nice for them. There used to be many Germans, but now the Germans were down. But the English—what could be better for them than Italy now: they had sun, they had warmth, they had abundance of everything, they had a charming people to deal with, and they had the *cambio!* Ecco! The other commercial travellers agreed. They appealed to the q-b if it was not so. And altogether I had enough of it.

"Oh, yes," said I, "it's very nice to be in Italy: especially if you are not living in an hotel, and you have to attend to things for yourself. It is very nice to be overcharged every time, and then insulted if you say a word. It's very nice to have the *cambio* thrown in your teeth, if you say two words to any Italian, even a perfect stranger. It's very nice to have. waiters and shop-people and railway porters sneering in a bad temper and being insulting in small, mean ways all the time. It's very nice to feel what they all feel against you. And if you understand enough Italian, it's very nice to hear what they say when you've gone by. Oh, very nice. —Very nice indeed!

I suppose the whisky had kindled this outburst in me. They sat dead silent. And then our bounder began, in his sugary deprecating voice:

"Why no! Why no! It is not true, Signore. No, it is not true. Why, England is the foremost nation in the world—"

"And you want to pay her out for it."

"But no, Signore. But no. What makes you say so? Why, we Italians are so good-natured. Noi Italiani siamo cosi buoni. Siamo cosi buoni."

They were the identical words of the schoolmistress.

"Buoni," said I. "Yes—perhaps. Buoni when it's not a question of the exchange and of money. But since it is always a question of *cambio* and *soldi* now, one is always, in a small way, insulted."

I suppose it must have been the whisky. Anyhow Italians can never bear hard bitterness. The jewellers looked distressed, the bounders looked down their noses, half exulting even now, and half sheepish, being caught. The third of the *commis voyageurs,* the gentle one, made large eyes and was terrified that he was going to be sick. He represented a certain Italian liqueur, and he modestly asked us to take a glass of it. He went with the waiter to secure the proper brand. So we drank—and it was good. But he, the giver, sat with large and haunted eyes. Then he said he would go to bed. Our bounder gave him various advice regarding sea-sickness. There was a mild swell on the sea. So he of the liqueur departed.

Our bounder thrummed on the table and hummed something, and asked the q-b if she knew the *Rosencavalier.* He always appealed to her. She said she did. And ah, he was passionately fond of music, said he. Then he warbled in a head voice a bit more. He only knew classical music, said he. And he mewed a bit of Moussorgsky. The q-b said Moussorgsky was her favourite musician, for opera. Ah, cried the bounder, if there were but a piano! —There is a piano, said his mate.—Yes, he replied, but it is locked up.— Then let us get the key, said his mate, with aplomb. The waiters, being men with the same feelings as our two, would give them anything. So the key was forthcoming. We paid our bills— mine about sixty francs. Then we went along the faintly rolling ship, up the curved staircase to the drawing. room. Our bounder unlocked the door of this drawing-room and switched on the lights.

It was quite a pleasant room, with deep divans upholstered in pale colours, and palm-trees standing behind little tables, and a black upright piano. Our bounder sat on the piano. stool and gave us an exhibition. He splashed out noise on the piano in splashes, like water splashing out of a pail. He lifted his head and shook his black mop of hair, and yelled out some fragments of opera. And he wriggled his large, bounder's back upon the piano-stool, wriggling upon his well-filled haunches. Evidently he had a great deal of feeling for music: but very little prowess. He yelped it out, and wriggled, and splashed the piano. His friend the other bounder, a quiet one in a pale suit, with stout limbs, older than the wriggler, stood by the piano whilst the young one exhibited. Across the space of carpet sat the two

197

brother jewellers, deep in a divan, their lean, semi-blond faces quite inscrutable. The q-b sat next to me, asking for this and that music, none of which the wriggler could supply. He knew four scraps, and a few splashes—not more. The elder bounder stood near him, quietly comforting, encouraging, and admiring him, as a lover encouraging and admiring his *ingénue* betrothed. And the q-b sat bright-eyed and excited, admiring that a man could perform so un-self-consciously self-conscious, and give himself away with such generous wriggles. For my part, as you may guess, I did not admire.

I had had enough. Rising, I bowed and marched off. The q-b came after me. Good-night, said I, at the head of the corridor. She turned in, and I went round the ship to look at the dark night of the sea.

Morning came with sunny pieces of cloud: and the Sicilian coast towering pale blue in the distance. How wonderful it must have been to Ulysses to venture into this Mediterranean and open his eyes on all the loveliness of the tall coasts. How marvellous to steal with his ship into these magic harbours. There is something eternally morning-glamorous about these lands as they rise from the sea. And it is always the Odyssey which comes back to one as one looks at them. All the lovely morning-wonder of this world, in Homer's day!

Our bounder was dashing about on deck, in one of those rain-coats gathered in at the waist and ballooning out into skirts below the waist. He greeted me with a cry of "It's a long, long way to Tipperary." "Very long," said I. "Goodbye, Piccadilly—" he continued. "Ciau," said I, as he dashed jauntily down the steps. Soon we saw the others as well. But it was morning, and I simply did not want to speak to them—except just good-day. For my life I couldn't say two more words to any of them this morning: except to ask the mild one if he had been sick. He had not.

So we waited for the great *Città di Trieste* to float her way into Palermo harbour. It looked so near—the town there, the great circle of the port, the mass of the hills crowding round. Panormus, the All-harbour. I wished the bulky steamer would hurry up. For I hated her now. I hated her swankiness, she seemed made for commercial travellers with cash.

I hated the big picture that filled one end of the state-room: an elegant and ideal peasant-girl, a sort of Italia, strolling on a lovely and ideal cliff's edge, among myriad blooms, and carrying over her arm, in a most sophisticated fashion, a bough of almond blossom and a sheaf of anemones. I hated the waiters, and the cheap elegance, the common *de luxe*. I disliked the people, who all turned their worst, cash-greasy sides outwards on this ship. Vulgar, vulgar post-war commercialism and dog-fish money-stink. I longed to get off. And the bloated boat edged her way so slowly into the port, and then more slowly still edged round her fat stern. And even then we were kept for fifteen minutes waiting for someone to put up the gangway for the first-class. The second-class, of course, were streaming off and melting like thawed snow into the crowds of onlookers on the quay, long before we were allowed to come off.

Glad, glad I was to get off that ship: I don't know why, for she was clean and comfortable and the attendants were perfectly civil. Glad, glad I was not to share the deck with any more commercial travellers. Glad I was to be on my own feet, independent. No, I would *not* take a carriage. I carried my sack on my back to the hotel, looking with a jaundiced eye on the lethargic traffic of the harbour front. It was about nine o'clock.

Later on, when I had slept, I thought as I have thought before, the Italians are not to blame for their spite against us. We, England, have taken upon ourselves for so long the role of leading nation. And if now, in the war or after the war, we have led them all into a real old swinery—which we have, notwithstanding all Entente cant—then they have a legitimate grudge against us. If you take upon yourself to lead, you must expect the mud to be thrown at you if you lead into a nasty morass. Especially if, once in the bog, you think of nothing else but scrambling out over other poor devils' backs. Pretty behaviour of great nations!

And still, for all that, I must insist that I am a single human being, an individual, not a mere national unit, a mere chip of l'Inghilterra or la Germania. I am not a chip of any nasty old block. I am myself.

In the evening the q-b insisted on going to the marionettes, for which she has a sentimental passion. So the three of us— we were with the American friend once more— chased through dark and tortuous side-streets and markets of Palermo in the night, until at last a friendly man led us to the place. The back streets of Palermo felt friendly, not huge and rather horrible, like Naples near the port.

The theatre was a little hole opening simply off the street. There was no one in the little ticket box, so we walked past the door-screen. A shabby old man with a long fennel-stalk hurried up and made us places on the back benches, and hushed us when we spoke of tickets. The play was in progress. A serpent-dragon was just having a tussle with a knight in brilliant brass armour, and my heart came into my mouth. The audience consisted mostly of boys, gazing with frantic interest on the bright stage. There was a sprinkling of soldiers and elderly men. The place was packed—about fifty souls crowded on narrow little ribbons of benches, so close one behind the other that the end of the man in front of me continually encroached and sat on my knee. I saw on a notice that the price of entry was forty centimes.

We had come in towards the end of the performance, and so sat rather bewildered, unable to follow. The story was the inevitable Paladins of France—one heard the names *Rinaldo! Orlando!* again and again. But the story was told in dialect, hard to follow

I was charmed by the figures. The scene was very simple, showing the interior of a castle. But the figures, which were about two-thirds of human size, were wonderful in their brilliant, glittering gold armour, and their martial prancing motions. All were knights— even the daughter of the king of Babylon. She was distinguished only by, her long hair. All were in the beautiful glittering armour, with helmets and visors that could be let down at will. I am told this armour has been handed down for many generations. It certainly is lovely. One actor alone was not in armour, the wizard Magicce, or Malvigge, the Merlin of the Paladins. He was in a long scarlet robe, edged with fur, and wore a three-cornered scarlet hat.

So we watched the dragon leap and twist and get the knight by the leg: and then perish. We watched the knights burst into the castle. We watched the wonderful armour-clashing embraces of the delivered knights, Orlando and his bosom friend and the little dwarf, clashing their armoured breasts to the breasts of their brothers and deliverers. We watched the would-be tears flow.—And then the statue of the witch suddenly go up in flames, at which a roar of exultation from the boys. Then it was over. The theatre was empty in a moment, but the proprietors and the two men who sat near us would not let us go. We must wait for the next performance.

My neighbour, a fat, jolly man, told me all about it. His neighbour, a handsome tipsy man, kept contradicting and saying it wasn't so. But my fat neighbour winked at me, not to take offence.

This story of the Paladins of France lasted three nights. We had come on the middle night—of course. But no matter—each night was a complete story. I am sorry I have forgotten the names of the knights. But the story was that Orlando and his friend and the little dwarf, owing to the tricks of that same dwarf, who belonged' to the Paladins, had been captured and immured in the enchanted castle of the ghastly old witch who lived on the blood of Christians. It was now the business of Rinaldo and the rest of the Paladins, by the help of Magicce the *good* wizard, to release their captured brethren from the ghoulish old witch.

So much I made out of the fat man's story, while the theatre was filling. He knew every detail of the whole Paladin cycle. And it is evident the Paladin cycle has lots of versions. For the handsome tipsy neighbour kept saying he was wrong, he was wrong, and giving different stories, and shouting for a jury to come and say who was right, he or my fat friend. A jury gathered, and a storm began to rise. But the stout proprietor with a fennel-wand came and quenched the noise, telling the handsome tipsy man he knew too much and wasn't asked. Whereupon the tipsy one sulked.

Ah, said my friend, couldn't I come on Friday? Friday was a great night. On Friday they were giving I Beati Paoli: The Blessed Pauls. He pointed to the walls where were the placards announcing The Blessed Pauls. These Pauls were evidently some awful secret society with masking hoods and daggers and awful eyes looking through the holes. I said were they assassins like the Black Hand? By no means, by no means. The Blessed Pauls were a society for the protection of the poor. Their business was to track down and murder the oppressive rich. Ah, they were a wonderful, a splendid society. Were they, said I, a sort of camorra? Ah, on the contrary—here he lapsed into a tense voice—they hated the camorra. These, the Blest Pauls, were the powerful and terrible enemy of the Grand Camorra. For the Grand Camorra oppresses the poor. And therefore the Pauls track down in secret the leaders of the Grand Camorra, and assassinate them, or bring them to the fearful hooded tribunal which utters the dread verdict of the Beati Paoli. And when once the Beati Paoli have decreed a man's death—all over. Ah, bellissimo, bellissimo! Why don't I come on Friday?

It seems to me a queer moral for the urchins thick-packed and gazing at the drop scene. They are all males: urchins or men. I ask my fat friend why there are no women—no girls. Ah, he says, the theatre is so small. But, I say, if there is room for all the boys and men, there is the same room for girls and women. Oh, no—not in this small theatre. Besides, this is nothing for women. Not that there is anything improper, he hastens to add. Not at all. But what should women and girls be doing at the marionette show? It was an affair for males.

I agreed with him really, and was thankful we hadn't a lot of smirking, twitching girls and lasses in the audience. This male audience was so tense and pure in its attention.

But hist! the play is going to begin. A lad is grinding a broken street-piano under the stage. The padrone yells *Silenzio!* with a roar, and reaching over, pokes obstreperous boys with his long fennel-stalk, like a beadle in church. When the curtain rises the piano stops, and there is dead silence. On swings a knight, glittering, marching with that curious hippety lilt, and gazing round with fixed and martial eyes. He begins the prologue, telling us where we are. And dramatically he waves sword and stamps his foot, and wonderfully sounds his male, martial, rather husky voice. Then the Paladins, his companions who are to accompany him, swing one by one on to the stage, till they are five in all, handsome knights, including the Babylonian Princess and the Knight of Britain. They stand in a handsome, glittering line. And then comes Merlin in his red robe. Merlin has a bright, fair, rather chubby face and blue eyes, and seems to typify the northern intelligence. He now tells them, in many words, how to proceed and what is to be done.

So then, the glittering knights are ready. Are they ready? Rinaldo flourishes his sword with the wonderful cry "Andiamo!" let us go—and the others respond: "Andiamo." Splendid word.

The first enemy were the knights of Spain, in red kirtles and half turbans. With these a terrible fight. First of all rushes in the Knight of Britain. He is the boaster, who, always in words, does everything. But in fact, poor Knight of Britain, he falls lamed. The four Paladins have stood shoulder to shoulder, glittering, watching the fray. Forth now steps another knight, and the fight recommences. Terrible is the smacking of swords, terrible the gasps from behind the dropped visors. Till at last the Knight of Spain falls—and the Paladin stands with his foot on the dead. Then loud acclamations from the Paladins, and yells of joy from the audience.

"*Silenzio!*" yells the padrone, flourishing the fennel-stalk.

Dead silence, and the story goes on. The Knight of Britain of course claims to have slain the foe: and the audience faintly, jeeringly hisses. "He's always the boaster, and he never does anything, the Knight of Britain," whispers my fat friend. He has forgotten my nationality. I wonder if the Knight of Britain is pure tradition, or if a political touch of today has crept in.

However, this fray is over—Merlin comes to advise for the next move. And are we ready? We are ready. *Andiamo!* Again the word is yelled out, and they set off. At first one is all engaged watching the figures: their brilliance, their blank, martial stare, their sudden, angular gestures. There is something extremely suggestive in them. How much better they fit the old legend-tales than living people would do. Nay, if we are going to have human beings on the stage, they should be masked and disguised. For in fact drama is enacted by symbolic creatures formed out of human consciousness: puppets if you like: but not human *individuals.* Our stage is all wrong, so boring in its personality.

Gradually, however, I found that my eyes were of minor importance. Gradually it was the voice that gained hold of, the blood. It is a strong, rather husky, male voice that acts direct on the blood, not on the mind. Again the old male Adam began to stir at the roots of my soul. Again the old, first-hand indifference, the rich, untamed male blood rocked down my veins. What does one care? What does one care for precept and mental dictation? Is there not the massive, brilliant, out-flinging recklessness in the male soul, summed up in the sudden word: *Andiamo!* Andiamo! Let us go on. Andiamo!—let us go hell knows where, but let us go on. The splendid recklessness and passion that knows no precept and no school-teacher, whose very molten spontaneity is its own guide.

I loved the voices of the Paladins—Rinaldo's voice, and Orlando's voice: the voice of men once more, men who are not to be tutored. To be sure there was Merlin making his long speeches in rather a chuntering, prosy tone. But who was he? Was he a Paladin and a splendour? Not he. A long-gowned chunterer. It is the reckless blood which achieves all, the piff-piff-piffing of the mental and moral intelligence is but a subsidiary help, a mere instrument.

The dragon was splendid: I have seen dragons in Wagner, at Covent Garden and at the Prinz-Regenten Theatre in Munich, and they were ridiculous. But this dragon simply frightened me, with his leaping and twisting. And when he seized the knight by the leg, my blood ran cold.

With smoke and sulphur leaps in Beelzebub. But he is merely the servant of the great old witch. He is black and grinning, and he flourishes his posterior and his tail. But he is curiously inefficacious: a sort of lackey of wicked powers.

The old witch with her grey hair and staring eyes, succeeds in being ghastly. With just a touch, she would be a tall, benevolent old lady. But listen to her. Hear her horrible female voice with its scraping yells of evil lustfulness. Yes, she fills me with horror. And I am staggered to find how I believe in her as *the* evil principle. Beelzebub, poor devil, is only one of her instruments.

It is her old, horrible, girning female soul which locks up the heroes, and which sends forth the awful and almost omnipotent malevolence. This old, ghastly woman-spirit is the very core of mischief. And I felt my heart getting as hot against her as the hearts of the lads in the audience were. Red, deep hate I felt of that symbolic old ghoul-female. Poor male Beelzebub is her loutish slave. And it takes all Merlin's bright-faced intelligence, and all the surging hot urgency of the Paladins, to conquer her.

She will never be finally destroyed—she will never finally die, till her statue, which is immured in the vaults of the castle, is burned. Oh, it was a very psycho-analytic performance altogether, and one could give a very good Freudian analysis of it. But behold this image of the witch: this white, submerged *idea* of woman which rules from the deeps of the unconscious. Behold, the reckless, untamable male knights will do for it. As the statue goes up in flame—it is only paper over wires—the audience yells! And yells again. And would God the symbolic act were really achieved. It is only little boys who yell. Men merely smile at the trick. They know well enough the white image endures.

So it is over. The knights look at us once more. Orlando, hero of heroes, has a slight inward cast of the eyes. This gives him that look of almost fierce good-nature which these people adore: the look of a man who does not think, but whose heart is all the time red hot with burning, generous blood-passion. This is what they adore.

So my knights go. They all have wonderful faces and are so splendidly glittering and male. I am sorry they will be laid in a box now.

There is a great gasp of relief. The piano starts its lame rattle. Somebody looking round laughs. And we all look round. And seated on the top of the ticket office is a fat, solemn urchin of two or three years, hands folded over his stomach, his forehead big and blank, like some queer little Buddha. The audience laughs with that southern sympathy: physical sympathy: that is what they love to feel and to arouse.

But there is a little after-scene: in front of the drop-curtain jerks out a little fat flat caricature of a Neapolitan, and from the opposite side jerks the tall caricature of a Sicilian. They jerk towards one another and bump into one another with a smack. And smack goes the Neapolitan, down on his posterior. And the boys howl with joy. It is the eternal collision between the two peoples, Neapolitan and Sicilian. Now goes on a lot of fooling between the two clowns, in the two dialects. Alas, I can hardly understand anything at all. But it sounds comic, and looks very funny. The Neapolitan of course gets most of the knocks. And there seems to be no indecency at all—unless once. The boys howl and rock with joy, and no one says Silenzio!

But it is over. All is over. The theatre empties in a moment. And I shake hands with my fat neighbour, affectionately, and in the right spirit. Truly I loved them all in the theatre: the generous, hot southern blood, so subtle and spontaneous, that asks for blood contact, not for mental communion or spirit sympathy. I was sorry to leave them.

INTRODUCTION to MEMOIRS OF THE FOREIGN LEGION

by Maurice Magnus

ON a dark, wet, wintry evening in November, 1919, I arrived in Florence, having just got back to Italy for the first time since 1914. My wife was in Germany, gone to see her mother, also for the first time since that fatal year 1914. We were poor; who was going to bother to publish me and to pay for my writings, in 1918 and 1919? I landed in Italy with nine pounds in my pocket and about twelve pounds lying in the bank in London. Nothing more. My wife, I hoped, would arrive in Florence with two or three pounds remaining. We should have to go very softly, if we were to house ourselves in Italy for the winter. But after the desperate weariness of the war, one could not bother.

So I had written to ND [Norman Douglas]; to get me a cheap room somewhere in Florence, and to leave a note at Cook's. I deposited my bit of luggage at the station, and walked to Cook's in the Via Tornabuoni. Florence was strange to me: seemed grim and dark and rather awful on the cold November evening. There was a note from D, who has never left me in the lurch. I went down the Lung' Arno to the address he gave.

I had just passed the end of the Ponte Vecchio, and was watching the first lights of evening and the last light of day on the swollen river as I walked, when I heard D's voice:

"Isn't that Lawrence? Why of course it is, of course it is, beard and all! Well, how are you, eh? You got my note? Well now, my dear boy, you just go on to the Cavelotti—straight ahead, straight ahead—you've got the number. There's a room for you there. We shall be there in half an hour. Oh, let me introduce you to M."

I had unconsciously seen the two men approaching, D tall and portly, the other man rather short and strutting. They were both buttoned up in their overcoats, and both had rather curly little hats. But D was decidedly shabby and a gentleman, with his wicked red face and tufted eyebrows. The other man was almost smart, all in grey, and he looked at first sight like an actor-manager, common. There was a touch of down-on-his-luck about him too. He looked at me, buttoned up in my old thick overcoat, and with my beard bushy and raggy because of my horror of entering a strange barber's shop, and he greeted me in a rather fastidious voice, and a little patronizingly. I forgot to say I was carrying a small hand-bag. But I realized at once that I ought, in this little grey-sparrow man's eyes—he stuck his front out tubbily, like a bird, and his legs seemed to perch behind him, as a bird's do—I ought to be in a cab. But I wasn't. He eyed me in that shrewd and rather impertinent way of the world of actor-managers: cosmopolitan, knocking shabbily round the world.

He looked a man of about forty, spruce and youngish in his deportment, very pink-faced, and very clean, very natty, very alert, like a sparrow painted to resemble a tom-tit. He was just the kind of man I had never met: little smart man of the shabby world, very much on the spot, don't you know.

"How much does it cost?" I asked D, meaning the room.

"Oh, my dear fellow, a trifle. Ten francs a day. Third rate, tenth rate, but not bad at the price. Pension terms of course—everything included—except wine."

"Oh no, not at all bad for the money," said M. "Well now, shall we be moving? You want the post-office, D?" His voice was precise and a little mincing, and it had an odd high squeak.

"I do," said D.

"Well then come down here—" M turned to a dark little alley.

"Not at all," said D. "We turn down by the bridge."

"This is quicker," said M——. He had a twang rather than an accent in his speech—not definitely American.

He knew all the short cuts of Florence. Afterwards I found that he knew all the short cuts in all the big towns of Europe.

I went on to the Cavelotti and waited in an awful plush and gilt drawing-room, and was given at last a cup of weird muddy brown slush called tea, and a bit of weird brown mush called jam on some bits of bread. Then I was taken to my room. It was far off, on the third floor of the big, ancient, deserted Florentine house. There I had a big and lonely, stone-comfortless room looking on to the river. Fortunately it was not very cold inside, and I didn't care. The adventure of being back in Florence again after the years of war made one indifferent.

After an hour or so someone tapped. It was D coming in with his grandiose air—now a bit shabby, but still very courtly.

"Why here you are—miles and miles from human habitation! I *told* her to put you on the second floor, where we are. What does she mean by it? Ring that bell. Ring it."

"No," said I, "I'm all right here."

"What!" cried D. "In this Spitzbergen! Where's that bell?"

"Don't ring it," said I, who have a horror of chambermaids and explanations.

"Not ring it! Well you're a man, you are! Come on then. Come on down to my room. Come on. Have you had some tea—filthy muck they call tea here? I never drink it."

I went down to D's room on the lower floor. It was a littered mass of books and type-writer and papers: D was just finishing his novel. M was resting on the bed, in his shirt sleeves: a tubby, fresh-faced little man in a suit of grey, faced cloth bound at the edges with grey silk braid. He had light blue eyes, tired underneath, and crisp, curly, dark brown hair just grey at the temples. But everything was neat and even finicking about his person.

"Sit down! Sit down!" said D, wheeling up a chair. "Have a whisky?"

"Whisky!" said I.

"Twenty-four francs a bottle—and a find at that," moaned D. I must tell that the exchange was then about forty-five lire to the pound.

"Oh D," said M, "I didn't tell you. I was offered a bottle of 1913 Black and White for twenty-eight lire."

"Did you buy it?"

"No. It's your turn to buy a bottle."

"Twenty-eight francs—my dear fellow!" said D, cocking up his eyebrows. "I shall have to starve myself to do it."

"Oh no you won't, you'll eat here just the same," said M.

"Yes, and I'm starved to death. Starved to death by the muck—the absolute muck they call food here. I can't face twenty-eight francs, my dear chap—can't be done, on my honour."

"Well look here, M. We'll both buy a bottle. And you can get the one at twenty-two, and I'll buy the one at twenty-eight."

So it always was, M indulged D, and spoilt him in every way. And of course D wasn't grateful. *Au contraire*! And M's pale blue smallish round eyes, in his cockatoo-pink face, would harden to indignation occasionally.

The room was dreadful. D never opened the windows: didn't believe in opening windows. He believed that a certain amount of nitrogen—I should say a great amount—is beneficial. The queer smell of a bedroom which is slept in, worked in, lived in, smoked in, and in which men drink their whiskies, was something new to me. But I didn't care. One had got away from the war.

We drank our whiskies before dinner. M was rather yellow under the eyes, and irritable; even his pink fattish face went yellowish.

"Look here," said D. "Didn't you say there was a turkey for dinner? What? Have you been to the kitchen to see what they're doing to it?"

"Yes," said M testily. "I forced them to prepare it to roast."

"With chestnuts—stuffed with chestnuts?" said D.

"They *said* so," said M.

"Oh but go down and see that they're doing it. Yes, you've got to keep your eye on them, got to. The most awful howlers if you don't. You go now and see what they're up to." D used his most irresistible grand manner.

"It's too late," persisted M, testy.

"It's *never* too late. You just run down and absolutely prevent them from boiling that bird in the old soup-water," said D. "If you need force, fetch me."

M went. He was a great epicure, and knew how things should be cooked. But of course his irruptions into the kitchen roused considerable resentment, and he was getting quaky. However, he went. He came back to say the turkey was being roasted, but without chestnuts.

"What did I tell you! What did I tell you!" cried D. "They are absolute! If you don't hold them by the neck while they peel the chestnuts, they'll stuff the bird with old boots, to save themselves trouble. Of course you should have gone down sooner, M."

Dinner was always late, so the whisky was usually two whiskies. Then we went down, and were merry in spite of all things. That is, D always grumbled about the food. There was one unfortunate youth who was boots and porter and waiter and all. He brought the big dish to D, and D always poked and pushed among the portions, and grumbled frantically, sotto voce, in Italian to the youth Beppo, getting into a nervous frenzy. Then M called the waiter to himself, picked the nicest bits off the dish and gave them to D, then helped himself.

The food was not good, but with D it was an obsession. With the waiter he was terrible—"Cos' è? Zuppa? Grazie. No, niente per me. *No—No*!—Quest' acqua sporca non bevo io. I don't drink this dirty water. What—What's that in it—a piece of dish clout? Oh holy Dio, I can't eat another thing this evening—"

And he yelled for more bread—bread being war-rations and very limited in supply—so M in nervous distress gave him his piece, and D threw the crumb part on the floor, anywhere, and called for another litre. We always drank heavy dark red wine at three francs a litre. D drank two-thirds, M drank least. He loved his liquors, and did not care for wine. We were noisy and unabashed at table. The old Danish ladies at the other end of the room, and the rather impecunious young Duca and family not far off were not supposed to understand English. The Italians rather liked the noise, and the young signorina with the high-up yellow hair eyed us with profound interest. On we sailed, gay and noisy, D telling witty anecdotes and grumbling wildly and only half whimsically about the food. We sat on till most people had finished—then went up to more whisky—one more perhaps—in M's room.

When I came down in the morning I was called into M's room. He was like a little pontiff in a blue kimono-shaped dressing-gown with a broad border of reddish purple: the blue was a soft mid-blue, the material a dull silk. So he minced about, in demi-toilette. His room was very clean and neat, and slightly perfumed with essences. On his dressing-table stood many cut-glass bottles and silver-topped bottles with essences and pomades and powders, and heaven knows what. A very elegant little prayer book lay by his bed—and a life of St. Benedict. For M was a Roman Catholic convert. All he had was expensive and finicking: thick leather silver-studded suit-cases standing near the wall, trouser-stretcher all nice, hair-brushes and clothes-brush with old ivory backs. I wondered over him and his niceties and little pomposities. He was a new bird to me.

For he wasn't at all just the common person he looked. He was queer and sensitive as a woman with D, and patient and fastidious. And yet he *was* common, his very accent was common, and D despised him.

And M rather despised me because I did not spend money. I paid for a third of the wine we drank at dinner, and bought the third bottle of whisky we had during M's stay. After all, he only stayed three days. But I would not spend for myself. I had no money to spend, since I knew I must live and my wife must live.

"Oh," said M. "Why, that's the very time to spend money, when you've got none. If you've got none, why try to save it? That's been my philosophy all my life; when you've got no money, you may just as well spend it. If you've got a good deal, that's the time to look after it." Then he laughed his queer little laugh, rather squeaky. These were his exact words.

"Precisely," said D. "Spend when you've nothing to spend, my boy. Spend *hard* then."

"No," said I. "If I can help it, I will never let myself be penniless while I live. I mistrust the world too much."

"But if you're going to live in fear of the world," said M, "what's the good of living at all? Might as well die."

I think I give his words almost verbatim. He had a certain impatience of me and of my presence. Yet we had some jolly times—mostly in one or other of their bedrooms, drinking a whisky and talking. We drank a bottle a day—I had very little, preferring the wine at lunch and dinner, which seemed delicious after the war famine. D would bring up the remains of the second litre in the evening, to go on with before the coffee came.

I arrived in Florence on the Wednesday or Thursday evening; I think Thursday. M was due to leave for Rome on the Saturday. I asked D who M was. "Oh, you never know what he's at. He was manager for Isadora Duncan for a long time—knows all the capitals of Europe: St. Petersburg, Moscow, Tiflis, Constantinople, Berlin, Paris—knows them as you and I know Florence. He's been mostly in that line—theatrical. Then a journalist. He edited the *Roman Review* till the war killed it. Oh, a many-sided sort of fellow."

"But how do you know him?" said I.

"I met him in Capri years and years ago—oh, sixteen years ago—and clean forgot all about him till somebody came to me one day in Rome and said: You're N.D. *I* didn't know who he was. But he'd never forgotten me. Seems to be smitten by me, somehow or other. All the better for me, ha-ha!—if he *likes* to run round for me. My dear fellow, I wouldn't prevent him, if it amuses him. Not for worlds."

And that was how it was. M ran D's errands, forced the other man to go to the tailor, to the dentist, and was almost a guardian angel to him.

"Look here!" cried D. "I *can't* go to that damned tailor. Let the thing wait, I can't go."

"Oh yes. Now look here N, if you don't get it done now while I'm here you'll never get it done. I made the appointment for three o'clock—"

"To hell with you! Details! Details! I can't stand it, I tell you."

D chafed and kicked, but went.

"A little fussy fellow," he said. "Oh yes, fussing about like a woman. Fussy, you know, fussy. I *can't stand* these fussy—" And D went off into improprieties.

Well, M ran round and arranged D's affairs and settled his little bills, and was so benevolent, and so impatient and nettled at the ungrateful way in which the benevolence was accepted. And D despised him all the time as a little busybody and an inferior. And I there between them just wondered. It seemed to me M would get very irritable and nervous at midday and before dinner, yellow round the eyes and played out. He wanted his whisky. He was tired after running round on a thousand errands and quests which I never understood. He always took his morning coffee at dawn, and was out to early Mass and pushing his affairs before eight o'clock in the morning. But what his affairs were I still do not know. Mass is all I am certain of.

However, it was his birthday on the Sunday, and D would not let him go. He had once said he would give a dinner for his birthday, and this he was not allowed to forget. It seemed to me M rather wanted to get out of it. But D was determined to have that dinner.

"You aren't going before you've given us that hare, don't you imagine it, my boy. I've got the smell of that hare in my imagination, and I've damned well got to set my teeth in it. Don't you imagine you're going without having produced that hare."

So poor M, rather a victim, had to consent. We discussed what we should eat. It was decided the hare should have truffles, and a dish of champignons, and cauliflower, and zabaioni—and I forget what else. It was to be on Saturday evening. And M would leave on Sunday for Rome.

Early on the Saturday morning he went out, with the first daylight, to the old market, to get the hare and the mushrooms. He went himself because he was a connoisseur.

On the Saturday afternoon D took me wandering round to buy a birthday present.

"I shall have to buy him something—have to—have to—" he said fretfully. He only wanted to spend about five francs. We trailed over the Ponte Vecchio, looking at the jewellers' booths there. It was before the foreigners had come back, and things were still rather dusty and almost at pre-war prices. But we could see nothing for five francs except the little saint-medals. D wanted to buy one of those. It seemed to me infra dig. So at last coming down to the Mercato Nuovo we saw little bowls of Volterra marble, a natural amber colour, for four francs.

"Look, buy one of those," I said to D, "and he can put his pins or studs or any trifle in, as he needs."

So we went in and bought one of the little bowls of Volterra marble.

M seemed so touched and pleased with the gift.

"Thank you a thousand times, N," he said. "That's charming! That's exactly what I want."

The dinner was quite a success, and, poorly fed as we were at the pension, we stuffed ourselves tight on the mushrooms and the hare and the zabaioni, and drank ourselves tight with the good red wine which swung in its straw flask in the silver swing on the table. A flask has two and a quarter litres. We were four persons, and we drank almost two flasks. D made the waiter measure the remaining half-litre and take it off the bill. But good, good food, and cost about twelve francs a head the whole dinner.

Well, next day was nothing but bags and suit-cases in M's room, and the misery of departure with luggage. He went on the midnight train to Rome: first class.

"I always travel first class," he said, "and I always shall, while I can buy the ticket. Why should I go second? It's beastly enough to travel at all."

"My dear fellow, I came up third the last time I came from Rome," said D. "Oh, not bad, not bad. Damned fatiguing journey anyhow."

So the little outsider was gone, and I was rather glad. I don't think he liked me. Yet one day he said to me at table: "How lovely your hair is—such a lovely colour! What do you dye it with?"

I laughed, thinking he was laughing too. But no, he meant it.

"It's got no particular colour at all," I said, "so I couldn't dye it that!"

"It's a lovely colour," he said. And I think he didn't believe me, that I didn't dye it. It puzzled me, and it puzzles me still.

But he was gone. D moved into M's room, and asked me to come down to the room he himself was vacating. But I preferred to stay upstairs.

M was a fervent Catholic, taking the religion alas, rather unctuously. He had entered the Church only a few years before. But he had a bishop for a god-father, and seemed to be very intimate with the upper clergy. He was very pleased and proud because he was a constant guest at the famous old monastery south of Rome. He talked of becoming a monk; a monk in that aristocratic and well-bred order. But he had not even begun his theological studies: or any studies of any sort. And D said he only chose the Benedictines because they lived better than any of the others.

But I had said to M, that when my wife came and we moved south, I would like to visit the monastery some time, if I might. "Certainly," he said. "Come when I am there. I shall be there in about a month's time. Do come! Do be sure and come. It's a wonderful place—oh, wonderful. It will make a great impression on you. Do come. Do come. And I will tell Don Bernardo, who is my *greatest* friend, and who is guest-master, about you. So that if you wish to go when I am not there, write to Don Bernardo. But do come when I am there."

My wife and I were due to go into the mountains south of Rome, and stay there some months. Then I was to visit the big, noble monastery that stands on a bluff hill like a fortress crowning a great precipice, above the little town and the plain between the mountains. But it was so icy cold and snowy among the mountains, it was unbearable. We fled south again, to Naples, and to, Capri. Passing, I saw the monastery crouching there above, world-famous, but it was impossible to call then.

I wrote and told M of my move. In Capri I had an answer from him. It had a wistful tone—and I don't know what made me think that he was in trouble, in monetary difficulty. But I felt it acutely—a kind of appeal. Yet he said nothing direct. And he wrote from an expensive hotel in Anzio, on the sea near Rome.

At the moment I had just received twenty pounds unexpected and joyful from America—a gift too. I hesitated for some time, because I felt unsure. Yet the curious appeal came out of the letter, though nothing was said. And I felt also I owed M that dinner, and I didn't want to owe him anything, since he despised me a little for being careful. So partly out of revenge, perhaps, and partly because I felt the strange wistfulness of him appealing to me, I sent him five pounds, saying perhaps I was mistaken in imagining him very hard up, but if so, he wasn't to be offended.

It is strange to me even now, how I knew he was appealing to me. Because it was all as vague as I say. Yet I felt it so strongly. He replied: "Your cheque has saved my life. Since I last saw you I have fallen down an abyss. But I will tell you when I see you. I shall be at the monastery in three days. Do come—and come alone." I have forgotten to say that he was a rabid woman-hater.

This was just after Christmas. I thought his "saved my life" and "fallen down an abyss" was just the American touch of "very, very—." I wondered what on earth the abyss could be, and I decided it must be that he had lost his money or his hopes. It seemed to me that some of his old buoyant assurance came out again in this letter. But he was now very friendly, urging me to come to the monastery, and treating me with a curious little tenderness and protectiveness. He had a queer delicacy of his own, varying with a bounce and a commonness. He was a common little bounder. And then he had this curious delicacy and tenderness and wistfulness.

I put off going north. I had another letter urging me—and it seemed to me that, rather assuredly, he was expecting more money. Rather cockily, as if he had a right to it. And that made me not want to give him any. Besides, as my wife said, what right had I to give away the little money we had, and we there stranded in the south of Italy with no resources if once we were spent up. And I have always been determined never to come to my last shilling—if I have to reduce my spending almost to nothingness. I have always been determined to keep a few pounds between me and the world.

I did not send any money. But I wanted to go to the monastery, so wrote and said I would come for two days. I always remember getting up in the black dark of the January morning, and making a little coffee on the spirit-lamp, and watching the clock, the big-faced, blue old clock on the campanile in the piazza in Capri, to see I wasn't late. The electric light in the piazza lit up the face of the campanile. And we were then, a stone's throw away, high in the Palazzo Ferraro, opposite the bubbly roof of the little duomo. Strange dark winter morning, with the open sea beyond the roofs, seen through the side window, and the thin line of the lights of Naples twinkling far, far off.

At ten minutes to six I went down the smelly dark stone stairs of the old palazzo, out into the street. A few people were already hastening up the street to the terrace that looks over the sea to the bay of Naples. It was dark and cold. We slid down in the funicular to the shore, then in little boats were rowed out over the dark sea to the steamer that lay there showing her lights and hooting.

It was three long hours across the sea to Naples, with dawn coming slowly in the east, beyond Ischia, and flushing into lovely colour as our steamer pottered along the peninsula, calling at Massa and Sorrento and Piano. I always loved hanging over the side and watching the people come out in boats from the little places of the shore, that rose steep and beautiful. I love the movement of these watery Neapolitan people, and the naïve trustful way they clamber in and out the boats, and their softness, and their dark eyes. But when the steamer leaves the peninsula and begins to make away round Vesuvius to Naples, one is already tired, and cold, cold, cold in the wind that comes piercing from the snow-crests away there along Italy. Cold, and reduced to a kind of stony apathy by the time we come to the mole in Naples, at ten o'clock—or twenty past ten.

We were rather late, and I missed the train. I had to wait till two o'clock. And Naples is a hopeless town to spend three hours in. However, time passes. I remember I was calculating in my mind whether they had given me the right change at the ticket-window. They hadn't—and I hadn't counted in time. Thinking of this, I got in the Rome train. I had been there ten minutes when I heard a trumpet blow.

"Is this the Rome train?" I asked my fellow-traveller.

"Si."

"The express?"

"No, it is the slow train."

"It leaves?"

"At ten past two."

I almost jumped through the window. I flew down the platform.

"The diretto!" I cried to a porter.

"Parte! Eccolo la!" he said, pointing to a big train moving inevitably away.

I flew with wild feet across the various railway lines and seized the end of the train as it travelled. I had caught it. Perhaps if I had missed it fate would have been different. So I sat still for about three hours. Then I had arrived.

There is a long drive up the hill from the station to the monastery. The driver talked to me. It was evident he bore the monks no good will.

"Formerly," he said, "if you went up to the monastery you got a glass of wine and a plate of maccaroni. But now they kick you out of the door."

"Do they?" I said. "It is hard to believe."

"They kick you out of the gate," he vociferated.

We twisted up and up the wild hillside, past the old castle of the town, past the last villa, between trees and rocks. We saw no one. The whole hill belongs to the monastery. At last at twilight we turned the corner of the oak wood and saw the monastery like a huge square fortress-palace of the sixteenth century crowning the near distance. Yes, and there was M just stepping through the huge old gateway and hastening down the slope to where the carriage must stop. He was bareheaded, and walking with his perky, busy little stride, seemed very much at home in the place. He looked up to me with a tender, intimate look as I got down from the carriage. Then he took my hand.

"So *very* glad to see you," he said. "I'm so *pleased* you've come."

And he looked into my eyes with that wistful, watchful tenderness rather like a woman who isn't quite sure of her lover. He had a certain charm in his manner; and an odd pompous touch with it at this moment, welcoming his guest at the gate of the vast monastery which reared above us from its buttresses in the rock, was rather becoming. His face was still pink, his eyes pale blue and sharp, but he looked greyer at the temples.

"Give me your bag," he said. "Yes do—and come along. Don Bernardo is just at Evensong, but he'll be here in a little while. Well now, tell me all the news."

"Wait," I said. "Lend me five francs to finish paying the driver—he has no change."

"Certainly, certainly," he said, giving the five francs. I had no news,—so asked him his.

"Oh, I have none either," he said. "Very short of money, that of course is *no* news." And he laughed his little laugh. "I'm so glad to be here," he continued. "The peace, and the rhythm of the life is so *beautiful*! I'm sure you'll love it."

We went up the slope under the big, tunnel-like entrance and were in the grassy courtyard, with the arched walk on the far sides, and one or two trees. It was like a grassy cloister, but still busy. Black monks were standing chatting, an old peasant was just driving two sheep from the cloister grass, and an old monk was darting into the little post-office which one recognized by the shield with the national arms over the doorway. From under the far arches came an old peasant carrying a two-handed saw.

And there was Don Bernardo, a tall monk in a black, well-shaped gown, young, good-looking, gentle, hastening forward with a quick smile. He was about my age, and his manner seemed fresh and subdued, as if he were still a student. One felt one was at college with one's college mates.

We went up the narrow stair and into the long, old, naked white corridor, high and arched. Don Bernardo had got the key of my room: two keys, one for the dark antechamber, one for the bedroom. A charming and elegant bedroom, with an engraving of English landscape, and outside the net curtain a balcony looking down on the garden, a narrow strip beneath the walls, and beyond, the clustered buildings of the farm, and the oak woods and arable fields of the hill summit: and beyond again, the gulf where the world's valley was, and all the mountains that stand in Italy on the plains as if God had just put them down ready made. The sun had already sunk, the snow on the mountains was full of a rosy glow, the valleys were full of shadow. One heard, far below, the trains shunting, the world clinking in the cold air. "Isn't it wonderful! Ah, the most wonderful place on earth!" said M. "What now could you wish better than to end your days here? The peace, the beauty, the eternity of it." He paused and sighed. Then he put his hand on Don Bernardo's arm and smiled at him with that odd, rather wistful smirking tenderness that made him such a quaint creature in my eyes.

"But I'm going to enter the order. You're going to let me be a monk and be one of you, aren't you, Don Bernardo?"

"We will see," smiled Don Bernardo. "When you have begun your studies."

"It will take me two years," said M. "I shall have to go to the college in Rome. When I have got the money for the fees—" He talked away, like a boy planning a new rôle.

"But I'm sure Lawrence would like to drink a cup of tea," said Don Bernardo. He spoke English as if it were his native language. "Shall I tell them to make it in the kitchen, or shall we go to your room?"

"Oh, we'll go to my room. How thoughtless of me! Do forgive me, won't you?" said M, laying his hand gently on my arm. "I'm so awfully sorry, you know. But we get so excited and enchanted when we talk of the monastery. But come along, come along, it will be ready in a moment on the spirit-lamp."

We went down to the end of the high, white, naked corridor. M had a quite sumptuous room, with a curtained bed in one part, and under the window his writing-desk with papers and photographs, and nearby a sofa and an easy table, making a little sitting-room, while the bed and toilet things, pomades and bottles were all in the distance, in the shadow. Night was fallen. From the window one saw the world far below, like a pool the flat plain, a deep pool of darkness with little twinkling lights, and rows and bunches of light that were the railway station.

I drank my tea, M drank a little liqueur, Don Bernardo in his black winter robe sat and talked with us. At least he did very little talking. But he listened and smiled and put in a word or two as we talked, seated round the table on which stood the green-shaded electric lamp.

The monastery was cold as the tomb. Couched there on the top of its hill, it is not much below the winter snow-line. Now by the end of January all the summer heat is soaked out of the vast, ponderous stone walls, and they become masses of coldness cloaking around. There is no heating apparatus whatsoever—none. Save the fire in the kitchen, for cooking, nothing. Dead, silent, stone cold everywhere.

At seven we went down to dinner. Capri in the daytime was hot, so I had brought only a thin old dust-coat. M therefore made me wear a big coat of his own, a coat made of thick, smooth black cloth, and lined with black sealskin, and having a collar of silky black sealskin. I can still remember the feel of the silky fur. It was queer to have him helping me solicitously into this coat, and buttoning it at the throat for me.

"Yes, it's a beautiful coat. Of course!" he said. "I hope you find it warm."

"Wonderful," said I. "I feel as warm as a millionaire."

"I'm so glad you do," he laughed.

"You don't mind my wearing your grand coat?" I said.

"Of course not! Of course not! It's a pleasure to me if it will keep you warm. We don't want to die of cold in the monastery, do we? That's one of the mortifications we will do our best to avoid. What? Don't you think? Yes, I think this coldness is going almost too far. I had that coat made in New York fifteen years ago. Of course in Italy—"he said It'ly—"I've never worn it, so it is as good as new. And it's a beautiful coat, fur and cloth of the very best. *And* the tailor." He laughed a little, self-approving laugh. He liked to give the impression that he dealt with the *best* shops, don't you know, and stayed in the *best* hotels, etc. I grinned inside the coat, detesting best hotels, best shops, and best overcoats. So off we went, he in his grey overcoat and I in my sealskin millionaire monster, down the dim corridor to the guests' refectory. It was a bare room with a long white table. M and I sat at the near end. Further down was another man, perhaps the father of one of the boy students. There is a college attached to the monastery.

We sat in the icy room, muffled up in our overcoats. A lay-brother with a bulging forehead and queer, fixed eyes waited on us. He might easily have come from an old Italian picture. One of the adoring peasants. The food was abundant—but alas, it had got cold in the long cold transit from the kitchen. And it was roughly cooked, even if it was quite wholesome. Poor M did not eat much, but nervously nibbled his bread. I could tell the meals were a trial to him. He could not bear the cold food in that icy, empty refectory. And his tisickyness offended the lay-brothers. I could see that his little pomposities and his "superior" behaviour and his long stay made them have that old monastic grudge against him, silent but very obstinate and effectual—the same now as six hundred years ago. We had a decanter of good red wine—but he did not care for much wine. He was glad to be peeling the cold orange which was dessert.

After dinner he took me down to see the church, creeping like two thieves down the dimness of the great, prison-cold white corridors, on the cold flag floors.

Stone cold: the monks must have invented the term. These monks were at Compline. So we went by our two secret little selves into the tall dense nearly-darkness of the church. M, knowing his way about here as in the cities, led me, poor wondering worldling, by the arm through the gulfs of the tomb-like place. He found the electric light switches inside the church, and stealthily made me a light as we went. We looked at the lily marble of the great floor, at the pillars, at the Benvenuto Cellini casket, at the really lovely pillars and slabs of different coloured marbles, all coloured marbles, yellow and grey and rose and green and lily white, veined and mottled and splashed: lovely, lovely stones—And Benvenuto had used pieces of lapis lazuli, blue as cornflowers. Yes, yes, all very rich and wonderful.

We tiptoed about the dark church stealthily, from altar to altar, and M whispered ecstasies in my ear. Each time we passed before an altar, whether the high altar or the side chapels, he did a wonderful reverence, which he must have practised for hours, bowing waxily down and sinking till his one knee touched the pavement, then rising like a flower that rises and unfolds again, till he had skipped to my side and was playing Cicerone once more. Always in his grey overcoat, and in whispers: me in the big black overcoat, millionairish. So we crept into the chancel and examined all the queer fat babies of the choir stalls, carved in wood and rolling on their little backs between monk's place and monk's place—queer things for the chanting monks to have between them, these shiny, polished, dark brown fat babies, all different, and all jolly and lusty. We looked at everything in the church—and then at everything in the ancient room at the side where surplices hang and monks can wash their hands.

Then we went down to the crypt, where the modern mosaics glow in wonderful colours, and sometimes in fascinating little fantastic trees and birds. But it was rather like a scene in the theatre, with M for the wizard and myself a sort of Parsifal in the New York coat. He switched on the lights, the gold mosaic of the vaulting glittered and bowed, the blue mosaic glowed out, the holy of holies gleamed theatrically, the stiff mosaic figures posed around us. To tell the truth I was glad to get back to the normal human room and sit on a sofa huddled in my overcoat, and look at photographs which M showed me: photographs of everywhere in Europe. Then he showed me a wonderful photograph of a picture of a lovely lady—asked me what I thought of it, and seemed to expect me to be struck to bits by the beauty. His almost sanctimonious expectation made me tell the truth, that I thought it just a bit cheap, trivial. And then he said, dramatic:

"That's my mother."

It looked so unlike anybody's mother, much less M's, that I was startled. I realized that she was his great stunt, and that I had put my foot in it. So I just held my tongue. Then I said, for I felt he was going to be silent forever:

"There are so few portraits, unless by the really great artists, that aren't a bit cheap. She must have been a beautiful woman."

"Yes, she *was*," he said curtly. And we dropped the subject.

He locked all his drawers *very* carefully, and kept the keys on a chain. He seemed to give the impression that he had a great many secrets, perhaps dangerous ones, locked up in the drawers of his writing-table there. And I always wonder what the secrets can be, that are able to be kept so tight under lock and key.

Don Bernardo tapped and entered. We all sat round and sipped a funny liqueur which I didn't like. M lamented that the bottle was finished. I asked him to order another and let me pay for it. So he said he would tell the postman to bring it up next day from the town. Don Bernardo sipped his tiny glass with the rest of us, and he told me, briefly, his story—and we talked politics till nearly midnight. Then I came out of the black overcoat and we went to bed.

In the morning a fat, smiling, nice old lay-brother brought me my water. It was a sunny day. I looked down on the farm cluster and the brown fields and the sere oak woods of the hill-crown, and the rocks and bushes savagely bordering it round. Beyond, the mountains with their snow were blue-glistery with sunshine, and seemed quite near, but across a sort of gulf. All was still and sunny. And the poignant grip of the past, the grandiose, violent past of the Middle Ages, when blood was strong and unquenched and life was flamboyant with splendours and horrible miseries, took hold of me till I could hardly bear it. It was really agony to me to be in the monastery and to see the old farm and the bullocks slowly working in the fields below, and the black pigs rooting among weeds, and to see a monk sitting on a parapet in the sun, and an old, old man in skin sandals and white bunched, swathed legs come driving an ass slowly to the monastery gate, slowly, with all that lingering nonchalance and wildness of the Middle Ages, and yet to know that I was myself, child of the present. It was so strange from M's window to look down on the plain and see the white road going straight past a mountain that stood like a loaf of sugar, the river meandering in loops, and the railway with glistening lines making a long black swoop across the flat and into the hills. To see trains come steaming, with white smoke flying. To see the station like a little harbour where trucks like shipping stood anchored in rows in the black bay of railway. To see trains stop in the station and tiny people swarming like flies! To see all this from the monastery, where the Middle Ages live on in a sort of agony, like Tithonus, and cannot die, this was almost a violation to my soul, made almost a wound.

Immediately after coffee we went down to Mass. It was celebrated in a small crypt chapel underground, because that was warmer. The twenty or so monks sat in their stalls, one monk officiating at the altar. It was quiet and simple, the monks sang sweetly and well, there was no organ. It seemed soon to pass by. M and I sat near the door. He was very devoted and scrupulous in his going up and down. I was an outsider. But it was pleasant—not too sacred. One felt the monks were very human in their likes and their jealousies. It was rather like a group of dons in the dons' room at Cambridge, a cluster of professors in any college. But during Mass they, of course, just sang their responses. Only I could tell some watched the officiating monk rather with ridicule—he was one of the ultra-punctilious sort, just like a don. And some boomed their responses with a grain of defiance against some brother monk who had earned dislike. It was human, and more like a university than anything. We went to Mass every morning, but I did not go to Evensong.

After Mass M took me round and showed me everything of the vast monastery. We went into the Bramante Courtyard, all stone, with its great well in the centre, and the colonnades of arches going round, full of sunshine, gay and Renaissance, a little bit ornate but still so jolly and gay, sunny pale stone waiting for the lively people, with the great flight of pale steps sweeping up to the doors of the church, waiting for gentlemen in scarlet trunk-hose, slender red legs, and ladies in brocade gowns, and page-boys with fluffed, golden hair. Splendid, sunny, gay Bramante Courtyard of lively stone. But empty. Empty of life. The gay red-legged gentry dead forever. And when pilgrimages do come and throng in, it is horrible artisan excursions from the great town, and the sordidness of industrialism.

We climbed the little watchtower that is now an observatory, and saw the vague and unshaven Don Giovanni among all his dust and instruments. M was very familiar and friendly, chattering in his quaint Italian, which was more wrong than any Italian I have ever heard spoken; very familiar and friendly, and a tiny bit deferential to the monks, and yet, and yet—rather patronizing. His little pomposity and patronizing tone coloured even his deferential yearning to be admitted to the monastery. The monks were rather brief with him. They no doubt have their likes and dislikes greatly intensified by the monastic life.

We stood on the summit of the tower and looked at the world below: the town, the castle, the white roads coming straight as judgment out of the mountains north, from Rome, and piercing into the mountains south, toward Naples, traversing the flat, flat plain. Roads, railway, river, streams, a world in accurate and lively detail, with mountains sticking up abruptly and rockily, as the old painters painted it. I think there is no way of painting Italian landscape except that way—that started with Lorenzetti and ended with the sixteenth century.

We looked at the ancient cell away under the monastery, where all the sanctity started. We looked at the big library that belongs to the State, and at the smaller library that belongs still to the abbot. I was tired, cold, and sick among the books and illuminations. I could not bear it any more. I felt I must be outside, in the sun, and see the world below, and the way out.

That evening I said to M: "And what was the abyss, then?"

"Oh well, you know," he said, "it was a cheque which I made out at Anzio. There should have been money to meet it, in my bank in New York. But it appears the money had never been paid in by the people that owed it me. So there was I in a very nasty hole, an unmet cheque, and no money at all in Italy. I really had to escape here. It is an *absolute* secret that I am here, and it must be, till I can get this business settled. Of course I've written to America about it. But as you see, I'm in a very nasty hole. That five francs I gave you for the driver was the last penny I had in the world: absolutely the last penny. I haven't even anything to buy a cigarette or a stamp." And he laughed chirpily, as if it were a joke. But he didn't really think it a joke. Nor was it a joke.

I had come with only two hundred lire in my pocket, as I was waiting to change some money at the bank. Of this two hundred I had one hundred left or one hundred and twenty-five. I should need a hundred to get home. I could only give M the twenty-five, for the bottle of drink. He was rather crestfallen. But I didn't want to give him money this time: because he expected it.

However, we talked about his plans: how he was to earn something. He told me what he had written. And I cast over in my mind where he might get something published in London, wrote a couple of letters on his account, told him where I thought he had best send his material. There wasn't a great deal of hope, for his smaller journalistic articles seemed to me very self-conscious and poor. He had one about the monastery, which I thought he might sell because of the photographs.

That evening he first showed me the Legion manuscript. He had got it rather raggedly typed out. He had a type-writer, but felt he ought to have somebody to do his typing for him, as he hated it and did it unwillingly. That evening and when I went to bed and when I woke in the morning I read this manuscript. It did not seem very good—vague and diffuse where it shouldn't have been—lacking in sharp detail and definite event. And yet there was something in it that made me want it done properly. So we talked about it, and discussed it carefully, and he unwillingly promised to tackle it again. He was curious, always talking about his work, even always working, but never *properly* doing anything.

We walked out in the afternoon through the woods and across the rocky bit of moorland which covers most of the hill-top. We were going to the ruined convent which lies on the other brow of the monastery hill, abandoned and sad among the rocks and heath and thorny bushes. It was sunny and warm. A barefoot little boy was tending a cow and three goats and a pony, a barefoot little girl had five geese in charge. We came to the convent and looked in. The further part of the courtyard was still entire, the place was a sort of farm, two rooms occupied by a peasant-farmer. We climbed about the ruins. Some creature was crying—crying, crying, crying with a strange, inhuman persistence, leaving off and crying again. We listened and listened—the sharp, poignant crying. Almost it might have been a sharp-voiced baby. We scrambled about, looking. And at last outside a little cave-like place found a blind black puppy crawling miserably on the floor, unable to walk, and crying incessantly. We put it back in the little cave-like shed, and went away. The place was deserted save for the crying puppy.

On the road outside however was a man, a peasant, just drawing up to the arched convent gateway with an ass under a load of brushwood. He was thin and black and dirty. He took off his hat, and we told him of the puppy. He said the bitch-mother had gone off with his son with the sheep. Yes, she had been gone all day. Yes, she would be back at sunset. No, the puppy had not drunk all day. Yes, the little beast cried, but the mother would come back to him.

They were the old-world peasants still about the monastery, with the hard, small bony heads and deep-lined faces and utterly blank minds, crying their speech as crows cry, and living their lives as lizards among the rocks, blindly going on with the little job in hand, the present moment, cut off from all past and future, and having no idea and no sustained emotion, only that eternal will-to-live which makes a tortoise wake up once more in spring, and makes a grasshopper whistle on in the moonlight nights even of November. Only these peasants don't whistle much. The whistlers go to America. It is the hard, static, unhoping souls that persist in the old life. And still they stand back, as one passes them in the corridors of the great monastery, they press themselves back against the whitewashed walls of the still place, and drop their heads, as if some mystery were passing by, some God-mystery, the higher beings, which they must not look closely upon. So also this old peasant—he was not old, but deep-lined like a gnarled bough. He stood with his hat down in his hands as we spoke to him and answered the short, hard, insentient answers, as a tree might speak.

"The monks keep their peasants humble," I said to M.

"Of course!" he said. "Don't you think they are quite right? Don't you think they should be humble?" And he bridled like a little turkey-cock on his hind legs.

"Well," I said, "if there's any occasion for humility, I do."

"Don't you think there is occasion?" he cried. "If there's one thing worse than another, it's this *equality* that has come into the world. Do you believe in it yourself?"

"No," I said. "I don't believe in equality. But the problem is, wherein does superiority lie."

"Oh," chirped M complacently. "It lies in many things. It lies in birth and in upbringing and so on, but it is chiefly in *mind*. Don't you think? Of course I don't mean that the physical qualities aren't *charming*. They are, and nobody appreciates them more than I do. Some of the peasants are *beautiful* creatures, perfectly beautiful. But that passes. And the mind endures."

I did not answer. M was not a man one talked far with. But I thought to myself, I *could* not accept M's superiority to the peasant. If I had really to live always under the same roof with either one of them, I would have chosen the peasant. If I had had to choose, I would have chosen the peasant. Not because the peasant was wonderful and stored with mystic qualities. No, I don't give much for the wonderful mystic qualities in peasants. Money is their mystery of mysteries, absolutely. No, if I chose the peasant it would be for what he *lacked* rather than for what he had. He lacked that complacent mentality that M was so proud of, he lacked all the trivial trash of glib talk and more glib thought, all the conceit of our shallow consciousness. For his mindlessness I would have chosen the peasant: and for his strong blood-presence. M wearied me with his facility and his readiness to rush into speech, and for the exhaustive nature of his presence. As if he had no strong blood in him to sustain him, only this modern parasitic lymph which cries for sympathy all the time.

"Don't you think yourself that you are superior to that peasant?" he asked me, rather ironically. He half expected me to say no.

"Yes, I do," I replied. "But I think most middle-class, most so-called educated people are inferior to the peasant. I do that."

"Of course," said M readily. "In their *hypocrisy*—" He was great against hypocrisy—especially the English sort.

"And if I think myself superior to the peasant, it is only that I feel myself like the growing tip, or one of the growing tips of the tree, and him like a piece of the hard, fixed tissue of the branch or trunk. We're part of the same tree: and it's the same sap," said I.

"Why, exactly! Exactly!" cried M. "Of course! The Church would teach the same doctrine. We are all one in Christ—but between our souls and our duties there are great differences."

It is terrible to be agreed with, especially by a man like M. All that one says, and means, turns to nothing.

"Yes," I persisted. "But it seems to me the so-called culture, education, the so-called leaders and leading-classes to-day, are only parasites—like a great flourishing bush of parasitic consciousness flourishing on top of the tree of life, and sapping it. The consciousness of to-day doesn't rise from the roots. It is just parasitic in the veins of life. And the middle and upper classes are just parasitic upon the body of life which still remains in the lower classes."

"What!" said M acidly. "Do you believe in the democratic lower classes?"

"Not a bit," said I.

"I should think not, indeed!" he cried complacently.

"No, I don't believe the lower classes can ever make life whole again, till they *do* become humble, like the old peasants, and yield themselves to real leaders. But not to great negators like Lloyd George or Lenin or Briand."

"Of course! of course!" he cried. "What you need is the Church in power again. The Church has a place for everybody."

"You don't think the Church belongs to the past?" I asked.

"Indeed I don't, or I shouldn't be here. No," he said sententiously, "the Church is eternal. It puts people in *their* proper place. It puts women down into their proper place, which is the first thing to be done—"

He had a great dislike of women, and was very acid about them. Not because of their sins, but because of their virtues: their economies, their philanthropies, their spiritualities. Oh, how he loathed women. He had been married, but the marriage had not been a success. He smarted still. Perhaps his wife had despised him, and he had not *quite* been able to defeat her contempt.

So, he loathed women, and wished for a world of men. "They talk about love between men and women," he said. "Why it's all a *fraud*. The woman is just taking all and giving nothing, and feeling sanctified about it. All she tries to do is to thwart a man in whatever he is doing. No, I have found my life in my *friendships*. Physical relationships are very attractive, of course, and one tries to keep them as decent and all that as one can. But one knows they will pass and be finished. But one's *mental* friendships last for ever."

"With me, on the contrary," said I. "If there is no profound blood-sympathy, I know the mental friendship is trash. If there is real, deep blood response, I will stick to that if I have to betray all the mental sympathies I ever made, or all the lasting spiritual loves I ever felt."

He looked at me, and his face seemed to fall. Round the eyes he was yellow and tired and nervous. He watched me for some time.

"Oh!" he said, in a queer tone, rather cold. "Well, my experience has been the opposite."

We were silent for some time.

"And you," I said, "even if you do manage to do all your studies and enter the monastery, do you think you will be satisfied?"

"If I can be so fortunate, I do really," he said. "Do you doubt it?"

"Yes," I said. "Your nature is worldly, more worldly than mine. Yet I should die if I had to stay up here."

"Why?" he asked, curiously.

"Oh, I don't know. The past, the past. The beautiful, the wonderful past, it seems to prey on my heart, I can't bear it."

He watched me closely.

"Really!" he said stoutly. "Do you feel like that? But don't you think it is a far preferable life up here than down there? Don't you think the past is far preferable to the future, with all this *socialismo* and these *communisti* and so on?"

We were seated, in the sunny afternoon, on the wild hill-top high above the world. Across the stretch of pale, dry, standing thistles that peopled the waste ground, and beyond the rocks was the ruined convent. Rocks rose behind us, the summit. Away on the left were the woods which hid us from the great monastery. This was the mountain top, the last foothold of the old world. Below we could see the plain, the straight white road, straight as a thought, and the more flexible black railway with the railway station. There swarmed the *ferrovieri* like ants. There was democracy, industrialism, socialism, the red flag of the communists and the red, white and green tricolor of the fascist! That was another world. And how bitter, how barren a world! Barren like the black cinder-track of the railway, with its two steel lines.

And here above, sitting with the little stretch of pale, dry thistles around us, our back to a warm rock, we were in the Middle Ages. Both worlds were agony to me. But here, on the mountain top was worst: The past, the poignancy of the not-quite-dead past.

"I think one's got to go through with the life down there—get somewhere beyond it. One can't go back," I said to him.

"But do you call the monastery going back?" he said. "I don't. The peace, the eternity, the concern with things that matter. I consider it the happiest fate that could happen to me. Of course it means putting physical things aside. But when you've done that—why, it seems to me perfect."

"No," I said. "You're too worldly."

"But the monastery is worldly too. We're not Trappists. Why the monastery is one of the centres of the world—one of the most active centres."

"Maybe. But that impersonal activity, with the blood suppressed and going sour—no, it's too late. It is too abstract—political maybe—"

"I'm sorry you think so," he said, rising. "I don't."

"Well," I said. "You'll never be a monk here, M. You see if you are."

"You don't think I shall?" he replied, turning to me. And there was a catch of relief in his voice. Really, the monastic state must have been like going to prison for him.

"You haven't a vocation," I said.

"I may not *seem* to have, but I hope I actually have."

"You haven't."

"Of course, if you're so sure," he laughed, putting his hand on my arm.

He seemed to understand so much, round about the questions that trouble one deepest. But the quick of the question he never felt. He had no real middle, no real centre bit to him. Yet, round and round about all the questions, he was so intelligent and sensitive.

We went slowly back. The peaks of those Italian mountains in the sunset, the extinguishing twinkle of the plain away below, as the sun declined and grew yellow; the intensely powerful mediaeval spirit lingering on this wild hill summit, all the wonder of the mediaeval past; and then the huge mossy stones in the wintry wood, that was once a sacred grove; the ancient path through the wood, that led from temple to temple on the hill summit, before Christ was born; and then the great Cyclopean wall one passes at the bend of the road, built even before the pagan temples; all this overcame me so powerfully this afternoon, that I was almost speechless. That hill-top must have been one of man's intense sacred places for three thousand years. And men die generation after generation, races die, but the new cult finds root in the old sacred place, and the quick spot of earth dies very slowly. Yet at last it too dies. But this quick spot is still not quite dead. The great monastery couchant there, half empty, but also not quite dead. And M and I walking across as the sun set yellow and the cold of the snow came into the air, back home to the monastery! And I feeling as if my heart had once more broken: I don't know why. And he feeling his fear of life, that haunted him, and his fear of his own self and its consequences, that never left him for long. And he seemed to walk close to me, very close. And we had neither of us anything more to say.

Don Bernardo was looking for us as we came up under the archway, he hatless in the cold evening, his black dress swinging voluminous. There were letters for M. There was a small cheque for him from America—about fifty dollars—from some newspaper in the Middle West that had printed one of his articles. He had to talk with Don Bernardo about this.

I decided to go back the next day. I could not stay any longer. M was very disappointed, and begged me to remain. "I thought you would stay a week at least," he said. "Do stay over Sunday. Oh do!" But I couldn't, I didn't want to. I could see that his days were a torture to him—the long, cold days in that vast quiet building, with the strange and exhausting silence in the air, and the sense of the past preying on one, and the sense of the silent, suppressed scheming struggle of life going on still in the sacred place.

It was a cloudy morning. In the green courtyard the big Don Anselmo had just caught the little Don Lorenzo round the waist and was swinging him over a bush, like lads before school. The Prior was just hurrying somewhere, following his long fine nose. He bade me goodbye; pleasant, warm, jolly, with a touch of wistfulness in his deafness. I parted with real regret from Don Bernardo.

M was coming with me down the hill—not down the carriage road, but down the wide old paved path that swoops so wonderfully from the top of the hill to the bottom. It feels thousands of years old. M was quiet and friendly. We met Don Vincenzo, he who has the care of the land and crops, coming slowly, slowly uphill in his black cassock, treading slowly with his great thick boots. He was reading a little book. He saluted us as we passed. Lower down a strapping girl was watching three merino sheep among the bushes. One sheep came on its exquisite slender legs to smell of me, with that insatiable curiosity of a pecora. Her nose was silken and elegant as she reached it to sniff at me, and the yearning, wondering, inquisitive look in her eyes, made me realize that the Lamb of God must have been such a sheep as this.

M was miserable at my going. Not so much at my going, as at being left alone up there. We came to the foot of the hill, on to the town highroad. So we went into a little cave of a wine-kitchen to drink a glass of wine. M chatted a little with the young woman. He chatted with everybody. She eyed us closely—and asked if we were from the monastery. We said we were. She seemed to have a little lurking antagonism round her nose, at the mention of the monastery. M paid for the wine—a franc. So we went out on the highroad, to part.

"Look," I said. "I can only give you twenty lire, because I shall need the rest for the journey—"

But he wouldn't take them. He looked at me wistfully. Then I went on down to the station, he turned away uphill. It was market in the town, and there were clusters of bullocks, and women cooking a little meal at a brazier under the trees, and goods spread out on the floor to sell, and sacks of beans and corn standing open, clustered round the trunks of the mulberry trees, and wagons with their shafts on the ground. The old peasants in their brown homespun frieze and skin sandals were watching for the world. And there again was the Middle Ages.

It began to rain, however. Suddenly it began to pour with rain, and my coat was wet through, and my trouser-legs. The train from Rome was late—I hoped not very late, or I should miss the boat. She came at last: and was full. I had to stand in the corridor. Then the man came to say dinner was served, so I luckily got a place and had my meal too. Sitting there in the dining-car, among the fat Neapolitans eating their macaroni, with the big glass windows steamed opaque and the rain beating outside, I let myself be carried away, away from the monastery, away from M, away from everything.

At Naples there was a bit of sunshine again, and I had time to go on foot to the Immacolatella, where the little steamer lay. There on the steamer I sat in a bit of sunshine, and felt that again the world had come to an end for me, and again my heart was broken. The steamer seemed to be making its way away from the old world, that had come to another end in me.

It was after this I decided to go to Sicily. In February, only a few days after my return from the monastery, I was on the steamer for Palermo, and at dawn looking out on the wonderful coast of Sicily. Sicily, tall, forever rising up to her gem-like summits, all golden in dawn, and always glamorous, always hovering as if inaccessible, and yet so near, so distinct. Sicily unknown to me, and amethystine-glamorous in the Mediterranean dawn: like the dawn of our day, the wonder-morning of our epoch.

I had various letters from M. He had told me to go to Girgenti. But I arrived in Girgenti when there was a strike of sulphur-miners, and they threw stones. So I did not want to live in Girgenti. M hated Taormina—he had been everywhere, tried everywhere, and was not, I found, in any good odour in most places. He wrote however saying he hoped I would like it. And later he sent the Legion manuscript. I thought it was good, and told him so. It was offered to publishers in London, but rejected.

In early April I went with my wife to Syracuse for a few days: lovely, lovely days, with the purple anemones blowing in the Sicilian fields, and Adonis-blood red on the little ledges, and the corn rising strong and green in the magical, malarial places, and Etna flowing now to the northward, still with her crown of snow. The lovely, lovely journey from Catania to Syracuse, in spring, winding round the blueness of that sea, where the tall pink asphodel was dying, and the yellow asphodel like a lily showing her silk. Lovely, lovely Sicily, the dawn-place, Europe's dawn, with Odysseus pushing his ship out of the shadows into the blue. Whatever had died for me, Sicily had then not died: dawn-lovely Sicily, and the Ionian sea.

We came back, and the world was lovely: our own house above the almond trees, and the sea in the cove below. Calabria glimmering like a changing opal away to the left, across the blue, bright straits, and all the great blueness of the lovely dawn-sea in front, where the sun rose with a splendour like trumpets every morning, and me rejoicing like a madness in this dawn, day-dawn, life-dawn, the dawn which is Greece, which is me.

Well, into this lyricism suddenly crept the serpent. It was a lovely morning, still early. I heard a noise on the stairs from the lower terrace, and went to look. M on the stairs, looking up at me with a frightened face.

"Why!" I said. "Is it you?"

"Yes," he replied. "A terrible thing has happened."

He waited on the stairs, and I went down. Rather unwillingly, because I detest terrible things, and the people to whom they happen. So we leaned on the creeper-covered rail of the terrace, under festoons of creamy bignonia flowers, and looked at the pale blue, ethereal sea.

"What terrible thing!" said I.

"When did you get back?" said he.

"Last evening."

"Oh! I came before. The contadini said they thought you would come yesterday evening. I've been here several days."

"Where are you staying?"

"At the San Domenico."

The San Domenico being then the most expensive hotel here, I thought he must have money. But I knew he wanted something of me.

"And are you staying some time?"

He paused a moment, and looked round cautiously.

"Is your wife there?" he asked, sotto voce.

"Yes, she's upstairs."

"Is there anyone who can hear?"

"No—only old Grazia down below, and she can't understand anyhow."

"Well," he said, stammering. "Let me tell you what's happened. I had to escape from the monastery. Don Bernardo had a telephone message from the town below, that the carabinieri were looking for an Americano—my name—Of course you can guess how I felt, up there! Awful! Well—! I had to fly at a moment's notice. I just put two shirts in a handbag and went. I slipped down a path—or rather, it isn't a path—down the back of the hill. Ten minutes after Don Bernardo had the message I was running down the hill."

"But what did they want you for?" I asked dismayed.

"Well," he faltered. "I told you about the cheque at Anzio, didn't I? Well, it seems the hotel people applied to the police. Anyhow," he added hastily, "I couldn't let myself be arrested up there, could I? So awful for the monastery!"

"Did they know then that you were in trouble?" I asked.

"Don Bernardo knew I had no money," he said. "Of course he had to know. Yes—he knew I was in *difficulty*. But, of course, he didn't know—well—*everything*." He laughed a little, comical laugh over the *everything*, as if he was just a little bit naughtily proud of it: most ruefully also.

"No," he continued, "that's what I'm most afraid of—that they'll find out everything at the monastery. Of course it's *dreadful*—the Americano, been staying there for months, and everything so nice and—, well you know how they are, they imagine every American is a millionaire, if not a multi-millionaire. And suddenly to be wanted by the police! Of course it's *dreadful*! Anything rather than a scandal at the monastery—anything. Oh, how awful it was! I can tell you, in that quarter of an hour, I sweated blood. Don Bernardo lent me two hundred lire of the monastery money—which he'd no business to do. And I escaped down the back of the hill, I walked to the next station up the line, and took the next train—the slow train—a few stations up towards Rome. And there I changed and caught the diretto for Sicily. I came straight to you—Of course I was in *agony*: imagine it! I spent most of the time as far as Naples in the lavatory." He laughed his little jerky laugh.

"What class did you travel?"

"Second. All through the night. I arrived more dead than alive, not having had a meal for two days—only some sandwich stuff I bought on the platform."

"When did you come then?"

"I arrived on Saturday evening. I came out here on Sunday morning, and they told me you were away. Of course, imagine what it's like! I'm in torture every minute, in torture, of course. Why just imagine!" And he laughed his little laugh.

"But how much money have you got?"

"Oh—I've just got twenty-five francs and five soldi." He laughed as if it was rather a naughty joke.

"But," I said, "if you've got no money, why do you go to the San Domenico? How much do you pay there?"

"Fifty lire a day. Of course it's *ruinous*—"

"But at the Bristol you only pay twenty-five—and at Fichera's only twenty."

"Yes, I know you do," he said. "But I stayed at the Bristol once, and I loathed the place. Such an offensive manager. And I couldn't touch the food at Fichera's."

"But who's going to pay for the San Domenico, then?" I asked.

"Well, I thought," he said, "you know all those manuscripts of mine? Well, you think they're some good, don't you? Well, I thought if I made them over to you, and you did what you could with them and just kept me going till I can get a new start—or till I can get away—"

I looked across the sea: the lovely morning-blue sea towards Greece.

"Where do you want to get away to?" I said.

"To Egypt. I know a man in Alexandria who owns newspapers there. I'm sure if I could get over there he'd give me an editorship or something. And of course money will come. I've written to —, who was my *greatest* friend, in London. He will send me something—"

"And what else do you expect?"

"Oh, my article on the monastery was accepted by *Land and Water*—thanks to you and your kindness, of course. I thought if I might stay very quietly with you, for a time, and write some things I'm wanting to do, and collect a little money—and then get away to Egypt—"

He looked up into my face, as if he were trying all he could on me. First thing I knew was that I could not have him in the house with me: and even if I could have done it, my wife never could.

"You've got a lovely place here, perfectly beautiful," he said. "Of course, if it had to be Taormina, you've chosen far the best place here. I like this side so much better than the Etna side. Etna always there and people raving about it gets on my nerves. And a *charming* house, charming."

He looked round the loggia and along the other terrace.

"Is it all yours?" he said.

"We don't use the ground floor. Come in here."

So we went into the salotto.

"Oh, what a beautiful room," he cried. "But perfectly palatial. Charming! Charming! *Much* the nicest house in Taormina."

"No," I said, "as a house it isn't very grand, though I like it for myself. It's just what I want. And I love the situation. But I'll go and tell my wife you are here."

"Will you?" he said, bridling nervously. "Of course I've never met your wife." And he laughed the nervous, naughty, jokey little laugh.

I left him, and ran upstairs to the kitchen. There was my wife, with wide eyes. She had been listening to catch the conversation. But M's voice was too hushed.

"M!" said I softly. "The carabinieri wanted to arrest him at the monastery, so he has escaped here, and wants me to be responsible for him."

"Arrest him what for?"

"Debts, I suppose. Will you come down and speak to him?"

M of course was very charming with my wife. He kissed her hand humbly, in the correct German fashion, and spoke with an air of reverence that infallibly gets a woman.

"Such a beautiful place you have here," he said, glancing through the open doors of the room, at the sea beyond. "So clever of you to find it."

"Lawrence found it," said she. "Well, and you are in all kinds of difficulty!"

"Yes, isn't it terrible!" he said, laughing as if it were a joke—rather a wry joke. "I felt dreadful at the monastery. So dreadful for them, if there was any sort of scandal. And after I'd been so well received there—and so much the Signor Americano—Dreadful, don't you think?" He laughed again, like a naughty boy.

We had an engagement to lunch that morning. My wife was dressed, so I went to get ready. Then we told M we must go out, and he accompanied us to the village. I gave him just the hundred francs I had in my pocket, and he said could he come and see me that evening? I asked him to come next morning.

"You're so awfully kind," he said, simpering a little.

223

But by this time I wasn't feeling kind.

"He's quite nice," said my wife. "But he's rather an impossible little person. And you'll see, he'll be a nuisance. Whatever do you pick up such dreadful people for?"

"Nay," I said. "You can't accuse me of picking up dreadful people. He's the first. And even he isn't dreadful."

The next morning came a letter from Don Bernardo addressed to me, but only enclosing a letter to M. So he was using my address. At ten o'clock he punctually appeared: slipping in as if to avoid notice. My wife would not see him, so I took him out on the terrace again.

"Isn't it beautiful here!" he said. "Oh, so beautiful! If only I had my peace of mind. Of course I sweat blood every time anybody comes through the door. You are splendidly private out here."

"Yes," I said. "But M, there isn't a room for you in the house. There isn't a spare room anyway. You'd better think of getting something cheaper in the village."

"But what can I get?" he snapped.

That rather took my breath away. Myself, I had never been near the San Domenico hotel. I knew I simply could not afford it.

"What made you go to the San Domenico in the first place?" I said. "The most expensive hotel in the place!"

"Oh, I'd stayed there for two months, and they knew me, and I knew they'd ask no questions. I knew they wouldn't ask for a deposit or anything."

"But nobody dreams of asking for a deposit," I said.

"Anyhow I shan't take my meals there. I shall just take coffee in the morning. I've had to eat there so far, because I was starved to death, and had no money to go out. But I had two meals in that little restaurant yesterday; disgusting food."

"And how much did that cost?"

"Oh fourteen francs and fifteen francs, with a quarter of wine—and such a poor meal!"

Now I was annoyed, knowing that I myself should have bought bread and cheese for one franc, and eaten it in my room. But also I realized that the modern creed says, if you sponge, sponge thoroughly: and also that every man has a "right to live," and that if he can manage to live well, no matter at whose expense, all credit to him. This is the kind of talk one accepts in one's slipshod moments; now it was actually tried on me, I didn't like it at all.

"But who's going to pay your bill at the San Domenico?" I said.

"I thought you'd advance me the money on those manuscripts."

"It's no good talking about the money on the manuscripts," I said. "I should have to give it to you. And as a matter of fact, I've got just sixty pounds in the bank in England, and about fifteen hundred lire here. My wife and I have got to live on that. We don't spend as much in a week as you spend in three days at the San Domenico. It's no good your thinking I can advance money on the manuscripts. I can't. If I was rich, I'd give you money. But I've got no money, and never have had any. Have you nobody you can go to?"

"I'm waiting to hear from—. When I go back into the village, I'll telegraph to him," replied M, a little crestfallen. "Of course I'm in torture night and day, or I wouldn't appeal to you like this. I know it's unpleasant for you—" and he put his hand on my arm and looked up beseechingly. "But what am I to do?"

"You must get out of the San Domenico," I said. "That's the first thing."

"Yes," he said, a little piqued now. "I know it is. I'm going to ask Pancrazio Melenga to let me have a room in his house. He knows me quite well—he's an awfully nice fellow. He'll do *anything* for me—*anything*. I was just going there yesterday afternoon when you were coming from Timeo. He was out, so I left word with his wife, who is a charming little person. If he has a room to spare, I know he will let me have it. And he's a *splendid* cook—splendid. By far the nicest food in Taormina."

"Well," I said. "If you settle with Melenga, I will pay your bill at the San Domenico, but I can't do any more. I simply can't."

"But what am I to *do*?" he snapped.

"I don't know," I said. "You must think."

"I came here," he said, "thinking you would help me. What am I to do, if you won't? I shouldn't have come to Taormina at all, save for you. Don't be unkind to me—don't speak so coldly to me—" He put his hand on my arm, and looked up at me with tears swimming in his eyes. Then he turned aside his face, overcome with tears. I looked away at the Ionian sea, feeling my blood turn to ice and the sea go black. I loathe scenes such as this.

"Did you telegraph to—?" I said.

"Yes. I have no answer yet. I hope you don't mind—I gave your address for a reply."

"Oh," I said. "There's a letter for you from Don Bernardo."

He went pale. I was angry at his having used my address in this manner.

"Nothing further has happened at the monastery," he said. "They rang up from the Questura, from the police station, and Don Bernardo answered that the Americano had left for Rome. Of course I did take the train for Rome. And Don Bernardo wanted me to go to Rome. He advised me to do so. I didn't tell him I was here till I had got here. He thought I should have had more resources in Rome, and of course I should. I should certainly have gone there, if it hadn't been for *you here*—"

Well, I was getting tired and angry. I would not give him any more money at the moment. I promised, if he would leave the hotel I would pay his bill, but he must leave it at once. He went off to settle with Melenga. He asked again if he could come in the afternoon: I said I was going out.

He came nevertheless while I was out. This time my wife found him on the stairs. She was for hating him, of course. So she stood immovable on the top stair, and he stood two stairs lower, and he kissed her hand in utter humility. And he pleaded with her, and as he looked up to her on the stairs the tears ran down his face and he trembled with distress. And her spine crept up and down with distaste and discomfort. But he broke into a few phrases of touching German, and I know he broke down her reserve and she promised him all he wanted. This part she would never confess, though. Only she was shivering with revulsion and excitement and even a sense of power, when I came home.

That was why M appeared more impertinent than ever, next morning. He had arranged to go to Melenga's house the following day, and to pay ten francs a day for his room, his meals extra. So that was something. He made a long tale about not eating any of his meals in the hotel now, but pretending he was invited out, and eating in the little restaurants where the food was so bad. And he had now only fifteen lire left in his pocket. But I was cold, and wouldn't give him any more. I said I would give him money next day, for his bill.

He had now another request, and a new tone.

"Won't you do *one more* thing for me?" he said. "Oh do! Do do this one thing for me. I want you to go to the monastery and bring away my important papers and some clothes and my important trinkets. I have made a list of the things here—and where you'll find them in my writing-table and in the chest of drawers. I don't think you'll have any trouble. Don Bernardo has the keys. He will open everything for you. And I beg you, *in the name of God*, don't let anybody else see the things. Not even Don Bernardo. Don't, whatever you do, let him see the papers and manuscripts you are bringing. If he sees them, there's an end to me at the monastery. I can *never* go back there. I am ruined in their eyes for ever. As it is—although Don Bernardo is the best person in the world and my dearest friend, still—you know what people are—especially monks. A little curious, don't you know, a little inquisitive. Well, let us hope for the best as far as that goes. But you will do this for me, won't you? I shall be so eternally grateful."

Now a journey to the monastery meant a terrible twenty hours in the train each way—all that awful journey through Calabria to Naples and northwards. It meant mixing myself up in this man's affairs. It meant appearing as his accomplice at the monastery. It meant travelling with all his "compromising" papers and his valuables. And all this time, I never knew what mischiefs he had really been up to, and I didn't trust him, not for one single second. He would tell me nothing save that Anzio hotel cheque. I knew that wasn't all, by any means. So I mistrusted him. And with a feeling of utter mistrust goes a feeling of contempt and dislike—And finally, it would have cost me at least ten pounds sterling, which I simply did not want to spend in waste.

"I don't want to do that," I said.

"Why not?" he asked, sharp, looking green. He had planned it all out.

"No, I don't want to."

"Oh, but I *can't* remain here as I am. I've got no clothes—I've got nothing to *wear*. I *must* have my things from the monastery. What can I do? What can I do? I came to you, if it hadn't been for you I should have gone to Rome. I came to you—Oh yes, you *will* go. You *will* go, won't you? You *will* go to the monastery for my things?" And again he put his hand on my arm, and the tears began to fall from his upturned eyes. I turned my head aside. Never had the Ionian sea looked so sickening to me.

"I don't *want* to," said I.

"But you *will*! You will! You *will* go to the monastery for me, won't you? Everything else is no good if you won't. I've nothing to wear. I haven't got my manuscripts to work on, I can't do the things I am doing. Here I live in a sweat of anxiety. I try to work, and I can't settle. I can't do anything. It's dreadful. I shan't have a minute's peace till I have got those things from the monastery, till I know they can't get at my private papers. You will do this for me! You will, won't you? Please do! Oh please do!" And again tears.

And I with my bowels full of bitterness, loathing the thought of that journey there and back, on such an errand. Yet not quite sure that I ought to refuse. And he pleaded and struggled, and tried to bully me with tears and entreaty and reproach, to do his will. And I couldn't quite refuse. But neither could I agree.

At last I said: "I don't want to go, and I tell you. I won't promise to go. And I won't say that I will not go. I won't say until to-morrow. To-morrow I will tell you. Don't come to the house. I will be in the Corso at ten o'clock."

"I didn't doubt for a minute you would do this for me," he said. "Otherwise I should never have come to Taormina." As if he had done me an honour in coming to Taormina; and as if I had betrayed *him*.

"Well," I said. "If you make these messes you'll have to get out of them yourself. I don't know why you are *in* such a mess."

"Any man may make a mistake," he said sharply, as if correcting me.

"Yes, a *mistake*!" said I. "If it's a question of a mistake."

So once more he went, humbly, beseechingly, and yet, one could not help but feel, with all that terrible insolence of the humble. It is the humble, the wistful, the would-be-loving souls to-day who bully us with their charity-demanding insolence. They just make up their minds, these needful sympathetic souls, that one is there to do their will. Very good.

I decided in the day I would *not* go. Without reasoning it out, I knew I *really* didn't want to go. I plainly didn't want it. So I wouldn't go.

The morning came again hot and lovely. I set off to the village. But there was M watching for me on the path beyond the valley. He came forward and took my hand warmly, clingingly. I turned back, to remain in the country. We talked for a minute of his leaving the hotel—he was going that afternoon, he had asked for his bill. But he was waiting for the other answer.

"And I have decided," I said, "I won't go to the monastery."

"You won't." He looked at me. I saw how yellow he was round the eyes, and yellow under his reddish skin.

"No," I said.

And it was final. He knew it. We went some way in silence. I turned in at the garden gate. It was a lovely, lovely morning of hot sun. Butterflies were flapping over the rosemary hedges and over a few little red poppies, the young vines smelt sweet in flower, very sweet, the corn was tall and green, and there were still some wild, rose-red gladiolus flowers among the watery green of the wheat. M had accepted my refusal. I expected him to be angry. But no, he seemed quieter, wistfuller, and he seemed almost to love me for having refused him. I stood at a bend in the path. The sea was heavenly blue, rising up beyond the vines and olive leaves, lustrous pale lacquer blue as only the Ionian sea can be. Away at the brook below the women were washing, and one could hear the chock-chock-chock of linen beaten against the stones. I felt M then an intolerable weight and like a clot of dirt over everything.

"May I come in?" he said to me.

"No," I said. "Don't come to the house. My wife doesn't want it."

Even that he accepted without any offence, and seemed only to like me better for it. That was a puzzle to me. I told him I would leave a letter and a cheque for him at the bank in the Corso that afternoon.

I did so, writing a cheque for a few pounds, enough to cover his bill and leave a hundred lire or so over, and a letter to say I could *not* do any more, and I didn't want to see him any more.

So, there was an end of it for a moment. Yet I felt him looming in the village, waiting. I had rashly said I would go to tea with him to the villa of one of the Englishmen resident here, whose acquaintance I had not made. Alas, M kept me to the promise. As I came home he appealed to me again. He was rather insolent. What good to him, he said, were the few pounds I had given him? He had got a hundred and fifty lire left. What good was that? I realized it really was not a solution, and said nothing. Then he spoke of his plans for getting to Egypt. The fare, he had found out, was thirty-five pounds. And where were thirty-five pounds coming from? Not from me.

I spent a week avoiding him, wondering what on earth the poor devil was doing, and yet *determined* he should not be a parasite on me. If I could have given him fifty pounds and sent him to Egypt to be a parasite on somebody else, I would have done so. Which is what we call charity. However, I couldn't.

My wife chafed, crying: "What have you done! We shall have him on our hands all our life. We can't let him starve. It is degrading, degrading, to have him hanging on to us."

"Yes," I said. "He must starve or work or something. I am not God who is responsible for him."

M was determined not to lose his status as a gentleman. In a way I sympathized with him. He would never be out at elbows. That is your modern rogue. He will not degenerate outwardly. Certain standards of a gentleman he *would* keep up: he would be well-dressed, he would be lavish with borrowed money, he would be as far as possible honourable in his small transactions of daily life. Well, very good. I sympathized with him to a certain degree. If he could find his own way out, well and good. Myself, I was not his way out.

Ten days passed. It was hot and I was going about the terrace in pyjamas and a big old straw hat, when suddenly, a Sicilian, handsome, in the prime of life, and in his best black suit, smiling at me and taking off his hat!

And could he speak to me. I threw away my straw hat, and we went into the salotto. He handed me a note.

"Il Signor M mi ha dato questa lettera per Lei!" he began, and I knew what was coming. Melenga had been a waiter in good hotels, had saved money, built himself a fine house which he let to foreigners. He was a pleasant fellow, and at his best now, because he was in a rage. I must repeat M's letter from memory—"Dear Lawrence, would you do me another kindness. *Land and Water* sent a cheque for seven guineas for the article on the monastery, and Don Bernardo forwarded this to me under Melenga's name. But unfortunately he made a mistake, and put Orazio instead of Pancrazio, so the post office would not deliver the letter, and have returned it to the monastery. This morning Melenga insulted me, and I cannot stay in his house another minute. Will you be so kind as to advance me these seven guineas, and I shall leave Taormina at once, for Malta."

I asked Melenga what had happened, and read him the letter. He was handsome in his rage, lifting his brows and suddenly smiling:

"Ma senta, Signore! Signor M has been in my house for ten days, and lived well, and eaten well, and drunk well, and I have not seen a single penny of his money. I go out in the morning and buy all the things, all he wants, and my wife cooks it, and he is very pleased, very pleased, has never eaten such good food in his life, and everything is splendid, splendid. And he never pays a penny. Not a penny. Says he is waiting for money from England, from America, from India. But the money never comes. And I am a poor man, signore, I have a wife and child to keep. I have already spent three hundred lire for this Signor M, and I never see a penny of it back. And he says the money is coming, it is coming—But when? He never says he has *got* no money. He says he is expecting. To-morrow—always to-morrow. It will come to-night, it will come to-morrow. This makes me in a rage. Till at last this morning I said to him I would bring nothing in, and he shouldn't have not so much as a drop of coffee in my house until he paid for it. It displeases me, Signore, to say such a thing. I have known Signor M for many years, and he has always had money, and always been pleasant, molto bravo, and also generous with his money. Si, lo so! And my wife, poverina, she cries and says if the man has no money he must eat. But he doesn't say he has no money. He says always it is coming, it is coming, to-day, to-morrow, to-day, to-morrow. E non viene mai niente. And this enrages me, Signore. So I said that to him this morning. And he said he wouldn't stay in my house, and that I had insulted him, and he sends me this letter to you, signore, and says you will send him the money. Ecco come!"

Between his rage he smiled at me. One thing however I could see: he was not going to lose his money, M or no M.

"Is it true that a letter came which the post would not deliver?" I asked him.

"Si signore, e vero. It came yesterday, addressed to me. And why, signore, why do his letters come addressed in my name? Why? Unless he has done something—?"

He looked at me enquiringly. I felt already mixed up in shady affairs.

"Yes," I said, "there is something. But I don't know exactly what. I don't ask, because I don't want to know in these affairs. It is better not to know."

"Gia! Gia! Molto meglio, signore. There will be something. There will be something happened that he had to escape from that monastery. And it will be some affair of the police."

Yes, I think so," said I. "Money and the police. Probably debts. I don't ask. He is only an acquaintance of mine, not a friend."

"Sure it will be an affair of the police," he said with a grimace. "If not, why does he use my name! Why don't his letters come in his own name? Do you believe, signore, that he has any money? Do you think this money will come?"

"I'm sure he's got no money," I said. "Whether anybody will send him any I don't know."

The man watched me attentively.

"He's got nothing?" he said.

"No. At the present he's got nothing."

Then Pancrazio exploded on the sofa.

"Allora! Well then! Well then, why does he come to my house, why does he come and take a room in my house, and ask me to buy food, good food as for a gentleman who can pay, and a flask of wine, and everything, if he has no money? If he has no money, why does he come to Taormina? It is many years that he has been in Italy—ten years, fifteen years. And he has no money. Where has he had his money from before? Where?"

"From his writing, I suppose."

"Well then why doesn't he get money for his writing now? He writes. He writes, he works, he says it is for the big newspapers."

"It is difficult to sell things."

"Heh! then why doesn't he live on what he made before? He hasn't a soldo. He hasn't a penny—But how! How did he pay his bill at the San Domenico?"

"I had to lend him the money for that. He really hadn't a penny."

"You! You! Well then, he has been in Italy all these years. How is it he has nobody that he can ask for a hundred lire or two? Why does he come to you? Why? Why has he nobody in Rome, in Florence, anywhere?"

"I wonder that myself."

"Sicuro! He's been all these years here. And why doesn't he speak proper Italian? After all these years, and speaks all upside-down, it isn't Italian, an ugly confusion. Why? Why? He passes for a signore, for a man of education. And he comes to take the bread out of my mouth. And I have a wife and child, I am a poor man, I have nothing to eat myself if everything goes to a mezzo-signore like him. Nothing! He owes me now three hundred lire. But he will not leave my house, he will not leave Taormina till he has paid. I will go to the Prefettura, I will go to the Questura, to the police. I will not be swindled by such a mezzo-signore. What does he want to do? If he has no money, what does he want to do?"

"To go to Egypt where he says he can earn some," I replied briefly. But I was feeling bitter in the mouth. When the man called M a mezzo-signore, a half-gentleman, it was so true. And at the same time it was so cruel, and so rude. And Melenga—there I sat in my pyjamas and sandals—probably he would be calling me also a mezzo-signore, or a quarto-signore even. He was a Sicilian who feels he is being done out of his money—and that is saying everything.

"To Egypt! And who will pay for him to go? Who will give him money? But he must pay me first. He must pay me first."

"He says," I said, "that in the letter which went back to the monastery there was a cheque for seven pounds—some six hundred lire—and he asks me to send him this money, and when the letter is returned again I shall have the cheque that is in it."

Melenga watched me.

"Six hundred lire—" he said.

"Yes."

"Oh well then. If he pays me, he can stay—" he said; he almost added: "till the six hundred is finished." But he left it unspoken.

"But am I going to send the money? Am I sure that what he says is true?"

"I think it is true. I think it is true," said he. "The letter *did* come."

I thought for a while.

"First," I said, "I will write and ask him if it is quite true, and to give me a guarantee."

"Very well," said Melenga.

I wrote to M, saying that if he could assure me that what he said about the seven guineas was quite correct, and if he would give me a note to the editor of *Land and Water*, saying that the cheque was to be paid to me, I would send the seven guineas.

Melenga was back in another half-hour. He brought a note which began:

"Dear Lawrence, I seem to be living in an atmosphere of suspicion. First Melenga this morning, and now you—" Those are the exact opening words. He went on to say that of course his word was true, and he enclosed a note to the editor, saying the seven guineas were to be transferred to me. He asked me please to send the money, as he could not stay another night at Melenga's house, but would leave for Catania, where, by the sale of some trinkets, he hoped to make some money and to see once more about a passage to Egypt. He had been to Catania once already—travelling *third class*!—but had failed to find any cargo boat that would take him to Alexandria. He would get away now to Malta. His things were being sent down to Syracuse from the monastery.

I wrote and said I hoped he would get safely away, and enclosed the cheque.

"This will be for six hundred lire," said Melenga.

"Yes," said I.

"Eh, va bene! If he pays the three hundred lire, he can stop in my house for thirty lire a day."

"He says he won't sleep in your house again."

"Ma! Let us see. If he likes to stay. He has always been a bravo signore. I have always liked him quite well. If he wishes to stay and pay me thirty lire a day—"

The man smiled at me rather greenly.

"I'm afraid he is offended," said I.

"Eh, va bene! Ma senta, signore. When he was here before—you know I have this house of mine to let. And you know the English signorina goes away in the summer. Oh, very well. Says M, he writes for a newspaper, he owns a newspaper, I don't know what, in Rome. He will put in an advertisement advertising my villa. And so I shall get somebody to take it. Very well. And he put in the advertisement. He sent me the paper and I saw it there. But no one came to take my villa. Va bene! But after a year, in the January, that is, came a bill for me for twenty-two lire to pay for it. Yes, I had to pay the twenty-two lire, for nothing—for the advertisement which Signore M put in the paper."

"Bah!" said I.

He shook hands with me and left. The next day he came after me in the street and said that M had departed the previous evening for Catania. As a matter of fact the post brought me a note of thanks from Catania. M was never indecent, and one could never dismiss him just as a scoundrel. He was not. He was one of these modern parasites who just assume their right to live and live well, leaving the payment to anybody who can, will, or must pay. The end is inevitably swindling.

There came also a letter from Rome, addressed to me. I opened it unthinking. It was for M, from an Italian lawyer, stating that enquiry had been made about the writ against M, and that it was for *qualche affaro di truffa*, some affair of swindling: that the lawyer had seen this, that and the other person, but nothing could be done. He regretted, etc. etc. I forwarded this letter to M at Syracuse, and hoped to God it was ended. Ah, I breathed free now he had gone.

But no. A friend who was with us dearly wanted to go to Malta. It is only about eighteen hours' journey from Taormina—easier than going to Naples. So our friend invited us to take the trip with her, as her guests. This was rather jolly. I calculated that M, who had been gone a week or so, would easily have got to Malta. I had had a friendly letter from him from Syracuse, thanking me for the one I had forwarded, and enclosing an I.O.U. for the various sums of money he had had.

So, on a hot, hot Thursday, we were sitting in the train again running south, the four and a half hours journey to Syracuse. And M dwindled now into the past. If we should see him! But no, it was impossible. After all the wretchedness of that affair we were in holiday spirits.

The train ran into Syracuse station. We sat on, to go the few yards further into the port. A tout climbed on the foot-board: were we going to Malta? Well, we couldn't. There was a strike of the steamers, we couldn't go. When would the steamer go? Who knows? Perhaps to-morrow.

We got down crestfallen. What should we do? There stood the express train about to start off back northwards. We could be home again that evening. But no, it would be too much of a fiasco. We let the train go, and trailed off into the town, to the Grand Hotel, which is an old Italian place just opposite the port. It is rather a dreary hotel—and many bloodstains of squashed mosquitoes on the bedroom walls. Ah, vile mosquitoes!

However, nothing to be done. Syracuse port is fascinating too, a tiny port with the little Sicilian ships having the slanting eyes painted on the prow, to see the way, and a coal boat from Cardiff, and one American and two Scandinavian steamers—no more. But there were two torpedo boats in the harbour, and it was like a festa, a strange, lousy festa.

Beautiful the round harbour where the Athenian ships came. And wonderful, beyond, the long sinuous sky-line of the long flat-topped table-land hills which run along the southern coast, so different from the peaky, pointed, bunched effect of many-tipped Sicily in the north. The sun went down behind that lovely, sinuous sky-line, the harbour water was gold and red, the people promenaded in thick streams under the pomegranate trees and hibiscus trees. Arabs in white burnouses and fat Turks in red fezzes and black alpaca long coats strolled also—waiting for the steamer.

Next day it was very hot. We went to the consul and the steamer agency. There was real hope that the brute of a steamer might actually sail that night. So we stayed on, and wandered round the town on the island, the old solid town, and sat in the church looking at the grand Greek columns embedded there in the walls.

When I came in to lunch the porter said there was a letter for me. Impossible! said I. But he brought me a note. Yes. M! He was staying at the other hotel along the front. "Dear Lawrence, I saw you this morning, all three of you walking down the Via Nazionale, but you would not look at me. I have got my visés and everything ready. The strike of the steamboats has delayed me here. I am sweating blood. I have a last request to make of you. Can you let me have ninety lire, to make up what I need for my hotel bill? If I cannot have this I am lost. I hoped to find you at the hotel but the porter said you were out. I am at the Casa Politi, passing every half-hour in agony. If you can be so kind as to stretch your generosity to this last loan, of course I shall be eternally grateful. I can pay you back once I get to Malta—"

Well, here was a blow! The worst was that he thought I had cut him—a thing I wouldn't have done. So after luncheon behold me going through the terrific sun of that harbour front of Syracuse, an enormous and powerful sun, to the Casa Politi. The porter recognized me and looked enquiringly. M was out, and I said I would call again at four o'clock.

It happened we were in the town eating ices at four, so I didn't get to his hotel till half-past. He was out—gone to look for me. So I left a note saying I had not seen him in the Via Nazionale, that I had called twice, and that I should be in the Grand Hotel in the evening.

When we came in at seven, M in the hall, sitting the picture of misery and endurance. He took my hand in both his, and bowed to the women, who nodded and went upstairs. He and I went and sat in the empty lounge. Then he told me the trials he had had—how his luggage had come, and the station had charged him eighteen lire a day for deposit—how he had had to wait on at the hotel because of the ship—how he had tried to sell his trinkets, and had to-day parted with his opal sleevelinks—so that now he only wanted seventy, not ninety lire. I gave him a hundred note, and he looked into my eyes, his own eyes swimming with tears, and he said he was sweating blood.

Well, the steamer went that night. She was due to leave at ten. We went on board after dinner. We were going second class. And so, for once, was M. It was only an eight hours' crossing, yet, in spite of all the blood he had sweated, he would not go third class. In a way I admired him for sticking to his principles. I should have gone third myself, out of shame of spending somebody else's money. He would not give way to such weakness. He knew that as far as the world goes, you're a first-class gentleman if you have a first-class ticket; if you have a third, no gentleman at all. It behoved him to be a gentleman. I understood his point, but the women were indignant. And I was just rather tired of him and his gentlemanliness.

It amused me very much to lean on the rail of the upper deck and watch the people coming on board—first going into the little customs house with their baggage, then scuffling up the gangway on board. The tall Arabs in their ghostly white woollen robes came carrying their sacks: they were going on to Tripoli. The fat Turk in his fez and long black alpaca coat with white drawers underneath came beaming up to the second class. There was a great row in the customs house: and then, simply running like a beetle with rage, there came on board a little Maltese or Greek fellow, followed by a tall lantern-jawed fellow: both seedy-looking scoundrels suckled in scoundrelism. They raved and nearly threw their arms away into the sea, talking wildly in some weird language with the fat Turk, who listened solemnly, away below on the deck. Then they rushed to somebody else. Of course, we were dying with curiosity. Thank heaven I heard men talking in Italian. It appears the two seedy fellows were trying to smuggle silver coin in small sacks and rolls out of the country. They were detected. But they declared they had a right to take it away, as it was foreign specie, English florins and half-crowns, and South American dollars and Spanish money. The customs-officers however detained the lot. The little enraged beetle of a fellow ran back and forth from the ship to the customs, from the customs to the ship, afraid to go without his money, afraid the ship would go without him.

At five minutes to ten, there came M: very smart in his little grey overcoat and grey curly hat, walking very smart and erect and genteel, and followed by a porter with a barrow of luggage. They went into the customs, M in his grey suède gloves passing rapidly and smartly in, like the grandest gentleman on earth, and with his grey suède hands throwing open his luggage for inspection. From on board we could see the interior of the little customs shed.

Yes, he was through. Brisk, smart, superb, like the grandest little gentleman on earth, strutting because he was late, he crossed the bit of flagged pavement and came up the gangway, haughty as you can wish. The carabinieri were lounging by the foot of the gangway, fooling with one another. The little gentleman passed them with his nose in the air, came quickly on board, followed by his porter, and in a moment disappeared. After about five minutes the porter reappeared—a red-haired fellow, I knew him—he even saluted me from below, the brute. But M lay in hiding.

I trembled for him at every unusual stir. There on the quay stood the English consul with his bull-dog, and various elegant young officers with yellow on their uniforms, talking to elegant young Italian ladies in black hats with stiff ospreys and bunchy furs, and gangs of porters and hotel people and onlookers. Then came a tramp-tramp-tramp of a squad of soldiers in red fezzes and baggy grey trousers. Instead of coming on board they camped on the quay. I wondered if all these had come for poor M. But apparently not.

So the time passed, till nearly midnight, when one of the elegant young lieutenants began to call the names of the soldiers: and the soldiers answered: and one after another filed on board with their kit. So, they were on board, on their way to Africa.

Now somebody called out—and the visitors began to leave the boat. Barefooted sailors and a boy ran to raise the gangway. The last visitor or official with a bunch of papers stepped off the gangway. People on shore began to wave handkerchiefs. The red-fezzed soldiers leaned like so many flower-pots over the lower rail. There was a calling of farewells. The ship was fading into the harbour, the people on shore seemed smaller, under the lamp, in the deep night—without one's knowing why.

So, we passed out of the harbour, passed the glittering lights of Ortygia, past the two lighthouses, into the open Mediterranean. The noise of a ship in the open sea! It was a still night, with stars, only a bit chill. And the ship churned through the water.

Suddenly, like a revenant, appeared M near us, leaning on the rail and looking back at the lights of Syracuse sinking already forlorn and little on the low darkness. I went to him.

"Well," he said, with his little smirk of a laugh. "Good-bye Italy!"

"Not a sad farewell either," said I.

"No, my word, not this time," he said. "But what an awful long time we were starting! A brutta mezz'ora for me, indeed. Oh, my word, I begin to breathe free for the first time since I left the monastery! How awful it's been! But of course, in Malta, I shall be all right. Don Bernardo has written to his friends there. They'll have everything ready for me that I want, and I can pay you back the money you so kindly lent me."

We talked for some time, leaning on the inner rail of the upper deck.

"Oh," he said, "there's Commander So-and-so, of the British fleet. He's stationed in Malta. I made his acquaintance in the hotel. I hope we're going to be great friends in Malta. I hope I shall have an opportunity to introduce you to him. Well, I suppose you will want to be joining your ladies. So long, then. Oh, for to-morrow morning! I never longed so hard to be in the British Empire—" He laughed, and strutted away.

In a few minutes we three, leaning on the rail of the second-class upper deck, saw our little friend large as life on the first-class deck, smoking a cigar and chatting in an absolutely first-class-ticket manner with the above mentioned Commander. He pointed us out to the Commander, and we felt the first-class passengers were looking across at us second-class passengers with pleasant interest. The women went behind a canvas heap to laugh, I hid my face under my hat-brim to grin and watch. Larger than any first-class ticketer leaned our little friend on the first-class rail, and whiffed at his cigar. So *dégagé* and so genteel he could be. Only I noticed he wilted a little when the officers of the ship came near.

He was still on the first-class deck when we went down to sleep. In the morning I came up soon after dawn. It was a lovely summer Mediterranean morning, with the sun rising up in a gorgeous golden rage, and the sea so blue, so fairy blue, as the Mediterranean is in summer. We were approaching quite near to a rocky, pale yellow island with some vineyards, rising magical out of the swift blue sea into the morning radiance. The rocks were almost as pale as butter, the islands were like golden shadows loitering in the midst of the Mediterranean, lonely among all the blue.

M came up to my side.

"Isn't it lovely! Isn't it beautiful!" he said. "I love approaching these islands in the early morning." He had almost recovered his assurance, and the slight pomposity and patronizing tone I had first known in him. "In two hours I shall be free! Imagine it! Oh what a beautiful feeling!" I looked at him in the morning light. His face was a good deal broken by his last month's experience, older looking, and dragged. Now that the excitement was nearing its end, the tiredness began to tell on him. He was yellowish round the eyes, and the whites of his round, rather impudent blue eyes were discoloured.

Malta was drawing near. We saw the white fringe of the sea upon the yellow rocks, and a white road looping on the yellow rocky hillside. I thought of St. Paul, who must have been blown this way, must have struck the island from this side. Then we saw the heaped glitter of the square facets of houses, Valletta, splendid above the Mediterranean, and a tangle of shipping and Dreadnoughts and watch-towers in the beautiful, locked-in harbour.

We had to go down to have passports examined. The officials sat in the long saloon. It was a horrible squash and squeeze of the first and second-class passengers. M was a little ahead of me. I saw the American eagle on his passport. Yes, he passed all right. Once more he was free. As he passed away he turned and gave a condescending affable nod to me and to the Commander, who was just behind me.

The ship was lying in Valletta harbour. I saw M, quite superb and brisk now, ordering a porter with his luggage into a boat. The great rocks rose above us, yellow and carved, cut straight by man. On top were all the houses. We got at last into a boat and were rowed ashore. Strange to be on British soil and to hear English. We got a carriage and drove up the steep highroad through the cutting in the rock, up to the town. There, in the big square we had coffee, sitting out of doors. A military band went by, playing splendidly in the bright, hot morning. The Maltese lounged about, and watched. Splendid the band, and the soldiers! One felt the splendour of the British Empire, let the world say what it likes. But alas, as one stayed on even in Malta, one felt the old lion had gone foolish and amiable. Foolish and amiable, with the weak amiability of old age.

We stayed in the Great Britain Hotel. Of course one could not be in Valletta for twenty-four hours without meeting M. There he was, in the Strada Reale, strutting in a smart white duck suit, with a white piqué cravat. But alas, he had no white shoes: they had got lost or stolen. He had to wear black boots with his summer finery.

He was staying in an hotel a little further down our street, and he begged me to call and see him, he begged me to come to lunch. I promised and went. We went into his bedroom, and he rang for more sodas.

"How wonderful it is to be here!" he said brightly. "Don't you like it immensely? And oh, how wonderful to have a whisky and soda! Well now, say when."

He finished one bottle of Black and White, and opened another. The waiter, a good-looking Maltese fellow, appeared with two syphons. M was very much the signore with him, and at the same time very familiar: as I should imagine a rich Roman of the merchant class might have been with a pet slave. We had quite a nice lunch, and whisky and soda and a bottle of French wine. And M was the charming and attentive host.

After lunch we talked again of manuscripts and publishers and how he might make money. I wrote one or two letters for him. He was anxious to get something under way. And yet the trouble of these arrangements was almost too much for his nerves. His face looked broken and old, but not like an old man, like an old boy, and he was really very irritable.

For my own part I was soon tired of Malta, and would gladly have left after three days. But there was the strike of steamers still, we had to wait on. M professed to be enjoying himself hugely, making excursions every day, to St. Paul's Bay and to the other islands. He had also made various friends or acquaintants. Particularly two young men,

Maltese, who were friends of Don Bernardo. He introduced me to these two young men: one Gabriel Mazzaiba and the other Salonia. They had small businesses down on the wharf. Salonia asked M to go for a drive in a motor-car round the island, and M pressed me to go too. Which I did. And swiftly, on a Saturday afternoon, we dodged about in the car upon that dreadful island, first to some fearful and stony bay, arid, treeless, desert, a bit of stony desert by the sea, with unhappy villas and a sordid, scrap-iron front: then away inland up long and dusty roads, across a bone-dry, bone-bare, hideous landscape. True, there was ripening corn, but this was all of a colour with the dust-yellow, bone-bare island. Malta is all a pale, softish, yellowish rock, just like bathbrick: this goes into fathomless dust. And the island is stark as a corpse, no trees, no bushes even: a fearful landscape, cultivated, and weary with ages of weariness, and old weary houses here and there.

We went to the old capital in the centre of the island, and this is interesting. The town stands on a bluff of hill in the middle of the dreariness, looking at Valletta in the distance, and the sea. The houses are all pale yellow, and tall, and silent, as if forsaken. There is a cathedral, too, and a fortress outlook over the sun-blazed, sun-dried, disheartening island. Then we dashed off to another village and climbed a church-dome that rises like a tall blister on the plain, with houses round and corn beyond and dust that has no glamour, stale, weary, like bone-dust, and thorn hedges sometimes, and some tin-like prickly pears. In the dusk we came round by St. Paul's Bay, back to Valletta.

The young men were very pleasant, very patriotic for Malta, very Catholic. We talked politics and a thousand things. M was gently patronizing, and seemed, no doubt, to the two Maltese a very elegant and travelled and wonderful gentleman. They, who had never seen even a wood, thought how wonderful a forest must be, and M talked to them of Russia and of Germany.

But I was glad to leave that bone-dry, hideous island. M begged me to stay longer: but not for worlds! He was establishing himself securely: was learning the Maltese language, and cultivating a thorough acquaintance with the island. And he was going to establish himself. Mazzaiba was exceedingly kind to him, helping him in every way. In Rabato, the suburb of the old town—a quiet, forlorn little yellow street—he found a tiny house of two rooms and a tiny garden. This would cost five pounds a year. Mazzaiba lent the furniture—and when I left, M was busily skipping back and forth from Rabato to Valletta, arranging his little home, and very pleased with it. He was also being very Maltese, and rather anti-British, as is essential, apparently, when one is not a Britisher and finds oneself in any part of the British Empire. M was very much the American gentleman.

Well, I was thankful to be home again and to know that he was safely shut up in that beastly island. He wrote me letters, saying how he loved it all, how he would go down to the sea—five or six miles' walk—at dawn, and stay there all day, studying Maltese and writing for the newspapers. The life was fascinating, the summer was blisteringly hot, and the Maltese were most attractive, especially when they knew you were not British. Such good-looking fellows, too, and do anything you want. Wouldn't I come and spend a month?—I did not answer—felt I had had enough. Came a postcard from M—: "I haven't had a letter from you, nor any news at all. I am afraid you are ill, and feel so anxious. Do write—" But no, I didn't want to write.

During August and September and half October we were away in the north. I forgot my little friend: hoped he was gone out of my life. But I had that fatal sinking feeling that he *hadn't* really gone out of it yet.

In the beginning of November a little letter from Don Bernardo—did I know that M had committed suicide in Malta? Following that, a scrubby Maltese newspaper, posted by Salonia, with a marked notice: "The suicide of an American gentleman at Rabato. Yesterday the American M M, a well-built man in the prime of life, was found dead in his bed in his house at Rabato. By the bedside was a bottle containing poison. The deceased had evidently taken his life by swallowing prussic acid. Mr. M had been staying for some months on the island, studying the language and the conditions, with a view to writing a book. It is understood that financial difficulties were the cause of this lamentable event."

Then Mazzaiba wrote asking me what I knew of M, and saying the latter had borrowed money which he, Mazzaiba, would like to recover. I replied at once, and then received the following letter from Salonia. "Valletta, 20 November, 1920. My dear Mr. Lawrence, some time back I mailed you our *Daily Malta Chronicle* which gave an account of the death of M. I hope you have received same. As the statements therein given were very vague and not quite correct, please accept the latter part of this letter as a more correct version.

"The day before yesterday Mazzaiba received your letter which he gave me to read. As you may suppose we were very much astonished by its general purport. Mazzaiba will be writing to you in a few days, in the meantime I volunteered to give you the details you asked for.

"Mazzaiba and I have done all in our power to render M's stay here as easy and pleasant as possible from the time we first met him in your company at the Great Britain Hotel. [This is not correct. They were already quite friendly with M before that motor-drive, when I saw these two Maltese for the first time.] He lived in an embarrassed mood since then, and though we helped him as best we could both morally and financially he never confided to us his troubles. To this very day we cannot but look on his coming here and his stay amongst us, to say the least of the way he left us, as a huge farce wrapped up in mystery, a painful experience unsolicited by either of us and a cause of grief unrequited except by our own personal sense of duty towards a stranger.

"Mazzaiba out of mere respect did not tell me of his commitments towards M until about a month ago, and this he did in a most confidential and private manner merely to put me on my guard, thinking, and rightly, too, that M would be falling on me next time for funds; Mazzaiba having already given him about £55 and would not possibly commit himself any further. Of course, we found him all along a perfect gentleman. Naturally, he hated the very idea that we or anybody else in Malta should look upon him in any other light. He never asked directly, though Mazzaiba (later myself) was always quick enough to interpret rightly what he meant and obliged him forthwith.

"At this stage, to save the situation, he made up a scheme that the three of us should exploit the commercial possibilities in Morocco. It very nearly materialized, everything was ready, I was to go with him to Morocco, Mazzaiba was to take charge of affairs here and to dispose of transactions we initiated there. Fortunately, for lack of the necessary funds the idea had to be dropped, and there it ended, thank God, after a great deal of trouble I had in trying to set it well on foot.

"Last July, the Police, according to our law, advised him that he was either to find a surety or to deposit a sum of money with them as otherwise at the expiration of his three months' stay he would be compelled to leave the place. Money he had none, so he asked Mazzaibato stand as surety. Mazzaiba could not as he was already guarantor for his alien cousins who were here at the time. Mazzaiba (not M) asked me and I complied, thinking that the responsibility was just moral and only exacted as a matter of form.

"When, as stated before, Mazzaiba told me that M owed him £55 and that he owed his grocer and others at Notabile (the old town, of which Rabato is the suburb) over £10, I thought I might as well look up my guarantee and see if I was directly responsible for any debts he incurred here. The words of his declaration which I endorsed stated that 'I hereby solemnly promise that I will not be a burden to the inhabitants of these islands, etc.,' and deeming that unpaid debts to be more or less a burden, I decided to withdraw my guarantee, which I did on the 23rd ult. The reason I gave to the police was that he was outliving his income and that I did not intend to shoulder any financial responsibility in the matter. On the same day I wrote to him up at Notabile saying that for family reasons I was compelled to withdraw his surety. He took my letter in the sense implied and no way offended at my procedure.

"M, in his resourceful way, knowing that he would with great difficulty find another guarantor, wrote at once to the police saying that he understood from Mr. Salonia that he (S) had withdrawn his guarantee, but as he (M) would be leaving the island in about three weeks' time (still intending to exploit Morocco) he begged the Commissioner to allow him this period of grace, without demanding a new surety. In fact he asked me to find him a cheap passage to Gib. in an ingoing tramp steamer. The police did not reply to his letter at all, no doubt they had everything ready and well thought out. He was alarmed in not receiving an acknowledgment, and, knowing full well what he imminently expected at the hands of the Italian police, he decided to prepare for the last act of his drama.

"We had not seen him for three or four days when he came to Mazzaiba's office on Wednesday, 3rd inst., in the forenoon. He stayed there for some time talking on general subjects and looking somewhat more excited than usual. He went up to town alone at noon as Mazzaiba went to Singlea. I was not with them in the morning, but in the afternoon about 4.30, whilst I was talking to Mazzaiba in his office, M again came in looking very excited, and, being closing time, we went up, the three of us, to town, and there left him in the company of a friend.

"On Thursday morning, 4th inst., at about 10 a.m., two detectives in plain clothes met him in a street at Notabile. One of them quite casually went up to him and said very civilly that the inspector of police wished to see him *re* a guarantee or something, and that he was to go with him to the police station. This was an excuse as the detective had about him a warrant for his arrest for frauding an hotel in Rome, and that he was to be extradited at the request of the authorities in Italy. M replied that as he was in his sandals he would dress up and go with them immediately, and, accompanying him to his house at No. 1 Strada S. Pietro, they allowed him to enter. He locked the door behind him, leaving them outside.

"A few minutes later he opened his bedroom window and dropped a letter addressed to Don Bernardo which he asked a boy in the street to post for him, and immediately closed the window again. One of the detectives picked up the letter and we do not know to this day if same was posted at all. Some time elapsed and he did not come out. The detectives were by this time very uneasy and as another police official came up they decided to burst open the door. As the door did not give way they got a ladder and climbed over the roof, and there they found M in his bedroom dying from poisoning, outstretched on his bed and a glass of water close by. A priest was immediately called in who had just time to administer Extreme Unction before he died at 11.45 a.m.

"At 8.0 a.m. the next day his body was admitted for examination at the Floriana Civil Hospital and death was certified to be from poisoning with hydrocyanic acid. His age was given as 44, being buried on his birthday (7th Novr.), with R. Catholic Rites at the expense of *His Friends in Malta.*

"Addenda: Contents of Don Bernardo's letter: —

"'I leave it to you and to Gabriel Mazzaiba to arrange my affairs. I cannot live any longer. Pray for me.'

Document found on his writing-table:

"'In case of my unexpected death inform American consul. "'I want to be buried first class, my wife will pay. My little personal belongings to be delivered to my wife. (Address.)

"'My best friend here, Gabriel Mazzaiba, inform him. (Address.)

"'My literary executor N D. (Address.)

"'All manuscripts and books for N D. I leave my literary property to N D—to whom half of the results are to accrue. The other half my debts are to be paid with: "'Furniture etc. belong to Coleiro, Floriana.

"'Silver spoons etc. belong to Gabriel Mazzaiba. (Address.).'

"The American Consul is in charge of all his personal belongings. I am sure he will be pleased to give you any further details you may require. By the way, his wife refused to pay his burial expenses, but five of his friends in Malta undertook to give him a decent funeral. His mourners were: The consul, the vice-consul, Mr. A., an American citizen, Gabriel Mazzaiba and myself.

"Please convey to Mrs. Lawrence an expression of our sincere esteem and high regard and you will kindly accept equally our warmest respects, whilst soliciting any information you would care to pass on to us regarding the late M. Believe me, My dear Mr. Lawrence, etc."

[Mrs. M refunded the burial expenses through the American consul about two months after her husband's death.]

When I had read this letter the world seemed to stand still for me. I knew that in my own soul I had said, "Yes, he must die if he cannot find his own way." But for all that, now I *realized* what it must have meant to be the hunted, desperate man: everything seemed to stand still. I could, by giving half my money, have saved his life. I had chosen not to save his life.

Now, after a year has gone by, I keep to my choice. I still would not save his life. I respect him for dying when he was cornered. And for this reason I feel still connected with him: still have this to discharge, to get his book published, and to give him his place, to present him just as he was as far as I knew him myself.

The worst thing I have against him, is that he abused the confidence, the kindness, and the generosity of unsuspecting people like Mazzaiba. He did not want to, perhaps. But he did it. And he leaves Mazzaiba swindled, distressed, confused, and feeling sold in the best part of himself. What next? What is one to feel towards one's strangers, after having known M? It is this Judas treachery to ask for sympathy and for generosity, to take it when given—and then: "Sorry, but anybody may make a mistake!" It is this betraying with a kiss which makes me still say: "He should have died sooner." No, I would not help to keep him alive, not if I had to choose again. I would let him go over into death. He shall and should die, and so should all his sort: and so they will. There are so many kiss-giving Judases. He

239

was not a criminal: he was obviously well intentioned: but a Judas every time, selling the good feeling he had tried to arouse, and had aroused, for any handful of silver he could get. A little loving vampire!

Yesterday arrived the manuscript of the Legion, from Malta. It is exactly two years since I read it first in the monastery. Then I was moved and rather horrified. Now I am chiefly amused; because in my mind's eye is the figure of M in the red trousers and the blue coat with lappets turned up, swinging like a little indignant pigeon across the drill yards and into the canteen of Bel-Abbès. He *is* so indignant, so righteously and morally indignant, and so funny. All the horrors of the actuality fade before the indignation, his little, tuppenny indignation.

Oh, M is a prime hypocrite. How loudly he rails against the *Boches*! *How* great his enthusiasm for the pure, the spiritual Allied cause. Just so long as he is in Africa, and it suits his purpose! His scorn for the German tendencies of the German legionaries: even Count de R. secretly leans towards Germany. "Blood is thicker than water," says our hero glibly. Some blood, thank God. Apparently not his own. For according to all showing he was, by blood, pure German: father and mother: even Hohenzollern blood!!! Pure German! Even his speech, his *mother-tongue*, was German and not English! And then the little mongrel—!

But perhaps something happens to blood when once it has been taken to America.

And then, once he is in Valbonne, lo, a change! Where now is sacred France and the holy Allied Cause! Where is our hero's fervour? It is *worse than* Bel-Abbès! Yes, indeed, far less human, more hideously cold. One is driven by very rage to wonder if he was really a spy, a German spy whom Germany cast off because he was no good.

The little *gentleman*! God damn his white-blooded gentility. The legionaries must have been gentlemen, that they didn't kick him every day to the lavatory and back.

"You are a journalist?" said the colonel.

"No, a *littérateur*" said M perkily.

"That is something more?" said the Colonel.

Oh, I would have given a lot to have seen it and heard it. The *littérateur*! Well, I hope this book will establish his fame as such. I hope the editor, if it gets one, won't alter any more of the marvellously staggering sentences and the joyful French mistakes. The *littérateur*!—the impossible little pigeon!

But the Bel-Abbès part is alive and interesting. It should be read only by those who have the stomach. Ugly, foul—alas, it is no uglier and no fouler than the reality. M himself was near enough to being a scoundrel, thief, forger, etc., etc.—what lovely strings of names he hurls at them!—to be able to appreciate his company. He himself was such a liar, that he was not taken in. But his conceit as a gentleman *keeping up appearances* gave him a real standpoint from which to see the rest. The book is in its way a real creation. But I would hate it to be published and taken at its face value, with M as a spiritual dove among vultures of lust. Let us first put a pinch of salt on the tail of this dove. What he did do in the way of vice, even in Bel-Abbès, I never chose to ask him.

Yes, yes, he sings another note when he is planted right among the sacred Allies, with never a German near. Then the gorgeousness goes out of his indignation. He takes it off with the red trousers. Now he is just a sordid little figure in filthy corduroys. There is no vice to purple his indignation, the little holy liar. There is only sordidness and automatic, passionless, colourless awful mud. When all is said and done, mud, cold, hideous, foul, engulfing mud, up to the waist, this is the final symbol of the Great War. Hear some of the horrified young soldiers. They dare hardly speak of it yet.

The Valbonne part is worse, really, than the Bel-Abbès part. Passionless, barren, utterly, coldly foul and hopeless. The ghastly emptiness, and the slow mud-vortex, the brink of it.

Well, now M has gone himself. Yes, and he would be gone in the common mud and dust himself, if it were not that the blood still beats warm and hurt and kind in some few hearts. M "hinted" at Mazzaiba for money, in Malta, and Mazzaiba gave it to him, thinking him a man in distress. He thought him a gentleman, and lovable, and in trouble! And Mazzaiba—it isn't his real name, but there he is, real enough—still has this feeling of grief for M. So much so that now he has had the remains taken from the public grave in Malta, and buried in his own, the Mazzaiba grave, so that they shall not be lost. For my part, I would have said that the sooner they mingled with the universal dust, the better. But one is glad to see a little genuine kindness and gentleness, even if it is wasted on the bones of that selfish little scamp of a M. He despised his "physical friendships—" though he didn't forego them. So why should anyone rescue his physique from the public grave? But there you are—there was his power: to arouse affection and a certain tenderness in the hearts of others, for himself. And on this he traded. One sees the trick working all the way through the Legion book. God knows how much warm kindness, generosity, was showered on him during the course of his forty-odd years. And selfish little scamp, he took it as a greedy boy takes cakes off a dish, quickly, to make the most of his opportunity while it lasted. And the cake once eaten: *buona sera*! He patted his own little paunch and felt virtuous. Merely physical feeling, you see! He had a way of saying "physical"—a sort of American way, as if it were spelt "fisacal"—that made me want to kick him.

Not that he was mean, while he was about it. No, he would give very freely: even a little ostentatiously, always feeling that he was being a *liberal gentleman*. Ach, the liberality and the gentility he prided himself on! *Ecco*! And he gave a large tip, with a little winsome smile. But in his heart of hearts it was always himself he was thinking of, while he did it. Playing his rôle of the gentleman who was awfully *nice* to everybody: so long as they were nice to him, or so long as it served his advantage. Just private charity!

Well, poor devil, he is dead: which is all the better.

He had his points, the courage of his own terrors, quick-wittedness, sensitiveness to certain things in his surroundings. I prefer him, scamp as he is, to the ordinary respectable person. He ran his risks: he had to be running risks with the police, apparently. And he poisoned himself rather than fall into their clutches. I like him for that. And I like him for the sharp and quick way he made use of every one of his opportunities to get out of that beastly army. There I admire him: a courageous, isolated little devil, facing his risks, and like a good rat, *determined* not to be trapped. I won't forgive him for trading on the generosity of others, and so dropping poison into the heart of all warm-blooded faith. But I am glad after all that Mazzaiba has rescued his bones from the public grave. I wouldn't have done it myself, because I don't forgive him his "fisacal" impudence and parasitism. But I am glad Mazzaiba has done it. And, for my part, I will put his Legion book before the world if I can. Let him have his place in the world's consciousness.

Let him have his place, let his word be heard. He went through vile experiences: he looked them in the face, braved them through, and kept his manhood in spite of them. For manhood is a strange quality, to be found in human rats as well as in hot-blooded men.

241

M carried the human consciousness through circumstances which would have been too much for me. I would have died rather than be so humiliated, I could never have borne it. Other men, I know, went through worse things in the war. But then, horrors, like pain, are their own anaesthetic. Men lose their normal consciousness, and go through in a sort of delirium. The bit of Stendhal which Dos Passos quotes in front of *Three Soldiers* is frighteningly true. There are certain things which are *so* bitter, *so* horrible, that the contemporaries just cannot know them, cannot contemplate them. So it is with a great deal of the late war. It was so foul, and humanity in Europe fell suddenly into such ignominy and inhuman ghastliness, that we shall *never* fully realize what it was. We just cannot bear it. We haven't the soul-strength to contemplate it.

And yet, humanity can only finally conquer by realizing. It is human destiny, since Man fell into consciousness and self-consciousness, that we can only go forward step by step through realization, full, bitter, conscious realization. This is true of all the great terrors and agonies and anguishes of life: sex, and war, and even crime. When Flaubert in his story—it is so long since I read it—makes his saint have to kiss the leper, and naked clasp the leprous awful body against his own, that is what we must at last do. It is the great command *Know Thyself*. We've got to *know* what sex is, let the sentimentalists wiggle as they like. We've got to know the greatest and most shattering human passions, let the puritans squeal as they like for screens. And we've got to know humanity's criminal tendency, look straight at humanity's great deeds of crime against the soul. We have to fold this horrible leper against our naked warmth: because life and the throbbing blood and the believing soul are greater even than leprosy. Knowledge, true knowledge is like vaccination. It prevents the continuing of ghastly moral disease.

And so it is with the war. Humanity in Europe fell horribly into a hatred of the living soul, in the war. There is no gainsaying it. We all fell. Let us not try to wriggle out of it. We fell into hideous depravity of hating the human soul; a purulent small-pox of the spirit we had. It was shameful, shameful, shameful, in every country and in all of us. Some tried to resist, and some didn't. But we were all drowned in shame. A purulent small-pox of the vicious spirit, vicious against the deep soul that pulses in the blood.

We haven't got over it. The small-pox sores are running yet in the spirit of mankind. And we have got to take this putrid spirit to our bosom. There's nothing else for it. Take the foul rotten spirit of mankind, full of the running sores of the war, to our bosom, and cleanse it there. Cleanse it not with blind love: ah no, that won't help. But with bitter and wincing realization. We have to take the disease into our consciousness and let it go through our soul, like some virus. We have got to realize. And then we can surpass.

M went where I could never go. He carried the human consciousness unbroken through circumstances I could not have borne. It is not heroism to rush on death. It is cowardice to accept a martyrdom to-day. That is the feeling one has at the end of Dos Passos' book. To let oneself be absolutely trapped? Never! I prefer M. He drew himself out of the thing he loathed, despised, and feared. He fought it, for his own spirit and liberty. He fought it open-eyed. He went through. They were more publicly heroic, they won war medals. But the lonely terrified courage of the isolated spirit which grits its teeth and stares the horrors in the face and *will* not succumb to them, but fights its way through them, *knowing* that it must surpass them: this is the rarest courage. And this courage M had: and the man in the Dos Passos book didn't *quite* have it. And so, though M poisoned himself, and I would not wish him *not* to have poisoned himself: though as far as warm life goes, I don't forgive him; yet, as far as the eternal and unconquerable spirit of man goes, I am with him through eternity. I am grateful to him, he beat out for me boundaries of human experience which I could not have beaten out for myself. The *human* traitor he was. But he was not traitor to the spirit. In the great spirit of human consciousness he was a hero, little, quaking and heroic: a strange, quaking little star.

Even the dead ask only for *justice*: not for praise or exoneration. Who dares humiliate the dead with excuses for their living? I hope I may do M justice; and I hope his restless spirit may be appeased. I do not try to forgive. The living blood knows no forgiving. Only the overweening spirit takes on itself to dole out forgiveness. But Justice is a sacred human right. The overweening spirit pretends to perch above justice. But I am a man, not a spirit, and men with blood that throbs and throbs and throbs can only live at length by being just, can only die in peace if they have justice. Forgiveness gives the whimpering dead no rest. Only deep, true justice.

There is M's manuscript then, like a map of the lower places of mankind's activities. There is the war: foul, foul, unutterably foul. As foul as M says. Let us make up our minds about it.

It is the only help: to realize, *fully*, and then make up our minds. The war was *foul*. As long as I am a man, I say it and assert it, and further I say, as long as I am a man such a war shall never occur again. It shall not, and it shall not. All modern militarism is foul. It shall go. A man I am, and above machines, and it shall go, forever, because I have found it vile, vile, too vile ever to experience again. Cannons shall go. Never again shall trenches be dug. They *shall* not, for I am a man, and such things are within the power of man, to break and make. I have said it, and as long as blood beats in my veins, I mean it. Blood beats in the veins of many men who mean it as well as I.

Man perhaps *must* fight. Mars, the great god of war, will be a god forever. Very well. Then if fight you must, fight you shall, and without engines, without machines. Fight if you like, as the Roman fought, with swords and spears, or like the Red Indian, with bows and arrows and knives and war paint. But never again shall you fight with the foul, base, fearful, monstrous machines of war which man invented for the last war. You shall not. The diabolic mechanisms are man's, and I am a man. Therefore they are mine. And I smash them into oblivion. With every means in my power, except the means of these machines, I smash them into oblivion. I am at war! I, a man, am at war!—with these foul machines and contrivances that men have conjured up. Men have conjured them up. I, a man, will conjure them down again. Won't I? —but I will! I am not one man, I am many, I am most.

So much for the war! So much for M's manuscript. Let it be read. It is not this that will do harm, but sloppy sentiment, and cant. Take the bitterness and cleanse the blood.

Now would you believe it, that little scamp M spent over a hundred pounds of borrowed money during his four months in Malta, when his expenses, he boasted to me, need not have been more than a pound a week, once he got into the little house in Notabile. That is, he spent at least seventy pounds too much. Heaven knows what he did with it, apart from "guzzling." And this hundred pounds must be paid back in Malta. Which it never will be, unless this manuscript pays it back. Pay the gentleman's last debts, if no others.

He had to be a gentleman. I didn't realize till after his death. I never suspected him of royal blood. But there you are, you never know where it will crop out. He was the grandson of an emperor. His mother was the illegitimate daughter of the German Kaiser: D says, of the old Kaiser Wilhelm I, Don Bernardo says, of Kaiser Frederick Wilhelm, father of the present ex-Kaiser. She was born in Berlin on the 31 October, 1845: and her portrait, by Paul, now hangs in a gallery in Rome. Apparently there had been some injustice against her in Berlin—for she seems once to have been in the highest society there, and to have attended at court. Perhaps she was discreetly banished by Wilhelm II, hence M's hatred of that monarch. She lies buried in the Protestant Cemetery in Rome, where she died in 1912, with the words *Filia Régis* on her tomb. M adored her, and she him. Part of his failings one can *certainly* ascribe to the fact that he was an only son, an adored son, in whose veins the mother imagined only royal blood. And she must have thought him so beautiful, poor thing! Ah well, they are both dead. Let us be just and wish them Lethe.

M himself was born in New York, 7th November, 1876; so at least it says on his passport. He entered the Catholic Church in England in 1902. His father was a Mr. L M, married to the mother in 1867.

So poor M had Hohenzollern blood in his veins: close kin to the ex-Kaiser William. Well, that itself excuses him a great deal: because of the cruel illusion of importance *manqué*, which it must have given him. He never breathed a word of this to me. Yet apparently it is accepted at the monastery, the great monastery which knows most European secrets of any political significance. And for myself, I believe it is true. And if he was a scamp and a treacherous little devil, he had also qualities of nerve and breeding undeniable. He faced his way through that Legion experience: royal nerves dragging themselves through the sewers, without giving way. But alas, for royal blood! Like most other blood, it has gradually gone white, during our spiritual era. Bunches of nerves! And whitish, slightly acid blood. And no bowels of deep compassion and kindliness. Only charity—a little more than kin, and less than kind.

Also, M! Ich grüsse dich, in der Ewigkeit. Aber hier, im Herzblut, hast du Gift und Leid nachgelassen—to use your own romantic language.

MORNINGS IN MEXICO

I

CORASMIN AND THE PARROTS

ONE says Mexico: one means, after all, one little town away South in the Republic: and in this little town, one rather crumbly adobe house built round two sides of a garden *patio:* and of this house, one spot on the deep, shady veranda facing inwards to the trees, where there are an onyx table and three rocking-chairs and one little wooden chair, a pot with carnations, and a person with a pen. We talk so grandly, in capital letters, about Morning in Mexico. All it amounts to is one little individual looking at a bit of sky and trees, then looking down at the page of his exercise book.

It is a pity we don't always remember this. When books come out with grand titles, like *The Future of America,* or *The European Situation,* it's a pity we don't immediately visualize a thin or a fat person, in a chair or in bed, dictating to a bob-haired stenographer or making little marks on paper with a fountain pen.

Still, it is morning, and it is Mexico. The sun shines. But then, during the winter, it always shines. It is pleasant to sit out of doors and write, just fresh enough and just warm enough. But then it is Christmas next week, so it ought to be just right.

There is a little smell of carnations, because they are the nearest thing. And there is a resinous smell of ocote wood, and a smell of coffee, and a faint smell of leaves, and of Morning, and even of Mexico. Because when all is said and done, Mexico has a faint, physical scent of her own, as each human being has. And this is a curious, inexplicable scent, in which there are resin and perspiration and sunburned earth and urine among other things.

And cocks are still crowing. The little mill where the natives have their own corn ground is puffing rather languidly. And because some women are talking in the entrance-way, the two tame parrots in the trees have started to whistle.

The parrots, even when I don't listen to them, have an extraordinary effect on me. They make my diaphragm convulse with little laughs, almost mechanically. They are a quite commonplace pair of green birds, with bits of bluey red, and round, disillusioned eyes, and heavy, overhanging noses. But they listen intently. And they reproduce. The pair whistle now like Rosalino, who is sweeping the *patio* with a twig broom; and yet it is so unlike him, to be whistling full vent, when any of us is around, that one looks at him to see. And the moment one sees him, with his black head bent rather drooping and hidden as he sweeps, one laughs.

The parrots whistle exactly like Rosalino, only a little more so. And this little-more-so is extremely sardonically funny. With their sad old long-jowled faces and their flat disillusioned eyes, they reproduce Rosalino and a little-more-so without moving a muscle. And Rosalino, sweeping the *patio* with his twig broom, scraping and tittering leaves into little heaps, covers himself more and more with the cloud of his own obscurity. He doesn't rebel He is powerless. Up goes the wild, sliding Indian whistle into the morning, very powerful, with an immense energy seeming to drive behind it. And always, always a little more than life-like.

245

Then they break off into a cackling chatter, and one knows they are shifting their clumsy legs, perhaps hanging on with their beaks and clutching with their cold, slow claws, to climb to a higher bough, like rather raggedy green buds climbing to the sun. And suddenly the penetrating, demonish mocking voices:

'Perro! Oh, Perro! Perr-rro I Oh, Perr-rro! Perro!'

They are imitating somebody calling the dog. *Perro* means dog. But that any creature should be able to pour such a suave, prussic-acid sarcasm over the voice of a human being calling a dog, is incredible. One's diaphragm chuckles involuntarily.

And one thinks: *Is it possible?* Is it possible that we are so absolutely, so innocently, so *ab ovo* ridiculous?

And not only is it possible, it is patent. We cover our heads in confusion.

Now they are yapping like a dog: exactly like Corasmin. Corasmin is a little fat, curly white dog who was lying in the sun a minute ago, and has now come into the veranda shade, walking with slow resignation, to lie against the wall near-by my chair. 'Yap-yap-yap! Wouf! Wouf! Yapyapyapyap!' go the parrots, exactly like Corasmin when some stranger comes into the *zaguán,* Corasmin and a little-more-so.

With a grin on my face I look down at Corasmin. And with a silent, abashed resignation in his yellow eyes, Corasmin looks up at me, with a touch of reproach. His little white nose is sharp, and under his eyes there are dark marks, as under the eyes of one who has known much trouble. All day he does nothing but walk resignedly out of the sun, when the sun gets too hot, and out of the shade, when the shade gets too cool And bite ineffectually in the region of his fleas.

Poor old Corasmin: he is only about six, but resigned, unspeakably resigned. Only not humble. He does not kiss the rod. He rises in spirit above it, letting his body lie.

'Perro! Oh, Perr-rro! Perr-rro! Perr-rr-rro!!' shriek the parrots, with that strange penetrating, antediluvian malevolence that seems to make even the trees prick their ears. It is a sound that penetrates one straight at the diaphragm, belonging to the ages before brains were invented. And Corasmin pushes his sharp little nose into his bushy tail, closes his eyes because I am grinning, feigns to sleep and then, in an orgasm of self-consciousness, starts up to bite in the region of his fleas.

'Perr-rro! Perr-rro!' And then a restrained, withheld sort of yapping. The fiendish rolling of the Spanish 'r', malevolence rippling out of all the vanished spiteful aeons. And following it, the small, little-curly-dog sort of yapping. They can make their voices so devilishly small and futile, like a little curly dog. And follow it up with that ringing malevolence that swoops up the ladders of the sunbeams right to the stars, rolling the Spanish 'r'.

Corasmin slowly walks away from the veranda, his head drooped, and flings himself down in the sun. No! He gets up again, in an agony of self-control, and scratches the earth loose a little, to soften his lie. Then flings himself down again.

Invictus! The still-unconquered Corasmini The sad little white curly pendulum oscillating ever slower between the shadow and the sun.

> *In the fell clutch of circumstance*
> *I have not winced nor cried aloud,*
> *Under the bludgeonings of chance*
> *My head is bloody, but unbowed.*

But that is human bombast, and a little too ridiculous even for Corasmin. Poor old Corasmin's clear yellow eyes! He is going to be master of his own soul, under all the vitriol those parrots pour over him. But he's not going to throw out his chest in a real lust of self-pity. That belongs to the next cycle of evolution.

I wait for the day when the parrots will start throwing English at us, in the pit of our stomachs. They cock their heads and listen to our gabble. But so far they haven't got it. It puzzles them. Castilian, and Corasmin, and Rosalino come more natural.

Myself, I don't believe in evolution, like a long string hooked on to a First Cause, and being slowly twisted in unbroken continuity through the ages. I prefer to believe in what the Aztecs called Suns: that is, Worlds successively created and destroyed. The sun itself convulses, and the worlds go out like so many candles when somebody coughs in the middle of them. Then subtly, mysteriously, the sun convulses again, and a new set of worlds begins to flicker alight.

This pleases my fancy better than the long and weary twisting of the rope of Time and Evolution, hitched on to the revolving hook of a First Cause. I like to think of the whole show going bust, *bang!* — and nothing but bits of chaos flying about. Then out of the dark, new little twinklings reviving from nowhere, nohow.

I like to think of the world going pop! when the lizards had grown too unwieldy, and it was time they were taken down a peg or two. Then the little humming birds beginning to spark in the darkness, and a whole succession of birds shaking themselves clean of the dark matrix, flamingoes rising upon one leg like dawn commencing, parrots shrieking about at midday, *almost* able to talk, then peacocks unfolding at evening like the night with stars. And apart from these little pure birds, a lot of unwieldy skinny-necked monsters bigger than crocodiles, barging through the mosses; till it was time to put a stop to them. When someone mysteriously touched the button, and the sun went bang, with smithereens of birds bursting in all directions. On a few parrots' eggs and peacocks' eggs and eggs of flamingoes smuggling in some safe nook, to hatch on the next Day, when the animals arose.

Up reared the elephant, and shook the mud off his back. The birds watched him in sheer stupefaction. What? *What in heaven's name is this wingless, beakless old perambulator?*

No good, oh birds! Curly, little white Corasmin ran yapping out of the undergrowth, the new undergrowth, till parrots, going white at the gills, flew off into the ancientest recesses. Then the terrific neighing of the wild horse was heard in the twilight for the first time, and the bellowing of lions through the night.

And the birds were sad. What is this? they said. A whole vast gamut of new noises. A universe of new voices.

Then the birds under the leaves hung their heads and were dumb. No good our making .a sound, they said. We are superseded.

The great big, booming, half-naked birds were blown to smithereens. Only the real little feathery individuals hatched out again and remained. This was a consolation. The larks and warblers cheered up, and began to say their little say, out of the old 'Sun', to the new sun. But the peacock, and the turkey, and the raven, and the parrot above all, they could not get over it. Because, in the old days of the Sun of Birds, they had been the big guns. The parrot had been the old boss of the flock. He was so clever.

Now he was, so to speak, up a tree. Nor dare he come down, because of the toddling little curly white Corasmin, and such-like, down below. He felt absolutely bitter. That wingless, beakless, featherless, curly, misshapen bird's nest of a Corasmin had usurped the face of the earth, waddling about, whereas his Grace, the heavy-nosed old Duke of a parrot, was forced to sit out of reach up a tree, dispossessed.

So, like the riff-raff up in the gallery at the theatre, aloft in the Paradiso of the vanished Sun, be began to whistle and jeer. *'Yap-yap!'* said his new little lordship of a Corasmin. 'Ye Gods!' cried the parrot. 'Hear him forsooth! *Yap-yap!* he says! Could anything be more imbecile? Yap-yap! Oh, Sun of the Birds, hark at that! *Yap-yap-yap!* Perro! *Perro! Perr-rro!* Oh, *Perr-rr-rro!'*

The parrot had found his cue. Stiff-nosed, heavy-nosed old duke of the birds, he wasn't going to give in and sing a new song, like those fool brown thrushes and nightingales. Let them twitter and warble. The parrot was a gentleman of the old school. He was going to jeer now! Like an ineffectual old aristocrat.

'Oh, Perr-rro! Perr-rro-o-o-!'

The Aztecs say there have been four Suns and ours is the fifth. The first Sun, a tiger, or a jaguar, a night-spotted monster of rage, rose out of nowhere and swallowed it, with all its huge, mercifully forgotten insects along with it. The second Sun blew up in a great wind: that was when the big lizards must have collapsed. The third Sun burst in water, and drowned all the animals that were considered unnecessary, together with the first attempts at animal men.

Out of the floods rose our own Sun, and little naked man. 'Hello!' said the old elephant. 'What's that noise?' And he pricked his ears, listening to a new voice on the face of the earth. The sound of man, and *words* for the first time. Terrible, unheard-of sound. The elephant dropped his tail and ran into the deep jungle, and there stood looking down his nose.

But little white curly Corasmin was fascinated. *'Come on! Perro! Perro!'* called the naked two-legged one. And Corasmin, fascinated, said to himself: 'Can't stand out against that name. Shall have to go!' so off he trotted, at the heels of the naked one. Then came the horse, then the elephant, spell-bound at being given a name. The other animals ran for their lives and stood quaking.

In the dust, however, the snake, the oldest dethroned king of all, bit his tail once more and said to himself: *'Here's another! No end to these new lords of creation! But I'll bruise his heel! Just as I swallow the eggs of the parrot, and lick up the little Corasmin-pups.'*

And in the branches, the parrot said to himself: *'Hello! What's this new sort of half-bird? Why, he's got Corasmin fretting at his heels! Must be a new sort of boss! Let's listen to him, and see if I can't take him off.'*

Perr-rro! Perr-rr-rro-oo! Oh, Perro!

The parrot had hit it.

And the monkey, cleverest of creatures, cried with rage when he heard men speaking. *'Oh, why couldn't I do it!'* he chattered. But no good, he belonged to the old Sun. So he sat and gibbered across the invisible gulf in time, which is the 'other dimension' that clever people gas about: calling it 'fourth dimension', as if you could measure it with a foot-rule, the same as the obedient other three dimensions.

If you come to think of it, when you look at the monkey, you are looking straight into the other dimension. He's got length and breadth and height all right, and he's in the same universe of Space and Time as you are. But there's another dimension. He's different. There's no rope of evolution linking him to you, like a navel string. No! Between you and him there's a cataclysm and another dimension. It's no good. You can't link him up. Never will. It's the other dimension.

He mocks at you and gibes at you and imitates you. Sometimes he is even more *like* you than you are yourself. It's funny, and you laugh just a bit on the wrong side of your face. It's the other dimension.

He stands in one Sun, you in another. He whisks his tail in one Day, you scratch your head in another. He jeers at you, and is afraid of you. You laugh at him and are frightened of him.

What's the length and the breadth, what's the height and the depths between you and me? says the monkey.

You get out a tape-measure, and he flies into an obscene mockery of you.

It's the other dimension, put the tape-measure away, it won't serve.

'Perro! Oh, Perr-rro!' shrieks the parrot.

Corasmin looks up at me, as much as to say:

'It's the other dimension. There's no help for it. Let us agree about it?

And I look down into his yellow eyes, and say:

'You're quite right, Corasmin, it's the other dimension. You and I, we admit it. But the parrot won't, and the monkey won't, and the crocodile won't, neither the earwig. They all wind themselves up and wriggle inside the cage of the other dimension, hating it. And those that have voices jeer, and those that have mouths bite, and the insects that haven't even mouths, they turn up their tails and nip with them, or sting. Just behaving according to their own dimension: which, for me, is the other dimension.'

And Corasmin wags his tail mildly, and looks at me with real wisdom in his eyes. He and I, we understand each other in the wisdom of the other dimension.

But the flat, saucer-eyed parrot won't have it. Just won't have it.

'Oh, Perro! Perr-rro! Perr-rro-o-o-o! Yap-yap-yap!'

And Rosalino, the Indian *mozo,* looks up at me with his eyes veiled by their own blackness. We won't have it either: he is hiding and repudiating. Between us also is the gulf of the other dimension, and he wants to bridge it with the foot-rule of the three-dimensional space. He knows it can't be done. So do I. Each of us knows the other knows.

But he can imitate me, even more than life-like. As the parrot can him. And I have to laugh at his me, a bit on the wrong side of my face, as he has to grin on the wrong side of his face when I catch his eye as the parrot is whistling *him.* With a grin, with a laugh we pay tribute to the other dimension. But Corasmin is wiser. In his clear, yellow eyes is the self-possession of full admission.

The Aztecs said this world, our Sun, would blow up from inside, in earthquakes. Then what will come, in the other dimension, when we are superseded?

2

WALK TO HUAYAPA

CURIOUS is the psychology of Sunday. Humanity enjoying itself is on the whole a dreary spectacle, and holidays are more disheartening than drudgery. One makes up one's mind: On Sundays and on *fiestas* I will stay at home, in the hermitage of the *patio,* with the parrots and Corasmin and the reddening coffee-berries. I will avoid the sight of people 'enjoying themselves' — or try to, without much success.

Then comes Sunday morning, with the peculiar looseness of its sunshine. And even if *you* keep mum, the better-half says: Let's go somewhere.

But, thank God, in Mexico at least one can't set off in the 'machine'. It is a question of a meagre horse and a wooden saddle; on a donkey; or what we called, as children, 'Shanks' pony' — the shanks referring discourteously to one's own legs.

We will go out of the town. 'Rosalino, we are going for a walk to San Felipe de las Aguas. Do you want to go, and carry the basket?'

'Come no, Señor?'

It is Rosalino's inevitable answer, as inevitable as the parrot's 'Perro!' *'Come no, Señor?'* — 'How not, Señor?'

The *Norte,* the north-wind, was blowing last night, rattling the worm-chewed window-frames.

'Rosalino, I am afraid you will be cold in the night.'

'Come no, Señor?'

'Would you like a blanket?'

'Come no, Señor?'

'With this you will be warm?'

'Come no, Señor?'

But the morning is perfect; in a moment we are clear out of the town. Most towns in Mexico, saving the capital, end in themselves, at once. As if they bad been lowered from heaven in a napkin, and deposited, rather foreign, upon the wild plain. So we walk round the wall of the church and the huge old monastery enclosure that is now barracks for the scrap-heap soldiery, and at once there are the hills.

'I will lift up my eyes unto the hills, whence cometh my strength.' At least one can always do *that,* in Mexico. In a stride, the town passes away. Before us lies the gleaming, pinkish-ochre of the valley flat, wild and exalted with sunshine. On the left, quite near, bank the stiffly pleated mountains, all the foot-hills, that press savannah-coloured into the savannah of the valley. The mountains are clothed smokily with pine, *ocote,* and, like a woman in a gauze *rebozo,* they rear in a rich blue fume that is almost cornflower-blue in the clefts. It is their characteristic that they are darkest blue at the top. Like some splendid lizard with a wavering, royal-blue crest down the ridge of his back, and pale belly, and soft, pinky-fawn claws, on the plain.

Between the pallor of the claws, a dark spot of trees, and white dots of a church with twin towers. Further away, along the foot-hills, a few scattered trees, white dot and stroke of a *bacienda,* and a green, green square of sugar-cane. Further off still, at the mouth of a cleft of a canyon, a dense little green patch of trees, and two spots of proud church.

'Rosalino, which is San Felipe?'

'Quien sabe, Señor?' says Rosalino, looking at the villages beyond the sun of the savannah with black, visionless eyes. In his voice is the inevitable flat resonance of aloofness, touched with resignation, as if to say: It is not becoming to a man to know these things. — Among the Indians it is not becoming to know anything, not even one's own name.

Rosalino is a mountain boy, an Indian from a village two days' walk away. But he has been two years in the little city, and has learnt his modicum of Spanish.

'Have you never been to any of these villages?'

'No, Señor, I never went.'

'Didn't you want to?'

'Come no, Señor?'

The Americans would call him a dumb-bell.

We decide for the farthest speck of a village in a dark spot of trees It lies so magical, alone, tilted in the fawn-pink slope, again as if the dark-green napkin with a few white tiny buildings had been lowered from heaven and left, there at the foot of the mountains, with the deep groove of a canyon slanting in behind. So alone and, as it were, detached from the world in which it lies, a spot.

Nowhere more than in Mexico does human life become isolated, external to its surroundings, and cut off tinily from the environment. Even as you come across the plain to a big city like Guadalajara, and see the twin towers of the cathedral peering around in loneliness like two lost birds side by side on a moor, lifting their white heads to look around in the wilderness, your heart gives a clutch, feeling the pathos, the isolated tininess of human effort. As for building a church with one tower only, it is unthinkable. There must be two towers, to keep each other company in this wilderness world.

The morning is still early, the brilliant sun does not burn too much. Tomorrow is the shortest day. The savannah valley is shadeless, spotted only with the thorny ravel of mesquite bushes. Down the trail that has worn grooves in the turf — the rock is near the surface — occasional donkeys with a blue-hooded woman perched on top come tripping in silence, twinkling, a shadow. Just occasional women taking a few vegetables to market. Practically no men. It is Sunday.

Rosalino, prancing behind with the basket, plucks up his courage to speak to one of the women passing on a donkey. 'Is that San Felipe where we are going?' — 'No, that is not San Felipe.' — 'What, then, is it called?' — 'It is called Huayapa.' —'Which, then, is San Felipe?' — 'That one' —and she points to her right.

They have spoken to each other in half-audible, crushed tones, as they always do, the woman on the donkey and the woman with her on foot swerving away from the basket-carrying Rosalino. They all swerve away from us, as if we were potential bold brigands. It really gets one's pecker up. The presence of the Señora only half reassures them. For the Señora, in a plain hat of bluey-green woven grass, and a dress of white cotton with black squares on it, is almost a monster of unusualness. *Prophet art thou, bird, or devil?* the women seem to say, as they look at her with keen black eyes. I think they choose to decide she is more of the last.

The women look at the woman, the men look at the man. And always with that same suspicious, inquiring, wondering look, the same with which Edgar Allan Poe must have looked at his momentous raven:

'Prophet art thou, bird, or devil?'

Devil, then, to please you! one longs to answer, in a tone of *Nevermore.*

Ten o'clock, and the sun getting hot. Not a spot of shade, apparently, from here to Huayapa. The blue getting thinner on the mountains, and an indiscernible vagueness, of too much light, descending on the plain.

The road suddenly dips into a little crack, where runs a creek. This again is characteristic of these parts of America. Water keeps out of sight. Even the biggest rivers, even the tiny brooks. You look across a plain on which the light sinks down, and you think: Dry! Dry! Absolutely dry! You travel along, and suddenly come to a crack in the earth, and a little stream is running in a little walled-in valley bed, where is a halfyard of green turf, and bushes, the *palo-blanco* with leaves, and with big white flowers like pure white, crumpled cambric. Or you may come to a river a thousand feet below, sheer below you. But not in this valley. Only the stream.

'Shade!' says the Señora, subsiding under a steep bank.

'Mucho calor!' says Rosalino, taking off his extra-jaunty straw hat, and subsiding with the basket.

Down the slope are coming two women on donkeys. Seeing the terrible array of three people sitting under a bank, they pull up.

'Adios!' I say, with firm resonance.

'Adios!' says the Señora, with diffidence.

'Adios!' says the reticent Rosalino, his voice the shadow of ours.

'Adios! Adios! Adios!' say the women, in suppressed voices, swerving, neutral, past us on their self-contained, sway-eared asses.

When they have passed, Rosalino looks at me to see if I shall laugh. I give a little grin, and he gives me back a great explosive grin, throwing back his head in silence, opening his wide mouth and showing his soft pink tongue, looking along his cheeks with his saurian black eyes, in an access of *farouche* derision.

A great hawk, like an eagle, with white bars at the end of its wings, sweeps low over us, looking for snakes. One can hear the hiss of its pinions.

'Gabilán,' says Rosalino.

'What is it called in the *idioma?'*

'Psia!' — He makes the consonants explode and hiss.

'Ah!' says the Señora. 'One hears it in the wings. *Psia!'*

'Yes,' says Rosalino, with black eyes of incomprehension.

Down the creek, two native boys, little herdsmen, are bathing, stooping with knees together and throwing water over themselves, rising, gleaming dark coffee-red in the sun, wetly. They are very dark, and their wet heads are so black, they seem to give off a bluish light, like dark electricity.

The great cattle they are tending slowly plunge through the bushes, coming upstream. At the place where the path fords the stream, a great ox stoops to drink. Comes a cow after him, and a calf, and a young bull. They all drink a little at the stream, their noses delicately touching the water. And then the young bull, horns abranch, stares fixedly, with some of the same Indian wonder-and-suspicion stare, at us sitting under the bank.

Up jumps the Señora, proceeds uphill, trying to save her dignity. The bull, slowly leaning into motion, moves across-stream like a ship unmoored. The bathing lad on the bank is hastily fastening his calico pantaloons round his ruddy-dark waist. The Indians have a certain rich physique, even this lad. He comes running short-step down the bank, uttering a bird-like whoop, his dark hair gleaming bluish. Stooping for a moment to select a stone, he runs athwart the bull, and aims the stone sideways at him. There is a thud, the ponderous, adventurous young animal swerves docilely round towards the stream. *'Becerro!'* cries the boy, in his bird-like, piping tone, selecting a stone to throw at the calf.

We proceed in the blaring sun up the slope. There is a white line at the foot of the trees. It looks like water running white over a weir. The supply of the town water comes this way. Perhaps this is a reservoir. A sheet of water! How lovely it would be, in this country, if there was a sheet of water with a stream running out of it! And those dense trees of Huayapa behind.

'What is that white, Rosalino? Is it water?'

'El blanco? Si, agua, Señora,' says that dumb-bell. Probably, if the Señora had said: Is it milk? he would have replied in exactly the same way: *Si es leche, Señora!* — Yes, it's milk.

Hot, silent, walking only amidst a weight of light, out of which one hardly sees, we climb the spurs towards the dark trees. And as we draw nearer, the white slowly resolves into a broken, whitewashed wall.

'Oh!' exclaims the Señora, in real disappointment. 'It isn't water! It's a wall!'

'*Si, Señora. Es panteón.*' (They call a cemetery a *panteón,* down here.)

'It is a cemetery,' announces Rosalino, with a certain ponderous, pleased assurance, and without afterthought. But when I suddenly laugh at the absurdity, he also gives a sudden broken yelp of laughter. — They laugh as if it were against their will, as if it hurt them, giving themselves away.

It was nearing midday. At last we got into a shady lane, in which were puddles of escaped irrigation-water. The ragged semi-squalor of a half-tropical lane, with naked trees sprouting into spiky scarlet flowers, and bushes with biggish yellow flowers, sitting rather wearily on their stems, led to the village.

We were entering Huayapa. *Iᵃ Calle de las Minas,* said an old notice. *Iᵃ Calle de las Minas,* said a new, brand-new notice, as if in confirmation *First Street of the Mines* And every street had the same old and brand-new notice: Ist Street of the Magnolia: 4th Street of Enriquez Gonzalez: very fine!

But the First Street of the Mines was just a track between the stiff living fence of organ cactus, with poinsettia trees holding up scarlet mops of flowers, and mango trees, tall and black, stonily drooping the strings of unripe fruit. The Street of the Magnolia was a rocky stream-gutter, disappearing to nowhere from nowhere, between cactus and bushes. The Street of the Vasquez was a stony stream-bed, emerging out of tall, wildly tall reeds.

Not a soul anywhere. Through the fences, half deserted gardens of trees and banana plants, each enclosure with a half-hidden hut of black adobe bricks crowned with a few old tiles for a roof, and perhaps a new wing made of twigs. Everything hidden, secret, silent. A sense of darkness among the silent mango trees, a sense of lurking, of unwillingness. Then actually some half-bold curs barking at us across the stile of one garden, a forked bough over which one must step to enter the chicken-bitten enclosure. And actually a man crossing the proudly labelled: Fifth Street of the Independence.

If there were no churches to mark a point in these villages, there would be nowhere at all to make for. The sense of nowhere is intense, between the dumb and repellent living fence of cactus. But the Spaniards, in the midst of these black, mud-brick huts, have inevitably reared the white twin-towered magnificence of a big and lonely, hopeless church; and where there is a church there will be a *plaza.* And a *plaza* is a zócalo, a hub. Even though the wheel does not go round, a hub is still a hub. Like the old Forum.

So we stray diffidently on, in the maze of streets which are only straight tracks between cactuses, till we see *Reforma,* and at the end of *Reforma*, the great church.

In front of the church is a rocky *plaza* leaking with grass, with water rushing into two big, oblong stone basins. The great church stands rather ragged, in a dense forlornness, for all the world like some big white human being, in rags, held captive in a world of ants.

On the uphill side of the *plaza,* a long low white building with a shed in front, and under the shed crowding, all the short-statured men of the *pueblo,* in their white cotton clothes and big hats. They are listening to something: but the silence is heavy, furtive, secretive. They stir like white-clad insects.

Rosalino looks sideways at them, and sheers away. Even we lower our voices to ask what is going on. Rosalino replies, *sotto voce,* that they are making *asuntos.* But what business? we insist. The dark faces of the little men under the big hats look round at us suspiciously, like dark gaps in the atmosphere. Our alien presence in this vacuous village, is like the sound of a drum in a churchyard. Rosalino mumbles unintelligibly. We stray across the forlorn yard into the church.

Thursday was the day of the Virgin of the Soledad, so the church is littered with flowers, sprays of wild yellow flowers trailing on the floor. There is a great Gulliver's Travels fresco picture of an angel having a joy-ride on the back of a Goliath. On the left, near the altar steps, is seated a life-size Christ *Iᵃ Calle de las Minas* undersized; seated upon a little table, wearing a pair of woman's frilled knickers, a little mantle of purple silk dangling from His back, and His face bent forward gazing fatuously at His naked knee, which emerges from the needlework frill of the drawers. Across from Him a living woman is half-hidden behind a buttress, mending something, sewing.

We sit silent, motionless, in the whitewashed church ornamented with royal blue and bits of gilt. A barefoot Indian with a high-domed head comes in and kneels with his legs close together, his back stiff, at once very humble and resistant. His cotton jacket and trousers are long-unwashed rag, the colour of dry earth, and torn, so that one sees smooth pieces of brown thigh, and brown back. He kneels in a sort of intense fervour for a minute, then gets up and childishly, almost idiotically, begins to take the pieces of candle from the candlesticks. He is the Verger.

Outside, the gang of men is still pressing under the shed. We insist on knowing what is going on. Rosalino, looking sideways at them, plucks up courage to say plainly that the two men at the table are canvassing for votes: for the Government, for the State, for a new governor, whatever it may be. Votes! Votes! Votes! The farce of it! Already on the wall of the low building, on which one sees, in blue letters, the word *Justizia,* there are pasted the late political posters, with the loud announcement: Vote For This Mark +. Or another: Vote For This Mark Θ

My dear fellow, this is when democracy becomes real fun. You vote for one red ring inside another red ring and you get a Julio Echegaray. You vote for a blue dot inside a blue ring, and you get a Socrate Ezequiel Tos. Heaven knows what you get for the two little red circles on top of one another.

Suppose we vote, and try. There's all sorts in the lucky bag. There might come a name like Peregrino Zenon Cocotilla.

Independence! Government by the People, of the People, for the People! We all live in the Calle de la Reforma, in Mexico.

On the bottom of the *plaza* is a shop. We want some fruit.

'*Hay frutas?* Oranges or bananas?' — '*No, Señor.*' - 'No fruits?' — '*No hay.*' — 'Can I buy a cup?' — '*No hay.*' — 'Can I buy a *jicara,* a gourd-shell that we might drink from?' '*No hay.*'

No hay means *there isn't any,* and it's the most regular sound made by the dumb-bells of the land.

'What is there, then?' A sickly grin. There are, as a matter of fact, candles, soap, dead and withered chiles, a few dried grasshoppers, dust, and stark, bare wooden pigeon-holes. Nothing, nothing, nothing. Next-door is another little hole of a shop. *Hay frutas?* — *No hay.* — *Qué hay?* - *Hay tepache!*

'*Para borracharse,*' says Rosalino, with a great grin.

Tepache is a fermented drink of pineapple rinds and brown sugar: to get drunk on, as Rosalino says. But mildly drunk. There is probably *mescal* too, to get brutally drunk on.

The village is exhausted in resource. But we insist on fruit. Where, *where* can I buy oranges and bananas? I see oranges on the trees, I see banana plants.

'Up there!' The woman waves with her hand as if she were cutting the air upwards.

'That way?'

'Yes.'

We go up the Street of Independence. They have got rid of us from *the plaza.*

Another black hut with a yard, and orange-trees beyond.

'Hay frutas?'

'No hay.'

'Not an orange, nor a banana?'

'No hay.'

We go on. *She* has got rid of us. We descend the black rocky steps to the stream, and up the other side, past the high reeds. There is a yard with heaps of maize in a shed, and tethered bullocks: and a bare-bosom, black-browed girl.

'Hay frutas?'

'No hay.'

'But yes! There are oranges — there!'

She turns and looks at the oranges on the trees at the back, and imbecilely answers:
'No hay.'

It is a choice between killing her and hurrying away.

We hear a drum and a whistle. It is down a rocky black track that calls itself The Street of Benito Juarez: the same old gent who stands for all this obvious Reform, and Vote for Θ.

A yard with shade round. Women kneading the maize dough, *masa,* for *tortillas.* A man lounging. And a little boy beating a kettledrum sideways, and a big man playing a little reedy wooden whistle, rapidly, endlessly, disguising the tune of *La Cucuracha.* They won't play a tune unless they can render it almost unrecognizable.

'Hay frutas?'

'No hay.'

'Then what is happening here?' A sheepish look, and no answer. 'Why are you playing music?' 'It is *a fiesta.'*

My God, a feast! That weary *masa,* a millstone in the belly. And for the rest, the blank, heavy, dark-grey barrenness, like an adobe brick. The drum-boy rolls his big Indian eyes at us, and beats on, though lulled with consternation. The flute man glances, is half appalled and half resentful, so he blows harder. The lounging man comes and mutters to Rosalino, and Rosalino mutters back, four words.

Four words in the *idioma,* the Zapotec language. We retire, pushed silently away.

'What language do they speak here, Rosalino?'

'The *idioma.'*

'You understand them? It is Zapoteca, same as your language?'

'Yes, Señor.'

'Then why do you always speak in Spanish to them?'

'Because they don't speak the *idioma* of my village.'

He means, presumably, that there are dialect differences.

Anyhow, he asserts his bit of Spanish, and says *Hay frutas?*

It was like a *posada.* It was like the Holy Virgin on Christmas Eve, wandering from door to door looking for a lodging in which to bear her child: Is there a room here? *No hay!*

The same with us. *Hay frutas? No hay!* We went down every straight ant-run of that blessed village. But at last we pinned a good-natured woman. 'Now tell us, *where* can we buy oranges? We see them on the trees. We want them to eat.'

'Go,' she said, 'to Valentino Ruiz. He has oranges. Yes, he has oranges, and he sells them? And she cut the air upwards with her hand.

From black hut to black hut went we, till at last we got to the house of Valentino Ruiz. And lo! it was the yard with the *fiesta.* The lounging man was peeping out of the gateless gateway, as we came, at us.

'It is the same place!' cried Rosalino, with a laugh of bashful agony.

But we don't belong to the ruling race for nothing. Into the yard we march.

'Is this the house of Valentino Ruiz? *Hay narajas?* Are there oranges?'

We had wandered so long, and asked so often, that the *masa* was made into *tortillas,* the *tortillas* were baked, and a group of people were sitting in a ring on the ground, eating them. It was *fiesta.*

At my question up jumped a youngish man, and a woman as if they had been sitting on a scorpion each.

'Oh, Señor,' said the woman, 'there are few oranges, and they are not ripe, as the Señor would want them. But pass this way.'

We pass up to the garden, past the pink roses, to a little orange-tree, with a few yellowish-green oranges.

'You see, they are not ripe as you will want them,' says the youngish man.

'They will do.' Tropical oranges are always green. These, we found later, were almost insipidly sweet.

Even then, I can only get three of the big, thick-skinned, greenish oranges. But I spy sweet limes, and insist on having five or six of these.

He charges me three cents apiece for the oranges: the market price is two for five cents: and one cent each for the *limas.*

'In my village,' mutters Rosalino when we get away, 'oranges are five for one cent.'

Never mind! It is one o'clock. Let us get out of the village, where the water will be safe, and eat lunch.

In the *plaza,* the men are just dispersing, one gang coming down the hill. They watch us as if we were a coyote, a *zopilote,* and a white she-bear walking together in the street.

'*Adios!*'

'*Adios!*' comes the low roll of reply, like a roll of cannon shot.

The water rushes downhill in a stone gutter beside the road. We climb up the hill, up the Street of the Camomile, alongside the rushing water. At one point it crosses the road unchannelled, and we wade through it. It is the village drinking supply.

At the juncture of the roads, where the water crosses, another silent white gang of men. Again: *Adios!* and again the low, musical, deep volley of *Adios!*

Up, up wearily. We must get above the village to be able to drink the water without developing typhoid.

At last, the last house, the naked hills. We follow the water across a dry maize-field, then up along a bank. Below is a quite deep gully. Across is an orchard, and some women with baskets of fruit.

'*Hay frutas?*' calls Rosalino, in a half-voice. He is getting bold.

'*Hay,*' says an old woman, in the curious half-voice. 'But not ripe.'

Shall we go down into the gully into the shade? No; someone is bathing among the reeds below, and the aqueduct water lies along in the gutter here above. On, on, till we spy a wild guava tree over the channel of water. At last we can sit down and eat and drink, on a bank of dry grass, under the wild guava tree.

We put the bottle of lemonade in the aqueduct to cool. I scoop out a big half-orange, the thick rind of which makes a cup.

'Look, Rosalino! The cup!'

'*La taza!*' he cries, soft-tongued, with a bark of laughter and delight.

And one drinks the soft, rather lifeless, warmish Mexican water. But it is pure.

Over the brink of the water-channel is the gully, and a noise — chock, chock! I go to look. It is a woman, naked to the hips, standing washing her other garments upon a stone. She has a beautiful full back, of a deep orange colour, and her wet hair is divided and piled. In the water a few yards up-stream two men are sitting naked, their brown-orange giving off a glow in the shadow, also washing their clothes. Their wet hair seems to steam blue-blackness. Just above them is a sort of bridge, where the water divides, the channel-water taken from the little river, and led along the top of the bank.

We sit under the wild guava tree in silence, and eat. The old woman of the fruit, with naked breast and coffee-brown naked arms, her under-garment fastened on one shoulder, round her waist an old striped *sarape* for a skirt, and on her head a blue *rebozo* piled against the sun, comes marching down the aqueduct with black bare feet, holding three or four *chirimoyas* to her bosom. *Chirimoyas* are green custard-apples.

She lectures us, in slow, heavy Spanish:

'This water, here, is for drinking. The other, below, is for washing. This, you drink, and you don't wash in it. The other, you wash in, and you don't drink it.' And she looked inquisitively at the bottle of lemonade, cooling.

'Very good. We understand.'

Then she gave us the *chirimoyas*. I asked her to change the *peso:* I had no change.

'No, Señor,' she said. 'No, Señor. You don't pay me. I bring you these, and may you eat well. But the *chirimoyas* are not ripe: in two or three days they will be ripe. Now, they are not. In two or three days they will be. Now, they are not.

You can't eat them yet. But I make a gift of them to you, and may you eat well. Farewell. Remain with God.'

She marched impatiently off along the aqueduct.

Rosalino waited to catch my eye. Then he opened his mouth and showed his pink tongue and swelled out his throat like a cobra, in a silent laugh after the old woman.

'But,' he said in a low tone, 'the *chirimoyas* are not good ones.'

And again he swelled in the silent, delighted, derisive laugh. He was right. When we came to eat them, three days later, the custard-apples all had worms in them, and hardly any white meat.

'The old woman of Huayapa,' said Rosalino, reminiscent.

However, she had got her bottle. When we had drunk the lemonade, we sent Rosalino to give her the empty wine-bottle, and she made him another sententious little speech. But to her the bottle was a treasure.

And I, going round the little hummock behind the wild guava tree to throw away the papers of the picnic, came upon a golden-brown young man with his shirt just coming down over his head, but over no more of him. Hastily retreating, I thought again what beautiful, suave, rich skins these people have; a sort of richness of the flesh. It goes, perhaps, with the complete absence of what we call 'spirit'.

We lay still for a time, looking at the tiny guavas and the perfect, soft, high blue sky overhead, where the hawks and the ragged-winged *zopilotes* sway and diminish. A long, hot way home. But *mañana es otro dia.* Tomorrow is another day. And even the next five minutes are far enough away, in Mexico, on a Sunday afternoon.

THE MOZO

ROSALINO really goes with the house, though he has been in service here only two months. When we went to look at the place, we saw him lurking in the *patio,* and glancing furtively under his brows. He is not one of the erect, bantam little Indians that stare with a black, incomprehensible, but somewhat defiant stare. It may be Rosalino has a distant strain of other Indian blood, not Zapotec. Or it may be he is only a bit different. The difference lies in a certain sensitiveness and aloneness, as if he were a mother's boy. The way he drops his head and looks sideways under his black lashes, apprehensive, apprehending, feeling his way, as it were. Not the bold male glare of most of the Indians, who seem as if they had never, never had mothers at all.

The Aztec gods and goddesses are, as far as we have known anything about them, an unlovely and unlovable lot. In their myths there is no grace or charm, no poetry. Only this perpetual grudge, grudge, grudging, one god grudging another, the gods grudging men their existence, and men grudging the animals. The goddess of love is a goddess of dirt and prostitution, a dirt-eater, a horror, without a touch of tenderness. If the god wants to make love to her, she has to sprawl down in front of him, blatant and accessible.

And then, after all, when she conceives and brings forth, what is it she produces? What is the infant-god she tenderly bears? Guess, all ye people, joyful and triumphant!

You never could.

It is a stone knife.

It is a razor-edged knife of blackish-green flint, the knife of all knives, the veritable Paraclete of knives. It is the sacrificial knife with which the priest makes a gash in his victim's breast, before he tears out the heart, to hold it smoking to the sun.

And the Sun, the Sun behind the sun, is supposed to suck the smoking heart greedily with insatiable appetite.

This, then, is a pretty Christmas Eve. Lo, the goddess is gone to bed, to bring forth her child. Lo! ye people, await the birth of the saviour, the wife of a god is about to become a mother.

Tarumm-tarah! Tarumm-tarah! blow the trumpets. The child is born. Unto us a son is given. Bring him forth, lay him on a tender cushion. Show him, then, to all the people. See! See! See him upon the cushion, tenderly new-born and reposing! Ah, *qué bonito!* Oh, what a nice, blackish, smooth, keen stone knife!

And to this day, most of the Mexican Indian women seem to bring forth stone knives. Look at them, these Sons of incomprehensible mothers, with their black eyes like flints, and their stiff little bodies as taut and as keen as knives of obsidian. Take care they don't rip you up.

Our Rosalino is an exception. He drops his shoulders just a little. He is a bit bigger, also, than the average Indian down here. He must be about five feet four inches. And he hasn't got the big, obsidian, glaring eyes. His eyes are smaller, blacker, like the quick black eyes of the lizard. They don't look at one with the obsidian stare. They are just

258

a bit aware that there is another being, unknown, at the other end of the glance. Hence he drops his head with a little apprehension, screening himself as if he were vulnerable.

Usually, these people have no correspondence with one at all. To them a white man or white woman is a sort of phenomenon; just as a monkey is a sort of phenomenon; something to watch, and wonder at, and laugh at, but not to be taken on one's own plane

Now the white man is a sort of extraordinary white monkey that, by cunning, has learnt lots of semi-magical secrets of the universe, and made himself boss of the show Imagine a race of big white monkeys got up in fantastic clothes, and able to kill a man by hissing at him, able to leap through the air in great hops, covering a mile in each leap, able to transmit his thoughts by a moment's effort of concentration to some great white monkey or monkeyess, a thousand miles away: and you have, from our point of view, something of the picture that the Indian has of us.

The white monkey has curious tricks. He knows, for example, the time. Now to a Mexican, and an Indian, time is a vague, foggy reality. There are only three times: *en la mañana, en la tarde, en la noche.* — in the morning, in the afternoon, in the night. There is even no midday, and no evening.

But to the white monkey, horrible to relate, there are exact spots of time, such as five o'clock, half past nine. The day is a horrible puzzle of exact spots of time.

The same with distance: horrible invisible distances called two miles, ten miles. To the Indians, there is near and far, and very near and very far. There is two days or one day. But two miles are as good as twenty to him, for he goes entirely by his feeling. If a certain two miles feels far to him, then it *is* far, it is *muy lejos!* But if a certain twenty miles *feels* near and familiar, then it is not far. Oh, no, it is just a little distance. And he will let you set off in the evening, for night to overtake you in the wilderness, without a qualm. It is not far.

But the white man has a horrible, truly horrible, monkey-like passion for invisible exactitudes. *Mañana,* to the native, may mean tomorrow, three days hence, six months hence, and never. There are no fixed points in life, save birth, and death, and the *fiestas.* The fixed points of birth and death evaporate spontaneously into vagueness. And the priests fix the *fiestas.* From time immemorial priests have fixed the *fiestas,* the festivals of the gods, and men have had no more to do with time. What should men have to do with time?

The same with money. These *centavos* and these *pesos,* what do they mean, after all? Little discs that have no charm. The natives insist on reckoning in invisible coins, coins that don't exist here, like *reales* or *pesetas.* If you buy two eggs for a *real,* you have to pay twelve and a half *centavos.* Since also half a *centavo* doesn't exist, you or the vendor forfeit the non-existent.

The same with honesty, the *meum* and the *tuum.* The white man has a horrible way of remembering, even to a *centavo,* even to a thimbleful of *mescal.* Horrible! The Indian, it seems to me, is not naturally dishonest. He is not naturally avaricious, has not even any innate cupidity. In this he is unlike the old people of the Mediterranean, to whom possessions have a mystic meaning, and a silver coin a mystic white halo, a *lueur* of magic.

To the real Mexican, no! He doesn't care. He doesn't even *like* keeping money. His deep instinct is to spend it at once, so that he needn't have it. He doesn't really want to keep anything, not even his wife and children. Nothing that he has to be responsible for. Strip, strip, strip away the past and the future, leave the naked moment of the present disentangled. Strip away memory, strip away forethought and care; leave the moment, stark and sharp and without consciousness, like the obsidian knife. The before and the after are the stuff of consciousness. The instant moment is for ever keen with a razor-edge of oblivion, like the knife of sacrifice.

But the great white monkey has got hold of the keys of the world, and the black-eyed Mexican has to serve the great white monkey, in order to live. He has to learn the tricks of the white monkey-show: time of the day, coin of money, machines that start at a second, work that is meaningless and yet is paid for with exactitude, in exact coin. A whole existence of monkey-tricks and monkey-virtues. The strange monkey-virtue of the white monkeys nosing round to *help,* to *save!* Could any trick be more unnatural? Yet it is one of the tricks of the great white monkey.

If an Indian is poor, he says to another: I have no food; give me to eat. Then the other hands the hungry one a couple of *tortillas.* That is natural. But when the white monkey comes round, they peer at the house, at the woman, at the children. They say: Your child is sick. *Si, Señor.* What have you done for it — *Nothing. What is to be done?*-You must make a poultice. I will show you how.

Well, it was very amusing, this making hot dough to dab on the baby. Like plastering a house with mud. But why do it twice? Twice is not amusing. The child will die. Well, then, it will be in Paradise. How nice for it! That's just what God wants of it, that it shall be a cheerful little angel among the roses of Paradise. What could be better?

How tedious of the white monkey coming with the trick of salvation, to rub oil on the baby, and put poultices on it, and make you give it medicine in a spoon at morning, noon, and night. Why morning and noon and night? Why not just anytime, anywhen? It will die tomorrow if you don't do these things today! But tomorrow is another day, and it is not dead now, so if it dies at another time, it must be because the other times are out of hand.

Oh, the tedious, exacting white monkeys, with their yesterdays and todays and tomorrows! Tomorrow is always another day, and yesterday is part of the encircling never. Why think outside the moment? And inside the moment one does not think. So why pretend to think? It is one of the white-monkey-tricks. He is a clever monkey. But he is ugly, and he has nasty, white flesh. We are not ugly, with screwed-up faces, and we have good warm-brown flesh. If we have to work for the white monkey, we don't care. His tricks are half-amusing. And one may as well amuse oneself that way as any other. So long as one is amused.

So long as the devil does not rouse in us, seeing the white monkeys for ever mechanically bossing, with their incessant tick-tack of work. Seeing them get the work out of us, the sweat, the money, and then taking the very land from us, the very oil and metal out of our soil.

They do it! They do it all the time. Because they can't help it. Because grasshoppers can but hop, and ants can carry little sticks, and white monkeys can go tick-tack, tick-tack, do this, do that, time to work, time to eat, time to drink, time to sleep, time to walk, time to ride, time to wash, time to look dirty, tick-tack, tick-tack, time, time, time! time! Oh, cut off his nose and make him swallow it.

For the *moment* is as changeless as an obsidian knife, and the heart of the Indian is keen as the moment that divides past from future, and sacrifices them both.

To Rosalino, too, the white monkey-tricks are amusing. He is ready to work for the white monkeys, to learn some of their tricks, their monkey-speech of Spanish, their tick-tack ways. He works for four *pesos* a month, and his food: a few *tortillas.* Four *pesos* are two American dollars: about nine shillings. He owns two cotton shirts, two pairs of calico pantaloons, two blouses, one of pink cotton, one of darkish flannelette, and a pair of sandals. Also, his straw hat that he has curled up to look very jaunty, and a rather old, Factory-made, rather cheap shawl, or plaid rug with fringe. *Et praeterea nihil.*

His duty is to rise in the morning and sweep the street in front of the house, and water it. Then he sweeps and waters the broad, brick-tiled verandas, and flicks the chairs with a sort of duster made of fluffy reeds. After which he walks behind the cook — she is very superior, had a Spanish grandfather, and Rosalino must address her as *Señora* — carrying the basket to market. Returned from the market, he sweeps the whole of the *patio,* gathers up the leaves and refuse, fills the pannier-basket, hitches it up on to his shoulders, and holds it by a band across his forehead, and thus, a beast of burden, goes out to deposit the garbage at the side of one of the little roads leading out of the city. Every *little* road leaves the town between heaps of garbage, an avenue of garbage blistering in the sun.

Returning, Rosalino waters the whole of the garden and sprinkles the whole of the *patio.* This takes most of the morning. In the afternoon, he sits without much to do. If the wind has blown or the day is hot, he starts again at about three o'clock, sweeping up leaves, and sprinkling everywhere with an old watering-can.

Then he retreats to the entrance-way, the *zaguán,* which, with its big doors and its cobbled track, is big enough to admit an ox-wagon. The *zaguán* is his home: just the doorway. In one corner is a low wooden bench about four feet long and eighteen inches wide. On this he screws up and sleeps, in his clothes as he is, wrapped in the old *sarape.*

But this is anticipating. In the obscurity of the *zaguán* he sits and pores, pores, pores over a school-book, learning to read and write. He can read a bit, and write a bit. He filled a large sheet of foolscap with writing: quite nice. But I found out that what he had written was a Spanish poem, a love-poem, with *no puedo olvidar* and *voy a cortar* — the rose, of course. He had written the thing straight ahead, without verse-lines or capitals or punctuation at all, just a vast string of words, a whole foolscap sheet full. When I read a few lines aloud, he writhed and laughed in an agony of confused feelings. And of what he had written he understood a small, small amount, parrot-wise, from the top of his head. Actually, it meant just words, sound, noise, to him: noise called *Castellano,* Castilian. Exactly like a parrot.

From seven to eight he goes to the night-school, to cover a bit more of the foolscap. He has been going for two years. If he goes two years more he will perhaps really be able to read and write six intelligible sentences: but only Spanish, which is as foreign to him as Hindustani would be to an English farm-boy. Then if he can speak his quantum of Spanish, and read it and write it to a very uncertain extent, he will return to his village two days' journey on foot into the hills, and then, in time, he may even rise to be an *alcalde,* or headman of the village, responsible to the Government. If he were *alcalde* he would get a little salary. But far more important to him is the glory: being able to boss.

He has a *paisano,* a fellow-countryman, to sleep with him in the *zaguán,* to guard the doors. Whoever gets into the house or *patio* must get through these big doors. There is no other entrance, not even a needle's eye. The windows to the street are heavily barred. Each house is its own small fortress. Ours is a double square, the trees and flowers in the first square, with the two wings of the house. And in the second patio, the chickens, pigeons, guinea-pigs, and the big heavy earthenware dish or tub, called an *apaxtle,* in which all the servants can bathe themselves, like chickens in a saucer.

By half past nine at night Rosalino is lying on his little bench, screwed up, wrapped in his shawl, his sandals, called *huaraches,* on the floor. Usually he takes off his *huaraches* when he goes to bed. That is all his preparation. In another corner, wrapped up, head and all, like a mummy in his thin old blanket, the *paisano,* another lad of about twenty, lies asleep on the cold stones. And at an altitude of five thousand feet, the nights can be cold.

Usually everybody is in by half past nine in our very quiet house. If not, you may thunder at the big doors. It is hard to wake Rosalino. You have to go close to him, and call. That will wake him. But don't touch him. That would startle him terribly. No one is touched unawares, except to be robbed or murdered.

'Rosalino! *están tocando!*' — 'Rosalino! they are knocking!'

At last there starts up a strange, glaring, utterly lost Rosalino. Perhaps he just has enough wit to pull the door-catch. One wonders where he was, and what he was, in his sleep, he starts up so strange and wild and lost.

The first time he had anything to do for me was when the van was come to carry the bit of furniture to the house. There was Aurelio, the dwarf *mozo* of our friends and Rosalino, and the man who drove the wagon. But there *should* have been also a *cargador*— a porter. 'Help them,' said I to Rosalino. 'You give a hand to help.' But he winced away, muttering, *'No quiero! —* I don't want to.'

The fellow, I thought to myself, is a fool. He thinks it's not his job, and perhaps he is afraid of smashing the furniture. Nothing to be done but to leave him alone.

We settled in, and Rosalino seemed to like doing things for us. He liked learning his monkey-tricks from the white monkeys. And since we started feeding him from our own meals, and for the first time in his life he had real soups, meat-stews, or a fried egg, he loved to do things in the kitchen. He would come with sparkling black eyes: *'Hé comido el caldo. Grazias!'* ('I have eaten the soup. Thank you.') — And he would give a strange, excited little yelp of a laugh.

Came the day when we walked to Huayapa, on the Sunday, and he was very thrilled. But at night, in the evening when we got home, he lay mute on his bench — not that he was really tired. The Indian gloom, which settles on them like a black marsh-fog, had settled on him. He did not bring in the water — let me carry it by myself.

Monday morning, the same black, reptilian gloom, and a sense of hatred. He hated us. This was a bit flabbergasting, because he had been so thrilled and happy the day before. But the revulsion had come. He didn't forgive himself for having felt free and happy with us. He had eaten what we had eaten, hard-boiled eggs and sardine sandwiches and cheese; he had drunk out of the orange-peel *taza,* which delighted him so much. He had had a bottle of *gaseosa,* fizz, with us, on the way home, in San Felipe.

And now, the reaction. The flint knife. He had been happy, *therefore* we were scheming to take another advantage of him. We had some devilish white monkey-trick up our sleeve; we wanted to get at his *soul,* no doubt, and do it the white monkey's damage. We wanted to get at his heart, did we? But his heart was an obsidian knife.

He hated us, and gave off a black steam of hate, that filled the *patio* and made one feel sick. He did not come to the kitchen, he did not carry the water. Leave him alone.

At lunch-time on Monday he said he wanted to leave. Why? He said he wanted to go back to his village.

Very well. He was to wait just a few days, till another *mozo* was found.

At this a glance of pure, reptilian hate from his black eyes.

He sat motionless on his bench all the afternoon, in the Indian stupor of gloom and profound hate. In the evening, he cheered up a little and said he would stay on, at least till Easter.

Tuesday morning. More stupor and gloom and hate. He wanted to go back to his village at once. All right! No one wanted to keep him against his will Another *mozo* would be found at once.

He went off in the numb stupor of gloom and bate, a very potent hate that could affect one in the pit of one's stomach with nausea.

Tuesday afternoon, and he thought he would stay.

Wednesday morning, and he wanted to go.

Very good. Inquiries made; another *mozo* was coming on Friday morning. It was settled.

Thursday was *fiesta*. Wednesday, therefore, we would go to market, the Niñia — that is the mistress — myself and Rosalino with the basket. He loved to go to market with the *patrones*. We would give him money and send him off to bargain for oranges, *pitahayas,* potatoes, eggs, a chicken, and so forth. This he simply loved to do. It put him into a temper to see us buying without bargaining, and paying ghastly prices.

He bargained away, silent almost, muttering darkly It took him a long time, but he had far greater success than even Natividad, the cook. And he came back in triumph, with much stuff and little money spent.

So again that afternoon, he was staying on The spell was wearing off.

The Indians of the hills have a heavy, intense sort of attachment to their villages; Rosalino had not been out of the little city for two years Suddenly finding himself in Huayapa, a real Indian hill-village, the black Indian gloom of nostalgia must have made a crack in his spirits. But he had been perfectly cheerful — perhaps too cheerful — till we got home.

Again, the Señorita had taken a photograph of him. They are all crazy to have their photographs taken. I had given him in envelope and a stamp, to send a photograph to his mother. Because in his village he had a widow mother, a brother, and a married sister. The family owned a bit of land, with orange-trees. The best oranges come from the hills, where it is cooler. Seeing the photographs, the mother, who had completely forgotten her son, as far as any keen remembering goes, suddenly, a cracker going off inside her, wanted him: at that very moment. So she sent an urgent message.

But already it was Wednesday afternoon. Arrived a little fellow in white clothes, smiling hard. It was the brother from the hills. Now, we thought, Rosalino will have someone to walk back with. On Friday, after the *fiesta,* he would go.

Thursday, he escorted us with the basket to the *fiesta.* He bargained for flowers, and for a *sarape* which he didn't get, for a carved *jicara* which he did get, and for a number of toys. He and the Niñia and the Señorita ate a great wafer of a pancake with sweet stuff on it. The basket grew heavy. The brother appeared, to carry the hen and the extra things. Bliss.

He was perfectly happy again. He didn't want to go on Friday; he didn't want to go at all. He wanted to stay with us and come with us to England when we went home.

So, another trip to the friend, the Mexican, who had found us the other *mozo.* Now to put off the other boy again: but then, they are like that.

And the Mexican, who had known Rosalino when he first came down from the hills and could speak no Spanish, told us another thing about him.

In the last revolution — a year ago — the revolutionaries of the winning side wanted more soldiers from the hills. The *alcalde* of the hill-village was told to pick out young men and send them down to the barracks in the city. Rosalino was among the chosen.

But Rosalino refused, said again *No quiero!* He is one of those, like myself, who have a horror of serving in a mass of men, or even of being mixed up with a mass of men.

He obstinately refused. Whereupon the recruiting soldiers beat him with the butts of their rifles till he lay unconscious, apparently dead.

Then, because they wanted him at once, and he would now be no good for some time, with his injured back, they left him, to get the revolution over without him.

This explains his fear of furniture-carrying, and his fear of being 'caught'.

Yet that little Aurelio, the friend's *mozo,* who is not above four feet six in height, a tiny fellow, fared even worse, He, too, is from the hills. In this village, a cousin of his gave some information to the *losing* side in the revolution. The cousin wisely disappeared.

But in the city, the winning side seized Aurelio, since he was the *cousin* of the delinquent. In spite of the fact that he was the faithful *mozo* of a foreign resident, he was flung into prison. Prisoners in prison are not fed. Either friends or relatives bring them food, or they go very, very thin. Aurelio had a married sister in town, but *she* was afraid to go to the prison lest she and her husband should be seized. The master, then, sent his new *mozo* twice a day to the prison with a basket; the huge, huge prison, for this little town of a few thousands.

Meanwhile the master struggled and struggled with the 'authorities' — friends of the people — for Aurelio's release. Nothing to be done.

One day the new *mozo* arrived at the prison with the basket, to find no Aurelio. A friendly soldier gave the message Aurelio had left. *'Adios a mi patrón. Me llevan.'* Oh, fatal words: *'Me llevan.'* — They are taking me off. The master rushed to the train: it had gone, with the dwarf; plucky little *mozo,* into the void.

Months later, Aurelio reappeared. He was in rags, haggard, and his dark throat was Swollen up to the ears. He had been taken off, two hundred miles into Vera Cruz State. He had been hung up by the neck, with a fixed knot, and left hanging for hours. Why? To make the cousin come and save his relative: put his own neck into a running noose. To make the absolutely innocent fellow confess: what? Everybody knew he was innocent. At any rate, to teach everybody better next time. Oh, brotherly teaching!

Aurello escaped, and took to the mountains. Sturdy little dwarf of a fellow, he made his way back, begging *tortillas* at the villages, and arrived, haggard, with a great swollen neck, to find his master waiting, and another 'party' in power. More friends of the people.

Tomorrow is another day. The master nursed Aurelio well, and Aurelio is a strong, if tiny, fellow, with big, brilliant black eyes that for the moment will trust a foreigner, but none of his own people. A dwarf in stature, but perfectly made, and very strong. And very, intelligent, far more quick and intelligent than Rosalino.

Is it any wonder that Aurelio and Rosalino, when they see the soldiers with guns on their shoulders marching towards the prison with some blanched prisoner between them — and one sees it every few days — stand and gaze in a blank kind of horror, and look at the *patrón,* to see if there is any refuge?

Not to be *caught!* Not to be *caught!* It must have been the prevailing motive of Indian-Mexico life since long before Montezuma marched his prisoners to sacrifice.

MARKET DAY

THIS is the last Saturday before Christmas. The next year will be momentous, one feels. This year is nearly gone. Dawn was windy, shaking the leaves, and the rising sun shone under a gap of yellow cloud. But at once it touched the yellow flowers that rise above the *patio* wall, and the swaying, glowing magenta of the bougainvillea, and the fierce red outbursts of the poinsettia. The poinsettia is very splendid, the flowers very big, and of a sure stainless red. They call them Noche Buenas, flowers of Christmas Eve. These tufts throw out their scarlet sharply, like red birds ruffling in the wind of dawn as if going to bathe, all their feathers alert. This for Christmas, instead of holly-berries. Christmas seems to need a red herald.

The yucca is tall, higher than the house. It is, too, in flower, hanging an arm's-length of soft creamy bells, like a yard-long grape-cluster of foam. And the waxy bells break on their stems in the wind, fall noiselessly from the long creamy bunch, that hardly sways.

The coffee-berries are turning red. The hibiscus flowers, rose-coloured, sway at the tips of the thin branches, in rosettes of soft red.

In the second *patio,* there is a tall tree of the flimsy acacia sort. Above itself it puts up whitish fingers of flowers, naked on the blue sky. And in the wind these fingers of flowers in the bare blue sky, sway, sway with the reeling, roundward motion of tree-tips in a wind.

A restless morning, with clouds lower down, moving also with a larger roundward motion. Everything moving. Best to go out in motion too, the slow roundward motion like the hawks.

Everything seems slowly to circle and hover towards a central point, the clouds, the mountains round the valley, the dust that rises, the big, beautiful, white-barred hawks, *gabilanes,* and even the snow-white flakes of flowers upon the dim *palo-blanco* tree. Even the organ cactus, rising in stock-straight clumps, and the candelabrum cactus, seem to be slowly wheeling and pivoting upon a centre, close upon it.

Strange that we should think in straight lines, when there are none, and talk of straight courses, when every course, sooner or later, is seen to be making the sweep round, swooping upon the centre. When space is curved, and the cosmos is sphere within sphere, and the way from any point to any other point is round the bend of the inevitable, that turns as the tips of the broad wings of the hawk turn upwards, leaning upon the air like the invisible half of the ellipse. If I have a way to go, it will be round the swoop of a bend impinging centripetal towards the centre. The straight course is backed out in wounds, against the will of the world.

Yet the dust advances like a ghost along the road, down the valley plain. The dry turf of the valley-bed, gleams like soft tin, sunlit and pinkish ochre, spreading wide between the mountains that seem to emit their own darkness, a dark-blue vapour translucent, sombring them from the humped crests downwards. The many-pleated, noiseless mountains of Mexico.

And away on the footslope lie the white specks of Huayapa, among its lake of trees. It is Saturday, and the white dots of men are threading down the trail over the bare humps to the plain, following the dark twinkle-movement of asses, the dark nodding of the woman's head as she rides between the baskets. Saturday and market-day, and morning, so the white specks of men, like sea-gulls on plough-land, come ebbing like sparks from the palo-blanco, over the fawn undulating of the valley slope.

They are dressed in snow-white cotton, and they lift their knees in the Indian trot, following the ass where the woman sits perched between the huge baskets, her child tight in the *rebozo,* at the brown breast. And girls in long, full, soiled cotton skirts running, trotting, ebbing along after the twinkle-movement of the ass. Down they come in families, in clusters, in solitary ones, threading with ebbing, running, barefoot movement noiseless towards the town, that blows the bubbles of its church-domes above the stagnant green of trees, away under the opposite fawn-skin hills.

But down the valley middle comes the big road, almost straight. You will know it by the tall walking of the dust, that hastens also towards the town, overtaking, overpassing everybody. Overpassing all the dark little figures and the white specks that thread tinily, in a sort of underworld, to the town.

From the valley villages and from the mountains the peasants and the Indians are coming in with supplies, the road is like a pilgrimage, with the dust in greatest haste, dashing for town. Dark-eared asses and running men, running women, running girls, running lads, twinkling donkeys ambling on fine little feet, under twin baskets with tomatoes and gourds, twin great nets of bubble-shaped jars, twin bundles of neat-cut faggots of wood, neat as bunches of cigarettes, and twin net-sacks of charcoal. Donkeys, mules, on they come, great pannier baskets making a rhythm under the perched woman, great bundles bouncing against the sides of the slim-footed animals. A baby donkey trotting naked after its piled-up dam, a white, sandal-footed man following with the silent Indian haste, and a girl running again on light feet.

Onwards, on a strange current of haste. And slowly rowing among the foot-travel, the ox-wagons rolling solid wheels below the high net of the body. Slow oxen, with heads pressed down nosing to the earth, swaying, swaying their great horns as a snake sways itself, the shovel-shaped collar of solid wood pressing down on their necks like a scoop. On, on between the burnt-up turf and the solid, monumental green of the organ cactus. Past the rocks and the floating *palo-blanco* flowers, past the towsled dust of the mesquite bushes. While the dust once more, in a greater haste than anyone, comes tall and rapid down the road, overpowering and obscuring all the little people, as in a cataclysm.

They are mostly small people, of the Zapotec race: small men with lifted chests and quick, lifted knees, advancing with heavy energy in the midst of dust. And quiet, small, round-headed women running barefoot, tightening their blue *rebozos* round their shoulders, so often with a baby in the fold. The white cotton clothes of the men so white that their faces are invisible places of darkness under their big hats. Clothed darkness, faces of night, quickly, silently, with inexhaustible energy advancing to the town.

And many of the *serranos,* the Indians from the hills, wearing their little conical black felt hats, seem capped with night, above the straight white shoulders. Some have come far, walking all yesterday in their little black hats and black-sheathed sandals. Tomorrow they will walk back. And their eyes will be just the same, black and bright and wild, in the dark faces. They have no goal, any more than the hawks in the air, and no course to run, any more than the clouds.

The market is a huge roofed-in place. Most extraordinary is the noise that comes out, as you pass along the adjacent street. It is a huge noise, yet you may never notice it. It sounds as if all the ghosts in the world were talking to one another, in ghost-voices, within the darkness of the market structure. It is a noise something like rain, or banana leaves in a wind. The market, full of Indians, dark-faced, silent-footed, hush-spoken, but pressing in in countless numbers The queer hissing murmurs of the Zapotec *idioma*, among the sounds of Spanish, the quiet, aside, voices of the Mixtecas.

To buy and to sell, but above all, to commingle. In the old world, men make themselves two great excuses for coming together to a centre, and commingling freely in a mixed, unsuspicious host. Market and religion. These alone bring men, unarmed, together since time began. A little load of firewood, a woven blanket, a few eggs and tomatoes are excuse enough for men, women, and children to cross the foot-weary miles of valley and mountain. To buy, to sell, to barter, to exchange. To exchange, above all things, human contact.

That is why they like you to bargain, even if it's only the difference of a *centavo*. Round the centre of the covered market where there is a basin of water, are the flowers: red, white, pink roses in heaps, many-coloured little carnations, poppies, bits of larkspur, lemon and orange marigolds, buds of madonna lilies, pansies, a few forget-me-nots. They don't bring the tropical flowers. Only the lilies come wild from the hills, and the mauve red orchids.

'How much this bunch of cherry-pie heliotrope?'

'Fifteen *centavos*.'

'Ten.'

'Fifteen.'

You put back the cherry-pie, and depart. But the woman is quite content. The contact, so short even, brisked her up.

'Pinks?'

'The red one, Señorita? Thirty *centavos*.'

'No. I don't want red ones. The mixed.'

'Ah!' The woman seizes a handful of little carnations of all colours, carefully puts them together. 'Look, Señorita! No more?'

'No, no more. How much?'

'The same. Thirty *centavos*.'

'It is much.'

'No, Señorita, it is not much. Look at this little bunch. It is eight centavos.' — Displays a scrappy little bunch. 'Come then, twenty-five.'

'No! Twenty-two.'

'Look!' She gathers up three or four more flowers, and claps them to the bunch. 'Two *reales*, Señorita.'

It is a bargain. Off you go with multicoloured pinks, and the woman has had one more moment of contact, with a stranger, a perfect stranger. An intermingling of voices, a threading together of different wills. It is life. The *centavos* are an excuse.

The stalls go off in straight lines, to the right, brilliant vegetables, to the left, bread and sweet buns. Away at the one end, cheese, butter, eggs, chicken, turkeys, meat. At the other, the native-woven blankets and rebozos, skirts, shirts, handkerchiefs. Down the far-side, sandals and leather things. The sarape men spy you, and whistle to you like ferocious birds, and call 'Señor! Señor! Look!' Then with violence one flings open a dazzling blanket, while another whistles more ear-piercingly still, to make you look at his blanket. It is the veritable den of lions and tigers, that spot where the *sarape* men have their blankets piled on the ground. You shake your head, and flee.

To find yourself in the leather avenue.

'Señor! Señor! Look! *Huaraches*! Very fine, very finely made! Look, Señor!'

The fat leather man jumps up and holds a pair of sandals at one's breast. They are of narrow woven strips of leather, in the newest Paris style, but a style ancient to these natives. You take them in your hand, and look at them quizzically, while the fat wife of the *huarache* man reiterates, 'Very fine work. Very fine. Much work!'

Leather men usually seem to have their wives with them.

'How much?'

'Twenty *reales*.'

'Twenty!' — in a voice of surprise and pained indignation.

'How much do you give?'

You refuse to answer. Instead you put the *huaraches* to your nose. The *huarache* man looks at his wife, and they laugh aloud.

'They smell,' you say.

'No, Señor, they don't smell!' — and the two go off into fits of laughter.

'Yes, they smell. It is not American leather.'

'Yes, Señor, it is American leather. They don't smell, Señor. No, they don't smell.' He coaxes you till you wouldn't believe your own nose.

'Yes, they smell.'

'How much do you give?'

'Nothing, because they smell.'

And you give another sniff, though it is painfully unnecessary. And in spite of your refusal to bid, the man and wife go into fits of laughter to see you painfully snifling.

You lay down the sandals and shake your head.

'How much do you offer?' reiterates the man, gaily.

You shake your head mournfully, and move away. The leather man and his wife look at one another and go off into another fit of laughter, because you smelt the *huaraches,* and said they stank.

They did. The natives use human excrement for tanning leather. When Bernal Diaz came with Cortés to the great market-place of Mexico City, in Montezuma's day, he saw the little pots of human excrement in rows for sale, and the leather-makers going round sniffing to see which was the best, before they paid for it. It staggered even a fifteenth-century Spaniard. Yet my leather man and his wife think it screamingly funny that I smell the *huaraches* before buying them. Everything has its own smell, and the natural smell of *huaraches* is what it is. You might as well quarrel with an onion for smelling like an onion.

The great press of the quiet natives, some of them bright and clean, many in old rags, the brown flesh showing through the rents in the dirty cotton. Many wild hillmen, in their little hats of conical black felt, with their wild, staring eyes. And as they cluster round the hat-stall, in a long, long suspense of indecision before they can commit themselves, trying on a new hat, their black hair gleams blue-black, and falls thick and rich over their foreheads, like gleaming bluey-black feathers.

And one is reminded again of the blue-haired Buddha, with the lotus at his navel.

But already the fleas are travelling under one's clothing.

Market lasts all day. The native inns are great dreary yards with little sheds, and little rooms around. Some men and families who have come from far, will sleep in one or other of the little stall-like rooms. Many will sleep on the stones, on the earth, round the market, anywhere. But the asses are there by the hundred, crowded in the inn-yards, drooping their ears with the eternal patience of the beast that knows better than any other beast that every road curves round to the same centre of rest, and hither and thither means nothing.

And towards nightfall the dusty road will be thronged with shadowy people and unladen asses and new-laden mules, urging silently into the country again, their backs to the town, glad to get away from the town, to see the cactus and the pleated hills, and the trees that mean a village. In some village they will lie under a tree, or under a wall, and sleep. Then the next day, home.

It is fulfilled, what they came to market for. They have sold and bought. But more than that, they have had their moment of contact and centripetal flow. They have been part of a great stream of men flowing to a centre, to the vortex of the market-place. And here they have felt life concentrate upon them, they have been jammed between the soft hot bodies of strange men come from afar, they have had the sound of strangers' voices in their ears, they have asked and been answered in unaccustomed ways.

There is no goal, and no abiding-place, and nothing is fixed, not even the cathedral towers. The cathedral towers are slowly leaning, seeking the curve of return. As the natives curved in a strong swirl, towards the vortex of the market. Then on a strong swerve of repulsion, curved out and away again, into space.

Nothing but the touch, the spark of contact. That, no more. That, which is most elusive, still the only treasure. Come, and gone, and yet the clue itself.

True, folded up in the handkerchief inside the shirt, are the copper *centavos,* and maybe a few silver *pesos.* But these too will disappear as the stars disappear at daybreak, as they are meant to disappear. Everything is meant to disappear. Every curve plunges into the vortex and is lost, re-emerges with a certain relief and takes to the open, and there is lost again.

Only that which is utterly intangible, matters. The contact, the spark of exchange. That which can never be fastened upon, for ever gone, for ever coming, never to be detained: the spark of contact.

Like the evening star, when it is neither night nor day. Like the evening star, between the sun and the moon, and swayed by neither of them. The flashing intermediary, the evening star that is seen only at the dividing of the day and night, but then is more wonderful than either.

INDIANS AND ENTERTAINMENT

WE go to the theatre to be entertained. It may be *The Potters,* it may be Max Reinhardt, *King Lear,* or *Electra.* All entertainment.

We want to be taken out of ourselves. Or not entirely that. We want to become spectators at our own show. We lean down from the plush seats like little gods in a democratic heaven, and see ourselves away below there, on the world of the stage, in a brilliant artificial sunlight, behaving comically absurdly, like Pa Potter, yet getting away with it, or behaving tragically absurdly, like King Lear, and not getting away with it: rather proud of not getting away with it.

We see ourselves: we survey ourselves: we laugh at ourselves: we weep over ourselves: we are the gods above of our own destinies. Which is very entertaining.

The secret of it all, is that we detach ourselves from the painful and always sordid trammels of actual existence, and become creatures of memory and of spirit-like consciousness. We are the gods and there's the machine, down below us. Down below, on the stage, our mechanical or earth-bound self stutters or raves, Pa Potter or King Lear. But however Potterish or Learian we may be, while we sit aloft in plush seats we are creatures of pure consciousness, pure spirit, surveying those selves of clay who are so absurd or so tragic, below.

Even a little girl trailing a long skirt and playing at being Mrs Paradiso next door, is enjoying the same sensation. From her childish little consciousness she is making Mrs Paradiso, creating her according to her own fancy. It is the little individual consciousness lording it, for the moment, over the actually tiresome and inflexible world of actuality. Mrs Paradiso in the flesh is a thing to fear. But if I can play at being Mrs Paradiso, why, then I am a little Lord Almighty, and Mrs Paradiso is but a creation from my consciousness.

The audience in the theatre is a little democracy of the ideal consciousness. They all sit there, gods of the ideal mind, and survey with laughter or tears the realm of actuality.

Which is very soothing and satisfying so long as you believe that the ideal mind is the actual arbiter. So long as you instinctively feel that there is some supreme, universal Ideal Consciousness swaying all destiny.

When you begin to have misgivings, you sit rather uneasily on your plush seat.

Nobody really believes that destiny is an accident. The very fact that day keeps on following night; and summer winter, establishes the belief in universal law, and from this to a belief in some great hidden mind in the universe is an inevitable step for us.

A few people, the so-called advanced, have grown uneasy in their bones about the Universal Mind. But the mass are absolutely convinced. And every member of the mass is absolutely convinced that he is part and parcel of this Universal Mind. Hence his joy at the theatre. His even greater joy at the cinematograph.

In the moving pictures he has detached himself even further from the solid stuff of earth. There, the people are truly shadows: the shadow-pictures are thinkings of his mind. They live in the rapid and kaleidoscopic realm of the abstract. And the individual watching the shadow-spectacle sits a very god, in an orgy of abstraction, actually dissolved into delighted, watchful spirit. And if his best girl sits beside him, she vibrates in the same ether, and triumphs in the same orgy of abstraction. No wonder this passion of dramatic abstraction becomes a lust.

That is our idea of entertainment.

You come to the Indian and ask him about his. He hasn't got one.

The Indians dance around the drum, singing. They have their great spectacular dances, Eagle dance, Corn dance. They have the dancing, singing procession between the fires at Christmas. They have their sacred races, down the long track.

White people always, or nearly always, write sentimentally about the Indians. Even a man like Adolf Bandelier. He was not a sentimental man. On the contrary. Yet the sentimentality creeps in, when he writes about the thing he knows best, the Indian.

So it is with all of them, anthropologists and myth-transcribers and all. There is that creeping note of sentimentality through it all, which makes one shrug one's shoulders and wish the Indians to hell, along with a lot of other bunk.

You've got to de-bunk the Indians, as you've got to debunk the Cowboy. When you've de-bunked the Cowboy, there's not much left. But the Indian bunk is not the Indian's invention. It is ours.

It is almost impossible for the white people to approach the Indian without either sentimentality or dislike. The common healthy vulgar white usually feels a certain native dislike of these drumming aboriginals. The highbrow invariably lapses into sentimentalism like the smell of bad eggs.

Why? — Both the reactions are due to the same feeling in the white man. The Indian is not in line with us. He's not coming our way. His whole being is going a different way from ours. And the minute you set eyes on him you know it. And then, there's only two things you can do. You can detest the insidious devil for having an utterly different way from our own great way. Or you can perform the mental trick, and fool yourself and others into believing that the befeathered and bedaubed darling is nearer to the true ideal gods than we are.

This last is just bunk, and a lie. But it saves our appearances. The former feeling, of instinctive but tolerant repulsion, the feeling of most ordinary farmers and ranchers and mere individuals in the west, is quite natural, it is only honesty to admit it.

270

The Indian way of consciousness is different from and fatal to our way of consciousness. Our way of consciousness is different from and fatal to the Indian. The two ways, the two streams are never to be united. They are not even to be reconciled. There is no bridge, no canal of connexion.

The sooner we realise, and accept, this, the better, and leave off trying, with fulsome sentimentalism, to render the Indian in our own terms.

The acceptance of the great paradox of human consciousness is the first step to a new accomplishment.

The consciousness of one branch of humanity is the annihilation of the consciousness of another branch. That is, the life of the Indian, his stream of conscious being, is just death to the white man. And we can understand the consciousness of the Indian only in terms of the death of our consciousness.

And let not this be turned into another sentimentalism. Because the same paradox exists between the consciousness of white men and Hindoos or Polynesians or Bantu. It is the eternal paradox of human consciousness. To pretend that all is one stream is to cause chaos and nullity. To pretend to express one stream in terms of another, so as to identify the two, is false and sentimental. The only thing you can do is to have a little Ghost inside you which sees both ways, or even many ways. But a man cannot *belong* to both ways, or to many ways. One man can belong to one great way of consciousness only. He may even change from one way to another. But he cannot go both ways at once. Can't be done. So that, to understand the Indian conception of entertainment, we have to destroy our own conception.

Perhaps the commonest entertainment among the Indians is singing round the drum, at evening, when the day is over. European peasants will sit round the fire and sing. But they sing ballads or lyrics, tales about individuals or individual, personal experience. And each individual identifies the emotion of the song with his own emotion.

Or the wild fishermen of the Outer Hebrides will sing in their intense, concentrated way, by the fire. And again, usually, the songs have words. Yet sometimes not. Sometimes the song has merely sounds, and a marvellous melody. It is the seal drifting in to shore on the wave, or the seal-woman, singing low and secret, departing back from the shores of men, through the surf, back to the realm of the outer beasts that rock on the waters and stare through glistening, vivid, mindless eyes.

This is approaching the Indian song. But even this is pictorial, conceptual far beyond the Indian point. The Hebridean still sees himself human, and *outside* the great naturalistic influences, which are the dramatic circumstances of his life.

The Indian, singing, sings without words or vision. Face lifted and sightless, eyes half closed and visionless, mouth open and speechless, the sounds arise in his chest, from the consciousness in the abdomen. He will tell you it is a song of a man coming home from the bear-hunt: or a song to make rain: or a song to make the corn grow: or even, quite modern, the song of the church bell on Sunday morning.

But the man coming home from the bear-hunt is any man, all men, the bear is any bear, every bear, all bear. There is no individual, isolated experience. It is the hunting, tired, triumphant demon of manhood which has won against the squint-eyed demon of all bears. The experience is generic, non-individual. It is an experience of the human bloodstream, not of the mind or spirit. Hence the subtle incessant, insistent rhythm of the drum, which is pulsated like the heart, and soulless, and unescapable. Hence the strange blind unanimity of the Indian men's voices. The experience is one experience, tribal, of the blood-stream. Hence, to our ears, the absence of melody. Melody is individualized emotion, just as orchestral music is the harmonizing again of many separate, individual emotions or experiences. But the real Indian song is non-individual, and without melody. Strange, clapping, crowing, gurgling sounds, in an unseizable subtle rhythm, the rhythm of the heart in her throes: from a parted entranced mouth, from a chest powerful and free, from an abdomen where the great blood-stream surges in the dark, and surges in its own generic experiences.

This may mean nothing to you. To the ordinary white ear, the Indian's singing is a rather disagreeable howling of dogs to a tom-tom. But if it rouses no other sensation, it rouses a touch of fear amid hostility. Whatever the spirit of man may be, the blood is basic.

Or take the song to make the corn grow. The dark faces stoop forward, in a strange race darkness. The eyelashes droop a little in the dark, ageless, vulnerable faces. The drum is a heart beating with insistent thuds. And the spirits of the men go out on the ether, vibrating in waves from the hot, dark, intentional blood, seeking the creative presence that hovers for ever in the ether, seeking the identification, following on down the mysterious rhythms of the creative pulse, on and on into the germinating quick of the maize that lies under the ground, there, with the throbbing, pulsing, clapping rhythm that comes from the dark, creative blood in man, to stimulate the tremulous, pulsating protoplasm in the seed-germ, till it throws forth its rhythms of creative energy into rising blades of leaf and stem.

Or take the round dances, round the drum. These may or not have a name. The dance, anyhow, is primarily a song. All the men sing in unison, as they move with the soft, yet heavy bird-tread which is the whole of the dance. There is no drama. With bodies bent a little forward, shoulders and breasts loose and heavy, feet powerful but soft, the men tread the rhythm into the centre of the earth. The drums keep up the pulsating heart-beat. The men sing in unison, though some will be silent for moments, or even minutes. And for hours, hours it goes on: the round dance.

It has no name. It has no words. It means nothing at all. There is no spectacle, no spectator.

Yet perhaps it is the most stirring sight in the world, in the dark, near the fire, with the drums going, the pine-trees standing still, the everlasting darkness, and the strange lifting and dropping, surging, crowing, gurgling, aah - h - h - ing! of the male voices.

What are they doing? Who knows? But perhaps they are giving themselves again to the pulsing, incalculable fall of the blood, which for ever seeks to fall to the centre of the earth, while the heart like a planet pulsating in an orbit, keeps up the strange, lonely circulating of the separate human existence.

But what we seek, passively, in sleep, they perhaps seek actively, in the round dance. It is the homeward pulling of the blood, as the feet fall in the soft, heavy rhythm, endlessly. It is the dark blood falling back from the mind, from sight and speech and knowing, back to the great central source where is rest and unspeakable renewal. We whites, creatures of spirit, look upon sleep and see only the dreams that lie as debris of the day, mere bits of wreckage from day-consciousness. We never realize the strange falling back of the dark blood into the downward rhythm, the rhythm of pure forgetting and pure renewal.

Or take the little dances round the fire, the mime dances, when two men put on the eagle feathers and take the shield on their arm, and dance the pantomime of a fight, a spear dance. The rhythm is the same, really, the drums keep up the heart-pulsation, the feet the peculiar bird-tread, the soft, heavy, birdlike step that treads as it were towards the centre of the earth. But there is also the subtle leaping towards each other of the two shield-sheltered naked ones, feathered with the power of an eagle. The leaping together, the coming close, the circling, wary, stealthy avoidance and retreat, always on the same rhythm of drum-beats, the same regular, heavy-soft tread of moccasined feet. It is the dance of the naked blood-being, defending his own isolation in the rhythm of the universe. Not skill nor prowess, not heroism. Not man to man. The creature of the isolated, circulating blood-stream dancing in the peril of his own isolation, in the overweening of his own singleness. The glory in power of the man of single existence. The peril of the man whose heart is suspended, like a single red star, in a great and complex universe, following its own lone course round the invisible sun of our own being, amid the strange wandering array of other hearts.

The other men look on. They may or may not sing. And they see themselves in the power and peril of the lonely heart, the creature of the isolated blood-circuit. They see also, subsidiary, the skill, the agility, the swiftness, the daunting onrush that make the warrior. It is practice as well as mystery.

Or take the big, spectacular dances, like the deer dance, the corn dance. The deer dance in the New Year. The people crowded on the roofs of the pueblo: women, children, old men, watching. The two lines of men, hunters, facing one another. And away at the stream which comes running swiftly from among the cotton-wood trees, the watchers, watching eagerly. At last, over the log bridge, two maidens leading the animals: two maidens in their black shawls and wide white deer-skin top-boots, dancing with a slow, delicate-footed rhythm, facing out, then facing in, and shaking their gourd rattles delicately, marking the rhythm as the drums mark it. Following the maidens, all the animals: men in two columns, and each man an animal, leaning forward each on two slim sticks which are his forelegs, with the deer-skin over him, the antlers branching from his head: or the buffalo hide, from whose shaggy mane his bent head peers out: or a black bear, or a wolf. There they come, the two long lines of wild animals: deer, buffalo, bear, wolf, coyote, and at the back, even tiny boys, as foxes, all stepping on those soft, pointed toes, and moving in slow silence under the winter sun, following the slow, swinging progress of the dancing maidens.

Everything is very soft, subtle, delicate. There is none of the hardness of representation. They are not representing something, not even playing. It is a soft, subtle *being* something.

Yet at the same time it is a game, and a very dramatic naïve spectacle. The old men trot softly alongside, laughing, showing all their wrinkles. But they are experiencing a delicate, wild inward delight, participating in the natural mysteries. They tease the little boys under the fox-skins, and the boys, peeping with their round black eyes, are shy and confused. Yet they keep on in the procession, solemnly, as it moves between the ranks of the wild hunters. And all eyes are round with wonder, and the mystery of participation. Amused, too, on the merely human side of themselves. The gay touch of amusement in buffoonery does not in the least detract from the delicate, pulsing wonder of solemnity, which comes from participating in the ceremony itself

There you have it all, the pantomime, the buffoonery, the human comicalness. But at the same time, quivering bright and wide-eyed in unchangeable delight of solemnity, you have the participating in a natural wonder. The mystery of the wild creatures led from their fastnesses, their wintry retreats and holes in the ground, docilely fascinated by the delicacy and the commanding wistfulness of the maidens who went out to seek them, to seek food in the winter, and who draw after them, in a following, the wild, the timid, the rapacious animals, following in gentle wonder of bewitchment, right into the haunts of men, right into the camp and up to the hunters. The two long lines of wild animals delicately and slowly stepping behind the slow gyration of the two dark-fringed maidens, who shake their gourd rattles in a delicate, quick, three-pulsed rhythm, and never change their wide dark eyes, under the dark fringe. It is the celebration of another triumph, the triumph of the magical wistfulness of women, the wonderful power of her seeking, her yearning, which can draw forth even the bear from his den.

Drama, we are told, has developed out of these ceremonial dances. Greek drama arose this way.

But from the Indian's ceremonial dance to the Greek's early religious ceremony is still a long step. The Greeks usually had some specified deity, some particular god to whom the ceremony was offered. And this god is the witness, the essential audience of the play. The ceremony is *performed* for the gratification of the god. And here you have the beginning of the theatre, with players and audience.

With the Indians it is different. There is strictly no god. The Indian does not consider himself as created, and therefore external to God, or the creature of God. To the Indian there is no conception of a defined God. Creation is a great flood, for ever flowing, in lovely and terrible waves. In everything, the shimmer of creation, and never the finality of the created. Never the distinction between God and God's creation, or between Spirit and Matter. Everything, everything is the wonderful shimmer of creation, it may be a deadly shimmer like lightning or the anger in the little eyes of the bear, it may be the beautiful shimmer of the moving deer, or the pine-boughs softly swaying under snow. Creation contains the unspeakably terrifying enemy, the unspeakably lovely friend, as the maiden who brings us our food in dead of winter, by her passion of tender wistfulness. Yet even this tender wistfulness is the fearful danger of the wild creatures, deer and bear and buffalo, which find their death in it.

There is, in our sense of the word, no God. But all is godly. There is no Great Mind directing the universe. Yet the mystery of creation, the wonder and fascination of creation shimmers in every leaf and stone, in every thorn and bud, in the fangs of the rattlesnake, and in the soft eyes of a fawn. Things utterly opposite are still pure wonder of creation, the yell of the mountain-lion, and the breeze in the aspen leaves. The Apache warrior in his war-paint, shrieking the war-cry and cutting the throats of old women, still he is part of the mystery of creation. He is godly as the growing corn. And the mystery of creation makes us sharpen the knives and point the arrows in utmost determination against him. It must be so. It is part of the wonder. And to every part of the wonder we must answer in kind.

The Indians accept Jesus on the Cross amid all the rest of the wonders. The presence of Jesus on the Cross, or the pitiful Mary Mother, does not in the least prevent the strange intensity of the war-dance. The brave comes home with a scalp. In the morning he goes to Mass. Two mysteries! The soul of man is the theatre in which every mystery is enacted. Jesus, Mary, the snake-dance, red blood on the knife: it is all the rippling of this untellable flood of creation, which, in a narrow sense, we call Nature.

There is no division between actor and audience. It is all one.

There is no God looking on. The only god there is, is involved all the time in the dramatic wonder and inconsistency of creation. God is immersed, as it were, in creation, not to be separated or distinguished. There can be no Ideal God.

And here finally you see the difference between Indian entertainment and even the earliest form of Greek drama. Right at the beginning of Old World dramatic presentation there was the onlooker, if only in the shape of the God Himself, or the Goddess Herself, to whom the dramatic offering was made. And this God or Goddess resolves, at last, into a Mind occupied by some particular thought or idea. And in the long course of evolution, we ourselves become the gods of our own drama. The spectacle is offered to us. And we sit aloft, enthroned in the Mind, dominated by some one exclusive idea, and we judge the show.

There is absolutely none of this in the Indian dance. There is no God. There is no Onlooker. There is no Mind. There is no dominant idea. And finally, there is no judgement: absolutely no judgement.

The Indian is completely embedded in the wonder of his own drama. It is a drama that has no beginning and no end, it is all-inclusive. It can't be judged, because there is nothing outside it, to judge it.

The mind is there merely as a servant, to keep a man pure and true to the mystery, which is always present. The mind bows down before the creative mystery, even of the atrocious Apache warrior. It judges, not the good and the bad, but the lie and the true. The Apache warrior in all his atrocity, is true to his own creative mystery. And as such, he must be fought. But he cannot be called a *lie* on the face of the earth. Hence he cannot be classed among the abominations, the cowards, and the liars: those who betray the wonder.

The Indian, so long as he is pure, has only two great negative commandments.

Thou shalt not lie.

Thou shalt not be a coward.

Positively, his one commandment is:

Thou shalt acknowledge the wonder.

Evil lies in lying and in cowardice. Wickedness lies in witch-craft; that is, in seeking to prostitute the creative wonder to the individual mind and will, the individual conceit.

And virtue? Virtue lies in the heroic response to the creative wonder, the utmost response. In the man, it is a valiant putting forth of all his strength to meet and to run forward with the wonder. In woman it is the putting forth of all herself in a delicate, marvellous sensitiveness, which draws forth the wonder to herself, and draws the man to the wonder in her, as it drew even the wild animals from the lair of winter.

You see this so plainly in the Indian races. Naked and daubed with clay to hide the nakedness, and to take the anointment of the earth; stuck over with bits of fluff of eagle's down, to be anointed with the power of the air, the youths and men whirl down the racing track, in relays They are not racing to win a race. They are not racing for a prize. They are not racing to show their prowess.

They are putting forth all their might, all their strength, in a tension that is half anguish, half ecstasy, in the effort to gather into their souls more and more of the creative fire, the creative energy which shall carry their tribe through the year, through the vicissitudes of the months, on, on, in the unending race of humanity along the track of trackless creation. It is the heroic effort, the sacred heroic effort which men must make and must keep on making. As if hurled from a catapult the Indian youth throws himself along the course, working his body strangely incomprehensibly. And when his turn comes again, he hurls himself forward with greater intensity, to greater speed, driving himself, as it were, into the heart of the fire. And the old men along the track encourage him, urge him with their green twigs, laughingly, mockingly, teasingly, but at the same time with an exquisite pure anxiety and concern.

And he walks away at last, his chest lifting and falling heavily, a strange look in his eyes, having run with the changeless god who will give us nothing unless we overtake him.

DANCE OF THE SPROUTING CORN

PALE, dry, baked earth, that blows into dust of fine sand. Low hills of baked pale earth, sinking heavily, and speckled sparsely with dark dots of cedar bushes. A river on the plain of drought, just a deft of dark, reddish-brown water, almost a flood. And over all, the blue, uneasy, alkaline sky.

A pale, uneven, parched world, where a motor-car rocks and lurches and churns in sand. A world pallid with dryness, inhuman with a faint taste of alkali. Like driving in the bed of a great sea that dried up unthinkable ages ago, and now is drier than any other dryness, yet still reminiscent of the bottom of the sea, sandhills sinking, and straight, cracked mesas, like cracks in the dry-mud bottom of the sea.

So, the mud church standing discreetly outside, just outside the pueblo, not to see too much. And on its façade of mud, under the timbered mud-eaves, two speckled horses rampant, painted by the Indians, a red piebald and a black one.

Swish! Over the logs of the ditch-bridge, where brown water is flowing full. There below is the pueblo, dried mud like mud-pie houses, all squatting in a jumble, prepared to crumble into dust and be invisible, dust to dust returning, earth to earth.

That they don't crumble is the mystery. That these little squarish mud-heaps endure for centuries after centuries, while Greek marble tumbles asunder, and cathedrals totter, is the wonder. But then, the naked human hand with a bit of new soft mud is quicker than time, and defies the centuries.

Roughly the low, square, mud-pie houses make a wide street where all is naked earth save a doorway or a window with a pale-blue sash. At the end of the Street, turn again into a parallel wide, dry street. And there, in the dry, oblong aridity, there tosses a small forest that is alive: and thud — thud — thud goes the drum, and the deep sound of men singing is like the deep soughing of the wind, in the depths of a wood.

You realise that you had heard the drum from the distance, also the deep, distant roar and boom of the singing, but that you had not heeded, as you don't heed the wind.

It all tosses like young, agile trees in a wind. This is the dance of the sprouting corn, and everybody holds a little, beating branch of green pine. Thud - thud — thud — thud — thud! goes the drum, heavily the men hop and hop and hop, sway, sway, sway, sway go the little branches of green pine. It tosses like a little forest, and the deep sound of men's singing is like the booming and tearing of a wind deep inside a forest. They are dancing the Spring Corn Dance.

This is the Wednesday after Easter, after Christ Risen and the corn germinated. They dance on Monday and on Tuesday. Wednesday is the third and last dance of this green resurrection.

You realize the long line of dancers, and a solid cluster of men singing near the drum. You realize the intermittent black-and-white fantasy of the hopping Koshare, the jesters, the Delight-Makers. You become aware of the ripple of bells on the knee-garters of the dancers, a continual pulsing ripple of little bells; and of the sudden wild, whooping yells from near the drum. Then you become aware of the seed-like shudder of the gourd-rattles, as the dance changes, and the swaying of the tufts of green pine-twigs stuck behind the arms of all the dancing men, in the broad green arm-bands.

Gradually come through to you the black, stable solidity of the dancing women, who poise like solid shadow, one woman behind each rippling, leaping male. The long, silky black hair of the women streaming down their backs, and the equally long, streaming, gleaming hair of the males, loose over broad, naked, orange-brown shoulders.

Then the faces, the impassive, rather fat, golden-brown faces of the women, with eyes cast down, crowned above with the green *tableta,* like a flat tiara. Something strange and noble about the impassive, barefoot women in the short black cassocks, as they subtly tread the dance, scarcely moving, and yet edging rhythmically along, swaying from each hand the green spray of pine-twig out — out — out, to the thud of the drum, immediately behind the leaping fox-skin of the men dancers. And all the emerald-green, painted *tabletas,* the flat wooden tiaras shaped like a castle gateway, rise steady and noble from the soft, slightly bowed heads of the women, held by a band under the chin. All the *tabletas* down the line, emerald green, almost steady, while the bright black heads of the men leap softly up and down, between.

Bit by bit you take it in. You cannot get a whole impression, save of some sort of wood tossing, a little forest of trees in motion, with gleaming black hair and gold-ruddy breasts that somehow do not destroy the illusion of forest.

When you look at the women, you forget the men. The bare-armed, bare-legged, barefoot women with streaming hair and lofty green tiaras, impassive, downward-looking faces, twigs swaying outwards from subtle, rhythmic wrists; women clad in the black, prehistoric short gown fastened over one shoulder, leaving the other shoulder bare, and showing at the arm-place a bit of pink or white undershirt; belted also round the waist with a woven woollen sash, scarlet and green on the hand-woven black cassock. The noble, slightly submissive bending of the tiara-ed head. The subtle measure of the bare, breathing, bird-like feet, that are flat, and seem to cleave to earth softly, and softly lift away. The continuous outward swaying of the pine-sprays.

But when you look at the men, you forget the women. The men are naked to the waist, and ruddy-golden, and in the rhythmic hopping leap of the dance their breasts shake downwards, as the strong, heavy body comes down, down, down, down, in the downward plunge of the dance. The black hair streams loose and living down their backs, the black brows are level, the black eyes look out unchanging from under the silky lashes. They are handsome, and absorbed with a deep rhythmic absorption, which still leaves them awake and aware. Down, down, down they drop, on the heavy, ceaseless leap of the dance, and the great necklaces of shell-cores spring on the naked breasts, the neck-shell flaps up and down, the short white kilt of woven stuff with the heavy woollen embroidery, green and red and black, opens and shuts slightly to the strong lifting of the knees: the heavy whitish cords that hang from the kilt-band at the side sway and coil for ever down the side of the right leg, down to the ankle, the bells on the red-woven garters under the knees ripple without end, and the feet, in buckskin boots furred round the ankle with a beautiful band of skunk fur, black with a white tip, come down with a lovely, heavy, soft precision, first one, then the other, dropping always plumb to earth. Slightly bending forward, a black gourd rattle in the right hand, a small green bough in the left, the dancer dances the eternal drooping leap, that brings his life down, down, down, down from the mind, down from the broad, beautiful shaking breast, down to the powerful pivot of the knees, then to the ankles, and plunges deep from the ball of the foot into the earth, towards the earth's red centre, where these men belong, as is signified by the red earth with which they are smeared.

And meanwhile, the shell-cores from the Pacific sway up and down, ceaselessly on their breasts.

Mindless, without effort, under the hot sun, unceasing, yet never perspiring nor even breathing heavily, they dance on and on. Mindless, yet still listening, observing. They hear the deep, surging singing of the bunch of old men, like a great wind soughing. They hear the cries and yells of the man waving his bough by the drum. They catch the word of

277

the song, and at a moment, shudder the black rattles, wheel, and the line breaks, women from men, they thread across to a new formation. And as the men wheel round, their black hair gleams and shakes, and the long fox-skin sways, like a tail. And always, when they form into line again, it is a beautiful long straight line, flexible as life, but straight as rain.

The men round the drum are old, or elderly. They are all in a bunch, and they wear day dress, loose cotton drawers, pink or white cotton shirt, hair tied up behind with the red cords, and banded round the head with a strip of pink rag, or white rag, or blue. There they are, solid like a duster of bees, their black heads with the pink rag circles all close together, swaying their pine-twigs with rhythmic, wind-swept hands, dancing slightly, mostly on the right foot, ceaselessly, and singing, their black bright eyes absorbed, their dark lips pushed out, while the deep strong sound rushes like wind, and the unknown words form themselves in the dark.

Suddenly the solitary man pounding the drum swings his drum round, and begins to pound on the other end, on a higher note, pang - pang - pang! instead of the previous brumm! brumm! brumm! of the bass note. The watchful man next the drummer yells and waves lightly, dancing on bird-feet. The Koshare make strange, eloquent gestures to the sky.

And again the gleaming bronze-and-dark men dancing in the rows shudder their rattles, break the rhythm, change into a queer, beautiful two-step, the long lines suddenly curl into rings, four rings of dancers, the leaping, gleaming-seeming men between the solid subtle, submissive blackness of the women who are crowned with emerald-green tiaras, all going subtly round in rings. Then slowly they change again, and form a star. Then again, unmingling, they come back into rows.

And all the while, all the while the naked Koshare are threading about. Of bronze-and-dark men-dancers there are some forty-two, each with a dark, crowned woman attending him like a shadow. The old men, the bunch of singers in shirts and tied-up black hair, are about sixty in number, or sixty-four. The Koshare are about twenty-four.

They are slim and naked, daubed with black and white earth, their hair daubed white and gathered upwards to a great knot on top of the head, whence springs a tuft of corn-husks, dry corn-leaves. Though they wear nothing but a little black square cloth, front and back, at their middle, they do not seem naked, for some are white with black spots, like a leopard, and some have broad black lines or zigzags on their smeared bodies, and all their faces are blackened with triangle or lines till they look like weird masks. Meanwhile their hair, gathered straight up and daubed white and sticking up from the top of the head with corn-husks, completes the fantasy. They are anything but natural. Like blackened ghosts of a dead corn-cob, tufted at the top.

And all the time, running like queer spotted dogs, they weave nakedly, through the unheeding dance, comical, weird, dancing the dance-step naked and fine, prancing through the lines, up and down the lines, and making fine gestures with their flexible hands, calling something down from the sky, calling something up from the earth, and dancing forward all the time. Suddenly as they catch a word from the singers, name of a star, of a wind, a name for the sun, for a cloud, their hands soar up and gather in the air, soar down with a slow motion. And again, as they catch a word that means earth, earth deeps, water within the earth, or red-earth-quickening, the hands flutter softly down, and draw up the water, draw up the earth-quickening, earth to sky, sky to earth, influences above to influences below, to meet in the germ-quick of corn, where life is.

And as. they dance, the Koshare watch the dancing men. And if a fox-skin is coming loose at the belt, they fasten it as the man dances, or they stoop and tie another man's shoe. For the dancer must not hesitate to the end.

And then, after some forty minutes, the drum stops. Slowly the dancers file into one line, woman behind man, and move away, threading towards their kiva, with no sound but the tinkle of knee-bells in the silence.

But at the same moment the thud of an unseen drum, from beyond, the soughing of deep song approaching from the unseen. It is the other half, the other half of the tribe coming to continue the dance. They appear round the kiva — one Koshare and one dancer leading the rows, the old men all abreast, singing already in a great strong burst.

So, from ten o'clock in the morning till about four in the afternoon, first one-half then the other. Till at last, as the day wanes, the two halves meet, and the two singings like two great winds surge one past the other, and the thicket of the dance becomes a real forest. It is the close of the third day.

Afterwards, the men and women crowd on the roofs of the two low round towers, the kivas, while the Koshare run round jesting and miming, and taking big offerings from the women, loaves of bread and cakes of blue-maize meal. Women come carrying big baskets of bread and guayava, on two hands, an offering.

And the mystery of germination, not procreation, but *putting forth,* resurrection, life springing within the seed, is accomplished. The sky has its fire, its waters, its stars, its wandering electricity, its winds, its fingers of cold. The earth has its reddened body, its invisible hot heart, its inner waters and many juices and unaccountable stuffs. Between them all, the little seed: and also man, like a seed that is busy and aware. And from the heights and from the depths man, the caller, calls: man, the knower, brings down the influences and brings up the influences, with his knowledge: man, so vulnerable, so subject, and yet even in his vulnerability and subjection, a master, commands the invisible influences and is obeyed. Commands in that song, in that rhythmic energy of dance, in that still-submissive mockery of the Kosbare. And he accomplishes his end, as master. He partakes in the springing of the corn, in the rising and budding and earing of the corn. And when he eats his bread at last, he recovers all he once sent forth, and partakes again of the energies he called to the corn, from out of the wide universe.

THE HOPI SNAKE DANCE

THE Hopi country is in Arizona, next the Navajo country, and some seventy miles north of the Santa Fe railroad. The Hopis are Pueblo Indians, village Indians, so their reservation is not large. It consists of a square track of greyish, unappetizing desert, out of which rise three tall arid mesas, broken off in ragged pallid rock. On the top of the mesas perch the ragged, broken, greyish pueblos, identical with the mesas on which they stand.

The nearest village, Walpi, stands in half-ruin high, high on a narrow rock-top where no leaf of life ever was tender. It is all grey, utterly grey, utterly pallid stone and dust, and very narrow. Below it all the stark light of the dry Arizona sun.

Walpi is called the 'first mesa'. And it is at the far edge of Walpi you see the withered beaks and claws and bones of sacrificed eagles, in a rock-cleft under the sky. They sacrifice an eagle each year, on the brink, by rolling him out and crushing him so as to shed

279

no blood. Then they drop his remains down the dry cleft in the promontory's farthest grey tip.

The trail winds on, utterly bumpy and horrible, for thirty miles, past the second mesa, where Chimopova is, on to the third mesa. And on the Sunday afternoon of 17th August black automobile after automobile lurched and crawled across the grey desert, where low, grey, sage-scrub was coming to pallid yellow. Black hood followed crawling after black hood, like a funeral cortège. The motor-cars, with all the tourists wending their way to the third and farthest mesa, thirty miles across this dismal desert where an odd water-windmill spun, and odd patches of corn blew in the strong desert wind, like dark-green women with fringed shawls blowing and fluttering, not far from the foot of the great, grey, up-piled mesa.

The snake dance (I am told) is held once a year, on each of the three mesas in succession. This year of grace 1924 it was to be held in Hotevilla, the last village on the farthest western tip of the third mesa.

On and on bumped the cars. The lonely second mesa lay in the distance. On and on, to the ragged ghost of the third mesa.

The third mesa has two main villages, Oraibi, which is on the near edge, and Hotevilla, on the far. Up scrambles the car, on all its four legs, like a black-beetle straddling past the school-house and store down below, up the bare rock and over the changeless boulders, with a surge and a sickening lurch to the sky-brim, where stands the rather foolish church.

Just beyond, dry, grey, ruined, and apparently abandoned, Oraibi, its few ragged stone huts. All these cars come all this way, and apparently nobody at home.

You climb still, up the shoulder of rock, a few more miles, across the lofty, wind-swept mesa, and so you come to Hotevilla, where the dance is, and where already hundreds of motor-cars are herded in an official camping-ground, among the piñon bushes.

Hotevilla is a tiny little village of grey little houses, raggedly built with undressed stone and mud around a little oblong *plaza,* and partly in ruins. One of the chief two-storey houses on the small square is a ruin, with big square window-holes.

It is a parched, grey country of snakes and eagles, pitched up against the sky. And a few dark-faced, short, thickly built Indians have their few peach trees among the sand, their beans and squashes on the naked sand under the sky, their springs of brackish water.

Three thousand people came to see the little snake dance this year, over miles of desert and bumps. Three thousand, of all sorts, cultured people from New York, Californians, onward-pressing tourists, cowboys, Navajo Indians, even Negroes; fathers, mothers, children, of all ages, colours, sizes of stoutness, dimensions of curiosity.

What had they come for? Mostly to see men hold *live rattlesnakes* in their mouths. *'I never did see a rattlesnake and I'm crazy to see one!'* cried a girl with bobbed hair.

There you have it. People trail hundreds of miles, avidly, to see this circus-performance of men handling live rattlesnakes that may bite them any minute — even do bite them. Some show, that!

There is the other aspect, of the ritual dance. One may look on from the angle of culture, as one looks on while Anna Pavlova dances with the Russian Ballet.

Or there is still another point of view, the religious. Before the snake dance begins, on the Monday, and the spectators are packed thick on the ground round the square, and in the window-holes, and on all the roofs, all sorts of people greedy with curiosity, a little speech is made to them all, asking the audience to be silent and respectful, as this is a sacred religious ceremonial of the Hopi Indians, and not a public entertainment. Therefore, please, no clapping or cheering or applause, but remember you are, as it were, in a church.

The audience accepts the implied rebuke in good faith, and looks round with a grin at the 'church'. But it is a good-humoured, very decent crowd, ready to respect any sort of feelings. And the Indian with his 'religion' is a sort of public pet.

From the cultured point of view, the Hopi snake dance is almost nothing, not much more than a circus turn, or the games that children play in the street. It has none of the impressive beauty of the Corn Dance at Santo Domingo, for example. The big pueblos of Zuni, Santo Domingo, Taos have a cultured instinct which is not revealed in the Hopi snake dance. This last is uncouth rather than beautiful, and rather uncouth in its touch of horror. Hence the thrill, and the crowd.

As a cultured spectacle, it is a circus turn: men actually dancing round with snakes, poisonous snakes, dangling from their mouths.

And as a religious ceremonial: well, you can either be politely tolerant like the crowd to the Hopis; or you must have some spark of understanding of the sort of religion implied.

'Oh, the Indians,' I heard a woman say, 'they believe we are all brothers, the snakes are the Indians' brothers, and the Indians are the snakes' brothers. The Indians would never hurt the snakes, they won't hurt any animal. So the snakes won't bite the Indians. They are all brothers, and none of them hurt anybody.'

This sounds very nice, only more Hindoo than Hopi. The dance itself does not convey much sense of fraternal communion. It is not in the least like St Francis preaching to the birds.

The animistic religion, as we call it, is not the religion of the Spirit. A religion of spirits, yes. But not of Spirit There is no One Spirit. There is no One God. There is no Creator.

There is strictly no God at all: because all is alive. In our conception of religion there exists God and His Creation: two things. We are creatures of God, therefore we pray to God as the Father, the Saviour, the Maker.

But strictly, in the religion of aboriginal America, there is no Father, and no Maker. There is the great living source of life: say the Sun of existence: to which you can no more pray than you can pray to Electricity. And emerging from this Sun are the great potencies, the invincible influences which make shine and warmth and rain. From these great interrelated potencies of rain and heat and thunder emerge the seeds of life itself, corn, and creatures like snakes. And beyond these, men, persons. But all emerge separately. There is no oneness, no sympathetic identifying oneself with the rest. The law of isolation is heavy on every creature.

Now the Sun, the rain, the shine, the thunder, they are alive. But they are not persons or people. They are alive. They are manifestations of living activity. But they are not personal Gods.

Everything lives. Thunder lives, and rain lives, and sunshine lives. But not in the personal sense.

How is man to get himself into relation with the vast living convulsions of rain and thunder and sun, which are conscious and alive and potent, but like vastest of beasts, inscrutable and incomprehensible. How is man to get himself into relation with these, the vastest of cosmic beasts?

It is the problem of the ages of man. Our religion says the cosmos is Matter, to be conquered by the Spirit of Man. The yogi, the fakir, the saint try conquest by abnegation and by psychic powers. The real conquest of the cosmos is made by science.

The American-Indian sees no division into Spirit and Matter, God and not-God. Everything is alive, though not personally so. Thunder is neither Thor nor Zeus. Thunder is the vast living thunder asserting itself like some incomprehensible monsters or some huge reptile-bird of the pristine cosmos.

How to conquer the dragon-mouthed thunder! How to capture the feathered rain!

We make reservoirs, and irrigation ditches and artesian wells. We make lightning conductors, and build vast electric plants. We say it is a matter of science, energy, force.

But the Indian says No! It all lives. We must approach it fairly, with profound respect, but also with desperate courage. Because man must conquer the cosmic monsters of living thunder and live rain. The rain that slides down from its source, and ebbs back subtly, with a strange energy generated between its coming and going, an energy which, even to our science, is of life: this, man has to conquer. The serpent-striped, feathery Rain

We made the conquest by dams and reservoirs and windmills. The Indian, like the old Egyptian, seeks to make the conquest from the mystic will within him, pitted against the Cosmic Dragon.

We must remember, to the animistic vision there is no perfect God behind us, who created us from his knowledge, and foreordained all things. No such God. Behind lies only the terrific, terrible, crude Source, the mystic Sun, the well-head of all things. From this mystic Sun emanate the Dragons, Rain, Wind, Thunder Shine, Light. The Potencies of Powers. These bring forth Earth, then reptiles, birds, and fishes.

The Potencies are not Gods. They are Dragons. The Sun of Creation itself is a dragon most terrible, vast, and most powerful, yet even so, less in being than we. The only gods on earth are men. For gods, like man, do not exist beforehand. They are created and evolved gradually, with aeons of effort, out of the fire and smelting of life. They are the highest thing created, smelted between the furnace of the Life-Sun, and beaten on the anvil of the rain, with hammers or thunder and bellows of rushing wind. The cosmos is a great furnace, a dragon's den, where the heroes and demi-gods, men, forge themselves into being. It is a vast and violent matrix, where souls form like diamonds in earth, under extreme pressure.

So that gods are the outcome, not the origin. And the best gods that have resulted, so far, are men. But gods frail as flowers; which have also the godliness of things that have won perfection out of the terrific dragon-clutch of the cosmos. Men are frail as flowers. Man is as a flower, rain can kill him or succour. him, heat can flick him with a bright tail, and destroy him: or, on the other hand, it can softly call him into existence, out of the egg of chaos. Man is delicate as a flower, godly beyond flowers, and his lordship is a ticklish business.

He has to conquer, and hold his own, and again conquer all the time. Conquer the powers of the cosmos. To us, science is our religion of conquest. Hence through science, we are the conquerors and resultant gods of our earth. But to the Indian, the so-called mechanical processes do not exist. All lives. And the conquest is made by the means of the living will.

This is the religion of all aboriginal America. Peruvian, Aztec, Athabascan: perhaps the aboriginal religion of all the word. In Mexico, men fell into horror of the crude, pristine gods, the dragons. But to the pueblo Indian, the most terrible dragon is still somewhat gentle-hearted.

This brings us back to the Hopi. He has the hardest task, the stubbornest destiny. Some inward fate drove him to the top of these parched mesas, all rocks and eagles, sand and snakes, and wind and sun and alkali. These he had to conquer. Not merely, as we should put it, the natural conditions of the place. But the mysterious life-spirit that reigned there. The eagle and the snake.

It is a destiny as well as another. The destiny of the animistic soul of man, instead of our destiny of Mind and Spirit. We have undertaken the scientific conquest of forces, of natural conditions. It has been comparatively easy, and we are victors. Look at our black motor-cars like beetles working up the rock-face at Oraibi. Look at our three thousand tourists gathered to gaze at the twenty lonely men who dance in the tribe's snake dance!

The Hopi sought the conquest by means of the mystic, living will that is in man, pitted against the living will of the dragon-cosmos. The Egyptians long ago made a partial conquest by the same means. We have made a partial conquest by other means. Our corn doesn't fail us: we have no seven years' famine, and apparently need never have. But the other thing fails us, the strange inward sun of life; the pellucid monster of the rain never shows us his stripes. To us, heaven switches on daylight, or turns on the shower-bath. We little gods are gods of the machine only. It is our highest. Our cosmos is a great engine. And we die of *ennui*. A subtle dragon stings us in the midst of plenty. *Ques vult perdere Deus, dementat prius.*

On the Sunday evening is a first little dance in the plaza at Hotevilla, called the Antelope dance. There is the hot, sandy, oblong little place, with a tuft of green cotton-wood boughs stuck like a plume at the south end, and on the floor at the foot of the green, a little lid of a trap-door. They say the snakes are under there.

They say that the twelve officiating men of the snake clan of the tribe have for nine days been hunting snakes in the rocks. They have been performing the mysteries for nine days, in the kiva, and for two days they have fasted completely. All these days they have tended the snakes, washed them with repeated lustrations, soothed them, and exchanged spirits with them. The spirit of man soothing and seeking and making interchange with the spirits of the snakes. For the snakes are more rudimentary, nearer to the great convulsive powers. Nearer to the nameless Sun, more knowing in the slanting tracks of the rain, the pattering of the invisible feet of the rain-monster from the sky. The snakes are man's next emissaries to the rain-gods. The snakes lie nearer to the source of potency, the dark, lurk-ing, intense sun at the centre of the earth. For to the cultured animist, and the pueblo Indian is such, the earth's dark centre holds its dark sun, our source of isolated being, round which our world coils its folds like a great snake. The snake is nearer the dark sun, and cunning of it.

They say — people say — that rattlesnakes are not travellers. They haunt the same spots on earth, and die there. It is said also that the snake priest (so-called) of the Hopi probably capture the same snakes year after year.

Be that as it may. At sundown before the real dance, there is the little dance called the Antelope Dance. We stand and wait on a house-roof. Behind us is tethered an eagle; rather dishevelled he sits on the coping, and looks at us in unutterable resentment. See him, and see how much 'brotherhood' the Indian feels with animals — at best the silent tolerance that acknowledges dangerous difference. We wait without event. There are no drums, no announcements. Suddenly into the *plaza,* with rude, intense movements, hurried a little file of men. They are smeared all with grey and black, and are naked save for little kilts embroidered like the sacred dance-kilts in other pueblos, red and green and black on a white fibre-cloth. The fox-skins hang behind. The feet of the dancers are pure ash-grey. Their hair is long.

The first is a heavy old man with heavy, long, wild grey hair and heavy fringe. He plods intensely forward in the silence, followed in a sort of circle by the other grey-smeared, long-haired, naked, concentrated men. The oldest men are first: the last is a short-haired boy of fourteen or fifteen. There are only eight men — the so-called antelope priests. They pace round in a circle, rudely, absorbedly, till the first heavy, intense old man with his massive grey hair flowing, comes to the lid on the ground, near the tuft of kiva-boughs. He rapidly shakes from the hollow of his right hand a little white meal on the lid, stamps heavily, with naked right foot, on the meal, so the wood resounds, and paces heavily forward. Each man, to the boy, shakes meal, stamps, paces absorbedly on in the circle, comes to the lid again, shakes meal, stamps, paces absorbedly on, comes a third time to the lid, or trap-door, and this time spits on the lid, stamps, and goes on. And this time the eight men file away behind the lid, between it and the tuft of green boughs. And there they stand in a line, their backs to the kivatuft of green; silent, absorbed, bowing a little to the ground.

Suddenly paces with rude haste another file of men. They are naked, and smeared with red 'medicine', with big black lozenges of smeared paint on their backs. Their wild heavy hair hangs loose, the old, heavy, grey-haired men go first, then the middle-aged, then the young men, then last, two short-haired, slim boys, schoolboys. The hair of the young men, growing after school, is bobbed round.

The grown men are all heavily built, rather short, with heavy but shapely flesh, and rather straight sides. They have not the archaic slim waists of the Taos Indians. They have archaic squareness, and a sensuous heaviness. Their very hair is black, massive, heavy. These are the so-called snake-priests, men of the snake clan. And tonight they are eleven in number.

They pace rapidly round, with that heavy wild silence of concentration characteristic of them, and cast meal and stamp upon the lid, cast meal and stamp in the second round, come round and spit and stamp in the third. For to the savage, the animist, to spit may be a kind of blessing, a communion, a sort of embrace.

The eleven snake-priests form silently in a row, facing the eight grey smeared antelope-priests across the little lid, and bowing forward a little, to earth. Then the antelope-priests, bending forward, begin a low, sombre chant, or call, that sounds wordless, only a deep, low-toned, secret Ay-a! Ay-a! Ay-a! And they bend from right to left, giving two shakes to the little, flat, white rattle in their left hand, at each shake, and stamping the right foot in heavy rhythm. In their right hand, that held the meal, is grasped a little skin bag, perhaps also containing meal.

They lean from right to left, two seed-like shakes of the rattle each time and the heavy rhythmic stamp of the foot, and the low, sombre, secretive chant-call each time. It is a strange low sound, such as we never hear, and it reveals how deep, how deep the men are in the mystery they are practising, how sunk deep below our world, to the world of snakes, and dark ways in the earth, where the roots of corn, and where the little rivers of unchannelled, uncreated life-passion run like dark, trickling lightning, to the roots of the corn and to the feet and loins of men, from the earth's innermost dark sun. They are calling in the deep, almost silent snake-language, to the snakes and the rays of dark emission from the earth's inward 'Sun'.

At this moment, a silence falls on the whole crowd of listeners. It is that famous darkness and silence of Egypt, the touch of the other mystery. The deep concentration of the priests' conquers for a few seconds our white-faced flippancy, and we hear only the deep Hah-ha! Hah-ha! speaking to snakes and the earth's inner core.

This lasts a minute or two. Then the antelope-priests stand bowed and still, and the snake-priests take up the swaying and the deep chant, that sometimes is so low, it is like a mutter underground, inaudible. The rhythm is crude, the swaying unison is all uneven. Culturally, there is nothing, if it were not for that mystic, dark-sacred concentration.

Several times in turn, the two rows of daubed, long-haired, insunk men facing one another take up the swaying and the chant. Then that too is finished. There is a break in the formation. A young snake-priest takes up something that may be a corn-cob — perhaps an antelope-priest hands it to him — and comes forward, with an old, heavy, but still shapely snake-priest behind him dusting his shoulders with the feathers, eagle-feathers presumably, which are the Indians' hollow prayer-sticks. With the heavy, stamping hop they move round in the previous circle, the young priest holding the cob curiously, and the old priest prancing strangely at the young priest's back, in a sort of incantation, and brushing the heavy young shoulders delicately with the prayer-feathers. It is the God-vibration that enters us from behind, and is transmitted to the hands, from the hands to the corn-cob. Several young priests emerge, with the bowed heads and the cob in their hands and the heavy older priests hanging over them behind. They tread round the rough curve and come back to the kiva, take perhaps another cob, and tread round again.

That is all. In ten or fifteen minutes it is over. The two files file rapidly and silently away. A brief, primitive performance.

The crowd disperses. They were not many people. There were no venomous snakes on exhibition, so the mass had nothing to come for. And therefore the curious immersed intensity of the priests was able to conquer the white crowd.

By afternoon of the next day the three thousand people had massed in the little *plaza*, secured themselves places on the roof and in the window-spaces, everywhere, till the small pueblo seemed built of people instead of stones. All sorts of people, hundreds and hundreds of white women, all in breeches like half-men, hundreds and hundreds of men who had been driving motor-cars, then many Navajos, the women in their full, long skirts and tight velvet bodices, the men rather lanky, long-waisted, real nomads. In the hot sun and the wind which blows the sand every day, every day in volumes round the corners, the three thousand tourists sat for hours, waiting for the show. The Indian policeman cleared the central oblong, in front of the kiva. The front rows of onlookers sat thick on the ground. And at last, rather early, because of the masses awaiting them, suddenly, silently, in the same rude haste, the antelope-priests filed absorbedly in, and made the rounds over the lid, as before. Today, the eight antelope-priests were very grey. Their feet ashed pure grey, like suède soft boots: and their lower jaw was pure suède grey, while the rest of their face was blackish. With that pale-grey jaw, they looked like corpse-faces with swathing-bands. And all their bodies ash-grey smeared, with smears of black, and a black cloth today at the loins.

They made their rounds, and took their silent position behind the lid, with backs to the green tuft: an unearthly grey row of men with little skin bags in their hands. They were the lords of shadow, the intermediate twilight, the place of afterlife and before-life, where house the winds of change; Lords of the mysterious, fleeting power of change.

Suddenly, with abrupt silence, in paced the snake-priests, headed by the same heavy man with solid grey hair like iron. Today they were twelve men, from the old one, down to the slight, short-haired, erect boy of fourteen. Twelve men, two for each of the six worlds, or quarters: east, north, south, west, above, and below. And today they were in a queer ecstasy. Their faces were black, showing the whites of the eyes. And they wore small black loin-aprons. They were the hot living men of the darkness, lords of the earth's inner rays, the black sun of the earth's vital core, from which dart the speckled snakes, like beams.

Round they went, in rapid, uneven, silent absorption, the three rounds. Then in a row they faced the eight ash-grey men, across the lid. All kept their heads bowed towards earth, except the young boys.

Then, in the intense, secret, muttering chant the grey men began their leaning from right to left, shaking the hand, one-two, one-two, and bowing the body each time from right to left, left to right, above the lid in the ground, under which were the snakes. And their low, deep, mysterious voices spoke to the spirits under the earth, not to men above the earth.

But the crowd was on tenterhooks for the snakes, and could hardly wait for the mummery to cease. There was an atmosphere of inattention and impatience. But the chant and the swaying passed from the grey men to the black-faced men, and back again, several times.

This was finished. The formation of the lines broke up. There was a slight crowding to the centre, round the lid. The old antelope-priest (so called) was stooping. And before the crowd could realize anything else a young priest emerged, bowing reverently, with the neck of a pale, delicate rattlesnake held between his teeth, the little, naïve, bird-like head of the rattlesnake quite still, near the black cheek, and the long, pale, yellowish, spangled body of the snake dangling like some thick, beautiful cord. On passed the black-faced young priest, with the wondering snake dangling from his mouth, pacing in the original circle, while behind him, leaping almost on his shoulders, was the oldest heavy priest, dusting the young man's shoulders with the feather-prayer-sticks, in an intense, earnest anxiety of concentration such as I have only seen in the old Indian men during a religious dance.

Came another young black-faced man out of the confusion, with another snake dangling and writhing a little. from his mouth, and an elder priest dusting him from behind with the feathers: and then another, and another: till it was all confusion, probably, of six, and then four young priests with snakes dangling from their mouths, going round, apparently, three times in the circle. At the end of the third round the young priest stooped and delicately laid his snake on the earth, waving him away, away, as it were, into the world. He must not wriggle back to the kiva bush.

And after wondering a moment, the pale, delicate snake steered away with a rattlesnake's beautiful movement, rippling and looping, with the small, sensitive head lifted like antennae, across the sand to the massed audience squatting solid on the ground around. Like soft, watery lightning went the wondering snake at the crowd. As he came nearer, the people began to shrink aside, half-mesmerized. But they betrayed no exaggerated fear. And as the little snake drew very near, up rushed one of the two black-faced young priests who held the snakestick, poised a moment over the snake, in the prayer-concentration of reverence which is at the same time conquest, and snatched the pale, long creature delicately from the ground, waving him in a swoop over the heads of the seated crowd, then delicately smoothing down the length of the snake with his left hand, stroking and smoothing and soothing the long, pale, bird-like thing; and returning with it to the kiva, handed it to one of the grey-jawed antelope-priests.

Meanwhile, all the time, the other young priests were emerging with a snake dangling from their mouths. The boy had finished his rounds. He launched his rattlesnake on the ground, like a ship, and like a ship away it steered. In a moment, after it went one of those two black-faced priests who carried snake-sticks and were the snake-catchers. As it neared the crowd, very close, he caught it up and waved it dramatically, his eyes glaring strangely out of his black face. And in the interim that youngest boy had been given a long, handsome bull-snake, by the priest at the hole under the kiva boughs. The bull-snake is not poisonous. It is a constrictor. This one was six feet long, with a sumptuous pattern. It waved its pale belly, and pulled its neck out of the boy's mouth. With two hands he put it back. It pulled itself once more free. Again he got it back, and managed to hold it. And then as he went round in his looping circle, it coiled its handsome folds twice round his knee. He stooped, quietly, and as quietly as if he were untying his garter, he unloosed the folds. And all the time, an old priest was intently brushing the boy's thin straight shoulders with the feathers. And all the time, the snakes seemed strangely gentle, naive, wondering and almost willing, almost in harmony with the man. Which of course was the sacred aim. While the boy's expression remained quite still and simple, as it were candid, in a candour where he and the snake should be in unison. The only dancers who showed signs of being wrought-up were the two young snake-catchers, and one of these, particularly, seemed in a state of actor-like uplift, rather ostentatious. But the old priests had that immersed, religious intentness which is like a spell, something from another world.

The young boy launched his bull-snake. It wanted to go back to the kiva. The snake-catcher drove it gently forward. Away it went, towards the crowd, and at the last minute was caught up into the air. Then this snake was handed to an old man sitting on the ground in the audience, in the front row. He was an old Hopi of the Snake clan.

Snake after snake had been carried round in the circles, dangling by the neck from the mouths of one young priest or another, and writhing and swaying slowly, with the small, delicate snake-head held as if wondering and listening. There had been some very large rattlesnakes, unusually large, two or three handsome bull-snakes, and some racers, whipsnakes. All had been launched, after their circuits in the mouth, all had been caught up by the young priests with the snake-sticks, one or two had been handed to old-snake clan men in the audience, who sat holding them in their arms as men hold a kitten. The most of the snakes, however, had been handed to the grey antelope-men who stood in the row with their backs to the kiva bush. Till some of these ash-smeared men held armfuls of snakes, hanging over their arms like wet washing. Some of the snakes twisted and knotted round one another, showing pale bellies.

Yet most of them hung very still and docile. Docile, almost sympathetic, so that one was struck only by their clean, slim length of snake nudity, their beauty, like soft, quiescent lightning. They were so clean, because they had been washed and anointed and lustrated by the priests, in the days they had been in the kiva.

At last all the snakes had been mouth-carried in the circuits, and had made their little outrunning excursion to the crowd, and had been handed back to the priests in the rear. And now the Indian policemen, Hopi and Navajo, began to clear away the crowd that sat on the ground, five or six rows deep, around the small *plaza*. The snakes were all going to be set free on the ground. We must clear away.

We recoiled to the farther end of the *plaza*. There, two Hopi women were scattering white corn-meal on the sandy ground. And thither came the two snake-catchers, almost at once, with their arms full of snakes. And before we who stood had realized it, the snakes were all writhing and squirming on the ground, in the white dust of meal, a couple of yards from our feet. Then immediately, before they could writhe clear of each other and steer away, they were gently, swiftly snatched up again, and with their arms full of snakes, the two young priests went running out of the *plaza*.

We followed slowly, wondering, towards the western, or north-western edge of the mesa. There the mesa dropped steeply, and a broad trail wound down to the vast hollow of desert brimmed up with strong evening light, up out of which jutted a perspective of sharp rock and further mesas and distant sharp mountains: the great, hollow, rock-wilderness space of that part of Arizona, submerged in light.

Away down the trail, small, dark, naked, rapid figures with arms held close, went the two young men, running swiftly down to the hollow level, and diminishing, running across the hollow towards more stark rocks of the other side. Two small, rapid, intent, dwindling little human figures. The tiny, dark sparks of men. Such specks of gods.

They disappeared, no bigger than stones, behind rocks in shadow. They had gone, it was said, to lay down the snakes before a rock called the snake-shrine, and let them all go free. Free to carry the message and thanks to the dragon-gods who can give and withhold. To carry the human spirit, the human breath, the human prayer, the human gratitude, the human command which had been breathed upon them in the mouths of the priests, transferred into them from those feather-prayer-sticks which the old wise men swept upon the shoulders of the young, snake-bearing men, to carry this back, into the vaster, dimmer, inchoate regions where the monsters of rain and wind alternated in beneficence and wrath. Carry the human prayer and will-power into the holes of the winds, down into the octopus heart of the rain-source. Carry the corn-meal which the women had scattered, back to that terrific, dread, and causeful clark sun which is at the earth's core, that which sends us corn out of the earth's nearness, sends us food or death, according to our strength of vital purpose, our power of sensitive will, our courage.

It is a battle, a wrestling all the time. The Sun, the nameless Sun, source of all things, which we call sun because the other name is too fearful, this, this vast dark protoplasmic sun from which issues all that feeds our life, this original One is all the time willing and unwilling. Systole, diastole, it pulses its willingness and its unwillingness that we should live and move on, from being to being, manhood to further manhood. Man, small, vulnerable man, the farthest adventurer from the dark heart of the first of suns, into the cosmos of creation. Man, the last god won into existence. And all the time, he is sustained and threated, menaced and sustained from the Source, the innermost sun-dragon. And all the time, he must submit and he must conquer. Submit to the strange beneficence from the Source, whose ways are past finding out. And conquer the strange malevolence of the Source, which is past comprehension also.

For the great dragons from which we draw our vitality are all the time willing and unwilling that we should have being. Hence only the heroes snatch manhood, little by little, from the strange den of the Cosmos.

Man, little man, with his consciousness and his will, must both submit to the great origin-powers of his life, and conquer them. Conquered by man who has overcome his fears, the snakes must go back into the earth with his messages of tenderness, of request, and of power. They go back as rays of love to the dark heart of the first of suns. But they go back also as arrows shot clean by man's sapience and courage, into the resistant, malevolent heart of the earth's oldest, stubborn core. In the core of the first of suns, whence man draws his vitality, lies poison as bitter as the rattlesnake's. This poison man must overcome, he must be master of its issue. Because from the first of suns come travelling the rays that make men strong and glad and gods who can range between the known and the unknown. Rays that quiver out of the earth as serpents do, naked with vitality. But each ray charged with poison for the unwary, the irreverent, and the cowardly. Awareness, wariness, is the first virtue in primitive man's morality. And his awareness must travel back and forth, back and forth, from the darkest origins out to the brightest edifices of creation.

And amid all its crudity, and the sensationalism which comes chiefly out of the crowd's desire for thrills, one cannot help pausing in reverence before the delicate, anointed bravery of the snake-priests (so called), with the snakes.

They say the Hopis have a marvellous secret cure for snake-bites. They say the bitten are given an emetic drink, after the dance, by the old women, and that they must lie on the edge of the cuff and vomit, vomit, vomit. I saw none of this. The two snake-men who ran down into the shadow came soon running up again, running all the while, and steering off at a tangent, ran up the mesa once more, but beyond a deep, impassable cleft. And there, when they had come up to our level, we saw them across the cleft distance washing, brown and naked, in a pool; washing off the paint, the medicine, the ecstasy, to come back into daily life and eat food. Because for two days they had eaten nothing, it was said. And for nine days they had been immersed in the mystery of snakes, and fasting in some measure.

Men who have lived many years among the Indians say they do not believe the Hopi have any secret cure. Sometimes priests do die of bites, it is said. But a rattlesnake secretes his poison slowly. Each time he strikes he loses his venom, until if he strikes several times, he has very little wherewithal to poison a man. Not enough, not half enough to kill. His glands must be very full charged with poison, as they are when he merges from winter-sleep, before he can kill a man outright. And even then, he must strike near some artery.

Therefore, during the nine days of the kiva, when the snakes are bathed and lustrated, perhaps they strike their poison away into some inanimate object. And surely they are soothed and calmed with such things as the priests, after centuries of experience, know how to administer to them.

We dam the Nile and take the railway across America. The Hopi smooths the rattlesnake and carries him in his mouth, to send him back into the dark places of the earth, an emissary to the inner powers.

To each sort of man his own achievement, his own victory, his own conquest. To the Hopi, the origins are dark and dual, cruelty is coiled in the very beginnings of all things, and circle after circle creation emerges towards a flickering, revealed Godhead. With Man as the godhead so far achieved, waveringly and for ever incomplete, in this world.

To us and to the Orientals, the Godhead was perfect to start with, and man makes but a mechanical excursion into a created and ordained universe, an excursion of mechanical achievement, and of yearning for the return to the perfect Godhead of the beginning.

To us, God was in the beginning, Paradise and the Golden Age have been long lost, and all we can do is to win back.

To the Hopi, God is not yet, and the Golden Age lies far ahead. Out of the dragon's den of the cosmos, we have wrested only the beginnings of our being, the rudiments of our Godhead.

Between the two visions lies the gulf of mutual negations. But ours was the quickest way, so we are conquerors for the moment.

The American aborigines are radically, innately religious. The fabric of their life is religion. But their religion is animistic, their sources are dark and impersonal, their conflict with their 'gods' is slow, and unceasing.

289

This is true of the settled pueblo Indian and the wandering Navajo, the ancient Maya, and the surviving Aztec. They are all involved at every moment, in their old, struggling religion.

Until they break in a kind of hopelessness under our cheerful, triumphant success. Which is what is rapidly happening. The young Indians who have been to school for many years are losing their religion, becoming discontented, bored, and rootless. An Indian with his own religion inside him *cannot* be bored. The flow of the mystery is too intense all the time, too intense, even, for him to adjust himself to circumstances which really are mechanical. Hence his failure. So he, in his great religious struggle for the Godhead of man, falls back beaten. The Personal God who ordained a mechanical cosmos gave the victory to his sons, a mechanical triumph.

Soon after the dance is over, the Navajo begin to ride down the Western trail, into the light. Their women, with velvet bodices and full, full skirts, silver and turquoise tinkling thick on their breasts, sit back on their horses and ride down the steep slope, looking wonderingly around from their pleasant, broad, nomadic, Mongolian faces. And the men, long, loose, thin, long-waisted, with tall hats on their brows and low-sunk silver belts on their hips, come down to water their horses at the spring. We say they look wild. But they have the remoteness of their religion, their animistic vision, in their eyes, they can't see as we see. And they cannot accept us. They stare at us as the coyotes stare at us: the gulf of mutual negation between us.

So in groups, in pairs, singly, they ride silently down into the lower strata of light, the aboriginal Americans riding into their shut-in reservations. While the white Americans hurry back to their motor-cars, and soon the air buzzes with starting engines, like the biggest of rattlesnakes buzzing.

A LITTLE MOONSHINE WITH LEMON

'Ye Gods, he doth bestride the narrow world
Like a Colossus... !'

THERE IS a bright moon, so that even the vines make a shadow, and the Mediterranean has a broad white shimmer between its dimness. By the shore, the lights of the old houses twinkle quietly, and out of the wall of the headland advances the glare of a locomotive's lamps. It is a feast day, St Catherine's Day, and the men are all sitting round the little tables, down below, drinking wine or vermouth.

And what about the ranch, the little ranch in New Mexico? The time is different there: but I too have drunk my glass to St Catherine, so I can't be bothered to reckon. I consider that there, too, the moon is in the south-east, standing, as it were, over Santa Fé, beyond the bend of those mountains of Picoris.

Sono io ! say the Italians. I am I! Which sounds simpler than it is.

Because which I am I, after all, now that I have drunk a glass also to St Catherine, and the moon shines over the sea, and my thoughts, just because they are fleetingly occupied by the moon on the Mediterranean, and ringing with the last farewell: *Dunque, Signore! di nuovo!* — must needs follow the moon-track south-west, to the great South-west, where the ranch is.

They say: *in vino veritas.* Bah! They say so much! But in the wine of St Catherine, my little ranch, and the three horses down among the timber. Or if it has snowed, the horses are gone away, and it is snow, and the moon shines on the alfalfa slope, between the pines, and the cabins are blind. There is nobody there. Everything shut up. Only the big pine tree in front of the house, standing still and unconcerned, alive.

Perhaps when I have a *Weh* at all, my *Heimweh* is for the tree in front of the house, the overshadowing tree whose green top one never looks at. But on the trunk one hangs the various odds and ends of iron things. It is so near. One goes out of the door, and the tree-trunk is there, like a guardian angel.

The tree-trunk, and the long work table, and the fence! Then beyond, since it is night, and the moon shines, for me at least, away beyond is a light, at Taos, or at Ranchos de Taos. Here, the castle of Noli is on the western skyline. But there, no doubt it has snowed, since even here the wind is cold. There it has snowed, and the nearly full moon blazes wolf-like, as here it never blazes; risen like a were-wolf over the mountains. So there is a faint hoar shagginess of pine trees, away at the foot of the alfalfa field, and a grey gleam of snow in the night, on the level desert, and a ruddy point of human light, in Ranchos de Taos.

And beyond, you see them even if you don't see them, the circling mountains, since there is a moon.

So, one hurries indoors, and throws more logs on the fire. One doesn't either. One hears Giovanni calling from below, to say good-night! He is going down to the village for a spell.

Vado giù Signor Lorenzo! Buona notte!

And the Mediterranean whispers in the distance, a sound like in a shell. And save that somebody is whistling, the night is very bright and still. The Mediterranean, so eternally young, the very symbol of youth! And Italy, so reputedly old, yet for ever so child-like and naïve! Never, never for a moment able to comprehend the wonderful, hoary age of America, the continent of the afterwards.

I wonder if I am here, or if I am just going to bed at the ranch. Perhaps looking in Montgomery Ward's catalogue for something for Christmas, and drinking moonshine and hot water, since it is cold. Go out and look if the chickens are shut up warm: if the horses are in sight: if Susan, the black cow, has gone to her nest among the trees, for the night. Cows don't eat much at night. But Susan will wander in the moon. The moon makes her uneasy. And the horses stamp around the cabins.

In a cold like this, the stars snap like distant coyotes, beyond the moon. And you'll see the shadow of actual coyotes, going across the alfalfa field. And the pine trees make little noises, sudden and stealthy, as if they were walking about. And the place heaves with ghosts. That place, the ranch, heaves with ghosts. But when one has got used to one's own home-ghosts, be they never so many, and so potent, they are like one's own family, but nearer than the blood. It is the ghosts one misses most, the ghosts there, of the Rocky Mountains, that never go beyond the timber and that linger, like the animals, round the water-spring. I know them, they know me: we go well together. But they reproach me for going away. They are resentful too.

Perhaps the snow is in tufts on the greasewood bushes. Perhaps the blue jay falls in a blue metallic cloud out of the pine trees in front of the house, at dawn, in the terrific cold, when the dangerous light comes watchful over the mountains, and touches the desert far-off, far-off, beyond the Rio Grande.

And I, I give it up. There is a choice of vermouth, Marsala, red wine or white. At the ranch, tonight, because it is cold,

I should have moonshine, not very good moonshine, but still warming: with hot water and lemon, and sugar, and a bit of cinnamon from one of those little red Schilling's tins. And I should light my little stove in the bedroom, and let it roar a bit, sucking the wind. Then dark to bed, with all the ghosts of the ranch cosily round me, and sleep till the very coldness of my emerged nose wakes me. Waking, I shall look at once through the glass panels of the bedroom door, and see the trunk of the great pine tree, like a person on guard, and a low star just coming over the mountain, very brilliant, like someone swinging an electric lantern.

Si vedrà la primavera.

Fiorann' i mandorlini -

Ah, well, let it be vermouth, since there's no moonshine with lemon and cinnamon. Supposing I called Giovanni, and told him I wanted:

'Un poco di chiar' di luna, con canella e limone...'

ETRUSCAN PLACES

1

CERVETERI

THE Etruscans, as everyone knows, were the people who occupied the middle of Italy in early Roman days, and whom the Romans, in their usual neighbourly fashion, wiped out entirely in order to make room for Rome with a very big R. They couldn't have wiped them all out, there were too many of them. But they did wipe out the Etruscan existence as a nation and a people. However, this seems to be the inevitable result of expansion with a big E, which is the sole *raison d'être* people like the Romans.

Now, we know nothing about the Etruscans except what we find in their tombs. There are references to them in Latin writers. But of first-hand knowledge we have nothing except what the tombs offer.

So to the tombs we must go: or to the museums containing the things that have been rifled from the tombs.

Myself, the first time I consciously saw Etruscan kings, in the museum at Perugia, I was instinctively attracted to them. And it seems to be that way. Either there is instant sympathy, or instant contempt and indifference. Most people despise everything B.C. that isn't Greek, for the good reason that it ought to be Greek if it isn't. So Etruscan things are put down as a feeble Graeco-Roman imitation. And a great scientific historian like Mommsen hardly allows that the Etruscans existed at all. Their existence was antipathetic to him. The Prussian in him was enthralled by the Prussian in the all-conquering Romans. So being a great scientific historian, he almost denies the very existence of the Etruscan people. He didn't like the idea of them. That was enough for a great scientific historian.

Besides, the Etruscans were vicious. We know it because their enemies and exterminators said so. Just as we knew the unspeakable depths of *our* enemies in the late war. Who isn't vicious to his enemy? To my detractors I am a very effigy of vice *À la bonne heure!*

However, those pure, clean-living, sweet-souled Romans, who smashed nation after nation and crushed the free soul in people after people, And were ruled by Messalina and Heliogabalus and such like snowdrops, they said the Etruscians were vicious. So *basta! Quand le maîparle, tout le monde se tait*. The Etruscans were vicious! The only vicious people on the face of the earth presumably. You and I, dear reader, we are two unsullied snowflakes, aren't we? We have every right to judge.

Myself, however, if the Etruscans were vicious, I'm glad they were. To the Puritan all things are impure as somebody says And those naughty neighbours of Romans at least escaped being Puritans.

But to the tombs, to the tombs! On a sunny April morning we set out for the tombs. From Rome, the eternal city, now in a black bonnet. It was not far to go — about twenty miles over the Campagna towards the sea, on the line to Pisa.

The Campagna, with its great green spread of growing wheat, is almost human again. But still there are damp empty tracts, where now the little narcissus stands in clumps, or covers whole fields. And there are places green and foam-white, all with camomile, on a sunny. morning in early April.

We are going to Cerveteri, which was the ancient Caere, or Cere, and which had a Greek name too, Agylla. It was a gay and gaudy Etruscan city when Rome put up her first few hovels: probably. Anyhow, there are tombs there now.

The inestimable big Italian railway-guide says the station is Palo, and Cerveteri is eight and a half kilometres away: about five miles. But there is a post-omnibus.

We arrive at Palo, a station in nowhere, and ask if there is a bus to Cerveteri. No! An ancient sort of wagon with an ancient white horse stands outside. Where does that go? To Ladispoli. We know we don't want to go to Ladispoli, so we stare at the landscape. Could we get a carriage of any sort? It would be difficult. That is what they always say: difficult! Meaning impossible. At least they won't lift a finger to help. Is there an hotel at Cerveteri? They don't know. They have none of them ever been, though it is only five miles away, and there are tombs. Well, we will leave our two bags at the station. But they cannot accept them. Because they are not locked. But when did a hold-all ever lock? Difficult! Well then, let us leave them, and steal if you want to. Impossible! Such a moral responsibility! Impossible to leave an unlocked small hold-all at the station. So much for the officials!

However, we try the man at the small buffet. He is very laconic, but seems all right. We abandon our things in a corner of the dark little eating-place, and set off on foot. Luckily it is only something after ten in the morning.

A flat, white road with a rather noble avenue of umbrella-pines for the first few hundred yards. A road not far from the sea, a bare, flattish, hot white road with nothing but a tilted oxen-wagon in the distance like a huge snail with four horns. Beside the road the tall asphodel is letting off its spasmodic pink sparks, rather at random, and smelling of cats. Away to the left is the sea, beyond the flat green wheat, the Mediterranean glistening flat and deadish, as it does on the low shores. Ahead are hills, and a ragged bit of a grey village with an ugly big grey building: that is Cerveteri. We trudge on along the dull road. After all, it is only five miles and a bit.

We creep nearer, and climb the ascent. Caere, like most Etruscan cities, lay on the crown of a hill with cliff-like escarpments. Not that this Cerveteri is an Etruscan city. Caere, the Etruscan city, was swallowed by the Romans, and after the fall of the Roman Empire it fell out of existence altogether. But it feebly revived, and today we come to an old Italian village, walled in with grey walls, and having a few new, pink, box-shaped houses and villas outside the walls.

We pass through the gateway, where men are lounging talking and mules are tied up, and in the bits of crooked grey streets look for a place where we can eat. We see the notice, *Vini e Cucina,* Wines and Kitchen; but it is only a deep cavern where mule-drivers are drinking blackish wine.

However, we ask the man who is cleaning the post-omnibus in the street if there is any other place. He says no, so in we go, into the cavern, down a few steps.

Everybody is perfectly friendly. But the food is as usual, meat broth, very weak, with thin macaroni in it: the boiled meat that made the broth: and tripe: also spinach. The broth tastes of nothing, the meat tastes almost of less, the spinach, alas! has been cooked over in the fat skimmed from the boiled beef It is a meal — with a piece of so-called sheep's cheese, that is pure salt and rancidity, and probably comes from Sardinia; and wine that tastes like, and probably is, the black wine of Calabria wetted with a good proportion of water. But it is a meal. We will go to the tombs.

Into the cavern swaggers a spurred shepherd wearing goat-skin trousers with the long, rusty brown goat's hair hanging shaggy from his legs. He grins and drinks wine, and immediately one sees again the shaggy-legged faun. His face is a faun-face, not deadened by morals. He grins quietly, and talks very subduedly, shyly, to the fellow who draws the wine from the barrels. It is obvious fauns are shy, very shy, especially of moderns like ourselves. He glances at us from a corner of his eye, ducks, wipes his mouth on the back of his hand, and is gone, clambering with his hairy legs on to his lean pony, swirling, and rattling away with a neat little clatter of hoofs, under the ramparts and away to the open. He is the faun escaping again out of the city precincts, far more shy and evanescent than any Christian virgin. You cannot hard-boil him.

It occurs to me how rarely one sees the faun-face now, in Italy, that one used to see so often before the war: the brown, rather still, straight-nosed face with a little black moustache and often a little tuft of black beard; yellow eyes, rather shy under long lashes, but able to glare with a queer glare, on occasion; and mobile lips that had a queer way of showing the teeth when talking, bright white teeth. It was an old, old type, and rather common in the South. But now you will hardly see one of these men left, with the unconscious, ungrimacing faun-face. They were all, apparently, killed in the war: they would be sure not to survive such a war. Anyway the last one I know, a handsome fellow of my own age — forty and a bit — is going queer and morose, crushed between war memories, that have revived, and remorseless go-ahead women-folk. Probably when I go South again he will have disappeared. They can't survive, the faun-faced men, with their pure outlines and their strange non-moral calm. Only the deflowered faces survive.

So much for a Maremma shepherd! We went out into the sunny April street of this Cerveteri, Cerevetus, the old Caere. It is a worn-out little knot of streets shut in inside a wall. Rising on the left is the citadel, the acropolis, the high place, that which is the arx in Etruscan cities. But now the high place is forlorn, with a big, weary building like a governor's palace, or a bishop's palace, spreading on the crest behind the castle gate, and a desolate sort of yard tilting below it, surrounded by ragged, ruinous enclosure. It is forlorn beyond words, dead, and still too big for the grey knot of inhabited streets below.

The girl of the cavern, a nice girl but a bad cook, has found us a guide, obviously her brother, to take us to the necropolis. He is a lad of about fourteen, and like everybody in this abandoned place shy and suspicious, holding off. He bids us wait while he runs away somewhere. So we drink coffee in the tiny cafe outside which the motor-omnibus reposes all day long, till the return of our guide and another little boy, who will come with him and see him through. The two boys cotton together, make a little world secure from us, and move on ahead of us, ignoring us as far as possible. The stranger is always a menace. B. and I are two very quiet-mannered harmless men. But that first boy could not have borne to go alone with us. Not alone! He would have been afraid, as if he were in the dark.

They led us out of the only gate of the old town. Mules and ponies were tied up in the sloping, forlorn place outside, and pack-mules arrived, as in Mexico. We turned away to the left, under the rock cliff from whose summit the so-called palace goes up flush, the windows looking out on to the world. It seems as if the Etruscans may once have cut this low rock-face, and as if the whole crown on which the wall-girt village of Cerveteri now stands may once have been the arx, the ark, the inner citadel and holy place of the city of Caere, or Agylla, the splendid Etruscan city, with its Greek quarters. There was a whole suburb of Greek colonists, from Ionia, or perhaps from Athens, in busy Caere when Rome was still a rather crude place. About the year 390 B.C. the Gauls came swooping down on Rome. Then the Romans hurried the Vestal Virgins and other women and children away to

Caere, and the Etruscans took care of them, in their rich city. Perhaps the refugee Vestals were housed on this rock. And perhaps not. The site of Caere may not have been exactly here. Certainly it stretched away on this same hilltop, east and south, occupying the whole of the small plateau, some four or five miles round, and spreading a great city thirty times as big as the present Cerveteri. But the Etruscans built everything of wood — houses, temples — all save walls for fortification, great gates, bridges, and drainage works. So that the Etruscan cities vanished as completely as flowers. Only the tombs, the bulbs, were underground. But the Etruscans built their cities, whenever possible, on a long narrow plateau or headland above the surrounding country, and they liked to have a rocky cliff for their base, as in Cerveteri. Round the summit of this cliff, this headland, went the enclosure wall, sometimes miles of the great cincture. And within the walls they liked to have one inner high place, the arx, the citadel. Then outside they liked to have a sharp dip or ravine, with a parallel hill opposite. And on the parallel hill opposite they liked to have their city of the dead, the necropolis. So they could stand on their ramparts and look over the hollow where the stream flowed among its bushes, across from the city of life, gay with its painted houses and temples, to the near-at-hand city of their dear dead, pleasant with its smooth walks and stone symbols, and painted fronts.

So it is at Cerveteri. From the sea-plain — and the sea was probably a mile or two miles nearer in, in Etruscan days — the land leaves the coast in an easy slope to the low-crowned cliffs of the city. But behind, turning out of the gate away from the sea, you pass under the low but sheer cliff of the town, down the stony road to the little ravine, full of bushes.

Down here in the gully, the town — village, rather — has built its wash-house, and the women are quietly washing the linen. They are good-looking women, of the old world, with that very attractive look of noiselessness and inwardness, which women must have had in the past. As if, within the woman, there were again something to seek, that the eye can never search out. Something that can be lost, but can never be found out.

Up the other side of the ravine is a steep, rocky little climb along a sharp path, the two lads scrambling subduedly ahead. We pass a door cut in the rock-face. I peep in to the damp, dark cell of what was apparently once a tomb. But this must have been for unimportant people, a little room in a cliff-face, now all deserted. The great tombs in the Banditaccia are covered with mounds, tumuli. No one looks at these damp little rooms in the low cliff-face, among the bushes. So I scramble on hastily, after the others.

To emerge on to the open, rough, uncultivated plain. It was like Mexico, on a small scale: the open, abandoned plain; in the distance little, pyramid-shaped mountains set down straight upon the level, in the not-far distance; and between, a mounted shepherd galloping round a flock of mixed sheep and goats, looking very small. It was just like Mexico, only much smaller and more human.

The boys went ahead across the fallow land, where there were many flowers, tiny purple verbena, tiny forget-me-nots, and much wild mignonette, that had a sweet little scent. I asked the boys what they called it. They gave the usual dumb-bell answer: 'It is a flower!' On the heaping banks towards the edge of the ravine the asphodel grew wild and thick, with tall flowers up to my shoulder, pink and rather spasmodic. These asphodels are very noticeable, a great feature in all this coast landscape. I thought the boys surely would have a name for it. But no! Sheepishly they make the same answer: '*È un fiore! Puzza!*' — It is a flower. It stinks! — Both facts being self-evident, there was no contradicting it. Though the smell of the asphodel is not objectionable, to me: and I find the flower, now I know it well, very beautiful, with its way of opening some pale, big, starry pink flowers, and leaving many of its buds shut, with their dark, reddish stripes.

Many people, however, are very disappointed with the Greeks, for having made so much of this flower. It is true, the word 'asphodel' makes one expect some tall and mysterious lily, not this sparky, assertive flower with just a touch of the onion about it. But for me, I don't care for mysterious lilies, not even for that weird shyness the mariposa lily has. And having stood on the rocks in Sicily, with the pink asphodel proudly sticking up like clouds at sea, taller than myself, letting off pink different flowercts with such sharp and vivid *éclat,* and saving up such a store of buds in ear, stripey, I confess I admire the flower. It has a certain reckless glory, such as the Greeks loved.

One man said he thought we were mistaken in calling this the Greek asphodel, as somewhere in Greek the asphodel is called yellow. Therefore, said this scholastic Englishman, the asphodel of the Greeks was probably the single daffodil.

But not it! There is a very nice and silky yellow asphodel on Etna, pure gold. And heaven knows how common the wild daffodil is in Greece. It does not seem a very Mediterranean flower. The narcissus, the polyanthus narcissus, is pure Mediterranean, and Greek. But the daffodil, the Lent lily!

However, trust an Englishman and a modem for wanting to turn the tall, proud, sparky, dare-devil asphodel into the modest daffodil! I believe we don't like the asphodel because we don't like anything proud and sparky. The myrtle opens her blossoms in just the same way as the asphodel, explosively, throwing out the sparks of her stamens. And I believe it was just this that the Greeks *saw.* They were that way themselves.

However, this is all on the way to the tombs: which lie ahead, mushroom-shaped mounds of grass, great mushroom-shaped mounds, along the edge of the ravine. When I say ravine, don't expect a sort of Grand Canyon. Just a modest, Italian sort of ravine-gully, that you could almost jump down.

When we come near we see the mounds have bases of stone masonry, great girdles of carved and bevelled stone, running round touching the earth in flexible, uneven lines, like the girdles on big, uneasy buoys half sunk in the sea. And they are sunk a bit in the ground. And there is an avenue of mounds, with a sunken path between, parallel to the ravine. This was evidently the grand avenue of the necropolis, like the million-dollar cemetery in New Orleans. *Absit omen!*

Between us and the mounds is a barbed-wire fence. There is a wire gate on which it says you mustn't pick the flowers, whatever that may mean, for there are no flowers. And another notice says, you mustn't tip the guide, as he is gratuitous.

The boys run to the new little concrete house just by, and bring the guide: a youth with red eyes and a bandaged hand. He lost a finger on the railway a month ago. He is shy, and muttering, and neither prepossessing nor cheerful, but he turns out quite decent. He brings keys and an acetylene lamp, and we go through the wire gate into the place of tombs.

There is a queer stillness and a curious peaceful repose about the Etruscan places I have been to, quite different from the weirdness of Celtic places, the slightly repellent feeling of Rome and the old Campagna, and the rather horrible feeling of the great pyramid places in Mexico, Teotihuacan and Cholula, and Mitla in the south; or the amiably idolatrous Buddha places in Ceylon. There is a stillness and a softness in these great grassy mounds with their ancient stone girdles, and down the central walk there lingers still a kind of homeliness and happiness. True, it was a still and sunny afternoon in April, and larks rose from the soft grass of the tombs. But there was a stillness and a soothingness in all the air, in that sunken place, and a feeling that it was good for one's soul to be there.

The same when we went down the few steps, and into the chambers of rock, within the tumulus. There is nothing left. It is like a house that has been swept bare: the inmates have left: now it waits for the next comer. But whoever it is that has departed, they have left a pleasant feeling behind them, warm to the heart, and kindly to the bowels.

They are surprisingly big and handsome, these homes of the dead. Cut out of the living rock, they are just like houses. The roof has a beam cut to imitate the roof-beam of the house. It is a house, a home.

As you enter, there are two small chambers, one to the right, one to the left, antechambers. They say that here the ashes of the slaves were deposited, in urns, upon the great benches of rock. For the slaves were always burned, presumably. Whereas at Cerveteri the masters were laid full-length, sometimes in the great stone sarcophagi, sometimes in big coffins of terra-cotta, in all their regalia. But most often they were just laid there on the broad rock-bed that goes round the tomb, and is empty now, laid there calmly upon an open bier, not shut in sarcophagi, but sleeping as if in life.

The central chamber is large; perhaps there is a great square column of rock left in the centre, apparently supporting the solid roof as a roof-tree supports the roof of a house. And all round the chamber goes the broad bed of rock, sometimes a double tier, on which the dead were laid, in their coffins, or lying open upon carved litters of stone or wood, a man glittering in golden armour, or a woman in white and crimson robes, with great necklaces round their necks, and rings on their fingers. Here lay the family, the great chiefs and their wives, the Lucumones, and their sons and daughters, many in one tomb.

Beyond again is a rock doorway, rather narrow, and narrowing upwards, like Egypt. The whole thing suggests Egypt: but on the whole, here all is plain, simple, usually with no decoration, and with those easy natural proportions whose beauty one hardly notices, they come so naturally, physically. It is the natural beauty of proportion of the phallic consciousness, contrasted with the more studied or ecstatic proportion of the mental and spiritual consciousness we are accustomed to.

Through the inner doorway is the last chamber, small and dark and culminative. Facing the door goes the stone bed on which was laid, presumably, the Lucumo and the sacred treasures of the dead, the little bronze ship of death that should bear him over to the other world, the vases of jewels for his arraying, the vases of small dishes, the little bronze statuettes and tools, the weapons, the armour: all the amazing impedimenta of the important dead. Or sometimes in this inner room lay the woman, the great lady, in all her robes, with the mirror in her hand, and her treasures, her jewels and combs and silver boxes of cosmetics, in urns or vases ranged alongside. Splendid was the array they went with, into death.

One of the most important tombs is the tomb of the Tarquins, the family that gave Etruscan kings to early Rome. You go down a flight of steps, and into the underworld home of the Tarchne, as the Etruscans wrote it. In the middle of the great chamber there are two pillars, left from the rock. The walls of the big living-room of the dead Tarquins, if one may put it so, are stuccoed, but there are no paintings. Only there are the writings on the wall, and in the burial niches in the wall above the long double-tier stone bed; little sentences freely written in red paint or black, or scratched in the stucco with the finger, slanting with the real Etruscan carelessness and fullness of life, often running downwards, written from right to left. We can read these debonair inscriptions, that look as if someone had just chalked them up yesterday without a thought, in the archaic Etruscan letters, quite easily. But when we have read them we don't know what they mean. *Avle — Tarchnas — Larthal — Clan.* That is plain enough. But what does it mean? Nobody knows precisely. Names, family names, family connexions, titles of the dead — we may assume so much. 'Aule, son of Larte Tarchna,' say the scientists, having got so far. But we cannot read one single sentence. The Etruscan language is a mystery. Yet in Caesar's day it was the everyday language of the bulk of the people in central Italy — at least, east-central. And many Romans spoke Etruscan as we speak French. Yet now the language is entirely lost. Destiny is a queer thing.

The tomb called the Grotta Bella is interesting because of the low-relief carvings and stucco reliefs on the pillars and the walls round the burial niches and above the stone death-bed that goes round the tomb. The things represented are mostly warriors' arms and insignia: shields, helmets, corselets, greaves for the legs, swords, spears, shoes, belts, the necklace of the noble: and then the sacred drinking bowl, the sceptre, the dog who is man's guardian even on the death journey, the two lions that stand by the gateway of life or death, the triton, or merman, and the goose, the bird that swims on the waters and thrusts its head deep into the flood of the Beginning and the End. All these are represented on the walls. And all these, no doubt, were laid, the actual objects, or figures to represent them, in this tomb. But now nothing is left. But when we remember the great store of treasure that every notable tomb must have contained: and that every large tumulus covered several tombs: and that in the necropolis of Cerveteri we can still discover hundreds of tombs: and that other tombs exist in great numbers on the other side of the old city, towards the sea; we can have an idea of the vast mass of wealth this city could afford to bury with its dead, in days when Rome had very little gold, and even bronze was precious.

The tombs seem so easy and friendly, cut out of rock underground. One does not feel oppressed, descending into them. It must be partly owing to the peculiar charm of natural proportion which is in all Etruscan things of the unspoilt, romanized centuries. There is a simplicity, combined with a most peculiar, free-breasted naturalness and spontaneity, in the shapes and movements of the underworld walls and spaces, that at once reassures the spirit. The Greeks sought to make an impression, and Gothic still more seeks to impress the mind. The Etruscans, no. The things they did, in their easy centuries, are as natural and as easy as breathing. They leave the breast breathing freely and pleasantly, with a certain fullness of life. Even the tombs. And that is the true Etruscan quality ease, naturalness and an abundance of life, no need to force the mind or the soul in any direction.

And death, to the Etruscan, was a pleasant continuance of life, with jewels and wine and flutes playing for the dance. It was neither an ecstasy of bliss, a heaven, nor a purgatory of torment. It was just a natural continuance of the fullness of life. Everything was in terms of life, of living.

Yet everything Etruscan, save the tombs, has been wiped out. It seems strange. One goes out again into the April sunshine, into the sunken road between the soft, grassy-mounded tombs, and as one passes one glances down the steps at the doorless doorways of tombs. It is so still and pleasant and cheerful. The place is so soothing.

B., who has just come back from India, is so surprised to see the phallic stones by the doors of many tombs Why it's like the Shiva lingam at Benares! It's exactly like the lingam stones in the Shiva caves and the Shiva temples!

And that is another curious thing. One can live one's life, and read all the books about India or Etruria, and never read a single word about the thing that impresses one in the very first five minutes, in Benares or in an Etruscan necropolis: that is, the phallic symbol. Here it is, in stone, unmistakable, and everywhere, around these tombs. Here it is, big and little, standing by the doors, or inserted, quite small, into the rock: the phallic stone! Perhaps some tumuli had a great phallic column on the summit: some perhaps by the door.

There are still small phallic stones, only seven or eight inches long, inserted in the rock outside the doors: they always seem to have been outside. And these small lingams look as if they were part of the rock. But no, B. lifts one out. It is cut, and is fitted into a socket, previously cemented in. B. puts the phallic stone back into its socket, where it was placed, probably five or six hundred years before Christ was born.

The big phallic stones that, it is said, probably stood on top of the tumuli, are sometimes carved very beautifully, sometimes with inscriptions. The scientists call them *cippus, cippi*. But surely the cippus is a truncated column used usually as a gravestone: a column quite squat, often square, having been cut across, truncated, to represent maybe a life cut short. Some of the little phallic stones are like this — truncated. But others are tall, huge and decorated, and with the double cone that is surely phallic. And little inserted phallic stones are not cut short.

By the doorway of some tombs there is a carved stone house, or a stone imitation chest with sloping lids like the two sides of the roof of an oblong house. The guide-boy, who works on the railway and is no profound scholar, mutters that every woman's tomb had one of these stone houses or chests over it — over the doorway, he says — and every man's tomb had one of the phallic stones, or lingams. But since the great tombs were family tombs, perhaps they had both.

The stone house, as the boy calls it, suggests the Noah's Ark without the boat part: the Noah's Ark box we had as children, full of animals. And that is what it is, the Ark, the *arx,* the womb. The womb of all the world, that brought forth all the creatures. The womb, the *arx*, where life retreats in the last refuge. The womb, the ark of the covenant, in which lies the mystery of eternal life, the manna and the mysteries. There it is, standing displaced outside the doorway of Etruscan tombs at Cerveteri.

And perhaps in the insistence on these two symbols, in the Etruscan world, we can see the reason for the utter destruction and annihilation of the Etruscan consciousness. The new world wanted to rid itself of these fatal, dominant symbols of the old world, the old physical world. The Etruscan consciousness was rooted quite blithely in these symbols, the phallus and the arx. So the whole consciousness, the whole Etruscan pulse and rhythm, must be wiped out.

Now we see again, under the blue heavens where the larks are singing in the hot April sky, why the Romans called the Etruscans vicious. Even in their palmy days the Romans were not exactly saints. But they thought they ought to be. They hated the phallus and the ark, because they wanted empire and dominion and, above all, riches: social gain. You cannot dance gaily to the double flute and at the same time conquer nations or rake in large sums of money. *Delenda est Gartago*. To the greedy man, everybody that is in the way of his greed is vice incarnate.

There are many tombs, though not many of the great mounds are left. Most have been levelled. There are many tombs: some were standing half full of water; some were in process of being excavated, in a kind of quarry-place, though the work for the time was silent and abandoned. Many tombs, many, many, and you must descend to them all, for they are all cut out below the surface of the earth: and where there was a tumulus it was piled above them afterwards, loose earth, within the girdle of stone. Some tumuli have been levelled, yet the whole landscape is lumpy with them. But the tombs remain, here all more or less alike, though some are big and some are small, and some are noble and some are rather mean. But most of them seem to have several chambers, beyond the antechambers. And all these tombs along the dead highway would seem to have been topped, once, by the beautiful roundness of tumuli, the great mounds of fruition, for the dead, with the tall phallic cone rising from the summit.

The necropolis, as far as we are concerned, ends on a waste place of deserted excavations and flood-water. We turn back, to leave the home of dead Etruscans. All the tombs are empty. All have been rifled. The Romans may have respected the dead, for a certain time, while their religion was sufficiently Etruscan to exert a power over them. But later, when the Romans started collecting Etruscan antiques — as we collect antiques today —there must have been a great sacking of the tombs. Even when all the gold and silver and jewels had been pilfered from the urns — which no doubt happened very soon after the Roman dominion — still the vases and the bronze must have remained in their places. Then the rich Romans began to collect vases, 'Greek' vases with the painted scenes. So these were stolen from the tombs. Then the little bronze figures, statuettes, animals, bronze ships, of which the Etruscans put thousands in the tombs, became the rage with the Roman collectors. Some smart Roman gentry would have a thousand or two choice little Etruscan bronzes to boast of. Then Rome fell, and the barbarians pillaged whatever was left. So it went on.

And still some tombs remained virgin, for the earth had washed in and filled the entrance way, covered the stone bases of the mounds; trees, bushes grew over the graves; you had only hilly, humpy, bushy waste country.

Under this the tombs lay silent, either ravaged, or, in a few wonderful cases, still virgin. And still absolutely virgin lay one of the tombs of Cerveteri, alone and apart from the necropolis, buried on the other side of the town, until 1836, when it was discovered: and, of course, denuded. General Galassi and the arch-priest Regolini unearthed it: so it is called the Regolini-Galassi tomb.

It is still interesting: a primitive narrow tomb like a passage, with a partition half-way, and covered with an arched roof, what they call the false arch, which is made by letting the flat horizontal stones of the roof jut out step by step, as they pile upwards, till they almost meet. Then big flat stones are laid as cover, and make the flat top of the almost Gothic arch: an arch built, probably, in the eighth century before Christ.

In the first chamber lay the remains of a warrior, with his bronze armour, beautiful and sensitive as if it had grown in life for the living body, sunk on his dust. In the inner chamber beautiful, frail, pale-gold jewellery lay on the stone bed, earrings where the ears were dust, bracelets in the dust that once was arms, surely of a noble lady, nearly three thousand years ago.

They took away everything. The treasure, so delicate and sensitive and wistful, is mostly in the Gregorian Museum in the Vatican. On two of the little silver vases from the Regolini-Galassi tomb is the scratched inscription — *Mi Larthia*. Almost the first written Etruscan words we know. And what do they mean, anyhow? 'This is Larthia' — Larthia being a lady?

Caere, even seven hundred years before Christ, must have been rich and full of luxury, fond of soft gold and of banquets, dancing, and great Greek vases. But you will find none of it now. The tombs are bare: what treasure they yielded up, and even to us Cerveteri has yielded a great deal, is in the museums. If you go you will see, as I saw, a grey, forlorn little township in tight walls — perhaps having a thousand inhabitants — and some empty burying places.

But when you sit in the post-automobile, to be rattled down to the station, about four o'clock in the sunny afternoon, you will probably see the bus surrounded by a dozen buxom, handsome women, saying good-bye to one of their citizenesses. And in the full, dark, handsome, jovial faces surely you see the lustre still of the life-loving Etruscans! There are some level Greek eyebrows. But surely there are other vivid, warm faces still jovial with Etruscan vitality, beautiful with the mystery of the unrifled ark, ripe with the phallic knowledge and the Etruscan carelessness!

2. TARQUINIA

IN Cervereti there is nowhere to sleep, so the only thing to do is to go back to Rome, or forwards to Cività Vecchia. The bus landed us at the station of Palo at about five o'clock: in the midst of nowhere: to meet the Rome train. But we were going on to Tarquinia, not back to Rome, so we must wait two hours, till seven.

In the distance we could see the concrete villas and new houses of what was evidently Ladispoli, a seaside place, some two miles away. So we set off to walk to Ladispoli, on the flat sea-road. On the left, in the wood that forms part of the great park, the nightingales had already begun to whistle, and looking over the wall one could see many little rose-coloured cyclamens glowing on the earth in the evening light.

We walked on, and the Rome tram came surging round the bend. It misses Ladispoli, whose two miles of branch line runs only in the hot bathing months. As we neared the first ugly villas on the road the ancient wagonette drawn by the ancient white horse, both looking sun-bitten almost to ghostliness, clattered past. It just beat us.

Ladispoli is one of those ugly little places on the Roman coast, consisting of new concrete villas, new concrete hotels, kiosks and bathing establishments; bareness and non-existence for ten months in the year, seething solid with fleshy bathers in July and August. Now it was deserted, quite deserted, save for two or three officials and four wild children.

B. and I lay on the grey-black lava sand, by the flat, low sea, over which the sky, grey and shapeless, emitted a flat, wan evening light. Little waves curled green out of the sea's dark greyness, from the curious low flatness of the water. It is a peculiarly forlorn coast, the sea peculiarly flat and sunken, lifeless-looking, the land as if it had given its last gasp, and was now for ever inert.

Yet this is the Tyrrhenian sea of the Etruscans, where their shipping spread sharp sails, and beat the sea with slave-oars, roving in from Greece and Sicily, Sicily of the Greek tyrants; from Cumae, the city of the old Greek colony of Campania, where the province of Naples now is; and from Elba, where the Etruscans mined their iron ore. The Etruscans sailed the seas. They are even said to have come by sea, from Lydia in Asia Minor, at some date far back in the dim mists before the eighth century B.C. But that a whole people, even a whole host, sailed in the tiny ships of those days, all at once, to people a sparsely peopled central Italy, seems hard to imagine. Probably ships did come — even before Ulysses. Probably men landed on the strange flat coast, and made camps, and then treated with the natives. Whether the newcomers were Lydians or Hittites with hair curled in a roll behind, or men from Mycenae or Crete, who knows. Perhaps men of all these sorts came, in batches. For in Homeric days a restlessness seems to have possessed the Mediterranean basin, and ancient races began shaking ships like seeds over the sea. More people than Greeks, or Hellenes, or Indo-Germanic groups, were on the move.

But whatever little ships were run ashore on the soft, deep, grey-black volcanic sand of this coast, three thousand years ago, and earlier, their mariners certainly did not find those hills inland empty of people. If the Lydians or Hittites pulled up their long little two-eyed ships on to the beach, and made a camp behind a bank, in shelter from the wet strong wind, what natives came down curiously to look at them? For natives there were, of that we may be certain. Even before the fall of Troy, before even Athens was dreamed of, there were natives here. And they had huts on the hills, thatched huts in clumsy groups most probably; with patches of grain, and flocks of goats and probably cattle. Probably it was like coming on an old Irish village, or a village in the Scottish Hebrides in Prince Charlie's day, to come upon a village of these Italian aborigines, by the Tyrrhenian sea, three thousand years ago. But by the time Etruscan history starts in Caere, some eight centuries B.C., there was certainly more than a village on the hill. There was a native city, of that we may be sure; and a busy spinning of linen and beating of gold, long before the Regolini-Galassi tomb was built.

However that may be, somebody came, and somebody was already here: of that we may be certain: and, in the first place, none of them were Greeks or Hellenes. It was the days before Rome rose up: probably when the first comers arrived it was the days even before Homer. The newcomers, whether they were few or many, seem to have come from the east, Asia Minor or Crete or Cyprus. They were, we must feel, of an old, primitive Mediterranean and Asiatic or Aegean stock. The twilight of the beginning of our history was the nightfall of some previous history, which will never be written. Pelasgian is but a shadow-word. But Hittite and Minoan, Lydian, Carian, Etruscan, these words emerge from shadow, and perhaps from one and the same great shadow come the peoples to whom the names belong.

The Etruscan civilization seems a shoot, perhaps the last, from the prehistoric Mediterranean world, and the Etruscans, newcomers and aborigines alike, probably belonged to that ancient world, though they were of different nations and levels of culture. Later, of course, the Greeks exerted a great influence. But that is another matter.

Whatever happened, the newcomers in ancient central Italy found many natives flourishing in possession of the land. These aboriginals, now ridiculously called Villanovans, were neither wiped out nor suppressed. Probably they welcomed the strangers, whose pulse was not hostile to their own. Probably the more highly developed religion of the newcomers was not hostile to the primitive religion of the aborigines: no doubt the two religions had the same root. Probably the aborigines formed willingly a sort of religious aristocracy from the newcomers: the Italians might almost do the same today. And so the Etruscan world arose. But it took centuries to arise. Etruria was not a colony, it was a slowly developed country.

There was never an Etruscan nation: only, in historical times, a great league of tribes or nations using the Etruscan language and the Etruscan script — at least officially — and uniting in their religious feeling and observances. The Etruscan alphabet seems to have been borrowed from the old Greeks, apparently from the Chalcidians of Cumae — the Greek colony just north of where Naples now is. But the Etruscan language is not akin to any of the Greek dialects, nor, apparently, to the Italic. But we don't know. It is probably to a great extent the language of the old aboriginals of southern Etruria, just as the religion is in all probability basically aboriginal, belonging to some vast old religion of the prehistoric world. From the shadow of the prehistoric world emerge dying religions that have not yet invented gods or goddesses, but live by the mystery of the elemental powers in the Universe, the complex vitalities of what we feebly call Nature. And the Etruscan religion was certainly one of these. The gods and goddesses don't seem to have emerged in any sharp definiteness.

But it is not for me to make assertions. Only, that which half emerges from the dim background of time is strangely stirring; and after having read all the learned suggestions, most of them contradicting one another; and then having looked sensitively at the tombs and the Etruscan things that are left, one must accept one's own resultant feeling.

Ships came along this low, inconspicuous sea, coming up from the Near East, we should imagine, even in the days of Solomon — even, maybe, in the days of Abraham. And they kept on coming. As the light of history dawns and brightens, we see them winging along with their white or scarlet sails. Then, as the Greeks came crowding into colonies in Italy, and the Phoenicians began to exploit the western Mediterranean, we begin to hear of the silent Etruscans, and to see them.

Just north of here Caere founded a port called Pyrgi, and we know that the Greek vessels flocked in, with vases and stuffs and colonists coming from Hellas or from Magna Graecia, and that Phoenician ships came rowing sharply, over from Sardinia, up from Carthage, round from Tyre and Sidon; while the Etruscans had their own fleets, built of timber from the mountains, caulked with pitch from northern Volterra, fitted with sails from Tarquinia, filled with wheat from the bountiful plains, or with the famous Etruscan articles of bronze and iron, which they carried away to Corinth or to Athens or to the ports of Asia Minor. We know of the great and finally disastrous sea-battles with the Phoenicians and the tyrant of Syracuse. And we know that the Etruscans, all except those of Caere, became ruthless pirates, almost like the Moors and the Barbary corsairs later on. This was part of their viciousness, a great annoyance to their loving and harmless neighbours, the law-abiding Romans —who believed in the supreme law of conquest.

However, all this is long ago. The very coast has changed since then. The smitten sea has sunk and fallen back, the weary land has emerged when, apparently, it didn't want to, and the flowers of the coast-line are miserable bathing-places such as Ladispoli and seaside Ostia, desecration put upon desolation, to the triumphant trump of the mosquito.

The wind blew flat and almost chill from the darkening sea, the dead waves lifted small bits of pure green out of the leaden greyness, under the leaden sky. We got up from the dark grey but soft sand, and went back along the road to the station, peered at by the few people and officials who were holding the place together till the next bathers came.

At the station there was general desertedness. But our things still lay untouched in a dark corner of the buffet, and the man gave us a decent little meal of cold meats and Wine and oranges. It was already night. The train came rushing in, punctually.

It is an hour or more to Città Vecchia, which is a port of not much importance, except that from here the regular steamer sails to Sardinia. We gave our things to a friendly old porter, and told him to take us to the nearest hotel. It was night, very dark as we emerged from the station.

And a fellow came furtively shouldering up to me.

'You are foreigners, aren't you?'

'Yes.'

'What nationality?'

'English.'

'You have your permission to reside in Italy — or your passport?'

'My passport I have — what do you want?'

'I want to look at your passport.'

'It's in the valise! And why? Why is this?'

'This is a port, and we must examine the papers of foreigners.'

'And why? Genoa is a port, and no one dreams of asking for papers.'

I was furious. He made no answer. I told the porter to go on to the hotel, and the fellow furtively followed at our side, half-a-pace to the rear, in the mongrel way these spy-louts have.

In the hotel I asked for a room and registered, and then the fellow asked again for my passport. I wanted to know why he demanded it, what he meant by accosting me outside the station as if I was a criminal, what he meant by insulting us with his requests, when in any other town in Italy one went unquestioned — and so forth, in considerable rage.

He did not reply, but obstinately looked as though he would be venomous if he could. He peered at the passport — though I doubt if he could make head or tail of it — asked where we were going, peered at B.'s passport, half excused himself in a whining, disgusting sort of fashion, and disappeared into the night. A real lout.

I was furious. Supposing I had not been carrying my passport — and usually I don't dream of carrying it — what amount of trouble would that lout have made me! Probably I should have spent the night in prison, and been bullied by half a dozen low bullies.

Those poor rats at Ladispoli had seen me and B. go to the sea and sit on the sand for half-an-hour, then go back to the train. And this was enough to rouse their suspicions, I imagine, so they telegraphed to Città Vecchia. Why are officials always fools? Even when there is no war on? What could they imagine we were doing?

The hotel manager, propitious, said there was a very interesting museum in Città Vecchia, and wouldn't we stay the next day and see it. 'Ah!' I replied. 'But all it contains is Roman stuff, and we don't want to look at that.' It was malice on my part, because the present regime considers itself purely ancient Roman. The man looked at me scared, and I grinned at him. 'But what do they mean,' I said, 'behaving like this to a simple traveller, in a country where foreigners are invited to travel!'

'Ah!' said the porter softly and soothingly. 'It is the Roman province. You will have no more of it when you leave the Provincia di Roma.' And when the Italians give the soft answer to turn away wrath, the wrath somehow turns away.

We walked for an hour in the dull street of Città Vecchia. There seemed so much suspicion, one would have thought there were several wars on. The hotel manager asked if we were staying. We said we were leaving by the eight-o'clock train in the morning, for Tarquinia.

And, sure enough, we left by the eight-o'clock train. Tarquinia is only one station from Città Vecchia — about twenty minutes over the flat Maremma country, with the sea on the left, and the green wheat growing luxuriantly, the asphodel sticking up its spikes.

We soon saw Tarquinia, its towers pricking up like antennae on the side of a low bluff of a hill, some few miles inland from the sea. And this was once the metropolis of Etruria, chief city of the great Etruscan League. But it died like all the other Etruscan cities, and had a more or less medieval rebirth, with a new name. Dante knew it, as it was known for centuries, as Corneto —Corgnetum or Cornetium — and forgotten was its Etruscan past. Then there was a feeble sort of wakening to remembrance a hundred years ago, and the town got Tarquinia tacked on to its Corneto: Corneto-Tarquinia. The Fascist regime, however, glorying in the Italian origins of Italy, has now struck out the Corneto, so the town is once more, simply, Tarquinia. As you come up in the motor-bus from the station you see the great black letters, on a white ground, painted on the wall by the city gateway: *Tarquinia.* So the wheel of revolution turns. There stands the Etruscan word — Latinized Etruscan — beside the medieval gate, put up by the Fascist power to name and unname.

But the Fascists, who consider themselves in all things Roman, Roman of the Caesars, heirs of Empire and world power, are beside the mark restoring the rags of dignity to Etruscan places. For of all the Italian people that ever lived, the Etruscans were surely the least Roman. Just as, of all the people that ever rose up in Italy, the Romans of ancient Rome were surely the most un-Italian, judging from the natives of today.

Tarquinia is only about three miles from the sea. The omnibus soon runs one up, charges through the widened gateway, swirls round in the empty space inside the gateway, and is finished. We descend in the bare place, which seems to expect nothing. On the left is a beautiful stone palazzo — on the right is a café, upon the low ramparts above the gate. The man of the *Dazio,* the town customs, looks to see if anybody has brought food-stuffs into the town — but it is a mere glance. I ask him for the hotel. He says: 'Do you mean to sleep?' I say I do. Then tells a small boy to carry my bag and takes us to Gentile's.

Nowhere is far off, in these small wall-girdled cities. In the warm April morning the stony little town seems half asleep. As a matter of fact, most of the inhabitants are out in the fields. and won't come in through the gates again till evening. The slight sense of desertedness is everywhere — even in the inn, when we have climbed up the stairs to it, for the ground floor does not belong. A little lad in long trousers, who would seem to be only twelve years old but who has the air of a mature man, confronts us with his chest out. We ask for rooms. He eyes us, darts away for the key, and leads us off upstairs another flight, shouting to a young girl, who acts as chambermaid, to follow on. He shows us two small rooms, opening off a big, desert sort of general assembly room common in this kind of inn. 'And you won't be lonely,' he said briskly, 'because you can talk to one another through the wall. *Toh! Lina!'* He lifts his finger and listens. *'Eh!'* comes through the wall, like an echo, with startling nearness and clearness. *'Fai presto!'* says Albertino. *'È pronto!'* comes the voice of Lina. *'Ecco!'* says Albertino to us. 'You hear!' We certainly did. The partition wall must have been butter-muslin. And Albertino was delighted, having reassured us we should not feel lonely nor frightened in the night.

He was, in fact, the most manly and fatherly little hotel manager I have ever known, and he ran the whole place. He was in reality fourteen years old, but stunted. From five in the morning till ten at night he was on the go, never ceasing, and with a queer, abrupt, sideways-darting alacrity that must have wasted a great deal of energy. The father and mother were in the background — quite young and pleasant. But they didn't seem to exert themselves. Albertino did it all. How Dickens would have loved him! But Dickens would not have seen the queer wistfulness, and trustfulness, and courage in the boy. He was absolutely unsuspicious of us strangers. People must be rather human and decent in Tarquinia, even the commercial travellers: who, presumably, are chiefly buyers of agricultural produce, and sellers of agricultural implements and so forth.

We sallied out, back to the space by the gate, and drank coffee at one of the tin tables outside. Beyond the wall there were a few new villas — the land dropped green and quick, to the strip of coast plain and the indistinct, faintly gleaming sea, which seemed somehow not like a sea at all.

I was thinking, if this were still an Etruscan city, there would still be this cleared space just inside the gate. But instead of a rather forlorn vacant lot it would be a sacred clearing, with a little temple to keep it alert.

Myself, I like to think of the little wooden temples of the early Greeks and of the Etruscans: small, dainty, fragile, and evanescent as flowers. We have reached the stage when we are weary of huge stone erections, and we begin to realize that it is better to keep life fluid and changing than to try to hold it fast down in heavy monuments. Burdens on the face of the earth are man's ponderous erections.

The Etruscans made small temples, like little houses with pointed roofs, entirely of wood. But then, outside, they had friezes and cornices and crests of terra-cotta, so that the upper part of the temple would seem almost made of earthenware, terra-cotta plaques fitted neatly, and alive with freely modelled painted figures in relief, gay dancing creatures, rows of ducks, round faces like the sun, and faces grinning and putting out a big tongue, all vivid and fresh and unimposing. The whole thing small and dainty in proportion, and fresh, somehow charming instead of impressive. There seems to have been in the Etruscan instinct a real desire to preserve the natural humour of life. And that is a task surely more worthy, and even much more difficult in the long run, than conquering the world or sacrificing the self or saving the immortal soul.

Why has mankind had such a craving to be imposed upon? Why this lust after imposing creeds, imposing deeds, imposing buildings, imposing language, imposing works of art? The thing becomes an imposition and a weariness at last. Give us things that are alive and flexible, which won't last too long and become an obstruction and a weariness. Even Michelangelo becomes at last a lump and a burden and a bore. It is so hard to see past him.

Across the space from the café is the Palazzo Vitelleschi, a charming building, now a national museum — so the marble slab says. But the heavy doors are shut. The place opens at ten, a man says. It is nine-thirty. We wander up the steep but not very long street, to the top.

And the top is a fragment of public garden, and a look-out. Two old men are sitting in the sun, under a tree. We walk to the parapet, and suddenly are looking into one of the most delightful landscapes I have ever seen: as it were, into the very virginity of hilly green country. It is all wheat — green and soft and swooping, swooping down and up, and glowing with green newness, and no houses. Down goes the declivity below us, then swerving the curve and up again, to the neighbouring hill that faces in all its greenness and long-running, immaculateness. Beyond, the hills ripple away to the mountains, and far in the distance stands a round peak, that seems to have an enchanted city on its summit.

Such a pure, uprising, unsullied country, in the greenness of wheat on an April morning! — and the queer complication of hills! There seems nothing of the modern world here — no houses, no contrivances, only a sort of fair wonder and stillness, an openness which has not been violated.

The hill opposite is like a distinct companion. The near end is quite steep and wild, with evergreen oaks and scrub, and specks of black-and-white cattle on the slopes of common. But the long crest is green again with wheat, running and drooping to the south. And immediately one feels: that hill has a soul, it has a meaning.

Lying thus opposite to Tarquinia's long hill, a companion across a suave little swing of valley, one feels at once that, if this is the hill where the living Tarquinians had their gay wooden houses, then that is the hill where the dead lie buried and quick, as seeds, in their painted houses underground. The two hills are as inseparable as life and death, even now, on the sunny, green-filled April morning with the breeze blowing in from the sea. And the land beyond seems as mysterious and fresh as if it were still the morning of Time.

But B. wants to go back to the Palazzo Vitelleschi: it will be open now. Down the street we go, and sure enough the big doors are open, several officials are in the shadowy courtyard entrance. They salute us in the Fascist manner; *alla romana!*

Why don't they discover the Etruscan salute, and salute us *all' etrusca!* But they are perfectly courteous and friendly. We go into the courtyard of the palace.

The museum is exceedingly interesting and delightful, to anyone who is even a bit aware of the Etruscans. It contains a great number of things found at Tarquinia, and important things.

If only we would realize it, and not tear things from their settings. Museums anyhow are wrong. But if one must have museums, let them be small, and above all, let them be local. Splendid as the Etruscan museum is in Florence, how much happier one is in the museum at Tarquinia, where all the things are Tarquinian, and at least have some association with one another, and form some sort of *organic* whole.

In an entrance room from the cortile lie a few of the long sarcophagi in which the nobles were buried. It seems as if the primitive inhabitants of this part of Italy always burned their dead, and then put the ashes in a jar, sometimes covering the jar with the dead man's helmet, sometimes with a shallow dish for a lid, and then laid the urn with its ashes in a little round grave like a little well. This is called the Villanovan way of burial, in the well-tomb.

The newcomers to the country, however, apparently buried their dead whole. Here, at Tarquinia, you may still see the hills where the well-tombs of the aboriginal inhabitants are discovered, with the urns containing the ashes inside. Then come the graves where the dead were buried unburned, graves very much like those of today. But tombs of the same period with cinerary urns are found near to, or in connexion. So that the new people and the old apparently lived side by side in harmony, from very early days, and the two modes of burial continued side by side, for centuries, long before the painted tombs were made.

At Tarquinia, however, the main practice seems to have been, at least from the seventh century on, that the nobles were buried in the great sarcophagi, or laid out on biers, and placed in chamber-tombs, while the slaves apparently were cremated, their ashes laid in urns, and the urns often placed in the family tomb, where the stone coffins of the masters rested. The common people, on the other hand, were apparently sometimes cremated, sometimes buried in graves very much like our graves of today, though the sides were lined with stone. The mass of the common people was mixed in race, and the bulk of them were probably serf-peasants, with many half-free artisans. These must have followed their own desire in the matter of burial: some had graves, many must have been cremated, their ashes saved in an urn or jar which takes up little room in a poor man's burial-place. Probably even the less important members of the noble families were cremated, and their remains placed in the vases, which became more beautiful as the connexion with Greece grew more extensive.

It is a relief to think that even the slaves — and the luxurious Etruscans had many, in historical times — had their remains decently stored in jars and laid in a sacred place. Apparently the 'vicious Etruscans' had nothing comparable to the vast deadpits which lay outside Rome, beside the great highway, in which the bodies of slaves were promiscuously flung.

It is all a question of sensitiveness. Brute force and overbearing may make a terrific effect. But in the end, that which lives lives by delicate sensitiveness. If it were a question of brute force, not a single human baby would survive for a fortnight. It is the grass of the field, most frail of all things, that supports all life all the time. But for the green grass, no empire would rise, no man would eat bread: for grain is grass; and Hercules or Napoleon or Henry Ford would alike be denied existence.

Brute force crushes many plants. Yet the plants rise again. The Pyramids will not last a moment compared with the daisy. And before Buddha or Jesus spoke the nightingale sang, and long after the words of Jesus and Buddha are gone into oblivion the nightingale still will sing. Because it is neither preaching nor teaching nor commanding nor urging. It is just singing. And in the beginning was not a Word, but a chirrup.

Because a fool kills a nightingale with a stone, is he therefore greater than the nightingale? Because the Roman took the life out of the Etruscan, was he therefore greater than the Etruscan? Not he! Rome fell, and the Roman phenomenon with it. Italy today is far more Etruscan in its pulse than Roman; and will always be so. The Etruscan element is like the grass of the field and the sprouting of corn, in Italy: it will always be so. Why try to revert to the Latin-Roman mechanism and suppression?

In the open room upon the courtyard of the Palazzo Vitelleschi lie a few sarcophagi of stone, with the effigies carved on top, something as the dead crusaders in English churches. And here, in Tarquinia, the effigies are more like crusaders than usual, for some lie flat on their backs, and have a dog at their feet; whereas usually the carved figure of the dead rears up as if alive, from the lid of the tomb, resting upon one elbow, and gazing out proudly, sternly. If it is a man, his body is exposed to just below the navel, and he holds in his hand the sacred *patera,* or *mundum,* the round saucer with the raised knob in the centre, which represents the round germ of heaven and earth. It stands for the plasm, also, of the living cell, with its nucleus, which is the indivisible God of the beginning, and which remains alive and unbroken to the end, the eternal quick of all things, which yet divides and sub-divides, so that it becomes the sun of the firmament and the lotus of the waters under the earth, and the rose of all existence upon the earth: and the sun maintains. its own quick, unbroken for ever; and there is a living quick of the sea, and of all the waters; and every living created thing has its own unfailing quick. So within each man is the quick of him, when he is a baby, and when he is old, the same quick; some spark, some unborn and undying vivid life-electron. And this is what is symbolized in the *patera,* which may be made to flower like a rose or like the sun, but which remains the same, the germ central within the living plasm.

And this *patera,* this symbol, is almost invariably found in the hand of a dead man. But if the dead is a woman her dress falls in soft gathers from her throat, she wears splendid jewellery, and she holds in her hand not the *mundum,* but the mirror, the box of essence, the pomegranate, some symbols of her reflected nature, or of her woman's quality. But she, too, is given a proud, haughty look, as is the man: for she belongs to the sacred families that rule and that read the signs.

These sarcophagi and effigies here all belong to the centuries of the Etruscan decline, after there had been long intercourse with the Greeks, and perhaps most of them were made after the conquest of Etruria by the Romans. So that we do not look for fresh, spontaneous works of art, any more than we do in modern memorial stones. The funerary arts are always more or less commercial. The rich man orders his sarcophagus while he is still alive, and the monument-carver makes the work more or less elaborate, according to the price. The figure is supposed be a portrait of the man who orders it, so we see well enough what the later Etruscans look like. In the third and second centuries B.C., at the fag end of their existence as a people, they look very like the Romans of the same day, whose busts we know so well. And often they are given the tiresomely haughty air of people who are no longer rulers indeed, only by virtue of wealth.

Yet, even when the Etruscan art is Romanized and spoilt; there still flickers in it a certain naturalness and feeling. The Etruscan *Lucumones,* or prince-magistrates, were in the first place religious seers, governors in religion, then magistrates, then princes. They were not aristocrats in the Germanic sense, not even patricians in the Roman. They were first and foremost leaders in the sacred mysteries, then magistrates, then men of family and wealth. So there is always a touch of vital life, of life-significance. And you may look through modern funerary sculpture in vain for anything so good even as the Sarcophagus of the Magistrate, with his written scroll spread before him, his strong, alert old face gazing sternly out, the necklace of office round his neck, the ring of rank on his finger. So he lies, in the museum at Tarquinia. His robe leaves him naked to the hip, and his body lies soft and slack, with the soft effect of relaxed flesh the Etruscan artists render so well, and which is so difficult. On the sculptured side of the sarcophagus the two death-dealers wield the hammer of death, the winged figures wait for the soul, and will not be persuaded away. Beautiful it is, with the easy simplicity of life. But it is late in date. Probably this old Etruscan magistrate is already an official under Roman authority: for he does not hold the sacred *mundum,* the dish, he has only the written scroll, probably of laws. As if he were no longer the religious lord or Lucumo. Though possibly, in this case, the dead man was not one of the Lucumones anyhow.

Upstairs in the museum are many vases, from the ancient crude pottery of the Villanovans to the early black ware decorated in scratches, or undecorated, called *bucchero,* and on to the painted bowls and dishes and amphoras which came from Corinth or Athens, or to those painted pots made by the Etruscans themselves more or less after the Greek patterns. These may or may not be interesting: the Etruscans are not at their best, painting dishes. Yet they must have loved them. In the early days these great jars and bowls, and smaller mixing bowls, and drinking cups and pitchers, and flat winecups formed a valuable part of the household treasure. In very early times the Etruscans must have sailed their ships to Corinth and to Athens, taking perhaps wheat and honey, wax and bronzeware, iron and gold, and coming back with these precious jars, and stuffs, essences, perfumes, and spice. And jars brought from overseas for the sake of their painted beauty must have been household treasures.

But then the Etruscans made pottery of their own, and by the thousand they imitated the Greek vases. So that there must have been millions of beautiful jars in Etruria. Already in the first century B. C. there was a passion among the Romans for collecting Greek and Etruscan painted jars from the Etruscans, particularly from the Etruscan tombs: jars and the little bronze votive figures and statuettes, the *sigilla Tyrrhena* of the Roman luxury. And when the tombs were first robbed, for gold and silver treasure, hundreds of fine jars must have been thrown over and smashed. Because even now, when a part-rifled tomb is discovered and opened, the fragments of smashed vases lie around.

As it is, however, the museums are full of vases. If one looks for the Greek form of elegance and convention, those elegant 'still-unravished brides of quietness', one is disappointed. But get over the strange desire we have for elegant convention, and the vases and dishes of the Etruscans, especially many of the black bucchero ware, begin to open out like strange flowers, black flowers with all the softness and the rebellion of life against convention, or red-and-black flowers painted with amusing free, bold designs. It is there nearly always in Etruscan things, the naturalness verging on the commonplace, but usually missing it, and often achieving an originality so free and bold, and so fresh, that we, who love convention and things 'reduced to a norm', call it a bastard art, and commonplace.

It is useless to look in Etruscan things for 'uplift'. If you want uplift, go to the Greek and the Gothic. If you want mass, go to the Roman. But if you love the odd spontaneous forms that are never to be standardized, go to the Etruscans. In the fascinating little Palazzo Vitelleschi one could spend many an hour, but for the fact that the very fullness of museums makes one rush through them.

3 THE PAINTED TOMBS OF TARQUINIA I

WE arranged for the guide to take us to the painted tombs, which are the real fame of Tarquinia. After lunch we set out, climbing to the top of the town, and passing through the south-west gate, on the level hillcrest. Looking back, the wall of the town, medieval, with a bit of more ancient black wall lower down, stands blank. Just outside the gate are one or two forlorn new houses, then ahead, the long, running table-land of the hill, with the white highway dipping and going on to Viterbo, inland.

'All this hill in front,' said the guide, 'is tombs! All tombs! The city of the dead.'

So! Then this hill is the necropolis hill! The Etruscans never buried their dead within the city walls. And the modem cemetery and the first Etruscan tombs lie almost close up to the present city gates. Therefore, if the ancient city of Tarquinia lay on this hill, it can have occupied no more space, hardly, than the present little town of a few thousand people. Which seems impossible. Far more probably, the city itself lay on that opposite hill there, which lies splendid and unsullied, running parallel to us.

We walk across the wild bit of hilltop, where the stones crop out, and the first rock-rose flutters, and the asphodels stick up. This is the necropolis. Once it had many a tumulus, and streets of tombs. Now there is no sign of any tombs: no tumulus, nothing but the rough bare hill-crest, with stones and short grass and flowers, the sea gleaming away to the right, under the sun, and the soft land inland glowing very green and pure.

But we see a little bit of wall, built perhaps to cover a water-trough. Our guide goes straight towards it. He is a fat, good-natured young man, who doesn't look as if he would be interested in tombs. We are mistaken, however. He knows a good deal, and has a quick, sensitive interest, absolutely unobtrusive, and turns out to be as pleasant a companion for such a visit as one could wish to have.

The bit of wall we see is a little hood of masonry with an iron gate, covering a little flight of steps leading down into the ground. One comes upon it all at once, in a rough nothingness of the hillside. The guide kneels down to light his acetylene lamp, and his old terrier lies down resignedly in the sun, in the breeze which rushes persistently from the south-west, over these long, exposed hilltops.

The lamp begins to shine and smell, then to shine without smelling: the guide opens the iron gate, and we descend the steep steps down into the tomb. It seems a dark little hole underground: a dark little hole, after the sun of the upper world! But the guide's lamp begins to flare up, and we find ourselves in a little chamber in the rock, just a small, bare little cell of a room that some anchorite might have lived in. It is so small and bare and familiar, quite unlike the rather splendid spacious tombs at Cerveteri.

But the lamp flares bright, we get used to the change of light, and see the paintings on the little walls. It is the Tomb of Hunting and Fishing, so called from the pictures on the walls, and it is supposed to date from the sixth century B.C. It is very badly damaged, pieces of the wall have fallen away, damp has eaten into the colours, nothing seems to be left. Yet in the dimness we perceive flights of birds flying through the haze, with the draught of the life still in their wings. And as we take heart and look closer we see the little room is frescoed all round with hazy sky and sea, with birds flying and fishes leaping, and little men hunting, fishing, rowing in boats. The lower part of the wall is all a blue-green of sea with a silhouette surface that ripples all round the room. From the sea rises a tall rock; off which a naked man, shadowy but still distinct, is beautifully and cleanly diving into the sea, while a companion climbs up the rock after him, and on the water a boat waits with rested oars in it, three men watching the diver, the middle man standing up naked, holding out his arms. Meanwhile a great dolphin leaps behind the boat, a flight of birds soars upwards to pass the rock, in the clear air. Above all, from the bands of colour that border the wall at the top hang the regular loops of garlands, garlands of flowers and leaves and buds and berries, garlands which belong to maidens and to women, and which represent the flowery circle of the female life and sex. The top border of the wall is formed of horizontal stripes or ribands of colour that go all round the room, red and black and dull gold and blue and primrose, and these are the colours that occur invariably. Men are nearly always painted a darkish red, which is the colour of many Italians when they go naked in the sun, as the Etruscans went. Women are coloured paler, because women did not go naked in the sun.

At the end of the room, where there is a recess in the wall, is painted another rock rising from the sea, and on it a man with a sling is taking aim at the birds which rise scattering this way and that. A boat with a big paddle oar is holding off from the rock, a naked man amidships is giving a queer salute to the slinger, a man kneels over the bows with his back to the others, and is letting down a net. The prow of the boat has a beautifully painted eye, so the vessel shall see where it is going. In Syracuse you will see many a two-eyed boat today come swimming in to quay. One dolphin is diving down into the sea, one is leaping out. The birds fly, and the garlands hang from the border.

It is small and gay and quick with life, spontaneous as only young life can be. If only it were not so much damaged, one would be happy, because here is the real Etruscan liveliness and naturalness. It is not impressive or grand. But if you are content with just a sense of the quick ripple of life, then here it is.

The little tomb is empty, save for its shadowy paintings. It had no bed of rock around it: only a deep niche for holding vases, perhaps vases of precious things. The sarcophagus on the floor, perhaps under the slinger on the end wall. And it stood alone, for this is an individual tomb, for one person only, as is usual in the older tombs of this necropolis.

In the gable triangle of the end wall, above the slinger and the boat, the space is filled in with one of the frequent Etruscan banqueting scenes of the dead. The dead man, sadly obliterated, reclines upon his banqueting couch with his flat wine-dish in his hand, resting on his elbow, and beside him, also half risen, reclines a handsome and jewelled lady in fine robes, apparently resting her left hand upon the naked breast of the man, and in her right holding up to him the garland — the garland of the female festive offering. Behind the man stands a naked slave-boy, perhaps with music, while another naked slave is just filling a wine-jug from a handsome amphora or wine-jar at the side.

On the woman's side stands a maiden, apparently playing the flute: for a woman was supposed to play the flute at classic funerals; and beyond sit two maidens with garlands, one turning round to watch the banqueting pair, the other with her back to it all. Beyond the maidens in the corner are more garlands, and two birds, perhaps doves. On the wall behind the head of the banqueting lady is a problematic object, perhaps a bird-cage.

The scene is natural as life, and yet it has a heavy archaic fullness of meaning. It is the death-banquet; and at the same time it is the dead man banqueting in the underworld; for the underworld of the Etruscans was a gay place. While the living feasted out of doors,

312

at the tomb of the dead, the dead himself feasted in like manner, with a lady to offer him garlands and slaves to bring him wine, away in the underworld. For the life on earth was so good, the life below could but be a continuance of it.

This profound belief in life, acceptance of life, seems characteristic of the Etruscans. It is still vivid in the painted tombs. There is a certain dance and glamour in all the movements, even in those of the naked slave men. They are by no means downtrodden menials, let later Romans say what they will. The slaves in the tombs are surging with full life.

We come up the steps into the upper world, the sea-breeze and the sun. The old dog shambles to his feet, the guide blows out his lamp and locks the gate, we set off again, the dog trundling apathetic at his master's heels, the master speaking to him with that soft Italian familiarity which seems so very different from the spirit of Rome, the strong-willed Latin.

The guide steers across the hilltop, in the clear afternoon sun, towards another little hood of masonry. And one notices there is quite a number of these little gateways, built by the Government to cover the steps that lead down to the separate small tombs. It is utterly unlike Cerveteri, though the two places are not forty miles apart. Here there is no stately tumulus city, with its highroad between the tombs, and inside, rather noble, many-roomed houses of the dead. Here the little one-room tombs seem scattered at random on the hilltop, here and there: though probably, if excavations were fully carried out, here also we should find a regular city of the dead, with its streets and crossways. And probably each tomb had its little tumulus of piled earth, so that even above-ground there were streets of mounds with tomb entrances. But even so, it would be different from Cerveteri, from Caere; the mounds would be so small, the streets surely irregular. Anyhow, today there are scattered little one-room tombs, and we dive down into them just like rabbits popping down a hole. The place is a warren.

It is interesting to find it so different from Cerveteri. The Etruscans carried out perfectly what seems to be the Italian instinct: to have single, independent cities, with a certain surrounding territory, each district speaking its own dialect and feeling at home in its own little capital, yet the whole confederacy of city-states loosely linked together by a common religion and a more-or-less common interest. Even today Lucca is very different from Ferrara, and the language is hardly the same. In ancient Etruria this isolation of cities developing according to their own idiosyncrasy, within the loose union of a so-called nation, must have been complete. The contact between the plebs, the mass of the people, of Caere and Tarquinii must have been almost null. They were, no doubt, foreigners to one another. Only the Lucumones, the ruling sacred magistrates of noble family, the priests and the other nobles, and the merchants, must have kept up an intercommunion, speaking 'correct' Etruscan, while the people, no doubt, spoke dialects varying so widely as to be different languages. To get any idea of the pre-Roman past we must break up the conception of oneness and uniformity, and see an endless confusion of differences.

We are diving down into another tomb, called, says the guide, the Tomb of the Leopards. Every tomb has been given a name, to distinguish it from its neighbours. The Tomb of the Leopards has two spotted leopards in the triangle of the end wall, between the roof-slopes. Hence its name.

The Tomb of the Leopards is a charming, cosy little room, and the paintings on the walls have not been so very much damaged. All the tombs are ruined to some degree by weather and vulgar vandalism, having been left and neglected like common holes, when they had been broken open again and rifled to the last gasp.

But still the paintings are fresh and alive the ochre-reds and blacks and blues and blue-greens are curiously alive and harmonious on the creamy yellow walls. Most of the tomb walls have had a thin coat of stucco, but it is of the same paste as the living rock, which is fine and yellow, and weathers to a lovely creamy gold, a beautiful colour for a background.

The walls of this little tomb are a dance of real delight. The room seems inhabited still by Etruscans of the sixth century before Christ, a vivid, life-accepting people, who must have lived with real fullness. On come the dancers and the music-players, moving in a broad frieze towards the front wall of the tomb, the wall facing us as we enter from the dark stairs, and where the banquet is going on in all its glory. Above the banquet, in the gable angle, are the two spotted leopards, heraldically facing each other across a little tree. And the ceiling of rock has chequered slopes of red and black and yellow and blue squares, with a roof-beam painted with coloured circles, dark red and blue and yellow. So that all is colour, and we do not seem to be underground at all, but in some gay chamber of the past.

The dancers on the right wall move with a strange, powerful alertness onwards. The men are dressed only in a loose coloured scarf; or in the gay handsome chlamys draped as a mantle. The *subulo* plays the double flute the Etruscans loved so much, touching the stops with big, exaggerated hands, the man behind him touches the seven-stringed lyre, the man in front turns round and signals with his left hand, holding a big wine-bowl in his right. And so they move on, on their long, sandalled feet, past the little berried olive-trees, swiftly going with their limbs full of life, full of life to the tips.

This sense of vigorous, strong-bodied liveliness is characteristic of the Etruscans, and is somehow beyond art. You cannot think of art, but only of life itself, as if this were the very life of the Etruscans, dancing in their coloured wraps with massive yet exuberant naked limbs, ruddy from the air and the sea-light, dancing and fluting along through the little olive-trees, out in the fresh day.

The end wall has a splendid banqueting scene. The feasters recline upon a checked or tartan couch-cover, on the banqueting couch, and in the open air, for they have little trees behind them. The six feasters are bold and full of life like the dancers, but they are strong, they keep their life so beautifully and richly inside themselves, they are not loose, they don't lose themselves even in their wild moments. They lie in pairs, man and woman, reclining equally on the couch, curiously friendly. The two end women are called *hetaerae,* courtesans; chiefly because they have yellow hair, which seems to have been a favourite feature in a woman of pleasure. The men are dark and ruddy, and naked to the waist. The women, sketched in on the creamy rock, are fair, and wear thin gowns, with rich mantles round their hips. They have a certain free bold look, and perhaps really are courtesans.

The man at the end is holding up, between thumb and fore-finger, an egg, showing it to the yellow-haired woman who reclines next to him, she who is putting out her left hand as if to touch his breast. He, in his right hand, holds a large wine-dish, for the revel.

The next couple, man and fair-haired woman, are looking round and making the salute with the right hand curved over, in the usual Etruscan gesture. It seems as if they too are saluting the mysterious egg held up by the man at the end; who is, no doubt, the man who has died, and whose feast is being celebrated. But in front of the second couple a naked slave with a chaplet on his head is brandishing an empty wine-jug, as if to say he is fetching more wine. Another slave farther down is holding out a curious thing like a little axe, or fan. The last two feasters are rather damaged. One of them is holding up a garland to the other, but not putting it over his head as they still put a garland over your head, in India, to honour you.

Above the banqueters, in the gable angle, the two great spotted male leopards hang out their tongues and face each other heraldically, lifting a paw, on either side of a little tree. They are the leopards or panthers of the underworld Bacchus, guarding the exits and the entrances of the passion of life.

There is a mystery and a portentousness in the simple scenes which go deeper than commonplace life. It seems all so gay and light. Yet there is a certain weight, or depth of significance that goes beyond aesthetic beauty.

If one once starts looking, there is much to see. But if one glances merely, there is nothing but a pathetic little room with unimposing, half-obliterated, scratchy little paintings in tempera.

There are many tombs. When we have seen one, up we go, a little bewildered, into the afternoon sun, across a tract of rough, tormented hill, and down again to the underground, like rabbits in a warren. The hilltop is really a warren of tombs. And gradually the underworld of the Etruscans becomes more real than the above day of the afternoon. One begins to live with the painted dancers and feasters and mourners, and to look eagerly for them.

A very lovely dance tomb is the *Tomba del Triclinio,* or *del Convito,* both of which mean: Tomb of the Feast. In size and shape this is much the same as the other tombs we have seen. It is a little chamber about fifteen feet by eleven, six feet high at the walls, about eight feet at the centre. It is again a tomb for one person, like nearly all the old painted tombs here. So there is no inner furnishing. Only the farther half of the rock-floor, the pale yellow-white rock, is raised two or three inches, and on one side of this raised part are the four holes where the feet of the sarcophagus stood. For the rest, the tomb has only its painted walls and ceiling.

And how lovely these have been, and still are! The band of dancing figures that go round the room still is bright in colour, fresh, the women in thin spotted dresses of linen muslin and coloured mantles with fine borders, the men merely in a scarf. Wildly the bacchic woman throws back her head and curves out her long, strong fingers, wild and yet contained within herself; while the broad-bodied young man turns round to her, lifting his dancing hand to hers till the thumbs all but touch. They are dancing in the open, past little trees, and birds are running, and a little fox-tailed dog is watching something with the naïve intensity of the young. Wildly and delightedly dances the next woman, every bit of her, in her soft boots and her bordered mantle, with jewels on her arms; till one remembers the old dictum, that every part of the body and of the *anima* shall know religion, and be in touch with the gods. Towards her comes the young man piping on the double flute, and dancing as he comes. He is clothed only in a fine linen scarf with a border, that hangs over his arms, and his strong legs dance of themselves, so full of life. Yet, too, there is a certain solemn intensity in his face, as he turns to the woman beyond him, who stoops in a bow to him as she vibrates her castanets.

She is drawn fair-skinned, as all the women are, and he is of a dark red colour. That is the convention, in the tombs. But it is more than convention. In the early days men smeared themselves with scarlet when they took on their sacred natures. The Red Indians still do it. When they wish to figure in their sacred and portentous selves they smear their bodies all over with red. That must be why they are called Red Indians. In the paste for all serious or solemn occasions, they rubbed red pigment into their skins. And the same today. And today, when they wish to put strength into their vision, and to see true, they smear round their eyes with vermilion, rubbing it into the skin. You may meet them so, in the streets of the American towns. It is a very old custom. The American Indian will tell you:

'The red paint, it is medicine, makes you see!' But he means medicine in a different sense from ours. It is deeper even than magic. Vermilion is the colour of his sacred or potent or god body. Apparently it was so in all the ancient world. Man all scarlet was his bodily godly self We know the kings of ancient Rome, who were probably Etruscans, appeared in public with their faces painted vermilion with minium. And Ezekiel says (23: 14, 15): 'She saw men pourtrayed upon the wall, the images of the Chaldeans pourtrayed with vermilion . . . all of them princes to look to, after the manner of the Babylonians of Chaldea, the land of their nativity.'

It is then partly a convention, and partly a symbol, with the Etruscans, to represent their men red in colour, a strong red. Here in the tombs everything is in its sacred or inner-significant aspect. But also the red colour is not so very unnatural. When the Italian today goes almost naked on the beach he becomes of a lovely dark ruddy colour, dark as any Indian. And the Etruscans went a good deal naked. The sun painted them with the sacred minium.

The dancers dance on, the birds run, at the foot of a little tree a rabbit crouches in a bunch, bunched with life. And on the tree hangs a narrow, fringed scarf, like a priest's stole; another symbol.

The end wall has a banqueting scene, rather damaged, but still interesting. We see two separate couches, and a man and a woman on each. The woman this time is dark-haired, so she need not be a courtesan. The Etruscans shared the banqueting bench with their wives; which is more than the Greeks or Romans did, at this period. The classic world thought it indecent for an honest woman to recline as the men did, even at the family table. If a woman appeared at all, she must sit up straight, in a chair.

Here, the women recline calmly with the men, and one shows a bare foot at the end of the dark couch. In front of the *lecti,* the couches, is in each case a little low square table bearing delicate dishes of food for the feasters. But they are not eating. One woman is lifting her hand to her head in a strange salute to the robed piper at the end, the other woman seems with the lifted hand to be saying No! to the charming maid, perhaps a servant, who stands at her side, presumably offering the *alabastron,* or ointment-jar, while the man at the end apparently is holding up an egg. Wreaths hang from the ivy-border above, a boy is bringing a wine-jug, the music goes on, and under the beds a cat is on the prowl, while an alert cock watches him. The silly partridge, however, turns his back, stepping innocently along.

This lovely tomb has a pattern of ivy and ivy berries, the ivy of the underworld Bacchus, along the roof-beam and in a border round the top of the walls. The roof-slopes are chequered in red and black, white, blue, brown, and yellow squares. In the gable angle, instead of the heraldic beasts, two naked men are sitting reaching back to the centre of an ivy-covered altar, arm outstretched across the ivy. But one man is almost obliterated. At the foot of the other man, in the tight angle of the roof, is a pigeon, the bird of the soul that coos out of the unseen.

This tomb has been open since 1830, and is still fresh. It is interesting to see, in Fritz Weege's book, *Etruskische Malerei,* a reproduction of an old water-colour drawing of the dancers on the right wall. It is a good drawing, yet, as one looks closer, it is quite often out, both in line and position. These Etruscan paintings, not being in our convention, are very difficult to copy. The picture shows my rabbit all spotted, as if it were some queer cat. And it shows a squirrel in the little tree in front of the piper, and flowers, and many details that have now disappeared.

But it is a good drawing, unlike some that Weege reproduces, which are so Flaxmanized and Greekified; and made according to what our great-grandfathers thought they *ought* to be, as to be really funny, and a warning for ever against thinking how things *ought* to be, when already they are quite perfectly what they are.

We climb up to the world, and pass for a few minutes through the open day. Then down we go again. In the Tomb of the Bacchanti the colours have almost gone. But still we see, on the end wall, a strange wondering dancer out of the mists of time carrying his zither, and beyond him, beyond the little tree, a man of the dim ancient world, a man with a short beard, strong and mysteriously male, is reaching for a wild archaic maiden who throws up her hands and turns back to him her excited, subtle face. It is wonderful, the strength and mystery of old life that comes out of these faded figures. The Etruscans are still there, upon the wall.

Above the figures, in the gable angle, two spotted deer are prancing heraldically towards one another, on either side the altar, and behind them two dark lions, with pale manes and with tongues hanging out, are putting up a paw to seize them on the haunch. So the old story repeats itself.

From the striped border rude garlands are hanging, and on the roof are little painted stars, or four-petalled flowers. So much has vanished! Yet even in the last breath of colour and form, how much life there is!

In the *Tomba del Morto,* the Tomb of the Dead Man, the banqueting scene is replaced by a scene, apparently, of a dead man on his bed, with a woman leaning gently over to cover his face. It is almost like a banquet scene. But it is so badly damaged! In the gable above, two dark heraldic lions are lifting the paw against two leaping, frightened, backward-looking birds. This is a new variation. On the broken wall are the dancing legs of a man, and there is more life in these Etruscan legs, fragment as they are, than in the whole bodies of men today. Then there is one really impressive dark figure of a naked man who throws up his arms so that his great wine-bowl stands vertical, and with spread hand and closed face gives a strange gesture of finality. He has a chaplet on his head, and a small pointed beard, and lives there shadowy and significant.

Lovely again is the *Tomba delle Leonesse,* the Tomb of the Lionesses. In its gable two spotted lionesses swing their bell-like udders, heraldically facing one another across the altar. Beneath is a great vase, and a flute-player playing to it on one side, a zither-player on the other, making music to its sacred contents. Then on either side of these goes a narrow frieze of dancers, very strong and lively in their prancing. Under the frieze of dancers is a lotus dado, and below that again, all round the room, the dolphins are leaping, leaping all downwards into the rippling sea, while birds fly between the fishes.

On the right wall reclines a very impressive dark red man wearing a curious cap, or head-dress, that has long tails like long plaits. In his right hand he holds up an egg, and in his left is the shallow wine-bowl of the feast. The scarf or stole of his human office hangs from a tree before him, and the garland of his human delight hangs at his side. He holds up the egg of resurrection, within which the germ sleeps as the soul sleeps in the tomb, before it breaks the shell and emerges again. There is another reclining man, much obliterated, and beside him hangs a garland or chain like the chains of dandelion-stems we used to make as children. And this man has a naked flute-boy, lovely in naked outline, coming towards him.

The *Tomba della Pulcella,* or Tomb of the Maiden, has faded but vigorous figures at the banquet, and very ornate couch-covers in squares and the key-pattern, and very handsome mantles.

The *Tomba dei Vasi Dipinti,* Tomb of the Painted Vases, has great amphorae painted on the side wall, and springing towards them is a weird dancer, the ends of his waist-cloth flying. The amphorae, two of them, have scenes painted on them, which can still be made out. On the end wall is a gentle little banquet scene, the bearded man softly touching the woman with him under the chin, a slave-boy standing childishly behind, and an alert dog under the couch. The *kylix,* or wine-bowl, that the man holds is surely the biggest on record; exaggerated, no doubt, to show the very special importance of the feast. Rather gentle and lovely is the way he touches the woman under the chin, with a delicate caress. That again is one of the charms of the Etruscan paintings: they really have the sense of touch; the people and the creatures are all really in touch. It is one of the rarest qualities, in life as well as in art. There is plenty of pawing and laying hold, but no real touch. In pictures especially, the people may be in contact, embracing or laying hands on one another. But there is no soft flow of touch. The touch does not come from the middle of the human being. It is merely a contact of surfaces, and a juxtaposition of objects. This is what makes so many of the great masters boring, in spite of all their clever composition. Here, in this faded Etruscan painting, there is a quiet flow of touch that unites the man and the woman on the couch, the timid boy behind, the dog that lifts his nose, even the very garlands that hang from the wall.

Above the banquet, in the triangle, instead of lions or leopards, we have the hippocampus, a favourite animal of the Etruscan imagination. It is a horse that ends in a long, flowing fish-tail. Here these two hippocampi face one another prancing their front legs, while their fish-tails flow away into the narrow angle of the roof. They are a favourite symbol of the seaboard Etruscans.

In the *Tomba del Vecchio,* the Tomb of the Old Man, a beautiful woman with her hair dressed backwards into the long cone of the East, so that her head is like a sloping acorn, offers her elegant, twisted garland to the white-bearded old man, who is now beyond garlands. He lifts his left hand up at her, with the rich gesture of these people, that must mean something each time.

Above them, the prancing spotted deer are being seized in the haunch by two lions. And the waves of obliteration, wastage of time and damage of men, are silently passing over all.

So we go on, seeing tomb after tomb, dimness after dimness, divided between the pleasure of finding so much and the disappointment that so little remains. One tomb after another, and nearly everything faded or eaten away, or corroded with alkali, or broken wilfully. Fragments of people at banquets, limbs that dance without dancers, birds that fly in nowhere, lions whose devouring heads are devoured away! Once it was all bright and dancing: the delight of the underworld; honouring the dead with wine, and flutes playing for a dance, and limbs whirling and pressing. And it was deep and sincere honour rendered to the dead and to the mysteries. It is contrary to our ideas; but the ancients had their own philosophy for it. As the pagan old writer says: 'For no part of us nor of our bodies shall be, which doth not feel religion: and let there be no lack of singing for the soul, no lack of leaping and of dancing for the knees and heart; for all these know the gods.'

Which is very evident in the Etruscan dancers. They know the gods in their very finger-tips. The wonderful fragments of limbs and bodies that dance on in a field of obliteration still know the gods, and made it evident to us.

But we can hardly see any more tombs. The upper air seems pallid and bodiless, as we emerge once more, white with the light of the sea and the coming evening. And spent and slow the old dog rises once more to follow after.

We decide that the *Tomba delle Iscrizioni,* the Tomb of the Inscriptions, shall be our last for today. It is dim but fascinating, as the lamp flares up, and we see in front of us the end wall, painted with a false door studded with pale studs, as if it led to another chamber beyond; and riding from the left, a trail of shadowy tall horsemen; and running in from the right, a train of wild shadowy dancers wild as demons.

The horsemen are naked on the four naked horses, and they make gestures as they come towards the painted door. The horses are alternately red and black, the red having blue manes and hoofs, the black, red ones, or white. They are tall archaic horses on slim legs, with necks arched like a curved knife. And they come pinking daintily and superbly along, with their long tails, towards the dark red death-door.

From the left, the stream of dancers leaps wildly, playing music, carrying garlands or wine-jugs, lifting their arms like revellers, lifting their live knees, and signalling with their long hands. Some have little inscriptions written near them: their names.

And above the false door in the angle of the gable is a fine design: two black, wide-mouthed, pale-maned lions seated back to back, their tails rising like curved stems, between them, as they each one lift a black paw against the cringing head of a cowering spotted deer, that winces to the death-blow. Behind each deer is a smaller dark lion, in the acute angle of the roof, coming up to bite the shrinking deer in the haunch, and so give the second death-wound. For the wounds of death are in the neck and in the flank.

At the other end of the tomb are wrestlers and gamesters; but so shadowy now! We cannot see any more, nor look any further in the shadows for the unconquerable life of the Etruscans, whom the Romans called vicious, but whose life, in these tombs, is certainly fresh and cleanly vivid.

The upper air is wide and pale, and somehow void. We cannot see either world any more, the Etruscan underworld nor the common day. Silently, tired, we walk back in the wind to the town, the old dog padding stoically behind. And the guide promises to take us to the other tombs tomorrow.

There is a haunting quality in the Etruscan representations. Those leopards with their long tongues hanging out: those flowing hippocampi; those cringing spotted deer, struck in flank and neck; they get into the imagination, and will not go out. And we see the wavy edge of the sea, the dolphins curving over, the diver going down clean, the little man climbing up the rock after him so eagerly. Then the men with beards who recline on the banqueting beds: how they hold up the mysterious egg! And the women with the conical head-dress, how strangely they lean forward, with caresses we no longer know! The naked slaves joyfully stoop to the wine-jars. Their nakedness is its own clothing, more easy than drapery. The curves of their limbs show pure pleasure in life, a pleasure that goes deeper still in the limbs of the dancers, in the big, long hands thrown out and dancing to the very ends of the fingers, a dance that surges from within, like a current in the sea. It is as if the current of some strong different life swept through them, different from our shallow current today: as if they drew their vitality from different depths that we are denied.

Yet in a few centuries they lost their vitality. The Romans took the life out of them. It seems as if the power of resistance to life, self-assertion, and overbearing, such as the Romans knew: a power which must needs be moral, or carry morality with it, as a cloak for its inner ugliness: would always succeed in destroying the natural flowering of life. And yet there still are a few wild flowers and creatures.

The natural flowering of life! It is not so easy for human beings as it sounds. Behind all the Etruscan liveliness was a religion of life, which the chief men were seriously responsible for. Behind all the dancing was a vision, and even a science of life, a conception of the universe and man's place in the universe which made men live to the depth of their capacity.

To the Etruscan all was alive; the whole universe lived; and the business of man was himself to live amid it all. He had to draw life into himself, out of the wandering huge vitalities of the world. The cosmos was alive, like a vast creature. The whole thing breathed and stirred. Evaporation went up like breath from the nostrils of a whale, steaming up. The sky received it in its blue bosom, breathed it in and pondered on it and transmuted it, before breathing it out again. Inside the earth were fires like the heat in the hot red liver of a beast. Out of the fissures of the earth came breaths of other breathing, vapours direct from the living physical underearth, exhalations carrying inspiration. The whole thing was alive, and had a great soul, or *anima:* and in spite of one great soul, there were myriad roving, lesser souls: every man, every creature and tree and lake and mountain and stream, was animate, had its own peculiar consciousness. And has it today.

The cosmos was one, and its *anima* was one; but it was made up of creatures. And the greatest creature was earth, with its soul of inner fire. The sun was only a reflection, or off-throw, or brilliant handful, of the great inner fire. But in juxtaposition to earth lay the sea, the waters that moved and pondered and held a deep soul of their own. Earth and waters lay side by side, together, and utterly different.

So it was. The universe, which was a single aliveness with a single soul, instantly changed, the moment you thought of it, and became a dual creature with two souls, fiery and watery, for ever mingling and rushing apart, and held by the great aliveness of the universe in an ultimate equilibrium. But they rushed together and they rushed apart, and immediately they became myriad: volcanoes and seas, then streams and mountains, trees, creatures, men. And everything was dual, or contained its own duality, for ever mingling and rushing apart.

The old idea of the vitality of the universe was evolved long before history begins, and elaborated into a vast religion before we get a glimpse of it. When history does begin, in China or India, Egypt, Babylonia, even in the Pacific and in aboriginal America, we see evidence of one underlying religious idea: the conception of the vitality of the cosmos, the myriad vitalities in wild confusion, which still is held in some sort of array: and man, amid all the glowing welter, adventuring, struggling, striving for one thing, life, vitality, more vitality: to get into himself more and more of the gleaming vitality of the cosmos. That is the treasure. The active religious idea was that man, by vivid attention and subtlety and exerting all his strength, could draw more life into himself, more life, more and more glistening vitality, till he became shining like the morning, blazing like a god. When he was all himself he painted himself vermilion like the throat of dawn, and was god's body, visibly, red and utterly vivid. So he was a prince, a king, a god, an Etruscan Lucumo; Pharaoh, or Belshazzar, or Ashurbanipal, or Tarquin; in a feebler *decrescendo,* Alexander, or Caesar, or Napoleon.

This was the idea at the back of all the great old civilizations. It was even, half-transmuted, at the back of David's mind, and voiced in the Psalms. But with David the living cosmos became merely a personal god. With the Egyptians and Babylonians and Etruscans, strictly there were no personal gods. There were only idols or symbols. It was the living cosmos itself, dazzlingly and gaspingly complex, which was divine, and which could be contemplated only by the strongest soul, and only at moments. And only the peerless soul could draw into itself some last flame from the quick. Then you had a king-god indeed.

There you have the ancient idea of kings, kings who are gods by vividness, because they have gathered into themselves core after core of vital potency from the universe, till they are clothed in scarlet, they are bodily a piece of the deepest fire. Pharaohs and kings of Nineveh, kings of the East, and Etruscan Lucumones, they are the living clue to the pure fire, to the cosmic vitality. They are the vivid key to life, the vermilion clue to the mystery and the delight of death and life. They, in their own body, unlock the vast treasure-house of the cosmos for their people, and bring out life, and show the way into the dark of death, which is the blue burning of the one fire. They, in their own bodies, are the life-bringers and the death-guides, leading ahead in the dark, and coming out in the day with more than sunlight in their bodies. Can one wonder that such dead are wrapped in gold; or were?

The life-bringers, and the death-guides. But they set guards at the gates both of life and death. They keep the secrets, and safeguard the way. Only a few are initiated into the mystery of the bath of life, and the bath of death: the pool within pool within pool, wherein, when a man is dipped, he becomes darker than blood, with death, and brighter than fire, with life; till at last he is scarlet royal as a piece of living life, pure vermilion.

The people are not initiated into the cosmic ideas, nor into the awakened throb of more vivid consciousness. Try as you may, you can never make the mass of men throb with full awakenedness. They *cannot* be more than a little aware. So you must give them symbols, ritual and gesture, which will fill their bodies with life up to their own full measure. Any more is fatal. And so the actual knowledge must be guarded from them, lest knowing the formulae, without undergoing at all the experience that corresponds, they may become insolent and impious, thinking they have the all, when they have only an empty monkey-chatter. The esoteric knowledge will always be esoteric, since knowledge is an experience, not a formula. But it is foolish to hand out the formulae. A little knowledge is indeed a dangerous thing. No age proves it more than ours. Monkey-chatter is at last the most disastrous of all things.

The clue to the Etruscan life was the Lucumo, the religious prince. Beyond him were the priests and warriors. Then came the people and the slaves. People and warriors and slaves did not think about religion. There would soon have been no religion left. They felt the symbols and danced the sacred dances. For they were always kept *in touch,* physically, with the mysteries. The 'touch' went from the Lucumo down to the merest slave. The blood-stream was unbroken. But 'knowing' belonged to the high-born, the pure-bred.

So, in the tombs we find only the simple, uninitiated vision of the people. There is none of the priest-work of Egypt. The symbols are to the artist just wonderforms, pregnant with emotion and good for decoration. It is so all the way through Etruscan art. The artists evidently were of the people, artisans. Presumably they were of the old Italic stock, and understood nothing of the religion in its intricate form, as it had come in from the East: though doubtless the crude principles of the official religion were the same as those of the primitive religion of the aborigines. The same crude principles ran through the religions of all the barbaric world of that time, Druid or Teutonic or Celtic. But the newcomers in Etruria held secret the science and philosophy of their religion, and gave the people the symbols and the ritual, leaving the artists free to use the symbols as they would; which shows that there was no priest-rule.

Later, when scepticism came over all the civilized world, as it did after Socrates, the Etruscan religion began to die, Greeks and Greek rationalism flooded in, and Greek stories more or less took the place of the old Etruscan symbolic thought. Then again the

321

Etruscan artists, uneducated, used the Greek stories as they had used the Etruscan symbols, quite freely, making them over again just to please themselves.

But one radical thing the Etruscan people never forgot, because it was in their blood as well as in the blood of their masters: and that was the mystery of the journey out of life, and into death; the death-journey, and the sojourn in the after-life. The wonder of their soul continued to play round the mystery of this journey and this sojourn.

In the tombs we see it; throes of wonder and vivid feeling throbbing over death. Man moves naked and glowing through the universe. Then comes death: he dives into the sea, he departs into the underworld.

The sea is that vast primordial creature that has a soul also, whose inwardness is womb of all things, out of which all things emerged, and into which they are devoured back. Balancing the sea is the earth of inner fire, of after-life, and before-life. Beyond the waters and the ultimate fire lay only the oneness of which the people knew nothing: it was a secret the Lucumones kept for themselves, as they kept the symbol of it in their hand.

But the sea the people knew. The dolphin leaps in and out of it suddenly, as a creature that suddenly exists, out of nowhere. He was not: and lo! there he is! The dolphin which gives up the sea's rainbows only when he dies. Out he leaps; then, with a head-dive, back again he plunges into the sea. He is so much alive, he is like the phallus carrying the fiery spark of procreation down into the wet darkness of the womb. The diver does the same, carrying like a phallus his small hot spark into the deeps of death. And the sea will give up her dead like dolphins that leap out and have the rainbow within them.

But the duck that swims on the water, and lifts his wings, is another matter: the blue duck, or goose, so often represented by the Etruscans. He is the same goose that saved Rome, in the night.

The duck does not live down within the waters as the fish does. The fish is the *anima*, the animate life, the very clue to the vast sea, the watery element of the first submission. For this reason Jesus was represented in the first Christian centuries as a fish, in Italy especially, where the people still thought in the Etruscan symbols. Jesus was the *anima* of the vast, moist ever-yielding element which was the opposite and the counterpart of the red flame the Pharaohs and the kings of the East had sought to invest themselves with.

But the duck has no such subaqueous nature as the fish. It swims upon the waters, and is hot-blooded, belonging to the red flame, of the animal body of life. But it dives under water, and preens itself upon the flood. So it became, to man, the symbol of that part of himself which delights in the waters, and dives in, and rises up and shakes its wings. It is the symbol of a man's own phallus and phallic life. So you see a man holding on his hand the hot, soft, alert duck, offering it to the maiden. So today the Red Indian makes a secret gift to the maiden of a hollow, earthenware duck, in which is a little fire and incense. It is that part of his body and his fiery life that a man can offer to a maid. And it is that awareness or alertness in him, that other consciousness, that wakes in the night and rouses the city.

But the maid offers the man a garland, the rim of flowers from the edge of the 'pool', which can be placed over the man's head and laid on his shoulders, in symbol that he is invested with the power of the maiden's mystery and different strength, the female power. For whatever is laid over the shoulders is a sign of power added.

Birds fly portentously on the walls of the tombs. The artist must often have seen these priests, the augurs, with their crooked, bird-headed staffs in their hand, out on a high place watching the flight of larks or pigeons across the quarters of the sky. They were reading the signs and the portents, looking for an indication, how they should direct the course of some serious affair. To us it may seem foolish. To them, hot-blooded birds flew through the living universe as feelings and premonitions fly through the breast of a man, or as thoughts fly through the mind. In their flight the suddenly roused birds, or the steady, far-coming birds, moved wrapped in a deeper consciousness, in the complex destiny of all things. And since all things corresponded in the ancient world, and man's bosom mirrored itself in the bosom of the sky, or *vice versa,* the birds were flying to a portentous goal, in the man's breast who watched, as well as flying their own way in the bosom of the sky. If the augur could see the birds flying *in his heart,* then he would know which way destiny too was flying for him.

The science of augury certainly was no exact science. But it was as exact as our sciences of psychology or political economy. And the augurs were as clever as our politicians, who also must practise divination, if ever they are to do anything worth the name. There is no other way when you are dealing with life. And if you live by the cosmos, you look in the cosmos for your clue. If you live by a personal god, you pray to him. If you are rational, you think things over. But it all amounts to the same thing in the end. Prayer, or thought, or studying the stars, or watching the flight of birds, or studying the entrails of the sacrifice, it is all the same process, ultimately: of divination. All it depends on is the amount of *true,* sincere, religious concentration you can bring to bear on your object. An act of pure attention, if you are capable of it, will bring its own answer. And you choose that object to concentrate upon which will best focus your consciousness. Every real discovery made, every serious and significant decision ever reached, was reached and made by divination. The soul stirs, and makes an act of pure attention, and that is a discovery.

The science of the augur and the haruspex was not so foolish as our modern science of political economy. If the hot liver of the victim cleared the soul of the haruspex, and made him capable of that ultimate inward attention which alone tells us the last thing we need to know, then why quarrel with the haruspex? To him, the universe was alive, and in quivering *rapport* To him, the blood was conscious: he thought with his heart. To him, the blood was the red and shining stream of consciousness itself Hence, to him, the liver, that great organ where the blood struggles and 'overcomes death', was an object of profound mystery and significance. It stirred his soul and purified his consciousness; for it was also his victim. So he gazed into the hot liver, that was mapped out in fields and regions like the sky of stars, but these fields and regions were those of the red, shining consciousness that runs through the whole animal creation. And therefore it must contain the answer to his own blood's question.

It is the same with the study of stars, or the sky of stars. Whatever object will bring the consciousness into a state of pure attention, in a time of perplexity, will also give back an answer to the perplexity. But it is truly a question of *divination.* As soon as there is any pretence of infallibility, and pure scientific calculation, the whole thing becomes a fraud and a jugglery. But the same is true not only of augury and astrology, but also of prayer and of pure reason, and even of the discoveries of the great laws and principles of science. Men juggle with prayer today as once they juggled with augury; and in the same way they are juggling with science. Every great discovery or decision comes by an act of divination. Facts are fitted round afterwards.

But all attempt at divination, even prayer and reason and research itself, lapses into jugglery when the heart loses its purity. In the impurity of his heart, Socrates often juggled logic unpleasantly. And no doubt, when scepticism came over the ancient world, the haruspex and the augur became jugglers and pretenders. But for centuries they held real sway. It is amazing to see, in Livy, what a big share they must have had in the building up of the great Rome of the Republic.

Turning from birds to animals, we find in the tombs the continual repetition of lion against deer. As soon as the world was created, according to the ancient idea, it took on duality. All things became dual, not only in the duality of sex, but in the polarity of action. This is the 'impious pagan duality'. It did not, however, contain the later pious duality of good and evil.

The leopard and the deer, the lion and the bull, the cat and the dove, or the partridge, these are part of the great duality, or polarity of the animal kingdom. But they do not represent good action and evil action. On the contrary, they represent the polarized activity of the divine cosmos, in its animal creation.

The treasure of treasures is the soul, which, in every creature, in every tree or pool, means that mysterious conscious point of balance or equilibrium between the two halves of the duality, the fiery and the watery. This mysterious point clothes itself in vividness after vividness from the right hand, and vividness after vividness from the left. And in death it does not disappear, but is stored in the egg, or in the jar, or even in the tree which brings forth again.

But the soul itself, the conscious spark of every creature, is not dual; and being the immortal, it is also the altar on which our mortality and our duality is at last sacrificed.

So as the key-picture in the tombs, we have over and over again the heraldic beasts facing one another across the altar, or the tree, or the vase; and the lion is smiting the deer in the hip and the throat. The deer is spotted, for day and night, the lion is dark and light the same.

The deer or lamb or goat or cow is the gentle creature with udder of overflowing milk and fertility; or it is the stag or ram or bull, the great father of the herd, with horns of power set obvious on the brow, and indicating the dangerous aspect of the beasts of fertility. These are the creatures of prolific, boundless procreation, the beasts of peace and increase. So even Jesus is the lamb. And the endless, endless gendering of these creatures will fill all the earth with cattle till herds rub flanks over all the world, and hardly a tree can rise between.

But this must not be so, since they are only half, even of the animal creation. Balance must be kept. And this is the altar we are all sacrificed upon: it is even death; just as it is our soul and purest treasure.

So, on the other hand from the deer, we have lionesses and leopards. These, too, are male and female. These, too, have udders of milk and nourish young; as the wolf nourished the first Romans: prophetically, as the destroyers of many deer, including the Etruscan. So these fierce ones guard the treasure and the gateway, which the prolific ones would squander or close up with too much gendering. They bite the deer in neck and haunch, where the great blood-streams run.

So the symbolism goes all through the Etruscan tombs. It is very much the symbolism of all the ancient world. But here it is not exact and scientific, as in Egypt. It is simple and rudimentary, and the artist plays with it as a child with fairy stories. Nevertheless, it is the symbolic element which rouses the deeper emotion, and gives the peculiarly satisfying quality to the dancing figures and the creatures. A painter like Sargent, for example, is so clever. But in the end he is utterly uninteresting, a bore. He never has an inkling of his own triviality and silliness. One Etruscan leopard, even one little quail, is worth all the miles of him.

4. THE PAINTED TOMBS OF TARQUINIA II

We sit at the tin tables of the café above the gate watching the peasants coming in the evening from the fields, with their implements and their asses. As they drift in through the gate the man of the Dazio, the town customs, watches them, asks them questions if they carry bundles, prods the pack on the ass, and when a load of brush-wood rolls up keeps it halted while he pierces the load with a long steel rod, carefully thrusting to see if he can feel hidden barrels of wine or demijohns of oil, bales of oranges or any other foodstuffs. Because all foodstuffs that come into an Italian town — many other things too, besides comestibles — must pay a duty, in some instances a heavy one.

Probably in Etruscan days the peasants came in very much the same, at evening, to the town. The Etruscans were instinctively citizens. Even the peasants dwelt within walls. And in those days, no doubt, the peasants were serfs very much as they are today in Italy, working the land for no wages, but for a portion of the produce; and working the land intensely, with that careful, almost passionate attention the Italian still gives to the soil; and living in the city, or village, but having straw huts out in the fields, for summer.

But in those days, on a fine evening like this, the men would come in naked, darkly ruddy-coloured from the sun and wind, with strong, insouciant bodies; and the women would drift in, wearing the loose, becoming smock of white or blue linen; and somebody, surely, would be playing on the pipes; and somebody, surely, would be singing, because the Etruscans had a passion for music, and an inner carelessness the modem Italians have lost. The peasants would enter the clear, clean, sacred space inside the gates, and salute the gay-coloured little temple as they passed along the street that rose uphill towards the arx, between rows of low houses with gay-coloured fronts painted or hung with bright terra-cottas. One can almost hear them still, calling, shouting, piping, singing, driving in the mixed flocks of sheep and goats, that go so silently, and leading the slow, white, ghost-like oxen with the yokes still on their necks.

And surely, in those days, young nobles would come splashing in on horseback, riding with naked limbs on an almost naked horse, carrying probably a spear, and cantering ostentatiously through the throng of red-brown, full-limbed, smooth-skinned peasants. A Lucumo, even, sitting very noble in his chariot driven by an erect charioteer, might be driving in at sundown, halting before the temple to perform the brief ritual of entry into the city. And the crowding populace would wait; for, the Lucumo of the old days, glowing ruddy in flesh, his beard stiffly trimmed in the Oriental style, the torque of gold round his neck, and the mantle or wrap bordered with scarlet falling in full folds, leaving the breast bare, he was divine, sitting on the chair in his chariot in the stillness of power. The people drew strength even from looking at him.

The chariot drew a little forward, from the temple: the Lucumo, sitting erect on his chair in the chariot, and bare-shouldered and bare-breasted, waits for the people. Then the peasants would shrink back in fear. But perhaps some citizen in a white tunic would lift up his arms in salute, and come forward to state his difficulty, or to plead for justice. And the Lucumo, seated silent within another world of power, disciplined to his own responsibility of knowledge for the people, would listen till the end. Then a few words — and the chariot of gilt bronze swirls off up the hill to the house of the chief, the citizens drift on to their houses, the music sounds in the dark streets, torches flicker, the whole place is eating, feasting, and as far as possible having a gay time.

It is different now. The drab peasants, muffled in ugly clothing, straggle in across the waste bit of space, and trail home, songless and meaningless. We have lost the art of living; and in the most important science of all, the science of daily life, the science of behaviour, we are complete ignoramuses. We have psychology instead. Today in Italy, in the hot Italian summer, if a navvy working in the street takes off his shirt to work with free, naked torso, a policeman rushes to him and commands him insultingly into his shirt again. One would think a human being was such a foul indecency altogether that life was feasible only when the indecent thing was as far as possible blotted out. The very exposure of female arms and legs in the street is only done as an insult to the whole human body. 'Look at that! It doesn't matter!'

Neither does it! But then, why did the torso of the workman matter?

At the hotel, in the dark emptiness of the place, there are three Japanese staying: little yellow men. They have come to inspect the salt works down on the coast below Tarquinia, so we are told, and they have a Government permit. The salt works, the extracting of salt from the pools shut off from the low sea, are sort of prisons, worked by convict labour. One wonders why Japanese men should want to inspect such places, officially. But we are told that these salt works are 'very important'.

Albertino is having a very good time with the three Japanese, and seems to be very deep in their confidence, bending over their table, his young brown head among the three black ones, absorbed and on the *qui vive.* He rushes off for their food — then rushes to us to see what we want to eat.

"What is there?'

'Er — c'è —, He always begins with wonderful deliberation, as if there was a menu fit for the Tsar. Then he breaks off suddenly, says: 'I'll ask the mamma!' — darts away — returns, and says exactly what we knew he'd say, in a bright voice, as if announcing the New Jerusalem: 'There are eggs — er — and beefsteak — er and there are some little potatoes.' We know the eggs and beefsteak well! However, I decide to have beefsteak once more, with the little potatoes — left over by good fortune from lunch — fried. Off darts Albertino, only to dart back and announce that the potatoes and beefsteak are finished ('by the Chinese,' he whispers), 'but there are frogs.' 'There are what?' *'Le rane,* the frogs!' 'What sort of frogs?' 'I'll show you!' Off he darts again, returns with a plate containing eight or nine pairs of frogs' naked hind-legs. B. looks the other way and I accept frogs — they look quite good. In the joy of getting the frogs safely to port, Albertino skips, and darts off: to return in a moment with a bottle of beer, and whisper to us all the information about the Chinese, as he calls them. They can't speak a word of Italian. When they want a word they take the little book, French and Italian. *Bread?* — eh? They want bread, Er! —Albertino gives little grunts, like commas and semicolons, which I write as *er!* Bread they want, eh? — er! — they take the little book — here he takes an imaginary little book, lays it on the tablecloth, wets his finger and turns over the imaginary leaves — *bread!* — er! — p — you look under 'p' — er! — *ecco! pane! — pane! —si capisce!* — bread! they want bread. Then wine! er! take the little book (he turns over imaginary little leaves with fervour) —er! here you are, *vino! — pane, e vino!* So they do! Every word! They looked out name! Er! you! Er! I tell him, *Albertino.* And so the boy continues, till I ask what about *Le rane?* Ah! Er! *Le rane!* Off he darts, and swirls back with a plate of fried frogs' legs, in pairs.

He is an amusing and vivacious boy, yet underneath a bit sad and wistful, with all his responsibility. The following day he darted to show us a book of views of Venice, left behind by the Chinese, as he persists in calling them, and asks if I want it. I don't. Then he shows us two Japanese postage stamps, and the address of one of the Japanese gentlemen, written on a bit of paper. The Japanese gentleman and Albertino are to exchange picture postcards. I insist that the Japanese are not Chinese. 'Er!' says Albertino. 'But the Japanese are also Chinese!' I insist that they are not, that they live in a different country. He darts off, and returns with a school atlas. 'Er! China is in Asia! Asia! Asia!' — he turns the leaves. He is really an intelligent boy, and ought to be going to school instead of running an hotel at the tender age of fourteen.

The guide to the tombs, having had to keep watch at the museum all night, wants to get a sleep after dawn, so we are not to start till ten. The town is already empty, the people gone out to the fields. A few men stand about with nothing doing. The city gates are wide open. At night they are closed, so that the *Dazio* man can sleep: and you can neither get in nor out of the town. We drink still another coffee — Albertino's morning dose was a very poor show.

Then we see the guide, talking to a pale young fellow in old corduroy velveteen knee-breeches and an old hat and thick boots: most obviously German. We go over, make proper salutes, nod to the German boy, who looks as if he'd had vinegar for breakfast — and set off. This morning we are going out a couple miles, to the farthest end of the necropolis. We have still a dozen tombs to look at. In all, there are either twenty-five or twenty-seven painted tombs one can visit.

This morning there is a stiff breeze from the south-west. But it is blowing fresh and clear, not behaving in the ugly way the *libeccio* can behave. We march briskly along the highway, the old dog trundling behind. He loves spending a morning among the tombs. The sea gives off a certain clearness, that makes the atmosphere doubly brilliant and exhilarating, as if we were on a mountain-top. The omnibus rolls by, from Viterbo. In the fields the peasants are working, and the guide occasionally greets the women, who give him a sally back again. The young German tramps firmly on: but his spirit is not as firm as his tread. One doesn't know what to say to him, he vouchsafes nothing, seems as if he didn't want to be spoken to, and yet is probably offended that we don't talk to him. The guide chatters to him in unfailing cheerfulness, in Italian: but after a while drops back with evident relief to the milder company of B., leaving me to the young German, who has certainly swallowed vinegar some time or other.

But I feel with him as with most of the young people of today: he has been sinned against more than he sins. The vinegar was given him to drink. Breaking reluctantly into German, since Italian seems foolish, and he won't come out in English, I find, within the first half-mile, that he is twenty-three (he looks nineteen), has finished his university course, is going to be an archaeologist, is travelling doing archaeology, has been in Sicily and Tunis, whence he has just returned; didn't think much of either place — *mehr Schrei wie Wert,* he jerks out, speaking as if he were throwing his words away like a cigarette-end he was sick of; doesn't think much of any place; doesn't think much of the Etruscans — *nicht viel wert;* doesn't, apparently, think much of me; knows a professor or two whom I have met; knows the tombs of Tarquinia very well, having been here, and stayed here, twice before; doesn't think much of them; is going to Greece; doesn't expect to think much of it; is staying in the other hotel not Gentile's, because it is still cheaper: is probably staying a fortnight, going to photograph all the tombs, with a big photographic apparatus — has the Government authority, like the Japs — apparently has very little money indeed, marvellously doing everything on nothing — expects to be a famous professor in a science he doesn't think much of — and I wonder if he always has enough to eat.

He certainly is a fretful and peevish, even if in some ways silent and stoical, young man. *Nicht viel wert!* — not much worth — doesn't amount to anything — seems to be his favourite phrase, as it is the favourite phrase of almost all young people today. Nothing amounts to anything, for the young.

Well, I feel it's not my fault, and try to bear up. But though it is bad enough to have been of the war generation, it must be worse to have grown up just after the war. One can't blame the young, that they don't find that anything amounts to anything. The war cancelled most meanings for them.

And my young man is not really so bad: he would even rather like to be *made* to believe in something. There is a yearning pathos in him somewhere.

We have passed the modern cemetery, with its white marble headstones, and the arches of a medieval aqueduct mysteriously spanning a dip, and left the highroad, following a path along the long hill-crest, through the green wheat that flutters and ripples in the sea-wind like fine feathers, in the wonderful brilliance of morning. Here and there are tassels of mauve anemones, bits of verbena, many daisies, tufts of camomile. On a rocky mound, which was once a tumulus, the asphodels have the advantage, and send up their spikes on the bright, fresh air, like soldiers clustered on the mount. And we go along this vivid green headland of wheat — which still is rough and uneven, because it was once all tumuli — with our faces to the breeze, the sea-brightness filling the air with exhilaration, and all the country still and silent, and we talk German in the wary way of two dogs sniffing at one another.

Till suddenly we turn off to an almost hidden tomb — the German boy knows the way perfectly. The guide hurries up and lights the acetylene lamp, the dog slowly finds himself a place out of the wind, and flings himself down: and we sink slowly again into the Etruscan world, out of the present world, as we descend underground.

One of the most famous tombs at this far-off end of the necropolis is the Tomb of the Bulls. It contains what the guide calls: *Un po' di pornografico!* — but a very little. The German boy shrugs his shoulders as usual: but he informs us that this is one of the oldest tombs of all, and I believe him, for it looks so to me.

It is a little wider than some tombs, the roof has not much pitch, there is a stone bed for sarcophagi along the side walls, and in the end wall are two doorways, cut out of the rock of the end and opening into a second chamber, which seems darker and more dismal. The German boy says this second chamber was cut out later, from the first one. It has no paintings of any importance.

We return to the first chamber, the old one. It is called the Tomb of the Bulls from the two bulls above the doorways of the end wall, one a man-faced bull charging at the *'po' di pornografico',* the other lying down serenely and looking with mysterious eyes into the room, his back turned calmly to the second bit of a picture which the guide says is not *'pornografico'* —'because it is a woman.' The young German smiles with his sour-water expression.

Everything in this tomb suggests the old East: Cyprus, or the Hittites, or the culture of Minos of Crete. Between the doorways of the end wall is a charming painting of a naked horseman with a spear, on a naked horse, moving towards a charming little palm-tree and a well-head or fountain-head, on which repose two sculptured, black-faced beasts, lions with queer black faces. From the mouth of the one near the palm-tree water pours down into a sort of altar-bowl, while on the far side a warrior advances, wearing a bronze helmet and shin-greaves, and apparently menacing the horseman with a sword which he brandishes in his left hand, as he steps up on to the base of the well-head. Both warrior and horseman wear the long, pointed boots of the East: and the palm-tree is not very Italian.

This picture has a curious charm, and is evidently symbolical. I said to the German: 'What do you think it means?' 'Ach, nothing! The man on the horse has, come to the drinking-trough to water his horse: no more!' 'And the man with the sword?' 'Oh, he is perhaps his enemy.' 'And the black-faced lions?' 'Ach nothing! Decorations of the fountain.' Below the picture are trees on which hang a garland and a neck-band. The border pattern, instead of the egg and dart, has the sign of Venus, so called, between the darts: a ball surmounted by a little cross. 'And that, is that a symbol?' I asked the German. 'Here no!' he replied abruptly. 'Merely a decoration!' — which is perhaps true. But that the Etruscan artist had no more feeling for it, as a symbol, than a modem house-decorator would have, that we cannot believe.

I gave up for the moment. Above the picture is a sentence lightly written, almost scribbled, in Etruscan. 'Can you read it?' I said to the German boy. He read it off quickly — myself, I should have had to go letter by letter. 'Do you know what it means?' I asked him. He shrugged his shoulders. 'Nobody knows.'

In the shallow angle of the roof the heraldic beasts are curious. The squat centre-piece, the so-called altar, has four rams' heads at the corners. On the right a pale bodied man with a dark face is galloping up with loose rein, on a black horse, followed by a galloping bull. On the left is a bigger figure, a queer galloping lion with his tongue out. But from the lion's shoulders, instead of wings, rises the second neck of a dark-faced, bearded goat: so that the complex animal has a second, backward-leaning neck and head, of a goat, as well as the first maned neck and menacing head of a lion. The tail of the lion ends in a serpent's head. So this is the proper Chimaera. And galloping after the end of the lion's tail comes a winged female sphinx.

'What is the meaning of this lion with the second head and neck?' I asked the German. He shrugged his shoulders, and said: 'Nothing!' It meant nothing to him, because nothing except the A B C of facts means anything to him. He is a scientist, and when he doesn't want a thing to have a meaning it is, *ipso facto*, meaningless.

But the lion with the goat's head springing backwards from its shoulders must mean something, because there it is, very vivid, in the famous bronze Chimaera of Arezzo, which is in the Florence museum, and which Benvenuto Cellini restored, and which is one of the most fascinating bronzes in the world. There, the bearded goat's head springs twisting backwards from the lion's shoulders, while the right horn of the goat is seized in the mouth of the serpent, which is the tail of the lion whipped forward over his back.

Though this is the correct Chimaera, with the wounds of Bellerophon in hip and neck, still it is not merely a big toy. It has, and was intended to have, an exact esoteric meaning. In fact, Greek myths are only gross representations of certain very clear and very ancient esoteric conceptions, that are much older than the myths: or the Greeks. Myths, and personal gods, are only the decadence of a previous cosmic religion.

The strange potency and beauty of these Etruscan things arise, it seems to me, from the profundity of the symbolic meaning the artist was more or less aware of The Etruscan religion, surely, was never anthropomorphic: that is, whatever gods it contained were not *beings,* but symbols of elemental powers, just symbols: as was the case earlier in Egypt. The undivided Godhead, if we can call it such, was symbolized by the *mundum,* the plasm-cell with its nucleus: that which is the very beginning; instead of, as with us, by a personal god, a person being the very end of all creation or evolution. So it is all the way through: the Etruscan religion is concerned with all those physical and creative powers and forces which go to the building up and the destroying of the soul: the soul, the personality, being that which gradually is produced out of chaos, like a flower, only to disappear again into chaos, or the underworld. We, on the contrary, say: In the beginning was the Word! — and deny the physical universe true existence. We exist only in the Word, which is beaten out thin to cover, gild, and hide all things.

The human being, to the Etruscan, was a bull or a ram, a lion or a deer, according to his different aspects and potencies. The human being had in his veins the blood of the wings of birds and the venom of serpents. All things emerged from the blood-stream, and the blood-relation, however complex and contradictory it might become, was never interrupted or forgotten. There were different currents in the blood-stream, and some always clashed: bird and serpent, lion and deer, leopard and lamb. Yet the very clash was a form of unison, as we see in the lion which also has a goat's head.

But the young German will have nothing of this. He is a modern, and the obvious alone has true existence for him. A lion with a goat's head as well as its own head is unthinkable. That which is unthinkable is non-existent, is nothing. So, all the Etruscan symbols are to him non-existent and mere crude incapacity to think. He wastes not a thought on them: they are spawn of mental impotence, hence negligible.

But perhaps also he doesn't want to give himself away, or divulge any secret that is going to make him a famous archaeologist later on. Though I don't think that was it. He was very nice, showing me details, with his flashlight, that I should have overlooked. The white horse, for example, has had its drawing most plainly altered: you can see the old outline of the horse's back legs and breast, and of the foot of the rider, and you can see how considerably the artist changed the drawing, sometimes more than once. He seems to have drawn the whole thing complete, each time, then changed the position, changed the direction, to please his feeling. And as there was no indiarubber to rub out the first attempts, there they are, from at least six hundred years before Christ: the delicate mistakes of an Etruscan who had the instinct of a pure artist in him, as well as the blithe insouciance which makes him leave his alterations for anyone to spy out, if they want to.

The Etruscan artists either drew with the brush or scratched, perhaps, with a nail, the whole outline of their figures on the soft stucco, and then applied their colour *alfresco.* So they had to work quickly. Some of the paintings seemed to me tempera, and in one tomb, I think the Francesco Giustiniani, the painting seemed to be done on the naked, creamy rock. In that case, the blue colour of the man's scarf is marvellously vivid.

The subtlety of Etruscan painting, as of Chinese and Hindu, lies in the wonderfully suggestive *edge* of the figures. It is not outlined. It is not what we call 'drawing'. It is the flowing contour where the body suddenly leaves off, upon the atmosphere. The Etruscan artist seems to have seen living things surging from their own centre to their own surface. And the curving and contour of the silhouette-edge suggests the whole movement of the modelling within. There is actually no modelling. The figures are painted in the flat. Yet they seem of a full, almost turgid muscularity. It is only when we come to the late Tomb of Typhon that we have the figure *modelled,* Pompeian style, with light and shade.

It must have been a wonderful world, that old world where everything appeared alive and shining in the dusk of contact with all things, not merely as an isolated individual thing played upon by daylight; where each thing had a clear outline, visually, but in its very clarity was related emotionally or vitally to strange other things, one thing springing from another, things mentally contradictory fusing together emotionally, so that a lion could be at the same moment also a goat, and not a goat. In those days, a man riding on a red horse was not just Jack Smith on his brown nag; it was a suave-skinned creature, with death or life in its face, surging along on a surge of animal power that burned with travel, with the passionate movement of the blood, and which was swirling along on a mysterious course, to some unknown goal, swirling with a weight of its own. Then also, a bull was not merely a stud animal worth so much, due to go to the butcher in a little while. It was a vast wonder-beast, a well-head of the great, furnace-like passion that makes the worlds roll and the sun surge up, and makes a man surge with procreative force; the bull, the herd-lord, the father of calves and heifers, of cows; the father of milk; he who has the horns of power on his forehead, symbolizing the warlike aspect of the horn of fertility; the bellowing master of force, jealous, horned, charging against opposition. The goat was in the same line, father of milk, but instead of huge force he had cunning, the cunning *consciousness* and self-consciousness of the jealous, hard-headed father of procreation. Whereas the lion was most terrible, yellow and roaring with a blood-drinking energy, again like the sun, but the sun asserting himself in drinking up the life of the earth. For the sun can warm the worlds, like a yellow hen sitting on her eggs. Or the sun can lick up the life of the world with a hot tongue. The goat says: let me breed for ever, till the world is one reeking goat. But then the lion roars from the other blood-stream, which is also in man, and he lifts his paw to strike, in the passion of the other wisdom.

So all creatures are potential in their own way, a myriad manifold consciousness storming with contradictions and oppositions that are eternal, beyond all mental reconciliation. We can know the living world only symbolically. Yet every consciousness, the rage of the lion, and the venom of the snake, *is,* and therefore is divine. All emerges out of the unbroken circle with its nucleus, the germ, the One, the god, if you like to call it so. And man, with his soul and his personality, emerges in eternal connexion with all the rest. The blood-stream is one, and unbroken, yet storming with oppositions and contradictions.

The ancients saw, consciously, as children now see unconsciously, the everlasting *wonder* in things. In the ancient world the three compelling emotions must have been emotions of wonder, fear, and admiration: admiration in the Latin sense of the word, as well as our sense; and fear in its largest meaning, including repulsion, dread, and hate: then arose the last, individual emotion of pride. Love is only a subsidiary factor in wonder and admiration.

But it was by seeing all things alert in the throb of interrelated passional significance that the ancients kept the wonder and the delight in life, as well as the dread and the repugnance. They were like children: but they had the force, the power and the sensual *knowledge* of true adults. They had a world of valuable knowledge, which is utterly lost to us. Where they were true adults, we are children; and vice versa.

Even the two bits of *'pornografico'* in the Tomb of the Bull are not two little dirty drawings. Far from it. The German boy felt this, as we did. The drawings have the same naïve wonder in them as the rest, the same archaic innocence, accepting life, knowing all about it, and *feeling* the meaning, which is like a stone fallen into consciousness, sending its rings ebbing out and out, to the extremes. The two little pictures have a symbolic meaning, quite distinct from a *moral* meaning — or an immoral. The words moral and immoral have no force. Some acts — what Dennis would call flagrant obscenity — the man-faced bull accepts calmly lying down; against other acts he charges with lowered horns. It is not judgement. It is the sway of passional action and reaction: the action and reaction of the father of milk.

There are beautiful tombs, in this far-off wheat-covered hill. The Tomb of the Augurs is very impressive. On the end wall is painted a doorway to a tomb, and on either side of it is a man making what is probably the mourning gesture, strange and momentous, one hand to the brow. The two men are mourning at the door of the tomb.

331

'No!' says the German. 'The painted door does not represent the door to the tomb, with mourners on either side. It is merely the painted door which later they intended to cut out, to make a second chamber to the tomb. And the men are not mourning.'

'Then what are they doing?'

Shrug!

In the triangle above the painted door two lions, a white-faced one and a dark-faced, have seized a goat or an antelope: the dark-faced lion turns over and bites the side of the goat's neck, the white-faced bites the haunch. Here we have again the two heraldic beasts: but instead of their roaring at the altar, or the tree, they are biting the goat, the father of milk-giving life, in throat and hip.

On the side walls are very fine frescoes of nude wrestlers, and then of a scene which has started a lot of talk about Etruscan cruelty. A man with his head in a sack, wearing only a skin-girdle, is being bitten in the thigh by a fierce dog which is held, by another man, on a string attached to what is apparently a wooden leash, this wooden handle being fastened to the dog's collar. The man who holds the string wears a peculiar high conical hat, and he stands, big-limbed and excited, striding behind the man with his head in the sack. This victim is by now getting entangled in the string, the long, long cord which holds the dog; but with his left hand he seems to be getting hold of the cord to drag the dog off from his thigh, while in his right hand he holds a huge club, with which to strike the dog when he can get it into striking range.

This picture is supposed to reveal the barbarously cruel sports of the Etruscans. But since the tomb contains an augur, with his curved sceptre, tensely lifting his hand to the dark bird that flies by: and the wrestlers are wrestling over a curious pile of three great bowls; and on the other side of the tomb the man in the conical pointed hat, he who holds the string in the first picture, is now dancing with a peculiar delight, as if rejoicing in victory or liberation: we must surely consider this picture as symbolic, along with all the rest: the fight of the blindfolded man with some raging, attacking element. If it were sport there would be onlookers, as there are at the sports in the Tomb of the Chariots; and here there are none.

However, the scenes portrayed in the tomb are all *so* real, that it seems they must have taken place in actual life. Perhaps there was some form of test or trial which gave a man a great club, tied his head in a sack, and left him to fight a fierce dog which attacked him, but which was held on a string, and which even had a wooden grip-handle attached to its collar, by which the man might seize it and hold it firm, while he knocked it on the head. The man in the sack has very good chances against the dog. And even granted the thing was done for sport, and not as some sort of trial or test, the cruelty is not excessive, for the man has a very good chance of knocking the dog on the head quite early. Compared with Roman gladiatorial shows, this is almost 'fair play'.

But it must be more than sport. The dancing of the man who held the string is too splendid. And the tomb is, somehow, too intense, too meaningful. And the dog — or wolf or lion —that bites the thigh of the man is too old a symbol. We have it very plainly on the top of the Sarcophagus of the Painted Amazons, in the Florence museum. This sarcophagus comes from Tarquinia — and the end of the lid has a carved naked man, with legs apart, a dog on each side biting him in the thigh. They are the dogs of disease and death, biting at the great arteries of the thigh, where the elementary life surges in a man. The motive is common in ancient symbolism. And the esoteric idea of malevolent influences attacking the great arteries of the thighs was turned in Greece into the myth of Actaeon and his dogs.

332

Another very fine tomb is the Tomb of the Baron, with its frieze of single figures, dark on a light background going round the walls. There are horses and men, all in dark silhouette, and very fascinating in drawing. These archaic horses are so perfectly satisfying *as* horses: so far more horse-like, to the soul, than those of Rosa Bonheur or Rubens or even Velazquez, though he comes nearer to these: so that one asks oneself, what, after all, is the horsiness of a horse? 'What is it that man sees, when he looks at a horse? — what is it that will never be put into words? For a man who secs, sees not as a camera does when it takes a snapshot, not even as a cinema-camera, taking its succession of instantaneous snaps; but in a curious rolling flood of vision, in which the image itself seethes and rolls; and only the mind *picks out* certain factors which *shall* represent the image seen. That is why a camera is so unsatisfactory: its eye is flat, it is related only to a negative thing inside the box: whereas inside our living box there is a decided positive.

We go from tomb to tomb, down into the dark, up again into the wind and brilliance; and the day rolls by. But we are moving, tomb by tomb, gradually nearer the city. The new cemetery draws near. We have passed the aqueduct, which crosses the dip, then takes an underground channel towards the town. Near the cemetery we descend into a big tomb, the biggest we have yet seen — a great underground cavern with great wide beds for sarcophagi and biers, and in the centre a massive square pillar or shaft on which is painted a Typhon — the seaman with coiled snake-legs, and wings behind his arms, his hands holding up the roof; two Typhons, another on the opposite face of the pillar, almost identical with the first.

In this place, almost at once, the Etruscan charm seems to vanish. The tomb is big, crude, somehow ugly like a cavern. The Typhon, with his reddish flesh and light-and-shade modelling, is clever, and might be modern, done for effect. He is rather Pompeian — and a little like Blake. But he is done from quite a new consciousness, external; the old inwardness has gone. Dennis, who saw him eighty years ago, thinks him far more marvellous than the archaic dancers. But we do not.

There are some curly-wig dolphins sporting over a curly border which, but for experience, we should not know was the sea. And there is a border of 'roses' really the sacred symbol of the 'one' with its central germ, here for the first time vulgarly used. There is also a fragment of a procession to Hades, which must have been rather fine in the Greco-Roman style. But the true archaic charm is utterly gone. The dancing Etruscan spirit is dead.

This is one of the very latest tombs: said to be of the second century B.C., when the Romans had long been masters of Tarquinia. Veii, the first great Etruscan city to be captured by Rome, was taken abbut 388 B.C., and completely destroyed. From then on, Etruria gradually weakened and sank, till the peace of 280 B.C., when we may say the military conquest of Etruria was complete.

So that the tombs suddenly change. Those supposed to be of the fifth century, like the Tomb of the Baron, with the frieze of horses and men, or the Tomb of the Leopards, are still perfectly Etruscan, no matter what touch of the Orient they may have, and perfectly charming. Then suddenly we come to the Tomb of Orcus, or Hell, which is given the fourth century as a date, and here the whole thing utterly changes. You get a great gloomy, clumsy, rambling sort of underworld, damp and horrid, with large but much-damaged pictures on the walls.

These paintings, though they are interesting in their way, and have scribbled Etruscan inscriptions, have suddenly lost all Etruscan charm. They still have a bit of Etruscan freedom, but on the whole they are Greco-Roman, half suggesting Pompeian, half

333

suggesting Roman things. They are more free than the paintings of the little old tombs; at the same time, all the motion is gone; the figures are stuck there without any vital flow between them. There is no touch.

Instead of the wonderful old silhouette forms we have modern 'drawing', often quite good. But to me it is an intense disappointment.

When the Roman took the power from the hands of the Etruscan Lucumones — in the fourth century B.C. — and made them merely Roman magistrates, at the best, the mystery of Etruria died almost at once. In the ancient world of king-gods, governing according to a religious conception, the deposition of the chiefs and the leading priests leaves the country at once voiceless and mindless. So it was in Egypt and Babylonia, in Assyria, in the Aztec and Maya lordships of America. The people are governed by the flower of the race. Pluck the flower and the race is helpless.

The Etruscans were not destroyed. But they lost their being. They had lived, ultimately, by the *subjective* control of the great natural powers. Their subjective power fell before the objective power of the Romans. And almost at once the true race-consciousness finished. The Etruscan knowledge became mere superstition. The Etruscan princes became fat and inert Romans. The Etruscan people became expressionless and meaningless. It happened amazingly quickly, in the third and second centuries B.C.

Yet the Etruscan *blood* continued to beat. And Giotto and the early sculptors seem to have been a flowering again of the Etruscan blood, which is always putting forth a flower, and always being trodden down again by some superior 'force'. It is a struggle between the endless patience of life and the endless triumph of force.

There is one other huge late tomb, the Tomb of the Shields, said to be of the third century. It contains many fragmentary paintings. There is a banqueting scene, with a man on the banqueting bench taking the egg from the woman, and she is touching his shoulder. But they might as well be two chairs from a 'suite'. There is nothing between them. And they have those 'important' sort of faces — all on the outside, nothing inside — that are so boring. Yet they are interesting. They might almost be done today, by an ultra-modern artist bent on being absolutely childlike and naïve and archaic. But after the real archaic paintings, these are empty. The air is empty. The egg is still held up. But it means no more to that man and woman than the chocolate Easter egg does to us. It has gone cold.

In the Tomb of Orcus begins that representation of the grisly underworld, hell and its horrors, which surely was reflected on to the Etruscans from the grisly Romans. The lovely little tombs of just one small chamber, or perhaps two chambers, of the earlier centuries give way to these great sinister caverns underground, and hell is fitly introduced.

The old religion of the profound attempt of man to harmonize himself with nature, and hold his own and come to flower in the great seething of life, changed with the Greeks and Romans into a desire to resist nature, to produce a mental cunning and a mechanical force that would outwit Nature and chain her down completely, completely, till at last there should be nothing free in nature at all, all should be controlled, domesticated, put to man's meaner uses. Curiously enough, with the idea of the triumph over nature arose the idea of a gloomy Hades, a hell and purgatory. To the peoples of the great natural religions the after-life was a continuing of the wonder-journey of life. To the peoples of the Idea the after-life is hell, or purgatory, or nothingness, and paradise is an inadequate fiction. But, naturally enough, historians seized on these essentially non-Etruscan evidences, in the Etruscan late tombs, to build up a picture of a gloomy, hellish, serpent-writhing, vicious Etruscan people who were quite rightly stamped out by the noble Romans. This myth is still not dead. Men *never* want to believe the evidence of their senses. They would far rather go on elaborating some 'classical' author. The whole science of history seems to be the picking of old fables and old lies into fine threads, and weaving them up again. Theopompus collected some scandalous tales, and that is quite enough for historians. It is written down, so that's enough. The evidence of fifty million gay little tombs wouldn't weigh a straw. In the beginning was the Word, indeed! Even the word of a Theopompus!

Perhaps the favourite painting for representing the beauties of the Etruscan tombs is the well-known head of a woman, seen in profile with wheat-ears for a head-wreath, or fillet. This head comes from the Tomb of Orcus, and is chosen because it is far more Greek-Roman than it is Etruscan. As a matter of fact, it is rather stupid and self-conscious — and modern. But it belongs to the classic Convention, and men can only see according to a Convention. We haven't exactly plucked our eyes out, but we've plucked out three-fourths of their vision.

After the Tomb of the Typhon one has had enough. There is nothing really Etruscan left. It is better to abandon the necropolis altogether, and to remember that almost everything we know of the Etruscans from the classic authors is comparable to the paintings in the late tombs. It refers only to the fallen, Romanized Etruscans of the decadence.

It is very pleasant to go down from the hill on which the present Tarquinia stands, down into the valley and up to the opposite hill, on which the Etruscan Tarquinii surely stood. There are many flowers, the blue grape-hyacinth and the white, the mauve tassel anemone, and, in a corner of a field of wheat, the big purple anemone, then a patch of the big pale pink anemone with the red, sore centre — the big-petalled sort. It is curious how the anemone varies. Only in this one place in Tarquinia have I found the whity-pink kind, with the dark, sore-red centre. But probably that is just chance.

The town ends really with the wall. At the foot of the wall is wild hillside, and down the slope is only one little farm, with another little house made of straw. The country is clear of houses. The peasants live in the city.

Probably in Etruscan days it was much the same, but there must have been far more people on the land, and probably there were many little straw huts, little temporary houses, among the green corn: and fine roads, such as the Etruscans taught the Romans to build, went between the hills: and the high black walls, with towers, wound along the hill-crest.

The Etruscans, though they grew rich as traders and metal-workers, seem to have lived chiefly by the land. The intense culture of the land by the Italian peasant of today seems like the remains of the Etruscan system. On the other hand, it was Roman, and not Etruscan, to have large villas in the country, with the great compound or 'factory' for the slaves, who were shut in at night, and in gangs taken out to labour during the day. The huge farms of Sicily and Lombardy and other parts of Italy must be a remains of this Roman system: the big *fattorie*. But one imagines the Etruscans had a different system: that the peasants were serfs rather than slaves: that they had their own small portions of land, which they worked to full pitch, from father to son, giving a portion of the produce to the masters, keeping a portion for themselves. So they were half-free, at least, and had a true life of their own, stimulated by the religious life of their masters.

The Romans changed it all. They did not like the country. In palmy days they built great villas with barracks for slaves, out in the country. But, even so, it was easier to get rich by commerce or conquest. So the Romans gradually abandoned the land, which fell into neglect and prepared the way for the Dark Ages.

The wind blows stiffer and stiffer from the south-west. There are no trees: but even the bushes bend away from it. And when we get to the crown of the long, lonely hill on which stood the Etruscan Tarquinii we are almost blown from our feet, and have to sit down behind a thicket of bushes, for a moment's shelter: to watch the great black-and-white cattle stepping slowly down to the drinking-place, the young bulls curving and playing. All along the hilltop the green wheat ruffles like soft hair. Away inland the green land looks empty, save for a far-off town perched on a hilltop, like a vision. On the next hill, towards the sea, Tarquinia holds up her square towers, in vain.

And we are sitting on what would be the arx of the vanished city. Somewhere here the augurs held up their curved staffs, and watched the birds move across the quarters of the city. We can do so much even today. But of the city I cannot find even one stone. It is so lonely and open.

One can go back up a different road, and in through another gate of the city of today. We drop quickly down, in the fierce wind, down to calm. The road winds up slowly from the little valley, but we are in shelter from the wind. So, we pass the first wall, through the first medieval gateway. The road winds inside the wall, past the *Dazio,* but there are no houses. A bunch of men are excitedly playing *morra,* and the shouts of the numbers came up like explosions, with wild excitement. The men glance at us apprehensively, but laugh as we laugh.

So we pass on through a second frowning gateway, inside the second circle of walls. And still we are not in the town. There is still a third wall, and a third massive gate. And then we are in the old part of the town, where the graceful little palazzos of the Middle Ages are turned into stables and barns, and into houses for poor peasants. In front of the lower storey of one little old palace, now a blacksmith's shop, the smith is shoeing a refractory mule, which kicks and plunges, and brings loud shouts from the inevitable little group of onlookers.

Queer and lonely and slummy the waste corners and narrow streets seem, forlorn, as if belonging to another age. On a beautiful stone balcony a bit of poor washing is drying. The houses seem dark and furtive, people lurking like rats. And then again rises another tall, sharp-edged tower, blank and blind. They have a queer effect on a town, these sharp, rigid, blind, meaningless towers, soaring away with their sharp edges into the sky, for no reason, beyond the house-roofs; and from the far distance, when one sees the little city down far off, suggesting the factory chimneys of a modern town.

They are the towers which in the first place were built for retreat and defence, when this coast was ravaged by sea-rovers, Norman adventurers, or Barbary pirates that were such a scourge to the Mediterranean. Later, however, the medieval nobles built towers just for pure swank, to see who should have the tallest, till a town like Bologna must have bristled like a porcupine in a rage, or like Pittsburg with chimney-stacks —square ones. Then the law forbade towers — and towers, after having scraped the heavens, begin to come down. There are some still, however, in Tarquinia, where age overlaps age.

5. VULCI

ANCIENT Etruria consisted of a league, or loose religious Confederacy of twelve cities, each city embracing some miles of country all around, so that we may say there were twelve states, twelve city-states, the famous *dodecapolis* of the ancient world, the Latin *duodecim populi Etruriae.* Of these twelve city-states, Tarquinii was supposed to be the oldest, and the chief. Caere is another city: and not far off, to the north, Vulci.

Vulci is now called Volci — though there is no city, only a hunting ground for treasure in Etruscan tombs. The Etruscan city fell into decay in the decline of the Roman Empire, and either lapsed owing to the malaria which came to fill this region with death, or else was finally wiped out, as Ducati says, by the Saracens. Anyhow there is no life there now.

I asked the German boy about the Etruscan places along the coast: Volci, Vetulonia, Populonia. His answer was always the same: 'Nothing! Nothing! There is nothing there!'

However, we determined to look at Volci. It lies only about a dozen miles north of Tarquinia. We took the train, one station only, to Montalto di Castro, and were rattled up to the little town on the hill, not far inland. The morning was still fairly early — and Saturday. But the town, or village, on the hill was very quiet and dead-alive. We got down from the bus in a sort of nowhere-seeming little piazza: the town had no centre of life. But there was a café, so in we went, asked for coffee, and where could we get a carriage to take us to Volci.

The man in the little café was yellow and slow, with the slow smile of the peasants. He seemed to have no energy at all: and eyed us lethargically. Probably he had malaria — though the fevers were not troubling him at the time. But it had eaten into his life.

He said, did we want to go to the bridge — the *Ponte?* I said yes, the *Ponte dell' Abbadia:* because I knew that Volci was near to this famous old bridge of the monastery. I asked him if we could get a light cart to drive us out. He said it would be difficult. I said, then we could walk: it was only five miles, eight kilometres. 'Eight kilometres!' he said, in the slow, laconic malarial fashion, looking at me with a glint of ridicule in his black eyes. 'It is at least twelve!'

'The book says eight!' I insisted stoutly. They always want to make distances twice as long, if you are to hire a carriage. But he watched me slowly, and shook his head. 'Twelve!' he said. 'Then we must have a carriage,' said I. 'You wouldn't find your way anyhow,' said the man. 'Is there a carriage?' He didn't know. There was one, but it had gone off somewhere this morning, and wouldn't be back till two or three in the afternoon. The usual story.

I insisted, was there no little cart, no *barrocino,* no *carretto?* He slowly shook his head. But I continued to insist, gazing at him fixedly, as if a carriage *must* be produced. So at last he went out, to look. He came back, after a time, shaking his head. Then he had a colloquy with his wife. Then he went out again, and was gone ten minutes.

A dusty little baker, a small man very full of energy, as little Italians often are, came in and asked for a drink. He sat down a minute and drank his drink, eyeing us from his floury face. Then he got up and left the shop again. In a moment the café man returned, and said that perhaps there was a *carretto.* I asked where it was. He said the man was coming.

The drive to the Ponte was apparently two hours — then the trip would be six hours. We should have to take a little food with us — there was nothing there.

A small-faced, weedy sort of youth appeared in the doorway: also malaria! We could have the *carretto.* 'For how much?'

'Seventy liras!' 'Too much!' said I. 'Far too much! Fifty, or nothing. Take it or leave it, fifty!' The youth in the doorway looked blank. The café man, always with his faint little sardonic smile, told the youth to go and ask. The youth went. We waited. Then the youth came back, to say all right! So! 'How long?' *'Subito!'* *Subito* means immediately, but it is as well to be definite. 'Ten minutes?' said I. 'Perhaps twenty!' said the youth. 'Better say twenty!' said the café man: who was an honest man, really, and rather pleasant in his silent way.

We went out to buy a little food, and the café man went with us. The shops in the place were just holes. We went to the baker. Outside stood a cart being loaded with bread, by the youth and the small, quicksilver baker. Inside the shop, we bought a long loaf, and a few bits of sliced sausage, and asked for cheese. There was no cheese — but they would get us some. We waited an infinite while. I said to the café man, who waited alongside, full of interest: 'Won't the *carretto* be ready?' He turned round and pointed to the tall, randy mare between the shafts of the bread-cart outside. 'That's the horse that will take you. When the bread is delivered, they will hitch her into the *carretto,* and the youth will drive you.' There was nothing for it but patience, for the baker's mare and the baker's youth were our only hope. The cheese came at last. We wandered out to look for oranges. There was a woman selling them on a low bench beside the road, but B., who was getting impatient, didn't like the look of them. So we went across to a little hole of a shop where another woman had oranges. They were tiny ones, and B. was rejecting them with impatient scorn. But the woman insisted they were sweet, sweet as apples, and full of juice. We bought four and I bought *a finocchio* for a salad. But she was right. The oranges were exquisite, when we came to eat them, and we wished we had ten.

On the whole, I think the people in Montalto are honest and rather attractive, but most of them slow and silent, It must be the malaria every time.

The café man asked if we would stay the night. We said, was there an inn? He said: 'Oh yes, several!' I asked where, and he pointed up the street. 'But,' said I, 'what do you want with several hotels here?' 'For the agents who come to buy agricultural produce,' he said. 'Montalto is the centre of a great agricultural industry, and many agents come, many!' However, I decided that, if we could, we would leave in the evening. There was nothing in Montalto to keep us.

At last the *carretto* was ready; a roomy, two-wheeled gig hung rather low. We got in, behind the dark, mulberry mare, and the baker's youth, who certainly hadn't washed his face for some days, started us on the trip. He was in an agony of shyness, stupefied.

The town is left behind at once. The green land, squares of leaden-dark olives planted in rows slopes down to the railway line, which runs along the coast parallel with the ancient Via Aurelia. Beyond the railway is the flatness of the coastal strip, and the whitish emptiness of the sea's edge. It gives a great sense of nothingness, the sea down there.

The mulberry mare, lean and spare, reaches out and makes a good pace. But very soon we leave the road and are on a wide, wide trail of pinkish clayey earth, made up entirely of ruts. In parts the mud is still deep, water stands in the fathomless mud-holes. But fortunately, for a week it hasn't rained, so the road is passable; most of the ruts are dry, and the wide trail, wide as a desert road which has no confines, is not difficult, only jolly. We run the risk of having our necks jerked out of their sockets by the impatient, long-striding mare.

The boy is getting over his shyness, now he is warmed up to driving, and proves outspoken and straightforward. I said to him: 'What a good thing the road is dry!' 'If it had been fifteen days ago,' he said, 'you couldn't have passed.' But in the late afternoon, when we were returning on the same road and I said: 'In bad wet weather we should have to come through here on horseback,' he replied: 'Even with the *carretto* you can get through.' 'Always?' said I. 'Always!' said he.

And that was how he was. Possibility or impossibility was just a frame of mind with him.

We were on the Maremma, that flat, wide plain of the coast that has been water-logged for centuries, and one of the most abandoned, wildest parts of Italy. Under the Etruscans, apparently, it was an intensely fertile plain. But the Etruscans seem to have been very clever drainage-engineers; they drained the land so that it was a waving bed of wheat, with their methods of intensive peasant culture. Under the Romans, however, the elaborate system of canals and levels of water fell into decay, and gradually the streams threw their mud along the coast and choked themselves, then soaked into the land and made marshes and vast stagnant shallow pools where the mosquitoes bred like fiends, millions hatching on a warm May day; and with the mosquitoes came the malaria, called the marsh fever in the old days. Already in late Roman times this evil had fallen on the Etruscan plains and on the Campagna of Rome. Then, apparently, the land rose in level, the sea-strip was wider but even more hollow than before, the marshes became deadly, and human life departed or was destroyed, or lingered on here and there.

In Etruscan days, no doubt, large tracts of this coast were covered with pine-forest, as are the slopes of the mountains that rise a few miles inland, and stretches of the coast, still farther north. The pleasant *pineta,* or open, sparse forest of umbrella-pines, once spread on and on, with tall arbutus and heather covering the earth from which the reddish trunks rose singly, as from an endless moor, and tufts of arbutus and broom making thickets. The pine-woods farther north are still delightful, so silent and bosky, with the umbrella roofs.

But the pine will not bear being soaked. So, as the great pools and marshes spread, the trees of Etruscan days fell for ever, and great treeless tracts appeared, covered with an almost impenetrable low jungle of bush and scrub and reeds, spreading for miles, and quite manless. The arbutus, that is always glossy green, and the myrtle, the mastic-tree, heaths, broom, and other spiny, gummy, coarse moorland plants rose up in dense luxuriance, to have their tops bent and whipped off by the everwhipping winds from the sea, so that there was a low, dark jungle of scrub, less than man-high, stretching in places from the mountains almost to the sea. And here the wild boar roamed in herds; foxes and wolves hunted the rabbits, the hares, the roebuck; the innumerable wild-fowl and the flamingoes walked the sickly, stricken shores of the great pools and the sea.

So the Maremma country lay for centuries, with cleared tracts between, and districts a little elevated, and therefore rich in produce, but for the most part a wilderness, where the herdsmen pastured sheep, if possible, and the buffaloes roamed unherded. In 1828, however, the Grand-duke Leopold of Tuscany signed the decree for the reclaiming of the Maremma, and lately the Italian Government has achieved splendid results — great tracts of farmland added on to the country's resources, and new farms struck up.

But still there are large tracts of moorland. We bowled along the grassy ruts, towards the distant mountains, and first all was wheat: then it was moorland, with great, grey-headed carrion-crows floating around in the bareness; then a little thicket of ilex-oak; then another patch of wheat; and then a desolate sort of farmhouse, that somehow reminded one of America, a rather dismal farm on the naked prairie, all alone.

The youth told me he had been for two years *guardiano,* or herdsman, at this place. The large cattle were lingering around the naked house, within the wire enclosure. But there was a notice that the place was shut off, because of foot-and-mouth disease. The driver saluted a dismal woman and two children as he drove by.

We made a good pace. The driver, Luigi, told me his father had been also a *guardiano,* a herdsman, in this district, his five sons following him. The youth would look round, into the distance, with that keen, far-off look of men who have always lived wild and apart, and who are in their own country. He knew every sign. And he was so glad to get out again, out of Montalto.

The father, however, had died, a brother had married and lived in the family house, and Luigi had gone to help the baker in Montalto. But he was not happy: caged. He revived and became alert once more out in the Maremma spaces. He had lived more or less alone all his life — he was only eighteen — and loneliness, space, was precious to him, as it is to a moorland bird.

The great hooded crows floated round, and many big meadow-larks rose up from the moor. Save for this, everything to us was silent. Luigi said that now the hunting season was closed: but still, if he had a gun, he could take a shot at those hooded crows. It was obvious he was accustomed to have a gun in his hand when he was out in the long, hot, malarial days, mounted on a pony, watching the herds of cattle roving on the Maremma. Cattle do not take malaria.

I asked him about game. He said there was much in the foothills there. And he pointed away ahead, to where the mountains began to rise, six or eight miles away. Now so much of the Maremma itself is drained and cleared, the game is in the hills. His father used to accompany the hunters in winter: they still arrive in winter-time, the hunters in their hunting outfit, with dogs, and a great deal of fuss and paraphernalia, from Rome or from Florence. And still they catch the wild boar, the fox, the *capriolo:* which I suppose means the roedeer rather than the wild goat. But the boar is the *pièce de resistance.* You may see his bristling carcass in the market-place in Florence, now and again, in winter. But, like every other wild thing on earth, he is becoming scarcer and scarcer. Soon the only animals left will be tame ones: man the tamest and most swarming. Adieu even to Maremma.

'There!' said the boy. 'There is the bridge of the monastery!' We looked into the shallow hollow of green land, and could just see a little, black sort of tower by some bushes, in the empty landscape. There was a long, straight ditch or canal, and digging evidently going on. It was the Government irrigation works.

We left the road and went bowling over rough grass, by tracts of poor-looking oats. Luigi said they would cut these oats for fodder. There was a scrap of a herdsman's house, and new wire fences along the embankment of the big irrigation canal. This was new to Luigi. He turned the mare uphill again, towards the house, and asked the urchin where he was to get through the wire fence. The urchin explained — Luigi had it in a moment. He was intelligent as a wild thing, out here in his own spaces.

'Five years ago,' he said, 'there was none of this' — and he pointed around. 'No canal, no fences, no oats, no wheat. It was all *maremma,* moorland, with no life save the hooded crows, the cattle and the herdsmen. Now the cattle are all going — the herds are only remnants. And the ranch-houses are being abandoned.' He pointed away to a large house some miles off, on the nearest hill-foot. 'There, there are no more cattle, no more herdsmen. The steam-plough comes and ploughs the earth, the machinery sows and reaps the wheat and oats, the people of the Maremma, instead of being more, are fewer. The wheat grows by machinery.'

We were on a sort of trail again, bowling down a slight incline towards a bushy hollow and a black old ruin with a tower. Soon we saw that in the hollow was a tree-filled ravine, quite deep. And over the ravine a queer bridge, curving up like a rainbow, and narrow and steep and fortified-seeming. It soared over the ravine in one high curve, the stony path nipped in like a gutter between its broken walls, and charging straight at the black lava front of the ruin opposite, which was once a castle of the frontier. The little river in the gully, the Fiora, formed the boundary between the Papal States and Tuscany, so the castle guarded the bridge.

We wanted to get down, but Luigi made us wait, while he ran ahead to negotiate. He came back, climbed in, and drove up between the walls of the bridge. It was just wide enough for the cart: just. The walls of the bridge seemed to touch us. It was like climbing up a soft of gutter. Far below, way down in a thicket of bushes, the river rushed: the Fiora, a mere torrent or rainstream.

We drove over the bridge, and at the far end the lava wall of the monastery seemed to shut us back, the mare's nose almost touched it. The road, however, turned to the left under an arched gateway. Luigi edged the mare round cleverly. There was just room to get her round with the *carretto,* out of the mouth of the bridge and under the archway, scraping the wall of the castle.

So! We were through. We drove a few yards past the ruin, and got down on a grassy place over the ravine. It was a wonderfully romantic spot. The ancient bridge, built in the first place by the Etruscans of Vulci, of blocks of black *tufo,* goes up in the air like a black bubble, so round and strange. The little river is in the bushy cleft, a hundred feet below. The bridge is in the sky, like a black bubble, most strange and lonely, with the poignancy of perfect things long forgotten. It has of course, been restored in Roman and medieval days. But essentially it is Etruscan, a beautiful Etruscan movement.

Pressing on to it, on this side, is the black building of the castle, mostly in ruins, with grass growing from the tops of the walls and from the black tower. Like the bridge, it is built of blocks of reddish black, spongy lava-stone, but its blocks are much squarer.

And all around is a peculiar emptiness. The castle is not entirely ruined. It is a sort of peasant farmstead. Luigi knows the people who live there. And across the stream there are patches of oats, and two or three cattle feeding, and two children. But all on this side, towards the mountains, is heathy, waste moorland, over which the trail goes towards the hills, and towards a great house among trees which we had seen from the distance. That is the *Badia,* or monastery, which gave the name to the bridge. But it has long been turned into a villa. The whole of this property belonged to Lucien Bonaparte, Prince of Canino, brother of Napoleon. He lived here after the death of his brother, as an Italian prince. In 1828 some oxen ploughing the land near the castle suddenly went through the surface of the earth, and sank into a tomb, in which were broken vases. This at once led to excavations. It was the time when the 'Grecian urn' was most popular. Lucien Bonaparte had no interest in vases. He hired an overseer to superintend the excavating, giving orders that every painted fragment must be saved, but that coarse ware must be smashed, to prevent the cheapening of the market. So that the work went savagely on, vases and basketfuls of broken pieces were harvested, the coarse, rough black Etruscan ware was smashed to pieces, as it was discovered, the overseer guarding the workmen with his gun over his knees. Dennis saw this still happening in 1846, when Lucien was dead. But the work was still going on, under the Princess's charge. And vainly Dennis asked the overseer to spare him some of the rough black ware. Not one! Smash they went to earth, while the overseer sat with his gun over his knees ready to shoot. But the bits of painted pottery were most skilfully fitted together, by the Princess's expert workmen, and she would sell some patera or amphora for a thousand crowns, which had been a handful of potsherds. The tombs were opened, rifled, and then filled in with earth again. All the landed proprietors with property in the neighbourhood carried on excavations, and endless treasure was exhumed. Within two months of the time when he started excavating, Lucien Bonaparte had got more than two thousand Etruscan objects out of tombs occupying a few acres of ground. That the Etruscans should have left fortunes to the Bonapartes seems an irony; but so it was. Vulci had mines indeed: but mostly of painted vases, those 'brides of quietness' which had been only too much ravished. The tombs have little to show now.

We ate our food, the mare cropping the grass. And I wondered, seeing youths on bicycles, four or five, come swooping down the trail across the stream, out of emptiness, dismount and climb the high curve of the bridge, then disappear into the castle. From the mountains a man came riding on an ass: a pleasant young man in corduroy velveteens. He was riding without a saddle. He had a word with Luigi, in the low, secretive tones of the country, and went on towards the bridge. Then across, two men on mules came trotting down to the bridge: and a peasant drove in two bullocks, whose horns pricked the sky from the tall poise of the bridge.

The place seemed very populous for so lonely a spot. And still, all the air was heavy with isolation, suspicion, guardedness. It was like being in the Middle Ages. I asked Luigi to go to the house for some wine. He said he didn't know if he could get it: but he went off, with the semi-barbaric reluctance and fear of approaching a strange place.

After a while he came back, to say the *dispensa* was shut, and he couldn't get any. 'Then,' said I, 'let us go to the tombs! Do you know where they are?' He pointed vaguely into the distance of the moorland, and said they were there, but that we should want candles. The tombs were dark, and no one was there. 'Then let us get candles from the peasants,' I said. He answered again, the *dispensa* was shut, and we couldn't get candles. He seemed uneasy and depressed, as the people always are when there is a little difficulty. They are so afraid and mistrustful of one another.

We walked back to the black ruin, through a dark gateway that had been portcullised, into a half-ruined black courtyard, curiously gloomy. And here seven or eight men were squatting or standing about, their shiny bicycles leaning against the ruined walls. They were queer-looking men, youngish fellows, smallish, unshaven, dirty; not peasants, but workmen of some sort, who looked as if they had been swept together among the rubbish. Luigi was evidently nervous of them: not that they were villains, merely he didn't know them. And he had one friend among them: a queer young fellow of about twenty, in a close-fitting blue jersey, a black, black beard on his rather delicate but *gamin* face, and an odd sort of smile. This young fellow came roving round us, with a queer, uneasy, half-smiling curiosity. The men all seemed like that, uneasy and as it were outcast, but with an unknown quality too. They were, in reality, the queer, poorest sort of natives of this part of the Maremma.

The courtyard of the castle was black and sinister, yet very interesting in its ruined condition. There were a few forlorn rat-like signs of peasant farming. And an outside staircase, once rather grand, went up to what was now apparently the inhabited quarter, two or three rooms facing the bridge.

The feeling of suspicion and almost of opposition, negative rather than active, was still so strong we went out again and on to the bridge. Luigi, in a dilemma, talked mutteringly to his black-bearded young friend with the bright eyes: all the men seemed to have queer, bright black eyes, with a glint on them such as a mouse's eyes have.

At last I asked him, flatly: 'Who are all those men?' He muttered that they were the workmen and navvies. I was puzzled to know *what* workmen and navvies, in this loneliness. Then he explained they were working on the irrigation works, and had come in to the *dispensa* for their wages and to buy things — it was Saturday afternoon — but that the overseer, who kept the *dispensa,* and who sold wine and necessaries to the workmen, hadn't come yet to open the place, so we couldn't get anything.

At least, Luigi didn't explain all this. But when he said these were the workmen from the irrigation diggings, I understood it all.

By this time, we and our desire for candles had become a feature in the landscape. I said to Luigi, why didn't he ask the *peasants.* He said they hadn't any. Fortunately at that moment an unwashed woman appeared at an upper window in the black wall. I asked her if she couldn't sell us a candle. She retired to think about it — then came back to say, surlily, it would be sixty centimes. I threw her a lira, and she dropped a candle. So!

Then the black-bearded young fellow glintingly said we should want more than one candle. So I asked the woman for another, and threw her fifty centimes — as she was contemplating giving me the change for the lira. She dropped another candle.

B. and I moved towards the *carretto,* with Luigi. But I could see he was still unhappy. 'Do you know where the tombs are?' I asked him. Again he waved vaguely: 'Over there!' But he was unhappy. 'Would it be better to take one of those men for a guide?' I said to him. And I got the inevitable answer: 'It is as you think.' 'If *you* don't know the tombs well,' I said to him, 'then find a man to come with us.' He still hesitated, with that dumb uncertainty of these people. 'Find a man anyhow,' I said, and off he went, feebly.

He came back in relief with the peasant, a short but strong *maremmano* of about forty, unshaven but not unclean. His name was Marco, and he had put on his best jacket to accompany us. He was quiet and determined-seeming — a brownish blond, not one of the queer black natives with the queer round soft contours. His boy of about thirteen came with him, and they two climbed on to the back of the *carretto.*

Marco gave directions, and we bowled down the trail, then away over a slight track, on to the heathy strong moorland. After us came a little black-eyed fellow on a bicycle. We passed on the left a small encampment of temporary huts made of planks, with women coming out to look. By the trail were huge sacks of charcoal, and the black charcoal-burners, just down from the mountains, for the week-end, stood aside to look at us. The asses and mules stood drooping.

This was the winter camp of the charcoal-burners. In a week or so, Marco told me, they would abandon this camp and go up into the mountains, out of reach of the fevers which begin in May. Certainly they looked a vigorous bunch, if a little wild. I asked Marco if there was much fever — meaning malaria. He said: 'Not much,' I asked him if he had had any attacks. He said: 'No, never.' It is true he looked broad and healthy, with a queer, subdued, explosive sort of energy. Yet there was a certain motionless, rather worn look in his face, a certain endurance and sallowness, which seemed like malaria to me. I asked Luigi, our driver, if he had had any fever. At first he too said no. Then he admitted he had had a touch now and then. Which was evident, for his face was small and yellowish, evidently the thing had eaten into him. Yet he too, like Marco, had a strong, *manly* energy, more than the ordinary Italians. It is evidently the thing, in these parts, to deny that the malaria has ever touched you.

To the left, out of the heath, rose great flattish mounds, great tumuli, bigger than those of Cerveteri. I asked Marco were those the tombs? He said those were the tumuli, Coccumella and Coccumelletta — but that we would go first to the river tombs.

We were descending a rocky slope towards the brink of the ravine, which was full of trees, as ever. Far away, apparently, behind us to the right, stood the lonely black tower of the castle, across the moorland whence we had come. Across the ravine was a long, low hill, grassy and moorland: and farther down the stream were the irrigation works. The country was all empty and abandoned-seeming, yet with that peculiar, almost ominous, poignancy of places where life has once been intense. 'Where do they say the city of Vulci was?' I asked Marco. He pointed across stream, to the long, low elevation along the opposite side of the ravine. I guessed it had been there — since the tombs were on this side. But it looked very low and undefended, for an Etruscan site: so open to the world! I supposed it had depended upon its walls, seawards, and the ravine inland. I asked Marco if anything was there; some sign of where the walls had gone round. He said: 'Nothing!' It has evidently not been a very large city, like Caere and Tarquinia. But it was one of the cities of the League, and very rich indeed, judging from the thousands of painted vases which have been found in the tombs here.

The rocky descent was too uneven. We got out of the cart, and went on foot. Luigi left the mare, and Marco led us on, down to a barb-wire fence. We should never, never have found the place ourselves. Marco expertly held the wire apart, and we scrambled through on to the bushy, rocky side of the ravine. The trees rose from the riverside, some leaves bright green. And we descended a rough path, past the entrance-passage to a tomb most carefully locked with an iron gate, and defended with barbed wire, like a hermit's cave with the rank vegetation growing up to choke it again.

Winding among rank vegetation and fallen rocks of the face of the ravine, we came to the openings of the tombs, which were cut into the face of the rock, and must have been a fine row once, like a row of rock-houses with a pleasant road outside, along the ravine. But now they are gloomy holes down which one must clamber through the excavated earth. Once inside, with the three candles — for the black-faced youth on the bicycle had brought a stump too — we were in gloomy wolves' dens of places, with large chambers opening off one another as at Cerveteri, damp beds of rock for the coffins, and huge grisly stone coffins, seven feet long, lying in disorder, among fallen rocks and rubble, in some of them the bones and man-dust still lying dismally. There was nothing to see but these black, damp chambers, sometimes cleared, sometimes with coarse great sarcophagi and broken rubbish and excavation-rubble left behind in the damp-grisly darkness.

Sometimes we had to wriggle into the tombs on our bellies, over the mounds of rubble, going down into holes like rats, while the bats flew blindly in our faces. Once inside, we clambered in the faint darkness over huge pieces of rock and broken stone, from dark chamber to chamber, four or five or even more chambers to a tomb, all cut out of the rock and made to look like houses, with the sloping roof-tilts and the central roof-beam. From these roofs hung clusters of pale brown furry bats, in bunches, like bunches of huge furry hops. One could hardly believe they were alive, till I saw the squat little fellow of the bicycle holding his candle up to one of the bunches, singeing the bats' hair, burning the torpid creatures, so the skinny wings began to flutter, and half-stupefied, half-dead bats fell from the clusters of the roof, then groped on the wing and began to fly low, staggering towards the outlet. The dark little fellow took pleasure in burning them. But I stopped him at it, and he was afraid, and left them alone.

He was a queer fellow — quite short, with the fat, soft, round curves, and black hair and sallow face and black bats' eyes of a certain type of this district. He was perhaps twenty years old, and like a queer burrowing dumb animal. He would creep into holes in the queerest way, with his queer, soft, round hind-quarters jutting behind: just like some uncanny animal. And I noticed the backs of his ears were all scaly and raw with sores; whether from dirt or some queer disease, who can say. He seemed healthy and alive enough, otherwise. And he seemed quite unconscious of his sore ears, with an animal unconsciousness.

Marco, who was a much higher type, knew his way about, and led us groping and wriggling and clambering from tomb to tomb, among the darkness and brokenness and bats and damp, then out among the fennel and bushes of the ravine top, then in again into some hole. He showed us a tomb whence only last year they had taken a big stone statue — he showed me where it had stood, there, in the innermost chamber, with its back to the wall. And he told me of all the vases, mostly broken pieces, that he too had lifted from the dirt, on the stone beds.

But now there is nothing, and I was tired of climbing into these gruesome holes, one after another, full of damp and great fallen rocks. Nothing living or beautiful is left behind — nothing. I was glad when we came to the end of the excavated tombs, and saw beyond only the ravine bank grown over with bushes and fennel and great weeds. Probably many a vase and many a stone coffin still lie hidden there — but let them lie.

We went back along the path the way we had come, to climb back to the upper level. As we came to the gangway leading to the locked tomb Marco told me that in here were paintings and some things left behind. Probably it was the famous François tomb with the paintings that are copied in the Vatican museum. It was opened by the excavator François in 1857, and is one of the very, very few painted tombs found at Vulci.

We tried in vain to get in. Short of smashing the lock, it was impossible. Of course, in these expeditions, one should arm oneself with official permits. But it means having officials hanging round.

So we climbed up to the open world, and Luigi made us get into the *carretto*. The mare pulled us jolting across towards the great tumuli, which we wanted to see. They are huge grassy-bushy mounds, like round, low hills. The band of stonework round the base, if it be there, is buried.

Marco led us inside the dense passage of brambles and bushes which leads to the opening into the tumulus. Already this passage is almost blocked up, overgrown. One has to crawl under the scratching brambles, like a rabbit.

And at last one is in the plain doorway of the tumulus itself. Here, even in 1829, two weird stone sphinxes guarded the entrance. Now there is nothing. And inside the passage or at the angles were lions and griffins on guard. What now shall we find as we follow the candlelight in the narrow, winding passage? It is like being in a mine, narrow passages winding on and on, from nowhere to nowhere. We had not any great length of candle left: four stumps. Marco left one stump burning at the junction of the passage as a signpost, and on and on we went, from nowhere to nowhere, stooping a little, our hats brushing the clusters of bats that hung from the ceiling as we went on, one after the other, pinned all the time in the narrow stone corridors that never led anywhere or did anything. Sometimes there was a niche in the wall — that was all.

There must, surely, be a central burial chamber, to which the passages finally lead. But we didn't find it. And Marco said there was no such thing — the tumulus was all passages and nothing but passages. But Dennis says that when the tumulus was opened in 1829 there were two small chambers in the heart of the mound, and rising from these, two shafts of masonry which passed up to the apex of the mound, and probably these supported great monuments, probably the phallic cippi. On the floor of the chamber were fragments of bronze and frail gold. But now there is nothing; the centre of the tumulus is no doubt collapsed.

It was like being buried inside some ancient pyramid. This was quite unlike any other Etruscan tomb we had seen: and if this tumulus was a tomb, then it must have been a very important person whose coffin formed the nut inside all this shell — a person important as a Pharaoh, surely. The Etruscans were queer people, and this tumulus, with no peripheral tombs, only endless winding passages, must be either a reminiscence of prehistoric days or of Egyptian pyramids.

When we had had enough of running along passages in nowhere we got out, scrambled through the bramble tangle, and were thankful to see clear heaven again. We all piled into the *carretto,* and the mare nobly hauled us up to the trail. The little dark fellow sailed ahead silently, on his bicycle, to open the gate for us. We looked round once more at the vast mound of the Coccumella, which strange dead hands piled in soft earth over two tiny death-chambers, so long ago: and even now it is weirdly conspicuous across the flat Maremma. A strange, strange nut indeed, with a kernel of perpetual mystery! And once it rose suave as a great beast, tipped with the budded monuments of the cippi! It is too problematic. We turn our back on it all as the *carretto* jolts over the tomb-rifled earth. There is something gloomy, if rather wonderful, about Vulci.

The charcoal-burners were preparing to wash their faces for Sunday, in the little camp. The women stood smiling as we drove by on the moor. 'Oh, how fat thou has got!' Luigi shouted to one plump and smiling woman. *'You* haven't though!' she shouted back at him. *'Tu pure no!'*

At the bridge we said good-bye to Marco and his boy, then we pulled over the arch once more. But on the other side Luigi wanted to drink. So he and I scrambled down to the spring, the old, thin-trickling spring, and drank cool water. The river rushed below: the bridge arched its black, soaring rainbow above, and we heard the shouts of mule-drivers driving the mules over the arch.

Once this old bridge carried an aqueduct, and it is curious to see the great stalactitic mass that hangs like a beard down the side facing the mountains. But the aqueduct is gone, the muddy stalactitic mass itself is crumbling. Everything passes!

So we climbed up and into the *carretto,* and away went the mare at a spanking pace. We passed the young man in velveteens, on the donkey — a peasant from the hills, Luigi said he was. And we met horsemen riding towards us, towards the hills, away from Montalto. It was Saturday afternoon, with a bright sea-wind blowing strong over the Maremma, and men travelling away from work, on horseback, on mules, or on asses. And some drove laden donkeys out to the hills.

'It would be a good life,' I said to Luigi, 'to live here, and have a house on the hills, and a horse to ride, and space: except for the malaria!'

Then, having previously confessed to me that the malaria was still pretty bad, though children often escaped it, but grown people rarely; the fever inevitably came to shake them sometimes; that Montalto was more stricken than the open country; and that in the time of rains the roads were impassable — one was cut off — now Luigi changed his tune: said there was almost no fever any more; the roads were always passable; in Montalto people came at bathing season to bathe in the sea, having little cane huts on the coast: the roads were always easily passable, easily! and that you never got fever at all if you were properly fed, and had a bit of meat now and then, and a decent glass of wine. He wanted me so much to come and have some abandoned house in the foothills; and he would look after my horses, and we would go hunting together — even out of season, for there was no one to catch you.

B. dozed lightly while we drove joltingly on. It was a dream too. I would like it well enough — if I were convinced about that malaria. And I would certainly have Luigi to look after the horses. He hasn't a grand appearance, but he is solitary and courageous and surely honest, solitary, and far more manly than the townsmen or the grubbing peasants.

So, we have seen all we could see of Vulci. If we want to see what the Etruscans buried there we must go to the Vatican, or to the Florence museum, or to the British Museum in London, and see vases and statues, bronzes, sarcophagi and jewels. In the British Museum lie the contents, for the most part, of the famous Tomb of Isis, where lay buried a lady whom Dennis thought was surely Egyptian, judging from her statue, that is stiff and straight, and from the statuette of 'Isis', the six ostrich eggs and other imported things that went to the grave with her: for in death she must be what she was in life, as exactly as possible. This was the Etruscan creed. How the Egyptian lady came to Vulci, and how she came to be buried there along with a lady of ancient Etruria, down in that bit of the Vulci necropolis now called Polledrara, who knows? But all that is left of her is now in the British Museum. Vulci has nothing. Anyhow she was surely not Egyptian at all. Anything of the archaic east Mediterranean seemed to Dennis Egyptian.

So it is. The site of Vulci was lost from Roman times till 1828. Once found, however, the tombs were rapidly gutted by the owners, everything precious was taken away, then the tombs were either closed again or abandoned. All the thousands of vases that the Etruscans gathered so lovingly and laid by their dead, where are they? Many are still in existence. But they are everywhere except at Vulci.

6. VOLTERRA

VOLTERRA is the most northerly of the great Etruscan cities of the west. It lies back some thirty miles from the sea, on a towering great bluff of rock that gets all the winds and sees all the world, looking out down the valley of the Cecina to the sea, south over vale and high land to the tips of Elba, north to the imminent mountains of Carrara, inward over the wide hills of the Pre-Apennines, to the heart of Tuscany.

You leave the Rome-Pisa tram at Cecina, and slowly wind up the valley of the stream of that name, a green, romantic, forgotten sort of valley, in spite of all the come-and-go of ancient Etruscans and Romans, medieval Volterrans and Pisans, and modern traffic. But the traffic is not heavy. Volterra is a sort of inland island, still curiously isolated, and grim.

The small, forlorn little train comes to a stop at the Saline de Volterra, the famous old salt works now belonging to the State, where brine is pumped out of deep wells. What passengers remain in the train are transferred to one old little coach across the platform, and at length this coach starts to creep like a beetle up the slope, up a cog-and-ratchet line, shoved by a small engine behind. Up the steep but round slope among the vineyards and olives you pass almost at walking-pace, and there is not a flower to be seen, only the beans make a whiff of perfume now and then, on the chill air, as you rise and rise, above the valley below, coming level with the high hills to south, and the bluff of rock with its two or three towers, ahead.

After a certain amount of backing and changing, the fragment of a train eases up at a bit of a cold wayside station, and is finished. The world lies below. You get out, transfer yourself to a small ancient motor-omnibus and are rattled up to the final level of the city, into a cold and gloomy little square, where the hotel is.

The hotel is simple and somewhat rough, but quite friendly, pleasant in its haphazard way. And what is more, it has central heating, and the heat is on, this cold, almost icy, April afternoon. Volterra lies only 1800 feet above the sea, but it is right in the wind, and cold as any Alp.

The day was Sunday, and there was a sense of excitement and fussing, and a bustling in and out of temporarily important persons, and altogether a smell of politics in the air. The waiter brought us tea, of a sort, and I asked him what was doing. He replied that a great banquet was to be given this evening to the new *podestà* who had come from Florence to govern the city, under the new regime. And evidently he felt that this was such a hugely important 'party' occasion we poor outsiders were of no account.

It was a cold, grey afternoon, with winds round the hard dark corners of the hard, narrow medieval town, and crowds of black-dressed, rather squat little men and pseudo-elegant young women pushing and loitering in the streets, and altogether that sense of furtive grinning and jeering and threatening which always accompanies a public occasion — a political one especially — in Italy, in the more out-of-the-way centres. It is as if the people, alabaster-workers and a few peasants, were not sure which side they wanted to be on, and therefore were all the more ready to exterminate anyone who was on the other side. This fundamental uneasiness, indecision, is most curious in the Italian soul. It is as if the people could never be wholeheartedly anything: because they can't trust anything. And this inability to trust is at the root of the political extravagance and frenzy. They don't trust themselves, so how can they trust their 'leaders' or their 'party'?

Volterra, standing sombre and chilly alone on her rock, has always, from Etruscan days on, been grimly jealous of her own independence. Especially she has struggled against the Florentine yoke. So what her actual feelings are, about this new-old sort of village tyrant, the *podestà,* whom she is banqueting this evening, it would be hard, probably, even for the Volterrans themselves to say. Anyhow the cheeky girls salute one with the 'Roman' salute, out of sheer effrontery: a salute which has nothing to do with me, so I don't return it. Politics of all sorts are anathema. But in an Etruscan city which held out so long against Rome I consider the Roman salute unbecoming, and the Roman *imperium* unmentionable.

It is amusing to see on the walls, too, chalked fiercely up: *Morte a Lenin!* though that poor gentleman has been long enough dead, surely even for a Volterran to have heard of it. And more amusing still is the legend permanently painted: *Mussolini ha sempre ragione!* Some are born infallible, some achieve infallibility, and some have it thrust upon them.

But it is not for me to put even my little finger in any political pie. I am sure every post-war country has hard enough work to get itself governed, without outsiders interfering or commenting. Let those rule who can rule.

We wander on, a little dismally, looking at the stony stoniness of the medieval town. Perhaps on a warm sunny day it might be pleasant, when shadow was attractive and a breeze welcome. But on a cold, grey, windy afternoon of April, Sunday, always especially dismal, with all the people in the streets, bored and uneasy, and the stone buildings peculiarly sombre and hard and resistant, it is no fun. I don't care about the bleak but truly medieval piazza: I don't care if the Palazzo Pubblico has all sorts of amusing coats of arms on it: I don't care about the cold cathedral, though it is rather nice really, with a glow of dusky candles and a smell of Sunday incense: I am disappointed in the wooden sculpture of the taking down of Jesus, and the basreliefs don't interest me. In short, I am hard to please.

The modern town is not very large. We went down a long, stony street, and out of the Porta dell'Arco, the famous old Etruscan gate. It is a deep old gateway, almost a tunnel, with the outer arch facing the desolate country on the skew, built at an angle to the old road, to catch the approaching enemy on his right side, where the shield did not cover him. Up handsome and round goes the arch, at a good height, and with that peculiar weighty richness of ancient things; and three dark heads, now worn featureless, reach out curiously and inquiringly, one from the keystone of the arch, one from each of the arch bases, to gaze from the city and into the steep hollow of the world beyond.

Strange, dark old Etruscan heads of the city gate, even now they are featureless they still have a peculiar, out-reaching life of their own. Ducati says they represented the heads of slain enemies hung at the city gate. But they don't hang. They stretch with curious eagerness forward. Nonsense about dead heads. They were city deities of some sort.

And the archaeologists say that only the doorposts of the outer arch, and the inner walls, are Etruscan work. The Romans restored the arch, and set the heads back in their old positions. (Unlike the Romans to set anything back in its old position!) While the wall above the arch is merely medieval.

But we'll call it Etruscan still. The roots of the gate, and the dark heads, these they cannot take away from the Etruscans. And the heads are still on the watch.

The land falls away steeply, across the road in front of the arch. The road itself turns east, under the walls of the modem city, above the world: and the sides of the road, as usual outside the gates, are dump-heaps, dump-heaps of plaster and rubble, dump-heaps of the white powder from the alabaster works, the waste edge of the town.

The path turns away from under the city wall, and dips down along the brow of the hill. To the right we can see the tower of the church of Santa Chiara, standing on a little platform of the irregularly-dropping hill. And we are going there. So we dip downwards above a Dantesque, desolate world, down to Santa Chiara, and beyond. Here the path follows the top of what remains of the old Etruscan wall. On the right are little olive-gardens and bits of wheat. Away beyond is the dismal sort of crest of modern Volterra. We walk along, past the few flowers and the thick ivy, and the bushes of broom and marjoram, on what was once the Etruscan wall, far out from the present city wall. On the left the land drops steeply, in uneven and unhappy descents.

The great hilltop or headland on which Etruscan 'Volterra', *Velathri, Vlathri,* once stood spreads out jaggedly, with deep-cleft valleys in between, more or less in view, spreading two or three miles away. It is something like a hand, the bluff steep of the palm sweeping in a great curve on the east and south, to seawards, the peninsulas of fingers running jaggedly inland. And the great wall of the Etruscan city swept round the south and eastern bluff, on the crest of steeps and cliffs, turned north and crossed the first finger, or peninsula, then started up hill and down dale over the fingers and into the declivities, a wild and fierce sort of way, hemming in the great crest. The modern town occupies merely the highest bit of the Etruscan city site.

The walls themselves are not much to look at, when you climb down. They are only fragments, now, huge fragments of embankment, rather than wall, built of uncemented square masonry, in the grim, sad sort of stone. One only feels, for some reason, depressed. And it is pleasant to look at the lover and his lass going along the top of the ramparts, which are now olive- orchards, away from the town. At least they are alive and cheerful and quick.

On from Santa Chiara the road takes us through the grim and depressing little suburb-hamlet of San Giusto, a black street that emerges upon the waste open place where the church of San Giusto rises like a huge and astonishing barn. It is so tall, the interior should be impressive. But no! It is merely nothing. The architects have achieved nothing, with all that tallness. The children play around with loud yells and ferocity. It is Sunday evening, near sundown, and cold.

Beyond this monument of Christian dreariness we come to the Etruscan walls again, and what was evidently once an Etruscan gate: a dip in the wall-bank, with the groove of an old road running to it.

Here we sit on the ancient heaps of masonry and look into weird yawning gulfs, like vast quarries. The swallows, turning their blue backs, skim away from the ancient lips and over the really dizzy depths, in the yellow light of evening, catching the upward gusts of wind, and flickering aside like lost fragments of life, truly frightening above those ghastly hollows. The lower depths are dark grey, ashy in colour, and in part wet, and the whole things looks new, as if it were some enormous quarry all slipping down.

This place is called *Le Balze* — the cliffs. Apparently the waters which fall on the heights of Volterra collect in part underneath the deep hill and wear away at some places the lower strata, so that the earth falls in immense collapses. Across the gulf, away from the town, stands a big, old, picturesque, isolated building, the *Badia* or Monastery of the Camaldolesi, sad-looking, destined at last to be devoured by *Le Balze,* its old walls already splitting and yielding.

From time to time, going up to the town homewards, we come to the edge of the walls and look out into the vast glow of gold, which is sunset, marvellous, the steep ravines sinking in darkness, the farther valley silently, greenly gold, with hills breathing luminously up, passing out into the pure, sheer gold gleams of the far-off sea, in which a shadow, perhaps an island, moves like a mote of life. And like great guardians the Carrara mountains jut forward, naked in the pure light like flesh, with their crests portentous: so that they seem to be advancing on us: while all the vast concavity of the west roars with gold liquescency, as if the last hour had come, and the gods were smelting us all back into yellow transmuted oneness.

But nothing is being transmuted. We turn our faces, a little frightened, from the vast blaze of gold, and in the dark, hard streets the town band is just chirping up, brassily out of tune as usual, and the populace, with some maidens in white, are streaming in crowds towards the piazza. And, like the band, the populace also is out of tune, buzzing with the inevitable suppressed jeering. But they are going to form a procession.

When we come to the square in front of the hotel, and look out from the edge into the hollow world of the west, the light is sunk red, redness gleams up from the far-off sea below, pure and fierce, and the hollow places in between are dark. Over all the world is a low red glint. But only the town, with its narrow streets and electric light, is impervious.

The banquet, apparently, was not till nine o'clock, and all was hubbub. B. and I dined alone soon after seven, like two orphans whom the waiters managed to remember in between whiles. They were so thrilled getting all the glasses and goblets and decanters, hundreds of them, it seemed, out of the big chiffonnier-cupboard that occupied the back of the dining-room and whirling them away, stacks of glittering glass, to the banquet-room: while out-of-work young men would poke their heads in through the doorway, black hats on, overcoats hung over one shoulder, and gaze with bright inquiry through the room, as though they expected to see Lazarus risen, and not seeing him, would depart again to the nowhere whence they came, A banquet is a banquet, even if it is given to the devil himself; and the *podestà* may be an angel of light.

Outside was cold and dark. In the distance the town band tooted spasmodically, as if it were short-winded this chilly Sunday evening. And we, not bidden to the feast, went to bed. To be awakened occasionally by sudden and roaring noises — perhaps applause — and the loud and unmistakable howling of a child, well after midnight.

Morning was cold and grey again, with a chilly and forbidding country yawning and gaping and lapsing away beneath us. The sea was invisible. We walked the narrow cold streets, whose high, cold, dark stone walls seemed almost to press together, and we looked in at the alabaster workshops, where workmen, in Monday-morning gloom and half-awakedness, were turning the soft alabaster, or cutting it out, or polishing it.

Everybody knows Volterra marble — so called — nowadays, because of the translucent bowls of it which hang under the electric lights, as shades, in half the hotels of the world. It is nearly as transparent as alum, and nearly as soft. They peel it down as if it were soap, and tint it pink or amber or blue, and turn it into all those things one does not want: tinted alabaster lampshades, light-bowls, statues, tinted or untinted, vases, bowls with doves on the rim, or vine-leaves, and similar curios. The trade seems to be going strong. perhaps it is the electric-light demand: perhaps there is a revival of interest in 'statuary'. Anyhow there is no love lost between a Volterran alabaster worker and the lump of pale Volterran earth he turns into marketable form. Alas for the goddess of sculptured form, she has gone from here also.

But it is the old alabaster jars we want to see, not the new. As we hurry down the stony street the rain, icy cold, begins to fall. We flee through the glass doors of the museum, which has just opened, and which seems as if the alabaster inside had to be kept at a low temperature, for the place is dead-cold as a refrigerator.

Cold, silent, empty, unhappy the museum seems. But at last an old and dazed man arrives, in uniform, and asks quite scared what we want. 'Why, to see the museum!' *'Ah! Ah! Ah sì— sì!'* It just dawns upon him that the museum is there to be looked at. *'Ah sì, sì, Signori!'*

We pay our tickets, and start in. It is really a very attractive and pleasant museum, but we had struck such a bitter cold April morning, with icy rain falling in the courtyard, that I felt as near to being in the tomb as I have ever done. Yet very soon, in the rooms with all those hundreds of little sarcophagi, ash-coffins, or urns, as they are called, the strength of the old life began to warm one up.

Urn is not a good word, because it suggests, to me at least, a vase, an amphora, a round and shapely jar: perhaps through association with Keats' *Ode to a Grecian Urn* — which vessel no doubt wasn't an urn at all, but a wine-jar — and with the 'tea-urn' of children's parties. These Volterran urns, though correctly enough used for storing the ashes of the dead, are not round, they are not jars, they are small alabaster sarcophagi. And they are a peculiarity of Volterra. Probably because the Volterrans had the alabaster to hand.

Anyhow here you have them in hundreds, and they are curiously alive and attractive. They are not considered very highly as 'art'. One of the latest Italian writers on Etruscan things, Ducati, says: 'If they have small interest from the artistic point of view, they are extremely valuable for the scenes they represent, either mythological or relative to the beliefs in the after-life.'

George Dennis, however, though he too does not find much 'art' in Etruscan things, says of the Volterran ash-chests: 'The touches of Nature on these Etruscan urns, so simply but eloquently expressed, must appeal to the sympathies of all — they are chords to which every heart must respond; and I envy not the man who can walk through this museum unmoved, without feeling a tear rise in his eye'

And recognizing ever and anon

The breeze of Nature no longer shakes dewdrops from our eyes, at least so readily, but Dennis is more alive than Ducati to that which is alive. What men mean nowadays by 'art' it would be hard to say. Even Dennis said that the Etruscans never approached the pure, the sublime, the perfect beauty which Flaxman reached. Today, this makes us laugh: the Greekified illustrator of Pope's *Homer!* But the same instinct lies at the back of our idea of 'art' still. Art is still to us something which has been well cooked — like a plate of spaghetti. An ear of wheat is not yet 'art'. Wait, wait till it has been turned into pure, into perfect macaroni.

For me, I get more real pleasure out of these Volterran ash-chests than out of — I had almost said, the Parthenon frieze. One wearies of the aesthetic quality — a quality which takes the edge off everything, and makes it seem 'boiled down'. A great deal of pure Greek beauty has this boiled-down effect. It is too much cooked in the artistic consciousness.

In Dennis's day a broken Greek or Greekish amphora would fetch thousands of crowns in the market, if it was the right 'period', etc. These Volterran urns fetched hardly anything. Which is a mercy, or they would be scattered to the ends of the earth.

As it is, they are fascinating, like an open book of life, and one has no sense of weariness with them, though there are so many. They warm one up, like being in the midst of life.

The downstairs rooms of ash-chests contain those urns representing 'Etruscan' subjects: those of sea-monsters, the sea-man with fish-tail, and with wings, the sea-woman the same: or the man with serpent-legs, and wings, or the woman the same. It was Etruscan to give these creatures wings, not Greek.

If we remember that in the old world the centre of all power was at the depths of the earth, and at the depths of the sea, while the sun was only a moving subsidiary body: and that the serpent represented the vivid powers of the inner earth, not only such powers as volcanic and earthquake, but the quick powers that run up the roots of plants and establish the great body of the tree, the tree of life, and run up the feet and legs of man, to establish the heart: while the fish was the symbol of the depths of the waters, whence even light is born: we shall see the ancient power these symbols had over the imagination of the Volterrans. They were a people faced with the sea, and living in a volcanic country.

Then the powers of the earth and the powers of the sea take life as they give life. They have their terrific as well as their prolific aspect.

Someone says the wings of the water-deities represent evaporation towards the sun, and the curving tails of the dolphin represent torrents. This is part of the great and controlling ancient idea of the come-and-go of the life-powers, the surging up, in a flutter of leaves and a radiation of wings, and the surging back, in torrents and waves and the eternal downpour of death.

Other common symbolic animals in Volterra are the beaked griffins, the creatures of the powers that tear asunder and, at the same time, are guardians of the treasure. They are lion and eagle combined, of the sky and of the earth with caverns. They do not allow the treasure of life, the gold, which we should perhaps translate as consciousness, to be stolen by thieves of life. They are guardians of the treasure: and then, they are the tearers asunder of those who must depart from life.

It is these creatures, creatures of the elements, which carry men away into death, over the border between the elements. So is the dolphin, sometimes; and so the hippocampus, the seahorse; and so the centaur.

The horse is always the symbol of the strong animal life of man: and sometimes he rises, a sea-horse, from the ocean: and sometimes he is a land creature, and half-man. And so he occurs on the tombs, as the passion in man returning into the sea, the soul retreating into the death-world at the depths of the waters: or sometimes he is a centaur, sometimes a female centaur, sometimes clothed in a lion-skin, to show his dread aspect, bearing the soul back, away, off into the other-world.

It would be very interesting to know if there were a definite connexion between the scene on the ash-chest and the dead whose ashes it contained. When the fish-tailed sea-god entangles a man to bear him off, does it mean drowning at sea? And when a man is caught in the writhing serpent-legs of the Medusa, or of the winged snake-power, does it mean a fall to earth; a death from the earth, in some manner; as a fall, or the dropping of a rock, or the bite of a snake? And the soul carried off by a winged centaur: is it a man dead of some passion that carried him away?

But more interesting even than the symbolic scenes are those scenes from actual life, such as boar-hunts, circus-games, processions, departures in covered wagons, ships sailing away, city gates being stormed, sacrifice being performed, girls with open scrolls, as if reading at school; many banquets with man and woman on the banqueting couch, and slaves playing music, and children around: then so many really tender farewell scenes, the dead saying good-bye to his wife, as he goes on the journey, or as the chariot bears him off, or the horse waits; then the soul alone, with the death-dealing spirits standing by with their hammers that gave the blow. It is as Dennis says, the breeze of Nature stirs one's soul. I asked the gentle old man if he knew anything about the urns. But no! no! He knew nothing at all. He had only just come. He counted for nothing. So he protested. He was one of those gentle, shy Italians too diffident even to look at the chests he was guarding. But when I told him what I thought some of the scenes meant he was fascinated like a child, full of wonder, almost breathless. And I thought again, how much more Etruscan than Roman the Italian of today is: sensitive, diffident, craving really for symbols and mysteries, able to be delighted with true delight over small things, violent in spasms, and altogether without sternness or natural will-to-power. The will-to-power is a secondary thing in an Italian, reflected on to him from the Germanic races that have almost engulfed him.

The boar-hunt is still a favourite Italian sport, the grandest sport of Italy. And the Etruscans must have loved it, for they represent it again and again, on the tombs. It is difficult to know what exactly the boar symbolized to them. He occupies often the centre of the scene, where the one who dies should be: and where the bull of sacrifice is. And often he is attacked, not by men, but by young winged boys, or by spirits. The dogs climb in the trees around him, the double axe is swinging to come down on him, he lifts up his tusks in a fierce wild pathos. The archaeologists say that it is Meleager and the boar of Calydon, or Hercules and the fierce brute of Erymanthus. But this is not enough. It is a symbolic scene: and it seems as if the boar were himself the victim this time, the wild, fierce fatherly life hunted down by dogs and adversaries. For it is obviously the boar who must die: he is not, like the lions and griffins, the attacker. He is the father of life running free in the forest, and he must die. They say too he represents winter: when the feasts for the dead were held. But on the very oldest archaic vases the lion and the boar are facing each other, again and again, in symbolic opposition.

Fascinating are the scenes of departures, journeyings in covered wagons drawn by two or more horses, accompanied by driver on foot and friend on horseback, and dogs, and met by other horsemen coming down the road. Under the arched tarpaulin tilt of the wagon reclines a man, or a woman, or a whole family: and all moves forward along the highway with wonderful slow surge. And the wagon, as far as I saw, is always drawn by horses, not by oxen.

This is surely the journey of the soul. It is said to represent even the funeral procession, the ash-chest being borne away to the cemetery, to be laid in the tomb. But the *memory* in the scene seems much deeper than that. It gives so strongly the feeling of a people who have trekked in wagons, like the Boers, or the Mormons, from one land to another.

They say these covered-wagon journeys are peculiar to Volterra, found represented in no other Etruscan places. Altogether the feeling of the Volterran scenes is peculiar. There is a great sense of *journeying:* as of a people which remembers its migrations, by sea as well as land. And there is a curious restlessness, unlike the dancing surety of southern Etruria: a touch of the Gothic.

In the upstairs rooms there are many more ash-chests, but mostly representing Greek subjects: so called. Helen and the Dioscuri, Pelops, Minotaur, Jason, Medea fleeing from Corinth, Oedipus, and the Sphinx, Ulysses and the Sirens, Eteocles and Polynices, Centaurs and Lapithae, the Sacrifice of Iphigenia — all are there, just recognizable. There are so many Greek subjects that one archaeologist suggested that these urns must have been made by a Greek colony planted there in Volterra after the Roman conquest.

One might almost as well say that *Timon of Athens* was written by a Greek colonist planted in England after the over-throw of the Catholic Church. These 'Greek' ash-chests are about as Grecian as *Timon of Athens* is. The Greeks would have done them so much 'better'.

No, the 'Greek' scenes are innumerable, but it is only just recognizable what they mean. Whoever carved these chests knew very little of the fables they were handling: and fables they were, to the Etruscan artificers of that day, as they would be to the Italians of this. The story was just used as a peg upon which the native Volterran hung his fancy, as the Elizabethans used Greek stories for their poems. Perhaps also the alabaster cutters were working from old models, or the memory of them. Anyhow, the scenes show nothing of Hellas.

Most curious these 'classic' subjects: so unclassic! To me they hint at the Gothic which lay unborn in the future, far more than at the Hellenistic past of the Volterran Etruscan. For, of course, all these alabaster urns are considered late in period, after the fourth century B.C. The Christian sarcophagi of the fifth century A.D. seem much more nearly kin to these ash-chests of Volterra than do contemporary Roman chests: as if Christianity really rose, in Italy, out of Etruscan soil, rather than out of Greco-Roman. And the first glimmering of that early, glad sort of Christian art, the free touch of Gothic within the classic, seems evident in the Etruscan scenes. The Greek and Roman 'boiled' soft of form gives way to a raggedness of edge and a certain wildness of light and shade which promises the later Gothic, but which is still held down by the heavy mysticism from the East.

Very early Volterran urns were probably plain stone or terra-cotta. But no doubt Volterra was a city long before the Etruscans penetrated into it, and probably it never changed character profoundly. To the end, the Volterrans burned their dead: there are practically no long sarcophagi of Lucumones. And here most of all one feels that the *people* of Volterra, or Velathri, were not Oriental, not the same as those who made most show at Tarquinia. This was surely another tribe, wilder, cruder, and far less influenced by the old Aegean influences. In Caere and Tarquinia the aborigines were deeply overlaid by incoming influences from the East. Here not! Here the wild and untamable Ligurian was neighbour, and perhaps kin, and the town of wind and stone kept, and still keeps, its northern quality.

So there the ash-chests are, an open book for anyone to read who will, according to his own fancy. They are not more than two feet long, or thereabouts, so the figure on the lid is queer and stunted. The classic Greek or Asiatic could not have borne that. It is a sign of barbarism in itself. Here the northern spirit was too strong for the Hellenic or Oriental or ancient Mediterranean instinct. The Lucumo and his lady had to submit to being stunted, in their death-effigy. The head is nearly life-size. The body is squashed small.

But there it is, a portrait-effigy. Very often, the lid and the chest don't seem to belong together at all. It is suggested that the lid was made during the lifetime of the subject, with an attempt at real portraiture: while the chest was bought ready-made, and apart. It may be so. Perhaps in Etruscan days there were the alabaster workshops as there are today, only with rows of ash-chests portraying all the vivid scenes we still can see: and perhaps you chose the one you wished your ashes to lie in. But more probably, the workshops were there, the carved ash-chests were there, but you did not select your own chest, since you did not know what death you would die. Probably you only had your portrait carved on the lid, and left the rest to the survivors.

So maybe, and most probably, the mourning relatives hurriedly *ordered* the lid with the portrait-bust, after the death of the near one, and then chose the most appropriate ash-chest. Be it as it may, the two parts are often oddly assorted: and so they were found with the ashes inside them.

But we must believe that the figure on the lid, grotesquely shortened, is an attempt at a portrait. There is none of the distinction of the southern Etruscan figures. The heads are given the 'imperious' tilt of the Lucumones, but here it becomes almost grotesque. The dead nobleman may be wearing the necklace of office and holding the sacred patera or libation-dish in his hand; but he will not, in the southern way, be represented ritualistically as naked to below the navel; his shirt will come to his neck: and he may just as well be holding the tippling wine-cup in his hand as the sacred patera; he may even have a wine-jug in his other hand, in full carousal. Altogether the peculiar 'sacredness', the inveterate symbolism of the southern Etruscans, is here gone. The religious power is broken.

It is very evident in the ladies: and so many of the figures are ladies. They are decked up in all their splendour, but the mystical formality is lacking. They hold in their hands winecups or fans or mirrors, pomegranates or perfume-boxes, or the queer little books which perhaps were the wax tablets for writing upon. They may even have the old sexual and death symbol of the pine-cone. But the *power* of the symbol has almost vanished. The Gothic actuality and idealism begins to supplant the profound *physical* religion of the southern Etruscans, the true ancient world.

In the museum there are jars and bits of bronze, and the pateras with the hollow knob in the middle. You may put your two middle fingers in the patera, and hold it ready to make the last libation of life, the first libation of death, in the correct Etruscan fashion. But you will not, as so many of the men on these ash-chests do, hold the symbolic dish upside down, with the two fingers thrust into the 'mundus'. The torch upside down means the flame has gone below, to the underworld. But the patera upside down is somehow shocking. One feels the Volterrans, or men of Velathri, were slack in the ancient mysteries.

At last the rain stopped crashing down icily in the silent inner courtyard; at last there was a ray of sun. And we had seen all we could look at for one day. So we went out, to try to get warmed by a kinder heaven.

There are one or two tombs still open, especially two outside the Porta a Selci. But I believe, not having seen them, they are of small importance. Nearly all the tombs that have been opened in Volterra, their contents removed, have been filled in again, so as not to lose two yards of the precious cultivable land of the peasants. There were many tumuli: but most of them are levelled. And under some were curious round tombs built of unsquared stones, unlike anything in southern Etruria. But then, Volterra is altogether unlike southern Etruria.

One tomb has been removed bodily to the garden of the archaeological museum in Florence: at least its contents have. There it is built up again as it was when discovered in Volterra in 1861, and all the ash-chests are said to be replaced as they stood originally. It is called the Inghirami tomb, from the famous Volterran archaeologist Inghirami.

A few steps lead down into the one circular chamber of the tomb, which is supported in the centre by a square pillar, apparently supposed to be left in the rock. On the low stone bed that encircles the tomb stand the ash-chests, a double row of them, in a great ring encircling the shadow.

The tomb belongs all to one family, and there must be sixty ash-chests, of alabaster, carved with the well-known scenes. So that if this tomb is really arranged as it was originally, and the ash-chests progress from the oldest to the latest counter-clockwise, as is said, one ought to be able to see certainly a century or two of development in the Volterran urns.

But one is filled with doubt and misgiving. Why, oh why, wasn't the tomb left intact as it was found, where it was found? The garden of the Florence museum is vastly instructive, if you want object-lessons about the Etruscans. But who wants object-lessons about vanished races? What one wants is a contact. The Etruscans are not a theory or a thesis. If they are anything, they are an *experience.*

And the experience is always spoilt. Museums, museums, museums, object-lessons rigged out to illustrate the unsound theories of archaeologists, crazy attempts to coordinate and get into a fixed order that which has no fixed order and will not be coordinated! It is sickening! Why must all experience be systematized? Why must even the vanished Etruscans be reduced to a system? They never will be. You break all the eggs, and produce an omelette which is neither Etruscan nor Roman not Italic nor Hittite, nor anything else, but just a systematized mess. Why can't incompatible things be left incompatible? If you make an omelette out of a hen's egg, a plover's, and an ostrich's, you won't have a grand amalgam or unification of hen and plover and ostrich into something we may call 'oviparity'. You'll have that formless object, an omelette.

So it is here. If you try to make a grand amalgam of Cerveten and Tarquinia, Vulci, Vetulonia, Volterra, Chiusi, Veii, then you won't get the essential *Etruscan* as a result, but a cooked-up mess which has no life-meaning at all. A museum is not a first-hand contact: it is an illustrated lecture. And what one wants is the actual vital touch. I don't want to be 'instructed'; nor do many other people.

They could take the more homeless objects for the museums, and still leave those that *have* a place in their own place: the Inghirami tomb here at Volterra.

But it is useless. We walk up the hill and out of the Florence gate, into the shelter under the walls of the huge medieval castle which is now a State prison. There is a promenade below the ponderous walls, and a scrap of sun, and shelter from the biting wind.

A few citizens are promenading even now. And beyond, the bare green country rises up in waves and sharp points, but it is like looking at the choppy sea from the brow of a tall ship; here in Volterra we ride above all.

And behind us, in the bleak fortress, are the prisoners. There is a man, an old man now, who has written an opera inside those walls. He had a passion for the piano: and for thirty years his wife nagged him when he played. So one day he silently and suddenly killed her. So, the nagging of thirty years silenced, he got thirty years of prison, and *still* is not allowed to play the piano. It is curious.

There were also two men who escaped. Silently and secretly they carved marvellous likenesses of themselves out of the huge loaves of hard bread the prisoners get. Hair and all, they made their own effigies lifelike. Then they laid them in the bed, so that when the warder's light flashed on them he should say to himself: 'There they lie sleeping, the dogs!'

And so they worked, and they got away. It cost the governor, who loved his household of malefactors, his job. He was kicked out. It is curious. He should have been rewarded, for having such clever children, sculptors in bread.

Also available from the Blackthorn Press

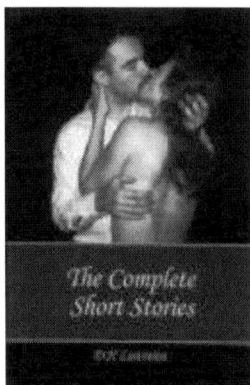

D H Lawrence *The Complete Short Stories*

All 67 of Lawrence's Short Stories in one volume

£19-95

ISBN 9780954630096

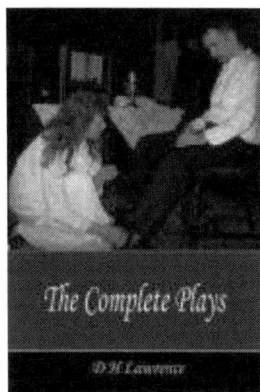

D H Lawrence *The Complete Plays*

All of Lawrence's six plays and two fragments.

£14-95

ISBN 9781906259129

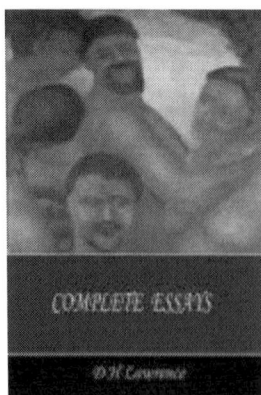

D H Lawrence *The Complete Essays*

All Lawrence's Essays in one volume

£19-95

ISBN 9781906259136

Available from all good bookshops or from Amazon.

Printed in Great Britain
by Amazon

80499591R00210